JUDGES AND RUTH

THE NIV
APPLICATION
COMMENTARY

From biblical text . . . to contemporary life

JUDGES AND RUTH

THE NIV
APPLICATION
COMMENTARY

From biblical text . . . to contemporary life

K. LAWSON YOUNGER JR.

ZONDERVAN®

ZONDERVAN.com/
AUTHORTRACKER
follow your favorite authors

The NIV Application Commentary: Judges, Ruth
Copyright © 2002 by K. Lawson Younger Jr.

Requests for information should be addressed to:
Zondervan, *Grand Rapids, Michigan 49530*

Library of Congress Cataloging-in-Publication Data

Younger, K. Lawson.
    Judges, Ruth / K. Lawson Younger.
        p. cm.—(The NIV application commentary)
    Includes bibliographical references and indexes.
    ISBN-10: 0-310-20636-7
    ISBN-13: 978-0-310-20636-1
    1. Bible. O.T. Judges—Commentaries. 2. Bible. O.T. Ruth—Commentaries. I. Title.
II. Series.
    BS1305.3.Y68 2001
    222' .3077—dc21   2001045574
                                                   CIP

This edition printed on acid-free paper.

Printed in the United States of America

16 17 /DCI/ 18 17 16 15 14 13

Contents

The NIV Application Commentary Series

When complete, the NIV Application Commentary
will include the following volumes:

To see which titles are available,
visit our web site at www.zondervan.com

NIV Application Commentary
Series Introduction

THE NIV APPLICATION COMMENTARY SERIES is unique. Most commentaries help us make the journey from our world back to the world of the Bible. They enable us to cross the barriers of time, culture, language, and geography that separate us from the biblical world. Yet they only offer a one-way ticket to the past and assume that we can somehow make the return journey on our own. Once they have explained the *original meaning* of a book or passage, these commentaries give us little or no help in exploring its *contemporary significance*. The information they offer is valuable, but the job is only half done.

Recently, a few commentaries have included some contemporary application as *one* of their goals. Yet that application is often sketchy or moralistic, and some volumes sound more like printed sermons than commentaries.

The primary goal of the NIV Application Commentary Series is to help you with the difficult but vital task of bringing an ancient message into a modern context. The series not only focuses on application as a finished product but also helps you think through the *process* of moving from the original meaning of a passage to its contemporary significance. These are commentaries, not popular expositions. They are works of reference, not devotional literature.

The format of the series is designed to achieve the goals of the series. Each passage is treated in three sections: *Original Meaning, Bridging Contexts,* and *Contemporary Significance.*

 THIS SECTION HELPS you understand the meaning of the biblical text in its original context. All of the elements of traditional exegesis—in concise form—are discussed here. These include the historical, literary, and cultural context of the passage. The authors discuss matters related to grammar and syntax and the meaning of biblical words. They also seek to explore the main ideas of the passage and how the biblical author develops those ideas.

After reading this section, you will understand the problems, questions, and concerns of the *original audience* and how the biblical author addressed those issues. This understanding is foundational to any legitimate application of the text today.

THIS SECTION BUILDS a bridge between the world of the Bible and the world of today, between the original context and the contemporary context, by focusing on both the timely and timeless aspects of the text.

God's Word is *timely*. The authors of Scripture spoke to specific situations, problems, and questions. The author of Joshua encouraged the faith of his original readers by narrating the destruction of Jericho, a seemingly impregnable city, at the hands of an angry warrior God (Josh. 6). Paul warned the Galatians about the consequences of circumcision and the dangers of trying to be justified by law (Gal. 5:2–5). The author of Hebrews tried to convince his readers that Christ is superior to Moses, the Aaronic priests, and the Old Testament sacrifices. John urged his readers to "test the spirits" of those who taught a form of incipient Gnosticism (1 John 4:1–6). In each of these cases, the timely nature of Scripture enables us to hear God's Word in situations that were *concrete* rather than abstract.

Yet the timely nature of Scripture also creates problems. Our situations, difficulties, and questions are not always directly related to those faced by the people in the Bible. Therefore, God's word to them does not always seem relevant to us. For example, when was the last time someone urged you to be circumcised, claiming that it was a necessary part of justification? How many people today care whether Christ is superior to the Aaronic priests? And how can a "test" designed to expose incipient Gnosticism be of any value in a modern culture?

Fortunately, Scripture is not only timely but *timeless*. Just as God spoke to the original audience, so he still speaks to us through the pages of Scripture. Because we share a common humanity with the people of the Bible, we discover a *universal dimension* in the problems they faced and the solutions God gave them. The timeless nature of Scripture enables it to speak with power in every time and in every culture.

Those who fail to recognize that Scripture is both timely and timeless run into a host of problems. For example, those who are intimidated by timely books such as Hebrews, Galatians, or Deuteronomy might avoid reading them because they seem meaningless today. At the other extreme, those who are convinced of the timeless nature of Scripture, but who fail to discern its timely element, may "wax eloquent" about the Melchizedekian priesthood to a sleeping congregation, or worse still, try to apply the holy wars of the Old Testament in a physical way to God's enemies today.

The purpose of this section, therefore, is to help you discern what is timeless in the timely pages of the Bible—and what is not. For example, how do the holy wars of the Old Testament relate to the spiritual warfare of the New? If Paul's primary concern is not circumcision (as he tells us in Gal. 5:6), what *is* he concerned about? If discussions about the Aaronic priesthood or Melchizedek seem irrelevant today, what is of abiding value in these passages? If people try to "test the spirits" today with a test designed for a specific first-century heresy, what other biblical test might be more appropriate?

Yet this section does not merely uncover that which is timeless in a passage but also helps you to see *how* it is uncovered. The authors of the commentaries seek to take what is implicit in the text and make it explicit, to take a process that normally is intuitive and explain it in a logical, orderly fashion. How do we know that circumcision is not Paul's primary concern? What clues in the text or its context help us realize that Paul's real concern is at a deeper level?

Of course, those passages in which the historical distance between us and the original readers is greatest require a longer treatment. Conversely, those passages in which the historical distance is smaller or seemingly nonexistent require less attention.

One final clarification. Because this section prepares the way for discussing the contemporary significance of the passage, there is not always a sharp distinction or a clear break between this section and the one that follows. Yet when both sections are read together, you should have a strong sense of moving from the world of the Bible to the world of today.

THIS SECTION ALLOWS the biblical message to speak with as much power today as it did when it was first written. How can you apply what you learned about Jerusalem, Ephesus, or Corinth to our present-day needs in Chicago, Los Angeles, or London? How can you take a message originally spoken in Greek, Hebrew, and Aramaic and communicate it clearly in our own language? How can you take the eternal truths originally spoken in a different time and culture and apply them to the similar-yet-different needs of our culture?

In order to achieve these goals, this section gives you help in several key areas.

(1) It helps you identify contemporary situations, problems, or questions that are truly comparable to those faced by the original audience. Because contemporary situations are seldom identical to those faced by the original audience, you must seek situations that are analogous if your applications are to be relevant.

(2) This section explores a variety of contexts in which the passage might be applied today. You will look at personal applications, but you will

also be encouraged to think beyond private concerns to the society and culture at large.

(3) This section will alert you to any problems or difficulties you might encounter in seeking to apply the passage. And if there are several legitimate ways to apply a passage (areas in which Christians disagree), the author will bring these to your attention and help you think through the issues involved.

In seeking to achieve these goals, the contributors to this series attempt to avoid two extremes. They avoid making such specific applications that the commentary might quickly become dated. They also avoid discussing the significance of the passage in such a general way that it fails to engage contemporary life and culture.

Above all, contributors to this series have made a diligent effort not to sound moralistic or preachy. The NIV Application Commentary Series does not seek to provide ready-made sermon materials but rather tools, ideas, and insights that will help you communicate God's Word with power. If we help you to achieve that goal, then we have fulfilled the purpose for this series.

The Editors

General Editor's Preface

I GREW UP IN THE SIXTIES, when one of the worst accusations you could make was to say to someone, "You're judging me."

I thought of that as I read Lawson Younger's excellent commentary on the biblical book of Judges, especially his discussion of what the word "judges" meant in the biblical context. As Younger points out, it meant something quite different from what it does now—not someone who decides cases in a court of law, but someone who helped deliver people from enemies and encouraged them to stay on the morally straight and narrow path. To put it another way, a biblical judge was a leader who helped save people from external and internal enemies.

Thus, I found myself reflecting on two questions: Does this book have anything to say to our modern discomfort with the concept of being morally judged? And, is there anything in the biblical understanding of "judges" that can help us cope with that discomfort?

I am not sure about the answer to the first question. Many have speculated wisely on why moral judgment became such a debated topic among anti-authoritarian, freedom-seeking Baby Boomers. It is fair to observe that they were not upset primarily with the idea of judgment itself since it occurs all the time and, indeed, is probably necessary for rational thinking to take place. Moreover, no one was more judgmental than the Boomers themselves when it came to decrying the injustices of the war in Vietnam, the dangers of nuclear weapons (and power), and the pervasive control of the growing multinational corporations and big government. Baby Boomers were more upset with who were the judges and with how that judging was done.

Is there, then, anything in the biblical understanding of judges that can help us cope with the modern discomfort with moral judgment? Absolutely! The core issue in Judges is not whether or not judging is done, but rather with who is God's viceroy in doing the judging—that is, the judges, then the kings, and after them the prophets. The Bible anticipated the Baby Boomer discomfort with individual judges. Although we often hold up the prominent judges in this book as models of ethical integrity—e.g., Samson and Gideon—closer examination doesn't warrant that "judgment." The judges were flawed men and women who delivered Israel only because they were doing the work of the true Judge. One understands the book of Judges only when the focus is put on the necessity of righteous living rather than on the "heroes" of the story.

Thus, the Baby Boomers were right, I think, to question the rights of individuals to judge others in a legal sense when it comes to morality. They were right on target in seeing that some universal moral law is at work, a law that the governments and businesses of the world tend to ignore. We cannot trust these individual judges to get in tune with that universal law. Matthew 7 makes it clear that this kind of judgment is reserved for the Lord alone.

Here is where the contribution of Judges becomes especially helpful today. The most important issue is for us to recognize that judgment gets done by God no matter what. God's people must figure out how that judgment is best communicated to the church and to the whole world. Who is the best vehicle for such judgment? Is it possible that the entrepreneurial and individualistic emphases of our culture make it even more improbable that individuals in any role can be judges? The temptations of power and the technology tend to accentuate the flawed nature of judges. Samson's flaws today would become too large to be offset by his good works. Perhaps we should put less emphasis on training individual leaders to be the "next Billy Graham" or the next "pope" or whatever, and develop instead a delivery system that focuses on the community of believers as the models of what God's standards for us are.

Perhaps the model here for us is not one of the Judges but Ruth. Why is it that when the great leaders of the biblical texts are listed, Ruth is rarely on the list? Not that she is ignored. Almost anyone who reads the story of Ruth notices an extraordinary person. But "leader" is not the label we usually affix to her name. We more often see Ruth as a model of a good citizen, ready to help any and all so that the "family" remains strong, faithful, effective.

Perhaps this is where the functions of protecting the community from external enemies and keeping us all aware of the righteousness demanded by God should lie today. Failure of individuals to do so in such a context does not have the disastrous consequences as the fall of a leader. Abuses of leadership can be handled by the overall strengths and commitments of the group. God's judgment—rather, God's righteousness—will reign as his flawed creation moves toward reconciliation.

Terry C. Muck

Author's Preface

IT IS IMPOSSIBLE TO COMPLETE a commentary on two books of the Bible without being immensely aware of one's indebtedness to the work of those who have gone before. I feel a tremendous sense of gratitude for all of their labor and insight from which I have benefited. In fact, twenty years ago, few commentaries attempted to explain how the different parts of the book of Judges fit together in order to make up the whole. Dissection and disjointed comment produced the same in the pulpit. Today this situation has changed. A number of outstanding works on the literary aspects of this book are available to enhance an understanding of the book. Most valuable for me have been the excellent monographs or commentaries of R. M. Polzin, B. G. Webb, L. Klein, R. H. O'Connell, and D. I. Block. Also beneficial to my study have been articles and essays by various scholars who have uncovered many of the book's internal structures. For the book of Ruth, I have greatly profited from the works of E. F. Campbell Jr., J. M. Sasson, R. L. Hubbard Jr., R. Westbrook, M. D. Gow, A. Berlin, F. W. Bush, and D. I. Block.

In the Original Meaning sections of this volume, the approach I have utilized in both Judges and Ruth is a canonical, rhetoric-type reading. There are basically two reasons for this. (1) This approach is best suited to uncover the coherent message of each book as it is developed within all the individual sections and within its place in the canon of Scripture. (2) It brings forth the most benefits from the text for the modern community of faith. While diachronic approaches serve an important function for scholarly inquiries into the Bible, they do not help explain the final form of the text nor do they facilitate teaching and preaching by the modern pastor or layperson.

Judges and Ruth, in many ways, are literary masterpieces. Partly because of the very nature of commentary writing and partly because of the nature of sermon making, this has not always been appreciated. It is not simply the content of each book that is important, it is how that content is communicated in each that is important.

I am also indebted to John H. Walton, Terry Muck, and Verlyn Verbrugge for their helpful criticisms, suggestions, and encouragements that improved this work on all levels. Finally, I must express my sincere gratitude to my wife, Patti, and my children, Kenneth, Andrew, and Rebecca, for their tolerance and patience at each stage in the commentary's production.

K. Lawson Younger Jr.
Trinity International University/Divinity School
May 15, 2001

Abbreviations

AB	Anchor Bible
ABD	*Anchor Bible Dictionary.* Edited by D. N. Freedman. 6 vols. New York: Doubleday, 1992.
ANETS	Ancient Near Eastern Texts and Studies
AOAT	Alter Orient und Altes Testament
ARM	Archives royales de Mari
ASV	American Standard Version
AUUSSU	Acta Universitatis Upsaliensis, Studia Semitica Upsaliensia
b.	Babylonian Talmud
B. Bat.	*Baba Batra*
BA	*Biblical Archaeologist*
BAR	*Biblical Archaeology Review*
BASOR	*Bulletin of the American Society of Oriental Research*
BBR	*Bulletin for Biblical Research*
Bib	*Biblica*
BibInt	*Biblical Interpretation*
BJRL	*Bulletin of the John Rylands Library*
BLS	Bible and Literature Series
BN	*Biblische Notizen*
BRev	*Bible Review*
BSac	*Bibliotheca sacra*
BST	The Bible Speaks Today
BT	*The Bible Translator*
BZ	*Biblische Zeitschrift*
BZAW	Beihefte zur Zeitschrift für die alttestamentliche Wissenschaft
CBC	Cambridge Bible Commentary
CBQ	*Catholic Biblical Quarterly*
COS	*The Context of Scripture.* Edited by W. W. Hallo and K. L. Younger Jr. 3 vols. Leiden: Brill, 1997–.
DDD	*Dictionary of Deities and Demons in the Bible.* Edited by K. van der Toorn, B. Becking, and P. W. van der Horst. Leiden: Brill, 1995.
EBC	*Expositor's Bible Commentary,* ed. F. E. Gaebelein (12 vols.; Grand Rapids: Zondervan, 1992)
ErIsr	*Eretz-Israel*

Abbreviations

FOTL	Forms of the Old Testament Literature
HALOT	*The Hebrew and Aramaic Lexicon of the Old Testament.* L. Koehler, W. Baumgartner, and J. J. Stamm. Translated and edited under the supervision of M. E. J. Richardson. 4 vols. Leiden: Brill, 1994–1999.
HAR	*Hebrew Annual Review*
HS	Hebrew Studies
HSM	Harvard Semitic Monographs
HTR	*Harvard Theological Review*
HUCA	*Hebrew Union College Annual*
IBHS	*An Introduction to Biblical Hebrew Syntax.* B. K. Waltke and M. O'Connor. Winona Lake, Ind.: Eisenbrauns, 1990.
ICC	International Critical Commentary
IDB	*The Interpreter's Dictionary of the Bible.* Edited by G. A. Buttrick and K. R. Crim. 4 vols. Nashville: Abindgon, 1962.
IDBSup	*Interpreter's Dictionary of the Bible: Supplementary Volume.* Edited by K. Crim. Nashville: Abingdon, 1976.
IEJ	*Israel Exploration Journal*
Int	*Interpretation*
JAAR	*Journal of the American Academy of Religion*
JANESCU	*Journal of Ancient Near Eastern Society of Columbia University*
JAOS	*Journal of the American Oriental Society*
JB	Jerusalem Bible
JBL	*Journal of Biblical Literature*
JETS	*Journal of the Evangelical Theological Society*
JPSV	Jewish Publication Society Version
JNES	*Journal of Near Eastern Studies*
JSS	*Journal of Semitic Studies*
JSOTSup	Journal for the Study of the Old Testament Supplement Series
JSOTMS	Journal for the Study of the Old Testament Monograph Series
KBL[2]	*Lexicon in Veteris Testamenti libros*, ed. Ludwig Koehler and Walter Baumgartner, 2d ed. (Leiden: Brill, 1967)
KAT	Kommentar zum Alten Testament
KJV	King James Version
LAS	*Letters from Assyrian Scholars to the Kings Esarhaddon and Assurbanipal.* Edited by S. Parpola. 2 vols.; AOAT 5; Neuchirchen-Vluyn: Neukirchen Verlag, 1970, 1983.
LXX	Septuagint (Greek translation of the Old Testament)
MT	Masoretic Text

NAC	New American Commentary
NASB	New American Standard Bible
NCB	New Century Bible
NEB	New English Bible
NIDOTTE	*New International Dictionary of Old Testament Theology and Exegesis.* Edited by W. VanGemeren. 5 vols. Grand Rapids: Zondervan, 1997.
NIV	New International Version
NIVAC	NIV Application Commentary
NRSV	New Revised Standard Version
OBO	Orbis biblicus et orientalis
OBT	Overtures to Biblical Theology
OLA	Orientalia lovaniensia analecta
Or	*Orientalia*
OTL	Old Testament Library
OTS	Old Testament Studies
PEQ	*Palestine Exploration Quarterly*
PNA	*The Prosopography of the Neo-Assyrian Empire.* Edited by S. Parpola, K. Radner, et al., Helsinki: The Neo-Assyrian Text Corpus Project, 1998–.
RAI	*Recontre Assyriologique Internationale*
RSV	Revised Standard Version
RTR	*Reformed Theological Review*
SAAB	*State Archives of Assyria Bulletin*
SBLDS	Society of Biblical Literature Dissertation Series
SEÅ	*Svensk exegetisk årsbok*
SBJT	*Southern Baptist Journal of Theology*
SJOT	*Scandinavian Journal of the Old Testament*
SOTBT	Studies in Old Testament Biblical Theology
SR	*Studies in Religion*
TBT	*The Bible Today*
TDOT	*Theological Dictionary of the Old Testament.* Edited by G. J. Botterweck and H. Ringgren. Translated by J. T. Willis, G. W. Bromiley, and D. E. Green. Grand Rapids: Eerdmans, 1974–.
ThWAT	*Theologisches Wörterbuch zum Alten Testament.* Edited by G. J. Botterweck and H. Ringgren. Stuttgart: Kohlhammer,1970–.
TOTC	Tyndale Old Testament Commentaries
TynBul	*Tyndale Bulletin*
TZ	*Theologische Zeitschrift*

Abbreviations

UF	*Ugarit-Forschungen*
USQR	*Union Seminary Quarterly Review*
VT	*Vetus Testamentum*
VTSup	Vetus Testamentum Supplement
WHJP	World History of the Jewish People
WTJ	*Westminster Theological Journal*
WZKM	*Weiner Zeitschrift für die Kunde des Morgenlandes*
ZAH	*Zeitschrift für Althebräistik*
ZAW	*Zeitschrift für die alttestamentliche Wissenschaft*
ZBAT	Zuricher Bibelkommentare zum Alten Testament
ZDPV	*Zeitschrift des deutschen Palästina-Vereins*

Introduction to Judges

The Composition of the Book of Judges

Title of the Book and Role of the Judges

THE ENGLISH TITLE for the book of Judges derives from the Latin *Liber Judicum*. The Latin stems from the Old Greek (LXX) *Kritai* ("Judges"). The English term *judges* implies the notion of individuals who adjudicate legal disputes or determine guilt or innocence in criminal cases. But it is quite apparent that such was not their primary task. The Hebrew title of the book is *šōpᵉṭîm*. The meaning of this term can be seen in 2:16–17: "Then the LORD raised up judges [*šōpᵉṭîm*], who saved them out of the hands of these raiders. Yet they would not listen to their judges but prostituted themselves to other gods and worshiped them."

Thus the judges (*šōpᵉṭîm*) are viewed as both "deliverers" or "saviors" of their people from their enemies and "instigators," "catalysts," or "stimuli" for godly living. In essence, their purpose was not judicial, but soteriological.[1] In fact, two of the judges are designated deliverers (*môšîaᶜ*): Othniel (3:9) and Ehud (3:15). A number of the activities of others are described through the use of the verb *yāšaᶜ* ("save, deliver"; cf. Shamgar, 3:31; Gideon, 6:15; 8:22; Tola, 10:1; Jephthah, 12:3; and Samson, 13:5).[2] Hence, this was apparently their role as leaders in external affairs, "restoring *shalom*, harmonious relations."[3]

But Judges 2:17 seems to imply clearly that these *šōpᵉṭîm* were also to be leaders in internal affairs regarding spiritual/moral matters. The verb *šāpaṭ* itself underscores this. Block has recently noted that *šāpaṭ* has the general meaning of "to rule, govern, exercise leadership" and thus can be used in more

---

1. D. I. Block, *Judges, Ruth* (NAC 6; Nashville: Broadman & Holman, 1999), 23.

2. Some scholars have argued on source-critical and form-critical grounds that the term *môšîaᶜ* is the older title used for these charismatic savior figures and that *šōpēṭ* is a secondary term used later when a redactor assumed a link between the "major" and "minor" judges. See, e.g., W. Beyerlin, "Gattung und Herkunft des Rahmens im Richterbuch," in *Tradition und Situation: Studien zur alttestamentlichen Prophetie, Festschrift A. Weiser*, ed. by E. Würthwein and O. Kaiser (Göttingen: Vandenhoeck & Ruprecht, 1963), 6–7. But such an approach blurs the literary function of the noncyclical judges (see more on this below).

3. T. L. J. Mafico, "Judge, Judging," *ABD*, 3:1104–5. While the root *špṭ* occurs in a number of cognate languages, the use of the nominal form in Phoenician and Punic may come closest to the biblical usage, where the term is used to designate high functionaries or rulers. See J. Hoftijzer and K. Jongeling, *Dictionary of the North-West Semitic Inscriptions* (Handbuch der Orientalistik 1/21; Leiden: Brill, 1995), 1182–83.

---

particular contexts to express "to judge" (i.e., to lead in internal affairs) and/or "to deliver" (i.e., to lead in external affairs).[4] Thus the *šōpᵉṭîm* should best be understood as "tribal rulers, leaders," rather than "judges," so that the name of the book is better rendered "The Book of Tribal Rulers."[5]

The success of the individual judges in the book is related to their success in delivering the people as well as in their spurring them by example to a proper relationship with God. The ultimate "judge" (*šōpēṭ*) is Yahweh (11:27). He is the One who gives the people into the hands of their oppressors; he is the One who raises up deliverers (i.e., the judges) for them; he is the One who brings his Spirit upon the deliverers and equips them for their tasks (3:10; 6:34; 11:29; 14:6, 19; 15:14).[6]

In another sense, each judge symbolizes an aspect of Israel, a weakness, a particular quality that leads to the narrative consequences of that episode and contributes to the resolution of the book. Thus the text supports the relevance of local events to the people as a whole. While individual judges are tribal leaders, they are identified as national leaders in order to emphasize God's dealings with the nation as a whole. Hence, on this basis, each of the judges may be seen as a symbol of Israel; furthermore, each serves to reveal a new aspect of the people's relationship to Yahweh.[7]

The book of Judges appears to deal with two types of judges, usually designated by scholars as "major" and "minor" judges (Block describes them as "primary" and "secondary"[8]). Both designations connote things that are not accurate to the book's narration. A more neutral designation is "cyclical" and "noncyclical" judges. It is important to remember that the functional distinctions between two types of judges should not be too sharply drawn.[9] The differences seem to be primarily twofold: (1) in the use of the narrative framework of the cycle for the development of the plot of each major (or cyclical) judge story, and (2) in the degree of narrative development attached to each of the major judge stories.

---

4. Block, *Judges, Ruth*, 23–24.

5. Ibid., 25.

6. It is interesting that the noun *šōpēṭ* is never used of any named individual in the book, except for Yahweh. The verbal form is used, but only with the following individuals: Othniel (3:10), Deborah (4:4), Tola (10:2), Jair (10:3), Jephthah (12:7), Ibzan (12:8, 9), Elon (12:11), Abdon (12:13, 14) and Samson (15:20; 16:31).

7. See A. Hauser, "Unity and Diversity in Early Israel Before Samuel," *JETS* 22 (1979): 289–303.

8. Block, *Judges, Ruth*, 54–55.

9. A. Malamat, "The Period of the Judges," in *Judges*, ed. B. Mazar (WHJP 3; Tel Aviv: Jewish History Publications, 1971), 131. He argues that the differences in the accounts derive primarily from the sources used by the narrator: family chronicles for the minor judges; folk narratives for the deliverer judges.

Authorship and Date of Composition

THE BOOK OF JUDGES is anonymous. It is apparent that the book is a collection of various blocks of material concerning the different judges. Some of the stories may have existed very early in oral or written form, but none of these blocks are attributed to any particular source in the text. Modern scholars have expended great amounts of time and energy in an attempt to identify these sources, but with limited success.[10]

The reference in 18:30 to "the time of the captivity of the land" seems to refer to the Exile (either 722 or 586 B.C.) and suggests that the final edition of the book came from the Exile or afterwards.[11] Thus the precise author and date are uncertain. But this should hardly deter the reader from understanding the book's message.

Purpose

THE BOOK OF JUDGES has a coherent message concerning the consequences of disobedience to God with the resultant moral degeneration that characterized the history of this period. Recently, Block has expressed this by describing the central theme of the book as "the Canaanization of Israel."[12] The book's selective presentation of the period is clearly designed to instruct the reader on the consequences of disobedience to God and his law.

Marius has divided the book of Judges along the theme of degeneracy, using different categories of perspective. Judges 1:1–2:5 is developed along

---

10. The majority of scholars understand the book as part of the Deuteronomistic History (though, in part, variously defined). For this popular way of viewing the book, see R. Boling, "Judges, Book of," in *ABD*, 3:1107–17. For an overview of the theory of the Deuteronomistic History, see S. L. McKenzie, "Deuteronomistic History," *ABD*, 2:160–68. For an evaluation of the scholarly discussion, see M. A. O'Brien, "Judges and the Deuteronomistic History," in *The History of Israel's Traditions: The Heritage of Martin Noth*, ed. S. L. McKenzie and M. P. Graham (JSOTSup 182; Sheffield: Sheffield Academic Press, 1994), 235–59. See also Block, *Judges, Ruth*, 44–50.

11. Or perhaps, as an alternative, the statement "until the time of the captivity of the land" should be linked with the next verse, which states that the Danites "continued to use the idols that Micah had made, all the time the house of God was in Shiloh." Thus "the captivity of the land" referred to in verse 30 is understood in relation to its fall, the historical context of this event being the Philistine ascendancy prior to the time of Saul. See J. Gordon McConville, *Grace in the End: A Study in Deuteronomic Theology* (SOTBT; Grand Rapids: Zondervan, 1993), 110. A variant of this view is seen in the attempt to emend 18:30 to read "ark" (ʾārôn) instead of "land" (ʾāreṣ) and to identify this event with the capture of the ark in the days of Eli by the Philistines (1 Sam. 4:21). See E. J. Young, *An Introduction to the Old Testament*, rev. ed. (Grand Rapids: Eerdmans, 1958), 180.

12. Block, *Judges, Ruth*, 57–59.

---

a *historical/military* perspective. Judges 2:6–3:6 utilizes a *religious* perspective. The cycles section (3:7–16:31) uses the *religious* perspective traced in individual lives. The final section of the book (17:1–21:25) represents all three perspectives in terms of "the spheres of cultus, family, and nation."[13] Israel as a nation expresses, in the final chapters, its fullest point of degeneracy in its corporate actions. It may be that Samson is "the epitome of degeneration,"[14] but the extension of that degeneration takes its widest scope in chapters 17–21, reaching its conclusion in the final chapter.

Interestingly, not every oppression that Israel suffers during the judges' era is fully narrated (or for that matter alluded to). This is manifest from 10:11–14, where the Lord refers to the oppressions of some peoples for which there is no corresponding narration in the book (e.g., Egyptians, Amorites, Sidonians, Maonites). It is also evident in the lack of plot development of the minor or noncyclical judges. The double introduction and double conclusion to the book are also written in order to add those things important to the interpretation and understanding of the purpose and to separate out those things that would detract from the primary message of the cycles section (see discussion of structure below). All and all, the author's didactic objective is well achieved.[15]

Chronology

THE PERIOD OF the judges began with the death of Joshua and ended with the coronation of Saul (i.e., the beginning of the monarchy). But if one simply adds the length of each judge's administration with its preceding oppression, the total comes to 410 years, a period far too extended to fit the time between Joshua and Saul. Therefore, scholars agree that the periods of some oppressions and judgeships overlap. This is to be expected since many (if not all) of the judges are local, tribal leaders, operating in geographically limited portions

---

13. J. Marius, *Representation in Old Testament Narrative Texts* (Leiden: Brill, 1998), 133–34.

14. Ibid., 134.

15. For many scholars the book of Judges is an apology for the monarchy. More specifically, it is a defense of the Judahite/Davidic monarchy, as opposed to the Saulide monarchy. See R. H. O'Connell, *The Rhetoric of the Book of Judges* (VTSup 63; Leiden: E. J. Brill, 1996); M. Brettler, "The Book of Judges: Literature As Politics," *JBL* 108 (1989): 395–418; and M. A. Sweeney, "Davidic Polemics in the Book of Judges," *VT* 47 (1997): 517–29. There are a number of good reasons why scholars have perceived this purpose for the book. However, while the book of Judges is concerned with and presents the general flow of the premonarchic political history of Israel, it is also clear that it is concerned with presenting Israel's spiritual state during this period with all of its ramifications, and that this is the primary purpose of the book. See the discussion of Block, *Judges, Ruth,* 66–67, and our discussion of the double conclusion's refrain below, pp. 30–33.

of Israel. The amount or degree of overlap is difficult to discern, and so the precise chronology of the period of the judges is unknown.[16] In addition, the book's uses of numbers in some instances are uncertain. For example, the book may use the number forty as a round number or figuratively to simply denote a generation.[17] It may not be intended to be understood literally.

Judges does not include an adequate historical presentation of all of the judges. In the case of the so-called "minor" (or noncyclical) judges, the writer chooses to give limited information. For example, the author relates that "Tola saved Israel." But from whom? Had Israel done evil in the eyes of the Lord as in other cases? How did he "save" Israel? The information is not forthcoming. Moreover, individuals such as Eli and Samuel, whom many scholars believe functioned as judges in Israel, are not included in the book. They are certainly part of the period of the judges (as 1 Sam. 12:11 clearly indicates for Samuel), yet the writer has not included them.[18] Thus it is important to remember that the book is very much a selective presentation designed to reinforce the author's didactic message.

The "Tribal League"

THE BOOK OF JUDGES presents Israel as constituting some sort of tribal confederacy or league. Such a confederation would facilitate important political, economic, social, and religious purposes. A brief overview of the tribal structure of ancient Israel will enhance an understanding of a number of passages in the book of Judges.

The family or house(hold) (*bêt ʾāb*, lit., "house of the father") was the fundamental unit of social structure. This unit was not simply the nuclear family (i.e., husband, wife/wives, and children) but had wider relational connections so that it could be used to designate a more extended family (i.e., husband, wife/wives, married children and grandchildren, all living in relatively close proximity to each other).[19] While an individual male warrior

---

16. For some suggested chronological arrangements, see A. Hill and J. Walton, *A Survey of the Old Testament* (Grand Rapids: Zondervan, 1991), 173–74; J. Bright, *A History of Israel*, 3d ed. (Philadelphia: Westminster, 1981), 178–81; and Block, *Judges, Ruth*, 59–63.

17. Note that the first four major/cyclical judges are credited with forty years of rest for the land (in the case of Ehud, double forty, i.e., eighty). The Philistine oppression (13:1) is forty years. Samson's judgeship is twenty years (half forty), as is the Canaanite oppression (4:3).

18. Perhaps their inclusion would have obscured his message. Also note that no precise information is given about the length of their judgeships.

19. Cf. the situation in the account of Abimelech and the *bêt ʾāb* of Gideon in the discussion of ch. 9 below.

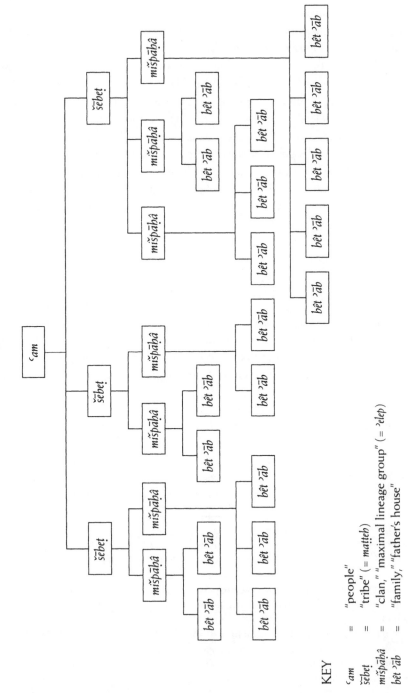

ISRAEL'S TRIBAL STRUCTURE

KEY

ʿam	=	"people"
šēbeṭ	=	"tribe" (= maṭṭeh)
mišpāḥâ	=	"clan," "maximal lineage group" (= ʾelep)
bêt ʾāb	=	"family," "father's house"

(*gibbôr*) might be the head of his own family (*bêt ʾab*), each family usually had a number of male warriors (cf. Josh. 7:14, 17).

The term that in most English versions is translated "clan" (*mišpaḥâ*) is more accurately a "maximal lineage group." It was a descent group that established ties of kinship between families or households (*bêt ʾāb*) through a common ancestor (who was no longer living), adding a protective and social function. It established vertical kinship solidarity. It appears that it was on the level of the *mišpaḥâ* that the law of the *gōʾēl* (kinsman-redeemer) functioned (see the introduction to Ruth).

The tribe (*šēbeṭ*) is more difficult to define, since social groups can be bound together in so many different ways: by descent, by residence, by common dialect, or by a common religion. In the Old Testament, tribes were generally certainly groups connected to one another by residence and descent as well as possibly dialect (see 12:6, where the Cisjordanian Ephraimites could not pronounce the word "shibboleth"). Studies of modern tribal societies demonstrate that Old Testament tribal culture was not necessarily an evolutionary stage following that of the band and preceding the state stage, but could represent a social form in its own right.[20] The term *šēbeṭ* may be applied to any kind of organization where there is unity at the center but freedom and variation at the periphery. In the Old Testament, therefore, a tribe seems to be the largest social unit for mutual defense against foreigners or other Israelite social units.[21]

Finally, several tribes combined to form the ethnic group, the *ʿam*, "people" (a root that implies internal blood relationship).[22] The book of Judges assumes that common descent from an eponymous ancestor provides the basis for Israel's ethnic unity. Expressions such as "Israel," the "sons of Israel" (or "Israelites"), "all Israel," and so on underscore the basic ethnic unity of the tribal confederation—at least as the book of Judges presents it.

Among numerous characteristics of tribal societies, one of the most important is that of vertical kinship solidarity within a segmentary system (i.e., rights, duties, privileges are inherited along the same segmentary lines that give clan and lineage solidarity). Examples of this from the Old Testament are: an emphasis on remembering genealogies, the kinsman-redeemer (*gōʾēl*) law, and landholding. Another important tribal characteristic is the importance of alliances. The covenant or treaty (*bᵉrît*) functioned not only as a

---

20. F. Lambert, "Tribal Influences in Old Testament Tradition," *SEÅ* 59 (1994): 33–58.

21. For further discussion, see S. Bendor, *The Social Structure of Ancient Israel: The Institution of the Family (Beit 'Ab) from the Settlement to the End of the Monarchy* (Jerusalem Biblical Studies 7; Jerusalem: Simor, 1996).

22. D. I. Block, *The Foundations of National Identity: A Study in Ancient Northwest Semitic Perspectives* (Ann Arbor, Mich.: University Microfilms, 1983), 1–83.

moral and religious document but also as a basis for tribal alliances within the confederacy or league.[23]

In clan ideology, it can be said fairly that the concept of abstract justice is lacking. All actions are based on specific loyalties, the lines of which are structurally determined. One supports one's fellow clansman in a dispute, regardless of moral questions. The only consideration is, "he is my fellow-clansman."[24] This fact concerning clan ideology is important to understand the loyalties in the case of Benjamin in Judges 19–20.

The *Ḥērem*

THE CONCEPT OF the *ḥērem* is important to understanding the book of Judges (especially the book's double introduction and double conclusion, where the term occurs). While the word is not used in the main section of the book, its concept and legal implications are present in a number of instances. The NIV usually translates the noun form as "devoted thing" and the verbal form as "totally destroy."

Although roughly 85 percent of its occurrences are in the context of warfare and destruction, its nonmilitary usage is informative. In Leviticus 27:21–29, a distinction is made between dedicating (*haqdîš*) and devoting (*haḥ°rîm*) in that the thing dedicated can be redeemed while that which is devoted cannot. The person devoted to Yahweh must be put to death (27:28–29). According to Exodus 22:20 [Heb. 19], a person who sacrifices to any god other than Yahweh alone "must be destroyed [*ḥrm*]."[25] This text links the *ḥērem* with the people's "internal identity" as Yahweh's people. Thus, the Old Testament *ḥērem*-narratives are stories connected with the notion of obedience/disobedience to Yahweh (i.e., the execution/nonexecution of the *ḥērem*).[26]

The essential delineation of the law of the *ḥērem* in military contexts is found in Deuteronomy 7. The prescriptive phrases (7:1–5, 11, 16, 25) and promises (7:20–22) echo precisely the terms of Exodus 23:20–33.[27] The implications of the *ḥērem* are clearly manifest: no covenant (treaty) with the inhabitants, no mercy, no intermarriage. Its purpose according to Deuteronomy 7 is to drive out (i.e., "dispossess") the Canaanites. The reasons appear

---

23. Concerning the twelve-tribe systems of Israel, see Z. Kallai, "The Twelve-Tribe Systems of Israel," *VT* 47 (1997): 53–90.

24. Lambert, "Tribal Influences," 46.

25. Cf. Deut. 13, which deals with a city involved in idolatry. In this case, the property is not forfeited to the priests but is to be destroyed along with the people (cf. also Ezra 10:8).

26. See Christa Schäfer-Lichtenberger, "Bedeutung und Funktion von *ḥerem* in biblisch-hebräischen Texten," *BZ* 38 (1994): 270–75.

27. J. P. U. Lilley, "Understanding the *ḥerem*," *TynBul* 44 (1993): 169–77, esp. 174.

to be threefold: judgment of the Canaanites, protection of the Israelites from Canaanite religious influence, and fulfillment of the patriarchal promises concerning the land. In Deuteronomy 20:16–17, *ḥērem* is defined by the clause "do not leave alive anything that breathes" (referring to humans in particular).

The kind of warfare attributed to Israel in the conquest of Canaan does not originate in a theology of "holy war" peculiar to Old Testament theology. Rather, it is a political ideology that Israel shared with other nations in the ancient Near East.[28] All wars waged by a country were "holy wars," dedicated to the glorification of its deity and the extension of the deity's land and reign.

Thus the term *ḥērem* seems to connote the uncompromising devotion of things without the possibility of recall or redemption.[29] It was not only applied to idolatrous objects but to things that could have been taken as plunder or people who could have been enslaved. In the case of its use in connection with people, it always implies their utter destruction. It is important to note that the use of the phrase "holy war" is an inadequate description often given to the *ḥērem*.[30]

In the book of Judges, *ḥērem* is first encountered in Judges 1:17, where it is applied by the Simeonites and Judahites in the possession of the Simeonite allotment. Deuteronomy 7 clearly provides the background to this application. While the term only occurs here in chapter 1, it is undoubtedly implied throughout the chapter by the Israelite tribes' attempts at possessing their allotments. The failure to implement the *ḥērem* is seen in the repetition of the phrases "did not drive out" (*yāraš*) and "live among" (*yāšab*) in the assessments of the individual tribes (see discussion of chapter 1 below).

Beside 1:17, the only other occurrence of *ḥērem* in the book of Judges is in 21:11, where it is applied selectively against Jabesh-Gilead as a means of securing wives for the surviving Benjamites. Even so, the concept is present in the total annihilation of the population of Laish by the Danites and in the civil war against Benjamin (Deut. 7 again providing the background). Ironically, Laish was not in Dan's allotment and should not have been subject to the *ḥērem* by them.

Moreover, the irony of the vow in the case of the civil war could not be greater. The Israelites were expected to *ḥērem* the Canaanites; they were not supposed to give their sons and daughters to the Canaanites. They do not do the former, and they do the latter. In the case of Benjamin, however, they

---

28. K. L. Younger Jr., *Ancient Conquest Accounts: A Study in Ancient Near Eastern and Biblical History Writing* (JSOTSup 98; Sheffield: Sheffield Academic Press, 1990), 235–36.

29. Cf. Lilley's conclusions, "Understanding the *ḥerem*," 176–77.

30. P. C. Craigie, *The Problem of War in the Old Testament* (Grand Rapids: Eerdmans, 1978).

ḥ*ērem* the Benjamites (if only 600 men are left, the ḥ*ērem* has certainly been applied!); and they vow that they will *never* give their daughters to the Benjamites. Right from the beginning of the book, the Israelites show little restraint in giving their *sons and daughters* to the Canaanites. But they tenaciously uphold their vow not to give their *daughters* to the Benjamites (a rash vow—shades of Jephthah's vow and daughter!). Note especially that the Benjamites are part of Israel, whereas the Canaanites are the real enemy.

The Structure of the Book of Judges

AS A PRELIMINARY to discussing the structure of the book of Judges, it is important to point out a basic literary assumption that the book makes. Judges assumes a basic familiarity with God's law—in particular, as contained in the book of Deuteronomy. The events recorded in Judges are interpreted and evaluated through the filter of Deuteronomy (if not more generally in the wider context of the Pentateuch as a whole). For example, the book assumes a knowledge of the ḥ*ērem*, of the covenant, of God's previous statements to the nation (particularly the blessings and curses of Deut. 28; cf. Lev. 26), and so on. Therefore, a close reading of the book of Deuteronomy before studying Judges is a positive move toward understanding the book.

The book of Judges has three main parts: a double introduction (1:1–2:5; 2:6–3:6), a double conclusion (17:1–18:31; 19:1–21:25), and a main section that is commonly called the "cycles" section (3:7–16:31).

The Double Introduction and Double Conclusion

THE BALANCE OF the double introduction by the double conclusion forms a type of inclusio.[31] The first introduction (A) is concerned with *foreign* wars of subjugation with the ḥ*ērem* being applied. In its counterpart, the second conclusion (A′) narrates *domestic* wars with the ḥ*ērem* being applied. The second introduction (B) relates the difficulties Israel had with *foreign* religious idols of the Canaanites. Its counterpart, the first conclusion (B′), describes the difficulties that Israel had with its own *domestic* idols. Thus the inclusio is clearly perceived as follows:

---

31. An inclusio is a literary unit that begins and ends with the same or similar word, phrase, clause, or subject matter. For the double introduction and double conclusion as an inclusio, see C. Exum, "The Centre Cannot Hold: Thematic and Textual Instabilities in Judges," *CBQ* 52 (1990): 410–31, esp. 413 and 429; and R. G. Boling, *Judges: Introduction, Translation and Commentary* (AB 6A; Garden City, N.Y.: Doubleday, 1975), 29–38; K. L. Younger Jr., "Judges 1 in Its Near Eastern Literary Context," in *Faith, Tradition, History: Essays on Old Testament Historiography in Its Near Eastern Context*, ed. A. R. Millard, J. K. Hoffmeier, and D. W. Baker (Winona Lake. Ind.: Eisenbrauns, 1994), 223–27.

A Foreign wars of subjugation with the *ḥērem* being applied (1:1–2:5)
  B Difficulties with foreign religious idols (2:6–3:6)
  B' Difficulties with domestic religious idols (17:1–18:31)
A' Domestic wars with the *ḥērem* being applied (19:1–21:25)

Besides its obvious relationship with the double conclusion, the double introduction initiates paradigms that create literary expectations for the main cycles section. Judges 1:1–2:5 introduces the reader to the pattern of Israel's increasing failure to drive out the Canaanites, which will be mirrored in the moral degeneration of the major judges' lives. It also reveals the geographic sequence pattern of Judah to Dan reflected in the major judge cycles (Othniel to Samson). Judges 2:6–3:6 introduces the reader to the all-important cyclic pattern, the framework of the cycles section. These paradigms lay the groundwork to the subsequent irony that permeates the book.

In the double conclusion (17:1–21:25), Israel's enemy is no longer external but internal. Cyclical time, which was introduced in 2:6–3:6 and has dominated the cycles section, is exhausted. The period is preeminently characterized by absence: "In those days Israel had no king."

The entire double conclusion is unified by the four-time repetition of a distinctive refrain: twice in full at the beginning and end of the double conclusion and twice in the center of the section[32] with an ellipsis of the refrain's second line (lit. trans. follows):

A In those days there was no king . . .
   Every man did what right in his own eyes (17:6)
  B In those days there was no king . . . (18:1)
  B' In those days there was no king . . . (19:1)
A' In those days there was no king . . .
   Every man did what was right in his own eyes (21:25)

The significance of the refrain is construed through the important statement in 8:23 ("I will not rule over you. . . . The LORD will rule over you"). Consequently, the first line of the refrain carries a double entendre: During the period of the judges there was no physical king, but more importantly there was no spiritual king![33] Thus the resultant "every man did what was right in

---

32. The two repetitions at the center of the double conclusion (i.e., 18:1a and 19:1a) are intrinsically bound together by a chiasm, *melek 'ên* versus *'ên melek* respectively.

33. Many biblical interpreters assume the reference in the formula is only to a human king and is the product of a promonarchical redaction. If one merely sees this as a promonarchical redaction, then one might miss the spiritual component that seems to be functioning to reinforce the proper theological understanding of the double conclusion. An example of this is found in the perspective asserted by J. A. Soggin, who writes, "It [the refrain] seems to be particularly ill-chosen for chs. 19–21: here the existence of an inter-tribal

his own eyes" is more profoundly linked to the previous chapters than is typically realized.

The war of occupation with which the book begins (Israel vs. the Canaanites) and the civil war with which it closes (Israel vs. Benjamin) bracket the book, reinforcing its theme.[34] Polzin explains it this way:

> If the book's first chapter begins with an effective psychological portrait of the process whereby Israel, after Joshua's death, progressively went from certainty to confusion . . . the book's finale [chs. 19–21] now completes with a flourish the paradoxical picture of confusion within certainty, obscurity in clarity, that has occupied its pages from the start . . . here [chs. 19–21] the narrator is intent upon intensifying the doubt and confusion in Israel with which he began his story in Judges 1.[35]

In summary, some of the strikingly similar parallels between the double introduction and the double conclusion can be seen in the following chart:[36]

Introduction 1 (1:1–2:5)	*Conclusion 2 (19:1–21:25)*
The Israelites asked the LORD, saying, "Who will be the first to go up and fight for us against the Canaanites?" The LORD answered, "Judah is to go. . . ." (1:1–2)	The Israelites . . . inquired of God . . . "Who of us shall go first to fight against the Benjamites?" The LORD replied, "Judah. . . ." (20:18)

assembly is actually affirmed, an assembly which judges the controversies that have broken out among the various members and whose decisions appear to be binding on all. Thus the phrase 'in those days . . . everyone did what seemed to him to be right' seems somewhat inappropriate to indicate what happened in that era, at least according to the opinion of the pro-monarchical redaction" (Soggin, *Judges: A Commentary* [OTL; Philadelphia: Westminster, 1981], 280).

Some interpreters assume the first line of the refrain refers to an idealized monarchy that redactionally supported the Davidic, as opposed to the Saulide, monarchy. See e.g., O'Connell, *The Rhetoric of the Book of Judges*, 268–69; Sweeney, "Davidic Polemics," 517–29. But the first line of the refrain need not imply a promonarchic, let alone pro-Davidic, polemic. See Block, *Judges, Ruth*, 475–76, 484. Contra Soggin, the first line is intimately tied to the second, which has obvious moral and spiritual overtones that even the presence of a Davidic king could not necessarily deter. See also note 13 above.

34. R. M. Polzin, *Moses and the Deuteronomist: A Literary Study of the Deuteronomic History, Part One: Deuteronomy, Joshua, Judges* (New York: Seabury, 1980), 200–202.

35. Ibid., 200, 202.

36. See D. W. Gooding, "The Composition of the Book of Judges," in *H. M. Orlinsky Memorial Volume* (Eretz Israel 16; Jerusalem: Israel Exploration Society, 1982), 70–79, esp. 76–78.

The story of how Othniel got his wife (1:11–15)	The story of how the remainder of the Benjamites got their wives (21:1–25)
The Benjamites fail to drive out the Jebusites from Jebus (1:21)	A Levite carefully avoiding the Jebusites in Jebus suffers terrible outrage in Gibeah of Benjamin (19:1–30)
Bochim: God's covenant; Israel's unlawful covenants with the Canaanites; Israel's weeping before the angel (messenger) of Yahweh (2:1–5)	Bethel: the ark of the covenant of God; Israel weeps and fasts before the Lord (20:26–29)
Introduction 2 (2:6–3:6)	*Conclusion 1 (17:1–18:31)*
The degeneration of the generations after the death of Joshua (2:6–19); God leaves certain nations "to test the Israelites to see whether they would obey the LORD's commands, which he had given . . . through Moses" (2:20–3:4)	A mother dedicates silver to the Lord for her son to make an idol! That son makes one of his own sons a priest in his idolatrous shrine, then replaces him with a Levite. That Levite is Moses' grandson. He and his sons become priests at Dan's shrine.

Finally, it should be noted that the double conclusion itself (17:1–18:31 and 19:1–21:25) has internal links. Thus in 17:1–18:31, the story's coherence revolves around a Levite in *Judah* moving to the hill country of *Ephraim* and then on to Dan. In 19:1–21:25, the story's coherence revolves around a Levite in *Ephraim* looking for his concubine in Bethlehem in *Judah*. Both passages end with a reference to Shiloh. Both conclusions begin by narrating the actions of individual Israelites (Micah and his mother in ch. 17, the Levite and his concubine in ch. 19) that consequently expand events on the tribal or national level (Dan in ch. 18, all the Israelite tribes in chs. 20–21). Moreover, both conclusions begin with a predicament (the curse of Micah's mother; the Levite's estrangement from his concubine) that seems to be solved almost immediately but turns out to have further complications and ramifications. These repeated patterns unify the chapters.[37]

---

37. P. Satterthwaite, "'No King in Israel': Narrative Criticism and Judges 17–21," *Tyn-Bul* 44 (1993): 75–88.

The Cycles Section

THE MAIN SECTION of Judges (3:7–16:31) contains six major judge stories built around a basic literary cycle. It also contains interspersed stories of minor judges, which occur in a one-two-three sequence. However, this main section (3:7–16:31) is not simply an anthology of judge stories and summary notices, but a long and complex narrative movement. The tendency to study and preach the major/cyclical judges in isolation from the overarching message of the cycles section has created many false impressions about these characters. Often these judges are held up as models after whom Christians should pattern their lives. But this is not the primary message that the book is communicating.[38]

Samson and Gideon are two clear examples. Samson is by far the best known of all the judges. Sermons and Sunday school lessons often concentrate on his various heroic deeds as positive attributes. But the picture from the context—especially when the entire cycles section is considered—is very different. Many of Samson's heroic feats are seen as blatant acts of disobedience to the Law, acts of a selfishly motivated man who cares little for his spiritual calling. Gideon too is frequently held up as a spiritual leader of the greatest sort with the famous fleece incidents interpreted as positive spiritual qualities. But again in the context of Judges, Gideon is far from this portrayal. Not only are the fleece incidents of negative spiritual quality, but before he is even dead, the Israelites are worshiping an idol that Gideon himself has made!

It is, therefore, important that the six major/cyclical judge narratives be read within the larger narrative complex of 3:7–16:31. Interpretation of the individual cycles should take into account both the distinctive features of that cycle and the function of that cycle within the larger literary context (i.e., the macrostructure) of the entire cycles section. To neglect this process of interpretation is to misunderstand the cycles section and produce the type of misreadings like those about Gideon and Samson mentioned above.

Moreover, the entire cycles section (3:7–16:31) should be read in the light of the double introduction's paradigms (as explained above). The linear movement towards a literary climax and moral nadir is a pattern that Introduction 1 (1:1–2:5) demonstrates. Introduction 1 also introduces the pattern of geographic arrangement that reinforces the linear movement. There is a rough geographic progression from south to north (Othniel, Ehud, Barak, Gideon) and from east to west (Jephthah, Samson). This may indicate that artistic considerations were operative in the sequencing of the cycles section

---

38. For further discussion of this abuse of the book, see Block, *Judges, Ruth*, 71–72.

(as opposed to a strict chronological arrangement).[39] The second paradigm—that is, the cyclical pattern itself (see discussion in the next paragraph)—is displayed in Introduction 2 (2:6–3:6). When both paradigms are recognized, the coherence of the message of the cycles section is manifest.

The major/cyclical judge cycle (introduced in 2:6–3:6) is composed of the following basic components:[40]

1. Israel does evil in the eyes of Yahweh.
2. Yahweh gives/sells them into the hands of oppressors.
3. Israel serves the oppressor for × years.
4. Israel cries out to Yahweh.
5. Yahweh raises up a deliverer (i.e., judge).
6. The Spirit of Yahweh is upon the deliverer.
7. The oppressor is subdued (reversal of component 2).
8. The land has "rest" for × years.

These cycle components do not occur in a fixed grid into which the rest of the narrative material is forced regardless of its content. In fact, except for the first cycle (the Othniel cycle), in all the remaining cycles the writer selects some framework statement of the paradigm to expand on, giving fuller elaboration: the nature of the oppression, the manner in which the deliverer is raised up, the way in which the deliverance is achieved, the judge's subsequent activity, the legacy of the judge. Thus the narrator enhances the literary quality of the overall work by giving depth and texture to the plots and also heightening the reader's interest with numerous surprising turns.[41] The framework components are varied in such a way as to indicate the changing state of Israel as seen in the succession of the major/cyclical judge cycles. The change is one of progressive deterioration in Israel's condition: in relation to Yahweh, in relation to its enemies, and in relation to its own internal stability.[42] In fact, the further into the cycles section one goes, the less consistent—generally speaking—are the components' occurrences.[43] By the time of Samson, the cycle has almost disappeared.

---

39. Interestingly, the order of four judges mentioned in 1 Sam. 12:9–11 is Jerub-Baal, Barak, Jephthah, and Samuel. Thus, since there is no clear indication in the book of Judges for chronological aspects beyond the number of years for certain items, the ordering principle may be governed by different criteria than simple chronology.

40. There is some disagreement among scholars concerning the number of framework components. Some count only five or six; others include as many as ten.

41. Block, *Judges, Ruth*, 149.

42. B. G. Webb, *The Book of the Judges: An Integrated Reading* (JSOTSup 46; Sheffield: Sheffield Academic Press, 1987), 175–76.

43. The Jephthah cycle is a blip in the pattern, for it includes many of the components.

This inconsistency and variations in the framework components can be illustrated through a few basic observations (which could be greatly expanded if space allowed). The "deliverer" in the Deborah and Barak story is not explicitly identified. The people do not remain faithful to Yahweh during Gideon's lifetime; rather, Gideon's own construction of a golden ephod becomes a snare both to him and to them. By the time of Jephthah, the list of Israel's apostasies is considerably expanded (10:6), and when the people first cry out, Yahweh refuses to deliver them. Neither the Jephthah story nor the Samson story depicts the land as regaining "rest," nor do the people of Samson's time bother to cry to Yahweh. Furthermore, Samson himself dies in captivity to the oppressor.[44] In other words, this unraveling of the cycle helps communicate the moral deterioration taking place during the period of the judges.

Accordingly, the "cycles" themselves in 3:6–16:31 (often considered part of the so-called Deuteronomistic framework) are arranged in such a way as to point to this decline in the character of the judges as illustrative of the chaos of the time. It is no happen-chance that the consistency of the pattern generally breaks down.[45] Cheryl Exum aptly remarks:

> Rather than attributing the lack of consistency in the framework pattern to careless redaction, I take it as a sign of further dissolution. The political and moral instability depicted in Judges is reflected in the textual instability. The framework deconstructs itself, so to speak, and the cycle of apostasy and deliverance becomes increasingly murky.[46]

Moreover, besides the cycles pattern that is observable in this main section (3:7–16:31), there are two linear movements: a literary movement towards a climax and a moral movement towards a nadir. The Samson cycle is both the literary climax and moral nadir of the cycles section.

The moral decline in the major/cyclical judges is generally reinforced through the amount of verbiage used for each judge. Othniel, the ideal judge, receives the least amount of verbiage; Ehud slightly more; Deborah/Barak more; Gideon more than Jephthah, less than Samson; Jephthah more than Deborah/Barak, less than Gideon or Samson;[47] and Samson, the worst judge

---

44. D. N. Fewell, "Judges," in *The Women's Bible Commentary*, ed. C. A. Newsom and S. H. Ringe (Louisville: Westminster/John Knox, 1992), 67.

45. Concerning this, see the excellent discussion of F. E. Greenspahn: "The Theology of the Framework of Judges," *VT* 36 (1986): 385–96. Greenspahn concludes that there is really no firm basis for describing the framework as Deuteronomistic (389–91, 395). Also, each judge may be seen as a microcosm of the nation. See A. Hauser, "Unity and Diversity in Early Israel," 289–303.

46. Exum, "The Centre Cannot Hold," 412.

47. Again, the Jephthah cycle is a blip in the pattern (cf. note 43, above).

and moral nadir of the major/cyclical judges, the most. Thus, the amount of verbiage attached to each major/cyclical judge is generally proportional to his or her spiritual or moral quality: the more moral, the less verbiage; the less moral, the greater the verbiage.

The moral decline in the relationship between Israel and Yahweh can also be seen in the characterization of the women of the book.[48] Acsah's practical shrewdness and resourcefulness in seizing the initiative from both Othniel and Caleb—the two male heroes of the story—introduces a motif that will recur at crucial points throughout the cycles section (3:6–16:31), particularly at 4:17–22 (Deborah and Jael), 9:53–54 (the "certain woman" of Thebez), and 16:14–21 (Delilah). While Acsah's actions will be commended because of her positive intentions, there is a deterioration until we reach Delilah, who is willing to take the initiative to bring down her man. Thus, the book evinces a clear degeneration from the outspoken (in a positive sense) Acsah (1:12–15), to Deborah and Jael (chs. 4–5), to the "[certain] woman" (9:53), to Jephthah's daughter (11:34–40), to Delilah (16:4–22), and finally to the dependent and silent women of chapters 19–21.

The male/female polarity is eminently important for the whole of Judges. Barak is eclipsed by Deborah as well as by Jael, the great victory song in Judges 5 comes from a woman, Jephthah is determined by the whore-virgin tension (= mother and daughter respectively!), the whoremonger Samson is fascinated by one Philistine woman after another (which among other things is a sign of an authority conflict with his parents), not to speak of the horrors and chaos brought upon the women in chapters 19–21.[49]

In some instances, scholars have argued that Gideon is the ideal judge.[50] Usually this is based on a belief that the Gideon cycle is central and therefore the ideal. It is also thought that Gideon evokes the memory of Moses and hence is another Moses type. But this evaluation of Gideon ignores the tremendous negative assessment of Gideon throughout and especially at the end of his cycle. He is the only judge who makes an idol and influences Israel to worship it *before* his death. In addition, the Gideon cycle is not completed until the end of the Abimelech account (Gideon = the judge, non-king; Abimelech = the king, non-judge). The macrostructure with its moral declivity argues

---

48. See Webb, *The Book of the Judges*, 31; K. R. R. Gros Louis, "The Book of Judges," in *Literary Interpretations of Biblical Narratives*, ed. K. R. R. Gros Louis (2 vols.; Nashville: Abingdon, 1974, 1982), 1:144–45; M. O'Connor, "The Women in the Book of Judges," *HAR* 10 (1986): 277–93.

49. J. P. Fokkelman, "Structural Remarks on Judges 9 and 19," in *"Sha'arei Talmon": Studies in the Bible, Qumran, and the Ancient Near East Presented to Shemaryahu Talmon*, ed. M. Fishbane and E. Tov with W. W. Fields (Winona Lake, Ind.: Eisenbrauns, 1992), 38, n. 11.

50. See, e.g., the popular *NIV Study Bible* notes (Grand Rapids: Zondervan, 1985), 327.

against Gideon's identification as the ideal judge. Othniel is clearly the ideal judge (for more, see 3:7–11).

But the Gideon cycle is pivotal in every sense. It is the beginning of the Out-group judges.[51] The In-group judges (Othniel, Ehud, Deborah/Barak) come from outstanding or acceptable backgrounds. While two of these In-group judge cycles (Ehud and Barak) manifest less than perfect characters, the Out-group judges exhibit "disturbing weaknesses, if not serious faults."[52] The Out-group judges (Gideon, Jephthah, and Samson) come from less than acceptable backgrounds. Gideon's father has made a Baal altar and an Asherah pole in Gideon's hometown. Jephthah is the son of a prostitute. Samson is from the renegade tribe of Dan. Moreover, there is a notable religious deterioration from Gideon on: Gideon/Abimelech (idolatry and the worship of Baal Berith) to Jephthah (human sacrifice) to Samson (doing what seems right in his own eyes, violating all his Nazirite vows).[53]

Revenge is a major motif of the Out-group judges. Note its presence in the Gideon/Abimelech cycle (severe revenge on the two towns of Succoth and Peniel, Jotham's prophetic allegory, retribution of Abimelech on the people of Shechem) and in the Jephthah cycle (the vengeance on the Ephraimites). It reaches a climax in the Samson cycle (revenge again and again on the Philistines, who are also dominated by revenge). An adjunct to this motif that begins in the Out-group judges is the movement toward civil war, which eventually becomes a reality at the end of the book. From Gideon on, Israelite society seems to become more and more fractured and chaotic.

The Gideon narrative is also pivotal because it is the first time that Israel's appeal to Yahweh will be met with a stern rebuke rather than immediate assistance. The response of Yahweh in the Jephthah cycle is even more severe; Yahweh is straightforwardly sarcastic in his response to Israel's continuing apostasy. In the Samson cycle, Israel does not appeal to Yahweh at all. From Gideon on, the major/cyclical judges evince significant character flaws. With the Gideon cycle and its sequel the pattern of declivity *within* the repeating pattern of the successive episodes comes sharply into focus.

In the cycles of the first three major/cyclical judges (the In-group judges), things return basically to the status quo that was in effect at the beginning of the cycle. But in the cycles of the last three major/cyclical judges (the Out-

---

51. For the In-group/Out-group distinction, see D. J. Chalcraft, "Deviance and Legitimate Action in the Book of Judges," in *The Bible in Three Dimensions: Essays in Celebration of Forty Years of Biblical Studies in the University of Sheffield*, ed. D. J. A. Clines, S. E. Fowl, and S. E. Porter (JSOTSup 87; Sheffield: Sheffield Academic Press, 1990), 177–207.

52. Exum, "The Centre Cannot Hold," 412.

53. B. Halpern, *The First Historians: The Hebrew Bible and History* (San Francisco: Harper & Row, 1988), 141 n. 9.

---

group judges), things are much worse in Israel than before the beginning of each cycle. By the end of the Gideon/Abimelech cycle, Israel has returned to worshiping the Baals and has begun to unravel internally.[54] It is only after Jephthah reintroduces a situation of instability into Israel (again originating internally, as in the Abimelech story) that the narrator brings to close the account of this deliverer (12:7). Finally, Samson has not delivered Israel (though killing a number of Philistines in his quests for personal revenge); he really only agitates the Philistines into making the oppression worse on Israel.

The motif of fire/burning plays an important role in the Out-group judges. In the case of Gideon, there is the incineration of the sacrifice, the use of three hundred torches, and so on. Jephthah burns his daughter, and the Ephraimites threaten to burn Jephthah's house over him. In the Samson cycle, the Philistines threaten to burn Samson's wife and father-in-law if she does not get the answer to Samson's riddle; three hundred foxes burn the shocks, standing grain, vineyards, and olive groves; the Philistines burn Samson's wife and father-in-law; the ropes with which the Judahites had tied Samson up become as "charred flax" in the presence of the Philistines (15:14); and the fresh bowstrings used in Delilah's first attempt to subdue Samson "snap ... as easily as a piece of string snaps when it comes close to a flame" (16:9).

Note also that the center cycles (Deborah/Barak; Gideon/Abimelech) manifest a propensity for pairs.[55] Deborah and Barak are paired against Jabin and Sisera. There is a pair of rhetorical questions used by Deborah to prompt Barak's military involvement against Sisera (4:6, 14). In addition, the Deborah/Barak cycle is conveyed in two parallel complementary accounts: a prose narration (ch. 4) and a poem (ch. 5). In the Deborah/Barak cycle there are parallel climaxes.

The complete cycle of Gideon/Abimelech manifests a goodly number of pairs. Gideon faces the pairs of Oreb and Zeeb (killed together on the west side of the Jordan) and Zebah and Zalmunna (killed together later on the east side of the Jordan). Other pairs or doublets include: two altar and offering scenes, two names for the hero (Gideon/Jerub-Baal), two different sizes of military force, two battles with surprise attacks, two tests of God by fleece and dew, two towns on which extreme reprisals are executed, and so on.

The Gideon/Abimelech cycle is also conveyed in two climaxes (although nonparallel): the account of Gideon (6:1–8:32) and the account of Abimelech

---

54. The Abimelech account, the sequel to Gideon and conclusion to the fourth cycle, introduces for the first time in the book an oppressor who is internal rather than external. The work of the cyclical/major judge, Gideon, is undone by the antijudge, "king" Abimelech, Gideon's son.

55. This "propensity for pairs" may help explain the preponderance of what have been dubbed "doublets" in the Gideon cycle.

(8:33–9:57). The Abimelech account is really a prolongation of the Gideon account, bringing to resolution a number of complications introduced in the Gideon narrative. Whereas the Gideon account contains a significant usage of the divine name Yahweh, in the Abimelech account the divine name Yahweh does not occur at all (only Elohim). While both narratives address the issue of the danger of kingship, neither condemns kingship as an institution.[56] But they both demonstrate the significant dangers of the wrong kind of kingship, one not patterned according to God's Law (Torah)—that is, one that is Canaanite in its essence. They accomplish this from two different directions: the Gideon narrative is subtle and implicit; the Abimelech story blunt and explicit. Even though Gideon attacks Baal worship and declares Yahweh's kingship, he subverts God's kingship with his own. Abimelech blatantly sets himself up as a king of a Canaanite city with the help of Baal/El.

Both accounts address the issue of infidelity, though the Gideon narrative addresses infidelity to Yahweh ("the Israelites ... did not remember the LORD their God, who had rescued them," 8:33–34), while the Abimelech narrative addresses infidelity to Gideon's family ("[the Israelites] failed to show kindness [*ḥesed*] to the family of Jerub-Baal [that is, Gideon]," 8:35). Finally, in many ways, Jotham's act of challenging the people of Shechem concerning their allegiance to Abimelech is analogous to Gideon's act of destroying the Baal altar and challenging the people of Ophrah concerning their allegiance to Baal.

There are other clear links between the two center cycles. The Deborah/Barak cycle begins with a prophetess (Deborah) ministering to Israel and ends with a woman, introduced late in the narrative, performing a mighty deed as an agent of Yahweh (Jael driving a tent peg into Sisera's skull). The Gideon and Abimelech cycle begins with a prophet (unnamed) challenging Israel (6:7–10) and ends with a woman, introduced late in the narrative, performing a mighty deed as the agent of Yahweh (the certain woman smashing Abimelech's skull with an upper millstone). Both evince Yahweh's sovereign control over circumstances in order to bring about victory (over Sisera or Abimelech) and poetic justice (vis-à-vis Barak or Abimelech).

Besides this propensity for pairing in the two middle cyclical judge narratives, it is also clear that there is a set of three pairings among the cyclical/major judges themselves. Othniel and Ehud form an initial pair. They exhibit the two most successful judges in terms of basic outline. They are also, by far, the two shortest narratives of the six cyclical judges; they are the only two designated by the term "savior/deliverer" (*môšîaʿ*); and they do their delivering in the southern end of the country. The Deborah/Barak cycle and the

---

56. See the discussion of G. E. Gebrandt, *Kingship According to the Deuteronomistic History* (SBLDS 87; Atlanta: Scholars Press, 1986), 123–29.

Gideon/Abimelech cycle form the second pairing (see above for discussion). They are the pivotal cycles with Deborah/Barak being the last of the In-group judges and Gideon/Abimelech being the first of the Out-group cycles. They do their delivering in the northern, Cisjordanian context. Finally, the third pairing is Jephthah and Samson. They evince the most serious character flaws of the six, and the oppressions they address are introduced together (10:6–8). They both feature agreements with leaders, vows to God undone by a female, and so on. In particular, one can see this in the matter of vows. In the case of Jephthah, his manipulative, rash vow is ignorantly fulfilled, whereas in the case of Samson, the God-ordained Nazirite vow is callously broken.

Finally, the three pairings of the cyclical judges can be seen in the type of oppressors/opponents with which they are associated, as the following chart illustrates:[57]

Judge Cycle	*Type of Oppressors*	*Names*
1. Othniel	single, named	Cushan-Rishathaim (*melek*)
2. Ehud	single, named	Eglon (*melek*)
3. Deborah/Barak	pair, named	Jabin (*melek*)/Sisera (*śar*)
4. Gideon/Abimelech	pairs, named	Oreb/Zeeb (*śārîm*); Zebah/Zalmunna (*mᵉlākîm*); Jotham/Gaal
5. Jephthah	single, unnamed	————
6. Samson	multiple, unnamed	————

While there is unquestionably this pairing process with its own internal links, there are also strong links between the pairs themselves. For example, the Ehud and Deborah/Barak cycles evince a number of links, the most obvious being the way in which the death scenes of the oppressors (Eglon and Sisera) are portrayed. Ehud and Jael are painted in similar colors as they execute the enemy leader. There is likewise great similarity between the discovery of the dead Eglon by his Moabite guards and the discovery of Sisera by the pursuing Barak.

There are also strong links between the Gideon/Abimelech cycle and the Jephthah cycle. On the one hand, there are bonds between the Gideon narrative and Jephthah's account. Both open with a confrontation between Yahweh

---

57. Interestingly, the book of Hebrews pairs these judges, with one pair being Gideon and Barak, the other pair being Samson and Jephthah; it leaves out the pair Othniel and Ehud. On the book of Hebrews usage, see the discussion of Samson below, pp. 325–28.

and Israel (6:7–10; 10:6–10). Both men begin as nobodies, become heroes (both characterized as *gibbôr ḥayil*), and end as despots. Both are empowered by the Spirit of Yahweh, which results in the immediate mobilization of troops (6:34–35; 11:29). Both follow up the divine empowerment with expressions of doubt (6:36–40; 11:30–31). Both win great victories over the enemy (7:19–25; 11:32–33). Both must deal with confrontations with the jealous Ephraimites after the battle has been won (8:1–3; 12:1–6). Both brutalize their own countrymen (8:4–17; 12:4–6).[58]

There are strong bonds between the Abimelech account and the Jephthah cycle. Both are children of secondary women (concubine, prostitute; 8:31; 11:1). Both are apparently disinherited by their half-brothers. Both recruit morally empty and reckless men to make up their armed gang (9:4; 11:3). Both are opportunists who negotiate their way into powerful leadership positions (9:1–6; 11:4–11). Both seal the agreement with their subjects in a formal ceremony at a sacred site (9:6; 11:11). Both turn out to be brutal rulers, slaughtering their own relatives (9:5; 11:34–40) and engaging their own countrymen in battle (9:26–57; 12:1–6). Both end up as tragic figures without a future (9:50–57; 11:34–35).[59] Thus Jephthah is in many ways a composite of the two characters of the previous cycle.

Modern scholarship in the main has tended to detach the minor/noncyclical judges from the narrative of the cycles section altogether. It has been divided over who counts as a noncyclical judge and what function or role such judges had. This lack of integration of the noncyclical ("minor") judges in the interpretation of the cycles section has contributed to the inability to comprehend its overarching message. The short notices concerning these judges are not only integral to the message of the cycles section, but also reinforce it. The moral declivity of the major/cyclical judges is also perceptible in the minor/noncyclical judges, as will be made clear in the exposition below.

Some scholars attempt to differentiate between "saving/delivering" judges and "nonsaving" or "administering" judges.[60] However, according to the description of Judges 2, part of the role of a judge included the responsibility of "delivering" Israel from the oppressors. Thus, those judges who do not deliver Israel are simply judges who do not live up to their responsibility. Two of the noncyclical judges (Shamgar and Tola) fulfill this role, although the oth-

---

58. See further the discussion of Block (*Judges, Ruth*, 342–43).

59. For a discussion of many of these, see L. R. Klein, *The Triumph of Irony in the Book of Judges* (BLS 13; Sheffield: Almond, 1988), 83–84.

60. Usually this is based on the observation that none of the five short notices in 10:1–5 and 12:8–15 refer to any external threat or military activity on the part of the judge, and thus these notices must represent generally peaceful interludes. See, for example, Webb, *The Book of the Judges*, 176.

ers do not.[61] Only in the case of Shamgar are the details provided (i.e., he saved Israel from the Philistines, etc.). If Eli and Samuel are included in this discussion, Eli evidently failed in his responsibility, while Samuel succeeded.

That there is no essential difference of the official role between the major/cyclical judges and the minor/noncyclical judges may be discerned both from the fact that the account of Jephthah closes with a pattern formula (12:7) used elsewhere in the minor/noncyclical judges (10:2, 3–5; 12:8–10, 13–15) and from the fact that Tola, a minor/noncyclical judge, is said to have arisen to deliver Israel (10:1)—a description elsewhere limited to the major/cyclical judge accounts.[62]

The initial minor/noncyclical judge formula uses the preposition "after" (*ʾaḥᵃrê*) all six times to introduce each noncyclical judge, usually in the phrase: "and after him. . . ." The one-two-three character of the noncyclical judge reports is also demonstrated by this formula:[63]

1.	Shamgar (3:31a)	"after him was . . ."	*wᵉʾaḥᵃrāyw hāyâ*[64]
2.	Tola (10:1a)	"And there arose after . . ."	*wayyāqom ʾaḥᵃrê*
	Jair (10:3a)	"And there arose after him"	*wayyāqom ʾaḥᵃrāyw*
3.	Ibzan (12:8a)	"And there judged after him"	*wayyišpōṭ ʾaḥᵃrāyw*
	Elon (12:11a)	"And there judged after him"	*wayyišpōṭ ʾaḥᵃrāyw*
	Abdon (12:13a)	"And there judged after him"	*wayyišpōṭ ʾaḥᵃrāyw*

The use of different verbs with the preposition (*ʾaḥᵃrê*) solidifies the one-two-three pattern. Thus this pattern is not fortuitous; rather, it is part of the literary movement that culminates in the climax of the Samson cycle.

Thus in every way, the cycles section of the book reflects a progressive degeneration. By the end of the story of Samson, the reader is left questioning the value of judgeship altogether. This is precisely what the narrator has planned so that his double conclusion to the book will be exactly the proper ending in which the issue of kingship is raised.

---

61. By the way, it is worth noting that Samson fails in saving Israel too. In fact, he doesn't really even attempt to "save" Israel.

62. O'Connell, *The Rhetoric of the Book of Judges*, 3. Cf. also A. J. Hauser, "The 'Minor Judges'— A Re-evaluation," *JBL* 94 (1975): 190–200, esp. 200; and E. T. Mullen Jr., "The 'Minor Judge': Some Literary and Historical Considerations," *CBQ* 44 (1982): 185–201, esp. 201.

63. This formula may be simply a device for signalling the next item for narration and is not indicative of chronology. See also the comment of Block, *Judges, Ruth*, 338 n. 871.

64. I recognize that the precise wording here is unique to the entire Hebrew Bible. But the use of "after" (*ʾaḥᵃrê*) as an introductory phrase of the minor judge still argues for Shamgar's inclusion in the minor judge list. In fact, the pattern revealed in the chart above showing the one-two-three pattern of the minor judges argues conclusively in favor of inclusion.

Bridging Contexts

INTERPRETIVE ISSUES. In bridging the ancient context to the modern, we must keep in mind a basic principle that, while important in the interpretation and application of any passage from the Old Testament, it is especially important in the interpretation and application of the book of Judges. The historical, literary context of this book must be fully understood and appreciated *before* any application can be employed. Observations about the literary or rhetorical structure of the book are not fortuitous; they are not simply "filler" to make this particular commentary a certain length!

The old adage "it's not just what you say; it's how you say it" applies here. It is not just what the book says that is important, it is how the writer has chosen to say it that is also important. Through the historical, literary structure the writer effectively communicated his message to the ancient audience; thus, to ignore it is to diminish the understanding of that message and its application in a modern situation. For example, to not perceive the literary structures in the episode about Othniel (3:7–11) is to lose much of the power of the message of that passage (see below).

Furthermore, to fail to put the individual cyclical ("major") judge narratives into their larger context within the cycles section of the book endangers the proper understanding of the particular cyclical judge narrative (e.g., see comments on the misinterpretation of the Gideon and Samson narratives above, pp. 34–37). The downward spiral of these judges must be kept in mind at each point in the cycles section.

Another danger to avoid is the common fallacy of moralizing the message of the Old Testament. Many sermons and much teaching on the book of Judges err by falling into the trap of simply turning the book's characters into heroes and villains: "Be like Gideon!" or "Don't be like Barak!" Such an approach removes the focus of the book from the intended main point, God, and thus misses the power of the passage.[65] This kind of preaching never pays any attention to the macrostructures and literary development of the message of the book. For if attention were paid to this, one would never, knowing the full development of the Gideon/Abimelech cycle, want a person to simply "be like Gideon."

We are not advocating that the actions of the various characters are irrelevant to the modern Christian. When Samson blatantly breaks his Nazirite vows, this action is theologically instructive to the modern reader—not in

---

65. Following the warning given by J. H. Walton, L. D. Bailey, and C. Williford, "Bible Based Curricula and the Crisis of Scriptural Authority," *Christian Education Journal* 13 (1993): 83–94.

the sense that we should take Nazirite vows and be careful not to break them, but in the sense that we should avoid the self-absorbed narcissism that Samson manifested in the process of which he carelessly broke his commitments to God.

The Old Testament historical books are not just there to teach us what happened in the past or to inform us about the nature of God in the abstract, but are also intended to shape our emotions and our actions. The Old Testament is not a philosophical or theological treatise, nor is it a systematic theology for use only in the classroom. The Old Testament narratives have a didactic intention to stimulate godly living through the stories of God's interaction with his people in the past.[66] The Word of God is intended to motivate us intellectually, emotionally, and spiritually to serve God. But to explicate this means that we must strive to implement a thorough investigation of the historical, literary context of the book in its canonical place.

Cultural, religious issues. On the surface, it appears that there is little connection between the ancient Israelite religious context and the contemporary religious scene. There is little danger today that people will worship Baal or Asherah or any of the various Canaanite deities. But there are three problems here.

(1) There is a general misunderstanding of the dangers of idolatry even in a modern context. Idolatry is not simply the making and worshiping of a graven image. Idolatry is the blurring or obscuring of the distinction between the living God who creates and the creation he has created (Ex. 20:4–6). Anything that is substituted or added to the worship of the one true God is idolatry. The myth of secularism is that idolatry cannot exist in a secular society, for secular society has no god at its heart whose reality makes other objects of worship into idols. But idolatry does exist in so-called secular society. Secularization has a constant, ever-present friend labeled by sociologists as sacralization—the development by which "people, things, events and processes are bestowed with 'sacred' status" (e.g., money, self, human sexuality, etc.).[67]

(2) There is a misunderstanding of the nature and especially the goals of ancient Baal and Asherah worship. Both deities were part of a wider fertility religion. Cults connected to fertility were concerned about securing for the worshiper a large family, large flocks and herds, and abundant crops, all of which are connected to material prosperity. Certainly, the materialistic emphasis of our modern culture corresponds to this (see comments on 2:6–3:6).

---

66. See T. Longman III, *Literary Approaches to Biblical Interpretation* (Grand Rapids: Zondervan, 1987), 70.

67. I. Provan, "To Highlight All Our Idols: Worshipping God in Nietzsche's World," *Ex Auditu* 15 (1999): 19–42.

(3) There is an unawareness that at the heart of idolatry is the concept of magic. While the cult image was seen to be the joint product of human and divine artisans, the human artisans were perceived to be acting on behalf of the gods in fashioning the statues, and any skill that they displayed was ultimately that of specific craft deities. Thus we end up with human artisans even disavowing that they have crafted the deity, for, in Esarhaddon's words, "the making of [images of] the gods and goddesses is your [i.e., Ashur's and Marduk's] right, it is in your hands."[68]

It is clear that statues could not "become divine" through mere human activity. The living presence of the god in the image was magically accomplished through the famous *pīt pî* or *mīs pî* ("opening of the mouth" or "washing of the mouth") ceremony.[69] This nocturnal ritual[70] was performed in the craftsman's workshop so that the work of human hands was thought to magically come alive. The cult image became the vessel for the deity. In fact, precise methods of production of cult images were followed in the ancient Near East. The statues had to be made of specific materials, and detailed procedures had to be followed in their manufacture. If these things were not done and done properly, the magical indwelling of the cult image by the deity could not take place. One Akkadian text reads: "This [statue?] without the mouth-opening ceremony [*pīt pî*] cannot smell incense, cannot eat food, and cannot drink water."

But once this ceremony had taken place, the cult image became the primary focus of the deity's presence on earth. Oppenheim puts it this way: "Fundamentally, the deity was considered present in its image.... The god moved with the image when it was carried off.... Only on the mythological level were the deities thought to reside in the cosmic localities."[71] This is why cult images/idols were taken away from a conquered people and deposited in the temple of the victorious god (cf. the famous and somewhat humorous story of the captured ark of the covenant in the temple of Dagon

68. Esarhaddon's "Renewal of the Gods," a text that describes at great length the renewal (or better, the "remaking") of the cult images. See R. Borger, *Die Inschriften Asarhaddons Königs von Assyrien* (AfO 9; Osnabrück: Biblio-Verlag, 1956), §53, AsBbA Rs. 2–38.

69. C. Walker and M. B. Dick, "The Induction of the Cult Image in Ancient Mesopotamia: The Mesopotamian *mīs pî* Ritual," in *Born in Heaven, Made on Earth: The Making of the Cult Image in the Ancient Near East,* ed. M. B. Dick (Winona Lake, Ind.: Eisenbrauns, 1999), 55–122.

70. This was "a performative ritual designed to dissociate the statue from its aspects of man-made artifact" (see T. N. D. Mettinger, *No Graven Image? Israelite Aniconism in Its Ancient Near Eastern Context* [Coniectanea Biblica, Old Testament Series 42; Stockholm: Almqvist & Wiksell, 1995], 41).

71. A. L. Oppenheim, *Ancient Mesopotamia,* 2d ed. (Chicago: Univ. of Chicago Press, 1977), 184.

in 1 Sam. 5–6). The terms ṣalmu or ṣelem ("image") could also be used to refer to the cult "symbol," which, on occasion, could even be understood as the deity itself.[72]

The presence of the deity in the statue was then maintained magically through offerings and the proper care of the statue. If improper attention was given to the cult image, the deity could withdraw of its own free will. In addition, the deity could be forced to withdraw through desecration of the physical object (this explains the purposeful overturning and destruction of cult images by conquering armies, who were too busy or lazy to carry them off).

Thus in the production of the idol, in the idol's embodiment by the deity, and in the maintenance of deity's indwelling of the idol, there was a significant degree of control exercised by the human manufacturers and worshipers through magical means. The second commandment (Ex. 20:4–6) addresses especially the issue of the cult image[73] since this is a *human manipulative attempt* that inverts the created order. Consequently, any human attempt to manipulate God, whether in thought, intent, or action, is a serious breech of the second commandment.

THE BOOK OF JUDGES has great contemporary significance. Recently I taught a Doctor of Ministry course to about twenty pastors from Canada and the western part of the United States. At the end of the course, to a person, they all expressed their surprise at how relevant the book of Judges is to the modern context. We live today in a Western society that has been dubbed by one scholar as "neo-pagan."[74] With the decline of the influence of Christianity during the nineteenth and twentieth centuries, the unbelief that underlies Western culture has become more predominant.[75] While it is chiefly in the philosophic and religious spheres that this is especially true, the impact on other areas has been fully felt at the beginning of the twenty-first century. The apostasy of the Israelites in their worship of Yahweh finds particular relevance to the modern problems of

---

72. Compare the Neo-Assyrian letter that states: "The *kizertu* is set up in the temple; they say about it: 'It is Nabû'" (*LAS* 318:6–7). Cf. also the Tanit signs, Baal Hammon signs, etc., in Phoenician contexts.

73. As opposed to the cosmic manifestations of the ancient Near Eastern deities, which are addressed in the first commandment (Ex. 20:3).

74. C. F. H. Henry, *Twilight of a Great Civilization: The Drift Toward Neo-Paganism* (Westchester, Ill.: Crossway, 1988).

75. This underlying unbelief is traceable in Western culture back to the Renaissance.

materialism, hedonism, and narcissism (see comments on 2:6–3:6). Carl Henry sums this up:

> These factors—the extensive loss of God through a commanding spread of atheism, the collapse of modern philosophical supports for human rights, the brutish dehumanization of life which beyond abortion and terrorism could encourage also a future acceptance even of nuclear war, and a striking shift of sexual behavior that welcomes not only divorce and infidelity but devious alternatives to monogamous marriage as well—attest that radical secularism grips the life of Western man more firmly than at any time since the pre-Christian pagan era. Still more disconcerting is the fact that modernity deliberately experiences this new immorality as an option superior to the inherited Judeo-Christian alternative. What underlies the atheistic commitment to novel sexual and marital and political patterns is a stultification of Biblical conscience, an irreligious redefinition of the good, a profane willset.[76]

While the overall message of Judges records increasing and devastating failures by the human participants with an almost depressing feeling coming upon the reader by the end of the narration,[77] it is important to recognize that the book reveals important truths about God and his sovereignty, grace, and faithfulness. At the end it is hard not to appreciate the great longsuffering of God toward his people and humanity in general. The appalling and dreadful degeneration exhibited in the downward spiral of the cycles section and the self-destructive behavior and depravity of the double conclusion only stress in contrast how much God loves. Were it not for his great everlasting compassion and patience, who would not be consumed?

---

76. Henry, *Twilight of a Great Civilization*, 27.

77. It is hard to preach or teach the double conclusion of the book (chs. 17–21) without feeling some of this depression.

Outline of Judges

Bibliography on Judges

Achtemeier, P. J. "Gods Made with Hands: The New Testament and the Problem of Idolatry." *Ex Auditu* 15 (1999): 43–61.

Alonso-Schökel, L. "Erzählkunst im Buche der Richter." *Bib* 42 (1961): 143–72.

Alter, R. *The Art of Biblical Narrative*. New York: Basic Books, 1981.

Alter, R., and F. Kermode, eds. *The Literary Guide to the Bible*. Cambridge, Mass.: Harvard Univ. Press, 1987.

Amit, Y. "Judges 4: Its Contents and Form." *JSOT* 39 (1987): 89–111.

_____. "The Story of Ehud (Judges 3:12–30): The Form and the Message." Pp. 97–123 in *Signs and Wonders: Biblical Texts in Literary Focus*. Ed. J. C. Exum. Decatur, Ga.: Scholars, 1989.

Auld, A. G. "Gideon: Hacking at the Heart of the Old Testament." *VT* 39 (1989): 257–67.

_____. *Joshua, Judges, and Ruth*. The Daily Study Bible. Philadelphia: Westminster, 1984.

Bal, M. *Murder and Difference: Gender, Genre, and Scholarship on Sisera's Death*. Trans. by M. Gumpert. Bloomington: Indiana Univ. Press, 1988.

Barré, M. L. "The Meaning of *pršdn* in Judges iii.22." *VT* 41 (1991): 1–11.

Beem, B. "The Minor Judges: A Literary Reading of Some Very Short Stories." Pp. 147–72 in *The Canon in Comparative Perspective: Scripture in Context IV*. Ed. K. L. Younger Jr., W. W. Hallo, and B. F. Batto. ANETS 11. Lewiston, N.Y.: Edwin Mellen, 1991.

Beyerlin, W. "Gattung und Herkunft des Rahmens im Richtersbuch." Pp. 6–7 in *Tradition und Situation: Studien zur alttestamentlichen Prophetie; Festschrift A. Weiser*. Ed. E. Würthwein and O. Kaiser. Göttingen: Vandenhoeck & Ruprecht, 1963.

Block, D. I. "Echo Narrative Technique in Hebrew Literature: A Study of Judges 19." *WTJ* 52 (1990): 325–41.

_____. "Empowered by the Spirit of God: The Work of the Holy Spirit in the Historiographic Writings of the Old Testament." *SBJT* 1 (1997): 42–61.

_____. *The Foundations of National Identity: A Study in Ancient Northwest Semitic Perspectives*. Ann Arbor, Mich.: University Microfilms, 1983.

_____. "'Israel'—'Sons of Israel': A Study in Hebrew Eponymic Usage." *Studies in Religion* 13 (1984): 301–26.

_____. *Judges, Ruth*. NAC 6. Nashville: Broadman & Holman, 1999.

_____. "The Period of the Judges: Religious Disintegration Under Tribal Rule." Pp. 41–45 in *Israel's Apostasy and Restoration: Essays in Honor of Roland K. Harrison*. Ed. A. Gileadi. Grand Rapids: Baker, 1988.

Boling, R. G. *Judges: Introduction, Translation and Commentary*. AB 6A. Garden City: N.Y.: Doubleday, 1975.

_____ . "Judges, Book of." *ABD*, 3:1107–17.

Brenner, A. "A Triangle and a Rhombus in Narrative Structure: A Proposed Integrative Reading of Judges IV and V." *VT* 40 (1990): 129–38.

Brettler, M. Z. "The Book of Judges: Literature as Politics." *JBL* 108 (1989): 395–418.

_____. *The Creation of History in Ancient Israel*. London and New York: Routledge, 1995.

Browne, E. "Samson: Riddle and Paradox." *TBT* 22 (1984): 161–67.

Brueggemann, W. "Social Criticism and Social Vision in the Deuteronomic Formula of Judges." Pp. 101–14 in *Die Botschaft und die Boten: Festschrift für Hans Walter Wolff zum 70. Geburtstag*. Ed. J. Jeremias and L. Perlitt. Neukirchen-Vluyn: Neukirchener Verlag, 1981.

Burney, C. F. *The Book of Judges with Introduction and Notes*. 1st ed. 1903; 2d ed. 1920. Repr., New York: Ktav, 1970.

Cahill, J., et al., "It Had to Happen—Scientists Examine Remains of Ancient Bathroom." *BAR* 17 (May/June 1991): 64–69.

Campbell, E. F., Jr. "Judges 9 and Archaeology." Pp. 263–67 in *Essays in Honor of David Noel Freedman in Celebration of his Sixtieth Birthday*. Ed. C. Meyers and M. O'Connor. Winona Lake, Ind.: Eisenbrauns, 1983.

_____. *Shechem II: Portrait of a Hill Country Vale*. ASOR Archaeology Reports 2. Atlanta: Scholars Press, 1991.

Chalcraft, D. J. "Deviance and Legitimate Action in the Book of Judges." Pp. 177–207 in *The Bible in Three Dimensions: Essays in Celebration of Forty Years of Biblical Studies in the University of Sheffield*. Ed. D. J. A. Clines, S. E. Fowl, and S. E. Porter. JSOTSup 87. Sheffield: Sheffield Academic, 1990.

Childs, B. S. *Introduction to the Old Testament As Scripture*. Philadelphia: Fortress, 1979.

Coogan, M. D. "A Structural and Literary Analysis of the Song of Deborah." *CBQ* 40 (1978): 143–66.

Craigie, P. C. *The Problem of War in the Old Testament*. Grand Rapids: Eerdmans, 1978.

_____. "A Reconsideration of Shamgar Ben Anath (Judg 3:31 and 5:6)." *JBL* 91 (1972): 239–40.

Crenshaw, J. L. *Samson: A Secret Betrayed, a Vow Ignored*. Macon, Ga.: Mercer Univ. Press, 1978.

Cundall, A. E. *Judges: An Introduction and Commentary*. Downers Grove, Ill.: InterVarsity, 1968.

Dearman, J. A. "Baal in Israel: The Contribution of Some Place Names and Personal Names to an Understanding of Early Israelite Religion." Pp.

173–91 in *History and Interpretation: Essays in Honour of John H. Hayes*. Ed. M. P. Graham, W. P. Brown, and J. K. Kuan. JSOTSup 173. Sheffield: Sheffield Academic Press, 1993.

Dumbrell, W. J. "'In Those Days There Was No King in Israel; Every Man Did What Was Right in His Own Eyes': The Purpose of the Book of Judges Reconsidered." *JSOT* 25 (1983): 23–33.

Emerton, J. A. "Some Comments on the Shibboleth Incident (Judges XII 6)." Pp. 149–57 in *Mélanges bibliques et orientaux en l'honneur de M. Mathias Delcor*. Ed. A. Caquot, S. Légasse, and M. Tardie. AOAT 215. Neukirchen-Vluyn: Neukirchener Verlag, 1985.

Eshel, H., and Z. Erlich, "Abimelech's First Battle with the Lords of Shechem and the Question of the Navel of the Land." *Tarbiz* 58 (1988–89): 111–16.

Exum, J. C. "Aspects of Symmetry and Balance in the Samson Saga." *JSOT* 19 (1981): 3–29.

_____. "The Centre Cannot Hold: Thematic and Textual Instabilities in Judges." *CBQ* 52 (1990): 410–31.

_____. "Feminist Criticism: Whose Interests Are Being Served?" Pp. 65–90 in *Judges and Method: New Approaches in Biblical Studies*. Ed. G. A. Yee. Minneapolis: Fortress, 1995.

_____. "Literary Patterns in the Samson Saga: An Investigation of Rhetorical Style in Biblical Prose." Ph.D. diss. Columbia University, 1976.

_____. "Promise and Fulfillment: Narrative Art in Judges 13." *JBL* 99 (1980): 43–59.

Faber, A. "Second Harvest: *šibbōlet* Revisited (Yet Again)." *JSS* 37 (1992): 1–10.

Fensham, F. C. "Literary Observations on Historical Narratives in Sections of Judges." Pp. 77–88 in *Storia e tradizioni di Israele: Scitti in onore di J. Alberto Soggin*. Ed. D. Garrone and F. Israel. Brescia: Paideia, 1991.

_____. "Shamgar ben Anath." *JNES* 20 (1961): 197–98.

Fewell, D. N. "Judges." Pp. 67–77 in *The Women's Bible Commentary*. Ed. C. A. Newsom and S. H. Ringe. Louisville: Westminster/John Knox, 1992.

Fewell, D. N., and D. M. Gunn, "Controlling Perspectives: Women, Men and the Authority of Violence in Judges 4 and 5." *JAAR* 58 (1990): 389–411.

Fields, W. W. "The Motif 'Night As Danger' Associated with Three Biblical Destruction Narratives." Pp. 17–32 in *"Shaʿarei Talmon": Studies in the Bible, Qumran, and the Ancient Near East Presented to Shemaryahu Talmon*. Ed. M. Fishbane and E. Tov with W. W. Fields. Winona Lake, Ind.: Eisenbrauns, 1992.

Fishbane, M. *Biblical Interpretation in Ancient Israel*. Oxford: Clarendon, 1986.

Fleming, D. E. "The Etymological Origins of the Hebrew *nābîʾ*: The One Who Invokes God." *CBQ* 55 (1993): 217–24.

Fokkelman, J. P. "The Song of Deborah and Barak: Its Prosodic Levels and Structure." Pp. 595–628 in *Pomegranates and Golden Bells: Studies in Biblical, Jew-*

ish, and Near Eastern Ritual, Law, and Literature in Honor of Jacob Milgrom. Ed. D. P. Wright, D. N. Freedman, and A. Hurvitz. Winona Lake, Ind.: Eisenbrauns, 1995.

_____. "Structural Remarks on Judges 9 and 19." Pp. 33–45 in *"Shaᶜarei Talmon": Studies in the Bible, Qumran, and the Ancient Near East Presented to Shemaryahu Talmon*. Ed. M. Fishbane and E. Tov with W. W. Fields. Winona Lake, Ind.: Eisenbrauns, 1992.

Fowler, M. "A Closer Look at the Temple of El-Berith at Shechem." *PEQ* 115 (1983): 49–53.

Freedman, D. N. "A Note on Judges 15,5." *Bib* 52 (1971): 535.

Freeman, J. A. "Samson's Dry Bones: A Structural Reading of Judges 13–16." Pp. 145–60 in vol. 2 of *Literary Interpretations of Biblical Narratives*. Ed. K. R. R. Gros Louis. 2 vols. Nashville: Abingdon, 1974, 1982.

Gal, Z. "The Settlement of Issachar: Some New Observations." *Tel Aviv* 9 (1982): 79–86.

Garsiel, M. *Biblical Names: A Literary Study of Midrashic Deriviations and Puns*. Trans. P. Hackett. Ramat-Gan: Bar-Ilan Univ. Press, 1991.

Gebrandt, G. E. *Kingship According to the Deuteronomistic History*. SBLDS 87. Atlanta: Scholars Press, 1986.

Gevirtz, S. "Jericho and Shechem: A Religio-Literary Aspect of City Destruction." *VT* 13 (1963): 52–62.

Gooding, D. W. "The Composition of the Book of Judges." Pp. 70–79 in *H. M. Orlinsky Memorial Volume*. Eretz Israel 16. Jerusalem: Israel Exploration Society, 1982.

Görg, M. "Zu den Kleiderbezeichnungen in Ri 14,12f." *BN* 68 (1993): 5–9.

Goslinga, C. J. *Joshua, Judges, Ruth*. Bible Student's Commentary. Grand Rapids: Eerdmans, 1986.

Gray, J. *Joshua, Judges and Ruth*. NCB. London: Thomas Nelson, 1967.

Greenspahn, F. E. "The Theology of the Framework of Judges." *VT* 36 (1986): 385–96.

Greenstein, E. L. "The Riddle of Samson." *Prooftexts* 1/3 (1981): 237–60.

Gros Louis, K. R. R. "The Book of Judges." Pp. 141–62 in vol. 1 of *Literary Interpretations of Biblical Narratives*. Ed. K. R. R. Gros Louis. 2 vols. Nashville: Abingdon, 1974, 1982.

Grottanelli, C. "Aspetti simbolici del latte nella bibbia." Pp. 381–97 in *Drinking in Ancient Societies: History and Culture of Drinks in the Ancient Near East. Papers of a Symposium Held in Rome, May 17–19, 1990*. Ed. L. Milano. Padova: Sargon, 1994.

_____. "The Story of Deborah and Barak: A Comparative Approach." *Studi e Materiali di Storia delle Religioni* N.S. 11 (1987): 311–16.

Gunn, D. M. "Joshua and Judges." Pp. 102–21 in *The Literary Guide to the Bible*. Ed. R. Alter and F. Kermode. Cambridge, Mass.: Harvard Univ. Press, 1987.

Gunn, D. M., and D. N. Fewell. *Narrative in the Hebrew Bible*. The Oxford Bible Series. Oxford: Oxford Univ. Press, 1993.

Hadley, J. M. "The Fertility of the Flock? The De-Personalization of Astarte in the Old Testament." Pp. 115–33 in *On Reading Prophetic Texts: Gender-Specific and Related Studies in Memory of Fokkelien van Dijk-Hemmes*. Ed. B. Becking and M. Dijkstra. Biblical Interpretation Series 18. Leiden: Brill, 1996.

Halpern, B. *The First Historians: The Hebrew Bible and History*. San Francisco: Harper & Row, 1988.

Handy, L. K. "Uneasy Laughter: Ehud and Eglon and Ethnic Humor." *SJOT* 6 (1992): 233–46.

Hauser, A. J. "The 'Minor Judges'—A Re-evaluation." *JBL* 94 (1975): 190–200.

_____. "Two Songs of Victory: A Comparison of Exodus 15 and Judges 5." Pp. 265–84 in *Directions in Biblical Hebrew Poetry*. Ed. E. Follis. Sheffield: JSOT Press, 1987.

_____. "Unity and Diversity in Early Israel Before Samuel." *JETS* 22 (1979): 289–303.

Hendel, R. "Aniconism and Anthropomorphism in Ancient Israel." Pp. 205–28 in *The Image and the Book: Iconic Cults, Aniconism, and the Veneration of the Holy Book in Israel and the Ancient Near East*. Ed. K. van der Toorn. Kampen: Kok, 1999.

Henry, C. F. H. *Twilight of a Great Civilization: The Drift Toward Neo-Paganism*. Westchester, Ill.: Crossway, 1988.

Hess, R. S. "Asherah or Asherata?" *Or* 65 (1996): 209–19.

_____. *Joshua. An Introduction and Commentary*. TOTC. Leicester: Inter-Varsity, 1996.

_____. "Non-Israelite Personal Names in the Narratives of the Book of Joshua." *CBQ* 58 (1996): 205–14.

_____. "Yahweh and His Asherah? Religious Pluralism in the Old Testament World." Pp. 13–42 in *One God, One Lord: Christianity in a World of Religious Pluralism*. Ed. A. D. Clarke and B. W. Winter. Grand Rapids: Eerdmans, 1993.

Hoffmeier, J. K. *Egypt in Israel: The Evidence for the Authenticity of the Exodus Tradition*. New York/Oxford: Oxford Univ. Press, 1997.

Howard, D. M., Jr. "Philistines." Pp. 231–50 in *Peoples of the Old Testament World*. Ed. A. J. Hoerth et al. Grand Rapids: Baker, 1994.

Hübner, U. "Mord auf dem Abort? Überlegungen zu Humor, Gewaltdarstellung und Realienkunde in Ri 3,12–30." *BN* 40 (1987): 130–40.

Hudson, D. M. "Living in a Land of Epithets: Anonymity in Judges 19–21." *JSOT* 62 (1994): 49–66.

Kallai, Z. "The Twelve-Tribe Systems of Israel." *VT* 47 (1997): 53–90.

Kaufmann, Y. *The Book of Judges*. Jerusalem: Kiryat Sepher, 1962 (Hebrew).

Klein, L. R. *The Triumph of Irony in the Book of Judges.* BLS 14. Sheffield: Almond, 1988.

Kraeling, E. G. H. "Difficulties in the Story of Ehud." *JBL* 54 (1935): 205–10.

Lambert, F. "Tribal Influences in Old Testament Tradition." *SEÅ* 59 (1994): 33–58.

Lasine, S. "Guest and Host in Judges 19: Lot's Hospitality in an Inverted World." *JSOT* 29 (1984): 37–59.

Layton, S. *Archaic Features of Canaanite Names in the Hebrew Bible.* HSM 47. Atlanta: Scholars, 1990.

Lewis, T. J. "The Identity and Function of El/Baal Berith." *JBL* 115 (1996): 401–23.

Lilley, J. P. U. "A Literary Appreciation of the Book of Judges." *TynBul* 17 (1967): 94–102.

_____. "Understanding the *ḥerem*." *TynBul* 44 (1993): 169–77.

Lindars, B. "Deborah's Song: Women in the Old Testament." *BJRL* 65 (1982–93): 158–75.

_____. *Judges 1–5: A New Translation and Commentary.* Ed. A. D. H. Mayes. Edinburgh: T. & T. Clark, 1995.

Longman, T., III. *Literary Approaches to Biblical Interpretation.* Grand Rapids: Zondervan, 1987.

Mafico, T. L. J. "Judge, Judging." *ABD*, 3:1104–5.

Maisler, B. "Shamgar ben ʿAnat." *PEQ* 66 (1934): 192–94.

Malamat, A. "The Period of the Judges." Pp. 129–63 in *Judges.* Ed. B. Mazar. WHJP 3. Tel Aviv: Jewish History Publications, 1971.

Marcus, D. "The Bargaining Between Jephthah and the Elders (Judges 11:4–11)." *JANES* 19 (1989): 95–110.

_____. *Jephthah and His Vow.* Lubbock: Texas Tech Univ. Press, 1986.

_____. "The Legal Dispute Between Jephthah and the Elders." *HAR* 12 (1990): 107–11.

_____. "Ridiculing the Ephraimites: The Shibboleth Incident (Judg 12:6)." *Maarav* 8 (1992): 95–105.

Marius, J. *Representation in Old Testament Narrative Texts.* Leiden: Brill, 1998.

Martin, J. D. *The Book of Judges.* CBC. Cambridge: Cambridge Univ. Press, 1975.

Mazar, A. "Bronze Bull Found in Israelite 'High Place' From the Time of the Judges." *BAR* 9 (September/October 1983): 34–40.

_____. "The Bull Site—An Iron Age I Open Cult Place." *BASOR* 247 (1982): 27–42.

McConville, J. G. *Grace in the End: A Study in Deuteronomic Theology.* SOTBT. Grand Rapids: Zondervan, 1993.

McKenzie, S. L. "Deuteronomistic History." *ABD*, 2:160–68.

Millard, A. R. "Back to the Iron Bed: Og's or Procrustes?" Pp. 193–203 in *Congress Volume: Paris 1992*. Ed. J. A. Emerton. VTSup 61. Leiden: Brill, 1995.

Miller, G. P. "Verbal Feud in the Hebrew Bible: Judges 3:12–30 and 19–21." *JNES* 55 (1996): 105–17.

Moore, G. F. *A Critical and Exegetical Commentary on Judges*. ICC. Edinburgh: T. & T. Clark, 1895.

Mosca, P. G. "Who Seduced Whom? A Note on Joshua 15:18//Judges 1:14." *CBQ* 46 (1984): 18–22.

Mullen, E. T., Jr. "Judges 1:1–36: The Deuteronomistic Reintroduction of the Book of Judges." *HTR* 77 (1984): 33–54.

_____. "The 'Minor Judge': Some Literary and Historical Considerations." *CBQ* 44 (1982): 185–201.

Murray, D. F. "Narrative Structure and Technique in the Deborah-Barak Story, Judges iv 4–22." Pp. 155–89 in *Studies in the Historical Books of the Old Testament*. Ed. J. A. Emerton. VTSup 30. Leiden: Brill, 1979.

Neef, H.-D. "Der Stil des Deboraliedes (Ri 5)." *ZAH* 8 (1995): 275–93.

Niditch, S. "Samson As Culture Hero, Trickster, and Bandit: The Empowerment of the Weak." *CBQ* 52 (1990): 608–24.

_____. "The 'Sodomite' Theme in Judges 19–20: Family, Community, and Social Disintegration." *CBQ* 44 (1982): 365–78.

Noort, E. "Joshua 24,28–31, Richter 2,6–9 und das Josuagrab: Gedanken zu einem Strassenbild." Pp. 109–33 in *Biblische Welten: Festschrift für Martin Metzger zu seinem 65. Geburtstag*. Ed. W. Zwickel. OBO 123. Fribourg: Edition universitaires/Göttingen: Vandenhoeck & Ruprecht, 1993.

O'Brien, M. A. "Judges and the Deuteronomistic History." Pp. 235–59 in *The History of Israel's Traditions: The Heritage of Martin Noth*. Ed. S. L. McKenzie and M. P. Graham. JSOTSup 182. Sheffield: Sheffield Academic Press, 1994.

O'Connell, R. H. "Deuteronomy vii 1–26: Asymmetrical Concentricity and the Rhetoric of Conquest." *VT* 42 (1992): 248–65.

_____ *The Rhetoric of the Book of Judges*. VTSup 63. Leiden: Brill, 1996.

O'Connor, M. "The Women in the Book of Judges." *HAR* 10 (1986): 277–93.

Ogden, G. S. "Jotham's Fable: Its Structure and Function in Judges 9." *BT* 46 (1995): 301–8.

Polzin, R. M. *Moses and the Deuteronomist: A Literary Study of the Deuteronomic History; Part One: Deuteronomy, Joshua, Judges*. New York: Seabury, 1980.

Provan, I. "To Highlight All Our Idols: Worshipping God in Nietzsche's World." *Ex Auditu* 15 (1999): 19–42.

Rainey, A. F. "The Military Camp Ground at Taanach by the Waters of Megiddo." *ErIsr* 15 (1981): 61*–66*.

_____. "Toponymic Problems." *Tel Aviv* 10 (1983): 46–48.

_____. "Who Is a Canaanite?" *BASOR* 304 (1996): 1–15.

Revell, E. J. "The Battle with Benjamin (Judges xx 29–48) and Hebrew Narrative Techniques." *VT* 35 (1985): 417–33.

Rosner, B. "Soul Idolatry: Greed As Idolatry in the Bible." *Ex Auditu* 15 (1999): 73–86.

Sasson, J. M. "Who Cut Samson's Hair? (And Other Trifling Issues Raised by Judges 16)." *Prooftexts* 8 (1988): 334–35.

Satterthwaite, P. E. "Narrative Artistry in the Composition of Judges xx 29ff." *VT* 42 (1992): 80–89.

_____. "'No King in Israel': Narrative Criticism and Judges 17–21." *TynBul* 44 (1993): 75–88.

Schäfer-Lichtenberger, C. "Bedeutung und Funktion von ḥērem in biblisch-hebräischen Texten." *BZ* 38 (1994): 270–75.

Schlossberg, H. *Idols for Destruction: Christian Faith and Its Confronation with American Society.* Nashville: Nelson, 1983.

Shupak, N. "New Light on Shamgar ben 'Anath." *Bib* 70 (1989): 517–25.

Smelik, W. F. *The Targum of Judges.* OTS 36. Leiden: Brill, 1995.

Soggin, J. A. "Ehud und 'Eglon: Bemerkingen zu Richter iii 11b–31." *VT* 29 (1989): 95–100.

_____. *Judges: A Commentary.* Trans. J. Bowden. OTL 7. Philadelphia: Westminster, 1981.

Stager, L. E. "Archaeology, Ecology, and Social History: Background Themes to the Song of Deborah." Pp. 221–33 in *Congress Volume: Jerusalem, 1986.* Ed. J. A. Emerton. VTSup 40. Leiden: Brill, 1988.

_____ "Shemer's Estate." *BASOR* 277/278 (1990): 93–108.

Streck, M. P., and St. Weninger, "Zur Deutung des hebräischen Namens ʿOṯnīʾēl." *BN* 96 (1999): 21–29.

Sweeney, M. A. "Davidic Polemics in the Book of Judges." *VT* 47 (1997): 517–29.

Tanner, J. P. "The Gideon Narrative As the Focal Point of Judges." *BSac* 149 (1992): 146–61.

_____. "Textual Patterning in Biblical Hebrew Narrative: A Case Study in Judges 6–8." Ph.D. diss. University of Texas, Austin, 1990.

Taylor, J. G. "The Bible and Homosexuality." *Themelios* 21/1 (1995): 4–9.

Trible, P. *Texts of Terror: Literary-Feminist Readings of Biblical Narratives.* OBT. Philadelphia: Fortress, 1984.

Waldman, N. M. "The Imagery of Clothing, Covering, and Overpowering." *JANES* 19 (1989): 161–70.

Walton, J., V. H. Matthews, and M. W. Chavalas. *The IVP Background Commentary: Old Testament.* Downers Grove, Ill.: InterVarsity, 2000.

Webb, B. G. *The Book of the Judges: An Integrated Reading.* JSOTSup 46. Sheffield: Sheffield Academic Press, 1987.

_____ "A Serious Reading of the Samson Story (Judges 13–16)." *RTR* 54 (1995): 110–20.

Westbrook, R. *Property and the Family in Biblical Law.* JSOTSup 113. Sheffield: Sheffield Academic Press, 1991.

Wilcock, M. *The Message of Judges.* BST. Downers Grove, Ill.: InterVarsity, 1992.

Willis, T. M. "The Nature of Jephthah's Authority." *CBQ* 59 (1997): 33–44.

Wilson, M. K. "As You Like It: The Idolatry of Micah and the Danites (Judges 17–18)." *RTR* 54 (1995): 73–85.

Wolf, Herbert. "Judges." Pp. 375–506 in *The Expositor's Bible Commentary*, vol. 3. Ed. F. E. Gaebelein. Grand Rapids: Zondervan, 1992.

Yee, G. "By the Hand of a Woman: The Metaphor of the Woman Warrior in Judges 4." *Semeia* 61 (1993): 99–132.

_____ . "Ideological Criticism: Judges 17–21 and the Dismembered Body." Pp. 146–70 in *Judges and Method: New Approaches in Biblical Studies.* Ed. G. A. Yee. Minneapolis: Fortress, 1995.

Younger, K. L., Jr. *Ancient Conquest Accounts: A Study in Ancient Near Eastern and Biblical History Writing.* JSOTSup 98. Sheffield: Sheffield Academic Press, 1990.

_____ . "The Configuring of Judicial Preliminaries: Judges 1:1–2:5 and Its Dependence on the Book of Joshua." *JSOT* 68 (1995): 75–92.

_____ . "Early Israel in Recent Biblical Scholarship." Pp. 176–206 in *The Face of Old Testament Studies: A Survey of Contemporary Approaches.* Ed. D. W. Baker and B. T. Arnold. Grand Rapids: Baker, 1999.

_____ . "Heads! Tails! Or the Whole Coin?! Contextual Method and Intertextual Analysis: Judges 4 and 5." Pp. 109–45 in *The Canon in Comparative Perspective: Scripture in Context IV.* Ed. K. L. Younger, W. W. Hallo, and B. F. Batto; Lewiston, N.Y.: Edwin Mellen, 1991.

_____ . "Judges 1 in Its Near Eastern Literary Context." Pp. 207–27 in *Faith, Tradition, History: Essays on Old Testament Historiography in Its Near Eastern Context.* Ed. A. R. Millard, J. K. Hoffmeier, and A. D. Baker. Winona Lake, Ind.: Eisenbrauns, 1994.

Zakovitch, Y. "The Sacrifice of Gideon (Jud 6,11–24) and the Sacrifice of Manoah (Jud 13)." *Shnaton* 1 (1975): 151–54; xxv (Hebrew; English summary).

Judges 1:1–2:5

❦

FTER THE DEATH of Joshua, the Israelites asked the
LORD, "Who will be the first to go up and fight for us
against the Canaanites?"

²The LORD answered, "Judah is to go; I have given the land
into their hands."

³Then the men of Judah said to the Simeonites their broth-
ers, "Come up with us into the territory allotted to us, to fight
against the Canaanites. We in turn will go with you into
yours." So the Simeonites went with them.

⁴When Judah attacked, the LORD gave the Canaanites and
Perizzites into their hands and they struck down ten thousand
men at Bezek. ⁵It was there that they found Adoni-Bezek and
fought against him, putting to rout the Canaanites and Perizzites. ⁶Adoni-Bezek fled, but they chased him and caught
him, and cut off his thumbs and big toes.

⁷Then Adoni-Bezek said, "Seventy kings with their thumbs
and big toes cut off have picked up scraps under my table.
Now God has paid me back for what I did to them." They
brought him to Jerusalem, and he died there.

⁸The men of Judah attacked Jerusalem also and took it.
They put the city to the sword and set it on fire.

⁹After that, the men of Judah went down to fight against
the Canaanites living in the hill country, the Negev and the
western foothills. ¹⁰They advanced against the Canaanites living in Hebron (formerly called Kiriath Arba) and defeated
Sheshai, Ahiman and Talmai.

¹¹From there they advanced against the people living in
Debir (formerly called Kiriath Sepher). ¹²And Caleb said, "I
will give my daughter Acsah in marriage to the man who
attacks and captures Kiriath Sepher." ¹³Othniel son of Kenaz,
Caleb's younger brother, took it; so Caleb gave his daughter
Acsah to him in marriage.

¹⁴One day when she came to Othniel, she urged him to ask
her father for a field. When she got off her donkey, Caleb
asked her, "What can I do for you?"

¹⁵She replied, "Do me a special favor. Since you have given
me land in the Negev, give me also springs of water." Then
Caleb gave her the upper and lower springs.

¹⁶The descendants of Moses' father-in-law, the Kenite, went up from the City of Palms with the men of Judah to live among the people of the Desert of Judah in the Negev near Arad.

¹⁷Then the men of Judah went with the Simeonites their brothers and attacked the Canaanites living in Zephath, and they totally destroyed the city. Therefore it was called Hormah. ¹⁸The men of Judah also took Gaza, Ashkelon and Ekron—each city with its territory.

¹⁹The LORD was with the men of Judah. They took possession of the hill country, but they were unable to drive the people from the plains, because they had iron chariots. ²⁰As Moses had promised, Hebron was given to Caleb, who drove from it the three sons of Anak. ²¹The Benjamites, however, failed to dislodge the Jebusites, who were living in Jerusalem; to this day the Jebusites live there with the Benjamites.

²²Now the house of Joseph attacked Bethel, and the LORD was with them. ²³When they sent men to spy out Bethel (formerly called Luz), ²⁴the spies saw a man coming out of the city and they said to him, "Show us how to get into the city and we will see that you are treated well." ²⁵So he showed them, and they put the city to the sword but spared the man and his whole family. ²⁶He then went to the land of the Hittites, where he built a city and called it Luz, which is its name to this day.

²⁷But Manasseh did not drive out the people of Beth Shan or Taanach or Dor or Ibleam or Megiddo and their surrounding settlements, for the Canaanites were determined to live in that land. ²⁸When Israel became strong, they pressed the Canaanites into forced labor but never drove them out completely. ²⁹Nor did Ephraim drive out the Canaanites living in Gezer, but the Canaanites continued to live there among them. ³⁰Neither did Zebulun drive out the Canaanites living in Kitron or Nahalol, who remained among them; but they did subject them to forced labor. ³¹Nor did Asher drive out those living in Acco or Sidon or Ahlab or Aczib or Helbah or Aphek or Rehob, ³²and because of this the people of Asher lived among the Canaanite inhabitants of the land. ³³Neither did Naphtali drive out those living in Beth Shemesh or Beth Anath; but the Naphtalites too lived among the Canaanite inhabitants of the land, and those living in Beth Shemesh and Beth Anath became forced laborers for them. ³⁴The Amorites

confined the Danites to the hill country, not allowing them to come down into the plain. [35]And the Amorites were determined also to hold out in Mount Heres, Aijalon and Shaalbim, but when the power of the house of Joseph increased, they too were pressed into forced labor. [36]The boundary of the Amorites was from Scorpion Pass to Sela and beyond.

[2:1]The angel of the LORD went up from Gilgal to Bokim and said, "I brought you up out of Egypt and led you into the land that I swore to give to your forefathers. I said, 'I will never break my covenant with you, [2]and you shall not make a covenant with the people of this land, but you shall break down their altars.' Yet you have disobeyed me. Why have you done this? [3]Now therefore I tell you that I will not drive them out before you; they will be ˌthornsˌ in your sides and their gods will be a snare to you."

[4]When the angel of the LORD had spoken these things to all the Israelites, the people wept aloud, [5]and they called that place Bokim. There they offered sacrifices to the LORD.

SECTIONS 1 (1:1–2:5) and 2 (2:6–3:6) of Judges are parallel and form a double introduction to the main section of the cycles (3:7–16:31). The first section narrates matters from the point of view of the Israelites, while the second does so from the point of view of Yahweh. The first section narrates the foreign wars of subjugation with the *ḥērem* being applied (see the introduction, pp. 30–31).

Judges 1 recapitulates, recasts, and extends the story of the process of Israel's taking possession of the land of Canaan.[1] While it is a complex narrative, this chapter utilizes material from the book of Joshua (esp. Josh. 13–19) to make explicit what is only implicit in Joshua.[2] Along with some expansions, it reflects the general success of Judah and the increasing failure of the other Israelite tribes, especially Dan, in the process of dispossessing the Canaanites from the individual tribal allotments.

---

1. On 1:1–2:5, see K. L. Younger Jr., "The Configuring of Judicial Preliminaries: Judges 1:1–2:5 and its Dependence on the Book of Joshua," *JSOT* 68 (1995): 75–92; and "Judges 1 in Its Near Eastern Literary Context," 207–27.

2. Josh. 10:1–5 is parallel to Judg. 1:4–7; Josh. 15:63 to Judg. 1:8, 21; Josh. 15:13–19 (cf. 14:6–15) to Judg. 1:10–15, 20; Josh. 13:2–3 to Judg. 1:18–19; Josh. 17:11–13 to Judg. 1:27–28; Josh. 16:10 to Judg. 1:29; Josh. 19:10–16 to Judg. 1:30; Josh. 19:24–31 to Judg. 1:31–32; Josh. 19:32–39 to Judg. 1:33; Josh. 19:41–48 to Judg. 1:34–35.

There are two major structural techniques used in the portrayal (augmented by some short narratives): (1) the use of a concentric layout that parallels the roles of the tribes of Judah and Joseph, and (2) a geographically arranged narration that presents the moral degeneration of Israel. The latter technique employs a four-stage pattern that builds to a literary climax and moral nadir in the Dan episode.

A   The assembled Israelites ask Yahweh, "Who will . . . go up. . . ?" (ʿālâ)
    (1:1–2a)

                              a   Prologue. Yahweh's promise (1:2b)
                                  b   Compromise. Judah/Simeon alliance
                                     (1:3)
                                      Up—'lord of Bezeq' (1:4–8)
                                  x   Judah's successful Wars including
                                      Calebites/Kenazzites & Kenites
B   Judah goes up   (1:4–16)
    (1:2b–21)   *Down*—Caleb, Othniel &
                                      Acsah (1:9–16)
                                  b′ Compromise. Judah/Simeon alliance
                                     (1:17)
                             a′ Codicil. Yahweh's presence with Judah, but
                                 with qualifications [1. positive, 2. negative]
                                 (1:18–21)

                              a   Ellipsis. Prologue. Yahweh's promise
                                  b   The House of Joseph (1:22)
                                    x   Wars of the house of Joseph
  B′ Joseph goes up   including (in addition to Man-
    (1:22–36)   asseh and Ephraim) Zebulun,
                                     Asher, Naphtali, Dan (1:23–34)
                                b′ The House of Joseph (1:35)
                           a′ Codicil (1:36)

A′ The Messenger of Yahweh goes up (ʿālâ) to indict the assembled
    Israelites (2:1–5)

Figure 1. The Concentric Structures of Judges 1

The concentric design of this section can be seen in Figure 1. The Israelite assembly in A (1:1–2a) anticipates the activities described in the larger units of B (1:2b–21) and B′ (1:22–36). By contrast, the Israelite assembly of A′

(2:1–5) reviews and evaluates the activities of B and B'.[3] In both instances, as Webb has observed, the key word is *ʿālâ* ("to go up"). It unifies this segment of text and demarcates the units of which it is composed.

The structure of Section B also follows a concentric design. In the first instance there is a prologue (a) in which Yahweh promises victory (1:2b). The codicil[4] (a'), in contrast to the prologue, confirms Yahweh's presence with Judah, but with qualifications both positive and negative (1:18–21). In the second instance, there is the alliance of Judah and Simeon (b), in which the Judahites obtain their allotment (1:3), and the alliance of Judah and Simeon (b'), in which the Simeonites obtain their allotment (1:17). In the third instance and the center of the entire section (x), Judah's successful wars are narrated (1:4–16). This unit is subdivided into an "up" movement (1:4–8) and a "down" movement (1:9–16).

Like Section B, the structure of Section B' follows a concentric design. In the first instance, there is a prologue (a) (implied by ellipsis) and a codicil (a'), in which a modification to the promise is noted (1:36). In the second instance, the beginning activities of the house of Joseph (b) are narrated positively (1:22), and the final activities of the house of Joseph (b') are narrated negatively (1:35). In the third instance and the center of the entire section (x), the wars of the house of Joseph are narrated (1:23–34). This unit is subdivided into the assessments of the other Cisjordanian (west bank) tribes.

Both sections B and B' narrate initial successes that are followed by failures. Moreover, B and B' serve to exegete the indictment of Israel by the messenger of Yahweh in 2:1–5.[5] The compositional parallel between the Judah and Joseph sections (B and B') within chapter 1 throws the treatment of the Canaanite informer in the Bethel campaign (first item in the Joseph section) into sharp relief against the treatment of the Canaanite "lord of Bezeq"[6] (Adoni-Bezek) in the Bezeq campaign (first item in the Judah section). This comparison helps us to perceive more clearly the basic shift that has already begun to take place at this point in the relationship between Israelites and Canaanites in spite of the fact that the second section, like the first, begins with a notable victory. With this overview of the chapter, it is now possible to expound the individual sections.

---

3. Webb, *The Book of the Judges*, 103.

4. A codicil is a short writing or addition to a will that modifies it in some way.

5. E. T. Mullen Jr., "Judges 1:1–36: The Deuteronomistic Reintroduction of the Book of Judges," *HTR* 77 (1984): 33–54, esp. 43.

6. Concerning the translation "lord of Bezeq," see S. Layton, *Archaic Features of Canaanite Names in the Hebrew Bible* (HSM 47; Atlanta: Scholars press, 1990), 117; and Younger, "The Configuring of Judicial Preliminaries," 78 n. 9. See standard commentaries for discussions of the variant Adoni-Zedek. At the present, it seems impossible to conclude that there is a wordplay in the name, as some commentators have suggested, since the precise meaning of *bezeq* is uncertain.

"Who Will . . . Go Up?" (1:1–2a)

SECTION A (1:1–2A) opens with an important phrase "after the death of Joshua." Most commentators claim that this phrase is a later addition. The phrase, however, can be compared with the beginning of the book of Joshua: "after the death of Moses."[7] Thus it may be "a stylistic way of recapitulating briefly the previous book before interpreting it further."[8] In this case, Judges recapitulates the position of Joshua (how much of the land Israel would occupy) before going on to the central question of Judges: *Why* could they not completely occupy the land?[9]

The phrase "the Israelites asked the LORD" (*š'l byhwh*) expresses the idea of obtaining a declaration of the divine will and is substantially the same as (lit.) "inquire of the judgment of the Urim" (*s'l bmšpṭ h'wrym*) in Numbers 27:21, in which the divine will is obtained through the Urim and Thummim of the high priest. Thus at the beginning of the narrative, the Israelites seek divine guidance in the proper manner as to "Who will be the first to go up [*'ālâ*] and fight for us against the Canaanites?" The idea contained in the term "first" is that of time, not rank. Hence, the question is who will be the first chronologically? While a series of campaigns by individual tribes is envisioned, the concept of a united Israel remains ("who will go up first *for us*!").

Judah Goes Up (1:2b–21)

SECTION B (SEE Fig. 1) opens with a prologue (1:2b)[10] that contains Yahweh's promise through an oracle of victory: "I have given the land into their hands." This is the same phrase that Yahweh used when he promised Joshua victory in the land (e.g., Josh. 6:2; 6:2; 10:8; 11:6). So far, so good.

The Judahites, however, immediately make a deal with the Simeonites (1:3). The alliance (b in Fig. 1) is a "natural" one since Judah and Simeon are

---

7. Also see the close parallels 2 Sam. 1:1 and 2:1. The latter contains the same question-answer sequence found in Judg. 1:1: "In the course of time [lit., afterwards], David inquired of the LORD: 'Shall I go up [*'ālâ*] to one of the towns of Judah?' he asked. The LORD said: 'Go up.'"

8. Polzin, *Moses and the Deuteronomist*, 148.

9. Ibid.

10. The difficulty in the handling of 1:2 is reflected in Webb's analysis, where he understands verse 2 as part of Section A (*Judges*, 103) and yet as forming the prologue to the description of Judah's activities in Section B (ibid., 90). It seems to me that 1:2a goes with A ("Who will . . . go up?" 1:1–2a) as part of the major chiasm of Introduction 1. It is not only the answer to the Israelites' inquiry of God but serves as a counter to the angel/messenger of the Lord in A' (2:1–5). Judg. 1:2b goes with the next section (B), "Judah goes up" (1:2b–21), functioning as part of the smaller chiasm. In a sense 1:3–21 is the exposition of the answer in 1:2, and 1:22–36 a further exposition of the question of 1:1. Nonetheless, 1:2b serves as a transitional prologue to 1:3–21, and I have included it in Section B to indicate this.

full blood brothers. Moreover, in certain ways it is pragmatic. Since Simeon's allotment of the Promised Land falls within Judah's allotment (Josh. 19:1–9), the practical advantages of Judah's proposal are obvious. But on a purely military level, it is utterly unnecessary: the largest tribe numerically (Judah) does not need one of the smallest tribes (Simeon) in order to defeat the Canaanites within its allotted area. It was God's intention that each tribe trust him in the process of conquering its allotment. Thus, by making this treaty, the two tribes undercut this process. Klein has eloquently expressed the moral or spiritual decline that is evident in Judah's proposal:

> Yahweh tells Israel (here Judah) specifically what to do, but Israel only partially heeds Yahweh's command: Judah immediately establishes a battle pact with his brother Simeon. Thus, from the outset, Israel exerts self-determination, evidencing automatic trust in *human* perception. These verses may be regarded as introducing the ironic configuration of the book—implicit difference in perception between Yahweh and Israel and Israel's insistence on following human perception.[11]

Even so, the Judahites and Simeonites will see general success in their campaigns since they are willing "to go up" and "fight" the Canaanites.

The campaigns of this section are divided into two major movements: "up" ("Judah went up [*ʿlh*]," (1:4–8) and "down" ("after that, the Judahites went down [*yrd*]," 1:9–16). In the upward movement the campaigns against Bezeq and Jerusalem are related, and in the downward movement those against Hebron, Debir, and Zephath/Hormah are reported.

The first episode in the "up" movement is that of the victory at Bezeq. In fulfillment of Yahweh's oracle above, the Canaanites and Perizzites[12] are given into the hands of the Judahites (1:4). The next three verses are devoted to a description of the lord of Bezeq's capture, mutilation, and death. The humiliation of the Canaanite ruler is dwelt upon with apparent relish. The climax is most certainly in the direct speech of verse 7: "Seventy kings with their thumbs and big toes cut off have picked up scraps under my table. Now God has paid me back for what I did to them." The lord of Bezeq admits that he has suffered only what he deserved. The brutality is justified (from the victim's own mouth!) as divine retribution.

Amazingly this is an enemy king, the embodiment of evil, and a Canaanite who has a limited comprehension of God (note that he uses *ʾĕlōhîm* [God], not Yahweh). Ironically, if the same measure of justice were placed on Israel,

---

11. Klein, *Triumph of Irony*, 23. Note Judah's subtle disobedience from the start.

12. If "Canaanites" are understood here as "urban dwellers" and "Perizzites" as "rural dwellers," then the two together may function as a merism and signify the inhabitants of the land in their totality.

Israel would face a similar fate as the "lord of Bezeq." Therefore, in God's judgment on the lord of Bezeq, his grace towards Israel is heightened. The last statements of verse 7 ("They brought him to Jerusalem, and he died there") are the links to the second episode in the "up" movement. The implication is that the Israelites brought him with them as they marched on Jerusalem.

The Judahites have great success in conquering Jerusalem too. Using the stereotypical statements characteristic of conquest accounts,[13] they capture and destroy it like Jericho, Ai, and Hazor in the book of Joshua.

The "down" movement contains three reports (1:9–10, 11–15, 16). It begins with another victory: the conquest of Hebron (see parallels in Josh. 11:21–22; 14:6–15; 15:13–14).[14] In that Sheshai, Ahiman, and Talmai are Anakites (see Josh. 15:14),[15] this heightens the success attributed to Judah.

The second report in the "down" movement is about the capture of Debir, though the narration centers on Caleb, Othniel, and Acsah (in contrast to the three Anakites in the previous verse?). Caleb performs his traditional role as a "leader" (*nasîʾ*) of Judah (Num. 13:1–2, 6; 34:18; cf. Josh. 14:6).[16] Othniel, closely related to Caleb (both were Kenizzites [1:13a][17]),

---

13. See Younger, *Ancient Conquest Accounts;* also "The Configuring of Judicial Preliminaries," 86, n. 31.

14. For the problem of multiple attributions of victory to different entities, see Younger, "Judges 1 in Its Near Eastern Literary Context," 226.

15. For a discussion of the names see R. S. Hess, "Non-Israelite Personal Names in the Narratives of the Book of Joshua," *CBQ* 58 (1996): 205–14.

16. Webb, *The Book of the Judges,* 233, n. 24.

17. Caleb is identified twice as "from the tribe of Judah" (Num. 13:6; 34:19). He is frequently designated as "the son of Jephunneh" (Num. 13:6; 14:6, 30, 38; 26:35; 32:12; 34:19; Deut. 1:36; Josh. 14:6, 13, 14; 15:13; 21:12; 1 Chron. 4:15; 6:56). Three times (Num. 32:12; Josh. 14:6, 14) he is given the further designation "the Kenizzite" (*qnzy*). This form is a gentilic (e.g., in the modern context, "the American, the German, the Russian, etc."; in the Old Testament context, "the Midianite, the Philistine, the Assyrian, etc."). Thus, it is an ethnic designation. Another way of forming a gentilic in ancient Semitic languages was the combination of the word for "son" (either singular or plural) and the name of an eponymous ancestor (e.g., "sons of Israel" = "Israelites"; "sons of Ammon" = "Ammonites"; etc.). Thus Othniel is designated "son of Kenaz" (*bn qnz*), hence "Kenizzite" (note that the JPSV translates *bn qnz* in every instance as "Kenizzite"). He is further designated as "Caleb's [younger] brother [*ʾaḥ*]" (e.g., Judg. 1;13), which probably means that Othniel was a younger relative or kinsman of Caleb (the Heb. word *ʾaḥ* has this range of meaning; see the discussion of levirate marriage in the introduction to Ruth). This explains why Caleb is called the son of Jephunneh and Othniel is called the son of Kenaz, and yet Othniel is called Caleb's brother, and Caleb is called "the Kenizzite." It also explains the apparent discrepancy in the Old Greek, where Othniel is described as Caleb's younger brother (LXX^A) and yet also designated as Caleb's nephew (LXX^B). As pointed out in the introduction, the tribe (*šēbeṭ*) can be bound together by any one of the following: descent, residence, dialect, or religion. While some scholars disagree, the best way of understanding these designations in association with the

is the champion of Judah capturing Debir. He is rewarded with marriage to Acsah.[18]

Hardly passive, Acsah grasps the opportunity to get more of "the land" (something neither her father nor her husband have considered). She has already received from her father "land in the Negev" as a dowry. Now she strengthens its value by obtaining adequate water rights. It is likely that a wife in ancient Israel retained some potential rights over her dowry, even though the dowry became part of the husband's property.[19] Ancient Near Eastern laws and marriage contracts support this.[20] However, Acsah's request is for additional land that especially includes springs. So her initiative is still extraordinary.

It is important to remember that the notion of "land" in the Old Testament carries spiritual connotations as God's blessing on the recipient of the land. The "inherited estate" (*naḥᵃlâ*) was not simply a tract of turf but a gift from God, an evidence of his grace, and therefore should not, under normal conditions, be sold. It was to be highly prized, and its alienation was to be voided if at all possible (cf. Naboth's concerns 1 Kings 21).

Acsah is the first woman mentioned in Judges, and her exceptional spiritual qualities are greatly extolled. She will take the initiative twice in this short narration. (1) She takes the initiative in relation to Othniel: "She urged him to ask her father for a field."[21] (2) She takes the initiative with Caleb. When Caleb asks her, "What's the matter?" he gives her the context and incentive to speak. Acsah does not wait on Othniel but rather takes up the matter directly with her father, procuring an enhancement for her land:

---

statements that connect Caleb and Othniel with the tribe of Judah is to see them as proselytes from a different ethnic group who count in the tribe of Judah (i.e., through at least residence and religion, though not descent). For an analogy one can compare the case of Rahab, who is not a Judahite by descent but nonetheless counted as a Judahite after her proselytizing to the faith of Israel.

18. Caleb's promise to give Acsah to whoever would take Debir (1:12) is pictured here in positive terms (i.e., the capturing of Deber in the conquest of the Promised Land, the inheritance of God). In contrast, Jephthah's vow is a grotesque and tragic "giving" of one's daughter (Judg. 11:30–31).

19. It is doubtful that Acsah "beguiled" her father at a moment of weakness, i.e., the capture of Debir (as argued by P. G. Mosca, "Who Seduced Whom? A Note on Joshua 15:18 // Judges 1:14," *CBQ* 46 [1984]: 18–22).

20. See R. Westbrook, *Property and the Family in Biblical Law* (JSOTSup 113; Sheffield: Sheffield Academic Press, 1991), 152–53.

21. There is no need to emend this (with LXX and most scholars) to "he urged her," since what immediately follows explains how she rather than Othniel actually does the asking (see Webb, *The Book of the Judges*, 233 n. 29; Hess, *Joshua: An Introduction and Commentary* [TOTC; Downers Grove, Ill: InterVarsity, 1996], 245 n. 2).

springs of water—"the upper and lower springs."[22] These sources of water were important in the Negev desert (see Ps. 126:4).

Once again, it is important to remember that the land in the Old Testament carried spiritual overtones. This is true here as well as in the story of the daughters of Zelophehad (Num. 27:1–11; 36:1–13; Josh. 17:3–6). The actions of all these women are strongly commended. The story demonstrates that the claim of the descendants of Othniel and Acsah to this land is based on a legal bequest by the original recipient of the territory. Acsah's request is not transitory but generational in its impact. She emerges as "an image of ideal Yahwist womanhood."[23]

In the more extended context of the book of Judges, Acsah serves as a contrast in two important ways. (1) As a positive paradigm of a daughter being given to an ideal hero, she is juxtaposed to the notice of Israel's apostasy of intermarriage with the inhabitants of the land (3:6). These Israelite daughters (in contrast to Acsah) are, in a sense, dispossessed since the gift of the land will never be theirs because of their intermarriages.[24]

(2) The contrast between Acsah and Delilah could not be more stark! Acsah was the wife of Othniel (who will be described later in the book as the ideal judge). She took the initiative to procure greater blessing for her husband and progeny through her request for more land and springs. In contrast, Delilah was the consort of Samson (the worst of the judges). She used her initiative to bring down her man, all for filthily gained money.

The third report in the "down" movement is the notice concerning the movement of the Kenites into the Negev of Arad (1:16). The phrase "the descendants of Moses' father-in-law, the Kenite" refers the reader back to Numbers 10:29–32, where Moses entreats Hobab, the son of Moses' father-in-law, to join the Israelites in the blessings of the land. Judges 1:16 is the fulfillment of the promise of Moses. Thus the Kenites went up (or perhaps syntactically better "had gone up") from the City of Palms (i.e., Jericho, cf. Deut. 34:3) with the men of Judah to live (*yāšab*) among the people in the Negev near Arad. The phrase "to live among" will play an important role in the narration that follows. Here it seems to have positive (or at least neutral) connotations. Later in the narrative it has negative nuances. Moreover, the mention of the Kenites in Judges 1:16 will serve to anticipate the role they will play in 4:11, 17 (in the days of Deborah, Barak, and Jael).

---

22. Perhaps more than he had intended to give. See Y. Kaufmann, *The Book of Judges* (Jerusalem: Kiryat Sepher, 1962; Hebrew), 80. Acsah's practical shrewdness and resourcefulness in seizing the initiative from both Othniel and Caleb (the two male heroes of the story) is commended (see the introduction, p. 37).

23. Klein, *Triumph of Irony*, 26.

24. Fewell, "Judges," 68.

Just as there was irony in the "up" movement (i.e., Yahweh's divine punishment is conveyed through the mouth of the Canaanite "lord of Bezeq"), so too there is irony in the "down" movement. Here Yahweh's grace is bestowed on Caleb, Othniel, Acsah, and the Kenites. Ironically, this grace of Yahweh is specially given to non-Israelites![25]

On the heels of unit x (see Fig. 1) with its various stories in up and down movements, comes the reoccurrence of the alliance of Judah and Simeon (b'). In this case it is the Simeonites who obtain their allotment (1:17). They attack the city of Zephath and "totally destroy" it (lit., *ḥrm*, see discussion in the introduction, pp. 28–30). The city is renamed Hormah (derived from *ḥērem*).[26] It is ironic that the Simeonites, a numerically insignificant tribe, are the only tribe in the narration of the occupation of the land (1:1–2:5) who obey Yahweh and implement the *ḥērem* thoroughly (1:17). Yet they will not be mentioned in the book of Judges again.

The codicil (a') confirms Yahweh's presence with Judah, since 1:19 states that "the LORD was with the men of Judah. They took possession of the hill country" (a direct reference back to 1:2b). While the victory seems complete with even Gaza, Ashkelon, and Ekron falling to the Judahites, the unit emends this with the last statements "but they were unable to drive [*yāraš*] the people from the plains [*ʿēmeq*], because they had iron chariots."[27] In light of this general success of the Judahites, the Benjamite failure in 1:21 contrasts starkly.

The House of Joseph (1:22–36)

THE PARALLEL JOSEPH section (B' in Fig. 1) depicts an ironic relationship to Yahweh. In the story of the capture of Bethel (1:23–26), the success of the Joseph tribes is marked by failure. Ironically, the Israelites show covenant loyalty (*ḥesed*) to the man of Bethel instead of loyalty (*ḥesed*) to Yahweh's will

---

25. D. M. Gunn and D. N. Fewell, *Narrative in the Hebrew Bible* (The Oxford Bible Series; Oxford: Oxford Univ. Press, 1993), 162–63.

26. Contrast the story of the total destruction and renaming of Laish by the Danites in Judg 18:27–30. On Hormah see also Num. 14:45; 21:1–3; Deut. 1:44; and Josh. 12:14; 15:30.

27. See the discussion of iron chariots in Judg. 4, below. These iron chariots (perhaps three or four thin plates hung over the front to protect the charioteer's legs, which his hauberk did not cover) were obviously heavier. Once they were moving, they would be hard for opponents, especially foot soldiers, to withstand. This was a technology the Israelites did not possess and understandably intimidated them. They are the reason for Judah's failure to take the plains where their military capability would be at its greatest. See A. R. Millard, "Back to the Iron Bed: Og's or Procrustes?" in *Congress Volume: Paris, 1992*, ed. J. A. Emerton (VTSup 61; Leiden: Brill, 1995), 193–203, esp. 194–95. Also see, Younger, "The Configuring of Judicial Preliminaries," 82 n. 21.

according to the covenant. Even in executing the *ḥērem*, the Joseph tribes, in effect, produce another Canaanite city. The exposition of the tribal allotments in this section will be given in more detail below.

Finally, in the scene at Bokim (A') (2:1–5), the "messenger of Yahweh" (NIV, "angel of the LORD") touts the disobedience and failure of the Israelites. The difference between Israelites and Canaanites is the difference in serving Yahweh or other gods. Yet Yahweh shows ironically his *ḥesed* (excess) toward Israel instead of the divine retribution (equity) that was measured out for the "lord of Bezeq."

JUDGES 1

(Literary and Moral Movements)

Literary Movement

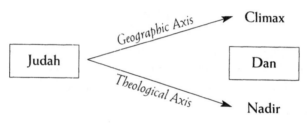

Moral Movement

Figure 2

A second technique in the structuring of Judges 1:1—2:5 is the use of geographic arrangement. Judges 1 utilizes its south-to-north geographic arrangement of the tribal episodes in order to foreshadow the geographic orientations of the judges cycle in 3:7–16:31. This arrangement builds the literary and moral movements that find their climax and nadir in the Dan episode (see Fig. 2).[28]

In like fashion, the cycles of the judges (3:6–16:31) have their climax and nadir in the person of Samson.[29] In fact, the "cycles" themselves in 3:6–16:31 are arranged in such a way as to point to the decline in the character of the judges as illustrative of the chaos of the time (see the discussion of the structure of Judges in the introduction).

---

28. B. S. Childs, *Introduction to the Old Testament As Scripture* (Philadelphia: Fortress, 1979), 259.
29. Webb, *The Book of the Judges*, 177–79; Exum, "The Centre Cannot Hold," 423–25.

The Four Stage Moral Decline in Judges 1
(with special reference to *yāraš*, *yāšab*, and *mas*)

1	Judah (1:2–20) +		INITIAL SUCCESS BOTH TRIBAL AND INDIVIDUAL.
	Simeon (1:17)	A	(*yāraš*) Judah drove out the Canaanites But did not drive out *in the plains (ˁemeq) because they had iron chariots*
		B	(*yāšab*) Kenites (descendents of Moses' father-in-law) live among the Judahites. (*yāšab*) No statement concerning Canaanites living among Judah or Simeon.
2	Benjamin (1:21)	A	(*yāraš*) Did not drive Jebusites out (*lōʾ hôrîš*)
		B	(*yāšab*) Jebusites live with the Benjaminites in …
	House of Joseph (1:22–26)		INITIAL "ARRANGEMENT" (AT BETHEL) THROUGH TRICKERY.
	Manasseh (1:27)	A	(*yāraš*) Did not drive Canaanites out (*lōʾ hôrîš*)
		B	(*yāšab*) Canaanites determined to live in …
		*	When Israel was strong, C+A (*mas*) they pressed the Canaanites into forced labor; (*yāraš*) but they never drove them out completely.
	Ephraim (1:29)	A	(*yāraš*) Did not drive Canaanites out (*lōʾ hôrîš*)
		B	(*yāšab*) Canaanites live among them
	Zebulun (1:30)	A	(*yāraš*) Did not drive Canaanites out (*lōʾ hôrîš*)
		B	(*yāšab*) Canaanites live among them
		C	(*mas*) *but became forced labor*
3	Asher (1:31–32)	A	(*yāraš*) Did not drive Canaanites out (*lōʾ hôrîš*)
		B	(*yāšab*) Asherites live among the Canaanites, the inhabitants of the land.
	Naphtali (1:33)	A	(*yāraš*) Did not drive Canaanites out (*lōʾ hôrîš*)
		B	(*yāšab*) Naphtalites live among the Canaanites, the inhabitants of the land;
		C	(*mas*) but two cities *became forced labor*
4	Dan (1:34)	A	(*yāraš*) No statement concerning driving out.
		B	(*yāšab*) No statement concerning Canaanites living among Danites. Instead, Danites are *oppressed/confined (lāḥaṣ)* and not even allowed to come *into the plains (ˁemeq)*
	House of Joseph (1:35)	*	(*yāšab*) Amorites determined to live in … C+B (*mas*) The hand of the House of Joseph bore down heavily *and the Amorites became forced labor.*
	Ironic conclusion (1:36)		Only border description is Amorite

A = "drive out" (*yāraš*);   B = "live" (*yāšab*);   C = "forced labor" (*mas*)   * = (*Parenthesis: Commentary*)

Figure 3

The process of subjugation is observable in a four-stage decline in Israelite spirituality. This is particularly evident in the use of the terms: *yā-raš*, *yāšab*, and *mas* (see Fig. 3). Judges 1:1–36 states that in many cases the subjugating tribe "did not drive out [*lōʾ hôrîš*]" the local population (vv. 19, 21, 27, 29, 30, 31, 33). In only one case is the excuse for this failure to drive out the Canaanites attributed to inferior Israelite armament (v. 19). Rather, the impact of the formula is to state that this was an intentional failure to wipe out the population. In fact, this point is explicitly made in the somewhat parenthetical statement of verse 28: "When Israel became strong, they pressed the Canaanites into forced labor [*mas*] but never drove them out completely."

Thus the writer/editor explains the failure to completely subjugate the Promised Land as "the deliberate violation of older injunctions which commanded the removal of the nations of Canaan."[30] This failure to drive out the nations climaxes in the case of the Danites through the ellipsis of this formula (*lōʾ hôrîš*). Not only do the Danites fail to drive out the inhabitants of their allotment; they are instead oppressed/confined by the Amorites and not allowed to come down into the plain (*ʿēmeq*)! Note that the only place where Judah could not drive out the Canaanites was the plain (*ʿēmeq*).

Additionally, in 1:1–36 the use of the verb "to live" (*yāšab*) illustrates this four-stage decline in Israelite spirituality. Beginning with Judah there is an absence of any statement concerning Canaanites living among Judah. Next, however, it is stated that the Canaanites live among the tribes of Benjamin, Manasseh, Ephraim, and Zebulun (although Zebulun subjects them to forced labor). But then it is stated that the tribes of Asher and Naphtali live among the Canaanites (although Naphtali subjects them to forced labor). Finally, the Danites are oppressed (*lāḥaṣ*,[31] within the same semantic field as *mas* ["forced labor"], cf. Ex. 3:9) by the Amorites. Note that the only border description given (1:36) is that of an Amorite border. Whose land is this? Webb correctly observes:

> By the time this note is introduced the focus of the narrative has shifted from conquest to co-existence. When the whole process of conquest and settlement has run its course, Israel dwells within "the border of the Amorite." The Amorites/Canaanites are still the inhabitants of the land among whom Israel dwells (see esp. 32a 33b). This note pro-

30. See M. Fishbane, *Biblical Interpretation in Ancient Israel* (Oxford: Clarendon, 1986), 203.
31. The introduction of *lāḥaṣ* is ominous, foreshadowing things to come (cf. 2:18; 4:3; 6:9; 10:12). On the other hand, *mas* has connections to the past. During the earlier Canaanite period, people were put under forced labor.

vides a final sardonic comment on the chapter as a whole, and on verses 22–35 in particular. Formally it is parallel to the notes appended to the Judah section.[32]

That Judges 1 emphasizes this moral decline is evident from a comparison with the narration in Joshua 13–19 of the tribal allotments and their allusions to *lōʾ hôrîš* and *yāšab*. Both accounts testify to the moral decline in Israel through the imposition of the tribal, geographic arrangement. A comparison of the amount of detail devoted to each tribe in Joshua 13–19 and in Judges 1 clearly demonstrates a similar pattern of declivity of description in both. Thus the account in Judges 1 corresponds in significant ways to the narration in Joshua 13–19 in both perspective (the moral degeneration of Israel) and content (the geographic tribal descriptions).[33]

The Messenger of Yahweh (2:1–5)

THE FINAL SECTION (A') is Judges 2:1–5. This unit clearly is connected with the preceding through the use of the verb "to go up" (*ʿālâ*) in 2:1 (cf. 1:1b, 2a, 3b, 4a, 16a, 22a). At the same time the unit serves as the thematic transition to Introduction 2 (2:6–3:5), with its emphasis on the Israelites' apostasy from Yahweh worship. This section essentially provides both a thematic and structural counterpart to 1:1–2a, which began Introduction 1 by asking Yahweh, "Who will be the first to go up and fight for us against the Canaanites?" (1:1b). Yahweh's reply was, "Judah is to go." Judges 2:1–5 confronts the Israelites with a comparable claim, "I brought you up out of Egypt" (2:1b), which implicitly rebukes the tribes for failing to dispossess the Canaanite nations and for worshiping their idols by alluding to Yahweh's covenant stipulations. Deuteronomy 7:7–24 correlates Yahweh's conquest of Egypt with

---

32. Webb, *The Book of the Judges*, 101. While at this point a number of scholars opt for a possible textual variant reading "Edomite," the reading "Amorite" seems to be preferred because of the literary context. There is a similar enigmatic territorial description at the end of the minor/noncyclical judge notices: "in the hill country of the Amalekites" (12:15).

33. Issachar is lacking in Judges. According to N. Naʾaman, one possible reason is the fact that Issachar's territory contains only one main site, Tel Rekhesh (Tell el-Mukharkhash), which presumably was destroyed sometime during the thirteenth to twelfth centuries B.C. Thus at the time of the united monarchy no significant towns existed in Issachar to be included as points of reference in a list of unconquered cities (*Borders and Districts in Biblical Historiography* [Jerusalem Biblical Studies 4; Jerusalem: Simor, 1986], 97).

Both the failure "to drive out" (*lōʾ hôrîš*) the Canaanites and their dwelling (*yāšab*) among the Israelites are presented in Judges 1 as Cisjordanian problems. In Joshua 13–19 these are portrayed as Transjordanian problems too (13:13). Naʾaman correctly observes that "since the Transjordan was regarded as an area not belonging to Canaan, one would never expect to find the Transjordanian tribes in a list of unconquered Canaanite cities west of the Jordan" (ibid., 97).

his assurance that Israel can conquer Canaan with his help. Moreover, Deuteronomy 7:1–5, 16, 25–26 specifically commands the Israelites to avoid treaties with the Canaanites and to destroy both the people and their idols.[34]

"The angel of the Lord[35] [went] up" (ʿālâ) from Gilgal. It is possible that Gilgal is the point from which all the "goings up" of Introduction 1 (i.e., ch. 1) have originated (cf. 1:16).[36] In 2:1, it is the angel of the Lord who goes up in order to give his verdict on the Israelites' "goings up." This repetitive "going up" (ʿālâ) in chapter 1 raises high expectations. Ironically, these expectations are dashed by Yahweh's reprimand, with the result that the Israelites weep at Bokim. The introduction of the name "Bokim" (lit., "weeping") in 2:1 is anticipatory of its explanation in verse 5. Thus these two verses function as a literary frame for this unit.

The indictment brought against the Israelites is that they have broken Yahweh's covenant (bᵉrît, treaty). They have ignored his prohibition against making any covenant (treaties) with "the people of this land" and his order to "break down their altars" (2:2a).[37] What seems especially offensive to Yahweh is the fact that Canaanite altars have been left standing, not only in those Canaanite enclaves with whose inhabitants the Israelites have entered into treaty, but also in areas that the Israelites themselves have occupied (see 6:25–32). This early disobedience of the Israelites to the covenant stipulations leads to the apostasy of Introduction 2 (2:6–3:6), as well as all of the apostasies throughout the accounts in the cycles section of 3:7–16:31. This continuity of the theme of apostasy should not be minimized.[38]

Interestingly, the Israelites are not indicted in 2:2 with failing to expel all the Canaanites but with entering into covenant (treaty) with them. In other words, the process of dispossession and occupation would have been completed in due course if the Israelites had fulfilled their obligations to Yahweh, but now their disobedience has put the completion of the Conquest in jeopardy (2:3). The question at the end of 2:2 is rhetorically loaded: "Why have you done this?" (i.e., "What in the world have you done?"). No answer is

---

34. O'Connell, *The Rhetoric of the Book of Judges*, 13.

35. "The angel of the LORD" is obviously an interpretive decision (which the NIV translators have made) for the Hebrew malʾak yhwh, "messenger/angel of Yahweh." Some scholars understand his identity to be that of a prophet (e.g., Kaufmann, *The Book of Judges*, 92). Webb uses the neutral translation of "messenger of Yahweh" (*The Book of the Judges*, 239 n. 81). In the end, since it is Yahweh himself who threatens the resultant action for Israel's failure to obey his words, the preferred understanding may be "the angel of Yahweh," though this is still not demanded by the text.

36. Webb, *The Book of the Judges*, 103.

37. See R. H. O'Connell, "Deuteronomy vii 1–26: Asymmetrical Concentricity and the Rhetoric of Conquest," *VT* 42 (1992): 248–65.

38. See Klein, *The Triumph of Irony*, 142, 144.

forthcoming, and the question emphatically stresses the Israelites' guilt (cf. Gen. 3:13 for the same grammatically constructed question).

Yahweh appeals to another of his earlier declarations: "Now therefore I tell you that I will not drive them out before you; they will be ⌐thorns¬ in your sides and their gods will be a snare to you." Yahweh simply reminds his audience of what he *has said* he would do in the kind of situation that has now materialized: He will not drive out the Canaanites. Thus, the Israelites may have to share the land indefinitely with these Canaanites. Moreover, these Canaanites will become thorns[39] in their sides.

Yahweh's decision to implement this threat is not narrated until 2:21. The speech of the angel of Yahweh in 2:1–5 is anticipatory of the divine speech of 2:20–22. Between these two speeches Israel lapses into apostasy (2:11–19), and this apostasy is anticipated by the final words of verse 3: "Their gods will be a snare [*môqēš*] to you." A passage from the Book of the Covenant (Ex. 23:32–33) forms the legal background for Judges 2:2–3 in general and 2:3d in particular: "Do not make a covenant with them or with their gods. Do not let them live in your land, or they will cause you to sin against me, because the worship of their gods will certainly be a snare [*môqēš*] to you." The Canaanite snare here, in turn, later becomes the snare (*môqēš*) of Gideon's ephod (8:27).

The reaction of the Israelites, as if to repudiate Yahweh's declarations in verse 3, is to weep and offer sacrifices to Yahweh (2:4–5). They may have failed in their obligations to Yahweh, but they have not yet forsaken him for other gods. The place is named Bokim ("weepers") by virtue of what happens there.[40]

PRIMARY MESSAGE. Judges 1:1–2:5 is a complex passage with a primary message and a number of secondary or subsidiary messages. In bridging the ancient context with the modern, it is critical to recognize that the fundamental message of the passage is conveyed through its literary structure. In spite of some initial successes, especially by the tribe

---

39. Lit., "They will be in [your] sides [*lᵉṣiddîm*]." The term *lᵉṣiddîm* is an abbreviated expression, an ellipsis, for *liṣnînîm bᵉṣiddêkem* ("thorns in your backs") in Num. 33:55 (cf. also Josh. 23:13). See Burney, *The Book of Judges with Introduction and Notes* (New York: Ktav, rept. 1970), 266.

40. The term *bkh* is frequently used in the Old Testament to describe weeping or mourning for the dead. It is used four more times in Judges: 11:37–38 (Jephthah's daughter bewailing her virginity and impending death); 14:16 (Samson's wife weeping because he has not told her the answer to his riddle); 20:23 (weeping over the dead as the result of the first battle at Gibeah); 21:2 (weeping over the extinction of Benjamin).

of Judah, the overall effect is an increasingly negative pattern.[41] Israel's failure to obey Yahweh's word concerning the ḥērem (see the introduction) produces the military failure recorded in this chapter. The four stages of increasing failure document the beginning of the "Canaanizing" of Israel.

Disobedience breeds disastrous failure. Why is Israel's disobedience to implement the ḥērem so devastating? Perhaps because of the ḥērem's link to the issue of covenantal love of God (Deut. 7). Perhaps because God really does know what's best for his people, and the implementation of the ḥērem would have brought the material and spiritual prosperity that God intended for Israel (cf. the specific blessings of Deut. 28). Had Israel implemented it consistently, the negative influence of the Canaanites would likely have been eliminated.

There can be no doubt concerning the difficulty in implementing the ḥērem. But this was God's commandment to Israel, specific to their historical context and specific to Israel's physical and spiritual situation. The lack of implementation can be directly attributed to a lack of belief and trust in God's commandments.

This lack of implementation of God's Word in the lives of the believing community because of a failure to believe and trust in God's commandments transcends all ages. In many instances throughout the two millennia of the church's history, the church as a whole has not realized some of Christ's most basic commandments: to love God, to love one another, to go and make disciples of all nations, and so on. Often the church has been content to be "Canaanized," to live as the world dictates.

It is important to note that a misapplication of this passage concerning the ḥērem and others like it is the teaching that makes this primarily apply to the issue of culture, as though this is simply an issue of Christian culture versus pagan culture. This often manifests itself in opinionated conflicts about particular cultural issues that the biblical text may be silent about. While culture is an issue (esp. as it may manifest ungodly worldviews) as it concerns the implementation of the ḥērem, it is secondary to the religious or spiritual issue. The ḥērem was not designed by God to eliminate the Canaanite culture per se but to eliminate the Canaanite religious influence. While it may be readily recognized that it is difficult in many instances to separate the two, there is nonetheless a distinction. The Israelite ḥērem commandments had close links to the issues of idolatry and the breaking of the second commandment (Ex. 22:20[19]; Deut. 7:26; 13:16–18[17–19]). That this is the case in Introduction 1 of Judges (1:1–2:5) is reinforced by Yahweh's con-

---

41. This pattern will be mirrored in the book of Judges as a whole. See Exum, "The Centre Cannot Hold," 413.

frontation of the nation in 2:1–5, where it is their failure on the religious front that is of primary concern.

In other words, the *ḥērem* was not concerned with the eradication of Canaanite clothing fashions, pottery styles, music, diet, and other types of particular cultural preferences. But it was deeply concerned with the eradication of the Canaanite religion: its gods/idols, altars, rituals, divinatory practices, uses of magic, worldview, and so on.

While the overall message concerns the increasing failure of Israel to obey Yahweh's word concerning the *ḥērem* and its resultant moral and spiritual degeneration, fortunately the passage also records the initial successes in the first stage of the four stages presented within the passage.

The basic successes in the beginning of the narration start with an inquiry of God. This is true in all ages. Without God's guidance any endeavor is doomed to failure. Since the inquiry is in accordance with God's will (i.e., that the Israelite tribes subjugate their allotments), there is explicit direction by God with the assurance that success will follow. This is an example of what the apostle John states: "This is the confidence we have in approaching God: that if we ask anything according to his will, he hears us. And if we know that he hears us—whatever we ask—we know that we have what we asked of him" (1 John 5:14–15).

Subsidiary messages. The vignettes that follow the inquiry describe the tribe of Judah's general success in occupying its allotment. All of these vignettes provide short lessons in themselves that bridge between the ancient and contemporary contexts.

(1) The segment about the lord of Bezeq (Adoni-Bezek) demonstrates that God is answering the Israelites' prayer for direction. God fulfills his promise in giving the Judahites victory over a harsh king who embodies the evil of Canaanite monarchy. God's fulfillment of his promises is a confidence that transcends the ages. Moreover, the theme of God's righteous retribution on evil is a message that transcends the ages.[42] It provides hope in a fallen world where evil seems to constantly prevail.

In fact, in the judgment on the lord of Bezeq (Adoni-Bezek), Yahweh's grace toward Israel is heightened, for the people do not deserve such a victory[43] (they have already sown the seeds of failure by having made an unnecessary treaty between Judah and Simeon). Thus, from the beginning, they seem

---

42. It is indeed ironic that it is this Canaanite monarch who acknowledges God's retribution on evil, for this theme of retribution turns up again in the book and is not always recognized, even by God's people.

43. This is also true in the most general sense: Israel did not "deserve" the land—the Israelites had not manifested great faith and obedience after coming out of Egypt and during the desert period!

prone to do things their way, not God's way. Judah's treaty with Simeon, while explicable from a certain human standpoint, is not God's will. Therefore, all of the victories that they achieve are the results of God's grace toward them.

(2) The narration concerning Judah contains three vignettes: the conquest of Hebron, the conquest of Debir, and the movement of the Kenites. In the second and third vignettes, Yahweh's grace is bestowed on individuals like Caleb, Othniel, Acsah, and the Kenites. In each instance, this grace is specially given to non-Israelites (see comments above). This theme— namely, that God gives grace to non-Israelites—is developed throughout the Old and New Testaments. Those who are not expected to evince faith do, and those who should show faith do not (cf. Rahab contrasted with Achan [Josh. 6–7], Elijah and the widow of Zarephath [1 Kings 17:7–24], Elisha and Naaman [2 Kings 5:1–19]; cf. also Luke 4:16–30). Such a lesson is a great encouragement to "Gentiles," especially in the church age.

In the first vignette, God's faithfulness to Judah is documented through the conquest of the city of Hebron, the very hub of the gigantic Anakites, the very ones who had discouraged the Israelite spies in Numbers 13. Such a victory is encouraging to God's people in every generation who may face what appear to be insurmountable obstacles.

The story of the capture of Debir with a gift given in exchange for its conquest anticipates the story of David's conquest of Jerusalem in 2 Samuel 5:6– 15. In both instances, the military commander promises a special reward to the warrior who captures the town. In 2 Samuel 5, David is based in Hebron and moves to Jerusalem. Hence, David may be trying to duplicate the Judges 1:11–13 account (cf. Josh. 15:15–17) by describing the capture of another town from a base at Hebron. In both cases, the captured town becomes the inheritance of those who captured it.[44]

Once again, it is important to remember that the concept of the "land" in the Old Testament carried spiritual overtones. This is true here with the story of Acsah's request for land and springs as well as in the story of the daughters of Zelophehad (Num. 27:1–11; 36:1–13; Josh. 17:3–6). The actions of all these women are strongly commended and serve as examples of faith.

In addition, Acsah's request for springs is parallel to Rebekah's meeting with Isaac (Gen. 24:61–67). Both accounts include:

- the female riding on an animal
- descent from the animal
- making a request
- receiving the desired result from the person who has authority or power in relationship to her

---

44. Hess, *Joshua*, 245.

Both accounts also involve an inheritance of the blessing ("land") that God had promised Abraham.

Acsah's request is also analogous in certain ways to that of Ruth. Both are non-Israelite women who have been "grafted" into the community of faith. Both have men who are outstanding in their personal qualities. Both make requests that involved God's blessings of inheritance (as connected to the land). Both received their requests.

(3) While there is relative success in Judah's endeavors at conquering its allotment, the other tribes fall into the second, third or fourth stages of the less than successful tribes in their application of God's directives (see Fig. 3 above). This culminates in Dan's complete and utter failure to possess its allotment (Stage 4).

The only vignette given in Stage 2 is the story of the capture of Bethel. While it records a successful conquest, the passage obviously contrasts with the previous vignettes of Stage 1, since the capture is accomplished through compromise and deceit. The end does not justify the means.

The phraseology of the two middle stages (i.e., Stages 2 and 3) is revealing. In Stage 2, it documents that the Israelites failed to drive out the Canaanites and that the Canaanites lived among the respective Israelite tribes. In Stage 3, the Israelites failed to drive out the Canaanites, and the respective Israelite tribes live among the Canaanites. These statements demonstrate the increasing lack of faith and commitment to the Lord on the part of God's people.

The failures in Stages 2 and 3 include either a lack of obedience ("not dispossessing/driving out") or compromise ("living among") or both. This can also be true in the modern context. If we examine our lives, the bulk of our failures—especially in spiritual matters, but not exclusively—are the results of outright disobedience to God's explicit, straightforward commandments, or of attempting to live in such a way that we blend into the world. Believers are under constant pressure to conform to the world's standards, and the desire not to be different is pronounced. Yet God has called us to different standards. To compromise is to endanger our very lives. Even on the corporate level this may be evident. Churches feel the pressure to conform to what other churches are doing (even though what these other churches are doing may not be scriptural).

(4) At the end of the day, Israel has broken the covenant. This is the indictment of the Lord in 2:1–5. God is especially angry with the people because they have not destroyed the Canaanite altars (even in the areas that they occupy). This is a direct violation of the *ḥerem* commandment. Moreover, God specifically indicts the Israelites for having entered into covenants (treaties) with the Canaanites. Having made peace with the enemy, they

have jeopardized the conquest of the land. Such an indictment of God's people bridges to many generations (cf. some of Christ's indictments against the churches in the book of Revelation).

In conclusion, in bringing this section into our modern world, the recognition of the passage's overall message as conveyed through its literary structure is vital. While the vignettes in the first portion of the passage provide some positive examples and encouragements, the remainder of the passage records the spiritual/moral declivity of the Israelites that culminates in the confrontation of the Israelites by the Lord in 2:1–5.

WHILE THE OVERALL message of this passage resonates in significant ways in the modern context, it is wrong to apply it on a national level (i.e., by equating either the United States of America or some other modern political entity with ancient Israel) and to interpret the national history of the United States or some other political entity as parallel to that of the nation of Israel in the period of the judges. No contemporary nation equates with the Israel of the Old Testament, who represents the people of God.[45]

Commonly, passages like Judges 1:1–2:5 are used to critique and criticize modern American culture as a degeneration from the godly Christian culture of America's beginnings. But this is a misreading of the basic political history of the United States and its founding fathers. This is most acute in the quoting of men like Thomas Jefferson and Benjamin Franklin in such a way as to give the impression that these men were "Christians" in the biblical sense of this term. In terms of their religious convictions as well as in their morals, both men were distinctly *not* Christians!

Thus, it is important that the proper correspondence to the passage is maintained. The church as God's people is the proper correspondence to biblical Israel. Yet this too raises problems of application, for there are distinctions between the two entities that must be maintained; otherwise the very nature of the church may be blurred.[46]

It would seem that the best application of the passage is first on the individual level, then on a more limited corporate level. In other words, how does the primary message of 1:1–2:5 about the lack of faith and disobedience

---

45. The very fact that there were "Great Awakenings" where people became true believers obviously indicates that in the early history of the United States there were many who were not believers.

46. E.g., the notion conveyed in Gal. 3:28 is a concept not found in the Old Testament.

regarding the implementation of the *ḥērem* and the consequent spiritual/moral degeneration speak to us about our own commitments and obedience to the Lord and his commandments to us? In what ways does the passage challenge us? If God's people failed in their allegiance to the Lord, how are we failing, and what are the consequences of our failures? These same questions can and should be asked on the corporate level with reference to local churches, to a denomination, or to the church as a whole.

Like ancient Israel, Christians also are in covenant relationship to God, albeit through a "better" covenant. Nevertheless, the stipulations of that covenant—"the law of love," as Paul puts it—require obedience. While the warfare in which Christians are engaged is not physical but spiritual, the necessity of walking by faith in loyalty to Christ's covenant is the only hope of victory.

Ḥērem. The natural question will likely arise: How are we to apply a passage like this one that centers around the implementation of the *ḥērem*? While it may seem obvious that we are not called to implement the *ḥērem* on our unbelieving neighbors, unfortunately many of the passages concerning the *ḥērem* have been misapplied by "Christians" throughout history to annihilate their enemies (the Crusades are a prime example of this type of misapplication).

The fact that must be remembered is conveyed in Ephesians 6:12: "For our struggle is not against flesh and blood, but against the rulers, against the authorities, against the powers of this dark world and against the spiritual forces of evil in the heavenly realms."[47] In other words, Christian warfare is spiritual, not physical. In the Old Testament, it was both physical and spiritual. But just because it is spiritual, not physical, does not mean that the warfare in the New Testament context is no less real. Thus, we are commanded to put on the full armor of God (Eph. 6:10–20) and engage in this spiritual warfare. The New Testament is replete with the use of military metaphors to describe our spiritual warfare. As Israel, in an overall sense, failed to implement the *ḥērem* because of a lack of faith and obedience, how are we failing in the implementation of Christ's commandments because of unbelief and disobedience? How are we failing to implement Ephesians 6:10–20 in our daily lives? In many ways, this is how Judges 1:1–2:5 applies to Christians today.

Many Christians become so consumed with the world that they simply do not believe they are really in a spiritual confrontation. They have compromised with the world and have forgotten the apostle's admonition "do not

---

47. For further discussion of the passage in Ephesians, see K. Snodgrass, *Ephesians* (NIVAC; Grand Rapids: Zondervan, 1996), 338–61.

love the world or anything in the world" (1 John 2:15). Judges 1:1–2:5 warns us of the dangers of not trusting in God's Word and heeding this admonition.

Subsidiary messages. The pragmatism of Judah's alliance with Simeon (1:2, 17) serves as a warning to Christians. The natural way is not necessarily God's way, for it can undercut his plan and lessen our dependence on him. Each tribe was responsible to conquer its own allotment, depending on God for the results. Note that Judah, because of its size, hardly needed Simeon to ensure the conquest of its allotment, and Simeon really did not need Judah to guarantee what God had promised he would do for them.

Fortunately, this passage also provides some good examples through the vignettes relating Judah's successes. The story about the defeat of the lord of Bezeq (Adoni-Bezek) shows that God answers prayer, fulfills his promises, and brings retribution on evil. Such stories engender confidence that God will do these same things in our own contexts.

The stories of the conquests of Hebron and Debir emphasize God's faithfulness and grace. The fact that Caleb and Othniel are non-Israelites only heightens this. The reality that God works "outside the circle" should encourage and challenge us. God often grafts into the community of faith individuals who become outstanding leaders.

For the Christian, Acsah represents a woman who will not be denied her full inheritance. She is a model resembling the women of the Gospels, who sought out Jesus and refused to be turned back by the crowds and by Jesus' own disciples. As a result, they found salvation, healing, and blessing for themselves and their families (see Matt. 9:20–22; 15:21–28; 26:7–13; Mark 7:24–30; 14:3–9; Luke 2:36–38; 7:11–15, 36–50; 8:43–48; 13:10–17; 18:1–5).[48]

Yet in spite of these few positive vignettes, the overall pattern of moral and spiritual failure prevails in Judges 1:1–2:5. Disobedience and compromise dominate the remainder of the passage and signal important warnings to the modern context. Ultimately, to apply this passage is to heed its warnings.

---

48. Hess, *Joshua*, 246.

Judges 2:6–3:6

❧

AFTER JOSHUA HAD dismissed the Israelites, they went to take possession of the land, each to his own inheritance. ⁷The people served the LORD throughout the lifetime of Joshua and of the elders who outlived him and who had seen all the great things the LORD had done for Israel.

⁸Joshua son of Nun, the servant of the LORD, died at the age of a hundred and ten. ⁹And they buried him in the land of his inheritance, at Timnath Heres in the hill country of Ephraim, north of Mount Gaash.

¹⁰After that whole generation had been gathered to their fathers, another generation grew up, who knew neither the LORD nor what he had done for Israel. ¹¹Then the Israelites did evil in the eyes of the LORD and served the Baals. ¹²They forsook the LORD, the God of their fathers, who had brought them out of Egypt. They followed and worshiped various gods of the peoples around them. They provoked the LORD to anger ¹³because they forsook him and served Baal and the Ashtoreths. ¹⁴In his anger against Israel the LORD handed them over to raiders who plundered them. He sold them to their enemies all around, whom they were no longer able to resist. ¹⁵Whenever Israel went out to fight, the hand of the LORD was against them to defeat them, just as he had sworn to them. They were in great distress.

¹⁶Then the LORD raised up judges, who saved them out of the hands of these raiders. ¹⁷Yet they would not listen to their judges but prostituted themselves to other gods and worshiped them. Unlike their fathers, they quickly turned from the way in which their fathers had walked, the way of obedience to the LORD's commands. ¹⁸Whenever the LORD raised up a judge for them, he was with the judge and saved them out of the hands of their enemies as long as the judge lived; for the LORD had compassion on them as they groaned under those who oppressed and afflicted them. ¹⁹But when the judge died, the people returned to ways even more corrupt than those of their fathers, following other gods and serving and worshiping them. They refused to give up their evil practices and stubborn ways.

²⁰Therefore the LORD was very angry with Israel and said, "Because this nation has violated the covenant that I laid down for their forefathers and has not listened to me, ²¹I will no longer drive out before them any of the nations Joshua left when he died. ²²I will use them to test Israel and see whether they will keep the way of the LORD and walk in it as their forefathers did." ²³The LORD had allowed those nations to remain; he did not drive them out at once by giving them into the hands of Joshua.

³:¹These are the nations the LORD left to test all those Israelites who had not experienced any of the wars in Canaan ²(he did this only to teach warfare to the descendants of the Israelites who had not had previous battle experience): ³the five rulers of the Philistines, all the Canaanites, the Sidonians, and the Hivites living in the Lebanon mountains from Mount Baal Hermon to Lebo Hamath. ⁴They were left to test the Israelites to see whether they would obey the LORD's commands, which he had given their forefathers through Moses.

⁵The Israelites lived among the Canaanites, Hittites, Amorites, Perizzites, Hivites and Jebusites. ⁶They took their daughters in marriage and gave their own daughters to their sons, and served their gods.

INTRODUCTION 2 (2:6–3:6) stresses the difficulties that Israel had with foreign religious idols. It provides a thematic summarizing outline of the spiritual background to the period of the judges.

This introduction returns chronologically to the beginning of the book (i.e., it is a flashback to the same characters and events as 1:1).[1] While Introduction 1 (1:1–2:5) narrates matters from the point of view of the Israelites, Introduction 2 (2:6–3:6) narrates them from the point of view of Yahweh. This dual introduction produces the potential for irony. We must never interpret 1:1–2:5 alone, for the writer has purposefully laid the one beside the other to produce the desired effect.

The developments described in Introduction 2, for the most part, coincide with those narrated in the bulk of the book. The details are contained not in 2:6–3:6 itself but in what follows. Introduction 2 is a narrative abstract,

---

1. Younger, "Judges 1 in Its Near Eastern Literary Context," 222–24; Klein, *The Triumph of Irony*, 12.

an outline of the plot. While Introduction 1 traces the linear (literary and moral) movements that will be observed in the main body of the book, Introduction 2 delineates the cyclical movement. It reduces suspense (we already "know" the story), but it does not necessarily hinder our ability to appreciate the detailed presentation of character, situation, and theme in the fully presented narrative that follows (3:7—16:31). Indeed, it may enhance it, as when one is given a summary of the plot of a complex drama before it is presented on the stage. In any case, suspense is not eliminated from individual episodes; rather, it is heightened via expectation.

The cycle introduced in this section (2:6—3:6) is obviously an imposed interpretive pattern of the events of the period of the judges reflecting the theological perspective of the narrator. Such cyclical patterns in the understanding of history are not unknown from other ancient and more modern cultures.[2] In a sense, it accurately portrays the human inclination toward sin, the angry work of God in punishing that sin,[3] the lament of those who find themselves under God's chastening hand, God's delivering them, and repose coming at the end. Such a pattern can often be observed on an individual as well as a corporate level in numerous contexts.

In 2:6—3:6, the theological perspective narrated is that of Yahweh. Thus it is evaluative, and the assessment is condemning. Israel has broken her covenant with Yahweh and has assimilated to the Canaanite culture ("lived among" is a key phrase in the description). This is most manifest in the Israelites' intermarriages with the Canaanites and the subsequent "serving" of their gods.

Interestingly, the only human individual who is named is Joshua. He is an ideal figure ("*the* servant of the LORD," 2:8). In contrast, the Israelites of this period are characterized en masse as religiously incontinent (*znh*, 2:17),[4]

---

2. An ancient example can be observed in Esarhaddon's Babylon inscriptions (R. Borger, *Inschriften Asarhaddons*, 12—15). J. A. Brinkman observes the following cyclical pattern in these inscriptions: "*divine alienation—devastation : divine reconciliation—reconstruction.*" Moreover, this cycle is used in Esarhaddon's Babylon inscriptions as "a religious explanation (answering the question 'why')" for the destruction of Babylon. See J. A. Brinkman, "Through a Glass Darkly: Esarhaddon's Retrospects on the Downfall of Babylon," in *Studies in Literature from the Ancient Near East: By Members of the American Oriental Society Dedicated to Samuel Noah Kramer*, ed. J. M. Sasson (New Haven, Conn.: American Oriental Society, 1984; = *JAOS* 103 [1983]): 35—42. For this cyclical pattern in Judges, see Polzin, *Moses and the Deuteronomist*, 140—50.

3. In the ancient Near Eastern context, a number of nations interpret their national oppression by a foreign power as the work of their god's angry reprises. For example, the Moabites understood their oppression by the Israelites as the result of Chemosh's anger with them (Mesha Inscription, line 5). See K. A. D. Smelik, "The Inscription of King Mesha," *COS*, 2.23.

4. Lit., incontinent means without self-restraint, especially in regard to sexual activity (the Heb. term *znh* has this nuance). It is used in a figurative description of the Israelites' religious orientations.

corrupt (*šḥḥ*, 2:19), and stubborn or obstinate (*qšh*, 2:19). These are the narrator's own evaluative terms; they reveal Yahweh's perspective.

In contrast to the depiction of the Israelites, Yahweh's emotional state is described directly: He becomes angry with the Israelites (v. 14), he is moved to pity by their groaning (v. 18), he becomes angry again (v. 20). This description of the ebb and flow of Yahweh's emotions draws our attention (admittedly in an unsubtle manner) to the depth of his personal attachment to Israel and to the reluctance with which he finally makes the decision to punish Israel (2:20–22). It stresses the long-suffering attribute of God. Thus the description has the effect of making that decision to punish Israel more understandable, and therefore acceptable, to the reader. The narrator's explicit condemnation of the Israelites serves the same end. The state of affairs in Israel is interpreted as the basis for Yahweh's reluctant but just judgment on his people (2:20–22). They have not come into secure possession of the land sworn to the fathers because of their persistent apostasy despite all of Yahweh's interventions.

The rhetorical structure of the second introduction (2:6–3:6) can be delineated as follows:

> Preface: From Joshua to "Another Generation" (2:6–10)
> Cyclical Pattern of History (2:11–19)
> Yahweh's Punishment: The Nations Left As Punishment (2:20–3:4)
> Summary Conclusion to the Whole Introduction (3:5–6)

Preface: From Joshua to "Another Generation" (2:6–10)

IN THESE VERSES, which are apparently dependent on Joshua 24:28–31,[5] there is a specific contrast between two different generations: the faithfulness of Joshua's day and the infidelity of the subsequent generation. The narrative is composed of four units:

> A dispersal of the people to their "inheritance" (2:6)
> > B the "obedience" of the people (2:7)
> A' the death of Joshua and his burial in his "inheritance" (2:8–9)
> > B' the "disobedience" of the next generation (2:10)

Both B and B' units end with references to "the great things the LORD had done for Israel." This pattern heightens the contrast between Joshua, the faithful servant of Yahweh, together with the people of his generation who "served" Yahweh, and the unfaithful generation who did not "know" Yahweh. "Serve" is richly contrasted with "did not know."

---

5. See W. Koopmans, *Joshua 24 As Poetic Narrative* (JSOTSup 93; Sheffield: Sheffield Academic Press, 1990), 363–69.

Joshua sent the people away to their inheritances in order to possess the land (what should have transpired instead of what is narrated in Judges 1:1–2:5). The people serve Yahweh in the generation of Joshua and the elders (who saw the great deeds that Yahweh had done). Joshua died and was buried in his inheritance in Timnath Heres[6] in the hill country of Ephraim. When that generation died, another generation arose.

The description of this second generation is stark (2:10). In contrast to the previous generation, they "knew neither the LORD nor what he had done for Israel." They did not have a relationship with him, nor did they even know about the mighty acts he had done on their behalf. The result is anticipated: They "did evil in the eyes of the LORD and served the Baals." This was an active choice on their part, as Joshua 24 reinforces.

The archaeological record tends to bear out this verdict. Any distinct ethnicity of the Israelites is almost impossible to determine from archaeological materials of the Iron I period (ca. 1200–1000 B.C.), since the Israelites themselves were not apt to make a difference, even though in at least religious things they were expected by God to do so. Unfortunately, the biblical text evinces an attitude of assimilation on the part of the Israelites, who were determined to make themselves indistinguishable from the other inhabitants of the hill country. The Israelites "lived" among the Canaanites (cf. Judg. 1 above), "intermarried" with them, and "served" their gods (3:5–6). Thus in religious matters, which lay at the heart of Israelite culture (as in most ancient cultures), most Israelites could not be distinguished from their neighbors.

Cyclical Pattern of History (2:11–19)

THIS NEXT SECTION introduces the narrative framework so that literary expectations are increased. There are three parts to this section: apostasy in Israel (2:11–13), Yahweh's anger—oppression as punishment (2:14–15), and Yahweh's compassion—deliverance by judges in spite of Israel's continued apostasies (2:16–19).

---

6. The matter of the alternate names Timnath-serah (Josh. 19:50; 24:30) and Timnath-heres (Judg. 2:9) is difficult. Timnath-heres means "portion of the sun," and Timnath-serah means "portion of excess." Some scholars argue that Timnath-serah is correct as in Joshua 19:50; 24:30; a scribe reversed the consonants (Boling, *Judges*, 72). Others argue that Timnath-heres is the orginal and that a scribe changed the spelling to Timnath-serah for polemically religious reasons (B. Lindars, *Judges 1–5: A New Translation and Commentary*, ed. A. D. H. Mayes [Edinburgh: T. & T. Clark, 1995], 96–97). The site is probably modern Khirbet Tibneh, about ten miles northwest of Bethel, sixteen miles southwest of Shechem. See E. Noort, "Joshua 24,28–31, Richter 2,6–9 und das Josuagrab. Gedanken zu einem Strassenbild," in *Biblische Welten: Festschrift für Martin Metzger zu seinem 65. Geburtstag*, ed. W. Zwickel (OBO 123; Fribourg: Edition universitaires/Göttingen: Vandenhoeck & Ruprecht, 1993), 109–33.

Apostasy in Israel (2:11–13). In this first part, the narrative relates Israel's apostasies by means of the following structure:

Then the Israelites did evil [*bāraʿ*] in the eyes of the LORD,
A and [they] served [*ʿābad*] the Baals.
    B They forsook [*ʿāzab*] the LORD, the God of their fathers,
        who had brought them out of Egypt.
            C They followed [lit., went after, *bālak ʾaḥᵃrê*] and
                worshiped [*šḥḥ*] various gods of the peoples around them.
            They provoked the LORD to anger [*kāʿas*]
    B' because they forsook [*ʿāzab*] him
A' and served [*ʿābad*] Baal and the Ashtoreths.

These statements fulfill the statement of the messenger/angel of Yahweh in 2:3. The initial statement that "the Israelites did evil in the eyes of the LORD" will be the opening declaration for every cyclical/major judge story in the book. The article on *bārāʿ* (lit., the evil) may imply both a specific and consummate evil, namely, apostasy from Yahweh (Ex. 20:3–6),[7] although it may simply be an articular usage with an abstract noun. Whatever the case, the following statements elaborate on this initial declaration and further define this apostasy from Yahweh.

The chiastic pattern A-B-C-B'-A' unifies the paragraph. The idea conveyed in the A, B and B', A' elements—that is, "forsaking/abandoning" (*ʿāzab*) Yahweh and "serving" (*ʿābad*) Baal—are really two sides of the same coin. They define more precisely "the evil" that the Israelites do in the eyes of Yahweh. These elements encircle C with its emphasis on false worship with the resultant anger of the Lord. The idea of "going or walking after other gods" (*bālak ʾaḥᵃrê*) clearly contrasts with the biblical idea of "walking with [*bālak ʾet*] the LORD." And the idea of "worshiping" (*šḥḥ*) these other gods is a blatant violation of Ex. 20:5, "You shall not bow down to [*šḥḥ*] them."

The term *šḥḥ* denotes the physical gesture of prostration before a superior and thus speaks of cultic homage and allegiance to a deity.[8] Thus, here it represents an abandoning of allegiance to Yahweh and the prostrating homage and allegiance given to "other gods" (which, of course, are not really gods at all). Furthermore, the appositional clause in B ("the God of their fathers, who brought them out of Egypt") heightens the apostasy. They have "forsaken" the true and living God, who had saved them from oppression, to

---

7. Cf. Block's discussion (*Judges, Ruth*, 123).
8. It is, as Block correctly notes (*Judges, Ruth*, 126), the opposite of what is often thought of today as "worship," i.e., standing before God with hands raised in praise (which is actually exaltation).

go after "other gods," who are nothing more than the "various gods of the peoples around them" and who cannot deliver, only oppress. The resultant anger of the Lord is entirely understandable!

The final and climatic statement of the paragraph, that they "served Baal and the Ashtoreths," is especially important. The word *ba'al* can be used in a secular sense of "lord, master, owner, citizen, or husband." When applied to a deity (often in the ancient Near East), it functioned as a title, "divine lord, master." It was also used as a reference to the Canaanite storm god[9] (see further discussion below).

The term "Ashtoreths" is a mistransliteration[10] by the NIV for the Hebrew *'aštārôt*, the plural of *'aštart*, that is, Astarte. Astarte was the popular (animal and human) fertility goddess and consort of Baal. She also was associated with war. She is often pictured in Egyptian iconography as riding a horse and carrying a bow and arrow or spear and shield.

There are only four verses in the Hebrew Bible that contain the combination Baal and Astarte (Judg. 2:13; 10:6; 1 Sam. 7:4; 12:10). Judges 2:13; 10:6; and 1 Samuel 12:10 also employ the parallelism of "forsake" (*'āzab*) and "serve" (*'ābad*). This is not fortuitous. The central question is the worship of Yahweh rather than the gods of the surrounding nations. This worship entails the recognition of Yahweh as king. Thus, Judges 2:13 and 10:6 emphasize the breaking of the oath of allegiance to Yahweh's kingship and recognition of the kingship of other gods ("forsake" Yahweh and "serve" Baals and Ashtoreths).

Many scholars believe that the Hebrew vocalization of Ashtoreth (*'aštōret*) found in 1 Kings 11:5, 33 and 2 Kings 23:13 is a deliberate scribal distortion of Astarte (*'aštart*), in which the vowels of the Hebrew word *bōšet* ("shame") were used in place of the normal vocalization for polemical reasons.[11] By contrast, other scholars argue that the vocalization is a natural Hebrew transcription of the Phoenician form Astarte and has nothing to do with *bōšet*. Hadley argues for a depersonalization or better dedeification of Astarte in the Old Testament,[12] in which case the vocalization with *bōšet* is understandable.

---

9. The storm deity's name divine name was "Hadad."

10. Perhaps under the influence of the vocalizations in 1 Kings 11:5, 33 and 2 Kings 23:13.

11. For an example of this, compare the use of Ish-Bosheth in 2 Sam. 2:10 for Esh-Baal (1 Chron. 8:33).

12. J. M. Hadley, "The Fertility of the Flock? The De-personalization of Astarte in the Old Testament," in *On Reading Prophetic Texts: Gender-Specific and Related Studies in Memory of Fokkelien van Dijk-Hemmes*, ed. B. Becking and M. Dijkstra (Biblical Interpretation Series 18; Leiden: Brill, 1996), 115–33, esp. 132.

The use of the plural of ʿaštārôt in Judges 2:13 and 10:6 is understood to be either a reference to various local manifestations of the goddess, an embodiment of the Canaanite cult, or a reference to polytheism in general (i.e., a term for female deities).

The plural form "Baals" (bᵉʿalîm) in verse 11, like the plural ʿaštārôt, is understood by different scholars to refer either to various local manifestations of the storm deity or to male deities in general.[13] The god Baal is primarily a storm god. In the Old Testament, Baal is also seen as a fertility deity. Bull imagery is sometimes used for Baal.[14] The fertility practices of the Baal cult were considered degrading by the supporters of Yahweh, and the worship of Baal is frequently referred to as harlotry and adultery (cf. 2:17). The intimate connection between myth and ritual in the life of an agricultural people greatly heighten this issue. Therefore, it is no accident that this historian of the judges' period (i.e., the writer of 2:6–3:6) finds in it the cause of national disaster. Apostasy in his view leads inevitably to moral corruption, and this in turn leads to the degeneracy that renders the people helpless before their foes.[15]

Yahweh's anger—oppression as punishment (2:14–15). In this second part, Yahweh's anger at the Israelites results in the oppressions that he brings on them as punishment. The clauses that Yahweh "handed . . . over" or "sold" the Israelites into the hands of oppressors or raiders are framework statements.[16] The NIV's translation of 2:14 obscures two important repetitions. The verse is better translated (cf. NRSV):

And the anger of Yahweh was kindled against Israel.[17]
And he gave them into the hand of plunderers [šōsîm],
and they plundered [šāsâ] them;
and he sold them into the hand of their enemies [ʾôyᵉbêhem] all around,
and they were not able to stand before their enemies [ʾôyᵉbêhem].

---

13. Cf. the careful discussion of J. A. Dearman, "Baal in Israel: The Contribution of Some Place Names and Personal Names to an Understanding of Early Israelite Religion," in *History and Interpretation: Essays in Honour of John H. Hayes*, ed. M. P. Graham, W. P. Brown, J. K. Kuan (JSOTSup 173; Sheffield: Sheffield Academic, 1993), 173–91.

14. A bull figurine discovered at the "Bull Site" (a reasonably certain Israelite cult installation of the period of the judges, dating to the twelfth century B.C.) is thought by most scholars to represent either El, Baal, or Yahweh. For a discussion of the site and the figurine, see A. Mazar, "'The Bull Site'—An Iron Age I Open Cult Place," *BASOR* 247 (1982): 27–42; idem, "Bronze Bull Found in Israelite 'High Place' from the Time of the Judges," *BAR* 9 (September/October 1983): 34–40.

15. Lindars, *Judges 1–5*, 96.

16. Both terms "sell" (mākar) and "hand over, give" (nātan) are economic expressions picturing Yahweh as transferring ownership of the apostasizing Israelites to the foreign oppressors.

17. Lit., "and the nose of Yahweh was kindled." This is a figurative way of expressing divine wrath and fury.

Thus through the repetitions of the verbal root *ššb* (plunder[18]) and the noun *ʾôyēb* (enemy), Yahweh's anger and discipline of Israel are greatly emphasized.

In verse 15, the NIV's "to defeat them" also misses the mark. The term is *rāʿâ* (misfortune, calamity) and is an obvious play on the term *raʿ* (evil) in verse 11a. Because the Israelites did "evil" (*raʿ*) in Yahweh's eyes and apostasized, the shocking reality for Israel was that their real enemy was God himself, who ensured that when they went out to battle, the outcome was a calamitous disaster. This is declared to be the promised result according to earlier solemn declarations of Yahweh (cf. Deut. 28:25–37; 31:16–21).

Yahweh's compassion—deliverance by judges in spite of Israel's continued apostasies (2:16–19). But in the third part, on account of the Israelites' groaning caused by the persecution of their oppressors, Yahweh has compassion on his people and raises up judges (i.e., "tribal rulers") to deliver them. Block observes:

> The fact that this statement follows immediately after the notice of Israel's dire straits suggests Yahweh's raising up of rulers represented a series of emergency measures to relieve the people of pain, which is rather remarkable. The narrator begins to speak of divine mercy without any hint of prior repentance. In this book Yahweh's actions will not typically be bound to any mechanical formula of blessing and/or retribution, based upon what human beings earn by their actions. Rather he intervenes on Israel's behalf solely on the basis of his compassion; the scene of Israelite distress moves the divine patron to action.[19]

Although the judges deliver the Israelites, their response is to return quickly to doing evil; they prostitute themselves[20] and worship and bow down to the gods of the land. They refuse to listen to the tribal rulers.[21] The text clearly implies that each successive generation experiences a greater degeneration in sin and corruption than with the previous one (2:19). Thus the picture is not just cyclical but downward. Israel is spiraling down into a spiritual abyss.

---

18. The root of this verb is probably connected to the infamous "Shasu"—Siniatic, nomadic raiders/plunderers mentioned in a number of Egyptian inscriptions.

19. Block, *Judges, Ruth*, 128.

20. Goodfriend suggests five reasons why Israel's spiritual infidelity is characterized as prostitution (*znh*) rather than adultery (*nʾp*): (1) *znh* implies iterative or habitual illicit behavior; (2) the motive is personal gain, not casual sex; (3) *znh* implies a multiplicity of sex partners; (4) the participle *zônâ* suggests a treacherous and hardened woman; and (5) *znh* refers only to illicit sex by a female partner. See E. A. Goodfriend, "Prostitution," *ABD*, 5:505–10.

21. See the discussion of the *šōpēṭ* ("judge") at the beginning of the introduction. This particular sentence in 2:17 is emphatic (lit.): "But to their tribal rulers (judges) they would not listen."

Yahweh's Punishment:
The Nations Left As Punishment
(2:20–3:4)

THE THIRD SECTION of Introduction 2 (2:20–3:4) is the resultant conclusion of this cyclical, downward pattern. Yahweh declares his punishment for Israelite unfaithfulness: The nations in the land will not be driven out but will be left. Yahweh's increased anger at Israel's pattern leads to this decision to leave the nations as punishment.

Yahweh's punishment is a fulfillment and expansion of his promise in 2:3. Both that passage and this one record the people's transgression of the covenant, their disobedience to Yahweh, and his vow to halt the progress of the subjugation of the land. In fact, all of this in Judges has been fore-shadowed already in Joshua 23:12–13. The promise that the inhabitants of the land will be "thorns in your sides" is expanded into the twofold rationale of Yahweh (Judg. 2:20–23; 3:4): first, to test Israel's adherence to the covenant (2:22; 3:1), and second, to add an instructive value to the pun-ishment (i.e., to teach warfare to the inexperienced descendents; 3:2). Irony is concentrated in the interpretation of the threefold repetition of "to test," to which Yahweh and Israel unquestionably attach differing perspectives (2:22; 3:1, 4).

The list of nations given in 3:3 corresponds roughly with the fuller list in Joshua 13:2–6 (sometimes referred to as "the land that remains"). The first nation listed (as in Josh. 13:2–3) is the "Philistines," who are ruled by five rulers (lit., "tyrants," $s^e ran\hat{i}m$).[22] Next on the list are the "Canaan-ites" and "Sidonians" (as in Josh. 13:3–4). Finally, while the "Hivites"[23] are not mentioned in Joshua 13, the general description of the Lebanon mountains from Mount Hermon to Lebo Hamath follows the pattern of Joshua 13:5.

Summary Conclusion
to the Whole Introduction (3:5–6)

THE LAST SECTION of Introduction 2 (3:5–6) is the final summary conclusion to the whole introduction. It stresses three things. (1) The Israelites "live among" the peoples of the land, they "intermarry" with the peoples there, and they "serve" their gods. Judges 3:5 is a stereotyped list of the peoples left in the land among whom the Israelites live (based on Deut. 7:1):

---

22. On the new Philistine inscription from Tel Miqnê/Ekron, see K. L. Younger, "The Ekron Inscription of Akhayus," *COS*, 2.42.

23. Possibly the same as the Horites (probably of Hurrian or Anatolian origin).

Deut. 7:1	Judg. 3:5
—	Canaanites
Hittites	Hittites
Girgashites	—
Amorites	Amorites
Canaanites	—
Perizzites	Perizzites
Hivites	Hivites
Jebusites	Jebusites

In spite of the slight difference in order, the lists are almost verbatim the same.[24] Only the Girgashites are missing from the Judges 3:5 list.

(2) Next is the Israelites' intermarriage with the peoples of the land (3:6). This concluding statement about these intermarriages serves two ironic functions in the book: (1) most immediate, it stands in contrast to Othniel, the initial and ideal judge (3:7–11), who is given the godly Acsah by Caleb (cf. 1:13); (2) it heightens the contrast with Conclusion 2, in which the Israelites take an oath not to give their daughters in marriage to the Benjamites (ch. 21; see discussion in the introduction).

(3) The Israelites "serve" the gods of all the peoples of the land. This, too, has ironic implications, since the same verb (*ᶜbd*) will be used to describe the oppression of Cushan-Rishathaim in the very next passage (3:7–11). This phrase climatically concludes the double introduction of Judges: The Israelites "served their gods!"

Bridging Contexts

FEW BOOKS PORTRAY so complete a picture of human depravity as does Judges. This section has a clear message concerning the apostasy of Israel from Yahweh and the subsequent cyclical process through which Yahweh disciplines Israel. Apostasy is the abandoning of allegiance to Yahweh in favor of allegiance to other gods, a clear violation of Yahweh's covenant with Israel. Ironically, Israel will continue a claim of association with Yahweh, yet their real commitments are elsewhere, to the gods of the Canaanites.

This message easily bridges between ancient and modern contexts.[25] True

---

24. See E. C. Hostetter, *Nations Mightier and More Numerous: The Biblical View of Palestine's Pre-Israelite Peoples* (Bibal Dissertation Series 3; North Richland Hills, Tex: Bibal, 1995), 29–31, 41–43.

25. As noted in the Bridging Contexts section of 1:1–2:5, it is important not to misapply this passage on the national level or simply on the cultural level. The prime issue is, once again, spiritual.

worship of the Lord requires an exclusive allegiance. An allegiance to any other thing is a transgression of his covenant, old or new. Unfortunately, there are many Christians today who want to be associated with Christ while their allegiance in everyday life is to another god. And, to say the least, there are many gods available in which people today do place their trust (see Contemporary Significance section). In this particular context, the worship of Baal is especially relevant. Baal was primarily a storm god, but this led secondarily to his worship as fertility deity. Fertility cults had obvious concerns with securing prosperity for the worshiper in terms of family, flocks, herds, and crops. In some ways this was the ancient equivalent to the modern health-and-wealth gospel, so popular in the North American context.

Sadly, in a number of instances where the Israelites continued to name Yahweh as their God, they syncretized his worship with aberrant forms based on their Canaanite neighbors' practices. The later story of Micah and his idolatry (ch. 17) illustrates this in graphic form. In the modern context, biblical faith is joined with any number of syncretistic forms, creating spiritual deviations of all kinds (cf. esp. the discussion of religious pluralism below). Another example is the propensity to fight the Lord's battles with the world's resources, strategies, and methods. Some local churches resemble corporate America more than the church of Jesus Christ as described in the New Testament. Integrity and accountability are not found in the everyday actions of the church.

There is little wonder that God becomes angry with the Israelites. We must remember that his anger is not unrighteous as ours often is. Rather, it is always consistent with his character, with all his attributes. It is his just response to flagrant spiritual adultery and involves his desire to bring Israel to repentance, not to punish (as our anger does). In the same way, there is little wonder that God is displeased and angry with many Christians today for their apostasy from his Word.

The passage begins with a contrast between generations. As a nation, Israel solemnly swore before Joshua to obey God (Josh. 24), yet only one generation later, they quickly turn to the gods of heathen nations and intermarry with the Canaanites. The statements that they "knew neither the LORD nor what he had done for Israel" (Judg. 2:10) are perhaps some of the more condemning in the Hebrew Bible. The contrast between the faithful generation and the unfaithful generation naturally raises the question of the passing on of the faith. With the intense interest in the raising of children among Christians, this passage has certain relevance.

Although Israel fails to drive out the Canaanites, God works through this to reveal his sovereignty: He trains the younger generation in warfare (3:1–2). And he can and does work in amazing ways in each generation. The sinfulness of one generation cannot stifle his work. Nevertheless, how we live does affect the next generation. The Israelites who turn to other gods do not consider the impact their actions will have on others.[26]

MODERN IDOLATRY. The message of apostasy from God has great contemporary significance. As mentioned in the introduction (see pp. 45–47), the myth of secularism is that there are no idols because there is no God. But if idolatry is worshiping the creation, or some part of it, instead of the Creator (cf. Rom. 1:18–23), then the process of sacralization (the process by which created things become central to life, invoking religious-like awe and submission) provides numerous examples of idolatry in modern contexts.

One object of sacralization is money and material possessions. This is the idol of Mammon (Matt. 6:24), which leads on to sins such as covetousness (named specifically as a form of idolatry in Eph. 5:5; Col. 3:5). Underlying this idol is the fundamental belief that utopia exists and that its essence is material well-being. Set in opposition to this approach to life are numerous biblical texts: for example, "one's life does not consist in the abundance of possessions" (Luke 12:15 NRSV); and "keep your lives free from the love of money and be content with what you have" (Heb. 13:5). "The Christian view of the world does not make economics coterminous with life, nor does it confuse wealth with moral worth, nor promote greed as a virtue."[27]

The biblical view sees creation as the possession of the Creator, not humanity's possession that can be endlessly manipulated and exploited. All creation belongs to God and is graciously provided to us as stewards. As Schlossberg has noted, this biblical view of wealth "seems odd only because we have adopted as normal a way of life that is hopelessly unable to produce what it promises and has demonstrated that inability to almost everyone."[28] Instead, it is the worship of this idol that is "odd," indeed truly insane, when one recognizes that it cannot bring well-being to its worshiper, but rather only mars human life in its often oppressive demands on our time and energy as workers and in its production within us of unrest and discontent. A quick survey of virtually any adult Sunday school class will reveal significant levels of unrest and discontent among Christians. It is ironic that the ultimate

26. Joash's idolatry likely had an impact on his son, Gideon, who, after saving Israel from the Midianite oppression, makes an idol that the nation worships (see Judg. 8).

27. Provan, "To Highlight All Our Idols," 31.

28. H. Schlossberg, *Idols for Destruction: Christian Faith and Its Confrontation with American Society* (Nashville: Nelson, 1983), 311.

end of the worship of this type of idol is destruction, for "insatiable greed placing infinite claims on finite resources can have no other end."[29]

Materialism with its pursuit of possessions and financial independence and security are probably the biggest obstacles to spiritual advancement. Everything in our culture, from commercials to our education, pushes us in the direction of advancing our standard of living for more comfort, pleasure, and self-confidence without any thought of the Creator. Thus we become our own deity, controlling our lives and manipulating things for our gratification. Ultimately, it is our greed that is the idol, with things being the means of its appeasement.

We must resist the rhetoric of advertisers and the devotees of this idol and their message that one is what one owns and consumes. We must not be conformed to the pattern of this world but be transformed by the renewal of our minds by the Holy Spirit (Rom. 12:2). This requires an intense involvement with God's Word and with other believers who are dedicated to growing in their faith and who resist succumbing to the pressures to worship this idol.

Religious pluralism. Another idol that dominates in the secular Western world is the pervasive relativism that permeates the whole of our culture. If in fact all things are relative, including truth, then no religion has any right or authority to claim any kind of absolute validity or truth. Consequently, no religion is in any shape to tell us what we must or must not believe and therefore what we can or cannot do. While it is not as recognized as the previously discussed idol of money and material possessions, this idol of religious pluralism nevertheless wields increasing power in our culture. P. J. Achtemeier puts it this way:

> As it functions in the religious sphere, pluralism dilutes the force of any one mode of thought, or, in our case, any one form of religious devotion. To say that pluralism has invaded the Christian faith is to state a truism. Seminary professors publicly express their unhappiness with the Gospel of John for having included such a blatantly exclusivistic word as that of Jesus: "No one comes to the Father but by me" (John 14:6). Preachers feel unduly constricted by having to preach only from the canonical texts, and study groups in churches turn to modern novels to find something worth pondering. To claim any kind of exclusive truth for the revelation of God in Jesus Christ is to incur the accusation of arrogance and lack of consideration for the truth that also resides in insights of other religious systems.[30]

---

29. Ibid., 139.
30. P. J. Achtemeier, "Idolatry in the New Testament," *Ex Auditu* 15 (1999): 43–61, esp. 57.

Achtemeier goes on to note that this is one of the advantages of idolatry. To worship the creature rather than the Creator leaves one a large array of entities in which one can invest religious significance.[31] When there are a number, not to say a multitude, of idols, one may choose those one finds most appealing or those that best meet one's "felt needs" or "one's inmost longings." When there is more than one god, no one god can lay absolute claim on our lives and thoughts.

Importantly, this means that when an individual is able to determine for himself or herself what is good and what is evil, that person is freed to act as one pleases in terms of one's own definitions.[32] It is against this appeal of advantage for idolatry that Paul tells the Corinthians that in the end, service rendered to idols is service rendered to demons (1 Cor. 10:20–21). If anyone doubts that the demonic is rampant in our culture, one need only contemplate the recent event at Columbine High School. As Paul makes clear, to indulge in idolatry is to be set loose by God and to be put at the mercy of the idols to whom we turn.[33]

The idol of the self. Finally, in this connection, it is worth mentioning the idol of the self. The self is set at the center of existence as a god; ultimate significance is found in godlike individual autonomy, in self-set goals and boundaries. The sacred is defined in the first instance in relation to the self. Self-expression and self-actualization are important themes in this religion, which is evident in our society from the advice columns of newspapers and magazines through to schools, where sometimes the point seems no longer to learn things but to "find oneself" and to be the best person that one can be. The narcissistic society constantly promotes the self over all others. It encourages at every turn the pursuit of personal happiness and gratification. It urges ignoring, and if necessary dispensing with, whatever and whoever stands in our way in this quest for personal satisfaction—whether it be husbands and wives, children, life in the womb, the aged, the poor, the mentally challenged, and so on. The idol of the self promotes sex as the autonomous individual's quest for self-fulfillment.

But, as Provan argues, "the narcissistic society, the society that worships the self, is not the 'good' or the 'great' society, but a deeply dysfuntional and wicked one."[34] Idols cannot liberate; they can only bring oppression. The

---

31. Ibid., 57. The fact is there is nothing in creation that cannot be made into a focus of idolatrous worship!

32. This is nothing short of "everyone doing what is right in one's own eyes" (cf. the refrain of the double conclusion in Judg. 17–21, which begins with the story of Micah's making an idol).

33. Achtemeier, "Idolatry in the New Testament," 58.

34. Provan, "To Highlight All Our Idols," 33.

oppressive, destructive fallout of the narcissistic society can be seen everywhere in modern Western culture. Interestingly, Christianity begins with a larger story than the individual story, with a much larger moral universe that has "the only true God at its center, whose worship is perfect freedom—including the freedom from the need to believe that we are gods and that we possess the power to attain salvation by our own exertions."[35] Provan sums it up well:

> The old gods are still with us. They have simply changed their clothes so that they merge more easily into the modern crowd. They still claim to provide meaning to life, to explain the universe, and to provide the basis for personal security. They still demand wholehearted commitment from their worshippers. Christians ought to be free of them; for a truly Christian view of the world provides the basis for such freedom.[36]

Finally, it is important to note that the gods behind the idols of this world are no less demonic than those that stand behind the worship of idols in other contexts (ancient or modern). Ultimately it is the god of this world, Satan himself, who stands behind these gods and demands allegiance with all of the oppressive overtones contained in that commitment.

The gravity of the human tragedy is that we are quite incapable even of enlightened self-interest. Our fallenness prevents us from seeing that false gods—none of whom can create, or bless, or love, or redeem—can do us no real good. Nor can we see that God, in jealously and fiercely opposing such idols and, indeed, any attempt to make the created into the divine, is actively pursuing our good.[37]

True knowledge. Moving now to a different issue in the application of this passage, it is noteworthy that the two statements that they "knew neither the LORD nor what he had done for Israel" (2:10) are challenging. How do these statements apply to our generation? Certainly, the general ignorance of the Bible's basic content is observable with the Christian community. This speaks to the latter statement. But what about the former? Do we really know the Lord? In what way(s) do we know him? Simply as Savior? How intimate is our relationship with him?

Just as God had expectations for the Israelites, so he has expectations for Christians today. Essentially, we must "know Christ" and "the power of his resurrection" (Phil. 3:10)—that is, "what mighty acts he has done for us." We need to experience his transforming power.

---

35. Ibid.

36. Ibid.

37. For some additional reflections on idolatry, see B. Rosner, "Soul Idolatry: Greed As Idolatry in the Bible," *Ex Auditu* 15 (1999): 73–86.

It is also clear from this text that the parents of the second-generation Israelites were not held responsible for their children's sins. It is the generation that "knew neither the LORD nor what he had done" that is held responsible, not their parents. Such an observation does not excuse irresponsible parenting by Christians. But the biblical text holds each individual ultimately responsible for his or her sin, failure to be in relationship to God, and failure to walk with God.

Unfortunately, there are those in evangelical circles that teach that Proverbs 22:6 offers a guarantee of salvation for the next generation—that is, that a child can be programmed so thoroughly as to determine his or her course. While certainly appealing—who doesn't want to ensure positive outcomes?—Judges 2:10ff. makes it clear that this is a simply wrong interpretation. It often produces unmerited guilt (i.e., if the child continues in rebellion and sin, it must be the parents' fault). In fact, each individual is saved not by one's parents' job in child rearing but by grace alone. Moreover, no matter how good a parent may be in child rearing, there will always be prodigals.[38]

Ultimately, all fail as parents, and only the grace of God can make the difference. We should do the best we can as parents, nurturing our children in the admonition of the Lord. But it is wrong for us to trust in our parenting skills. We must trust in the Spirit's work in the lives of our children.

---

38. For some uplifting stories about modern prodigals, see Ruth B. Graham, *Prodigals [and Those Who Love Them]* (Grand Rapids: Baker, 1991), esp. 105–18. For a discussion of our point here, see J. C. Dobson, *Parenting Isn't for Cowards* (Dallas: Word, 1987), 185–88.

Judges 3:7–11

‖

THE ISRAELITES DID evil in the eyes of the LORD; they forgot the LORD their God and served the Baals and the Asherahs. ⁸The anger of the LORD burned against Israel so that he sold them into the hands of Cushan-Rishathaim king of Aram Naharaim, to whom the Israelites were subject for eight years. ⁹But when they cried out to the LORD, he raised up for them a deliverer, Othniel son of Kenaz, Caleb's younger brother, who saved them. ¹⁰The Spirit of the LORD came upon him, so that he became Israel's judge and went to war. The LORD gave Cushan-Rishathaim king of Aram into the hands of Othniel, who overpowered him. ¹¹So the land had peace for forty years, until Othniel son of Kenaz died.

IN STEREOTYPICAL STATEMENTS that repeat the previous section's outline (2:6–3:6), the first cyclical judge narrative begins. The complete cycle of framework statements occurs only in the Othniel story. The plot of the Othniel narrative is formed chiefly through these framework statements. After this cycle, each cycle will lack more and more of the framework statements (see the introduction). Thus, although for the first time there is a particular enemy and a particular judge, there are no plot expansions or developments:¹ no dialogue, no reported speech of any kind, no dramatization of events, no scenic presentation, no descriptions of any character flaws, and so on. Such narrative expansions will characterize the next five cycles. Consequently, their absence here is significant. Nothing distracts the reader from the clear message of God's intervention through the deliverer (môšîaᶜ)² he raises up.

Thus from a literary standpoint, it appears as if the writer wishes to establish the pattern with a formally correct example—a paragon of the paradigm—before using traditions and other data, which may be more interesting as stories but are more difficult to fit into the scheme. Hence Block concludes: "This brief account functions as a paradigmatic model against which the rest must be interpreted."³ The Othniel account serves

---

1. O'Connell, *The Rhetoric of the Book of Judges*, 82–83; Webb, *The Book of the Judges*, 127.

2. Only Othniel and Ehud are designated *môšîaᶜ* (deliverer). Othniel, however, was the only one without fault. See O'Connell's discussion (*The Rhetoric of the Book of Judges*, 83 n. 34).

3. Block, *Judges, Ruth*, 149.

literarily as a foil to the other judge cycles—especially to the climactic Samson cycle.

While the narration may seem on the surface dull and colorless, a closer reading reveals that this is not entirely accurate. There are a number of features within this short text that give it a deeper level of sophistication and enhance the communication of this cycle's message. These features contribute to that message by highlighting Othniel as Yahweh's means of saving Israel.

As is the case with all six cyclical judge narratives, the initial framework statement is: "The Israelites did evil in the eyes of the LORD" (3:7). This documents Israelite apostasy.[4] The next two statements occur only in Introduction 2, the Othniel cycle, and the Jephthah cycle: They "served the Baals and the Asherahs," and "the anger of the LORD burned against Israel."[5] The statement that "they forgot the LORD their God" is unique to the Othniel section.[6]

The statement that the Israelites served the Baals and Asherahs is reminiscent of Introduction 2's assertion that the Israelites served "Baal and the Ashtoreths [i.e., the Astartes]" (2:13), although here it is not Astarte but Asherah that is in view. Asherah was a fertility goddess[7] and was regularly represented by an upright wooden pole (frequently denounced in the Hebrew Bible). The only clearly identifiable representation of Asherah in Israel is found on the tenth-century cult stand from Taanach.[8] Here she is represented anthropomorphically as a nude female holding the lions' ears in tier four of the cult stand. That this is the goddess Asherah is not disputed. In other instances that are less certain the goddess may be represented iconographically with anthropomorphic and vegetative imagery and could be associated with lion imagery.

Some scholars feel that there are textual references to the goddess Asherah in inscriptions from Kuntillet ʿAjrud and Khirbet el-Qôm.[9] Other

---

4. For a discussion of this framework statement, see the comments on 2:6–3:6 (p. 88).

5. Besides Introduction 2 (2:6–3:6) and the Othniel cycle (3:7–11), these statements are only found in the Jephthah cycle (10:6a, 7a).

6. Block correctly notes that the idea here is not a case of temporary amnesia but a more intentional and active nuance akin to the notion of "abandoning" (ʿzb) (*Judges, Ruth*, 151).

7. See N. Wyatt, "Asherah," in *DDD*, cols. 183–95.

8. R. Hendel, "Aniconism and Anthropomorphism in Ancient Israel," in *The Image and the Book: Iconic Cults, Aniconism, and the Veneration of the Holy Book in Israel and the Ancient Near East*, ed. by K. van der Toorn (Kampen: Kok, 1999), 205–28.

9. For the inscriptions, see P. K. McCarter, "Kuntillet ʿAjrud," *COS*, 2.47; and "Khirbet el-Qom," *COS*, 2.52. For a discussion of these texts in connection with the worship of Asherah, see R. S. Hess, "Yahweh and His Asherah? Religious Pluralism in the Old Testament World," in *One God, One Lord: Christianity in a World of Religious Pluralism*, ed. A. D. Clarke and B. W. Winter (Grand Rapids: Eerdmans, 1993), 13–42; idem, "Asherah or Asherata?" *Or* 65 (1996): 209–19.

scholars understand the references in these inscriptions to be to the cult image, not the goddess.[10] Interestingly, at the beginning of the Out-group judge cycles (i.e., the fourth cycle), Gideon is instructed to tear down his father's altar to Baal and cut down the Asherah pole beside it (6:25).

Deservedly, Yahweh becomes angry with Israel. Fittingly, he sells (*mkr*) them into the hands of an oppressor,[11] Cushan-Rishathaim (see discussion below). Justly, Yahweh subjects those who have served (*ᶜbd*) foreign Baals and Asherahs to serve (*ᶜbd*) this foreign king for eight years.

On account of this oppression, the Israelites cry out (*zᶜq*) to Yahweh. This outcry is not to be interpreted as a penitential plea, as though the Israelites have repented. Rather, it is a simple anguishing cry of pain (i.e., "a yelp of pain") of people in a distressing situation in need of deliverance. Thus, it is a cry for help, for rescue from a dire predicament, and is addressed to someone who it is hoped will intervene. That the element of repentance is lacking can be graphically seen in 10:14, where when the Israelites cry out (*zᶜq*) to Yahweh, he retorts sarcastically, "Go and cry out [*zᶜq*] to the gods you have chosen. Let them save [*hôšiaᶜ*] you when you are in trouble [*ṣārâ*]."[12] As noted above, Yahweh intervenes on Israel's behalf solely on the basis of his compassion for the Israelites in the midst of their distress, not on the basis of their repentance.

The introduction of Othniel[13] is heightened by a number of items that are clear in the Hebrew text (obscured by the NIV translation; for each of these items see Fig. 1). (1) The name Cushan-Rishathaim is mentioned twice (v. 8) before the introduction of Othniel (v. 9), and then twice after Othniel's introduction (v. 10). Thus the name serves a compositional function with wider thematic implications.[14]

---

10. See most recently J. A. Emerton, "'Yahweh and his Asherah: The Goddess or Her Symbol?" *VT* 49 (1999): 315–57. For the opposite view, see P. Xella, "Le dieu et 'sa' déesse: l'utilisation des suffixes pronominaux avec des théonymes d'Ebla à Ugarit et à Kuntillet 'Ajrud," *UF* 27 (1995): 599–610.

11. See the discussion of this framework statement on p. 90, n. 16.

12. On the significance of this framework statement, see the discussion of Block, *Judges, Ruth*, 148. The Old Testament usage of *zᶜq* (or its alternate spelling *ṣᶜq*) does not of itself imply repentance. See W. Brueggemann, "Social Criticism and Social Vision in the Deuteronomic Formula of Judges," *Die Botschaft und die Boten: Festschrift für Hans Walter Wolff zum 70. Geburtstag*, ed. by J. Jeremias and L. Perlitt (Neukirchen-Vluyn: Neukirchener Verlag, 1981), 101–14, esp. 108–9.

13. For the name Othniel, see M. P. Streck and St. Weninger, "Zur Deutung des hebräischen Namens ᶜOṯnīʾēl," *BN* 96 (1999): 21–29.

14. Boling, *Judges*, 80–81. See also Webb, *The Book of the Judges*, 128. Interestingly, Cushan-Rishathaim is mentioned twice as many times as Othniel.

⁷The Israelites did evil in the eyes of Yahweh.
And they forgot Yahweh their God.
And they served the Baals and Asherahs.

⁸And the anger of Yahweh was kindled against Israel.
And he <u>sold them into the hand of</u> <u>Cushan-Rishathaim</u>,
<u>king</u> of Aram Naharaim.
And the Israelites served <u>Cushan-Rishathaim</u> eight years.

⁹Then the Israelites cried to Yahweh,

and Yahweh raised up a savior for the Israelites
—and he saved them—   *pivotal phrase*
Othniel the Kenizzite, the younger kinsman of Caleb.

¹⁰The Spirit of Yahweh came upon him;
and he judged Israel.

He went out to war;
and Yahweh <u>gave</u> <u>Cushan-Rishathaim</u>, <u>king</u> of Aram, <u>into his hand</u>;
and his hand prevailed over <u>Cushan-Rishathaim</u>.

¹¹So the land had rest forty years.
Othniel the Kenizzite died.

Figure 1

(2) Along these same lines, Cushan-Rishathaim is called a "king" (*melek*) twice: once before the introduction of Othniel and once afterward.[15]

(3) The NIV's phrase "who saved them" (lit., "and he saved them") is syntactically parenthetical and is centrally positioned. Thus, there is a purposed ambiguity: Is it Yahweh or Othniel who "saves" them? The implication is both. Obviously, Othniel is involved in saving Israel. But ultimately it is Yahweh who accomplishes this through Othniel.

---

15. This mention of the fact that Cushan-Rishathaim is a "king" on both sides of Othniel's introduction is understood by a number of interpreters as an indication that Othniel represents the embodiment of an institution, namely, "judgeship." Thus the clash between Othniel and Cushan-Rishathaim is a clash between two institutions: kingship (represented in Cushan-Rishathaim), which brings punishment, and judgeship (represented in Othniel), which brings deliverance. See Webb, *The Book of the Judges*, 128; O'Connell, *The Rhetoric of the Book of Judges*, 83–84; Boling, *Judges*, 80–81.

(4) In the Hebrew text, there are precisely eight lines before the clause "and he saved them" and eight lines after it.[16] This heightens the emphasis on the phrase and its implied double subject. Othniel works so in tandem with Yahweh that they merge together as one.

(5) The use of the verbal phrases "to sell into the hand"/"to give into the hand" are usually employed in the cyclic framework statements to describe Yahweh's action of disciplining Israel through an oppressor (as also here in 3:8a). Only in the Othniel cycle is this phrase "to give into the hand" used to describe Yahweh's delivering the oppressor into the hand of the judge. In this way, Othniel is uniquely described as accomplishing the complete reversal of Cushan-Rishathaim's oppression.

The enemy that Othniel defeats is Cushan-Rishathaim, king of Aram Naharaim (for proposed identifications, see below). The name means "dark, doubly wicked!" and is clearly a pejorative (parents do not typically name their children such!).[17] There seems to have been a play on words with his original name (and/or a title?), which may have sounded like "Cushan-Rishathaim." The obvious implication is that he is evil, really bad—hence, the worst of the oppressors. The very name of this oppressor is used to invoke fear in the original readers' minds.

In addition, according to the text, he comes from Aram Naharaim.[18] Located in the area between the Euphrates and Habur rivers in northern

---

16. Webb, *The Book of the Judges*, 244.

17. Some other examples of pejorative names in the biblical text are: Bera ("in/with evil") and Birsha ("in/with wickedness") (Gen. 14:2), and Ish-Bosheth (2 Sam. 2:8). See also the belittling of the name of the Canaanite king in "lord of Bezeq" above (1:5). Also, compare the name Mahlon and Killion in Ruth 1:2 (see commentary). The case of Birsha is particularly interesting insofar as it comes from the same consonantal root (rš‘) and thus echoes Rishathaim ("doubly wicked").

18. Some scholars feel that the term Naharaim is a later erroneous gloss. They are inclined to this opinion because (1) the term Naharaim only occurs once in the story (in v. 10 the designation is simply Aram without the term Naharaim) and (2) because the word Aram may be an easy corruption for Edom (a possibility since only one letter mistake is necessary). See J. Gray, *Joshua, Judges and Ruth* (NCB; London: Thomas Nelson, 1967), 260–61; Burney, *Judges*, 68. For examples of this confusion see 2 Sam. 8:12–13; 1 Chron. 18:11; 2 Chron. 20:2. Nevertheless, the place name is well attested in the MT tradition, and the term Naharin was a designation for the Hurrian kingdom of Mitanni in the Eighteenth Dynasty of Egypt (e.g., Thutmose III's inscriptions). The term Naharaim is even found in v. 10 in a few Hebrew manuscripts. The term Aram was only applied to the region after the Aramean incursions during the decline of the Middle Assyrian empire. See W. T. Pitard, "An Historical Overview of Pastoral Nomadism in the Central Euphrates Valley," in *"Go to the Land I Will Show You": Studies in Honor of Dwight W. Young*, ed. J. Coleson and V. Matthews (Winona Lake, Ind.: Eisenbrauns, 1996), 293–308; and G. M. Schwartz, "The Origins of the Aramaeans in Syria and Northern Mesopotamia: Research Problems and Potential

Mesopotamia,[19] this would make Cushan-Rishathaim the oppressor who comes the greatest distance to oppress Israel.[20] Again this may underscore his severity. The Israelites, who choose to serve (ʿbd) foreign gods (3:7), are made to serve (ʿbd) a foreign tyrant (3:8). This type of retributive justice is noticed throughout the book (cf., e.g., 1:7).

But Othniel "overpowered him" (lit., "his hand was strong upon Cushan-Rishathaim"). This evinces the complete overwhelming of the foe. For Othniel, there is no need for deceptive stratagems, outside help, special vows, and so on. It is a simple, straightforward victory through the Spirit of Yahweh's empowerment.

The lack of mention of any character flaw immediately alerts the reader to his model qualities. Many commentators have noted that the narrator writes nothing negative about this man. This appears to be intentional.[21] O'Connell sums up this depiction as follows:

> The characterization of Othniel is unique among the deliverer accounts in that his is the only portrayal that lacks negative aspects. Nothing is said in this account that could be construed as negatively characterizing Othniel's motives or devotion to YHWH. Without exception, all the subsequent (non-Judahite) deliverers will evince some flaw of character that is paralleled, on an escalated level, by the negative portrayal of the deliverer's tribe or nation.[22]

Therefore, Othniel appears as the paragon by which the other major or cyclical judges are assessed. He functions in the macrostructure of the cycles section as the "ideal" judge. It is important also to remember that this ideal judge is a non-Israelite in ethnic origin, though as a proselyte he counts

---

Strategies," in *To the Euphrates and Beyond: Archaeological Studies in Honour of Maurits N. van Loon,* ed. O. M. C. Haex, H. H. Curvers, and P. M. M. G. Akkermans (Rotterdam and Brookfield: A. A. Balkema, 1989), 275–91.

19. It is difficult because of the designation Aram Naharaim and the uncertainty of date to know whether this designation indicates that Cushan-Rishathaim was of Hurrian origin or not (see previous note). For Hurrian movements into Canaan, see N. Naʾaman, "The Hurrians and the End of the Middle Bronze Age in Palestine," *Levant* 26 (1994): 175–87; R. Hess, "Hurrians and Other Inhabitants of Late Bronze Age Palestine," *Levant* 29 (1997): 153–56.

20. Block states: "He was the most powerful of all the enemies of Israel named in the book. For him to have extended his tentacles as far as Judah in southern Canaan meant he was a world-class emperor, who held Canaan in his grip for at least eight years" (*Judges, Ruth,* 152). It may be a bit too much to characterize Cushan-Rishathaim as "a world-class emperor."

21. Block, *Judges, Ruth,* 149; Webb, *The Book of the Judges,* 128. The lack of verbiage at this point is a significant indication of his outstanding quality (see the discussion concerning structure in the introduction).

22. O'Connell, *The Rhetoric of the Book of Judges,* 83.

within the tribe of Judah (as we are reminded in 1:13). Technically, Othniel, Acsah, and Caleb were Kenizzites who by faith commitment have been included in Israel—in particular, the tribe of Judah.[23]

In the larger narrative context, this short narrative about Othniel is set *in direct contrast* to the preceding Israelites who have taken Canaanite daughters to be their wives (3:6). Othniel has an "Israelite" wife, Acsah (previously introduced in 1:11–15), who served as his incentive for capturing Kiriath Sepher and who pressed her father for a field. As the daughter of Caleb, who acts with initiative for positive spiritual outcomes (see pp. 67–68 above), she elevates Othniel's ideal judgeship.[24] Again this is especially true when contrasted to the last major judge's woman, Delilah.

There is a certain appropriateness that the first judge should be a Judahite. Judah was the first to go up to fight the Canaanites (1:1–2), and they had the best record against the Canaanites of any Israelite tribe (ch. 1). Thus the reader is not surprised by Yahweh's choosing of Othniel. The confidence we feel at this point (even the workings of the divine mind are within our grasp) is going to be subtly transformed in subsequent episodes. There will be one surprise after the other. Things will turn out to be not as straightforward as the introduction and the Othniel episodes have led us to believe.

Finally, the identity of Cushan-Rishathaim is difficult and debated. Some of the proposals are:[25] (1) Cushan-Rishathaim is Irsu from Egypt, a Semitic usurper described as a Syrian.[26] (2) Cushan-Rishathaim is an otherwise unknown Cushan who came from Edom. Since Othniel was from the south country (Judah), some scholars have supposed that this threat came from Edom (Aram and Edom are easily confused in Hebrew, and in Hab. 3:7, Cushan appears in parallelism with Midian).[27] (3) Cushan-Rishathaim is Tushratta, a king of Mitanni.[28] (4) Cushan-Rishathaim is Artatama II, a

---

23. See the extended footnote on this issue on p. 66, n. 17.

24. Block notes that the larger context of 1:11–15 is assumed in this story (*Judges, Ruth*, 150).

25. See also the discussion of Lindars, *Judges 1–5*, 131–34.

26. A. Malamat, "Cushan Rishathaim and the Decline of the Near East Around 1200 B.C.," *JNES* 13 (1954): 231–42. Also see J. Bright, *A History of Israel*, 3d ed. (Philadelphia: Westminster, 1981), 179. Bright states: "But since a district of Qusana-ruma (Kûshân-rōm) is known in northern Syria (Aram) from a list of Ramesses III, the invasion may well have come from that quarter, possibly early in the twelfth century during the confusion attending the fall of the Nineteenth Dynasty. . . . But we cannot be certain."

27. Boling, *Judges*, 81–82. See also now B. Oded, "Cushan-Rishathaim (Judges 3:8–10): An Implicit Polemic," in *Texts, Temples, and Traditions: A Tribute to Menahem Haran*, ed. M. V. Fox (Winona Lake, Ind.: Eisenbrauns, 1996), 89*–94* (Heb. with Eng. summary). But see footnote 18 above.

28. H. Hansler, "Die historische Umwelt des Richter 3, 8–10," *Bib* 11 (1930): 391–418; 12 (1931) 3–26; 271–96, 395–410.

Mitannian monarch.[29] (5) Cushan-Rishathaim is Sharri Kushkh, a Hittite ruler of Carchemish.[30] (6) Cushan-Rishathaim is the ruler of a group of displaced Hurrians seeking a new homeland rather than a foreign conqueror trying to enlarge his empire.[31] The second proposal is the most popular in current scholarly literature.[32]

All of these proposals, however, are speculative. At the end of the day, we simply must admit that we do not know the identity of this individual. The problem is complicated because we lack enough chronological data in the book of Judges to accurately date the episode (see the introduction, pp. 24–25). It is also compounded by the fact that the name is a hebraized pejorative wordplay, which, without extrabiblical evidence, makes any attempt to analyze and identify the name enigmatic.

PRELIMINARY COMMENTS. As one attempts to bridge the ancient context with the modern in the cycles section of the book of Judges, there are some essentials to keep in mind. (1) As a preliminary to the interpretation and application of each cycle, it is important to place the particular cycle under consideration within the larger macrostructure of the cycles section (see the introduction, pp. 34–37). This ensures that the cycle will be seen in its proper context within the downward spiral that is the moral movement of the cycles section. This will also ensure that the individual judges will be properly evaluated in relationship to one another in the larger context.

(2) Each cycle's narrative works on two levels: a human plane and a divine plane. The story of the actions of the Israelites and the particular judge active in each cycle will contribute to the downward spiral observed in the cycles section. In these human actions there will be a level at which the text may be applied to the modern context. But there is also a level at which Yahweh is at work. Thus, there is a theme running throughout each individual cycle within the section, a theme of the glorification of Yahweh.[33] In each instance, in spite of the growing human failure to obey and worship the Lord, God will

---

29. W. H. Shea, "Cushan-Rishathaim," *Catastrophism and Ancient History* 14/2 (1992): 126–37.

30. Ibid., 126–37.

31. T. Muck, private communication.

32. For those scholars that perceive any historical core to the story. Many scholars believe the episode to be a contrived fiction. But the repeated traditions concerning Othniel as a Judahite (albeit Kenizzite) hero argue for caution in assuming the entire episode to be a fiction.

33. O'Connell, *The Rhetoric of the Book of Judges*, 83.

act to save Israel, his people, and thus demonstrate his great compassion and grace to humankind. In other words, each cycle in some way reflects this glorification of God.

(3) Although the Othniel cycle is short and sterile, the portrait of this judge emerges in graphic clarity once its structural features are recognized. As the first major judge cycle, it gives a successful cycle, a demonstration of how it could be. While Othniel is a man of positive spiritual character, demonstrated earlier by his faith in Yahweh in the conquest of Debir (1:11–15), the narrative is more about Yahweh's saving of Israel through Othniel than about who Othniel is. It is in this that he serves as an example of faith and godliness.

In other words, through this literary structuring more attention is drawn to Yahweh's character than to the individual judge. This contributes greatly to the theme of Yahweh's glorification. Yahweh is portrayed as justly subjecting the Israelites who served Baals and Asherahs (3:7b) to serving a foreign king, Cushan-Rishathaim (3:8b). When his people cry to him, Yahweh is further glorified by raising up a deliverer entirely on the basis of his compassion and not because of any repentance on the part of Israel. Moreover, Yahweh allows his Spirit to come on Othniel to judge Israel; finally, he gives Cushan-Rishathaim into Othniel's hand. In no other cycle is Yahweh's involvement so *explicitly* stated at every stage in the cycle. And in no other cycle will Yahweh's glorification be so complete, for in every other cycle there will be something—or numerous things—that distract the reader from fully appreciating the glorification of Yahweh.

Othniel, the ideal judge. On the human level, Othniel evinces the kind of devotion and service of the Lord that results in this type of glorification of Yahweh. In a world where it is often difficult to find true godly role models, Othniel serves as a breath of fresh air. He is depicted in this capacity in a number of important facets.

(1) In the larger context Othniel is the antithesis of the Israelites who are marrying unbelieving Canaanites (3:5–6). He marries a believer, a godly woman, Acsah (1:13). This is important, for the influence of a marriage partner can be spiritually positive or detrimental. Both the Old and New Testaments contain clear injunctions for believers to marry believers, not unbelievers. This clear teaching of the law (esp. Deuteronomy) is certainly a tenet promoted in Judges.

(2) Othniel overcomes a background that might be considered limiting (he is a Kenizzite) in order to become the ideal judge of Israel. Not being biologically Israelite may be considered by some to marginalize an individual, preventing such a person from attaining certain ranks. But Yahweh promoted Othniel because of his faithfulness.

(3) Othniel overcomes the worst of the oppressors. As evil and intimidating as the enemy was (at the very least as the name reflects the apex of evil), Othniel trusts in Yahweh, who can overcome even the greatest of foes. Thus the narrative is an encouragement that God can overcome any problem that challenges his people.

(4) Othniel performs this deliverance in tandem with Yahweh; they act as one. This gives evidence that Othniel truly walks with God so that his action reflects God's desired action. For the Christian, we are expected to walk in the light as he is in the light (1 John 1:7) so that we may have fellowship with one another and the blood of Christ, his Son, may purify us from all sin. In this way, we overcome the world (1 John 5:4—5).

FOR THE TEN YEARS that I taught an undergraduate Old Testament literature class at LeTourneau University, I conducted an informal survey when we came to the book of Judges. I asked the students who among them had heard of "Samson"; there was an almost unanimous response of "yes." When I followed up with the question who among them had heard of "Othniel," only a few could answer "yes." It is a great irony that the worst of the judges in moral character and success in delivering Israel is the best-known judge, while the ideal judge is the least known.

The Scriptures give numerous examples of men and women who walked with God, but Othniel stands out because of his simplicity. In spite of those things that might hold Christians back, Othniel serves as an example of one who was not limited by his background (Kenizzite). Background should not limit our service to Christ. No matter what human deficiencies, we can be faithful to God's calling in our lives. In the book of Judges, besides possibly Joshua (Judg. 2:8), Othniel is the only male who is so positively pictured (i.e., walking with God so completely).[34]

In an age when many choose a different path, not uncommonly bringing on themselves oppression that is the result of sin (i.e., like a Cushan-Rishathaim), it is wonderful to see a model like Othniel who simply walks in tandem with God and overcomes evil. While it is inferential from the text, it is apparent that like any godly believer throughout the ages, Othniel loved his fellow Israelites. He could not stand by and watch them suffer. In other words, his motives were not self-seeking but others-seeking. He acted (and this is important to emphasize) in accordance with the Lord's will—Yahweh raised up a "deliverer," a "savior" (*môšîaʿ*). If we walk with God and our

---

34. Acsah (Othniel's wife) and Deborah are the only females so positively portrayed.

eyes are on others' needs rather than our own self-interests, we will want to act in accordance with God's will. The simplicity and faithfulness of Othniel is in radical contrast to the complexity and self-gratification of the final judge of the book of Judges, Samson. The message is not that we "be an Othniel." Rather, we should demonstrate faithfulness to God's call for us, whatever that may be.

Ultimately, this initial judge serves to bring glory to God. While the human character is Othniel, this passage is not a biography about him.[35] Instead, the human character highlights God's involvement in the affairs of his people. In Othniel's day God punished evil, had compassion on his people, and brought deliverance and rest; Othniel was simply God's tool to accomplish that salvation. So too today, God still acts to punish evil, but he has compassion on his people and will bring deliverance and rest.

---

35. Actually, none of the cyclical judge accounts are biographies.

Judges 3:12–30

❧

ONCE AGAIN THE Israelites did evil in the eyes of the
LORD, and because they did this evil the LORD gave
Eglon king of Moab power over Israel. ¹³Getting the
Ammonites and Amalekites to join him, Eglon came and
attacked Israel, and they took possession of the City of Palms.
¹⁴The Israelites were subject to Eglon king of Moab for eighteen years.

¹⁵Again the Israelites cried out to the LORD, and he gave
them a deliverer—Ehud, a left-handed man, the son of Gera
the Benjamite. The Israelites sent him with tribute to Eglon
king of Moab. ¹⁶Now Ehud had made a double-edged sword
about a foot and a half long, which he strapped to his right
thigh under his clothing. ¹⁷He presented the tribute to Eglon
king of Moab, who was a very fat man. ¹⁸After Ehud had presented the tribute, he sent on their way the men who had carried it. ¹⁹At the idols near Gilgal he himself turned back and
said, "I have a secret message for you, O king."

The king said, "Quiet!" And all his attendants left him.

²⁰Ehud then approached him while he was sitting alone in
the upper room of his summer palace and said, "I have a message from God for you." As the king rose from his seat, ²¹Ehud
reached with his left hand, drew the sword from his right thigh
and plunged it into the king's belly. ²²Even the handle sank in
after the blade, which came out his back. Ehud did not pull
the sword out, and the fat closed in over it. ²³Then Ehud went
out to the porch; he shut the doors of the upper room behind
him and locked them.

²⁴After he had gone, the servants came and found the doors
of the upper room locked. They said, "He must be relieving
himself in the inner room of the house." ²⁵They waited to the
point of embarrassment, but when he did not open the doors
of the room, they took a key and unlocked them. There they
saw their lord fallen to the floor, dead.

²⁶While they waited, Ehud got away. He passed by the
idols and escaped to Seirah. ²⁷When he arrived there, he blew
a trumpet in the hill country of Ephraim, and the Israelites
went down with him from the hills, with him leading them.

²⁸"Follow me," he ordered, "for the LORD has given Moab, your enemy, into your hands." So they followed him down and, taking possession of the fords of the Jordan that led to Moab, they allowed no one to cross over. ²⁹At that time they struck down about ten thousand Moabites, all vigorous and strong; not a man escaped. ³⁰That day Moab was made subject to Israel, and the land had peace for eighty years.

AFTER INTRODUCTION 2 (2:6–3:6) and the Othniel cycle, where all of the components of the judges cycle have been present, the reader's expectation is for more of the same. And although the narrator begins with the familiar statement, "once again the Israelites did evil in the eyes of the LORD," this story will quickly surprise us with its satirical irony.¹ While many of the cycle components are present (mainly as narrative framework statements at the beginning and end of the story), it is in the detailed elaborations that the humor, sarcasm, and irony reside. Instead of the enigmatic Cushan-Rishathaim, we are faced with the massive bodily presence of Eglon.

The formal structure of the Ehud cycle² consists of a narrative frame at the beginning (3:12–15a) and end (3:30) with the story of Ehud's deliverance (3:15b–29) related in three units. Unit 1 focuses on the presentation of tribute (3:15b–3:18), Unit 2 on the assassination of Eglon by Ehud (3:19–3:26a), and Unit 3 on the liberation from Moabite oppression (3:26b–29). Each of these units is demarcated by an A–B–A' pattern with repetition of key words in the first and last elements. The B element in each unit ties the action of the entire story together through sacrificial overtones (see below).

Introduction (3:12–15a)

THE BEGINNING NARRATIVE frame sets the circumstances for Ehud's work. The text emphasizes through repetition that not only was Israel doing evil in the

---

1. For the satirical aspects of the story, see M. Z. Brettler, *The Creation of History in Ancient Israel* (London and New York: Routledge, 1995), 79–90, 190–97; L. K. Handy, "Uneasy Laughter: Ehud and Eglon and Ethnic Humor," *SJOT* 6 (1992): 233–46; J. A. Soggin, "'Ehud und 'Eglon: Bemerkingen zu Richter iii 11b–31," *VT* 29 (1989): 95–100; R. Alter, *The Art of Biblical Narrative* (New York: Basic Books, 1981), 39–40.

2. See in particular Webb, *The Book of the Judges*, 128–32; O'Connell, *The Rhetoric of the Book of Judges*, 84–100; Y. Amit, "The Story of Ehud (Judges 3:12–30): The Form and the Message," in *Signs and Wonders: Biblical Texts in Literary Focus*, ed. J. C. Exum (Decatur, Ga.: Scholars Press, 1989), 97–123.

eyes of the Lord, but because of that evil, Yahweh "gave Eglon king of Moab power over Israel." The Hebrew for this phrase is unique to the Ehud cycle. In the other major judge cycles, the description is either Yahweh gave (*ntn*) or sold (*mkr*) the Israelites into the hands of their oppressors. Only here does the writer say that Yahweh actively "gave . . . power" to or strengthened (*ḥzq*) the oppressor against Israel.

After gathering as allies the Ammonites and Amalekites (peoples who will be involved in other later oppressions of Israel), Eglon attacks Israel, and together they take possession (*yrš*) of "the City of Palms" (i.e., Jericho, cf. 1:16).[3] Ironically, it is the Israelites who are supposed to be taking possession (*yrš*) of the land. And it is Jericho (veiled here by the term "the City of Palms") that Eglon and company have confiscated! Has the work of Joshua 6 been undone?!!!

It is also ironic that earlier, in Moses' day, the Moabites under King Balak attempted to overcome Israel by hiring Balaam to curse them (Num. 22–24). And although the Moabites along with the Midianites had involved the Israelites in adultery and idolatry (Num. 25), the Moabites ultimately failed to thwart Israel. But now Moab through the addition of these allies has gained success over the Israelites.

While the duration of the oppression to despotic Eglon is mentioned (eighteen years), the description of the oppression is painted in subtle terms through a series of contrasts. Thus, the references to the "City of Palms," to Eglon's fatness, and to the cool upper chamber of his palace expose "the vast differences between the lives of the Moabites and the conquered Israelites—inside versus outside, cool versus hot, fatness versus barrenness, palms versus hills."[4]

The cyclic description continues with Israel's crying out to Yahweh in stress and pain (not repentance). Yahweh, as in the Othniel account, raises up a savior/deliverer (*môšîaʿ*, 3:14, cf. v. 9): Ehud, the son of Gera, a Benjamite. Through the use of these framework statements, the writer starts off the Ehud story just like the Othniel cycle, raising the readers' expectations for more of the same. But quickly this all changes.

This savior is left-handed (lit., "a man restricted in his right hand," 3:15). The phrase used here has created problems for centuries. One interpretation understands this as a physical deformity; that is, that Ehud's left-handedness is the result of a physical abnormality.[5] However, this is probably taking the

---

3. The city itself may not have been occupied at the time in which the story is set. It has been suggested that this was a temporary occupation of the oasis at ʾAin es-Sultan.

4. Gros Louis, "The Book of Judges," 147.

5. See, e.g., Webb, *The Book of the Judges*, 131; Soggin, *Judges*, 50; idem, "ʾEhud und ʿEglon," 96–97; L. Alonso-Schökel, "Erzählkunst im Buche der Richter," *Bib* 42 (1961): 143–72, esp. 148–49. Note also the Targum's translation "withered" and the Syriac's "crippled."

phrase too literally. In 20:16 there are seven hundred picked troops, (lit.) "their right hands restricted" (same phrase as 3:15), who "could sling a stone at a hair and not miss." As Halpern notes, "This excludes physical deformity: it would be comical to invent elite brigades organized on such a principle."[6] Moreover, only if Ehud has use of his right hand can he, by using his left, surprise Eglon. Ehud's plot only works if he appears normal to the Moabite guards.

Another interpretation understands this phrase to mean "ambidextrous" (i.e., skilled in the use of both hands). The Greek Old Testament translates the phrase by a word meaning "ambidextrous" (in both LXX[A] and LXX[B]). Block has recently argued for this meaning.[7] But this seems unlikely for this is a most odd way of expressing ambidextrity ("a man restricted in his right hand")! It is doubtful whether ambidextrity would ever be expressed by describing restriction of the use of one of the hands. Rather, it is expressed positively with the use of both. Note, for example, 1 Chronicles 12:2, which describes, positively, warriors who "were able to shoot arrows or to sling stones right-handed or left-handed." Thus it seems that the phrase in 3:15a simply means "left-handed" (esp. if it refers to artificially induced left-handedness through training).

But this left-handed savior is ironically a Benjamite ("son of the right hand").[8] Left-handedness, generally considered peculiar and unnatural in antiquity, was conspicuously recurrent in this tribe (see 20:16; cf. 1 Chron. 12:2). Such left-handedness may have been artificially induced (binding the right arms of the young children) so as to produce superior warriors. Left-handed persons may have had distinct advantages in physical combat, especially in regard to ancient armaments and defenses.[9] From a literary standpoint, Ehud's left-handedness is explicitly noted because it explains how he smuggles his dagger in. The palace guards, assuming he is right-handed, would have checked only his left side for weapons.

Presentation of Tribute (3:15b–18)

IN UNIT 1 the focus is on the presentation of tribute with the repetition of the verb "send" (*šlḥ*) marking off this unit.

---

6. B. Halpern, *The First Historians*, 41.

7. Block, *Judges, Ruth*, 161. See also H. N. Rösel, "Zur Ehud-Erzählung," *ZAW* 89 (1977): 270–72, esp. 270.

8. The word translated "Benjamite" is *ben-hayᵉmînî* rather than the more typical *ben-yᵉmînî*. This phraseology suggests that the irony of the situation was not missed by the author (Block, *Judges, Ruth*, 160).

9. Halpern, *The First Historians*, 40–43.

A The Israelites send (*šlḥ*) a gift to Eglon (3:15b)
  B Setting the stage for the assassination (3:16–18a)—"presenting
    the sacrifice"
A′ Ehud sends (*šlḥ*) away those who have carried the gift (3:18b)

The Israelites "send" their savior/deliverer Ehud with tribute to Eglon.
This provides the opportunity for Ehud to take a daring personal initiative.
It cannot be overemphasized that Ehud willingly takes a great personal risk
here. His initiative effectively decides the issue before he rallies the Israelites
and engages the Moabites on the field of battle. The slaying of Eglon will pre-
figure the slaying of the Moabites.

Ehud crafts a double-edged dagger[10] that is a *gōmed* in length. The NIV translates *gōmed* "about a foot and a half," with a note that the Hebrew is "a cubit."
This is incorrect. Ehud's dagger was more likely about a foot in length.[11] His
improvisation is undoubtedly a prefiguring of the improvising of other weapons:
Shamgar's oxgoad (3:31), Jael's tent peg (4:22), Gideon's jars and torches (7:20),
the certain woman's millstone (9:53), and Samson's donkey jawbone (15:15).
But here as opposed to the other instances, Ehud's action is deliberate and calculated. He takes time and effort to fashion his weapon—perhaps even, as
some commentators have suggested, making the length appropriate to the
size of Eglon. Finally, he devises a means of getting the implement into Eglon's
presence: He straps it to his right thigh under his clothing. To sum up, the dagger is short enough to hide under his clothing, long enough to do in Eglon, and
double-edged to ensure the fatality of one quick thrust.[12]

Sacrificial overtones are emphasized in section B (3:16–18a). The story
as a whole plays on the notion of sacrifice; while pretending to bring

---

10. The term *ḥereb*, translated "sword" by the NIV, can refer to an item as small as a razor-
blade knife (Ezek. 5:1) to a long sword. Hence in this context "dagger" is the preferred
translation.

11. The term *gōmed* is used only in Judg. 3:16. If it equaled a "cubit" (*ʾammâ*), then it
would be 44.4 cm or 17.5 inches (based on the Egyptian "royal cubit"). But since *ʾammâ* is
used 245 times in the Hebrew Bible, in addition to many extrabiblical occurrences, this raises
significant doubt that a *gōmed* was roughly synonymous with an *ʾammâ*. Just as a *pym* (1 Sam.
13:21) was two-thirds of a shekel, so the *gōmed* may have been two-thirds of an *ʾammâ* (hence
29.6 cm. or 11.6 inches). See D. J. Wiseman, "Weights and Measures," *IBD*, 3:1636; also
G. Cornfeld and G. J. Botterweck, *Die Bible und ihre Welt: Eine Enzyklopädie* (6 vol.; Munich:
Deutscher Taschenbuch Verlag, 1972), 3:564. In the most recent study of the problem,
Hartman argues that the blade of the dagger was a *gōmed*, roughly equivalent to one "fist"
(another measure used in the ancient Near East), i.e., 10.95 cm. (4.32 inches) in length.
Adding 10 cm. for the hilt, the dagger was 21 cm. (8.27 inches) in length. See T. A. G. Hart-
man, "גמד in Richter 3,16 oder die Pygmäen im Dschungel der Längermasse," *ZAH* 13
(2000): 188–93. In any case, it is doubtful that the dagger was a cubit in length.

12. Alter, *The Art of Biblical Narrative*, 39.

tribute/"offering" to Eglon, it is actually Eglon, the "fatted calf/bull," who becomes the offering. In fact, verses 17–18, in saying that Ehud offers tribute, employ an expression typically used of offering a sacrifice.[13] Indeed, the sacrificial knife and partial disembowelment of the "animal" are depicted in graphic detail (see below).

Ehud presents the tribute (*minḥâ*, "offering") to Eglon, who the text intentionally notes is "very fat." This tribute is most likely agricultural produce. The addition of the next statement concerning Eglon's rotund physique on the heels of the statement concerning the tribute seems clearly to imply this.

After presenting this tribute to Eglon, Unit 1 concludes with the statement that Ehud "sends" (*šlḥ*) on their way the other Israelite tribute bearers. The Israelites send Ehud to Eglon (A); Ehud sends the Israelites on their way (A').

The Assassination of Eglon (3:19–26b¹)

WITH THE STAGE now set, Unit 2 focuses on the act of the assassination of Eglon by Ehud. This unit, like Unit 1, is framed by a repetition of key words that delineate the unit.

A Ehud returns from the idols/sculptured stones (*happᵉsîlîm*) (3:19a)
   B Execution of the plot of assassination (3:19b–26a): "executing
      the main sacrifice"
A' Ehud passes beyond the idols/sculptured stones (*happᵉsîlîm*) (3:26b¹)

This unit opens with the assertion that "at the idols near Gilgal," Ehud turns back. By returning alone Ehud adds a degree of plausibility to his claim that he has a "secret message/thing." A number of different suggestions have been made for *happᵉsîlîm*, the term translated "idols" in the NIV. Beside this meaning, commentators have suggested "quarries,"[14] "boundary stones,"[15] and "sculptured stones."[16] The translation "idols"[17] may be preferred since

---

13. Brettler, *The Creation of History in Ancient Israel*, 192 n. 27. See also Amit, "The Story of Ehud (Judges 3:12–30)," 97–123.

14. See Amit, "The Story of Ehud (Judges 3:12–30)," 102, 112–18; see also the KJV and JPSV translations.

15. Perhaps a type of *kudurru* (boundary stone); see Burney, *Judges*, 71. However, note the comments of Block, *Judges, Ruth*, 163.

16. G. F. Moore, *A Critical and Exegetical Commentary on Judges* (ICC; Edinburgh: T. & T. Clark, 1895), 94, 100; Webb, *The Book of the Judges*, 131.

17. E. G. H. Kraeling, "Difficulties in the Story of Ehud," *JBL* 54 (1935): 205–10, esp. 206; Block, *Judges, Ruth*, 163; O'Connell, *The Rhetoric of the Book of Judges*, 90. O'Connell points out that "whatever may have been the meaning of הפסילים in the traditional account of Ehud, its recontextualization, so as to be interpreted in the light of deuteronomic standards, suggests that it should now be taken to refer to idols (cf. Deut. 4:16–18; 23; 7:25; 12:3)" (p. 90 n. 50).

Ehud returns immediately with a "secret message" that Eglon perceives is an oracle (obtained at the idols, at least in Eglon's thinking?).[18] If this is correct, then Ehud may have used Eglon's pagan misconceptions to undermine him. Whatever their precise identity, these objects mark the limits of Eglon's effective control. Later in the narrative, once Ehud passes these objects in 3:26, he has "escaped" and can openly muster the Israelite militia.

The focus on the execution of the plot (3:19b–26a)—"executing the main sacrifice"—is heightened by satire and irony, the principal target of which is Eglon ("young calf/bull"). This name is derived from *ʿegel* (calf/bull) and may be a diminutive or affectionate, familiar form. The name perhaps also plays on the term *ʿāgōl* (round, rotund).[19] Ironically, then, the name suggests that Eglon is a fatted calf ready for slaughter. Four times he is designated as "king [*melek*] of Moab" (3:12, 14, 15, 17) and then, climactically in 3:19, Ehud addresses him as "O king."[20] Through this use of this term, like Cushan-Rishathaim in the previous judge cycle, Eglon functions as the embodiment of an evil institution.

Again, sacrificial overtones are emphasized in section B. The satire centers mainly on Eglon's famed obesity. Eglon has fattened himself on the tribute he has extorted from Israel. While his obesity symbolizes his greed, it also hints at his vulnerability to Ehud's swift left-handed thrust of the blade (3:21).[21] Eglon has become plump, defenseless, stupid game. Gullibly, he is taken in by the wily Ehud. Like a dumb animal, he is completely unaware of the danger. Being so greedy to receive the "secret message/thing" that Ehud offers him, he dismisses his bodyguard (3:19)[22]; then he rises from his throne to receive this secret "message from God" (*dᵉbar ʾᵉlōhîm*) (3:20).[23]

---

18. The assumption that Eglon knows about Ehud's movements, although we are not told this, is reasonable in view of the compressed narrative style (Webb, *The Book of the Judges*, 246 n. 29).

19. M. Garsiel, *Biblical Names: A Literary Study of Midrashic Deriviations and Puns*, trans. P. Hackett (Ramat-Gan, Israel: Bar-Ilan University, 1991), 215.

20. This is not the more usual and polite use of "my lord" (*ᵃdōnî*) as in 1 Sam. 24:8 [9]; 26:17; 29:8; 2 Sam. 4:8; 13:33; etc.

21. It is interesting that the text dwells on the contrasting physical characteristics of Ehud ("left-handed") and Eglon ("very fat").

22. Ehud's deception would work best if he were a person of nonimposing physical appearance. Hence Eglon had no particular reason to retain the guards in the throne room since there did not appear to be a reason to suspect any danger from this man. While we cannot obviously say anything definitive about Ehud's physical statue, it is not too much of a stretch to say he must have been rather "ordinary."

23. The Hebrew word *dābār* is ambiguous and can mean "word," "message," "thing," or "matter." The shifting modifiers ("secret") and ("of God") deliberately elevate this ambiguity. In fact, Ehud is clever in his use of the divine names. He uses "God" (*ʾᵉlōhîm*) when he speaks to Eglon, so as to not raise suspicions. He will use the covenantal name the "LORD" (*Yahweh*) when he calls up the Israelite troops (3:28).

Ehud's words, like his double-edged dagger, have a double meaning: the one that Eglon naively accepts, and the one that the reader already knows, namely, that "the secret [thing] from God" is "the dagger"! Eglon is led to anticipate a divine revelation, a secret word or oracle from Elohim, while Ehud actually has a deadly secret of human origin that will be the means of divine dispatch for the Moabite king.

The actual description of the murder/sacrifice is given in grotesque detail, which unfortunately the NIV translation obscures.[24] Verse 22 should read:

And even the handle [*niṣṣāb*] entered after the blade;
and the fat [*ḥēleb*] closed in over the blade,
because he did not remove the dagger from his belly;
and the excrement [*parš'dōn*][25] came out.

Thus, Ehud stabs Eglon with even the hilt of the dagger penetrating the belly. The term translated "fat" (*ḥēleb*) is the sacrificial term used for the choicest parts of the sacrifice, the entrails (see Lev. 3–6). And at this climatic moment without the dagger being removed, Eglon's anal sphincter explodes.[26] Concerning this message/thing from God, Eglon got the point!

The scatological satire continues with the comic scene of 3:24–25, in which Eglon's servants belatedly discover their master's corpse. Ehud has shut the doors and locked them.[27] The courtiers erroneously assume that their corpulent monarch is taking his leisurely time in relieving himself in the chamber

---

24. The verse contains four clauses. The last and climatic clause is transferred to second place by the NIV and mistranslated.

25. The term *happarš'dōnâ* is a hapax legomenon. The NIV translates "his back," but this is unlikely on a number of grounds. Many modern commentators understand this hapax (*parš'dōn*) as meaning "excrement." See M. L. Barré, "The Meaning of *pršdn* in Judges iii.22," *VT* 41 (1991): 1–11. While this is not free from difficulties (in particular, the uses of the initial and final *h*), it seems to be the best explanation within the context. Some past commentators have emended the text to read *pereš* (feces) (e.g., Moore, *Judges*, 97–98; Rösel, "Ehud-Erzählung," 272). O'Connell has suggested understanding *pršdn* as "anus" with the final *h* being a *h*-locative (i.e., "at the anus"). That the sentence contains a scatological type reference is clear in the context since it enables an explanation of the guards' hesitation.

26. See Halpern, *The First Historians*, 40 and 69 n. 3. See the discussion in note 25 above. The loss of excrement on such occasions is not unusual. Note in Sennacherib's inscriptions the description of the Elamite nobility in the midst of the battle of Halule: "When I saw that they had voided their excrement [in their chariots], I left them alone." See A. K. Grayson, "The Walters Art Gallery Sennacherib Inscription, *Archiv für Orientforschung* 20 (1963): 83–96, esp. 94–95, line 100.

27. Halpern gives a detailed description of the palace based on archaeological evidence and proposes a means of escape for Ehud (*The First Historians*, 43–58). However, see Brettler, *The Creation of History in Ancient Israel*, 191 n. 11.

toilet.[28] And the odor from the accidental discharge from the anal sphincter further decoys the guards to tarry while Ehud escapes. Halpern puts it this way:

> We may imagine them whiling away their time with quips on quotidian reality—inferior Israelites, cuisine at the court, the king's constipation. As moments mounted into embarrassing minutes, the delicate matter of disturbing their liege pressed ever more on their minds.[29]

These courtiers, like their ruler, are held up to satirical humor[30] for their credulity. They are as gullible and helpless against the wily Ehud as their master. To their humiliation they only gradually realize the "foul" play. Having waited and waited (to the point of embarrassment), they finally fetch a key and unlock the door, only to find their lord fallen to the floor, dead![31]

While deception is critical to the achievement of the murder, it is also crucial to the escape. Ehud's deception counts on the locked doors (3:23), duping the guards and allowing him to escape all the way to Seirah (3:26). The unit closes with the assertion that while they wait, Ehud passes by the "idols" (*happᵉsîlîm*, 3:26b[1]).[32]

Liberation from Moabite Oppression (3:26b²–29)

UNIT 3 FOCUSES on the liberation from Moabite oppression. Like the previous two units, it is framed by a repetition of key words that define the unit.

A Ehud "escapes" (*mlṭ*) to Seirah (3:26b²)
  B The victory of the Israelites over the Moabites (3:27–29a)—
  "executing the other sacrifices"
A′ No one "escapes" (*mlṭ*) (3:29b)

---

28. For toilets in ancient Israel, see J. Cahill et al., "It Had to Happen—Scientists Examine Remains of Ancient Bathroom," *BAR* 17 (May/June 1991): 64–69; U. Hübner, "Mord auf dem Abort? Überlegungen zu Humor, Gewaltdarstellung und Realienkunde in Ri 3,12–30," *BN* 40 (1987): 130–40.

29. Halpern, *The First Historians*, 60.

30. Some scholars see sexual overtones in the scene of the execution of Eglon. See, e.g., Alter, *The Art of Biblical Narrative*, 38–41; G. P. Miller, "Verbal Feud in the Hebrew Bible: Judges 3:12–30 and 19–21," *JNES* 55 (1996): 105–17. However, it seems that most of these so-called sexual innuendos can be easily and more properly explained in the context of the scatological overtones (which are clearly present).

31. The killing of Eglon and the discovery of his corpse is anticipatory of the killing of Sisera by Jael and the discovery of Sisera by Barak in 4:22. The discovery scenes use the same basic structure. In light of this, the irony of Barak's leadership of Israel is heightened since he is paralleled to the gullible, incompetent Moabite guards.

32. See note 17 above.

The unit starts with the escape (*mlṭ*) of Ehud to Seirah, where he blows the trumpet in the hill country of Ephraim and stimulates the Israelites to seize the moment of victory. Ehud's rallying words, "Follow me . . . for the LORD has given Moab, your enemy, into your hands" is not just battlefield rhetoric.[33] Based on the narrative, it is a reference to the tangible grounds for such assurance: The Moabite despot has already been given into the hand of Ehud and is dead. Thus Ehud now stands revealed as Yahweh's chosen "savior/deliverer" (cf. 3:15). Moreover, the words demonstrate that for Ehud the entire process has been a matter of trust in Yahweh and assurance of Yahweh's deliverance (see more on this below).

With the Israelites capturing the fords of the Jordan River, passage of escape for the Moabites is effectively cut off. While this relatively straightforward piece of action brings the successful defeat of Moab, it is only possible because of the entire series of adeptly executed deceptions that have gone before. The seizing of the fords of the Jordan will recur in the Gideon and Jephthah narratives (7:24–8:3; 12:1–6). In every instance there is Ephraimite involvement.

The Moabite troops fare no better than their potentate. In fact, as stated above, Eglon's demise foreshadows their own demise. Hence, as Eglon was "sacrificed," so his troops will be "sacrificed." These troops are described as "all vigorous and strong." As a number of commentators correctly point out, the term translated "vigorous" (*šāmēn*) normally means "fat" or "stout." Thus it is reminiscent of Eglon, who was "fat." These stout warriors are "struck down [i.e., sacrificed]" under the hand of Israel (3:30) just as their stout monarch has already been struck down (i.e., sacrificed) under the hand of Ehud. The Israelites strike down the round number of ten thousand Moabites, which is the same number already given for the Canaanites under the command of "the lord of Bezeq," whom the Judahites struck down (1:4).

English translations typically obscure the repetition of the word "hand" (*yād*) in this story. An observation of its use emphasizes the connection between the murder of Eglon and the slaughter of his troops:[34]

---

33. Webb notes that the use of the perfect tense here, "has given," is not simply an instance of the customary use of the past tense to assure the troops that the victory is as good as won, but a reference to the tangible grounds for such assurance in this particular case: The Moabite tyrant has already been given into the hand of Ehud and lies dead in his chamber.

34. Alonso-Schökel, "Erzählkunst im Buche der Richter," 149–50; D. M. Gunn, "Joshua and Judges," in *The Literary Guide to the Bible*, ed. R. Alter and F. Kermode (Cambridge, Mass.: Harvard Univ. Press, 1987), 115.

3:15a   Ehud is restricted in his right hand (*yād*)

3:15b   The Israelites send tribute by Ehud's hand (*yād*)

3:21   Ehud reaches with his left hand (*yād*)

3:28   Yahweh has given their enemies (Moab) into their hands (*yād*)

3:30   So Moab was struck down by the hand (*yād*) of Israel.

Besides unifying the Ehud episode, the usage of *yād* emphasizes the active agency of the deliverance. Israel's deliverance did not come through passivity but through active involvement, first of Ehud and then of the Israelites. The unit closes with the statement that "not one of them escaped [*mlṭ*]," in contrast to Ehud, who did escape (*mlṭ*, 3:26b[2]).

While there is great humor and satire of Eglon in particular and the Moabites in general, it is important to remember that Eglon, his courtiers, and his troops are not all bungling buffoons (they have controlled this region of Israel for the past eighteen years!). This comments, in no small way, on the Israelites' spiritual condition, which brought this situation on them. But while Eglon and his men oppress Israel for this relatively lengthy period,[35] they are no match for the savior/deliverer (*môšîaʿ*) whom Yahweh raises up. Eglon has served his purpose (3:12); now he is removed with humorous ease. God's sovereign control of the circumstances is maintained throughout the story.

Conclusion (3:30)

THE NARRATIVE FRAMEWORK statement in 3:30 concludes the story: "Moab was made subject to Israel, and the land had peace for eighty years."[36] Both statements are standard elements of the major judge cycles (for the first sentence, see 3:10, 30a; 4:23; 8:28a; 11:33b; for the second, see 3:11a, 30b; 5:31b; 8:28b).

The Ehud narrative is the only cyclical/major judge story to relate the death of the enemy ruler/leader *before* the battle. In the parallel with Jael's actions in Judges 4–5, the death of the enemy ruler/leader is narrated *after* the battle. This is true also in the case of Gideon (actually twice: 7:25; 8:21). The Jephthah account has no narration of the death of the ruler/leader before or after the battle, only the relating of a second battle in which the Ephraimites are put to death. In the case of Samson, there is no battle at all, and the death of the rulers/leaders is narrated in conjunction with the death of Samson.

---

35. Note that it matches the Ammonite oppression in length (Judg. 10:8b).

36. The significance of the usage of the number eighty (obviously twice forty) is difficult to determine.

AS PREVIOUSLY MENTIONED, as a preliminary to the interpretation and application of each cycle, it is important to place the particular cycle under consideration within the larger macrostructure of the cycles section (see the introduction, pp. 34–43). In this way the cycle will be interpreted in its proper overall context within the downward moral movement of this section.

Increase in negative attributes. Each of the cyclical/major judges except Othniel, the first one, presents us with the same difficulty in evaluation: the complexity of their characterization. In the case of Othniel, there is only a positive characterization—hence the process of bridging the contexts is not difficult. But starting with Ehud, there is a mixture of positive and negative attributes, with a decline of the positive and an increase in the negative as the reader goes deeper into the cycles. This is, of course, linked to the very structure of the cycles section and enhances the communication of its central message of moral declivity within the period of the judges. It serves to underscore Yahweh's mighty deliverances in spite of the growing shortcomings of human agents.

In this case, Ehud is clearly not of the moral character of Othniel. He resorts to a complex process of deception in order to accomplish his task of deliverance. Nevertheless, Ehud is not the doubtful, manipulative Barak, whose characterization is more negative than Ehud's (see comments on ch. 4). Thus, for example, Ehud delivers Israel by effectively removing the leader of the enemy of God's people; Barak will win a victory, but the leader of the enemy will escape him.

It is also important to remember that each cycle narrative works on the divine and human levels. While on one level the actions of the Israelites and the judge of each cycle contribute applications to the modern context, there is also on another level a way in which Yahweh works that sees application in present-day situations. The theme of the glorification of Yahweh is present in all six cycles. Each one in some way reflects this glorification. "By means of satire, the narrative ridicules Israel's enemy king and his court and glorifies Israel's hero Ehud and God Yahweh."[37]

The apparent absence/silence of Yahweh. The Ehud narrative raises a theological tension that will be felt throughout the remaining cyclical judge narratives—the tension between the character/actions of the judge and the depiction of Yahweh's involvement.[38] How can Yahweh, the holy God, use

---

37. O'Connell, *The Rhetoric of the Book of Judges*, 100.

38. This is not a tension found in the Othniel cycle, where the human agent and the divine will merge so comprehensively.

men who manifest such horrible, sinful character traits and do such awful things? In the case of this second major judge cycle, it is difficult to explain Yahweh's choice of "Ehud the Benjamite" (certainly with the same assurance that one can explain the choice of Othniel). Why doesn't God raise up another knight in shining armor like Othniel? Why does he use a devious, left-handed assassin like Ehud? In fact, why doesn't he use another Judahite instead of a Benjamite (especially in view of the narration in chs. 1, 17–18)?

While the choice of a Benjamite may be explained on mainly formal grounds (i.e., Benjamin after Judah, as in ch. 1), this does not relieve the tension created by the character of Ehud. Because of the same type of plot development, Jael's action in killing Sisera in Judges 4–5 will create this same tension. This tension is not easily explained, and commentators have struggled with it throughout the history of interpretation.

This can be illustrated in the case of the Ehud cycle by looking at the different ways that scholars have attempted to deal with the apparent absence/silence of Yahweh with regard to Ehud's plan and its execution. Some have inferred from Yahweh's absence/silence that he was not in accord with Ehud's deceptive tactics.[39] Other scholars have argued that this absence/silence is intended by the narrator so that the reader will infer that it is Yahweh himself who prevents complications from arising in Ehud's plot. Thus Amit surmises that the narrator leaves gaps in the stages of narrative development but accumulates data concerning various "coincidences" that help Ehud's plan so that the reader will sense Yahweh's part in the plot.[40] Along similar lines, Webb concludes that "Ehud has been 'raised up'; his deceptions have been providentially directed and guaranteed, although even Ehud himself may not have been aware of it at the time."[41]

Thus, two different interpretations can be given for the same observation in the text. (1) Some scholars have dealt with the tension by arguing that while God does not condone Ehud's methods (i.e., this is not his preferred way), he nevertheless uses the human agent to accomplish the deliverance of his people. Thus Block concludes:

> The narrator's silence on the role of God in the assassination of Eglon is deafening. Prior to verse 28 there is no hint of any spiritual sensitivity in Ehud's heart nor any sense of divine calling. On the

---

39. E.g., Klein, *Triumph of Irony*, 38.

40. Amit, "The Story of Ehud (Judges 3:12–30)," 120. O'Connell notes that while the attribution of Ehud's success is reflected in the cycle framework statements, the inference that God helped Ehud probably existed already in the traditional account (see O'Connell, *The Rhetoric of the Book of Judges*, 85 n. 41).

41. Webb, *The Book of the Judges*, 132.

contrary, Ehud operates like a typical Canaanite of his time—cleverly, opportunistically, and violently, apparently for his own glory. But the narrator appears not to be concerned at all about the morality of the affair. He simply describes what happened from his point of view, and in so doing reminds the readers that in the dark days of the governors the tools available to God are crude.[42]

(2) There can be no doubt that this account (as the other cyclical judge accounts) emphasizes that God is able to use flawed individuals to accomplish his purposes without approving of their flaws. But is the narrator unconcerned about the morality of the affair? Is he simply describing what happens in order to remind his readers that the tools available to God are crude in the days of the judges? I find this difficult to accept from both the immediate context as well as a canonical reading. How does one know that these "tools" (i.e., the judges) are "crude" if there is no moral evaluation within the stories? The stories in the Former Prophets—Joshua, Judges, Samuel, Kings—are morally didactic. Canonically, the Law (esp. as expressed in Deuteronomy) serves as the filter for evaluating the actions of the individuals within the stories. While it is easy to fall into the trap of moralizing these stories, it is also easy to underestimate their didactic value, for they are not mere chronicles.

Accordingly, it is possible—and perhaps preferable—to see the Ehud story operating on both the human and divine levels. Thus, Ehud is undoubtedly not an Othniel. He depends on his own crafty, stealthy, deceptive plot to assassinate Eglon. He is treacherous and brutal. His characterization is an important element in the larger context of the book. Yet God uses him in spite of his flaws in order to emphasize his mercy and compassion on his people (even though they are not serving him and have not repented). Moreover, God manifests his justice in judging wickedness and oppression as evidenced in Eglon and the Moabites.

The faith of Ehud. Block's interpretation, however, raises another question. Are we only to see Ehud's faith and any evidence of his spirituality in the last lines of the story, where he calls out the Israelites and expresses faith and confidence that Yahweh has delivered the Moabites into their hands?[43] Some argue that Ehud manifests faith in the process of the "sacrifice" of

---

42. Block, *Judges, Ruth*, 171.

43. In fact, Block questions even this line, stating: "How genuine his declaration was we may only speculate. The role of the cult images at Gilgal in this story raises questions about the singularity of his spiritual devotion" (*Judges, Ruth*, 170). To me, this is overstating the evidence. Even if the proper understanding of the term *happᵉsîlîm* is "idols/cult images" (see discussion above), the text never states or implies that Ehud worshiped or consulted them for an oracle. The tension in the text is with Ehud's method—his deception and brutality—not with a supposed idolatrous tendency.

Eglon. That is, Ehud depends on God for his access to the king—a risky business, to say the least. If the palace guards had just happened to inspect Ehud's other thigh and find his weapon, he would have been executed on the spot. Hence, in a sense, God sanctions Ehud's courage by allowing his enemy to fall to his scheme. Yet, although Ehud must trust in God for the success of the plot, that plot is hardly on the same level of integrity as the story of Othniel's deliverance of Israel.

Nevertheless, Ehud is willing to take the personal risk without personal assurance(s) from God that it will succeed. In this way, he stands in contrast to most of the remaining cyclical/major judges (i.e., Barak, Gideon, Jephthah), who increasingly look for more and more assurance(s) and guarantee(s) that they will succeed and are less and less willing to risk things without such assurance.[44] His devious methods are not endorsed or condoned by God (i.e., this is scarcely God's preferred method), but God works through and in spite of the judge's weaknesses in order to accomplish the saving of Israel.[45] Moreover, at the end of the day, the glory belongs to God.

Satire. Finally in the Ehud narrative, there is another tension—namely, its use of satire to narrate the execution and destruction of the oppressor and his troops. But one must remember that this satire is at the expense of the enemy of God. Eglon has oppressed the Israelites for eighteen years. He and his minions have robbed and abused God's people this entire time. Consequently, God raises up Ehud to deliver Israel, to save the nation from any more of the Moabite monarch's exploitations. God brings his judgment on Eglon through the crafty Ehud. Likewise, God will judge any exploiter or abuser of his people in his timing (cf., e.g., the death of Herod in Acts 12:1–23).

DIVINE LEVEL. This passage emphasizes the work of God in saving his people. This story (as many others throughout the Bible) demonstrates the length to which God will go in order to deliver humankind. In spite of moral flaws in the deliverer, God accomplishes the salvation of Israel. This serves, in turn, to demonstrate his mercy and compassion, since Israel has not repented. But God hears the cry of pain and anguish among his people and acts on their behalf.

---

44. The case of Samson is different because he is apathetic to saving Israel and seeks no assurance for this reason. But Barak wants assurance (wants Deborah to come along), Gideon wants lots of assurance through various signs, and Jephthah will attempt to manipulate God's assurance through his rash, calculating vow.

45. All of these judges will manifest to some degree faith in Yahweh (otherwise there is a problem with the writer of Hebrews' understanding of them; cf. Heb. 11:32).

The judgment of God's enemies in the past assures God's people that he will judge his enemies in the future. Those who exploit, abuse, and seek to humiliate his people run the risk of humiliation by God. Eglon in particular and the Moabites in general have for eighteen years exploited Israel, God's people. The oppression brings Israel to the point of crying out to Yahweh (not in repentance, but in stress and pain; see comments on p. 102). In compassion on his people, God raises up a judge who is willing without any assurances to risk his very life to save Israel. Israel cannot be saved from Eglon without judgment on Eglon.

Although Ehud's deceptive plot and murder of Eglon may not have been God's preferred means, it does not signify that the Lord cannot turn this to accomplish Israel's deliverance. Throughout the biblical texts God accomplishes his judgments often using individuals far less godly than Ehud (e.g., the Assyrians and Babylonians as the mechanisms for his judgments on the northern kingdom of Israel and the southern kingdom of Judah respectively; cf. also Habakkuk's complaints in Hab. 1–2 with reference to God's judgments). We can take encouragement that God will, in his timing, judge the wicked of this world, though sometimes this may be accomplished through other wicked people.

Human level. On the human level, our context is quite different today from Israel's day. As mentioned before, we do not face the task of physical and spiritual warfare as in Ehud's case. Nevertheless, the question arises: How are we to wage spiritual warfare against those who abuse, exploit, and persecute the church? For Christians in certain parts of the world today, this is not a hypothetical question but a real and practical one.

As discussed in the Contemporary Significance section of 1:1–2:5, the concept of warfare is different between the Old and New Testaments. Nevertheless, while the warfare in which Christians are engaged is spiritual, not physical, the necessity of walking by faith in loyalty to Christ's covenant is the only hope of victory. We are certainly not to fashion our own daggers as Ehud did, but rather to engage the world with a better weapon already supplied—the sword of the Spirit, the word of God (Eph. 6:17). This sword is "living and active. Sharper than any double-edged sword, it penetrates even to dividing soul and spirit, joints and marrow" (Heb. 4:12). This is not to allegorize the passage and equate Ehud's dagger with the Word of God (i.e., the Bible). Rather, it is to acknowledge the role that the truth of that Word plays in the answer to the question posed above in the modern context.

Certainly the positive message of Ehud is in his willingness to risk it all for God (see Bridging Contexts section). This is a lesson we can benefit from. So many Christians are hampered by an unwillingness to take any risk for God—to share their faith, to stand up for righteousness and justice, even to speak a word of encouragement to the downtrodden—simply because we fear what others might say or think about us. Ehud evinces the kind of boldness of action for God that should spur us to action in these types of situations.

Still, Ehud's method of deception cannot be condoned as the ideal way to accomplish God's will. While it heightens the suspense and functions to expose Eglon and the Moabites to greater satire, it poses a significant theological problem. While deceptive methods (whether in evangelistic methods, church-growth methods, political involvements, etc.) may work, this should not be interpreted as God's condoning of such things. The ideal way is the way of integrity, the way in which God worked through Othniel to accomplish his deliverance of Israel in the first cycle.

Judges 3:31

❦

A FTER EHUD CAME Shamgar son of Anath, who struck
down six hundred Philistines with an oxgoad. He too
saved Israel.

THE FIRST MINOR JUDGE is introduced with the initial noncyclical/minor judge formula (see the
introduction, p. 43).[1] This brief account (made
up of one verse consisting of three Hebrew sen-
tences) follows the story of Ehud and continues that story's satirical tone.
Ehud delivered Israel through a single-handed act of diplomatic treachery.
So too the next judge, Shamgar, delivers Israel through a single-handed act
with an agricultural implement. Again the enemy is not only defeated but
made to look utterly ridiculous as the reader's attention is drawn to the improvised weapon. This also is anticipatory of the improvised weapon of Jael in
Judges 4–5.

Webb takes the oxgoad to be a makeshift weapon, which in turn indicates
that Shamgar is not a professional warrior.[2] But if other commentators are correct that "son of Anath" (*ben ᶜanāt*) is an indication of association with a professional army group known as *ben ᶜAnat* in ancient Near Eastern sources,[3] then
Shamgar is a professional soldier, perhaps a mercenary[4] (see below).

While Ehud employed great planning and deception, Shamgar seems to
act almost impulsively (a prepared warrior would not normally use an
oxgoad). While both required dexterity, Ehud relied on stealth to murder
Eglon, Shamgar on brute strength to impale six hundred Philistines (cf. Samson in 15:15). Six hundred warriors was a common troop configuration (cf.
the six hundred warriors sent by the tribe of Dan to conquer Laish [18:11];
see also 1 Sam. 13:15; 14:2; 27:2; 2 Sam. 15:18).

---

1. Note esp. the one-two-three sequence discussed there.

2. Webb, *The Book of the Judges*, 132.

3. See, e.g., N. Shupak, "New Light on Shamgar ben ᶜAnat," *Bib* 70 (1989): 517–25.

4. Craigie adduces examples of the phrase *ben ᶜanāt* from Mari, Ugarit, and Egypt, in
which it functions as a description of the person as one dedicated to the service of the
goddess Anath. Since Anath was a goddess of war, the phrase could denote a mercenary.
See P. C. Craigie, "A Reconsideration of Shamgar Ben Anath (Judg 3:31 and 5:6)," *JBL* 91
(1972): 239–40; see also Boling, *Judges*, 89.

Interestingly, the term "oxgoad" (*malmad*) is formed on the causative stem of *lmd* ("learn")—literally, an "instrument of instruction or learning."[5] Thus there may be a play on words involved in the choice of the oxgoad. Shamgar "teaches" the Philistines a thing or two. They, like Eglon, got the point of the lesson!

The final sentence ("he too saved Israel") emphasizes Shamgar's link to Ehud as another savior of Israel. The same verbal construction also occurs in the parenthetical statement of 3:9, where "he [Othniel/Yahweh] saved them" (see discussion on 3:9).[6]

The identity of Shamgar is obscure. The only scholarly agreement is that Shamgar son of Anath was not an Israelite. But on the other problems surrounding his identity, there is no consensus. There are two issues involved: the derivation and meaning of the name Shamgar, and the significance of the epithet *ben ʿanāt*. (1) According to some scholars "Shamgar" is Hurrian.[7] Others have argued for a Canaanite derivation[8] or a Mesopotamian derivation.[9]

(2) The epithet *ben ʿanāt* is clearly Semitic. There are two different ways of explaining it. Some interpreters understand this to be a description of Shamgar's place of origin, that is, Beth Anath (Josh. 19:32–39; Judg. 1:33).[10] Other commentators see this as an appellation referring to the Canaanite goddess of war, Anat. In general, her cult was widespread among professional soldiers in the ancient Near East in the early twelfth century B.C.

But worship of Anat was particularly widespread in Egypt, where the pharaohs had adopted it. Such worship was introduced as early as the Fifteenth Dynasty (c. 1634–1610 B.C.), but the adoption of military-type Asiatic

---

5. Klein, *Triumph of Irony*, 39. The word is a biblical hapax but is used in postbiblical Hebrew to describe a pointer or guiding instrument (M. Jastrow, *A Dictionary of the Targumim, the Talmud Babli and Yerushalmi, and the Midrashic Literature* [Brooklyn: Pardes, 1950], 793). Hence in the construction in 3:31 (*malmad habbāqār*) it means "the guiding instrument/pointer of the cattle."

6. See also the ambiguous statement concerning Tola in 10:1.

7. B. Maisler, "Shamgar ben ʿAnat," *PEQ* 66 (1934): 192–94; Craigie, "A Reconsideration of Shamgar," 239.

8. Soggin, *Judges*, 57. He argues that the name could be West Semitic (and therefore possibly Canaanite), if it is a *shaphel* form of *mgr* = "submit," citing a seal inscription that includes the theophoric name *mgrʾl*. This would make it a reduced theophoric name, i.e., "the god brings into submission."

9. F. C. Fensham, "Shamgar ben Anath," *JNES* 20 (1961): 197–98. Fensham even translates "ben Anath" as "son of a Ḥanaean," suggesting that Shamgar was related to a seminomadic group of Ḥanaeans (from the Mesopotamian city of Ḥanat), who migrated to Palestine.

10. See Gray, *Joshua, Judges, and Ruth*, 216; Bright states: "Presumably he was a city king of Beth-anath in Galilee, perhaps the head of a confederacy, who by throwing back the Philistines saved himself—and Israel" (Bright, *A History of Israel*, 179).

deities was especially pronounced among the militant pharaohs (Thutmose III, Amenhotep II, Ramesses II).[11] An inscription from Wadi Hammâmât, dated in the third year of Ramesses IV (1166–1190 B.C.), reads: "ʿprw of the troop of ʿAn[ath] eight hundred men." Working on the assumption that the same troop had fought against the Sea Peoples during the reign of Ramesses III (1198–1166 B.C.), Shupak suggests that Shamgar may have been one of these ʿprw, some of whom have Hurrian names.

In addition to the Egyptian evidence, there is other evidence that the epithet *ben ʿanāt* is a military designation. An inscription arrowhead from El-Khadr (dated to c. 1100 B.C.) reads: ʿbdlbʾt bn ʿnt (ʿAbd-Labiʾt Bin-ʿAnat).[12] As Hamilton notes, the term "Bin-ʿAnat" can either be the name of the father of ʿAbd-Labiʾt or may indicate that the latter is a member of an archers' guild.[13] From this evidence, it is possible to posit a West Semitic origin for the phrase.[14] Whatever the case, the evidence demonstrates that *ben ʿanāt* may designate some type of military unit. Shupak concludes that the evidence points to the figure of Shamgar son of Anath as having a real basis in the historical setting of the beginning of the Iron Age.[15]

The fact that Shamgar is paired in the Song of Deborah with Jael, a Kenite, seems to confirm his non-Israelite origins. Like Othniel, the first cyclical/major judge, Shamgar, the first noncyclical/minor judge, is a non-Israelite. He is the only noncyclical judge to save Israel from a specific oppressor (Tola will "save Israel," but from whom is left blank). He is the only noncyclical judge for which there is any information concerning how he does it (though admittedly scanty). If the role of judge as described in the introduction is applied to the minor judges, Shamgar seems to be the most successful in fulfilling the role. If the parallel to Othniel (first major judge, first minor judge) is considered, then it is possible to see Shamgar as a type of ideal noncyclical judge.

---

11. Stadelmann, *Syrisch-Palestinensische Gottheiten in Ägypten* (Probleme der Ägyptologie 5; Leiden: Brill, 1967), 20ff.; 135ff.; Jaroslav Černý, *Ancient Egyptian Religion* (Westport, Conn.: Greenwood, 1979), 126.

12. See G. Hamilton, "The El Khadr Arrowheads," *COS*, 2.84.

13. Ibid., n. 6. See also F. M. Cross, "Newly Found Inscriptions in Old Canaanite and Early Phoenician Scripts," *BASOR* 238 (1980): 1–20, esp. 7. For occurrences of the term on another arrowhead and elsewhere, cf. W. W. Hallo and H. Tadmor, "A Lawsuit from Hazor," *IEJ* 27 (1977): 1–11, esp. 4–5. See also B. Beem, "The Minor Judges: A Literary Reading of Some Very Short Stories," in *The Canon in Comparative Perspective. Scripture in Context IV*, ed. K. L. Younger Jr., W. W. Hallo, and B. F. Batto (ANETS 11; Lewiston, N.Y.: Edwin Mellen, 1991), 147–72, esp. 158–62.

14. See note 8 above. Note also a new Philistine inscription that reads: *bnʿnt* (ben ʿAnat). See S. Gitin, T. Dothan, and J. Naveh, "A Royal Dedicatory Inscription from Ekron," *IEJ* 47 (1997): 1–16, esp. 13–14.

15. Shupak, "New Light on Shamgar ben ʿAnat," 523.

It is clear from the text of Judges so far that Yahweh will deliver the Israel from their oppressors. However, it is also clear that his methods may not be so easy to predict or explain. The fact that the initial and ideal major judge was a non-Israelite should raise our eyebrows; the fact that Shamgar as the initial minor judge is also a non-Israelite should raise them that much the more. And the account of Deborah and Barak (plus the non-Israelite Jael) is just on the narrative horizon.

Shamgar's mighty exploit is similar to that of two other individuals: Samson and Shammah. Samson slew a thousand Philistines with the jawbone of a donkey (15:14–17); Shammah is one of David's heroes listed in 2 Samuel 23:8–23; note verses 11–12:

> Next to him was Shammah son of Agee the Hararite. When the Philistines banded together at a place where there was a field full of lentils, Israel's troops fled from them. But Shammah took his stand in the middle of the field. He defended it and struck the Philistines down, and the LORD brought about a great victory.

Certainly, such exploits were important for the ancient Israelites to remember because in each instance the credit for the victory is Yahweh's, at least in the cases of Shamgar and Shammah (for Samson, see the discussion below).

SEE THE COMMENTS at the end of the last three minor judges (12:8–15) (pp. 278–79 below).

SEE THE COMMENTS at the end of the last three minor judges (12:8–15) (p. 280 below).

Judges 4:1–5:31

A FTER EHUD DIED, the Israelites once again did evil in the eyes of the LORD. ²So the LORD sold them into the hands of Jabin, a king of Canaan, who reigned in Hazor. The commander of his army was Sisera, who lived in Harosheth Haggoyim. ³Because he had nine hundred iron chariots and had cruelly oppressed the Israelites for twenty years, they cried to the LORD for help.

⁴Deborah, a prophetess, the wife of Lappidoth, was leading Israel at that time. ⁵She held court under the Palm of Deborah between Ramah and Bethel in the hill country of Ephraim, and the Israelites came to her to have their disputes decided. ⁶She sent for Barak son of Abinoam from Kedesh in Naphtali and said to him, "The LORD, the God of Israel, commands you: 'Go, take with you ten thousand men of Naphtali and Zebulun and lead the way to Mount Tabor. ⁷I will lure Sisera, the commander of Jabin's army, with his chariots and his troops to the Kishon River and give him into your hands.'"

⁸Barak said to her, "If you go with me, I will go; but if you don't go with me, I won't go."

⁹"Very well," Deborah said, "I will go with you. But because of the way you are going about this, the honor will not be yours, for the LORD will hand Sisera over to a woman." So Deborah went with Barak to Kedesh, ¹⁰where he summoned Zebulun and Naphtali. Ten thousand men followed him, and Deborah also went with him.

¹¹Now Heber the Kenite had left the other Kenites, the descendants of Hobab, Moses' brother-in-law, and pitched his tent by the great tree in Zaanannim near Kedesh.

¹²When they told Sisera that Barak son of Abinoam had gone up to Mount Tabor, ¹³Sisera gathered together his nine hundred iron chariots and all the men with him, from Harosheth Haggoyim to the Kishon River.

¹⁴Then Deborah said to Barak, "Go! This is the day the LORD has given Sisera into your hands. Has not the LORD gone ahead of you?" So Barak went down Mount Tabor, followed by ten thousand men. ¹⁵At Barak's advance, the LORD routed Sisera and all his chariots and army by the sword, and

Sisera abandoned his chariot and fled on foot. ¹⁶But Barak
pursued the chariots and army as far as Harosheth Haggoyim.
All the troops of Sisera fell by the sword; not a man was left.

¹⁷Sisera, however, fled on foot to the tent of Jael, the wife of
Heber the Kenite, because there were friendly relations
between Jabin king of Hazor and the clan of Heber the Kenite.

¹⁸Jael went out to meet Sisera and said to him, "Come, my
lord, come right in. Don't be afraid." So he entered her tent,
and she put a covering over him.

¹⁹"I'm thirsty," he said. "Please give me some water." She
opened a skin of milk, gave him a drink, and covered him up.

²⁰"Stand in the doorway of the tent," he told her. "If someone comes by and asks you, 'Is anyone here?' say 'No.'"

²¹But Jael, Heber's wife, picked up a tent peg and a hammer
and went quietly to him while he lay fast asleep, exhausted. She
drove the peg through his temple into the ground, and he died.

²²Barak came by in pursuit of Sisera, and Jael went out to
meet him. "Come," she said, "I will show you the man you're
looking for." So he went in with her, and there lay Sisera with
the tent peg through his temple—dead.

²³On that day God subdued Jabin, the Canaanite king,
before the Israelites. ²⁴And the hand of the Israelites grew
stronger and stronger against Jabin, the Canaanite king, until
they destroyed him.

[The Setting of the Song]

⁵⁼¹On that day Deborah and Barak son of Abinoam sang
this song:*

I. Stanza

Strophe 1

¹²"When the princes in Israel take the lead,
    when the people willingly offer themselves—
    praise the LORD!
³"Hear this, you kings! Listen, you rulers!
    I will sing to the LORD, I will sing;
    I will make music to the LORD, the God of Israel.

---

*Note that although this Song of Deborah and Barak is set up differently from the NIV,
the translation used here is the NIV.

Strophe 2

⁴"O LORD, when you went out from Seir,
    when you marched from the land of Edom,
  the earth shook, the heavens poured,
    the clouds poured down water.
⁵The mountains quaked before the LORD, the One of Sinai,
    before the LORD, the God of Israel.

A

II. Stanza

Strophe 3

⁶"In the days of Shamgar son of Anath,
    in the days of Jael, the roads were abandoned;
  travelers took to winding paths.

Strophe 4

⁷Village life in Israel ceased,
    ceased until I, Deborah, arose,
  arose a mother in Israel.

Strophe 5

⁸When they chose new gods,
    war came to the city gates,
  and not a shield or spear was seen
    among forty thousand in Israel.

III. Stanza

Strophe 6

⁹My heart is with Israel's princes,
    with the willing volunteers among the people.
    Praise the LORD!
¹⁰"You who ride on white donkeys,
    sitting on your saddle blankets,
    and you who walk along the road,
  consider ¹¹the voice of the singers at the
        watering places.
    They recite the righteous acts of the LORD,
    the righteous acts of his warriors in Israel.

B

Strophe 7

"Then the people of the LORD
    went down to the city gates.
12'Wake up, wake up, Deborah!
    Wake up, wake up, break out in song!
Arise, O Barak!
    Take captive your captives, O son of Abinoam.'
13"Then the men who were left
    came down to the nobles;
the people of the LORD
    came to me with the mighty.

IV. Stanza

Strophe 8

14Some came from Ephraim, whose roots were
        in Amalek;
    Benjamin was with the people who
        followed you.
From Makir captains came down,
    from Zebulun those who bear a
        commander's staff.
15The princes of Issachar were with Deborah;
    yes, Issachar was with Barak,
    rushing after him into the valley.

C

Strophe 9

In the districts of Reuben
    there was much searching of heart.
16Why did you stay among the campfires
    to hear the whistling for the flocks?
In the districts of Reuben
    there was much searching of heart.

Strophe 10

17Gilead stayed beyond the Jordan.
    And Dan, why did he linger by the ships?
Asher remained on the coast
    and stayed in his coves.
18The people of Zebulun risked their very lives;
    so did Naphtali on the heights of the field.

V. Stanza

Strophe 11

¹⁹"Kings came, they fought;
    the kings of Canaan fought
  at Taanach by the waters of Megiddo,
    but they carried off no silver, no plunder.

Strophe 12

²⁰From the heavens the stars fought,
    from their courses they fought against Sisera.
²¹The river Kishon swept them away,
    the age-old river, the river Kishon.

Strophe 13

  March on, my soul; be strong!
²²Then thundered the horses' hoofs—
    galloping, galloping go his mighty steeds.

Strophe 14

²³'Curse Meroz,' said the angel of the LORD.
    'Curse its people bitterly,
  because they did not come to help the LORD,
    to help the LORD against the mighty.'

D

VI. Stanza

Strophe 15

²⁴"Most blessed of women be Jael,
    the wife of Heber the Kenite,
    most blessed of tent-dwelling women.
²⁵He asked for water, and she gave him milk;
    in a bowl fit for nobles she brought him curdled milk.

Strophe 16

²⁶Her hand reached for the tent peg,
    her right hand for the workman's hammer.
  She struck Sisera, she crushed his head,
    she shattered and pierced his temple.

Strophe 17

²⁷ At her feet he sank,
    he fell; there he lay.
  At her feet he sank, he fell;
    where he sank, there he fell—dead.

VII. Stanza

E

Strophe 18

²⁸ "Through the window peered Sisera's mother;
    behind the lattice she cried out,
  'Why is his chariot so long in coming?
    Why is the clatter of his chariots delayed?'

Strophe 19

²⁹ The wisest of her ladies answer her;
    indeed, she keeps saying to herself,
³⁰ 'Are they not finding and dividing the spoils:
    a girl or two for each man,
    colorful garments as plunder for Sisera,
    colorful garments embroidered,
    highly embroidered garments for my neck—
  all this as plunder?'

Strophe 20

³¹ "So may all your enemies perish, O LORD!
    But may they who love you be like the sun
    when it rises in its strength."

[Narrative Frame Conclusion]

    Then the land had peace forty years.

THE BIBLICAL ACCOUNT of the judge cycle of Deborah and Barak comes in two parts—a prose narrative (ch. 4) and a lengthy poem (ch. 5). The prose provides a logical account with a carefully constructed point. The Song of Deborah and Barak provides an emotional and more figurative account.

The Narrative of Deborah and Barak (4:1–24)

THE NARRATIVE OF Judges 4 is a well-composed unity.[1] Its opening prologue
(4:1–3) and concluding epilogue (4:23–24) form a type of inclusio, so that
the items in the prologue are readdressed in the epilogue. The main story is
organized into two parts (4:4–16 and 4:17–22), and these are subdivided into
two scenes each (4:4–10 + 4:11–16; and 4:17–21 + 4:22).

Prologue (4:1–3). This prologue relates the background to the story
using two narrative frame statements:

A The Israelites do evil in the eyes of Yahweh (4:1)
  B Yahweh gives them into the hand of Jabin, king of Canaan, who
    lives at Hazor and who oppresses them through Sisera (4:2–3)

The opening statement that "the Israelites once again did evil in the eyes
of the LORD" is the exact same wording as the opening to the Ehud narrative.[2]
Ehud's judgeship did not prevent the cyclical recurrence. Rather, the Israelites
return to their apostasy (the Song of Deborah will reveal that they worship
"new gods," 5:8). As expected, Yahweh sells them into the hand of an oppressor. The oppressor is once again a foreign monarch (*melek*), "Jabin, a king of
Canaan, who reigned in Hazor."[3] But immediately the prologue introduces
Jabin's commander, Sisera, who will be the up-front antagonist in the story.
Jabin blends into the background; the text mentions his name twice (4:7, 17),
and the epilogue resolves matters through a threefold repetition of his name.
Thus, he is always in the background while Sisera is in the forefront.

The two pieces of information recounted about Sisera are important to the
plot and will be alluded to again in the body of the narrative (4:13, 16). (1) He
dwells in Harosheth Haggoyim.[4] (2) He has nine hundred iron chariots at his

---

1. D. F. Murray, "Narrative Structure and Technique in the Deborah-Barak Story, Judges
iv 4–22," in *Studies in the Historical Books of the Old Testament*, ed. J. A. Emerton (VTSup 30; Leiden:
Brill, 1979), 155–89; Y. Amit, "Judges 4: Its Contents and Form," *JSOT* 39 (1987): 89–111.

2. The phrase "after Ehud died" is probably better translated as a pluperfect, "after Ehud
had died."

3. Not to be confused with the Jabin, the king of Hazor, in Josh. 11. The name "Jabin"
may possibly be a "dynastic name," similar to "Ramesses" in Egypt, "Henry" in English history, and "Louis" in French history. See K. L. Younger Jr. "Heads! Tails! Or the Whole
Coin?! Contextual Method and Intertextual Analysis: Judges 4 and 5," in *The Canon in Comparative Perspective. Scripture in Context IV*, ed. K. L. Younger, W. W. Hallo, and B. F. Batto
(Lewiston, N.Y.: Edwin Mellen, 1991), 133 n. 90.

4. The precise location of the town is unknown. The name Harosheth Haggoyim probably means "cultivated field of the Gentiles." See further A. F. Rainey, "Toponymic Problems," *Tel Aviv* 10 (1983): 46–48; idem, "The Military Camp Ground at Taanach by the
Waters of Megiddo," *ErIsr* 15 (1981): 61*–66*. The name may play a literary role as an inti-
mation of the involvement of the nations (*gôyīm*).

disposal.[5] Especially difficult for infantry, these "iron chariots" were a technology that Israel did not possess, and they therefore pose a great intimidation to them.[6]

Contrary to what is commonly stated, ancient chariots were not like modern tanks. They were not used to break through enemy lines.[7] Instead, they were used for pursuit and slaughter of the fleeing enemy. They were primarily a killing platform. Against a fleeing enemy on an open plain they were very effective.

Sisera's name is clearly non-Semitic, probably of Anatolian origin.[8] He is apparently a mercenary in charge of Jabin's chariot corps. On account of these chariots, Sisera is able to oppress[9] the Israelites for twenty years, resulting in the Israelites' crying out to Yahweh.

Part 1 (4:4–16). With the background established, it is now possible to investigate Part 1: Deborah :: Sisera + Barak. Here the focus is on Deborah and Sisera with Barak as an inclusion on the basis of Deborah's first prophecy.

Scene 1 (4:4–10) subdivides into the introductory circumstances (4:4–5) for Deborah and the plot development (4:6–10) based on this. The introduction of Deborah will parallel the introduction of Heber in the next scene. Four basic points are made here: Deborah ("honey bee") is a prophetess, the wife of Lappidoth (4:4a); she is judging Israel at that time (4:4b); her dwelling is under the Palm of Deborah in the hill country of Ephraim, where she sits (4:5a);[10] and Israel goes up to her for judgments (4:5b). These same basic informational-type items were included in the introduction of Sisera (4:2–3).

---

5. Boling suggests that these were esp. sturdy chariots constructed with iron fittings (Boling, "Judges, Book of," 3:1109). Millard thinks they were chariots with perhaps three or four thin plates hung over the front to protect the charioteer's legs, which his hauberk did not cover (Millard, "Back to the Iron Bed," 194–95). Cf. also 1:19 above.

6. For more on the archaeological background to Judges 4–5, see L. E. Stager, "Archaeology, Ecology, and Social History: Background Themes to the Song of Deborah," in *Congress Volume: Jerusalem, 1984*, ed. J. A. Emerton (VTSup 40; Leiden: Brill, 1988), 221–33.

7. Cf. Judg. 1:19.

8. Some have argued that perhaps this explains the origin of iron technology. However, for a more recent critique within the Hittite context, see S. Košak, "The Gospel of Iron," in *Kaniššuwar: A Tribute to Hans G. Güterbock on His Seventy-Fifth Birthday*, ed. H. A. Hoffner and G. A. Beckman (Chicago: Univ. of Chicago Press, 1986), 125–35.

9. The same verb (*lḥṣ*) is used here as in 1:34, where the Amorites confine (*lḥṣ*) the Danites to the hill country.

10. This location (between Ramah and Bethel) was relatively far away from Hazor. Kedesh Naphtali, Barak's home, was close to Hazor. This heightens the irony that the one far away is the one who takes the initiative to deliver those whose "general" lives near the palace of the oppressor king and the home of the oppressing general, Sisera. The mention of Ephraim is also significant because it links the Deborah and Barak cycle to Ehud (the hill country of Ephraim was where Ehud sounded his trumpet and led the volunteers to victory at the fords, 3:27).

It is her role as prophetess that is catalytic in this narrative.[11] A prophet was primarily a spokesperson or mouthpiece for the deity, a conduit for communication (see esp. Ex. 4:15–16; 7:1–2).[12] As a prophetess, Deborah stands in a long tradition starting with Miriam (Ex. 15:20) and continuing throughout the Old Testament.

The clauses "[she] was leading [judging, *špṭ*] Israel at that time" (4:4b) and "the Israelites came to her to have their disputes decided [lit., for judgments, *mšpṭ*]" (4:5b) seem to imply either that Deborah functions as a "judge" in the same sense as the others mentioned in the book,[13] or that she acts as a legal functionary rendering judicial decisions.[14] The former is unlikely, since it is Barak, not Deborah, who is the designated deliverer and who ought to have served as the main character of the account.[15] Block argues against the former, stating, "one wonders why the narrator would have inserted this parenthetical reference to the settlement of relatively petty civil disputes when the issue in the chapter is a national crisis."[16] He suggests that 4:4b is better understood as "she was governing [cf. NIV, leading] Israel at that time" and that 4:5b refers to the Israelites' going up to her "for the judgment" (namely, that she would give them the divine answer to their cries).[17]

The plot development in Scene 1 (4:6–10) will correspond in many ways to that in the plot development of Scene 2 (4:12–16). For Scene 1 the structure is clear:

A The command of Deborah and the response of Barak (4:6–9)

  a Deborah commands Barak to gather an army, assuring him of victory (4:6–7)

  b Barak requires Deborah's presence (4:8)

  c Barak wins his request but loses glory (4:9)

B Barak deploys the troops (4:10)

  a Barak calls (*zʿq*) the troops to Kedesh (4:10a¹)

  b Barak goes up (*ʿlh*) with the troops (4:10a²–b)

---

11. O'Connell, *The Rhetoric of the Book of Judges*, 107–8.

12. For a discussion of the etymology of the term, see D. E. Fleming, "The Etymological Origins of the Hebrew *nābîʾ*: The One Who Invokes God," *CBQ* 55 (1993): 217–24.

13. E.g., A. E. Cundall states: "Deborah was the savior of her people and the only woman in the distinguished company of the Judges" (*Judges: An Introduction and Commentary* [Downers Grove, Ill.: InterVarsity, 1968], 82 [see also p. 95]).

14. E.g., Soggin, *Judges*, 72.

15. O'Connell, *The Rhetoric of the Book of Judges*, 107–8. See also Block, who gives twelve arguments against Deborah being understood as a "judge" in the delivering sense of the word.

16. Block, *Judges, Ruth*, 197.

17. Ibid.

In 4:6, Barak ("lightning"), the son of Abinoam of Kedesh Naphtali, is introduced (note that Deborah "sends" for him and then "commands" him). Clearly she is the one who is taking the initiative, not Barak. From the introduction of Deborah in 4:4 on, the narrator surprises the reader with numerous twists in the plot. Deborah is not what we would expect. The fact that she holds a position of authority and takes the initiative in relation to the prospective male hero is surprising. Moreover, Deborah stands as God's envoy, the means by which God issues his call to Barak.

As Barak initially proves to be reluctant to serve Yahweh, Deborah also acts as a foil to further Barak's negative characterization. Twice Deborah anticipates Barak's reluctance to follow her instructions from Yahweh by using the rhetorical construction *hălō' yhwh* ("has not Yahweh?") (4:6, 14). The first time (4:6) literally reads: "Has not Yahweh, the God of Israel, commanded, go?" (cf. the NIV: "The LORD, the God of Israel, commands you: 'Go.'"). Thus, this is not her opinion about his calling and how things ought to work out but the sure word of Yahweh.

Deborah's charge to Barak in 4:6–7 indicates that he is destined for a role comparable to that played by Othniel in 3:7–11. His response, however, to Deborah's command from Yahweh with its great assurance of victory[18] is hardly the stuff of an Othniel or even an Ehud: "If you go with me, I will go; but if you don't go with me, I won't go" (4:8). While his motive for expressing his desire for Deborah to accompany him is not indicated in the narrative, some interpreters see this as a sign of cowardice.[19] But note what the Old Greek (LXX) adds, "for I [Barak] never know what day the angel of the Lord will give me success." This seems to suggest that Barak desires Deborah's presence as a source of oracular inquiry.[20] Block argues that "the request to be accompanied by the prophet [*sic*] is a plea for the presence of God."[21] O'Connell notes that by conditioning his obedience to Yahweh on Deborah's willingness to accompany him, "Barak was effectively denying her the authority that Yahweh had conferred upon her as a prophetess (4:4a)."[22]

Deborah's response that she will go seems to allay the problem of Barak's hesitation. But then she issues another prophecy: ". . . the honor will not be yours,

---

18. Is there some irony in Yahweh's command to take ten thousand men in light of the use of this figure in earlier contexts? To the original reader this must have raised an eyebrow since the figure was used to describe the number of Canaanite and Moabite dead. Is God assuring Barak (that much the more that), in spite of the figure, that he is to be trusted? With God's involvement, the figure is not a symbol of defeat, but victory.

19. B. Lindars, "Deborah's Song: Women in the Old Testament," *BJRL* 65 (1982–83): 158–75, esp. 161, 164.

20. Note Boling's discussion (*Judges*, 96).

21. Block, *Judges, Ruth*, 199.

22. O'Connell, *The Rhetoric of the Book of Judges*, 108.

for the LORD will hand Sisera over to a woman" (4:9). The reader has only one woman to suspect as the possible fulfillment—Deborah. But the ironic twist is just over the horizon. Thus, while Barak will win a notable victory, his insistence that Deborah accompany him instantly diminishes his heroic stature. With the assurance of Deborah (and hence God's) presence, Barak deploys the troops (4:10). He calls (z^cq) the troops to Kedesh and then goes up (^clh) with them.

Scene 2 (4:11–16), like Scene 1, contains introductory circumstances (4:11) and a plot development (4:12–16). In the introductory circumstances, Heber the Kenite is introduced. He has previously left the other Kenites in Judah (1:16) and has made his dwelling, like Deborah, under a great tree in Zaanannim near Kedesh (Barak's home). This sudden introduction of Heber is anticipatory. Ironically, it is not Heber who will be of aid to Israel's cause—as we might expect, based on 1:16. Instead, it will be his wife, Jael, since Heber has not only "left" his Kenite clan in Judah but has "friendly relations" with Jabin (the use of *šālôm*, lit., peace, does not necessitate a formal treaty, 4:17).

The plot development in Scene 2 (4:12–16) corresponds in many ways to that in Scene 1 (4:6–10).

> B' Sisera deploys the troops (4:12–13)
>> a' Sisera hears that Barak has gone up (^clh) (4:12)
>> b' Sisera calls (z^cq) the troops to Wadi-Kishon (4:13)
> A' The command of Deborah and the response of Barak (4:14–16)
>> a' Deborah commands Barak to go into battle, assuring him of victory (4:14a)
>> b' Barak goes down to fight (4:14b)
>> c' Barak wins the battle but loses Sisera (4:15–16)

Sisera, whose military intelligence has discovered Barak's military movements (i.e., that he has gone up [^clh]),[23] calls up (z^cq) his troops to the wadi Kishon. Sisera's deployment in B' (4:12–13) corresponds to Barak's deployment in B (4:10). The narrative leaves the impression in these verses that Sisera is functioning on his own (or Jabin's) initiative, but the reader knows from verse 7 that Yahweh is setting the stage for the showdown.

For the second time, Deborah anticipates Barak's reluctance to follow her instructions from Yahweh by using the rhetorical construction *hălō' yhwh* ("has not Yahweh?" 4:14; cf. 4:6 above): "Has not the LORD gone ahead of you?" This underscores the certainty of the victory but serves to heighten Barak's reluctance without great assurance.[24]

---

23. Perhaps Sisera learns of Barak's movements through Heber. This would only enrich the irony of what is to transpire.

24. These two instances of assurance foreshadow the two assurances through the fleece incidents of Gideon (see below). O'Connell notes also the use of the term *qûm* (arise) twice

Interestingly, Deborah's announcement in 4:14a that "this is the day the LORD has given Sisera into your hands" seems to suggest that, on the basis of Barak's performance of Yahweh's instructions, perhaps Sisera will be given into Barak's hands after all despite the limitation predicted in 4:9. However, the reference to Sisera is only a metonymy (subject [military commander] for adjunct [his chariots and troops]). Barak apparently takes Deborah's words literally for he will vainly pursue Sisera to the end. But in reality Sisera does not control things, nor does Barak control the outcome. God controls the battle and the results: Sisera will be the victim of a woman.

Perhaps stimulated by the assurance, this time Barak's response is appropriate. Barak goes down to fight with the ten thousand men following and wins the battle, but he loses Sisera (in accordance with Deborah's prophecy). Yahweh was the one who routs Sisera and his army with its iron chariots.[25] Ironically, Barak will pursue the chariots and army as far as Harosheth Haggoyim (Sisera's home), certainly with the expectation that he will get Sisera (and the honor connected to this). The humor here is at the Israelite general's expense. He expends tremendous effort to pursue the enemy from the Kishon to Harosheth Haggoyim, but all for naught.

Part 2 (4:17–22). In Part 2 the focus is on Jael and Sisera with Barak as an inclusion on the basis of Deborah's second prophecy (hence: Jael :: Sisera + Barak). Like Part 1, Part 2 is composed of two scenes with introductory circumstances and plot developments.

Scene 1 (4:17–21) opens with introductory circumstances (4:17) in which there is a reintroduction of Sisera (this time as a fugitive) and an explanation of Sisera's new location. Having escaped the battle Sisera flees to the tent of Jael, the wife of Heber the Kenite, because there are friendly relations between Jabin and Heber.[26] The introductory circumstances of Scene 1 will be paralleled by the introductory circumstances of Scene 2 (the reintroduction of Barak).

---

in the narrative (4:9, 14). It is used in 4:9b to describe the action of only Deborah when she arises (*qûm*) to go with Barak after rebuking him for his reluctance to follow Yahweh's instructions. Later, it is used again by Deborah, who prompts Barak to arise (*qûm*) and follow Yahweh into battle (4:14a), so that Barak comes to be seen as a deliverer who will not "be raised up to save" apart from the initiatives and actions of a woman (*The Rhetoric of the Book of Judges*, 108).

25. The Song of Deborah below will detail Yahweh's intervention in poetic terms.

26. The situation appears to be one in which there is no treaty, but good relations prevailing between the urban center of Hazor and tent-dwelling people of Heber. Hence, Sisera flees to the tent of Jael the Kenite. The text explicitly states that there was šālôm between the two parties. Even if no formal treaty existed, the state of šālôm probably means that a fugitive could find asylum with the other party (see D. J. Wiseman, "'Is It Peace?'—Covenant and Diplomacy," *VT* 32 [1982]: 314).

The plot development in Scene 1 corresponds in many ways to that in that of Scene 2 (4:22) below. The structure is:

A Jael entreats Sisera to come into her tent (4:18a)
   B Sisera enters asking for aid (4:18b−20)
      C Jael kills Sisera (4:21)

Jael intentionally goes out to meet Sisera and entreats him to come into her tent as a place of safety. Her words "Don't be afraid" disarm the Canaanite warlord. Having entered her tent, he makes his own entreaty: "I'm thirsty.... Please give me some water." The commander of the Canaanite hosts continues to issue commands, this time to a woman. Jael demonstrates ancient Near Eastern hospitality in giving him milk[27] and covering him up. These actions disarm Sisera even more. He issues his last command to the woman, which is rich in irony:

"Stand in the doorway of the tent.
If someone [ʾîš] comes by and asks you,
'Is anyone [ʾîš] here?'
say 'No [ʾên].'"

The someone/anyone (lit., "man" [ʾîš]) who comes to the door of the tent is, of course, Barak. And the "man" (ʾîš) within the tent is Sisera, dead by the time Barak arrives. Murray observes:

The confrontation is not now of two leaders at the head of vast armies, but of two men in the presence of a woman; and one word put with dreadful irony into the mouth of Sisera who has so cravenly abandoned his position of leadership, adumbrates the impending fate of them both: (ʾên) [lit., "nothing, no-one"].[28]

Sisera, now completely mollified, falls asleep as a result of the exhaustion of the battle and escape. Then Jael, having set her victim at ease, picks up a tent peg and hammer and drives the peg through Sisera's temple into the ground.

Scene 2 (4:22), relatively brief, contains an introductory circumstance (v. 22a¹) and plot development (v. 22a²-b). After the reintroduction of Barak as pursuer (Barak's new location assumed), the plot development has the following structure corresponding to Scene 1 above:

A′ Jael entreats Barak to come into her tent (4:22a²)
   B′ Barak responds by entering (4:22b¹)
      C′ Jael presents the slain Sisera to Barak (22b²)

---

27. Perhaps Jael ("mountain goat") gave him goat's milk.
28. Murray, "Narrative Structure and Technique in the Deborah-Barak Story," 180.

Poor Barak, no doubt like Sisera exhausted from the pursuit, is met by Jael, who comes out to meet him as she did Sisera. Jael likewise entreats Barak to enter the tent; Barak does so.[29] The dead Sisera lies on the ground—the tent peg climatically and ironically through his head.

The ironic juxtaposition of victor and vanquished in the same tent of Jael is significant. The woman has in effect conquered them both: Sisera, by depriving him of his life, and Barak, by depriving him of the honor that should have been his as the chosen deliverer. Interestingly, the true identity of the "woman" is delayed as long as possible so that the irony is nicely turned against the reader.[30] The result of this delay is to enhance the impact, when it comes, of the revelation that Yahweh's choice fell not merely on a woman, nor even on an Israelite prophetess (as we were led to expect), but on "Jael, the wife of Heber the Kenite."

To the attentive reader, the similarities between Jael's murder of Sisera and Ehud's assassination of Eglon are transparent. Both narratives feature a murder scene followed by a discovery scene. Both Ehud and Jael use false premises to set up the murder (Ehud's claim to have a "word from God"; Jael's seeming assurance of asylum). Ehud murders Eglon and the attendants discover their dead master; Jael murders Sisera and Barak discovers the dead Canaanite commander. In both narratives the murder and discovery scenes play much more significant roles than the battle scenes.[31] While in the Ehud narrative the murder takes place before the battle, in the Barak story it follows it.

Jael's murder of Sisera is narrated in the same vivid style as Ehud's murder of Eglon; each separate movement is described precisely (cf. 4:21 with 3:20–22). As Ehud's manipulation of Eglon and his courtiers serves to satirize Eglon and his men for their gullibility, so Jael's manipulation of Sisera by means of verbal ambiguity satirizes him for his gullibility. Ehud thrusts (tq^c) his sword into Eglon's belly; Jael drives (tq^c) her tent peg ($y\bar{a}t\bar{e}d$) into Sisera's head.[32] Finally, Barak's discovery of the dead Sisera is likewise narrated in the same style as the courtiers' discovery of the dead Eglon. The courtiers discover "their lord" ($^{3a}d\bar{o}n\hat{e}hem$) "fallen" ($n\bar{o}p\bar{e}l$) on the "ground" ($^3ar\d{s}\hat{a}$) "dead" ($m\bar{e}t$); Barak discovers "Sisera" ($s\hat{i}s^er\bar{a}^3$) "fallen" ($n\bar{o}p\bar{e}l$) "dead" ($m\bar{e}t$).

The result of all this is to ironically picture Barak playing a role analogous to that of Eglon's courtiers (who were ridiculed in 3:24–25). He has lost the

29. Though undoubtedly not like Sisera, who entered expecting refuge, Barak is unsure of possible danger and expects the worst.

30. Polzin, *Moses and the Deuteronomist*, 163.

31. For more explication of this, see Block, *Judges, Ruth*, 201.

32. Alter (*The Art of Biblical Narrative*, 41) points out that the words "drive" (tq^c) and "peg" ($y\bar{a}t\bar{e}d$) will recur in the Samson story, where Delilah will fasten (tq^c) Samson's hair with a pin ($y\bar{a}t\bar{e}d$) (16:14). Hence, Samson appears in the same position as Sisera!

honor to a woman. He can only stand and stare. It is his punishment for trying to manipulate Yahweh and his prophetess, Deborah (4:8). This certainly foreshadows Jephthah, who will bring on himself significant judgment for trying to manipulate Yahweh directly. Just as the vow and its fulfillment is the axis along which tension is developed and resolved in the Jephthah story, so the bargain struck in 4:8–9 (Deborah will go with Barak, but Yahweh will sell Sisera into the hand of a woman) is the axis along which tension is developed and resolved here.[33]

The Barak narrative involves two men and two women. The women are commanding the men, who lose out when they make demands of the women. Thus:

    (1) a woman commands (or invites—in the imperative) a man:
        Deborah → Barak   Jael → Sisera
    (2) the man responds to the command (invitation):
        Barak → Deborah   Sisera → Jael
    (3) the man loses his objective (or realizes his loss):
        Sisera (life)   Barak (glory)

Finally, Jael emerges as the real heroine of the narrative. But this is ironic too. She is hardly an orthodox hero. Rather, she shares the unorthodox qualities of Ehud and of Shamgar. Like Ehud, Jael is a lone assassin who accomplishes her ends by deception. Like him she dispatches her victim when the two of them are alone in a private chamber (hers, in this case, rather than her victim's). Moreover, like Shamgar she improvised a weapon from a domestic implement. Like Shamgar, Jael is a non-Israelite. Shamgar, if a Canaanite, was a member of Israel's archenemies. Likewise, Jael is a member of a Kenite splinter group, which is at "peace" with Jabin, the king of Canaan, Israel's archenemy (4:11, 17)! Her action is morally ambiguous, but her courage and the sheer virtuosity of her performance are sufficient to silence criticism on that score (5:24). The crowning aspect of her unorthodoxy as a hero is her sex: Yahweh sells Sisera into the hand of a woman.[34]

Epilogue (4:23–24). The epilogue relates two narrative frame statements in response to the prologue (4:1–3):

    B' God subdues Jabin, king of Canaan, before Israel (4:23)
    A' The Israelites do right by destroying Jabin (4:24)

The NIV's translation of the last sentence "until they destroyed him" obscures the threefold mention of "Jabin, king of Canaan" in the Hebrew text.

---

33. Webb, *The Book of the Judges*, 137.
34. Ibid.

This threefold mentioning seems to stress that with the destruction of his army at the Kishon and the death of Sisera, his commander, Jabin becomes isolated in Hazor and is eventually overcome by the Israelites, who thus finally establish their supremacy over the Canaanites in the north.

The Song of Deborah (5:1–31)

IN THE CASE of the battle against Sisera, the prose provides a logical account with a carefully constructed point. The Song of Deborah,[35] however, provides an emotional and more figurative account with special themes and purposes.

This song poses one of the most difficult passages in the Old Testament. Its date, authorship, text, unity, vocabulary, and structure have been debated by scholars for centuries. A detailed discussion of all these issues and the opinions of other scholars would easily produce a book in and of itself.[36] For the purposes of this commentary, attention will be given to the more evident matters. A general discussion of the synthesis of the song and the narrative will follow.

Notwithstanding the difficulties of this song, recent scholarship has helped to discern its basic structure.[37] Besides the narrative frame giving the setting (5:1) and conclusion (5:31d), there are five acts, made up of seven stanzas, which are comprised of twenty strophes.[38] Furthermore, there is a

---

35. I am using the traditional heading as a descriptive for the song (as in *The NIV Study Bible*). The statement in 5:1, "On that day Deborah and Barak son of Abinoam sang this song," provides the narrative setting for the song and does not speak directly to the issues of authorship. There are a number of reasons according to the traditional view why Deborah is seen as responsible for the song's composition (see Block, *Judges, Ruth*, 214–15), not least of which is the significant use of the first-person singular pronouns. But because of the poetic nature of the song, one must be cautious of attributing authorship on such grounds. See footnote 42.

36. One of the most recent analyses argues that the distribution of stylistic characteristics throughout the entire song indicate that it was composed at one time, as a unit. See H.-D. Neef, "Der Stil des Deboraliedes (Ri 5)," *ZAH* 8 (1995): 275–93. Neef dates the song's composition around 1025 B.C. See now also Block, *Judges, Ruth*, 211–18.

37. Two important analyses that underlie the exposition here are J. P. Fokkelman, "The Song of Deborah and Barak: Its Prosodic Levels and Structure," in *Pomegranates and Golden Bells: Studies in Biblical, Jewish, and Near Eastern Ritual, Law, and Literature in Honor of Jacob Milgrom*, ed. D. P. Wright, D. N. Freedman, and A. Hurvitz (Winona Lake, Ind.: Eisenbrauns, 1995), 595–628; and M. D. Coogan, "A Structural and Literary Analysis of the Song of Deborah," *CBQ* 40 (1978): 143–66. For bibliography on the song, which is massive, see Younger, "Heads, Tails or the Whole Coin?!" 136–37, 143–46.

38. Fokkelman's analysis ("The Song of Deborah and Barak," 626–28) yields twenty strophes and seven stanzas. On a higher level, he sees the poem having three sections (vv. 2–8, 9–23, 24–31). But it seems clear to me that there are five acts on a level between the stanzas and Fokkelman's sections.

developmental, narrowing shift from a focus on the nation to a focus on the ten tribes to a focus on two female individuals. The nation is the focus of Acts A and B (Stanzas I–III); the tribal focus is seen in Acts C and D (Stanzas IV–V); and the two women are the focus of Act E (Stanzas VI–VII). The following figure presents the poem's poetic structures:

The Prose Setting of the Song (5:1)

  A Initial Call to Praise and Report of Need (5:2–8) (Stanzas I and II; Strophes 1–5)
      Invocation to praise (*brk*) Yahweh (5:2)
      Exhortation to pay attention (5:3)
      Cause for praise: Yahweh's epiphany (5:4–5)
      Cause for praise: the state of affairs before the victory (5:6–8)

  B Renewal of Call to Praise Because of the Volunteers (5:9–13) (Stanza III; Strophes 6–7)
      Invocation to praise (*brk*) Yahweh (5:9)
      Exhortation to pay attention (5:10)
      Cause for praise and response of the people: then they went down to battle (5:11)
      Cause for praise and response of the people: then they went down to battle (5:12–13)

    C The Recognition of the Tribes Who Participated and Who Did Not (5:14–18) (Stanza IV; Strophes 8–10)

  D The Battle (5:19–22) + Transition (5:23) (Stanza V; Strophes 11–14)
      The Battle (5:19–22)
      Transition: the curse of Meroz (5:23)

  E Jael's Deed and Sisera's Mother and Climatic Conclusion (5:24–31c) (Stanzas VI–VII; Strophes 15–20)
      Jael's deed (5:24–27)
      Sisera's mother (5:28–30)
      Climatic conclusion (5:31a–c)

The Prose Frame Conclusion (5:31d)

The first Act (A) (5:2–8). After the prose setting of the song (5:1), the first Act (A) begins. An initial call to praise contains a report of Israel's need (5:2–8).[39]

---

39. Kempinski points out the important fact that "the references to Israel are numerous especially in vv. 1–11. Such an archaic song, even if put into written form in the early

This Act (Stanzas I–II), while corresponding in certain ways to the concluding Act in E (5:24–31c), has a parallel structure to Act B. It opens with an invocation to praise (*brk*) Yahweh (5:2).[40] The first line of verse 2 that the NIV
translates "When the princes in Israel take the lead" is perhaps better translated
"because hair was unbound in Israel," or "When locks were loosened in Israel."[41]

The Act continues with an exhortation especially addressed to royalty,
that is, to kings and rulers (5:3), to pay attention. In light of the use of king
(*melek*) in the book of Judges so far, this reference is to foreign monarchs and
is similar to the invocation in Psalm 2:2, 10. In other words, the princes and
kings of the non-Israelite communities around them are ordered to listen, so
that they are the first receivers of this communication. However, they are
mere witnesses—they certainly will keep their mouths shut after the devastating defeat some of them have just suffered. But having encouraged this
audience to respond in praise of Yahweh, the "lyrical I" now exclaims (lit.):
"I myself to Yahweh, I myself will sing!"[42]

Two causes for praise are given in Act A. (1) In Strophe 2 of Stanza I
(5:4–5) the singers draw attention to Yahweh's epiphany,[43] which itself has
a concentric structure:

a Yahweh marched from Seir/Edom (v. 4a-b)[44]
  b the earth shook (v. 4c)
    c the heavens poured (*ntp*—v. 4d)
    c' the clouds poured (*ntp*—v. 4e)
  b' the mountains shook (v. 5a)
a' before Yahweh of Sinai, Israel's God (v. 5b-c).[45]

---

monarchic period, could not be altered so greatly as to add the name 'Israel' to almost every
line in these verses" ("Review of Gösta Ahlström, *Who Were the Israelites?" IEJ* 41 [1991]: 297–
99). In fact, the name Israel occurs eight times in the poem, all in verses 1–11. See D. Block,
"'Israel'—'Sons of Israel': A Study in Hebrew Eponymic Usage," *SR* 13 (1984): 301–26.

40. The word *brk* is often translated "bless." It means "to fortunately empower." When
used to describe what a human being does to God, it has the meaning "to declare or acknowledge the origin or source of fortunate empowerment," hence, "to praise."

41. The difficulty lies in the term *pᵉrāʿôt*, which has a clear Akkadian cognate (*pirtu*, hair)
and occurs in a similar context. See W. W. Hallo, "The Cultic Setting of Sumerian Poetry,"
RAI 17 (1969): 132.

42. Fokkelman points out the use of the "lyrical I" ("The Song of Deborah and Barak,"
601). In the context, according to 5:1, this "I" would be Deborah (note that the verb *watāšar*
in this verse is feminine singular, referring to Deborah; cf. also 5:7). See footnote 35.

43. An epiphany is a revelatory manifestation esp. of a divine being.

44. Seir is used as a synonym for Edom.

45. The last line of each strophe in Stanza I (vv. 3c and 5b) ends with the phrase "the
LORD, the God of Israel." Note the great similarity of the epiphany in this strophe and
epiphanies in Ps. 68:7–8[8–9] and Hab. 3:3.

(2) In Stanza II (5:6–8) the state of affairs before the victory anticipates Yahweh's action as in the epiphany (5:4–5). The parallelism of verse 6 temporalizes the events:

In the days of Shamgar son of Anath,
in the days of Jael.

The mention of Shamgar, son of Anath (see 3:31), is a reminder (resumptive repetition) that a non-Israelite—who used a peasant tool rather than a conventional weapon—delivered Israel. The mention of Jael is anticipatory since she too, being a non-Israelite (cf. 4:17), will use domestic implements rather than a conventional weapon to deliver Israel. This will be resumed in Act E, Stanza VI.

Unfortunately, verses 6b–7a are difficult, being variously translated. The following is a composite:

the roads/caravans ($^{\circ}r\bar{a}\d{h}\hat{o}t$)[46] were abandoned/ceased ($\d{h}\bar{a}dal$),
    and those travelling
    went on winding paths ($^{\circ}r\bar{a}\d{h}\hat{o}t$).
Village life/warriors[47] ceased ($\d{h}\bar{a}dal$),
    they ceased ($\d{h}\bar{a}dal$) in Israel.

Regardless of the different translations, the picture is clearly one of oppression.

But God's actions behind the scene are documented: "until I, Deborah, arose, arose a mother in Israel." The description of the time continues:

When they chose new gods,[48]
    war came to the city gates.
and not a shield or spear was seen
    among forty thousand in Israel.

Israel's choices concerning "new gods" was the thing that brought military humiliation and servitude, including the very weapons of war (shield and spear) necessary to overcome the oppression. This stresses Yahweh's victorious intervention all the more.

---

46. The former seems preferred since it is reused with this meaning in v. 6d.

47. "Warriors" seems preferred in the context with the word's reuse in verse 11c. Note the NRSV, which translates the last two lines: "The peasantry prospered in Israel, they grew fat on plunder." Thus, these two lines would allude to a time of victory, not oppression. This translation is based on understanding $\d{h}\bar{a}dal$ as being from a second root $\d{h}dl$ meaning "to grow fat." However, this does not seem to fit the context as well.

48. The line is difficult syntactically. See Block, *Judges, Ruth*, 226–27, although his solution is somewhat forced.

The second Act (B) (5:9–13). This second Act, comprised of Stanza III, is parallel in structure to the first Act.[49] As in that Act, there is an invocation to praise (*brk*) Yahweh (v. 9), inspired by those who volunteered. An exhortation to pay attention is given to those who ride on donkeys[50] (v. 10). There are two causes for praise and response of the people (vv. 11 and 12–13). (1) The voice of the singers (or the report of the recruiters)[51] at the watering places concerning Yahweh's righteous deeds and those of his warriors stimulates a response: "Then [*ʾāz*] the people of the LORD went down [*yrd*] [to battle] at the gates" (5:11). (2) The leaderships of Deborah and then Barak are invoked to conduct the campaign that stimulates a response: "Then [*ʾāz*] the remnant went down [*yrd*] [to battle] against the nobles" (5:12–13).

Both strophes of this Act feature enveloping structures. Strophe 6 (5:9–11c) is framed by references to the people of "Israel" (i.e., the princes of "Israel" [v. 9a] and the warriors in "Israel" [v. 11c]). Strophe 7 is framed by references to "the people of the LORD" going down (*yrd*) (v. 11d-e and v. 13c-d). This strophe also includes an address to Deborah and Barak as a pair. It is a double appeal and cry of encouragement on the threshold of the battle.

The third Act (C) (5:14–18). The third and central Act of the song (C) is a complete stanza (Stanza IV) comprised of three strophes (vv. 14–15c, 15d–16, 17–18). It is a recognition of the tribes who participated and who did not (5:14–18). This seems to be a focal point of the song. It begins with a list of those who participated: Ephraim,[52] Benjamin, Makir (a subdivision of Manasseh, perhaps the part for the whole), Zebulun, and Issachar. This is given in the first strophe of the Act (Strophe 8). Note that Deborah and Barak are paired once again in verse 15a-b. Then a list of those who did not participate is given: Reuben, Gilead (i.e., Gad), Dan,[53] and Asher. This list comprises Strophe 9 and most of Strophe 10.

Strophe 9 is a particular taunt of Reuben and contains an inclusio (vv. 15d-e and 16c-d). While there was some reflective concern expressed, the Reubenite pastoralists seemed indifferent to the plight of the other sedentary tribes. The three other nonparticipant tribes are listed at the beginning of Strophe 10 (v. 17a-d). A possible political explanation (given by a number of commentators) for the reluctance on the part of Dan and Asher to join the

---

49. See O'Connell, *The Rhetoric of the Book of Judges*, 113–14.

50. This may have subtle royal overtones since rulers often rode on donkeys. The NIV's "white" donkeys is doubtful; "tawny" is a better translation of the term.

51. The exact meaning of *mᵉḥaṣṣîm* is uncertain.

52. The phrase "whose roots were in Amalek" might better be "thither into the valley."

53. For the best detailed explanation of Dan and the phrase "why did he linger by the ships?" see A. F. Rainey, "Who Is a Canaanite?" *BASOR* 304 (1996): 1–15.

fight against the Canaanites is that they did not dare to jeopardize their economic future, which was dependent on Phoenician commerce and shipping. The noninvolvement of the bulk of the Transjordanian tribes may be simply a matter of apathy as a result of geography. The last verse of this strophe returns to the participating tribes of Zebulun and Naphtali, who are especially praised for their bravery (v. 18).

Although they are theoretically united by their worship of Yahweh and the covenant with him, the Israelites manifest a serious deficiency of political and military solidarity.[54] The nonparticipant tribes refused to sacrifice their individual interest and well-being for the sake of the nation and are severely rebuked.

Act C gives a full picture of the mobilization of the tribes before the battle. In addition, it is evaluative in every way of the individual tribal involvement.[55] From the vantage point of hindsight, each group is weighed and classified as being either a positive or a negative factor in the preparation. This assessment is moral and spiritual, although the poet gives the appraisal without using adjectives such as "good" or "bad" even once.[56] His weighing is that of a historiographer writing on a period of national history. Fokkelman adeptly sums up the importance of the poet's assessment:

> The importance of passing judgment is indeed so central that the act of passing judgment permeates the whole poem. It is a ferment that has penetrated every stanza. And it has given the poet a set of positions that are fertile material for shaping and charging his structures dynamically.[57]

The fourth Act (D) (5:19–23). The fourth Act of the Song of Deborah (Stanza V) expounds the battle and presents a transition: the curse of Meroz. First the battle is described (5:19–22). As with so many battles in the ancient Near East, an army was often composed of troops from numerous small vassal states with their kinglets or chiefs leading them. While the Canaanite kings joined to Sisera fought, they had no success, no plunder. The text clearly discloses that plunder or booty was their aim (v. 19d).

---

54. This same picture is observable in the famous Merneptah Stela, which contains the earliest extrabiblical reference to Israel. See J. K. Hoffmeier, "The (Israel) Stela of Merneptah," *COS*, 2.6; idem, *Egypt in Israel: The Evidence for the Authenticity of the Exodus Tradition* (New York/Oxford: Oxford Univ. Press, 1997), 27–31.

55. The noninvolvement of certain tribes may allude to some type of military confederation within early Israel. That is, there must be a basis on which tribes can be chastened for their noninvolvement, which seems to imply a tribal, military-type confederation.

56. Fokkelman, "The Song of Deborah and Barak," 614.

57. Ibid., 615.

At this point, the poetry paints a magnificent portrait of divine intervention, in which a storm of epic proportions overwhelms the technologically superior Canaanite charioteers. The overflowing Kishon River "swept them away." The combination of skies and water is a link back to the epiphany of Act A, Strophe 2 (5:4–5, esp. 4c-d). The power with which the victory is now marching forward (Strophe 13) is ironically matched by the energy with which the enemy flees. Their power now goes completely into the loud pounding of the hoofs, which is balanced by the treading of the victors. The final scene of the battle (Strophe 14) is that of the chaos of the horses galloping wildly over the field, missing their riders or free of their chariots. The galloping is made audible by the poet in the wonderful onomatopoeia, *dabᵃrôt, dabᵃrôt* (v. 22).[58]

It is interesting that not one single line of the poem shows the Israelites directly involved in the hard and dangerous work of warfare. Certainly Stanza V would have been the appropriate place. But the poet seems to purposely choose not to give such a depiction in order to allow all the honor to go to Yahweh.

The transition of the curse of Meroz (Strophe 14) is pronounced by the angel (or messenger, *malᵓak*) of Yahweh (5:23; cf. 2:1).[59] The repetition of the imperative "curse" and the reintroduction of the divine name, Yahweh, disclose the poet's point of view clearly: Every soldier, battalion, or community that commits himself/itself to warfare is helping Yahweh; all are needed.

Though initially the curse seems out of place (belonging with the evaluation of the tribal participants/nonparticipants in Stanza IV, 5:14–18), it is actually well placed. In the Gideon narrative, two cities (Succoth and Peniel) refused to aid Gideon's army after the initial battle while Gideon was in pursuit of the remaining Midianites. They received a curse (8:7, 9), which was meted out after Gideon's successful return (8:16–17). If one considers this parallel of the Gideon narrative to the Song of Deborah, Meroz may be such an Israelite city[60] that failed to aid the pursuing forces of Barak when they needed it rather than when the initial call to go to war went out.

This supposition is supported by the placement in the text of the curse on Meroz and the general movement of the poem. This curse is framed by

---

58. W. G. E. Watson, *Classical Hebrew Poetry. A Guide to Its Techniques* (JSOTSup 26; Sheffield: JSOT Press, 1984), 234–36. For a different interpretation, see Block, *Judges, Ruth,* 237–38.

59. This *malᵓak yhwh* seems to refer to the angelic figure who appears to perform both a leadership and protective function in leading Israel through the desert and into the land of Canaan (Ex. 14:19; 23:20; 32:34; 33:2; Judg. 2:1–5). See H.-D. Neef, "Meroz: Jdc 5,23a," *ZAW* 107 (1995): 118–22.

60. Ibid.

the rout of the Canaanites and the climactic act of Jael's killing Sisera. From
the placement of the curse it is plausible to interpret the failure of Meroz as
one of denying immediate aid to the pursuing Israelite warriors rather than
as a failure for mustering troops at the beginning of the campaign. The seriousness of the curse logically follows, comparing Succoth and Peniel, as
opposed to the simple recognition and possible taunting of the absent tribes.[61]
Thus the curse provides the perfect transition from the battle of the kings to
the fleeing king, Sisera. Meroz did not aid Yahweh in the pursuit; but Jael,
the wife of a Kenite did, and she is praised (lit., "blessed") as fervently as
Meroz is cursed. In a sense, Meroz represents those Israelites who have taken
their stand on the side of the Canaanites; Jael (in the next stanza) represents
those non-Israelites who have taken their stand on the side of Israel.[62]

The fifth Act (E) (5:24–31). The fifth and final Act is a double portrait
of Jael's deed and Sisera's mother, which lead to the climactic conclusion of
this song. The image of Jael's killing of Sisera is the first portrait (5:24–27).
With intensity equal to that of the curse of Meroz, blessing is proclaimed for
Jael. In fact, she is made the receiving end of blessing, which is given to only
one other character in the poem, God himself! All of Stanza VI details the
reason: She slew Sisera. Jael's resourcefulness and courage in doing this are
the basis for admiration and praise. The unrestrained praise of Jael is analogous to that given to Mary in Luke 1:42.

Jael's action should be evaluated in light of the *ḥērem*—the utter destruction of the enemies of God (see the introduction, pp. 28–30). It provides a conclusion to the battle scene with the defeat of the enemy leader. The fact that
Jael is a non-Israelite is especially underscored by the repetition of "the wife
of Heber the Kenite" and by the reference to her as a "tent-dwelling" woman.
This heightens the contrast even more between Jael and the Israelite tribes and
city of Meroz.[63] Jael would not typically be expected to get involved. Not only
is she unrelated to the warring parties, but normally would be about her pacific
feminine, tent-dwelling duties. But she has risked everything to execute the
enemy of God and to aid God's people. By contrast, the Israelite tribes and
city of Meroz, who could be expected to participate and render aid, did not.

As only poetry can do, the scene shifts suddenly, without transition, into
the tent of Jael. Sisera requests water—ironically the very thing that has just

---

61. Following this logic, Neef's argument seems correct, namely that Meroz lay in immediate proximity to the territory where the battle of Deborah and Barak transpired (i.e., in
the region between Mount Tabor and the Kishon River, the south Jezreel Plain). See ibid.

62. Block, *Judges, Ruth*, 239.

63. Her act is praiseworthy and unique because she is not an Israelite (5:24b reminds the
reader); her act, however, makes her an Israelite, poetically speaking. In this respect, she is
parallel to another non-Israelite woman, Ruth.

destroyed his army! The request also contains a taunt—the mighty commander of the army of the kings of Canaan is forced to appeal for water from a simple tent-woman! Jael gives him milk[64] instead. Moreover, she brings it to him in a bowl fit for nobility. Her hospitality disarms her victim. It is implicitly a motherly kind of act.

By its very nature, poetry is ambiguous and impressionistic, and the final scene of Sisera's death is surrounded by ambiguous and impressionistic language. In Strophe 16, Jael is shown in constant and flowing action,[65] as though zoomed in by the camera, drawing closer attention to the inescapable and gory details of the murder. The poem paints Jael in terms of the head-smashing, victorious monarch.[66] Consequently, her praiseworthy deed can be described in terms of the victorious conquering leader—and not just a conqueror of Sisera but everything embodied in him, the enemy Canaanites.[67]

Finally, the shortening of the lines in Strophe 17 (v. 27) describe the action with a tantalizingly slow sequence of verbs that present his "fall":[68]

Between her feet he bowed, he fell, he lay.
Between her feet he bowed, he fell,
where he bowed,
there he fell,
slain.[69]

The second portrait of Act E (Stanza VII, Strophes 18–19) is a taunt of Sisera's mother (5:28–30). One moment the reader is in the tent of Jael, the next in Sisera's mother's house. The image of this noble woman in her palace with royal retainers presents a sharp contrast to Jael, the rustic wife of Heber the Kenite living in her tent.[70]

---

64. Poetically specified as "curdled milk" (ḥemʾâ), a type of curds/yogurt. See C. Grottanelli, "Aspetti simbolici del latte nella bibbia," in *Drinking in Ancient Societies: History and Culture of Drinks in the Ancient Near East. Papers of a Symposium Held in Rome, May 17–19, 1990*, ed. L. Milano (Padova: Sargon, 1994), 381–97, esp. 391–96; idem, "The Story of Deborah and Barak: A Comparative Approach," *Studi e Materiali di Storia delle Religioni* N.S. 11 (1987): 311–16.

65. Strophe 16 is the only syndetic one of the stanza (i.e., the only one that uses the *waw* conjunction) to emphasize the narrative, sequential flow of Jael's action.

66. J. K. Hoffmeier, "Some Egyptian Motifs Related to Warfare and Enemies and Their Old Testament Counterparts," in *Egyptological Miscellanies: A Tribute to Professor Ronald J. Williams*, ed. J. K. Hoffmeier & E. S. Meltzer (Ancient World 6; Toronto: Univ. of Toronto Press, 1983), 156–74.

67. K. L. Younger Jr., "Heads! Tails! Or the Whole Coin?!" 131.

68. A. J. Hauser, "Two Songs of Victory: A Comparison of Exodus 15 and Judges 5," in *Directions in Biblical Hebrew Poetry*, ed. E. Follis (Sheffield: JSOT Press, 1987), 265–84, esp. 278–79.

69. Cf. the description of the death of Eglon. See Webb, *The Book of the Judges*, 135–37.

70. Block, *Judges, Ruth*, 242.

The scene overflows with dramatic irony. Running synchronously with Stanza VI, the picture shifts to Sisera's mother looking out of the window, anxiously awaiting the return of her son. She remains nameless in the text, which implies that she identifies totally with her son. She wants *his* chariot to *come* quickly, as on all the other occasions when he returned victoriously. But now "it [the chariot] hesitates" (lit. trans., an interesting personification).

The single voice of the mother now merges with the voice of her wisest attendant (5:30). They are allowed to speak six full lines. They intend to ask one another a rhetorical question presupposing an affirmative answer ("Surely are they not finding and dividing the spoils?"). But because of the previous two Stanzas (V–VI), the audience, having knowledge of the outcome of the battle and Sisera's death, are enabled and invited to read the clause with an ironic twist: No, "they will certainly not find any spoil or divide it!"[71]

The lady and her attendants fantasize about a huge amount of booty (ironically including women) as the cause for his delay; they never (openly) suspect the possibility of his demise. The last word of the first line and the last word of the sixth line create an inclusio "spoils" (*šalāl*) and "plunder" (*šālāl*). This reveals the ladies' orientation: "plundered stuff." The item that opens the list highlights a greed and nationalistic mentality that totally override the gender aspect.[72]

The Israelite women who are expected to be taken captive by Sisera as the highest prize are depicted in the vulgar and macho frame of mind that has characterized soldiers of all ages. These Israelite women are no more than *raḥam raḥ⁽a⁾mātayim* "one or two broads/babes" (the NIV translates the line "a girl or two").[73] The heartlessness in the line is even more pronounced with a literal translation: *raḥam raḥ⁽a⁾mātayim l⁽e⁾rō⁾š geber* ("a womb, a pair of wombs for the head of each warrior/man"). Thus Israelite women are reduced to mere items of plunder. Ironically, the persons speaking are themselves women. Block sums up this irony well:

> One might have expected a refined woman like Sisera's mother to be more sensitive to the vulnerability of women in the violent world of male warfare. At the very least she could have used a more neutral expression like *na⁽a⁾rāh*, "girl, damsel," or *⁾āmāh*, "maid, handmaid." Her preference for this overtly sexual expression reflects the reali-

---

71. Fokkelman, "The Song of Deborah and Barak," 623.

72. See D. N. Fewell and D. M. Gunn, "Controlling Perspectives: Women, Men and the Authority of Violence in Judges 4 and 5," *JAAR* 58 (1990) 389–411.

73. Fokkelman, "The Song of Deborah and Barak," 624. He further notes "Whether *raḥam* with its *pataḥ* vowels means "womb" (elsewhere *reḥem*) or "darling" does not matter very much; what counts is the humiliating, reducing point of view" (624 n. 68).

ties of war: to victorious soldiers the women of vanquished foes represent primarily objects for their sexual gratification, another realm to conquer.[74]

The other treasured prize of war that Sisera's mother mentions is the rich, colorful garments that were typically plundered from the defeated army's tents and dead bodies. In this, her greed for such booty is unmistakable.

Yet, through parallel structuring, the poet emphasizes the last word of verses 27 and 30: "dead" (*šādûd*) and "plunder" (*šālāl*). Thus, in a sense, this scene continues the taunt of Sisera because he is unable to fulfill the expectations of his mother. He has become the plunder (*šādûd*) (v. 27).

The climactic conclusion (5:31a-c) is a double invocation for God to bring such a judgment to pass on all who defy him (cf. David's words to Goliath in 1 Sam. 17) and for God to bring blessing on those who love him. Block notes that the concluding lines reflect a consciousness of the covenant blessings and curses as spelled out in Leviticus 26 and Deuteronomy 28.[75] This double invocation, therefore, is a fitting conclusion to the extraordinary poem known as the Song of Deborah.

The "strength" (*gbwrh*) of the sun that goes out (*yṣ'*) is a daily reminder to the audience of the deity who goes out (*yṣ'*) to support his people with his strength. The root *gbr* occupies important positions in the poem. It is placed at the end of Stanzas III and V, which encircle the muster of the tribes. Together with the word "kings" it is almost the only concrete indication of the enemy. Thus the power of the enemy has met "its master in the magnetic field of poetic power."[76]

The conclusion to the Deborah and Barak cycle occurs in 5:31d with the common narrative frame statement: "Then the land had peace forty years."

Synthesis of the Two Accounts

THE STORY OF the Deborah and Barak cycle is recounted in both prose and poetry. Such a prose-poetic double accounting was not unusual in the ancient Near East. The narrative and poem of Judges 4 and 5 seem parallel and yet different. Scholars have long debated the relationship between the two.[77] For both chapters their individual emphases and purposes determine their selectivity of material. In the case of the battle against Sisera, the prose account

---

74. Block, *Judges, Ruth*, 243.

75. Ibid.

76. Fokkelman, "The Song of Deborah and Barak," 625. For a similar use of the root *gbr*, see 2 Sam. 1.

77. See K. L. Younger Jr., "Heads! Tails! Or the Whole Coin?!" 109–45.

provides a logical account with a carefully constructed point. The song, however, provides an emotional and more figurative account with special themes and purposes. The two are complementary in relationship.[78] This is important when dealing with divergent data between the two. The significant places of divergence are in their descriptions of tribal participation, Sisera's death, Jabin's presence, geographic references, and the description of the battle.

The Barak narrative is much less interested in who fought in the battle than it is in Barak's hesitation and its results: "He who hesitates loses!" But the purpose of the Song of Deborah is to acknowledge and praise Yahweh and those who participated. The song, therefore, presents three groups: those who did not respond (5:15d–17), those who did respond (5:14–15a), and those who distinguished themselves in battle (5:18).

IT IS IMPORTANT—as a preliminary to the interpretation and application of this cycle—to place it within the larger macrostructure of the cycles section (see the introduction, pp. 34–43). This ensures that the cycle will be interpreted in its proper overall context within the moral declivity movement of the cycles. Thus Barak is not the judge that Ehud was and certainly not the judge that Othniel was. But he will be unquestionably better in fulfilling the role of "judge" (*šōpēṭ*) than Gideon (see comments on chs. 6–7).

Glorification of Yahweh. It is also important to remember that each cycle narrative works on two levels: human and divine. (1) On the human level, the characters of Deborah, Barak, Jael, the tribal participants/nonparticipants, and Sisera's mother evince positive and negative qualities that serve to bridge the ancient context to the modern context (see below). (2) On the divine level, there is the continuing theme of the glorification of Yahweh. In this passage, both in the prose account and in the poem, Yahweh is glorified through his work on Israel's behalf. His sovereignty in accomplishing this is intensified by the fact of the shortage of dedicated Israelites from which he might work. The hesitancy of Barak and the noninvolvement of a number of Israelite tribes emphasize this situation. This problem will become worse in the successive cycles.

The cycle's satirization of the military commander Sisera as an agent of Jabin's oppressive foreign kingship is in contrast to the glorification of Yahweh, who controls all circumstances that lead to Israel's deliverance—both

---

78. See also the mention of this event in 1 Sam. 12:9–11.

those of the temporal order in the prose portrayal and those of the cosmic order, with which Jael's actions are consonant, in the hymnic portrayal. This oppression of Jabin and Sisera (especially with Sisera's iron chariots) is a significant trial and affliction for the Israelites. Like the previous oppressions, it is brought on the Israelites by God in order to chasten them, and it once again stresses his justice. God is utterly consistent in dealing with apostasy. He will not allow the Israelites to do as they please without certain repercussions in accordance with his covenant with them. But God is also compassionate; he does not overpunish. He uses his prophetess to raise up the deliverer. In spite of spiritual failings on the part of this deliverer, God brings about Israel's deliverance, ultimately using a non-Israelite tent-woman to bring judgment on the enemy leader.

Deborah. It is significant that the role over against the powerful monarch Jabin is Deborah, the prophetess—a person whom Jabin and Sisera would have mockingly derided as a leader. But in her weakness in a patriarchal world, Deborah proves to be God's answer. As his prophetess she will commission God's general, Barak, the counterpart to Sisera. And she will willingly and with great faith initiate the process of the demise of the mighty Canaanite king and his military commander.

It should be added that Deborah also stands in the commissioning position in the narrative structure that the angel of the Lord does in the Gideon narrative that follows. God is proving here what he proves many times over: He uses the weaker things (or what the world considers the weaker things) in order to confound the wise and mighty. He will bring down the arrogant and abusive Jabin and Sisera in his timing.

Barak. If Ehud was no Othniel, then Barak is no Ehud. Barak's unwillingness to go and fight even though he has tangible assurance through God's prophetess is serious. While this fact documents the continuation of the moral declivity of the major/cyclical judges, it especially reveals the reluctance to believe God's promise. Even though Barak gains the victory, he expends much time and energy trying to obtain the prize he has already forfeited. This is one of the sad truths testified to in the Bible as well as throughout the history of the church. God in his goodness is constantly looking for opportunities to give good gifts to men and women. Yet because of their lack of faith, they forfeit these blessings that God would freely give.

In the case of Barak, he loses the opportunity to truly be used of God. True, he does win the battle, and this is a testimony to his faith (this is why he is listed in Heb. 11:32). But this is not completely what God had in mind to give him. When Christians fail to trust God, demanding assurance when God, in fact, has already spoken, they lose out on the opportunity to be used by him to the fullest extent.

Jael. In the case of Jael, as in the previous case of Ehud, the interpretation of the narrative absence of Yahweh is understood differently by scholars. Some argue that the absence of Yahweh's involvement in Jael's actions indicates that her deeds "have been lifted from a Canaanite notebook."[79] Block maintains:

> The narration offers no hint of any spiritual motivation on her part or any concern for Israel. She acts entirely on her own and for her own (mysterious) reasons. Her actions are not only deviant and violent but socially revolutionary, challenging prevailing views of female roles in general and the relationship of husband and wife in particular. However, just because the author records her deeds does not mean he approves of them. It simply adds to the mystery of divine providence, demonstrating implicitly what the following verses explicitly affirm: God is able to incorporate the free activities of human beings into his plan for his own glory and for the salvation of his people.[80]

O'Connell, by contrast, argues that the lack of plot complication (i.e., this problem-free development leading to Jael's success in killing Sisera), like the lack of plot complication in the Ehud story, indicates that it is Yahweh who has control of the circumstances leading to the success in both cases.[81] He puts it this way:

> As in the Ehud account, Jael cannot claim final credit for success in humiliating Israel's enemy. The two foreshadowings of Jael in 4:9 and 4:11 seem designed to demonstrate YHWH's control over events in the story. That is, before anyone (character or reader) knew her name or understood her significance, YHWH is seen to have predicted the outcome of Jael's actions through Deborah (4:9) and to have set up the conditions for her humiliation of Sisera (and, unwittingly, Barak) by positioning her tent beside that of her husband on the route by which Sisera would escape (cf. 4:11, 17). Thus, as with Ehud, the strategies of Jael are seen to work in concert with those of YHWH. What is more, the humiliating effect that Jael's assassination of Sisera has upon Barak (4:22) comes as the result of a strategy outside Jael's interest (and probably awareness) and demonstrates that YHWH, who predicted her

---

79. Block, *Judges, Ruth,* 209.

80. Ibid., 209–10. This comment seems to be based on the narrative alone (i.e., ch. 4) without integrating the statements concerning Jael in the song of ch. 5. However, note that later in his commentary Block argues that the author's intention in the Jael/Sisera scene is to "glorify God whose mysterious but providential hand produces the victory" (p. 241 n. 446).

81. O'Connell, *The Rhetoric of the Book of Judges,* 110.

actions and positioned her tent, was the one ultimately in control of the circumstances leading to Jael's success.[82]

As with Shamgar, deliverance comes from an unexpected source and in an unexpected manner. Jael, the wife of Heber the Kenite, is the person who is the ultimate human hero(ine) of the story. She takes the initiative to do what needs to be done.

It is noteworthy that in the deliverances in these cycles the enemy leadership must be effectively dealt with.[83] Ideally, as with Othniel, the leadership can be simply overwhelmed. In the case of Ehud, he personally deals with the leadership. Here Barak is ineffective in successfully dealing with Sisera, so God uses Jael to accomplish this.

Jael risks her own life to deliver a people that she is not even a part of. She could easily have remained uninvolved. Her husband's treaty with Jabin meant that Sisera was not a threat. In fact, if she aided Sisera in his escape, perhaps this would be rewarded. After all, Jabin is still intact as the king of the region, and there is no guarantee that the Israelites will defeat him (note 4:24, which clearly implies a more prolonged process that eventually culminates in Jabin's demise). Sisera's defeat may be only a temporary setback. With all these factors, Jael's involvement is remarkable—again for a people with whom she is not directly associated.[84]

Like Ehud, Jael accomplishes the victory over God's enemy. Her willingness to risk her life is in greatly heightened contrast to the Israelite tribes who choose to remain at home, to play it safe.

The context of the Song of Deborah. The praise of Yahweh in song is a unique element to any of the other cycles. In the Song of Deborah, the focus is first on the nation of Israel, then on the ten tribes that either did or did not participate, and then on the two women. But throughout the entire song, it is Yahweh who is acknowledged and praised for his great work. Were it not for him, there would have been no deliverance. Manifold are his deliverances throughout the ages.

The epiphany of Yahweh is unique to this cycle; it pictures Yahweh as triumphant over Baal since Yahweh is pictured as in control of the storm (Baal was commonly pictured by storm imagery). Since this epiphany of

---

82. Ibid., 112–13.

83. This motif can already be observed in the book of Joshua in the dealing with the various Canaanite kings/leaders (Josh. 8:29; 10:16–27, 28, 30, 37, 38–39; 11:10, 12, 17).

84. Some interpreters argue that Jael was an Israelite. But it seems on the parallel with Shamgar in the Song of Deborah and the association with the Kenite clan that it is more likely that she was a non-Israelite. The name (*yᶜl*) does not contain the Yahwistic theophoric element.

Yahweh announces to the kings of Canaan that Yahweh, not their god Baal, reigns supreme, it does the same for the Israelites, whose fascination with Baal brought on the present crisis.

The Song of Deborah especially emphasizes the positive involvement of some of the tribes and Jael. The negative assessment of other tribes (and in particular the city of Meroz) who did not participate in the battle against Sisera and the Canaanites is a comment on God's outlook and expectations for his people. In this case, noninvolvement equates with self-centeredness.

The issue of participation is raised in the song with evaluative, theological implications. Those who do not participate in the battle against Sisera are guilty of apathy and of indirect support of the enemies of God (and by implication their gods). The Lord expects his people to participate in the advancement of his kingdom. Noninvolvement because of self-centeredness is as unacceptable today as in Deborah/Barak/Jael's time.

The scene of Sisera's mother is a powerful image that only poetry can communicate with this kind of effectiveness. The demise of Sisera and the portrayal of his mother are clear comments on God's determination to judge the wicked. This stanza frees the reader from any positive sympathetic feelings toward Sisera and negative feelings toward Jael. The horrors that Sisera (directly) and his mother (indirectly) have mercilessly dispensed on others come back on them. The mother's thoughts about Sisera's plundering and raping of helpless, innocent women reveal what he has done innumerable times in the past. But this time he will not humiliate a single woman; instead, a single woman—a Kenite woman—will humiliate him and turn him into the plunder. The justice is, to a certain extent, retributive—but not completely. What Sisera receives is not really an adequate end to what he has perpetrated, any more than the death of Hitler was adequate justice to what he executed on the Jews.

While in the present church age context we are not encouraged to be *exactly* like Jael, her action nevertheless serves to give hope that justice will ultimately come on the wicked. With all the injustice in the world, some of it meted out on Christians, it is comforting to know that God has made things right in the past and will make them right in the future.

The imprecation at the end of the poem (5:31a-b) climaxes the emotions of those who love God and hate evil. To God evil and wickedness—especially as manifested in Sisera—is an abomination. Yet his faithfulness to generations to come is evident to those who love him, as Deuteronomy 7:9–10 makes clear:

Know therefore that the LORD your God is God; he is the faithful God, keeping his covenant of love to a thousand generations of those who love him and keep his commands. But

> those who hate him he will repay to their face by destruction;
> he will not be slow to repay to their face those who hate him.[85]

GOD'S SOVEREIGNTY. God demonstrates that he will not give up on his people. Even though this is the third time they have apostasized, he deals with them in utter consistency. He will not allow them to do as they please. On account of his rich compassion, he will not leave them in prolonged oppression. While there is a decrease in the quality of the type of individuals whom he can use, he nevertheless is able to bring deliverance to his people. In fact, he uses those who in the ancient world were deemed insufficient to the task.

The entire account is deliberately constructed to emphasize the deliverance provided by Yahweh. He is the One pulling the strings, raising generals, deploying armies (even the enemy is indirectly controlled by him), dictating strategy, and effecting the victory. In the end both the narrative and the song celebrate the saving work of Yahweh. The double accounting in prose and poetry stress God's sovereignty over human events. This passage thus encourages us to perceive God's sovereignty over history and our own lives. Whether it is in his chastening, in his compassionate deliverance, in his financial provision, or in his leading and guiding decisions, God is sovereign over life, and he is at work bringing his plan to fruition.

Willing vessels. Often God uses the weaker things of this world to confound the wise. Certainly in using Deborah to raise up Barak and in using Jael to bring down the mighty Sisera, we see examples of this. He continues to work in this manner today. He brings deliverance from unexpected sources and in unexpected manners.

When he wants to use us, we need to be willing. We may not feel adequate to the task. We may feel that because of our past, God cannot use us. We may feel ungifted in what he is calling us to do. In one way or another we feel inhibited to serve. When we as Christians do not trust God in these contexts, we lose out on the opportunity for God to work through us. We lose out on his good gifts. And worse, we may find ourselves expending all kinds of time and energy hopelessly trying to make up the difference. We want to have the assurance up front that the risk will be worth it, that we will

---

85. Cf. Ex. 20:5–6.

succeed. But God has often already given the assurance in his Word and wants us to be involved so that he may work to accomplish his plan.

Deborah's willingness to be God's spokesperson in calling Barak to deliver his people illustrates the faithfulness that God is seeking. Moreover, her willingness to go with Barak after his request demonstrates her bravery in the midst of great personal danger. There is nothing in the text that indicates any warrior status or abilities on the part of Deborah.[86] She does not fight in the battle; she only pronounces to Barak God's reassurance of victory and exhortation to engage. Hence she is no Xena. In fact, the text seems to present the opposite: She is simply a prophetess, the wife of a man named Lappidoth.

Needing assurances. In the person of the deliverer, Barak, there is an important message for modern contexts. His unwillingness to believe God's Word through the prophetess serves a strong warning. His demand for tangible assurance of God's presence and guarantee of victory in order to believe and obey is not uncharacteristic of many believers today. Perhaps it is a matter of being products of the "scientific" age that demands physical proof before belief. However, this passage (and a number of others like it) demonstrate that this is not a recent problem (see more on this issue of tangible assurance in the Gideon section, where the issue is clearest in Judges).

In his goodness, God is constantly looking for opportunities to give good gifts to men and women. Yet because of their lack of faith, they forfeit these blessings that God would freely give. This is true in so many ways. For example, James 1:5–8 states:

> If any of you lacks wisdom, he should ask God, who gives generously to all without finding fault, and it will be given to him. But when he asks, he must believe and not doubt, because he who doubts is like a wave of the sea, blown and tossed by the wind. That man should not think he will receive anything from the Lord; he is a double-minded man, unstable in all he does.

Hence, help is readily obtainable from "the giving God." To those who lack wisdom, this valuable resource is available for the asking. James assumes his readers will feel the need for wisdom, not just knowledge. God will not only provide wisdom but will do so generously, not grudgingly. However, God's provision has some prerequisites. To receive God's wisdom in trials, the believer must be wise in asking. One must ask in faith and not doubt (i.e.,

---

86. Neither Deborah nor Jael are involved in the actual combat in the battle between Sisera and Barak. Their roles are on either end of the battle (Deborah before the actual fighting takes place; Jael after the major part of the battle is over). Thus, neither one is a warrior figure (contra G. Yee, "By the Hand of a Woman: The Metaphor of the Woman Warrior in Judges 4," *Semeia* 61 [1993]: 99–132).

vacillate). God wants us to believe that he is and that he is the rewarder of those who diligently seek him. When Christians do not trust God for the gifts he promises, not only do they lose those gifts, but they also may expend much time and energy hopelessly trying to make up the difference, just as Barak did.

Praise of Yahweh. In the end, however, God will do his work whether we are involved in it or not. Moreover, regardless of whether we are involved, he will receive the praise and glory for what he has done. For without him we are nothing, and there will be no salvation.

It is in the person of Jael that God's effective deliverance of Israel is completed. It is remarkable that Jael becomes involved at all, especially for a people with whom she was not directly associated. Didactically, she serves to illustrate the type of involvement that God is seeking. Obviously, we are not called in the present context to do in Sisera-types with tent pegs. Again, the New Testament's warfare is solely spiritual. But Jael's type of willing involvement is needed today. The fact that she is so directly contrasted with the nonparticipant tribes in the Song of Deborah accentuates this.

Praise of Yahweh is hardly limited to Old Testament contexts like this. God's mighty acts of deliverance continue to be worked on behalf of the undeserving. Israel's apostasy brought God's punishing oppression; in fact, as the poem makes clear, the involvement with "new gods" only underscores how undeserving Israel really was. It is God's amazing willingness to deliver us—certainly no more deserving than Israel—that ought to stimulate great praise of him in our midst.

It is interesting that the ancient poet perceived God's involvement in this deliverance on the cosmic level. To this poet, God's revelation through his epiphany in nature was a vital part of the deliverance. The Lord demonstrates his divinity over against whatever things are worshiped, whether in the context of ancient Israel or today. Too often we are so bound in our world today to a naturalistic interpretation of things that even we forget to recognize God's hand in the natural elements, especially in the divine timing of these natural phenomena.

To participate or not to participate. Participation in the kingdom of God is praiseworthy. Nonparticipation is shameful, perhaps in some cases abominable. This is especially true when his people's lack of involvement is based on their self-centered, self-serving interest and apathy. Christianity is not a spectator sport; it requires involvement. Just as God is holy, passionate, and zealous for righteousness, he expects his people to be the same. Just as God desires that none should perish and works so great a salvation on humanity's behalf, so he wants this same desire in his people for the lost. When we choose not to participate in what he has ordained as part of the establishment of his kingdom, we become supporters of another program, a program that is not of God, a program dictated by the gods of this world.

No acquittal of the guilty. How does one apply the scene of Sisera's mother? In one way, it is a sad, tragic scene. But in the larger scope of the poem as a whole and the cycle in which it is found, it provides an important evaluative balance to the events that have transpired, especially those in the tent of Jael. It prevents the reader from simply concluding that Sisera is an innocent victim. In different circumstances, Sisera would not have hesitated to victimize a Jael any less than he would have hesitated to victimize a Deborah or any other woman.[87] His track record is graphically testified to by his own mother—who, in fact, is not only perfectly content with this but apparently has encouraged this in her son. The poem's presentation of her thought processes serves to show that her son's life-emphases are like hers: plunder and self-gratification. Such wickedness at the expense of others will not go unjudged (Deut. 7:10). God does not acquit the guilty (Ex. 34:7).

---

87. With the fall of Berlin in 1945 to the Soviet army, an estimated 100,000 rapes of women occurred by Russian troops in the conquered city. There is no way of knowing the astounding number of Russian women raped by German troops during the Nazi occupation of Russian territory.

Judges 6:1–8:32

🌿

Introduction to the Gideon/Abimelech Cycle

THE GIDEON/ABIMELECH CYCLE is pivotal, being the beginning of the presentation of the Out-group judges (see the discussion in the introduction, pp. 38–39). It recounts the first time that Israel's appeal to Yahweh is met with a stern rebuke rather than immediate assistance and thus signals the beginning of a sharper declivity in the cycles. This cycle is conveyed in two major parts: the account of Gideon (6:1–8:32) and the account of Abimelech (8:33–9:57). The Abimelech account is really a prolongation of the Gideon account, bringing to resolution a number of complications spawned in the Gideon narrative. Thus it is the sequel to the Gideon narrative.

Both accounts address the issue of infidelity and religious deterioration. Revenge plays a major motif in both narratives: severe revenge on the two towns of Succoth and Peniel, Jotham's prophetic allegory, and Abimelech's retribution on the people of Shechem. Like the other middle cycle (Deborah/Barak), there is a propensity for pairings (again see comments in the introduction, pp. 39–40).

The Gideon Narrative (6:1–8:32). The narrative about Gideon (6:1–8:32) divides into five sections and is developed along concentric lines.[1] Thematic parallels exist between the first (A) and fifth (A') sections and between the second (B) and fourth (B') sections. The third section (C) stands alone. The narrative contains a series of mini-climaxes that lead to the ultimate climax in 8:22–32 (A'). Thus the symmetrical pattern is:

A Prologue to Gideon (6:1–10)
  B God's plan of deliverance through the call of Gideon—the story of two altars (6:11–32)
  B1 The first altar—call and commissioning of Gideon (6:11–24)
  B2 The second altar—the charge to clean house (6:25–32)
    C Gideon's personal faith struggle (6:33–7:18)
      a The Spirit-endowed Gideon mobilizes four tribes against the Midianites, though lacking confidence in God's promise (6:33–35)

---

1. See J. P. Tanner, "The Gideon Narrative as the Focal Point of Judges," *BSac* 149 (1992): 146–61; idem, "Textual Patterning in Biblical Hebrew Narrative: A Case Study in Judges 6–8" (Ph.D. diss.; Univ. of Texas, Austin, 1990).

   b Gideon seeks a sign from God with the two fleecings
      to confirm the promise that Yahweh will give Midian
      into his hand (6:36–40)
      c With the fearful Israelites having departed, God
         directs Gideon to go down to the water for the
         further reduction of his force (7:1–8)
      c' With fear still in Gideon himself, God directs
         Gideon to go down to the enemy camp to overhear
         the enemy (7:9–11)
   b' God provides a sign to Gideon with the dream of the
      Midianite and its interpretation to confirm the
      promise that Yahweh will give Midian into his hand
      (7:12–14)
 a' The worshiping Gideon mobilizes his force of three
    hundred for a surprise attack against the Midianites, fully
    confident in God's promise (7:15–18)
B' God's deliverance from the Midianites—the story of two battles
   (7:19–8:21)
   B1' The first battle (Cisjordan) (7:19–8:3)
   B2' The second battle (Transjordan) (8:4–21)
A' Epilogue to Gideon (8:22–32)

Judges 6:1–10

   ¹Again the Israelites did evil in the eyes of the LORD, and
for seven years he gave them into the hands of the Midianites.
²Because the power of Midian was so oppressive, the Israelites
prepared shelters for themselves in mountain clefts, caves and
strongholds. ³Whenever the Israelites planted their crops, the
Midianites, Amalekites and other eastern peoples invaded the
country. ⁴They camped on the land and ruined the crops all
the way to Gaza and did not spare a living thing for Israel,
neither sheep nor cattle nor donkeys. ⁵They came up with
their livestock and their tents like swarms of locusts. It was
impossible to count the men and their camels; they invaded
the land to ravage it. ⁶Midian so impoverished the Israelites
that they cried out to the LORD for help.
   ⁶When the Israelites cried to the LORD because of Midian,
⁸he sent them a prophet, who said, "This is what the LORD,
the God of Israel, says: I brought you up out of Egypt, out of
the land of slavery. ⁹I snatched you from the power of Egypt

and from the hand of all your oppressors. I drove them from before you and gave you their land. ¹⁰I said to you, 'I am the LORD your God; do not worship the gods of the Amorites, in whose land you live.' But you have not listened to me."

THE FIRST SECTION (A) gives the introduction and setting that lead up to the appearance of Gideon (6:1–10). The typical narrative frame statements are encountered as in previous cycles, but this time there is more development on the condition of the oppression.[2] The familiar cycle opening component, "Again the Israelites did evil in the eyes of the LORD," stands in abrupt contrast to the praise of Yahweh that has just been sung in the previous chapter. This component stresses the fickleness of the Israelites, who lack resistance to the lures of the other gods.

The description of the oppression pictures a reversal of lifestyles. The settled Israelites revert to living in caves as nomadic groups often do in the context of the southern Levant. By contrast, the nomadic Midianites come and plop all over the land. The sequence of verb forms in 6:3–5 "captures stylistically the wave after wave of pillage and destruction."[3] The Midianites, together with the Amalekites (cf. 3:13) and some easterners (lit., "Qedemites"), are like locusts on the land. Climactically it is described in 6:6: "Midian ... impoverished [lit., made small] the Israelites."

Accordingly, the Israelites cry to Yahweh (with, of course, no hint at true repentance).[4] This is as they have done in the past, but things are different this time; Yahweh sends a prophet (6:8a). The prophet, the only one in Judges, parallels the appearance of Deborah the prophetess (both appear at precisely the same point in the plot). But his function contrasts sharply with hers: He is not setting in motion the process of deliverance but is formally indicting the Israelites for a breach of the covenant and telling them that they have forfeited all right to deliverance (6:10b). The language is reminiscent of the covenant renewed at Shechem in Joshua 24, with Yahweh's integrity and Israel's guilt upheld throughout.[5] This Israelite covenantal unfaithfulness

---

2. The narrative development seems to be clearly based on Lev. 26 and Deut. 28.

3. Webb, *The Book of the Judges*, 145.

4. This becomes clear from the fact that while they are crying out to Yahweh, they are continuing to worship Baal at cult sites like the one in Ophrah that belonged to Gideon's father, Joash (Judg. 6:25–32).

5. Obscured by the NIV translation is the sevenfold usage of first-person singular pronouns in a framing construction that emphasizes Yahweh's integrity. See M. Eskhult, *Studies in Verbal Aspect and Narrative Technique in Biblical Hebrew Prose* (AUUSSU 12; Uppsala: Uppsala Univ. Press, 1990), 78 n. 54.

will foreshadow their unfaithfulness in the Abimelech story, which ironically takes place at Shechem (8:31; 9:1–5, 25–49).

Nevertheless, Yahweh's response is not the expected one. Is Yahweh beginning to lose patience with the Israelites? The appearance and message of the "prophet" caution against drawing any simple equation between calling on Yahweh and repentance (this is developed further in 10:10–16).[6] It makes clear that the appeal is not a device by which Israel can automatically secure its future. The relationship between Yahweh and Israel is not a mechanical process in which Israel can manipulatively call on Yahweh and he instantaneously responds. Moreover, this formal indictment (Heb. *rîb*) of Israel through the prophet turns out to be a verbal element in the name Jerub-Baal (see comments on 6:32).

WITH THE GIDEON/ABIMELECH cycle there is a marked moral decline within the people of Israel. Following on the heels of the Song of Deborah, the fickleness of the Israelites is stressed by the opening line. They lack the ability or willingness (or both) to resist the lures of the gods of the peoples around them. This fickleness, no matter how much Yahweh exerts himself on their behalf, is a problem that transcends time. In spite of God's gracious blessings, it is not unusual to find believers becoming enthralled and enamored with the lures of this present age.

However, persisting in apostasy is risky business. The reversal of habitats between the Midianites and Israelites emphasizes the severity of the chastening discipline of Yahweh. In this instance it becomes retributive. Those who would embrace the materialism and philosophies of the world today may find a reversal in their fortunes.

The response of Yahweh to the Israelites' cry is quite different from the first three cycles. By sending a prophet to confront the people and indicting them for their covenant unfaithfulness, he puts their deliverance in jeopardy. Clearly, Yahweh implies that there comes a time when his patience turns to judgment.

This passage also continues the theme of manipulation that was started in the last cycle. Yahweh will not instantaneously and robotically respond to his people's cry. This is especially true when that cry is not sincere, when God's people continue in their idolatry, and when that cry has manipulative intentions.

---

6. Again it should be emphasized that the clause "Israel cried out to Yahweh" does not mean a repentance on the Israelites' part.

THOSE WHO LACK the resolve to resist the lures of the world will likely face the disasters and destructions that these lures often bring. They may find that God is their opponent, not their friend. Certainly, fickleness in loyalty to the things of God occurs in the church today. When Christians run after the same gods as their non-Christian counterparts, they should not be surprised when God does not hear their prayers or react in the way they think he should.

It is interesting that God formally indicts. Such language places the relationship into the forensic, legal context, where doubt is removed and clarity added to the description of what is wrong in the relationship. That God still indicts his people is clear through various New Testament passages; note, for example, Revelation 2–3, where several churches are indicted for their failures to God's covenant. The Holy Spirit carries on this same process within the individual believer.

In a practical sense, this passage addresses a common problem in the area of prayer. We turn to God in a moment of need, even when we have not been walking in his ways. Yet we expect God to answer our prayers because (and often for no other reason) we are in need! Over and over the Bible (including the book of Judges) addresses this issue of manipulation in prayer (cf. , e.g., James 4:1–6). Relationship with God is never a mechanical process.

Judges 6:11–32

¹¹The angel of the LORD came and sat down under the oak in Ophrah that belonged to Joash the Abiezrite, where his son Gideon was threshing wheat in a winepress to keep it from the Midianites. ¹²When the angel of the LORD appeared to Gideon, he said, "The LORD is with you, mighty warrior."

¹³"But sir," Gideon replied, "if the LORD is with us, why has all this happened to us? Where are all his wonders that our fathers told us about when they said, 'Did not the LORD bring us up out of Egypt?' But now the LORD has abandoned us and put us into the hand of Midian."

¹⁴The LORD turned to him and said, "Go in the strength you have and save Israel out of Midian's hand. Am I not sending you?"

¹⁵"But Lord," Gideon asked, "how can I save Israel? My clan is the weakest in Manasseh, and I am the least in my family."

¹⁶The LORD answered, "I will be with you, and you will strike down all the Midianites together."

¹⁷Gideon replied, "If now I have found favor in your eyes, give me a sign that it is really you talking to me. ¹⁸Please do not go away until I come back and bring my offering and set it before you."

And the LORD said, "I will wait until you return."

¹⁹Gideon went in, prepared a young goat, and from an ephah of flour he made bread without yeast. Putting the meat in a basket and its broth in a pot, he brought them out and offered them to him under the oak.

²⁰The angel of God said to him, "Take the meat and the unleavened bread, place them on this rock, and pour out the broth." And Gideon did so. ²¹With the tip of the staff that was in his hand, the angel of the LORD touched the meat and the unleavened bread. Fire flared from the rock, consuming the meat and the bread. And the angel of the LORD disappeared. ²²When Gideon realized that it was the angel of the LORD, he exclaimed, "Ah, Sovereign LORD! I have seen the angel of the LORD face to face!"

²³But the LORD said to him, "Peace! Do not be afraid. You are not going to die."

²⁴So Gideon built an altar to the LORD there and called it The LORD is Peace. To this day it stands in Ophrah of the Abiezrites.

²⁵That same night the LORD said to him, "Take the second bull from your father's herd, the one seven years old. Tear down your father's altar to Baal and cut down the Asherah pole beside it. ²⁶Then build a proper kind of altar to the LORD your God on the top of this height. Using the wood of the Asherah pole that you cut down, offer the second bull as a burnt offering."

²⁷So Gideon took ten of his servants and did as the LORD told him. But because he was afraid of his family and the men of the town, he did it at night rather than in the daytime.

²⁸In the morning when the men of the town got up, there was Baal's altar, demolished, with the Asherah pole beside it cut down and the second bull sacrificed on the newly built altar!

²⁹They asked each other, "Who did this?"

When they carefully investigated, they were told, "Gideon son of Joash did it."

³⁰The men of the town demanded of Joash, "Bring out your son. He must die, because he has broken down Baal's altar and cut down the Asherah pole beside it."

³¹But Joash replied to the hostile crowd around him, "Are you going to plead Baal's cause? Are you trying to save him? Whoever fights for him shall be put to death by morning! If Baal really is a god, he can defend himself when someone breaks down his altar." ³²So that day they called Gideon "Jerub-Baal," saying, "Let Baal contend with him," because he broke down Baal's altar.

STRUCTURALLY, SECTION B (see introductory comments to 6:1–9:57) relates God's plan of deliverance by means of the call of Gideon through stories about two altars that Gideon raises for Yahweh (6:11–32). This section will have significant correspondences to section B', which narrates the deliverance of Israel from the Midianites through the two victorious battles of Gideon (7:19–8:21). It is interesting to note that items like a winepress and a rock play roles in both sections (cf. 6:11, 20 with 7:25; 8:2).

The section has two units (6:11–24, 25–32), in which the climax is the building of an altar to Yahweh. In order to explain his plan for the deliverance of Israel, Yahweh resorts to a theophany (a manifestation or appearance of God) to communicate his choice to Gideon. Gideon is the only judge in the book of Judges who is called by God personally through a theophany.

"The angel of the LORD" appears to Gideon and exclaims: "The LORD is with you, mighty warrior [*gibbôr ḥeḥāyil*]" (6:12). There is great irony in this statement by the angel of Yahweh. (1) Gideon is hiding from the Midianites, threshing wheat in a winepress.[7] (2) Gideon's name (*gidᶜôn*) means "hacker" (derived from the verb *gdᶜ*, to hack, break to pieces). But Gideon is characterized by fearfulness and reluctance, although Yahweh's words are correct (i.e., he will be a great warrior at the end; see 8:4–21).

Numerous commentators have noted similarities between Gideon's call and those of Moses in Exodus 3 and Joshua in Joshua 1.

---

7. Gideon's fear of the Midianites (6:11) will be paralleled by his fear of the people of his village (6:27).

Comparison of Gideon, Moses and Joshua[8]

	Gideon (Judg. 6)	Moses (Ex. 3)	Joshua (Josh. 1)
Circumstances	Hiding from the enemy, working for his father Joash, who is clan head and priest of a pagan shrine	Working for his father-in-law, Jethro, whose flocks Moses is tending when Yahweh's angel appears to him	After the death of Moses, in camp at Abel-Shittim
Authorization	Have I not sent you?	and I will send you	Now, rise up . . . you . . . you, have I not charged you?
Objection	Protest of inadequacy: With what shall I . . . my family is weakest. I am the least in the house of my father.	Protest of inadequacy: Who [am] I . . . that I should bring the sons of Israel out of Egypt?	(none)
Affirmation	for I will be with you	for I will be with you	. . . I will be with you
Sign	give me a sign	this [will be] a sign	(none)
Theophany	Fire theophany, which induces fear in the one who is called. This proof of the divine presence is withheld until the end, so that the recognition of the messenger becomes the climax of the scene.	Fire theophany, which induces fear in the one who is called. This proof of the divine presence is given unsolicited at the outset.	(none)

8. Adapted from Klein, *Triumph of Irony,* 51.

(cont.)	Gideon (Judg. 6)	Moses (Ex. 3)	Joshua (Josh. 1)
New material	——	——	Be strong and courageous; only be strong and very courageous; be strong and courageous; be not afraid nor discouraged.

Gideon's response to God's call, however, is not quite like that of Moses. In the dialogue with the angel of the Lord, Gideon will mount a three-point opposition, which, in each case, anticipates later plot complications.[9]

(1) His response to the angel of the Lord's initial call is a dull, cynical question and diatribe about God's treatment of the nation (6:13). Gideon shows an ignorance to the problem in Israel—"[doing] evil in the eyes of the LORD," 6:1; Israel has apostasized again, and this is why the Midianites have come.[10] Moreover, Gideon's question is cynical because it shows little awareness of all the recent mighty acts of God on behalf of the sinful nation and implies that Yahweh is not a god, that he does not defend his people, and that he does not contend for Israel (cf. ironically 6:31). Gideon evinces some knowledge of the past but a highly selective and distorted one. He manifests a dispassionate disregard for Yahweh's primary concern about Israel's covenantal disloyalty (anticipating 6:25–32; 8:24–27).

(2) Although Yahweh encourages Gideon ("Go in the strength you have and save Israel out of Midian's hand. Am I not sending you?" 6:14), Gideon's objection in 6:15 is an attempt to evade personal responsibility for the conquest because of his clan's (*ʾelep*) smallness[11] (anticipating 7:2–8; but cf. Deut. 7:17–24).

(3) After Yahweh's assurance ("I will be with you, and you will strike down all the Midianites together"), Gideon's request for a sign in 6:17 discloses his preoccupation with tangible manifestations of the divine (anticipating

---

9. O'Connell, *The Rhetoric of the Book of Judges*, 149, n. 184.

10. This interpretation is reinforced in the context by the preceding indictment of the Israelites by the prophet. These preceding verses enhance the negative tone of Gideon's response.

11. In spite of Gideon's argument here, it is clear that from the standpoint of his father, Joash, who appears to have been a man of considerable wealth and standing in the community, this is not entirely accurate—at least in the impression that it attempts to convey.

6:36–37, 39; 7:10–15; and esp. 8:24–27). Gideon does not really perceive to whom he is talking (he calls the angel of the Lord "sir" [*ᵓadōnî*] twice, 6:13, 15). His complaint that God has not acted to save Israel will be answered by God's call and commissioning of Gideon himself.

While the theophany is especially reminiscent of the call of Moses (Ex. 3:7–10), Gideon is no Moses.[12] Like Moses, there is a problem with the will. But in the case of Gideon, there are additional problems of perception (of the presence of the Lord and the reason for Israel's distress) and faith (Gideon will have a much harder time with trust in Yahweh than Moses, as the narrative will show). Indeed, the contrast of characterizations introduced in 6:11–24 between Yahweh's patience and Gideon's impetuosity form the background to Gideon's compensatory ruthlessness portrayed toward those who, like himself, doubted his ability to capture Yahweh's opponents (cf. 8:5–9, 13–17).[13]

Significantly, Gideon's commission comes not by the prophet (contrast Barak), nor by any human agency, but by Yahweh himself through a theophany. Yahweh and Gideon will be in almost constant dialogue with one another in the sequence of events leading up to the battle (6:25, 36, 39; 7:2, 4, 7, 9). This will prove ironic in light of the final outcome of the Gideon cycle.

In 6:17, Gideon begins his requests for signs.[14] The NIV's "give me a sign" is more accurately translated "perform a sign for me." Gideon's request for the angel of the Lord to wait for him to prepare an offering (*minḥâ*, lit., a "meal or cereal offering," though here used simply as a general term for offering) is anticipatory of Manoah's offering in 13:15–23. Like Manoah's offering there is a clear attempt on Gideon's part to detain God.[15] Gideon's offering is apparently based entirely on his own evaluation of what is appropriate. That he is preparing a meal for the gods/a god is evident from the nature and size of the offering.[16]

Nevertheless, in spite of Gideon's motives, the Lord accepts the sacrifices with miraculous fire[17] coming from the rock to consume the meat and bread—an outcome totally unexpected by Gideon. Gideon's highly emo-

---

12. Klein develops the comparisons in her analysis of the passage (*Triumph of Irony*, 51).

13. O'Connell, *The Rhetoric of the Book of Judges*, 149 n. 184.

14. These requests all occur before the first battle. In keeping with the narrative's tendency toward pairs, there will be a pair of requests for signs by Gideon. The first request is narrated here, and the second request for a sign occurs in the pair of fleece incidents below.

15. For some similarities between the sacrifice of Gideon and the sacrifice of Manoah, see Y. Zakovitch, "The Sacrifice of Gideon (Jud 6,11–24) and the Sacrifice of Manoah (Jud 13)," *Shnaton* 1 (1975): 151–54, xxv (Hebrew; English summary); A. G. Auld, "Gideon: Hacking at the Heart of the Old Testament," *VT* 39 (1989): 257–67, esp. 257–58.

16. Block, *Judges, Ruth*, 263.

17. The miraculous fire introduces a motif that will recur throughout the Gideon/Abimelech cycle (6:26; 7:16, 20; 9:15, 20, 49).

tional but illogical conclusion—namely, the fear of death as a result of seeing the angel of the Lord (again, mirrored in Manoah's false conclusion)[18]—serves to confirm his unbelief in spite of his own words and claim that a sign will remedy this. Only God's declaration of "peace" (šālôm) and his promise that Gideon will not die can relieve this highly emotional but illogical conclusion (much like Manoah's wife does in the case of Manoah). At this the theophany ends (6:21).

Hence, Gideon builds an altar (the first in the narration) and names it: "Yahweh-Shalom" ("The LORD is Peace").[19] He constructs it in "Ophrah of the Abiezrites." This serves a double function. Combined with 6:11 ("Ophrah that belonged to Joash the Abiezrite"), it forms an inclusio around the account of Gideon's call. At the same time, it effects the transition to the next scene (6:25–32) by anticipating the issue to be resolved there, namely, the rivalry between Yahweh and Baal as symbolized by the juxtaposition of their two altars.[20]

In the second unit of the section (6:25–32), events transpire that reach a climax in the building of a second altar to Yahweh in Ophrah. Before the story can proceed to describe Gideon's deliverance of Israel from the Midianites, a pair of abnormalities needs to be dealt with.[21] The first is an objective issue, the presence of a pagan cult installation in Gideon's own backyard. The second is a subjective problem, Gideon's persistent resistance to God's call.

God's command to Gideon (6:25) contains two demands—a negative one, followed by a positive one. (1) He must tear down his father's altar to Baal and cut down the Asherah pole that is beside it (note the pair of idolatrous items).[22] Yahweh's command to Gideon is a reverberation of his commands in Deuteronomy 7:5 and 12:3. In both texts, the verb "to cut, hack" (gdᶜ) occurs in a form that echoes Gideon's name (tᵉgaddēᶜûn).

When the narrator gives us this information about the Baal altar and the Asherah pole, he subtly acknowledges the fact that while Israel was crying out and appealing to Yahweh for help, there was an altar to Baal at Ophrah. An implied question follows: If there is one in Ophrah (a small rural site), were there not others throughout the land? No wonder Yahweh's response in 6:8–10 was to indict Israel through the prophet's speech.

---

18. In this phrase there is an echo of the Jacob story at the Jabbok (Gen. 32:23–33), but there are also major differences between the stories overall.

19. For the socioreligious practice of building altars in open contexts, cf. the "Bull site" in Manasseh, an open cult place of Iron Age I (Mazar, "The Bull Site," 27–42).

20. Webb, *The Book of the Judges*, 148–49.

21. Block, *Judges, Ruth*, 265.

22. This pair of deities was mentioned earlier in the first of the in-group judges, Othniel (Judg. 3:7). Here they are mentioned in connection with the very household of the first of the out-group judges.

(2) Gideon must build an altar to Yahweh and sacrifice the second bull[23] as a burnt offering. By his command to Gideon to destroy the pagan altar and rebuild a proper altar to Yahweh on this pagan site, Yahweh seems to be ordering him to reclaim this apostate shrine locale by himself. Not only was the site desecrated through its destruction, but further defilement was brought on it through the sacrifice of the bull that was used to destroy it.

Fearing the repercussions of the destruction of the Baal altar and Asherah pole, Gideon takes ten of his servants and carries out Yahweh's orders under cover of night. Block observes: "The reader cannot help but be disappointed that the real motivation for his hasty obedience was not an eagerness to obey God but fear of the consequences from the citizens of Ophrah if he should tear down the altar of Baal in broad daylight."[24] Even with such motives, Gideon does what God commands. He demolishes the Baal altar, cuts down the Asherah pole, builds a proper altar to Yahweh, and sacrifices the second bull on the new altar.

The next morning the utter outrage and hostility of the town is riveted on Gideon. This reflects the true spiritual condition of the nation. Gideon knows that his own family and the people of his own village will come to the defense of these pagan idols before they defend him, their kinsman and fellow citizen. The people demand Joash, his father, to hand over his son so that they can execute him (6:30).[25] Joash's decision is a ploy to save face and to save Gideon at the same time by referring the case to higher authority: "If Baal really is god, he can defend himself when someone breaks down his altar" (6:31). The townspeople back down, and Gideon, who has the Lord with him, surfaces as a champion, a "mighty warrior" (*gibbôr ḥeḥāyil*)—as the angel of the Lord pronounced at the beginning of the section (6:11).

Gideon receives a new name: Jerub-Baal ("Let/May Baal contend/indict"). In one sense, it designates him as living proof of Baal's impotence. Thus

---

23. The syntax of the first clause in v. 25 is not entirely clear, and the mention of a "second" bull seems problematic (why mention the "second" when only one bull is offered?). Some scholars have resolved this by understanding the phrase "the second bull" as a later scribal insertion. Others have attempted to explain the phrase as meaning "bull of high rank" (see Block's discussion, *Judges, Ruth*, 266). However, the reference to "the second bull" may well serve a literary function in the narrative through the binary force of the passage: second altar to Yahweh, second bull (i.e., the number two bull that is seven years old—the perfect sacrifice in this instance).

24. Block, *Judges, Ruth*, 267.

25. It is ironic that the sentence which should have been imposed on the idolaters (Deut. 13:1–18 [Heb. 13:2–19]) is pronounced on the one who destroyed the idol. The irony in Israel's response to Gideon's actions will be heightened in the later narrative where the Israelites demand the Benjamites to hand over the men who had done the crime in Gibeah (20:12–13)

Gideon begins his career by driving the deity Baal from the field of battle (Baal cannot contend with him). But he now must face the challenge of driving the human foe, the Midianites, from the field of battle. At the same time, the name also reminds the reader of the indictment (*rîb*) brought by the prophet at the beginning of the Gideon/Abimelech cycle (6:8–10). Ironically, judge Gideon ("hacker"), the son of apostate Joash, wears this Baal-name ("Let/May Baal contend/indict"), a name that occurs with increasing frequency in chapters 7 and 8 and beyond.

GOD'S GRACE. The story of Gideon's call and the building of the two altars introduces us to the first of the Out-group judges and reveals a declivity not yet encountered in the stories of the cyclical/major judges. On the divine level, it is amazing that Yahweh acts at all on Israel's behalf. Not only has Israel continued in their apostasizing, but in spite of the Lord's confrontation through his prophet, Israel has not repented. Even the household of the deliverer whom Yahweh calls worships the deities of the land of Canaan.

Nevertheless, God's grace is evident in his action of calling a deliverer for Israel, that is, Gideon. And that grace is manifest in the fact that no other judge (*šōpēṭ*) in the book of Judges is called by God personally through a theophany. While we may be inclined to think that this is an indication of Gideon's spirituality, we quickly realize that this is not the case. As the cycle continues, it is clear that on the divine level God once again is glorified: first, in even involving himself in the deliverance, and second, in the actual story of the deliverance. Thus the very call of Gideon underscores God's tremendous grace toward Israel (not to mention to Gideon, too).

Gideon's response. Gideon's initial response to the angel of the Lord's call is theologically correct in its basic assertions, but it is wrong in its tone and in its awareness of the correct evaluation of the present situation. Instead of acknowledging Israelite responsibility for the present crisis, as the narrator does in 6:1, Gideon blames God. Thus, he demonstrates an ignorance of Yahweh's covenant with Israel. The Israelites' sins have brought these things upon them; they are the cause of their problems, not God. Moreover, Gideon's incorrect evaluation is, no doubt, the result of the pagan situation in his village. Like many others in Israel at this time, this village has its own cult center where other gods are worshiped. Although Gideon is aware of some of the traditions of Yahweh (6:13), for all practical purposes he and his family are worshipers of Baal and Asherah! Gideon's problems lie in his lack of knowledge of God's word, in his perception of God's involvement in the life of the nation, in his willingness to serve, and in his faith.

In this sense, Gideon is an example of those who know what God has done in the past, who have memorized the creed, but who find it belied by present reality. To Gideon, stories of past deliverance are irrelevant in light of the Midianite crisis. To him, God may have worked long ago, but he no longer cares about Israel. Biblical faith has lost its relevance to the present situation.

Therefore, it is essential that before he embarks on God's mission of deliverance, Gideon must destroy the idolatry in his own household. Note this simple fact of polytheism: Pagan deities have no problem tolerating the simultaneous worship of more than one god! But Yahweh, the only true and living God, does (Ex. 20:1–7; Deut. 6:4)! Consequently, more serious than the oppression of the Midianites is the Israelites' bondage to the spiritual forces of the land—and this includes Gideon's own family.

While even his name, Gideon ("hacker"), seems to indicate a judge of strength, his activity at the time of his call and the subsequent processes demonstrate that he is hardly living up to the meaning of that name. In addition, the great similarity between Gideon's call and that of Moses and Joshua as the narrator presents it, in the end, only emphasizes the contrasts between these three (rather than the similarities).

Gideon's lack of faith will be especially apparent in his propensity for signs. This begins with his initial offering to Yahweh and will continue up to the first battle. Gideon's preoccupation with tangible manifestations of the divine will eventually be his undoing. Unfortunately, Gideon's propensity for signs and preoccupation with the tangible in religious matters is manifest today among some of those who name Christ (see more on this below).

In the initial dialogue, Yahweh twice specifically declares that he will be with Gideon (6:12, 16).[26] Yet Gideon's reply, "If now I have found favor in your eyes, give a sign that it is really you talking to me," demonstrates a spiritual dullness and lack of belief. What does God have to do? Then Gideon wants to bring an offering, an offering that appears to be based more on the notion of feeding the gods than on proper sacrifice and worship of Yahweh. Thus Gideon's ignorance of God's law extends to what proper sacrifice and worship is. Needless to say, this same ignorance can be found today in many church contexts.

Return to the past. Taking the larger structure of the cycles section into consideration, while Gideon obviously does not equate to an Othniel, Ehud, or even Barak, neither is he a Jephthah or a Samson. Thus, in building the

---

26. Note the interchange of subject for these two clauses: "the LORD" and "I."

first altar to Yahweh, Gideon draws witness to Yahweh's call through the theophany. Despite fearing the people of his village, Gideon obeys Yahweh's commands to "hack" down the Asherah pole, to destroy the Baal altar, and to build an altar to Yahweh (the second altar, 6:25−32). This endangers his life, but his father, Joash, rescues him—albeit through a ploy that questions the divinity of Baal: "If Baal really is a god, he can defend himself when someone breaks down his altar" (6:31). While this makes Gideon living proof of Baal's impotence as a deity, he nevertheless serves with a Baal-name (Jerub-Baal), and its frequency is truly ironic. While service to the Lord begins with a break with the past (in religious and moral matters, cf. Phil. 3:1−14; Heb. 12:1), the dangers of a return to the past are great.

DIVINE LEVEL. On the divine level, this section of the Gideon/Abimelech cycle emphasizes the grace of Yahweh. The very call of Gideon in spite of the national and familial apostasy is truly astonishing. In spite of the commitments of so many Christians to other gods—such as the gods of religious pluralism and modern, non-Christian worldviews—it is remarkable that God still calls and works out his plan. God's compassion for his people with all of their grave transgressions and weaknesses provides once again the impetus to deliver Israel. Moreover, God surprises us by remaining faithful in the midst of persistent cynicism and doubt.

Human level. On the human level, this section emphasizes a number of important points. It certainly teaches us how important it is to remember the mighty acts of God, especially those in the recent past. The human tendency is to forget these, which is all the more reason to make every effort to remember them. Why is this important? Because it informs our perception. The story of Gideon's call serves as a notable illustration of the dangers of not remembering God's mighty acts. The product can be cynicism and an inability to perceive God. It can lead to an ignorance and misunderstanding of God's Word and why things happen in the world.

For example, many Christians are ignorant of the Scriptures' teachings concerning suffering and pain. While such teaching is complex, there are certain principles that enable the believer to understand and face the difficulties of life differently from the unbeliever—and a proper biblical perspective is fundamental. Within some circles of Christianity, there is a cynicism concerning Christ's ability to intervene and make any difference in daily life. No matter what reasons may be given, such cynicism is ultimately the result of an ignorance of Scripture.

Again and again throughout both Testaments the sovereignty of God over human events is maintained, not to mention his willing intervention to accomplish *his* will. There is a desperate need in many Christian circles to develop eyes to see and ears to hear God, that is, the ability to perceive God. At the same time, we must evaluate and test our perceptions by the Word of God, to ensure that those perceptions are consistent with what Scripture teaches about God.

A need for signs. In some ways, today's society is incredibly gullible, easily taken in by the smooth marketing agent's pitch or the politician's good looks and promises. But in many other regards, contemporary society demands evidence, proof, signs, documentation, and/or verification. This is certainly true in religious quarters. People want to see divine manifestations before they will believe and follow. They demand first-class miracles, as if to say: "If Christ would appear before me now, then I would believe in him and follow him." It is doubtful, however, whether they would. For with many of these folk "even if one came back from the dead, they would not believe" (Luke 16:19–31). We need not be surprised when some do not respond to God's call. The failure to see what God is doing applies not just to a failure to see his revelation, but also to a failure to see the evidence he leaves behind that points to his revelation.

This was not exactly Gideon's problem; he was willing to believe (in that he already accepted God's existence and work). He simply demanded the assurances of success before acting on what God had revealed to him as his will. Gideon's problem was a matter of willingness because of his tremendous, obsessive fear. Gideon is no Mel Gibson, for he is faint-hearted, not braveheart! It is astounding how many times God states that he will be with Gideon and that he will defeat the Midianites, and yet how unbelieving Gideon is in spite of these statements. He must have evidence that demands a verdict!

Unfortunately, preoccupation with the tangible manifestations of the divine with the need for signs is manifest today among Christians on a level equal to that of Gideon. This does not mean that God does not give evidence of his presence and work. Certainly he does. But the *preoccupation* with such *tangible* manifestations is a serious and dangerous spiritual problem. In the case of Gideon, it prevented him from simply taking God at his word, trusting in the straightforward assertion of that message to him.

Such preoccupation with tangible manifestations can inhibit positive action for the cause of Christ, just as it did in the case of Gideon. God's willingness to go as far as he did in giving Gideon these signs only manifested how little faith Gideon had in the Lord's word. An unwillingness to act unless there are tangible signs can unnecessarily delay the implementation of God's revealed will. To ask for a sign when God has already revealed his will reflects an immature faith and perhaps, in certain circumstances, a greater willingness to disobey than to obey. For example, when God has clearly stated his will that believers not marry unbelievers, to ask God for a sign whether one should marry an unbelieving potential spouse is problematic and reflects on the spirituality of the one proposing such a sign.

Obedience. But putting Gideon into the larger context of the cycles section, Gideon's obedience to God's command to destroy the Baal altar and Asherah pole and build a new altar to him is noteworthy. In spite of his preoccupation with the tangible signs and in spite of perhaps working out of fear, Gideon did obey God's command. Obedience to this command was an important precursor to the deliverance of the nation through Gideon. Such obedience *ought* to be replicated in the lives of believers, especially those in leadership positions, regardless of their doubts and/or fears.

Moreover, before we can truly serve God, it is often necessary to deal with our own lives, our own backgrounds, in such a way as to bring proper and full glory to God when we do serve. Doubting people can be used of God, especially when they are obedient in spite of their doubts and fears!

Judges 6:33 – 7:18

³³Now all the Midianites, Amalekites and other eastern peoples joined forces and crossed over the Jordan and camped in the Valley of Jezreel. ³⁴Then the Spirit of the LORD came upon Gideon, and he blew a trumpet, summoning the Abiezrites to follow him. ³⁵He sent messengers throughout Manasseh, calling them to arms, and also into Asher, Zebulun and Naphtali, so that they too went up to meet them.

³⁶Gideon said to God, "If you will save Israel by my hand as you have promised—³⁷look, I will place a wool fleece on the threshing floor. If there is dew only on the fleece and all the ground is dry, then I will know that you will save Israel by my hand, as you said." ³⁸And that is what happened. Gideon rose early the next day; he squeezed the fleece and wrung out the dew—a bowlful of water.

³⁹Then Gideon said to God, "Do not be angry with me. Let me make just one more request. Allow me one more test with the fleece. This time make the fleece dry and the ground covered with dew." ⁴⁰That night God did so. Only the fleece was dry; all the ground was covered with dew.

⁷:¹Early in the morning, Jerub-Baal (that is, Gideon) and all his men camped at the spring of Harod. The camp of Midian

was north of them in the valley near the hill of Moreh. ²The
LORD said to Gideon, "You have too many men for me to
deliver Midian into their hands. In order that Israel may not
boast against me that her own strength has saved her,
³announce now to the people, 'Anyone who trembles with fear
may turn back and leave Mount Gilead.'" So twenty-two
thousand men left, while ten thousand remained.

⁴But the LORD said to Gideon, "There are still too many
men. Take them down to the water, and I will sift them for
you there. If I say, 'This one shall go with you,' he shall go;
but if I say,'This one shall not go with you,' he shall not go."

⁵So Gideon took the men down to the water. There the
LORD told him, "Separate those who lap the water with their
tongues like a dog from those who kneel down to drink."
⁶Three hundred men lapped with their hands to their mouths.
All the rest got down on their knees to drink.

⁷The LORD said to Gideon, "With the three hundred men
that lapped I will save you and give the Midianites into your
hands. Let all the other men go, each to his own place." ⁸So
Gideon sent the rest of the Israelites to their tents but kept
the three hundred, who took over the provisions and trumpets
of the others.

Now the camp of Midian lay below him in the valley. ⁹During that night the LORD said to Gideon, "Get up, go down
against the camp, because I am going to give it into your
hands. ¹⁰If you are afraid to attack, go down to the camp with
your servant Purah ¹¹and listen to what they are saying. Afterward, you will be encouraged to attack the camp." So he and
Purah his servant went down to the outposts of the camp.
¹²The Midianites, the Amalekites and all the other eastern
peoples had settled in the valley, thick as locusts. Their camels
could no more be counted than the sand on the seashore.

¹³Gideon arrived just as a man was telling a friend his
dream. "I had a dream," he was saying. "A round loaf of barley
bread came tumbling into the Midianite camp. It struck the
tent with such force that the tent overturned and collapsed."

¹⁴His friend responded, "This can be nothing other than
the sword of Gideon son of Joash, the Israelite. God has given
the Midianites and the whole camp into his hands."

¹⁵When Gideon heard the dream and its interpretation, he
worshiped God. He returned to the camp of Israel and called

out, "Get up! The LORD has given the Midianite camp into your hands." ¹⁶Dividing the three hundred men into three companies, he placed trumpets and empty jars in the hands of all of them, with torches inside.

¹⁷"Watch me," he told them. "Follow my lead. When I get to the edge of the camp, do exactly as I do. ¹⁸When I and all who are with me blow our trumpets, then from all around the camp blow yours and shout, 'For the LORD and for Gideon.'"

STRUCTURALLY, SECTION C (see introductory comments to 6:1–9:57) is clearly demarcated by the framing of the two mobilizations of troops by Gideon (a, 6:33–35; a', 7:15–18). The two sign incidents (b, 6:36–40; b', 7:12–14) are narrated on both sides of two presentations of God's dealing with fear among the Israelites and Gideon (c, 7:1–8; c', 7:9–11).

God's promise and Gideon's problem of faith are the crucial matters in tension within 6:33–7:18. Five times the promise of Yahweh's saving Israel through Gideon's hands is reiterated (6:36; 7:2, 7, 9, 14–15). Moreover, the repetition of "fear" (*yārē*) in the two innermost episodes of the structure (7:3, 10) singles this out for attention.[27]

With the narration of Gideon's call and name change complete, 6:33–35 resumes the description of the oppression of the Midianites and their alliances. Like the Moabites (and their allies) in 3:13 and the massively armed Canaanites in 4:12, this horde presents an almost insurmountable challenge to the undermanned Israelites. Reminscent of Ehud (blowing the trumpet) and Barak (calling out the troops, especially in Zebulun and Naphtali), Gideon, upon whom the Spirit of Yahweh has come (lit., "clothed"),[28] musters the Israelites from Manasseh, Asher, Zebulun, and Naphtali (6:34–35).

The reader's expectations for the same type of deliverance as in the earlier cycles are quickly dashed in 6:36–40. Gideon suddenly confronts God with the need for a "sign," a proof that God will really save Israel through him. Note that God has already said that he would, and Gideon knows it ("as you have promised," 6:36). Thus, while the phrase "the Spirit of the LORD came

---

27. Tanner, "The Gideon Narrative As the Focal Point of Judges," 158.

28. The choice of the term in 6:34 builds a contrastive wordplay between the Spirit's "clothing" Gideon and the article of "clothing" (i.e., the ephod) that Gideon later produces (8:27). See also next note.

upon [i.e., clothed, *lābaš*]²⁹ Gideon" sounds spiritually positive, it is important to recognize the irony built into the context. Block observes:

> This [the Spirit of Yahweh's "clothing" of Gideon] should not be interpreted too differently from every other instance in which the Spirit is described as having come/rushed upon its object. This expression, reminiscent of Num 24:3 (in which case Balaam, the Mesopotamian prophet, experiences the same phenomenon) does not presuppose *any particular level of spirituality on the part of the recipient* [emphasis mine]. To the contrary, this divine intrusion into human experience seems to graphically describe YHWH's arresting of men ill-disposed toward resolving Israel's problems and his equipping of them for the saving task.³⁰

Block's case is reinforced by the observation that the Spirit of Yahweh "comes/clothes/is strong" upon the Out-group judges more frequently than upon the In-group judges (five times vs. one time).³¹ It is especially clear from the usages in the Jephthah narrative and the Samson episodes that the phrase does not necessarily carry a positive comment on the individual's spirituality. In the case of Jephthah, after the Spirit "comes upon" him, he advances for battle against the Ammonites and immediately utters his rash, manipulative vow. In the case of Samson (where ironically the majority of uses occur), after the Spirit "is strong upon" him, Samson tears a lion in two (14:6). In the next instance (14:19), he murders thirty Philistines to get their sets of clothing to fulfill his deal with his "companions" at his wedding and returns in great anger to his father's house. In the final case (15:14), he kills one

---

29. Waldman has demonstrated that the Spirit's clothing of Gideon reflects a well-known ancient Near Eastern idiom that describes an individual as clothed/covered/overwhelmed by a divine or demonic force. See N. M. Waldman, "The Imagery of Clothing, Covering, and Overpowering," *JANES* 19 (1989): 161–70. See also previous note.

30. D. I. Block, "The Period of the Judges: Religious Disintegration Under Tribal Rule," in *Israel's Apostasy and Restoration: Essays in Honor of Roland K. Harrison*, ed. A. Gileadi (Grand Rapids: Baker, 1988), 52.

31. *In-Group judges*: Othniel (3:10): "The Spirit of the LORD came upon him" (*hyh ʿl*, lit., "was upon"). *Out Group judges*: Gideon (6:34): "The Spirit of the LORD came upon Gideon" (*lbš ʾt*, lit., "clothed"); Jephthah (11:29): "Then the Spirit of the LORD came upon Jephthah" (*hyh ʿl*, lit., "was upon"); Samson (14:6): "The Spirit of the LORD came upon him in power" (*ṣlḥ ʿl*, lit., "rushed upon"); (14:19), "The Spirit of the LORD came upon him in power" (*ṣlḥ ʿl*, lit., "rushed upon"); (15:14), "The Spirit of the LORD came upon him in power" (*ṣlḥ ʿl*, lit., "rushed upon). JPSV translates *ṣlḥ* as "gripped." See also 1 Sam. 10:6, 10; 11:6; 16:13; 18:10. Perhaps in a contrastive context, note Abimelech (9:23): "God sent an evil spirit between Abimelech and the citizens of Shechem" (*šlḥ byn*). I treat 13:25 as a different and special case. The vocabulary and syntax are uniquely different from the other instances in the book of Judges and hence the meaning is altogether different in this context.

thousand Philistines with the jawbone of an ass (an unclean implement) and then utters his first narcissistic prayer.

It is easy for Christians who are more familiar with the New Testament concepts of "indwelling" and "filling" to read these back into the Old Testament. These do not really equate. To be filled with the Spirit in the New Testament speaks to spirituality, that is, the one who is filled is controlled by the Spirit with the consequent actions being spiritual activities (Eph. 5:18b–20). In the Old Testament the notion is that of empowerment for a particular task, though it is apparent that the recipient might misuse this empowerment (e.g., 14:19). The New Testament equivalent is perhaps closer to the idea of giftedness, where the recipient can use his or her gifts to positive results or misuse or abuse those gifts.

Therefore, in the case of Gideon, the Spirit's work reflects God's sovereign will to set things in motion for the deliverance he has planned, not Gideon's condition of faith or spirituality. Although Gideon has much popular support and has a considerable fighting force at his disposal, he hesitates. His almost immediate "fleecing" of God speaks to his unbelief, his lack of spirituality. In fact, the fleece incidents are Gideon's second request for a sign from God (cf. the earlier request in 6:17). And this second sign request needs to be doubly confirmed! It is not enough that God makes the fleece wet and the ground dry; Gideon needs it the other way around. And sadly, unlike Yahweh, Gideon will not be true to his word after the first fleece incident ("then I will know that you will save Israel by my hand, as you said" v. 37). Therefore, in spite of the polite entreaty, we should not be blind to the manner in which Gideon is trying to manipulate God.[32]

Contrary to popular interpretation, these fleecings have nothing to do with discovering or determining God's will. The divine will is perfectly and absolutely clear in Gideon's own mind (note the wording in v. 36). These "signs" reveal his lack of faith. As Exum rightly notes: "No character in the book receives more divine assurance than Gideon and none displays more doubt. Gideon is, significantly, the only judge to whom God speaks directly, though this privilege does not allay his faintheartedness."[33]

Hence, despite being clear about God's will, being "clothed/empowered" by the Spirit of God, and being confirmed as a divinely chosen leader by the overwhelming response of his countrymen to his own summons to battle, Gideon uses every means available to try to get out of the mission to which he has been called.[34]

---

32. In this light, it is informative to compare Gideon's fleecings with Jephthah's vow. Both are manipulative; both are utterly unnecessary.

33. Exum, "The Centre Cannot Hold," 416.

34. Block, *Judges, Ruth*, 273.

It is not insignificant that throughout the pericope concerning the fleecings the divine personal, covenantal name of Yahweh is missing. Instead, the rather generic designation Elohim ("God") is used. Apparently Gideon has difficulty distinguishing between Yahweh, the God of the Israelites, and God in a general sense.[35] This fleecing process is nothing short of a pagan divinatory test of the deity. In the ancient Near East, there were many different divination processes invoked to inquire of the deities. Gideon's fleece incidents are examples of "impetrated divination"—divination by various techniques of asking a question and directly evoking a response.[36]

Particularly important here is the way Gideon utilizes the occurrence of normal versus abnormal activity as an indicator of the deity's answer. Gideon's procedure demonstrates that the first night he was content to use the oracle simply to give God the opportunity to communicate if he has changed his mind (which, of course, he has not). Thus the "normal" (absorbent fleece, wet; impervious threshing floor, dry) is set up as a "yes" answer (i.e., God *will* deliver by his hand). The lack of faith is clearly demonstrated when the normal occurrence is insufficient and he has to reverse the indicators (with effusive apology) and pose the oracle again with the "abnormal" (fleece, dry; threshing floor, wet) as the "yes" answer.[37]

Perhaps one may inquire of Baal this way, but this is not the way to treat the God of Israel. Remarkably, Yahweh responds to Gideon's tests. As Block rightly observes, Yahweh "is more anxious to deliver Israel than to quibble with this man's semipagan notions of deity."[38] On this basis, one may argue that the narrator includes this pericope to construct a sharper picture of Gideon's unbelief and questionable religious practices (thus his religious deviance in 8:27 is not as surprising). Finally, on the basis of the structure of this section (b, 6:36–40 :: b', 7:12–14), it should be observed that just as Yahweh uses the pair of fleecings with their pagan divinatory overtones to encourage Gideon to deliver Israel, he will also use two Midianites—one relating his dream, the other interpreting it (also with pagan divinatory overtones)—to encourage and motivate Gideon to action. What great lengths God is going in order to save Israel from the hand of Midian!

---

35. Ibid.

36. For a brief but helpful discussion of divination, especially in the Mesopotamian context, see A. K. Guinan, "Divination," in *COS*, 1:421–26. For a discussion of the proof by token type of divination, see M. Dijkstra, "KTU 1.6 (= CTA).III.1FF. and the So-called Zeichenbeweiss," *VT* 35 (1985): 105–9.

37. John Walton, personal communication.

38. Block, *Judges, Ruth*, 273. In addition, Gideon admits that he is testing God, and this reminds the reader of Israel's testing of God in the desert (Ex. 17:2, 7; Num. 14:22; Ps. 78:18, 41, 56; 95:9; 106:14).

The two central episodes (c and c') deal with the issue of "fear." The double reduction (7:1–8) of Gideon's fighting force begins with the removal of all the "fearful" Israelites (7:1–3). According to Deuteronomy 20:8, this was a Yahweh-commanded reduction for morale reasons.[39] The result is a 22,000-man reduction. Interestingly, this reduction of the "fearful" (*yārē'*) or "trembling" (*ḥārad*) Israelites takes place at the spring of Harod (the name derives from a verb *ḥārad*, to tremble; hence "the spring of trembling").

Then God directs Gideon to go down to the water for the further reduction of his remaining 10,000 man force (7:4–8).[40] Commentators are divided in their understanding of the process of reduction. Some argue that the criteria for elimination are based on positive components; others, that elimination is based on negative criteria. For example, Boling argues that this is a test of alertness and that it is difficult to watch out for the enemy if one kneels down and laps water directly from the spring.[41]

It seems best, however, to understand the process as based on purely arbitrary criteria. Whether the process of selection is based on positive or negative evaluative criteria is not as important as the reduction in number to an extremely small force—three hundred men. But along with this drastic reduction in his forces comes a further word of reassurance: "With the three hundred men that lapped I will save you and give the Midianites into your hands" (7:7). The reason for the reductions is stated explicitly in 7:2: "in order that Israel may not boast against me that her own strength has saved her." This motive will, unfortunately, be undercut, as we will see.

In addition, the reductions certainly are a way in which Yahweh is able to undermine any self-confidence that Gideon may have as the result of the fleece incidents. Gideon attempts to gain some security from his self-conceived divinatory signs with the fleece. While God acquiesced to that request, he immediately counters by putting Gideon in an even more vulnerable position through the troop reductions so that Yahweh himself will receive all the glory for the coming victory.

In the second central episode (7:9–11), Yahweh, knowing that Gideon himself is still fearful, directs him to go down to the enemy camp to overhear the enemy. This provides Gideon with the second instance of confirmation

---

39. Deut. 20:8 states: "Then the officers shall add, 'Is any man afraid or fainthearted? Let him go home so that his brothers will not become disheartened too.'" It is ironic in this context that one of the tests for eliminating unnecessary Israelite warriors (viz., "fear") is the very problem that affects the leader, Gideon, himself.

40. For the complex textual difficulties in 7:6, see O'Connell, *The Rhetoric of the Book of Judges*, 467–69.

41. Boling, *Judges*, 145. Of course, wild animals drink from springs this way all the time with alertness to what is around them.

that God will give the Midianites into his hands. The statement in 7:10, "If you are afraid to attack . . . ," demonstrates that, in fact, Gideon is still afraid. God graciously supplies Gideon with Purah as a companion, and the pair goes down to the Midianite camp at night (cf. Gideon's action with his servants in 6:25–27).

At this point (7:12–14), the narrator's repetition of the description of the hordes of the Midianites and other allied peoples as a swarm of "locusts" (cf. 6:3–5) and as numerous as the sand of the seashore (cf. Josh. 11:4) heightens the danger and the motif of fear. Gideon and his servant arrive at the Midianite camp at the precise moment (emphasized in the Hebrew syntax)[42] that a Midianite is relating his dream to his comrade. God has clearly devised his own sign for Gideon. Now, through a Midianite's dream retold and interpreted by another Midianite[43]—a dream and its interpretation[44] that Gideon will be in the exact place to overhear (imagine the complexity and probability here, especially with the size of the Midianite camp)—Gideon hears the exact same words that Yahweh had already spoken to him: "God has given the Midianites and the whole camp into his hands" (7:14; cf. 6:16, 36).

The irony is rich. Hearing the promise directly from Yahweh did not convince Gideon (his fleece signs really didn't either), but hearing it from the lips of a Midianite soldier does convince him.[45] The dream report and its interpretation also demonstrate that the feared Midianites are in fact in a state of near panic through the ominous dream that Yahweh has given them. There will be no real fight since they are already "given" into Gideon's hands before the battle begins.

In 7:15–18, it is evident that this reported dream has its intended effect on Gideon: He worships God (7:15). Gideon now musters his small band of men with the confidence that Yahweh will truly give them the victory. At this moment, he believes God. Dividing the three hundred into three companies, he places trumpets and empty jars in the hands of all of them with torches inside, and he instructs them to follow his lead. They are to shout "for the LORD *and for Gideon*" (emphasis added).[46]

---

42. The construction *w^ehinnēh* + subj. + ptc. = "just then."

43. Note the use of another "pair."

44. The dream is absurd: A round loaf of barley bread tumbles into the Midianite camp, smashing into the tent with such force that it overturns and collapses. The divinatory type interpretation (remember, this is a Midianite doing the interpreting) happens to match perfectly Yahweh's earlier words.

45. In light of this, Barak's lack of faith seems like nothing compared to Gideon's.

46. This phrase *lyhwh wlgd^cwn* ("for Yahweh and for Gideon") is no doubt literarily anticipatory of things to come. It is paralleled syntactically to a new inscription discovered at Ekron that reads: *lb^cl wlpdy* ("for Ba^cal and for Padi"). Interestingly, the editors of this inscrip-

After this final "sign" of encouragement through the dream and its interpretation as related by the two Midianites, all dialogue between Yahweh and Gideon ceases. After worshiping God as the result of this final sign, Gideon will not worship God again. Rather than having a wonderful song of Yahweh's glorification after the battle (cf. ch. 5), there will only be Gideon's increasing usurpation of God's glory for the victory in the battle and its outcomes.

Bridging Contexts

DIVINE LEVEL. On the divine level, the section stresses Yahweh's sovereignty and omnipotence, demonstrated both in the fleecings and in the dream and its interpretation. Gideon's manipulative, divinatory attempts to secure Yahweh's involvement (rather foolish when one considers that Yahweh has innumerable times stated to Gideon that he will be with him and give him victory) will be undercut by the sovereign Lord, who reduces the army twice in such a way that victory on purely human grounds will be impossible. The constant emphasis on the vastness of the Midianite army underscores this. Any number of things could go wrong with Gideon's strategy—as ingenious as it is. Unless Yahweh is in control of the events and especially the disposition of the Midianites in the camp, things could easily turn out another way.[47] The description of the battle in the next section will reinforce this fact.

Human level. On a human level, what is stressed repeatedly in this section is Gideon's fear and sense of inadequacy for the task—his lack of willingness to trust Yahweh's word. Consequently, he is in constant need of reassurance and moral support. Gideon is apparently a man of great potential and perhaps natural ability but lacks significantly in faith.

The fleece incidents are far from being a model for the discernment of God's will. As we have already discussed, these are expressions of doubt and lack of faith. By his own admission, Gideon already knew God's will and promise, for this had been carefully articulated to him by the angel of the Lord (6:14–16). His problem is his lack of willingness to trust the Lord, to take him at his word. Thus, the fleece incidents are about Gideon's unbelief

---

tion discuss the syntax of "for 'Divine Name' and for 'Royal Name.'" In light of this new inscription one must wonder if the narrator is using a stock phrase to make a subtle royal illusion in the text. See S. Gitin and M. Cogan, "A New Type of Dedicatory Inscription from Ekron," *IEJ* 49 (1999): 193–202. See also C. R. Krahmalkov, "The Foundation of Carthage, 814 B.C.: The Douïmès Pendant Inscription," *JSS* 26 (1981): 85–86. He interprets this form as the soldier's oath of allegiance to God and ruler.

47. Surprise night attacks do not always succeed. Much depends on the vigilance and disposition of the enemy.

and stubbornness in response to God's call. In such cases, God is not obligated to respond, and if he does, it is only by grace. Those who use this passage as a means of discerning God's will are simply misapplying Scripture.

Reduction of the army. The reduction of Gideon's army is a familiar story often told from the perspective of emphasizing God's ability to deliver whether by many or by few. While it is certainly true that God can do this, such an explanation falls short of doing justice to the text. The context is dealing with a struggle of fear and doubt within Gideon himself, which has important application to the modern context.

The reductions of Gideon's army contextually fall precisely between his unfounded request for a fleece and God's exposure of his fear. Those reductions have a threefold intention. (1) They enhance the glorification of God (7:2).

(2) They put Gideon in a position where his fear is exposed. God is interested in helping Gideon to overcome his fear, to deal with this emotion through faith. But God is interested in more than just Gideon—he wants to deliver Israel. Therefore, he manifests great patience in dealing with Gideon, not only to aid him in overcoming his fear, but perhaps more importantly to save Israel from the hand of the Midianites. While Gideon has sought to gain security by his self-conceived sign with the fleece, and though God acquiesced to that request, Yahweh immediately counters by putting Gideon in an even more vulnerable position. After all, if Gideon struggled to trust God with 32,000 Israelites against a Midianite force of 135,000 (see 8:10), how will he react when he has only a force of 300?[48] The problem at its heart is manipulation. Gideon wants to have the emotional and psychological assurance that God will really give the victory. Indeed, the fleecings were utterly unnecessary since God had already given his word.

(3) Given the spiritual independence and waywardness of the nation, if the forces massed under Gideon were to defeat the Midianites without the reductions, the Israelites might credit themselves rather than Yahweh with defeating the enemy. Yahweh recognizes this and removes this possibility (although Gideon will eventually usurp it anyway).

Gideon tests God with signs (the fleece incidents), and God answers him to dispel his fear. Yet God quickly dissolves the assurances Gideon may have had from the fleece incidents in order to demonstrate to him his real problem and its answer. It is only with God's own sign, with all of its complexity and irony, that Gideon finally follows the Lord. Hearing the promise directly from Yahweh was not convincing enough for Gideon, nor were Gideon's fleece signs. But hearing it from the lips of a Midianite soldier is convincing! It is ironic that it is at this point that Gideon "worships" the Lord. What does it take for us to believe?

48. Tanner, "The Gideon Narrative As the Focal Point of Judges," 159.

GOD'S SOVEREIGNTY. The narrator leaves readers with a penetrating message: God must bring his servants to a moment when all human confidence is stripped away, when they sit silently in humble adoration of his God as the One who is totally sufficient against all odds to accomplish his divine will. Then and only then are they ready to move forward to taste God's victory.

Sometimes God has to take us through such experiences to expose our fear and lack of trust in him. In spite of Gideon's fear and lack of trust, God uses Gideon to save Israel. God must break down the walls we have constructed to hide our fears and lack of trust in him. He must remove the pillars of our allusions that hold us from belief. If we continue to depend on other things for our security and confidence, he must remove these to bring us to the point of true dependence on him alone. He brings Gideon to the point where he either must trust God or reject him altogether.

But God's awesome sovereignty (cf. comments on *weḥinnēh* [just then] as Gideon arrives at the camp to hear the dream and its interpretation) startles Gideon into a new way of seeing the situation. God's sovereignty is not simply a doctrine of theology for theologians to debate, but most important it is the very means God uses to reveal himself to us again and again. We are forced to consider that the timing and the event cannot be by chance; it can only be the hand of the Lord, who is sovereignly arranging matters. When he does this and we have eyes to see, we cannot help but have the same reaction as Gideon—worship. He is God.

Engendering faith. It is impossible to engender faith without the Word of God. General revelation demonstrates that there is a God (Rom. 1:18–23), but only the Word of God reveals his attributes, his character, and his person. It is difficult, if not impossible, to have faith in someone that you don't know or barely know. It is extremely hard to trust someone that you misunderstand or are misinformed about. Gideon's ignorance about the Word of God was a strong factor in his inability to trust Yahweh, for he had misconceptions about Yahweh and misunderstood the very nature and character of God. If we do not inculcate the Word of God in our lives (Rom. 10:17), we will manifest the same unbelief—even stubbornness to believe—that Gideon did.

Gideon was apparently a man of great potential and natural ability but lacking in faith. He was timid in the midst of potential. It took God's call, signs, and arranging of events to change his heart. Are we the same? Perhaps God wants to use us in some way: teach a Sunday school class, sing in the choir, minister to the sick, or be a counselor to youth or the down-and-out. But we are timid. Can God really use us? We want assurance. In fact, we demand it. Are we delaying God's plan? Are we really trusting him if he must give evidence after evidence that he desires our participation? Fortunately, he does not leave us wallowing in our potential. And when he brings us to trust in him and serve him, there is worship of him.

Judges 7:19–8:21

[19]Gideon and the hundred men with him reached the edge of the camp at the beginning of the middle watch, just after they had changed the guard. They blew their trumpets and broke the jars that were in their hands. [20]The three companies blew the trumpets and smashed the jars. Grasping the torches in their left hands and holding in their right hands the trumpets they were to blow, they shouted, "A sword for the LORD and for Gideon!" [21]While each man held his position around the camp, all the Midianites ran, crying out as they fled.

[22]When the three hundred trumpets sounded, the LORD caused the men throughout the camp to turn on each other with their swords. The army fled to Beth Shittah toward Zererah as far as the border of Abel Meholah near Tabbath. [23]Israelites from Naphtali, Asher and all Manasseh were called out, and they pursued the Midianites. [24]Gideon sent messengers throughout the hill country of Ephraim, saying, "Come down against the Midianites and seize the waters of the Jordan ahead of them as far as Beth Barah."

So all the men of Ephraim were called out and they took the waters of the Jordan as far as Beth Barah. [25]They also captured two of the Midianite leaders, Oreb and Zeeb. They killed Oreb at the rock of Oreb, and Zeeb at the winepress of Zeeb. They pursued the Midianites and brought the heads of Oreb and Zeeb to Gideon, who was by the Jordan.

[8:1]Now the Ephraimites asked Gideon, "Why have you treated us like this? Why didn't you call us when you went to fight Midian?" And they criticized him sharply.

[2]But he answered them, "What have I accomplished compared to you? Aren't the gleanings of Ephraim's grapes better than the full grape harvest of Abiezer? [3]God gave Oreb and Zeeb, the Midianite leaders, into your hands. What was I able to do compared to you?" At this, their resentment against him subsided.

[4]Gideon and his three hundred men, exhausted yet keeping up the pursuit, came to the Jordan and crossed it. [5]He said to

the men of Succoth, "Give my troops some bread; they are worn out, and I am still pursuing Zebah and Zalmunna, the kings of Midian."

⁶But the officials of Succoth said, "Do you already have the hands of Zebah and Zalmunna in your possession? Why should we give bread to your troops?"

⁷Then Gideon replied, "Just for that, when the LORD has given Zebah and Zalmunna into my hand, I will tear your flesh with desert thorns and briers."

⁸From there he went up to Peniel and made the same request of them, but they answered as the men of Succoth had. ⁹So he said to the men of Peniel, "When I return in triumph, I will tear down this tower."

¹⁰Now Zebah and Zalmunna were in Karkor with a force of about fifteen thousand men, all that were left of the armies of the eastern peoples; a hundred and twenty thousand swordsmen had fallen. ¹¹Gideon went up by the route of the nomads east of Nobah and Jogbehah and fell upon the unsuspecting army. ¹²Zebah and Zalmunna, the two kings of Midian, fled, but he pursued them and captured them, routing their entire army.

¹³Gideon son of Joash then returned from the battle by the Pass of Heres. ¹⁴He caught a young man of Succoth and questioned him, and the young man wrote down for him the names of the seventy-seven officials of Succoth, the elders of the town. ¹⁵Then Gideon came and said to the men of Succoth, "Here are Zebah and Zalmunna, about whom you taunted me by saying, 'Do you already have the hands of Zebah and Zalmunna in your possession? Why should we give bread to your exhausted men?'" ¹⁶He took the elders of the town and taught the men of Succoth a lesson by punishing them with desert thorns and briers. ¹⁷He also pulled down the tower of Peniel and killed the men of the town.

¹⁸Then he asked Zebah and Zalmunna, "What kind of men did you kill at Tabor?"

"Men like you," they answered, "each one with the bearing of a prince."

¹⁹Gideon replied, "Those were my brothers, the sons of my own mother. As surely as the LORD lives, if you had spared their lives, I would not kill you." ²⁰Turning to Jether, his oldest son, he said, "Kill them!" But Jether did not draw his sword, because he was only a boy and was afraid.

²¹Zebah and Zalmunna said, "Come, do it yourself. 'As is the man, so is his strength.'" So Gideon stepped forward and killed them, and took the ornaments off their camels' necks.

STRUCTURALLY, SECTION B' (see introductory comments to 6:1—9:57) has two units. Each section features a victory in battle against the Midianites (7:19—8:3; 8:4—21), and in each of these, a pair of Midianite rulers is executed. One battle occurs on the west side of the Jordan, the other on the east side.

The First Battle: Cisjordan (7:19–8:3)

ON THE WEST side of the Jordan, Gideon and his men reach the Midianite camp at just the right time: the changing of the guard. Once again the narrator shows that Yahweh's sovereign hand is at work in the victory. The blowing of the trumpets, the breaking of the jars, the flashing of the torches, and the shouting of the men ("a sword for the LORD and for Gideon," 7:20) all proliferate utter chaos and horror in the Midianite camp. Yahweh's role is emphasized again in 7:22a: "The LORD caused the men throughout the camp to turn on each other with their swords" (lit., "Yahweh set a sword each man on his comrade," cf. 1 Sam. 14:20).

The pursuit of the defeated Midianites is narrated in two stages. In the initial stage (7:22b–23), the troops from Naphtali, Asher, and all Manasseh are called out to pursue the Midianites along a route described in verse 22b. In the second stage (7:24–25), Gideon calls out[49] the troops of Ephraim, who "seize the waters of the Jordan" (reminiscent of Ehud in 3:27–28).

At this point, the climax of the first battle is reached with the Ephraimites' capture and execution of the pair of Midianite leaders (*śārîm*): Oreb ("Raven") and Zeeb ("Wolf"). The setting for the execution is interesting: Oreb on a rock, Zeeb at a winepress (7:25). Ironically, a winepress and rock in Ophrah were the setting for Gideon's call to deliver the Israelites from the Midianites (6:11–20).

The brief epilogue that follows (8:1–3) this battle demonstrates Gideon's diplomatic skills (contrast Jephthah's lack of diplomacy, 12:1–6). Gideon

---

49. Some interpreters understand Gideon's mobilization of the Israelites in both stages of the pursuit to be indications of his reliance on human strength and strategy rather than his reliance on God's guidance. For example, see Klein, *Triumph of Irony*, 57–58; Block, *Judges, Ruth*, 283–84. However, on the basis of analogy with the story of the pursuit in the Ehud cycle, this may not be correct.

successfully averts the threat of civil war by quelling intertribal jealousies of the Ephraimites that have been provoked in the course of the campaign. Gideon's reply to the Ephraimites implies that they have accomplished much more than he and the other Israelites in the initial attack (8:2).[50] While this satisfies the Ephraimite contention, it is a psychological rather than a theological argument.[51] Accordingly, now with the external threat removed and internal peace restored, the reader naturally anticipates the narrative frame component: "and the land had peace for X years."

The Second Battle: Transjordan (8:4–21)

HOWEVER, QUITE UNEXPECTEDLY, the story is resumed in 8:4. If the narrative ended roughly with 8:3, Gideon would be considered one of the heroic judges of ancient Israel,[52] notwithstanding his problem with fear and lack of faith. However, the narration continues, and the portrayal of Gideon becomes bleaker and bleaker. The moment that he and his men cross the Jordan, a whole new Gideon emerges.

In contrast to the "first" Gideon, who was a timid "hacker" and who succeeded by the grace of God, this "second" Gideon is a forceful, resourceful, avenging "hacker," whose very success breeds even worse failure. Like an animal on the prowl, his pronounced purpose is to capture "Zebah and Zalmunna, the kings of Midian" (8:5),[53] and he presses towards this goal with frenzied determination despite the hunger and exhaustion of his three hundred men (in this, he foreshadows Saul, cf. 1 Sam. 14). While the refusal of the (military?) leaders (*śārîm*) of Succoth and Penuel/Peniel to give him support may be faulty,[54] Gideon's threats of revenge are totally

---

50. Gideon's generous and timely compliment to the Ephraimites (8:2) that "the gleaning of Ephraim's grapes [is] better than the full grape harvest of Abiezer" is not just a clever allusion to their slaughter of Zeeb at a winepress (7:25), but also recalls the beginning of the story, where Gideon himself is skulking in another winepress (6:11).

51. Block, *Judges, Ruth*, 286. Block also notes that Gideon refers to God as Elohim rather than Yahweh and is silent on Yahweh's call of him as the leader to deliver Israel.

52. No doubt this is where certain preachers and teachers stop in their reading of the Gideon account!

53. The names Zebah and Zalmunna appear to be pejoratives or distortions, like Cushan-Rishathaim in 3:8. Zebah means "sacrifice," and Zalmunna means "shelter/protection refused." The names obviously apply to the kings' outcomes. Zebah and Zalmunna are designated "kings" (*m^elākîm*), while Oreb and Zeeb are designated "leaders" (*śārîm*). This creates a link with the previous Deborah/Barak cycle, where Jabin is designated as "king" (*melek*) and Sisera as "commander" (*śar*).

54. The question that the leaders (*śārîm*) of Succoth ask is literally: "Is the palm [*kap*] of Zebah and Zalmunna now in your hand [*yād*]?" This refers to the ancient Near Eastern military practice of counting the dead on the battlefield by the number of hands (cut off). Thus

uncalled for.[55] While he declares that this pair of kings will be given into his hand by Yahweh just as Oreb and Zeeb were (8:7), there are no indications of Yahweh's involvement in this second battle. In fact, the statements of God's involvement, so prominent in the build-up to and description of the first battle, are entirely lacking here (cf. 8:11–12 with 7:21–22). As Boling observes:

> Here the chief protagonist is not Jerubbaal ("Let-Baal-sue," i.e., God's man!) but Gideon (Hacker). There is no participation by Yahweh, nor reference to him, except in Gideon's own usage (8:7, 19).[56]

Gideon's timidity has completely evaporated. There will be no more diplomacy, only demands of support from the two towns on his route. Gideon's personal resourcefulness, which in the first battle had been subordinated to Yahweh's will, has full domination now. Clearly what he now achieves is by his own strength of character and tactical skill. Using a route that the Midianite remnant does not anticipate, Gideon brings down on them a furious attack. Yahweh's silence and noninvolvement in this second battle and subsequent events is a foreshadowing of the Jephthah narrative, in which Yahweh's silence and noninvolvement is paramount.

On return from this battle, Gideon "seizes" a young man (or perhaps the term *naʿar* should be understood as "an official") and coerces him to write down the names of the seventy-seven officials (*śārîm*) of Succoth, the elders (*zᵉqēnîm*) of the town. He then tortures his own countrymen—by flogging them with desert thorns and briers—and he pulls down the tower of Penuel, killing the men of the city. Gideon is simply taking the law into his own hands as soon as events have permitted him a reasonable pretense and situation to do so. His actions against Succoth and Penuel[57] anticipate the similar but more brutal actions of his son Abimelech against

---

they are asking: "Have you already defeated Zebah and Zalmunna so that they are no longer a threat (with the implication that he may not succeed in this)?" This reaction of the Transjordanians contrasts sharply with their Cisjordanian countrymen, who responded immediately to Gideon's summons in 7:23.

55. In the case of Succoth, Gideon glibly invokes the name of Yahweh and threatens to take the law into his own hands by beating (rather than NIV, "tear") their bodies with switches of desert thorns (*qôṣîm*) and briars (*barqānîm*), like a man beats grain on the threshing floor. In the case of Penuel, he declares his intention to tear down their defensive tower. For these plants, see K. L. Younger Jr., "בַּרְקָן," *NIDOTTE*, 1:770–71; idem, "קוֹץ," *NIDOTTE*, 3:907.

56. Boling, *Judges*, 158.

57. Webb states: "Gideon is the first judge to turn the sword against his compatriots" (*The Book of the Judges*, 158). The domestic clashes continue with Abimelech, Jephthah, and Samson. Along with Gideon's ephod and the theme of monarchy, they set the stage, so to speak, for the double conclusion with its domestic wars and atrocities (Judg. 17–21).

Shechem and Thebez (cf. in particular Gideon's action against the tower of Penuel [8:17], with Abimelech's action against the tower of Shechem [9:46–49]). They also foreshadow those of Jephthah against Ephraim (12:1–6).

At length Gideon's motivation is revealed in the dialogue in 8:18–19: revenge. Zebah and Zalmunna had been responsible for the death of his brothers.[58] This is a personal vendetta that Gideon has been prosecuting with such ruthless determination in Transjordan.[59] Zebah and Zalmunna are executed, not because they are the enemies of Yahweh (as in the case of Oreb and Zeeb earlier), but because of Gideon's personal vengeance.[60]

Jether, Gideon's firstborn, who is unexpectedly introduced at this point (8:20), serves as an antithesis to his father and points up the contrast between Gideon as he was and Gideon as he now is. The father's earlier insecurity is now mirrored in the son, who hesitates when he is told to kill the prisoners, "because he ... was afraid [yr']" (8:20). Gideon, by way of contrast, is now a man of "strength" (g⁽bûrâ, 8:21, cf. 6:12) and has the appearance of a king's son (8:18). Jether also serves as a foil for Abimelech in Judges 9. Jether, the firstborn, is hesitant to slay the two "real" foreign kings; Abimelech, the last-mentioned son, is not hesitant to execute all of his brothers, some of whom may not have been adults.

As in the initial battle, a series of incidents builds the suspense; again it is Gideon and his three hundred who take the encamped enemy by surprise; again the enemy is thrown into a panic, routed, and pursued; and again the capture and execution of a pair of Midianite leaders functions as the climax.

However, in this second battle narrative there are major differences between it and the first. The pair of leaders this time are kings (m⁽lākîm, 8:5, 12) instead of leaders/commanders (śārîm, 7:25). Yahweh is not involved in this battle. Nor does Yahweh have to motivate Gideon before the battle; rather, he is so highly desirous of revenge that he stalks the enemy a great distance in order to attack them. In the first battle, Gideon was a fearful

---

58. Although there has been no mention of a battle at Tabor in the Gideon cycle, the seven years of hostilities alluded to in 6:1–5 may provide a possible context. Boling argues that the question in 8:18 "is intended to be as startling as it sounds" (*Judges*, 157). The explanation for Gideon's behavior is held back until the climax so that it might strike the reader with greatest force.

59. The two Midianite kings are defiant to the very end, unlike the lord of Bezeq in 1:5–7, who recognized Yahweh's justice being applied in his case. However, these executions are the work of Gideon's private vengeance.

60. Block calls Gideon's use of the oath "as the LORD lives," "a glib reference to Yahweh to sanctify his personal vendetta" (*Judges, Ruth*, 295).

young man; in the second, a ruthless hunter. Finally, these "kings" are captured and executed by Gideon himself rather than by Ephraimites.[61]

Gideon is clearly a man who is not without resources or resourcefulness. The strategies employed in the two defeats of the Midianites on both sides of the Jordan are apparently his own. His calling up of reserves in 7:23 and his deployment of the Ephraimite militia along the Jordan to cut off the enemy's escape in 7:24–25 also show a considerable military competence. Thus his self-deprecating words in 6:15 should not be taken at face value. In fact, the angel of the Lord addresses him as a "mighty warrior" (*gibbôr ḥeḥāyil,* 6:12). While not necessarily a professional soldier, Gideon is not a man devoid of resources or the natural potential for leadership.

A CONTRAST IN GIDEON. This section could not have two more different outcomes. In the first battle we see a trusting Gideon; as a result, Yahweh gives him the victory over the Midianite horde. In the second battle we see a revenge-driven Gideon, who wins a battle through his own cunning without Yahweh's involvement.

That Yahweh gives him the victory in the first battle is made explicit by the statement in 7:22 that "the LORD caused the men throughout the camp to turn on each other with their swords." This is why the writer of the book of Hebrews can ascribe faith to Gideon because Gideon thoroughly trusted Yahweh for victory in this battle (Heb. 11:32). This is the victory over the Midianites that Yahweh has wanted to give to Gideon from the beginning; in the next battle, however, Yahweh is absent.

Like all the stories of the cyclical judges, this narrative acknowledges that if anything positive happens in the lives of God's people, it is by his grace and not because they deserve it. Evidence of any positive disposition toward Yahweh on the part of the Israelites as a whole or even Gideon in particular is meager. But on account of his great compassion, being moved by the cry of his people over their distress caused by the enemy, Yahweh intervenes to rescue Israel. That this is completely Yahweh's doing is more than clear from the double reduction in preparation for the battle and his work in confusing the enemy to accomplish the victory.

Decreasing spirituality. One of the greatest obstacles to God's work among his people and in the world is their faithlessness. Gideon is one of

---

61. There is also a contrast in the dialogue of Gideon with the Ephraimites after the first battle, which results in no further action (8:1–3), and his dialogue with the leaders of the two Israelite cities (8:4–9), which results in vengeful overreaction (8:13–17).

these faithless persons. He refuses at first to follow the call of God. Only after he has presumptuously subjected Yahweh to a series of tests and after he has witnessed Yahweh's gracious answers—ironically, ultimately in the mouth of a Midianite—does he finally accept the call to deliver his people.

At the end of the first battle, Gideon demonstrates wisdom in his dealing with the Ephraimites. A gentle answer turns away wrath (Prov. 15:1), and Gideon applies this principle in his answer to the Ephraimites. Even though they are wrong in their attitude in sharply criticizing him, he wisely pays them a compliment rather than incite them to battle with a true but stinging reply to put them in their place. This is in direct contrast to how Jephthah will handle a similar situation in his day—fight it out!

However, Gideon "crosses the line" when he crosses over (ʿābar)[62] the Jordan. If the narrative about Gideon had ended in 8:3, Gideon, despite his character flaws as exposed in 6:11–8:3, would appear as a heroic judge, on the par with some of the previous major judges. But the narrative continues, and the degeneration of Gideon is documented. Motivated by revenge, Gideon's excesses are spelled out in the extreme reprisals on his own countrymen. While the cities did not give support, the punishment is unduly severe and sets a precedence for the later excesses of Jephthah. Also, the foil of Jether harks back to the more timid earlier Gideon, but now he is a mighty warrior who does not need God to help him.

GLORY TO GOD. We can be thankful that we have the example of Gideon's obedience and victory over the Midianites. The story of God's working through his call of Gideon to accomplish the victory in the Cisjordanian battle is an encouragement to Christians that God can use us to accomplish beneficial results for the kingdom of Christ. Positive examples of faith can enhance the application of faith in our lives. Marvelous is the victory when it is solely of God. Gideon and his puny three hundred were not the reason for the victory in this battle; rather, they were simply used by God to achieve *his* victory. When we trust God and see his great victory, so often in spite of us, we need to give him the glory.

The spirit of revenge. Unfortunately, the motive of revenge is too common in the annals of human history and in present-day conflicts. There are parts of the world where generations wait for the day when revenge can be

---

62. The term ʿābar can be used to designate a violation or transgression of God's law or covenant.

meted out on those who (in some cases) generations ago may have oppressed or taken advantage of their ancestors. Human nature looks for the opportunity to "make things right." The problem is that human nature is extremely sinful (cf. Jer. 17:9), and we rarely make anything "right."

Even in the little things of life—such as driving to work—we can find ourselves meting out revenge (mostly in the form of verbal expressions of a special kind for those who cut us off in traffic). But on a higher level where significant wrongs may have been incurred, we (yes, even Christians) sometimes look for ways "to get even." In the business world, this can take form in covert and overt repressions of our nemesis. Unfortunately, sometimes these forms become extreme and violent.

Such ways of revenge cannot be justified any more than Gideon's extreme measures of reprisal can be justified. God did not call Gideon to exercise revenge; he called him to deliver his people. He did do the latter, it is true, but he also did the former. Trusting God is not just trusting him for deliverance, but also for dealing in a positive way with those who may have wronged us. Only when we do this will the cycle of reprisal and counter-reprisal stop.

Gideon's torturous reprisals against Succoth and Penuel were an excessive response to people who doubted Gideon's ability to achieve the victory and feared the possible reprisals of Zebah and Zalmunna. In not supporting Gideon, the people of Succoth and Penuel end up receiving a similar fate to what they would have received if they had supported Gideon and Zebah and Zalmunna had brought reprisals on them. Yet note that Gideon's actions are the opposite of how God earlier acted toward him when he was full of doubt and fear. God showed incredible compassion and patience in dealing with his inordinate and obsessive fear and doubt. Yet Gideon showed no compassion or patience to the people of either city who were no different from him in terms of their doubt and fear.[63]

This is reminiscent of the parable of the unmerciful servant, who, after having been forgiven of the enormous debt to his master, showed no mercy on a fellow servant who owed him a small sum (Matt. 18:21–35). As we grow in Christ, we need to remember how the Lord has treated us (and how he still treats us!) and show this to others in like manner. Moreover, on the personal level, we are called on to forgive. This is difficult—our very nature rebels against such a thought. But more than God's way, it is saving. It frees us to live in a different manner.

---

63. This does not excuse the people of Succoth and Penuel from helping Gideon and his men; they should have helped. But Gideon's response is one of vengeance, and it is disgusting in light of where he had come from.

Judges 8:22−32

²²The Israelites said to Gideon, "Rule over us—you, your son and your grandson—because you have saved us out of the hand of Midian."

²³But Gideon told them, "I will not rule over you, nor will my son rule over you. The LORD will rule over you." ²⁴And he said, "I do have one request, that each of you give me an earring from your share of the plunder." (It was the custom of the Ishmaelites to wear gold earrings.)

²⁵They answered, "We'll be glad to give them." So they spread out a garment, and each man threw a ring from his plunder onto it. ²⁶The weight of the gold rings he asked for came to seventeen hundred shekels, not counting the ornaments, the pendants and the purple garments worn by the kings of Midian or the chains that were on their camels' necks. ²⁷Gideon made the gold into an ephod, which he placed in Ophrah, his town. All Israel prostituted themselves by worshiping it there, and it became a snare to Gideon and his family.

²⁸Thus Midian was subdued before the Israelites and did not raise its head again. During Gideon's lifetime, the land enjoyed peace forty years.

²⁹Jerub-Baal son of Joash went back home to live. ³⁰He had seventy sons of his own, for he had many wives. ³¹His concubine, who lived in Shechem, also bore him a son, whom he named Abimelech. ³²Gideon son of Joash died at a good old age and was buried in the tomb of his father Joash in Ophrah of the Abiezrites.

Original Meaning

THE FINAL SECTION A' (see introductory comments to 6:1−9:57) narrates the conclusion to Gideon's life after the two victories (8:22−32). The Gideon cycle formally concludes at 8:28, which states that the enemy was subdued before the Israelites and the land had rest for forty years (cf. 3:10b−11, 30; 4:23; 5:31). Thus, 8:29−32 is an epilogue on Gideon's life and a transition to Abimelech, who is the complement to the Gideon account.

Immediately after the slaughter of the last pair of kings, Gideon's countrymen offer him dynastic rule. It only stands to reason in their thinking that the slayer of kings has ipso facto achieved a kingly status. Besides, Zebah and

Zalmunna called him someone "with the bearing of a prince" (i.e., royalty). Gideon has reached his zenith of power with this offer of kingship. But verse 22 is more than just an dynastic offer to Gideon; it also states the reason (in the Israelites' thinking): "because you have saved [$yš^c$] us out of the hand of Midian."

Throughout the Gideon account, it has been forcefully stated or implied that it is Yahweh who saves ($yš^c$) Israel, not Gideon or the Israelites themselves (cf. 7:2, which explains the reason for the second troop reduction in these terms). Therefore, the Israelites make three errors in their proposition. (1) As Gideon correctly notes, he cannot be king over them, since Yahweh is already supposed to be king over them.[64]

> I will not rule [$mšl$] over you,
> nor will my son rule [$mšl$] over you.
> The LORD will rule [$mšl$] over you.

The threefold repetition of "rule" ($mšl$) makes Gideon's reply emphatic.

(2) Though Gideon does not mention this, Yahweh is the One who has saved Israel, not him. Yet Gideon does not correct their mistake regarding who has saved them. By allowing that statement to stand, he endorses it de facto. It is particularly ironic that Gideon allows this to stand when even a Midianite soldier knew it was Yahweh who was delivering Midian into Gideon's hand.[65] It is also ironic that from the moment he crossed the Jordan, Gideon acted more and more like a king, especially in his dispensing of summary punishments on those who resisted his authority. In crossing the Jordan he had already exceeded his commission and begun to move toward the kind of rule that is now formally offered to him.[66] Even the Midianite kings recognize the kingly posture of Gideon in 8:18b: (lit.) "men like you [Gideon], just like the form of the king's sons."

(3) According to the Israelites' logic, the one who has saved them should be their king. The text shows that the Israelites do exactly the opposite of what their own thesis requires, for their deliverer has been Yahweh. This is

---

64. Nevertheless, Gideon's answer is the interpretive key for the double conclusion's refrain "in those days there was no king. . . ." It demonstrates that the term *melek* ("king") has a double entrende: not only is there a lack of a human monarch, but more importantly in the context of the covenant theocracy, there is no spiritual king (which, of course, should be Yahweh!). This heightens the second part of the refrain "and every man did what was right in his own eyes," which is far more comprehensible when one understands *melek* to refer to the Lord. Simply having a human king does not deter people from "doing what is right in their own eyes."

65. Gunn, "Joshua and Judges," 114.
66. Webb, *The Book of the Judges*, 152.

summed up in the next section, in 8:34: The Israelites "did not remember the LORD their God, who had rescued them."

Not only does Gideon let the Israelites' erroneous statement stand, he counters with his own request: Let "each of you give me an earring from your share of the plunder."[67] The spontaneous response of the Israelites is weighty: about 42.5 pounds (19.38 kilograms) of gold.[68] Gideon then makes this gold into an ephod, which immediately becomes a "snare" or lure (*môqēs*) not only to himself and his family but to "all Israel," leading to the establishment of an all-Israel idolatrous cult in Ophrah, the very place where Gideon began his career by tearing down the idolatrous altar of Baal (6:25–32).

Gideon's concocting of an ephod from the Midianite (Ishmaelite) golden earrings is analogous to Aaron's casting the golden calf from the Egyptians' golden earrings (Ex. 32:1–8).[69] Both Gideon and Aaron's idols served as illegitimate cult objects for Israel to worship after a miraculous deliverance that Yahweh worked on Israel's behalf. If Gideon is somewhat like Moses in his calling, he is definitely like Aaron in this act.

The precise nature of "the ephod" in this passage is unclear. The Hebrew term *'ēpôd* simply means "a garment" (as clearly suggested by its Akkadian cognate *epattu*, which is used in Old Assyrian texts to refer to the costly garments worn by high officials or garments clothing cult images of the gods).[70] In the Old Testament, *'ēpôd* often refers to the high-priestly garment with the breastplate (e.g., Ex. 28:6–21), but it can also refer to a general priestly type garment (cf. 1 Sam. 2:18; 22:18; 2 Sam. 6:14). Perhaps Gideon's ephod refers to a high-priestly type garment with an unusual degree of gold ornamentation or to a replica of the high-priestly garment made of pure gold.[71] However,

---

67. The parenthetical statement at the end of verse 24 notes that it was "the custom of the Ishmaelites to wear gold earrings." The term "Ishmaelites" is probably used as a parallel designation or a metonymy in general for "the Midianites, Amalekites and other eastern peoples" (6:3, 33; 7:12; 8:10; cf. Gen. 37:25–36; 39:1). In fact, the designation "the eastern peoples" (*bʰnê qedem*) is used as a summarizing appositive: "Midian and Amalek, the easterners"; see Boling, *Judges*, 124–25.

68. For the shekel weight (11.4 grams or .4 ounces), see R. Kletter, *Economic Keystones: The Weight System of the Kingdom of Judah* (JSOTSup 276; Sheffield: Sheffield Academic Press, 1998).

69. See Gunn's discussion and note the prohibition of Deut. 17:17 against a king amassing for himself silver and gold ("Joshua and Judges," 114).

70. *CAD*, E, 183. Interestingly, the Old Assyrian *epattu* is equivalent to Hittite *ipantu*. One Hittite text refers to an *ipantu* of silver (i.e., "a garment of silver"). This could indicate that silver was used for the garment's ornamentation or that the garment itself was made out of silver fibers. See H. A. Hoffner Jr., "Hittite Equivalents of Old Assyrian *kumrum* and *epattum*," *WZKM* 86 (1996): 154–56.

71. As suggested by A. E. Cundall, *Judges: An Introduction and Commentary* (Downers Grove, Ill.: InterVarsity, 1968), 123. Compare the Hittite garment (*ipantu*) described in the previous note.

the amount of gold and the verbs used to describe Gideon's action ("made," "set up") mitigate against this understanding.[72] Here, "ephod" is perhaps used figuratively to represent not only the garment that clothed a sacred image but also the image over which the garment was draped.[73]

Since in biblical texts there is a connection between the ephod and the Urim and Thummim used by the high priest for obtaining divine guidance, it is possible that Gideon's ephod had divinatory intentions. Webb concludes that Gideon's request for materials to make an ephod is a logical sequel to his assertion that Yahweh shall rule Israel. Thus he argues: "If Yahweh is to rule he must be inquired of, and it is apparently with the intention of facilitating such inquiry that Gideon makes an ephod and puts it in Ophrah where Yahweh had appeared to him and an altar to Yahweh now stood."[74] In this way, the ephod became Gideon's permanent fleece.

The unusual use of the term calls attention to it, suggesting further implications. Earlier in the narrative, Gideon was clothed with Yahweh's Spirit; here "ephod" suggests he symbolically clothes the idol (and perhaps by extension, himself) with another "value": gold. Klein argues:

> The Yahwist value, his spirit, is not truly *within* Gideon and he drops the Yahwist mantle for one of gold. Furthermore, though Gideon refuses the title of leader, the object he has made from the gold is one associated with kingship. Most telling is the reference to "all Israel" playing the harlot after the ephod, worshipping a tangible in shape (idol) or value (gold) instead of the intangible source. Although the booty Gideon collects is passed "through" fire (melted), the purpose is not holy purification but reshaping for human glorification. The ephod does not memorialize Yahweh or even the people of Israel: it is Gideon's ephod and an ironic realization of Yahweh's warning against self-glorification (7:2).[75]

Although the narrator does not reveal the nature of the image, some interpreters argue that it seems most likely that Gideon reconstructed the shrine to Baal that he had torn down earlier at Yahweh's command (6:25–32).[76] This does fit the response of the Israelites, who "prostitute themselves" (*znh*) to it and for whom it becomes a "snare" (*môqēš*). However, there is no indication that either altar to Yahweh is destroyed, and it seems

---

72. Klein, *Triumph of Irony*, 64; Block, *Judges, Ruth*, 300.

73. Block, *Judges, Ruth*, 300. For similar interpretations, see Klein, *Triumph of Irony*, 64–65; Boling, *Judges*, 158; Gray, *Joshua, Judges and Ruth*, 299.

74. Webb, *The Book of the Judges*, 152–53.

75. Klein, *Triumph of Irony*, 64–65.

76. Block, *Judges, Ruth*, 300.

better to understand the ephod as a syncretism of Yahwism and idolatrous practices.

Nevertheless, the irony and perversion of Gideon's actions should not be overlooked. Instead of glorifying Yahweh, who has clothed him with his Spirit (6:34), and properly worshiping him in a victory song as in the previous cycle, Gideon creates his own image and clothes it with pagan materials.[77] If Yahweh's altar effectively replaced Baal's altar at Ophrah, then Gideon's cult image, the ephod, effectively replaces the Asherah cult image. Thus, in addition to the foregoing discussion, Gideon's creation of the ephod was sinful in several ways:

(1) Gideon has no business creating an ephod because this is a priestly task. Gideon is not a Levite. He does not ask God whether to build the ephod but rather creates it for self-gratification. Underlying Gideon's desire to fill the office is a dull perception of the highest function of one man in relation to others.

(2) Gideon makes Ophrah a place of worship (see more on this below). If anything, the ephod should have been made by a priest and then used in the tabernacle in the worship of Yahweh. But Gideon places the ephod in his hometown of Ophrah.[78] He fully intends for the ephod to bring himself and his family glory. This undercuts the true worship of Yahweh at the tabernacle at Shiloh. Not only has Gideon robbed God of the full credit for the victory over the Midianites, but through the making of the ephod he robs God of the full and undivided worship due him at the tabernacle.

(3) Gideon makes the ephod on the basis of faulty human logic. On the reasoning that if Yahweh is to rule he must be inquired of, Gideon's apparent intention is the facilitating of such inquiry through the production of an ephod. Since Yahweh appeared to him in Ophrah and Gideon has already built an altar to Yahweh there, it logically follows in Gideon's thinking that this is the place to put the ephod. But this on-the-surface act of piety is based on ignorance of God's law, and the results are devastating for Gideon, his family, and the nation.[79]

---

77. Perhaps the image is supposed to represent Gideon himself, clothed with the Spirit of Yahweh.

78. As a replacement for the Baal altar and Asherah pole? In effect, the altar of Yahweh and Gideon's ephod served this purpose.

79. The motif of ignorance of God's law and its devastating results will recur in the Jephthah and Samson cycles. The Out-group judges show ignorance of the law (Torah) again and again. In the cases of Gideon and Jephthah, there may have been some right motivations (though tainted here and there with improper ones). In the case of Samson, he is ignorant and doesn't seem to care.

(4) The ephod became a snare (*môqēš*) to Gideon and his house. The term *môqēš* is used for the fowler's bait or lure. As Klein points out, the ephod

> symbolizes the lure to power that Gideon, as an Israelite, has rejected. It remains a snare to Gideon's family, which includes his son by a She-chemite concubine. Abimelech, more Canaanite than Israelite, is famil-iar with the idea of kingship; and since it had been offered his father and was symbolically evident in the trappings of his father's leader-ship—the ephod—Abimelech went after the bait. Most significantly, the ephod is a snare, a lure to worship a *tangible* in which the people have invested *value* and *form*. This ephod introduces a motif which gains in significance in the remaining narratives: Israel's increasing secession from ethical Yahweh worship to worship of humanity's self-determined values, its own creations. This motif represents a shift from "merely" worshipping the local gods with which the Israelites come into contact. Israel is no longer the innocent of the desert who is easily seduced into apostasy. Grown more confident, more worldly, more sophisticated, Israel creates its own trap, its own lure from Yahweh.[80]

(5) Gideon's sin causes others to sin. His false step toward self-gratifica-tion leads multitudes of people astray. The people come to Ophrah to wor-ship Gideon's ephod, not to seek and honor God. Thus, Gideon's faith is turned into a superstition.

(6) The ephod cult image prepared the Israelites for a rapid return to the worship of Baal. No sooner has Gideon died than the Israelites prostitute themselves again to the Baals (8:33).

At the beginning of the Gideon story, Ophrah is the hub of a clan cult, a family affair. At the end, it is a center for national religious prostitution (under Gideon's oversight). Thus things have come full circle. The final irony of the story is that Gideon, champion of Yahweh against Baal, presides over the national apostasy that after his death will become full-scale Baal worship again (the Israelites reject Yahweh outright and make Baal-Berith their god, 8:33). Therefore, Gideon's challenge to Baal has been answered in full, and Gideon himself has contributed significantly to the answer. The name Jerub-Baal has acquired an ironic twist: Baal has indeed taken up his own cause (6:31–32) with the unknowing participation of his adversary.

Hard on the heels of the description of Gideon's idol production[81] comes ironically the stereotyped frame components:

---

80. Klein, *Triumph of Irony*, 65.

81. Gideon's production, from plundered gold, of an illegitmate cult object that later becomes an object of Israel's (Manasseh's) cultic deviation foreshadows the scenario involv-

> Thus Midian was subdued before the Israelites
> and did not raise its head again ...
> [and] the land enjoyed peace forty years. (8:28)

While the cycle seems to be ending, in reality the seeds for its continuation are sown on either side of these statements. The introduction of the ephod worship above and now the narration in an epilogue (8:29–32), which relate the birth and naming of Abimelech, set the stage for the complementary sequel that follows. Even with the death of Gideon the story is not over. The conflict between Israel and Yahweh has not been resolved. In fact, we are basically back to where we began.

In the epilogue we read that "Jerub-Baal son of Joash went back home to live" (8:29),[82] which seems to imply that Gideon retires into private life in an attempt to honor his commitment that Yahweh, not he, is to rule Israel. This retirement presumably takes place soon after he has installed the ephod in Ophrah. However, the details of Gideon's family life contradict his action. Although he declines kingship outwardly (8:23), his actions show that he craves this honor for himself. He acquires a considerable harem, which produces seventy sons (8:30).[83] The accumulation of wives was common among ancient Near Eastern monarchs, but a specific violation of the model for kingship in Deuteronomy 17:14–20. Additionally, to support such a harem and its "seventy" sons, one must have the resources of a king! Thus Gideon's lifestyle contradicts his words.

Furthermore, as though a harem of about fourteen women or more is not enough,[84] Gideon also has a Shechemite concubine, who gives birth to a

---

ing Micah's making from stolen silver the private cult objects that the Danites come to worship in Judg. 17–18. See O'Connell, *The Rhetoric of the Book of Judges*, 153.

82. Block understands this as a subtle indication of Gideon's rule as king (*Judges, Ruth,* 300–301).

83. Cf. the seventy vassal kings of the lord of Bezeq in 1:7 and the seventy sons/grandsons of Abdon in 12:14. The number "seventy" may have been used in the ancient Near East as symbolic of an ideal or perfect royal household. For example, the Samalian Aramaic inscription of Panamuwa refers to the killing of the "seventy brothers of his father" (see K. L. Younger Jr., "The Panamuwa Inscription," *COS*, 2.37). Cf. also 2 Kings 10:1–11, which mentions the execution of the seventy sons of Ahab. In this case, the number plays an "actual" role in the story since in Judg. 9:5, Abimelech will murder his "seventy brothers" with the help of "seventy empty and reckless men," hired with "seventy pieces of silver" donated by the Shechemites to Abimelech. For further discussion, see J. C. de Moor, "Seventy!" in *"Und Mose schrieb dieses Lied auf": Studien zum Alten Testament und zum Alten Orient. Festschrift für Oswald Loretz zur Vollendung seines 70. Lebensjahres mit Beiträgen von Freunden, Schülern und Kollagen,* ed. M. Dietrich and I. Kottsieper (AOAT 250; Münster: Ugarit Verlag, 1998), 199–203; and F. C. Fensham, "The Numeral Seventy in the Old Testament and the Family of Jerubbaal, Ahab, Panammuwa and Athirat," *PEQ* 109 (1977): 113–15.

84. Jacob had two wives plus two concubines, who gave birth to twelve sons; David had eight wives plus concubines that gave birth to nineteen sons. Thus it seems reasonable to posit that Gideon must have had, at the least, fourteen and perhaps as many as thirty wives!

son whom Gideon names Abimelech (8:31). While not explicitly stated in the text, it is nevertheless a clear inference this Shechemite concubine is a non-Israelite (i.e., a Canaanite). Abimelech's own carefully worded argument of 9:2 makes this clear. With Gideon, we have a cyclical/major judge who, in clear contradiction to Yahweh's commandment, is having conjugal relations with a Canaanite! And then he has the audacity to name the child Abimelech. Concerning the ironic twist in Abimelech's name, Block comments: "In spite of his pious comment, 'I will not rule over you' (8:23), all of these actions suggest the opposite. He behaves like an oriental king, a status memorialized in the name of his son, Abimelech ('my father is king')."[85]

In the birth and naming of Abimelech there is a further ironic contradiction between Gideon's public pronouncements and private practice. In fact, Gideon's pronouncement that "my son will not rule over you" has a special prognostication: Gideon says more than he knows for, in fact, his son will rule (*mšl*) over them (cf. 9:2, 6, 22).

Gideon's death and burial are recorded in 8:32. The deaths and burials are recorded for all the judges starting with Gideon (whether cyclical/major or noncyclical/minor judges). With the death and burial of Gideon, the stage is now open for his dynastic successor. Having lived his final days as an oriental ruler, Gideon has unleashed after his death the struggle for his "throne."

IN MANY WAYS, Gideon is enigmatic. He had some theological knowledge that Israel's government was to be a theocracy. Yahweh was to be the ruler, the king. So when the offer of dynastic rule comes to Gideon, he rightly declines the offer and proclaims that Yahweh is to rule over Israel. But then he implicitly accepts their assessment that he has saved them out of the hand of Midian, when he very well knows otherwise. Thus he usurps Yahweh's victory for himself. He takes glory away from God and attributes it to himself. Gideon is the direct cause why the Israelites fail to remember Yahweh their God, who has rescued them (8:34)! When we take credit for something that God did, we usurp God's place and cause others to not remember the Lord who has done good things for them. We cause others to lose their vision of God.

Gideon's request for some of the plunder of gold indicates that he recognizes his opportunity. Why not get some personal benefit out of these

---

85. Block, "The Period of the Judges: Religious Disintegration Under Tribal Rule," 50. There may be an even deeper level of wordplay in the name; see J. P. Fokkelman, "Structural Remarks on Judges 9 and 19," 33–45, esp. 33–34.

willing souls? Besides, has he not risked his life—especially with only three hundred men—to save these people? A little donation to help offset his personal investment would not be too much to expect.

When God has done a mighty act on our behalf, the glory belongs to him. No other judge before or after him receives a donation of the plunder. Gideon has no right to make this request. Although he has answered the Israelites correctly concerning the issue of dynastic rule, his actions contradict his answer. Very simply, Gideon is a hypocrite.

In the next section, we will see that the Israelites do not show kindness to the house of Jerub-Baal. Perhaps, the Israelites feel (wrongly, of course) that they have done enough for Gideon and his family by giving some of the plunder to him when he made his request.

Perhaps the most incredible thing in this narrative is Gideon's production of the ephod. The "wrongness" of its construction is registered above. In making this idol, Gideon causes others to sin and ensnares his own family. The devastation this causes is only hinted at here. It will take another (lengthy) story to elucidate its outcomes.

HYPOCRISY. We can have our theology right and yet live as hypocrites. This is not to say that it is okay to have wrong theology (that's another problem that this text does not directly address). But our lifestyle should match our words. There is perhaps nothing that causes people to turn away from Christianity more than the hypocrisy of some of those who profess Christ. People make enough excuses not to trust in Christ without those in the church giving them ammunition!

In not correcting the people as they give him credit for the victory over the Midianites, Gideon takes what did not belong to him—God's glory. He causes others not to give God the credit. What a contrast to the Song of Deborah, in which Yahweh receives the honor and praise that he is due and which is sung just before the Gideon account. When God works through us, whether in a formal or informal ministry situation, we must give him the honor and glory. The deep-rooted pride of achievement can blur our vision as to how we got to where we are. God has gifted men and women, and therefore whatever they accomplish ultimately redounds to his credit. The athlete, the intellectual, the businessman, the preacher— all owe their achievements and accomplishments to God's endowment. Gideon should have been content with being used to help accomplish the defeat of the Midianites. Instead, he denies God and seizes the acclaim of his countrymen.

The apostle Paul challenges us: "So whether you eat or drink or whatever you do, do it all for the glory of God" (1 Cor. 10:31). Whether it is a promotion, an accomplishment, a recognition, or a success, the Lord should be the first to receive the glory. To glorify God is the whole duty of humankind. Jesus prayed, "I have brought you glory on earth by completing the work you gave me to do. And now, Father, glorify me in your presence with the glory I had with you before the world began" (John 17:4–5). Gideon and his puny three hundred did not win the battle; the Lord did. Thus all boasting should have been in the Lord (Jer. 9:23–24; 1 Cor. 1:31; 2 Cor. 10:17).

Cause of sin. This passage is also a warning about being the cause of sin among the body of believers. God knows that sin will come. Nonetheless, one should not be the cause of any stumbling in the body, for God takes the source of sin in the body seriously. This warning crosses the centuries. God holds the source of such sin totally accountable. The church today is, on the one hand, prone to pay too little attention to the details concerning doctrinal teachings in God's revelation. This response puts the community at risk. Often practical mistakes ensue because theological errors stand behind them. On the other hand, practical errors may occur, even with "correct" theology. When this happens, it immediately undercuts the theology. It causes others to sin. The sequel to the story of Gideon (i.e., the story of Abimelech) will document the repercussions of Gideon's sin. As with him, when we cause others to sin, the destructive consequences wreak havoc throughout our families, our communities, or our nation.

Those who are called to leadership in the kingdom of God face a constant temptation to exchange the divine agenda for personal ambition. Ironically, the more impressive one's achievements for God, the greater the temptation. Gideon began to behave as if the victory had been achieved by "the sword of Gideon" rather than by "the sword of the Lord." Unfortunately, Lord Acton's famous saying that "power corrupts, and absolute power corrupts absolutely" is often true in the church. Too often in their dealings with others, Christian preachers, teachers, leaders, elders, and deacons exhibit their egos rather than the person of Christ.

This text makes it clear that Gideon was able to resist the obvious temptation to rule over the Israelites, at least in his initial reaction. But he fell prey to something more subtle, which eventually brought about the same damage. Often it is not the obvious temptation that brings about our demise into sin, but the subtle, more nuanced, and more sophisticated temptation that is our undoing. Vigilance for both is the Christian's call.

Judges 8:33–9:57

※

NO SOONER HAD Gideon died than the Israelites again prostituted themselves to the Baals. They set up Baal-Berith as their god and ³⁴did not remember the LORD their God, who had rescued them from the hands of all their enemies on every side. ³⁵They also failed to show kindness to the family of Jerub-Baal (that is, Gideon) for all the good things he had done for them.

⁹:¹Abimelech son of Jerub-Baal went to his mother's brothers in Shechem and said to them and to all his mother's clan, ²"Ask all the citizens of Shechem, 'Which is better for you: to have all seventy of Jerub-Baal's sons rule over you, or just one man?' Remember, I am your flesh and blood."

³When the brothers repeated all this to the citizens of Shechem, they were inclined to follow Abimelech, for they said, "He is our brother." ⁴They gave him seventy shekels of silver from the temple of Baal-Berith, and Abimelech used it to hire reckless adventurers, who became his followers. ⁵He went to his father's home in Ophrah and on one stone murdered his seventy brothers, the sons of Jerub-Baal. But Jotham, the youngest son of Jerub-Baal, escaped by hiding. ⁶Then all the citizens of Shechem and Beth Millo gathered beside the great tree at the pillar in Shechem to crown Abimelech king.

⁷When Jotham was told about this, he climbed up on the top of Mount Gerizim and shouted to them, "Listen to me, citizens of Shechem, so that God may listen to you. ⁸One day the trees went out to anoint a king for themselves. They said to the olive tree, 'Be our king.'

⁹"But the olive tree answered, 'Should I give up my oil, by which both gods and men are honored, to hold sway over the trees?'

¹⁰"Next, the trees said to the fig tree, 'Come and be our king.'

¹¹"But the fig tree replied, 'Should I give up my fruit, so good and sweet, to hold sway over the trees?'

¹²"Then the trees said to the vine, 'Come and be our king.'

¹³"But the vine answered, 'Should I give up my wine, which cheers both gods and men, to hold sway over the trees?'

¹⁴"Finally all the trees said to the thornbush, 'Come and be our king.'

¹⁵"The thornbush said to the trees, 'If you really want to anoint me king over you, come and take refuge in my shade; but if not, then let fire come out of the thornbush and consume the cedars of Lebanon!'

¹⁶"Now if you have acted honorably and in good faith when you made Abimelech king, and if you have been fair to Jerub-Baal and his family, and if you have treated him as he deserves—¹⁷and to think that my father fought for you, risked his life to rescue you from the hand of Midian ¹⁸(but today you have revolted against my father's family, murdered his seventy sons on a single stone, and made Abimelech, the son of his slave girl, king over the citizens of Shechem because he is your brother)—¹⁹if then you have acted honorably and in good faith toward Jerub-Baal and his family today, may Abimelech be your joy, and may you be his, too! ²⁰But if you have not, let fire come out from Abimelech and consume you, citizens of Shechem and Beth Millo, and let fire come out from you, citizens of Shechem and Beth Millo, and consume Abimelech!"

²¹Then Jotham fled, escaping to Beer, and he lived there because he was afraid of his brother Abimelech.

²²After Abimelech had governed Israel three years, ²³God sent an evil spirit between Abimelech and the citizens of Shechem, who acted treacherously against Abimelech. ²⁴ God did this in order that the crime against Jerub-Baal's seventy sons, the shedding of their blood, might be avenged on their brother Abimelech and on the citizens of Shechem, who had helped him murder his brothers. ²⁵In opposition to him these citizens of Shechem set men on the hilltops to ambush and rob everyone who passed by, and this was reported to Abimelech.

²⁶Now Gaal son of Ebed moved with his brothers into Shechem, and its citizens put their confidence in him. ²⁷After they had gone out into the fields and gathered the grapes and trodden them, they held a festival in the temple of their god. While they were eating and drinking, they cursed Abimelech. ²⁸Then Gaal son of Ebed said, "Who is Abimelech, and who is Shechem, that we should be subject to him? Isn't he Jerub-Baal's son, and isn't Zebul his deputy? Serve the men of

Hamor, Shechem's father! Why should we serve Abimelech?
²⁹If only this people were under my command! Then I would
get rid of him. I would say to Abimelech, 'Call out your whole
army!'"

³⁰When Zebul the governor of the city heard what Gaal
son of Ebed said, he was very angry. ³¹Under cover he sent
messengers to Abimelech, saying, "Gaal son of Ebed and
his brothers have come to Shechem and are stirring up the
city against you. ³²Now then, during the night you and
your men should come and lie in wait in the fields. ³³In the
morning at sunrise, advance against the city. When Gaal
and his men come out against you, do whatever your hand
finds to do."

³⁴So Abimelech and all his troops set out by night and took
up concealed positions near Shechem in four companies.
³⁵Now Gaal son of Ebed had gone out and was standing at the
entrance to the city gate just as Abimelech and his soldiers
came out from their hiding place.

³⁶When Gaal saw them, he said to Zebul, "Look, people
are coming down from the tops of the mountains!"

Zebul replied, "You mistake the shadows of the mountains
for men."

³⁷But Gaal spoke up again: "Look, people are coming down
from the center of the land, and a company is coming from the
direction of the soothsayers' tree."

³⁸Then Zebul said to him, "Where is your big talk now,
you who said, 'Who is Abimelech that we should be subject to
him?' Aren't these the men you ridiculed? Go out and fight
them!"

³⁹So Gaal led out the citizens of Shechem and fought
Abimelech. ⁴⁰Abimelech chased him, and many fell wounded
in the flight—all the way to the entrance to the gate. ⁴¹Abim-
elech stayed in Arumah, and Zebul drove Gaal and his brothers out of Shechem.

⁴²The next day the people of Shechem went out to the
fields, and this was reported to Abimelech. ⁴³So he took his
men, divided them into three companies and set an ambush in
the fields. When he saw the people coming out of the city, he
rose to attack them. ⁴⁴ Abimelech and the companies with him
rushed forward to a position at the entrance to the city gate.
Then two companies rushed upon those in the fields and

struck them down. ⁴⁵All that day Abimelech pressed his attack against the city until he had captured it and killed its people. Then he destroyed the city and scattered salt over it.

⁴⁶On hearing this, the citizens in the tower of Shechem went into the stronghold of the temple of El-Berith. ⁴⁷When Abimelech heard that they had assembled there, ⁴⁸he and all his men went up Mount Zalmon. He took an ax and cut off some branches, which he lifted to his shoulders. He ordered the men with him, "Quick! Do what you have seen me do!" ⁴⁹So all the men cut branches and followed Abimelech. They piled them against the stronghold and set it on fire over the people inside. So all the people in the tower of Shechem, about a thousand men and women, also died.

⁵⁰Next Abimelech went to Thebez and besieged it and captured it. ⁵¹Inside the city, however, was a strong tower, to which all the men and women—all the people of the city—fled. They locked themselves in and climbed up on the tower roof. ⁵²Abimelech went to the tower and stormed it. But as he approached the entrance to the tower to set it on fire, ⁵³a woman dropped an upper millstone on his head and cracked his skull.

⁵⁴Hurriedly he called to his armor-bearer, "Draw your sword and kill me, so that they can't say, 'A woman killed him.'" So his servant ran him through, and he died. ⁵⁵When the Israelites saw that Abimelech was dead, they went home.

⁵⁶Thus God repaid the wickedness that Abimelech had done to his father by murdering his seventy brothers. ⁵⁷God also made the men of Shechem pay for all their wickedness. The curse of Jotham son of Jerub-Baal came on them.

Original Meaning

THE COMPLEMENTARY SEQUEL to the Gideon story is the story of his son Abimelech (introduced in the epilogue to the Gideon story). In many regards, the story is a prolongation of the Gideon account, resolving a number of issues raised by that account. Almost everything in this story can be used as an argument for "the position that Judges 9 is not an independent narrative, but a part of, and the crown of, the Gideon act"[1] (for further comments see the introduction, pp. 37–41).

1. Fokkelman, "Structural Remarks on Judges 9 and 19," 38.

The Abimelech account, as the sequel to Gideon and conclusion to the fourth cycle, introduces for the first time in Judges an oppressor who is internal rather than external. Thus the work of the cyclical/major judge, Gideon, is undone by the antijudge, "king" Abimelech, Gideon's son. The theme of the account is clearly that of retribution: God causes the evil that Abimelech and the men of Shechem did to rebound upon their own heads (9:56–57).[2] While there is a general critique of kingship, the account is obviously a rejection of Abimelech's particular style of kingship. As Webb observes,[3] Abimelech's crime is not that he becomes king, nor is the Shechemites' crime that they make him king. The issue is their treacherous acts against Gideon, the person God chose to be his agent of deliverance from the Midianites. The issue is primarily spiritual, not political.

The Abimelech account contains a prologue (8:33–35), followed by two parts: Part 1: Abimelech's rise (9:1–24) and Part 2: Abimelech's decline (9:25–57). Each of these two parts has a threefold division with interlinks between the divisions. Thus the Abimelech narrative (8:33–9:57) displays the following structure:

Prologue (8:33–35)

Part 1: Abimelech's Rise (9:1–24)
    A Abimelech's Treachery Against the House of Jerub-Baal (9:1–6)
    B Jotham's Four-Part Plant Fable and Conditional Curse (9:7–21)
      a. The Fable (9:7–15)
      b The Curse (9:16–21)
    C The Narrator's First Assertion (9:22–24)

Part 2: Abimelech's Demise (9:25–57)
    A Shechem's Two Acts of Treachery Against Abimelech (9:25–41)
    B The Fable's Fulfillment: Abimelech's Three Acts of Repression (9:42–55)
      a. First Act of Repression (9:42–45)
      b. Second Act of Repression (9:46–49)
      c. Third Act of Repression (9:50–55)
    C The Narrator's Second Assertion (9:56–57)

---

2. Webb, *The Book of the Judges*, 154.
3. Ibid., 159.

The Prologue (8:33–35)

THE PROLOGUE PROVIDES a context for understanding this complex and lengthy passage. No sooner has Gideon died than the Israelites again prostitute themselves after the Baals. In fact, a particular "Baal" is now introduced. The Israelites set Baal-Berith (lit., "lord or master of the covenant") as their god and do not remember Yahweh. Lewis has recently discussed the identity and function of Baal-Berith (also called El-Berith in 9:46).[4] He argues that preference should be given to the deity El-Berith. It is more likely that the phrase *ba῾al b᷾rît* (lit., "lord of the covenant") served as an epithet of the god El-Berith, a patron god who has established a kinship bond with the "citizens/lords of Shechem" (*ba῾alê š᷾kem*).[5]

Thus the narrator's choice of using Baal-Berith is to play on the "Baals" of the previous sentence and to create an ironic twist on the idea of covenant. Covenant faithfulness was the problem at the beginning of the cycle (cf. 6:7–10) and is still the problem after the death of Gideon. The parallelism of the statements of 8:34 and 35 is informative in comparing the Israelites' covenantal unfaithfulness to Yahweh to their covenantal unfaithfulness to Gideon's household.

> [The Israelites] did not remember the LORD their God, who had rescued them from the hands of all their enemies on every side.

> They also failed to show gratitude [*῾āśâ ḥesed*, lit., "deal faithfully with"] to the family of Jerub-Baal (that is, Gideon) for all the good [*ṭôb*] he had done for them.

In other words, the Israelites have forgotten Yahweh's past mighty saving acts on their behalf and have displaced Yahweh, their covenant God, with this "Baal of the Covenant," reversing the order of divine-human relationships. This lack of remembrance will be clearly demonstrated in the remainder of the account, which exhibits no knowledge of or any allegiance to Yahweh at all.[6] They have also failed to remember Yahweh's human agent in the deliverance, Gideon, and have acted in disloyalty to his family, in contradiction to relational norms (*ḥesed*).[7]

There can be no doubt that Gideon's ephod has contributed greatly to this rapid return to "Baalism" and the resultant unfaithfulness to his family. The statement in 8:35 that Jerub-Baal ("Let Baal contend") was none other than

---

4. T. J. Lewis, "The Identity and Function of El/Baal Berith," *JBL* 115 (1996): 401–23.

5. It is possible that the Shechemite deity El Berith is represented by one of the bronze idols discovered in excavations at Shechem (ibid., 423).

6. Polzin, *Moses and the Deuteronomist*, 174.

7. Cf. 1:24, where the phrase *῾āśâ ḥesed* (to show loyalty/faithfulness) occurs.

Gideon ("Hacker") is only a grim reminder of the major judge's failure against Baalism. The worship of Baal has overrun the very ones whom God delivered from Midian. The complete lack of the mention of the name "Gideon" in Judges 9 is a significant choice and omission; only "Jerub-Baal" occurs (9:1, 2, 5 [2x], 16, 19, 24, 57). The narrator also brings a Baal motif into his story by regularly calling Abimelech's supporters "citizens" (lit., *ba'alê š'kem*, the masters/lords of Shechem). To the original hearers, the repetition in sound of *ba'al*, even though in these occurrences[8] the god is not in view, must have had the effect of reminding them of the tremendous Baalism permeating Israel at this time.

On top of this, it is from the temple of Baal-Berith that the citizens/lords take the "seventy shekels of silver" to finance the slaughter of Gideon's seventy sons (see below). Obviously, the number of shekels corresponds to the number of victims, indicating that the value of each human life to Abimelech was only worth one shekel.

The Rise of Abimelech (9:1–24)

PART 1, WHICH relates the rise of Abimelech, has a threefold division, with interlinks between the divisions (vv. 1–6, 7–21, 22–24).

The first division (9:1–6) narrates Abimelech's treachery against the house of Jerub-Baal (9:1–6). As O'Connell recognizes,[9] it has a series of components that will be repeated as the story progresses to its climax in 9:53–55.

   a. People/citizens' action: Abimelech comes to Shechem accompanied by his "brothers." He claims closer genealogical ties with Shechem than those of the current ruler and incites its lords to conspire with him against the sons of Jerub-Baal. The citizens/lords of Shechem trust the conspirator (9:1–2)

   b. Report: Abimelech's offer is told to the citizens/lords of Shechem (9:3a)

---

8. The use is extensive: 9:2, 3, 6, 7, 23 (2x), 24, 25, 26, 39, 46, 47, 51 (reference not to Shechem but Thebez). Note that in 9:57 the naming is changed from "the citizens/nobles of Shechem" (*ba'alê š'kem*) to "the men of Shechem" (*'anšê š'kem*). Fokkelman argues that this may have been to honor God, who is the agent there and has let nemesis take its course in order to fulfill Jotham's curse ("Structural Remarks on Judges 9 and 19," 35 n. 7). Note the similar expression in Josh. 24:11 and 1 Sam. 23:11–12. In both Judg. 9 and 1 Sam. 23 it describes a group or assembly that makes decisions for Shechem and Keilah. Such an expression occurs at Amarna and Ugarit, where it refers to a group distinguished from the king or chief leader (Moran, *The Amarna Letters*, 175, n. 5). The usage is also observable in Phoenician and Old Aramaic inscriptions.

9. O'Connell, *The Rhetoric of the Book of Judges*, 143–46.

c. The citizens' hearts are inclined toward Abimelech, since he is their brother (9:3b)

d. People/citizens supporting violence: They give Abimelech seventy pieces of silver from the temple of Baal-Berith (9:4a)

e. Leading to an entrance: Abimelech hires reckless men, who follow him; he enters his father's home at Ophrah (9:4b–5a[1])

f. Fatality/depopulation: Abimelech kills his (paternal) brothers, the seventy sons of Jerub-Baal, on a single stone (9:5a[2])

Jotham, the youngest son, escapes by hiding (9:5b)

Citizens/lords of Shechem and Beth Millo make Abimelech king by the great tree and pillar in Shechem (9:6)

Abimelech goes to Shechem with a purpose. He addresses two groups in order to enlist them in his plot: his mother's brothers (*^{3a}ḥê ^{3}immô*) in Shechem and all his mother's clan (*kol-mišpaḥat bêt-^{3a}bî ^{3}immô*, lit., "all the clan of his mother's father's house"). Thus he appeals to the immediate family as well as the complete extended family or clan. The first group with its maternal orientation was foreshadowed in Gideon's words of 8:19. The second was foreshadowed in Gideon's reply to Yahweh that "my clan[10] is the weakest/poorest in Manasseh, and I am the least/youngest in my family [*bêt ^{3}abî*, lit., my father's house]" (6:15).

Putting it mildly, Abimelech is not happy with his position as an outsider, and he is dominated by a ruthless craving to change his marginal existence (cf. Jephthah later). He deliberately splits his next-of-kin into two irreconcilable groups: the mother's side, whom he uses to raise him to the throne, and the father's side, whom he, with deep hatred, murders in the most gruesome execution imaginable. The scene is inconceivable—one victim after another after another on the same single stone. Body upon body upon body dispatched with unspeakable horror. Again and again and again until all seventy (save one) have been eliminated from possible usurpation of "his throne."[11] He is inspired by his father in the desire to be king, but at the same time he rejects, hates, and despises his father.[12]

---

10. The words translated "clan" are different (*^{3}elep* in 6:15 and *mišpaḥâ* in Judg. 9:1) but are synonyms (cf. their usages in 1 Sam. 10:19, 21).

11. Abimelech was certainly of the spiritual mold of Lamech (Gen. 4:23–24). Note that the number seventy is used in this murderous vignette too. Moreover, there are a number of similarities and differences between Abimelech's murder of his brothers and Jehu's murder of the sons of Ahab (2 Kings 10). See Block, *Judges, Ruth*, 312–13.

12. The total disregard for the fifth commandment ("honor your father and mother") is evident.

Abimelech's invocation to his relatives to remember (*zākar*) that he is their brother (i.e., of the same stuff as they) stands in opposition to the Israelites forgetting (*lōʾ zākar*, lit., "did not remember") the true God in 8:34.

The contrast between Abimelech's and Jotham's thinking is heightened by the fable and its curse. In Abimelech's encouragement to the citizens/lords of Shechem to make him king, he appeals to human logic: (1) By contrasting the seventy to the one, he infers that monarchy (lit., "one man") is better (*ṭôb*) than oligarchy (highly debatable in light of the results in his case!); (2) he argues that the factor of kinship is a good principle to act on politically ("remember, I am your flesh and blood," 9:2). In light of other passages, especially a number of passages in 2 Samuel, this is also a highly questionable basis for such action. The use of "better/good" (*ṭôb*) in 9:2 is ironically in direct contrast to "good" (*ṭôb*) in 8:35. Gideon had done "good"; Abimelech's "good" is to murder the seventy sons of Gideon.

Abimelech will not speak again in the story until almost the very end (9:48, 54). In all of these speeches, he commands others to take pains on his behalf. The first (9:2) and the last (9:54) reveal Abimelech's preoccupation with his image. In the case of this first speech, he is concerned with his "electability" image.

The citizens/lords of Shechem trust the conspirator and give him seventy shekels of silver (about 1.75 pounds or .798 kilograms) to hire reckless adventurers (lit., "men empty and audaciously reckless," cf. 11:3). With their aid Abimelech murders his (paternal) brothers, the seventy sons of Jerub-Baal, on a single stone. But one of these sons, Jotham (the youngest son), escapes by hiding. With seemingly all opposition removed, Abimelech is made king (*melek*) by the citizens/lords of Shechem and Beth Millo[13] by the great tree and pillar[14] in Shechem (9:6).

The second division (9:7−21) contains Jotham's four-part plant fable and conditional curse. After 9:6, Abimelech has lost all initiative. In fact, as already stated, he will not speak again until the end of the story (9:48, 54). The one who seemed so strong through all his machinations will, in the end, be quickly swept aside.

Jotham, the lone survivor of the Ophrah massacre, appears on the scene in 9:7 to confront the men of Shechem with the evil they have done.[15] Invoking the men of Shechem to listen, he appeals to a higher moral plane—the issues of honor, integrity, honesty, and a divine standard of justice—and

---

13. Beth Millo may refer to an earth-filled platform on which walls and other large structures were built, perhaps here identical to the stronghold in 9:46 (Boling, *Judges*, 171).

14. Cf. NRSV, "by the oak of the pillar" (cf. Josh. 24:26).

15. Jether, Gideon's eldest child (8:20), and Jotham, his youngest son, stand in contrast to their father and Abimelech. Thus Jether vs. Gideon is parallel to Jotham vs. Abimelech.

calls on God to witness their response. He adapts a four-part plant fable to his purpose (9:7–15), but the main point of the speech is not in the fable itself but in its application to the present situation in the form of a curse (9:16–20).

There is a close functional parallel, then, between the speech of Jotham and the speech of the prophet[16] in the Gideon narrative (6:7–10). The prophet brings an indictment against the Israelites in the name of Yahweh; Jotham brings an indictment against the men of Shechem in the name of Jerub-Baal. The fable and its application have many covenantal overtones. Ironically, Jotham's speech is delivered in a city that has a reputation for covenantal ceremonies (cf. Josh. 8 and 24) and boasts a temple to El-Berith ("god of the covenant").

In the context of the passage, not only is Jotham's speech crucial, so is his very name. Jotham is a combination of the short form of the divine name Yahweh and the short form of the term *tāmîm*, with the resultant meaning of "Yahweh is perfect, blameless, honest, has integrity."[17] One of the key words in Jotham's speech is also this *tāmîm*.

Yahweh is blameless concerning the events that have transpired, as the prophet at the beginning of the cycle argues (6:7–10). He has acted with integrity and honesty. Abimelech and the people of Shechem (yes, even the Israelites throughout the cycle) have been dishonest, have lacked integrity, and are not blameless but guilty. Yahweh's indictment through the prophet has proved true, and Jotham's speech serves to highlight this all the more.

The fable itself (9:7–15) is relatively straightforward. The setting is related in 9:7, in which Jotham takes his place on the top of Mount Gerizim and shouts down to the Shechemites. In the fable, the trees go out to anoint a king over them. They approach four different plants (the first three of which have significant value in the Palestinian agricultural context, producing valuable products for human beings).[18] Each is offered the kingship, but the first three have a declining response: the olive tree (9:8–9), the fig tree (9:10–11), and the vine (9:12–13).[19] Finally, the trees make an offer to the thornbush (9:14),

---

16. Webb, *The Book of the Judges*, 155–56.

17. HALOT, 375.

18. For the olive tree and the vine, see Rafael Frankel, *Wine and Oil Production in Antiquity in Israel and Other Mediterranean Countries* (JSOTMS 10; Sheffield: Sheffield Academic Press, 1999).

19. The identity of these three is not important to the fable, since it is the fourth item that is the climax and focus of the fable. Two features—the breaking of an established rhetorical pattern and a content variation (i.e., the offer is not made to a valued member of the forest family)—have a significant rhetorical function. They indicate that verses 14–15 are the most important part, the rhetorical climax or focus of Jotham's presentation. See G. S. Ogden, "Jotham's Fable: Its Structure and Function in Judges 9," *BT* 46 (1995): 301–8, esp. 303.

whose response is parabolic (9:15). "If you really want to anoint me king over you, come and take refuge in my shade."[20]

This is a physical absurdity: How can trees get under the smidgen of shade supplied by a thornbush? And worse, to attempt to do so would only bring the pain of being pricked by its thorns. "But if not, then let fire come out of the thornbush[21] and consume the cedars of Lebanon!" This is another physical absurdity: How can fire come out of a thornbush and burn up an entire forest? Jotham's implied thrust, however, is this: Since the trees (i.e., the citizens/lords of Shechem) have done the absurdity of trying to make the thornbush (i.e., Abimelech) their king, then perhaps fire will come out of the thornbush and consume the trees and forest!

Jotham's application of the fable is contained in a curse (9:16–20). Verse 15 serves as the structuring basis for verses 16–20. The curse is conditional (though rhetorical). The conditional clause is stated twice (interrupted by a parenthetical history of the relationship between Gideon and the Shechemites). The clause contains two possible situations: (1) "if you [i.e., citizens/lords of Shechem] have acted honorably and in good faith when you made Abimelech king," and (2) "if you have been fair to Jerub-Baal and his family." The parenthetical aside demonstrates that the implied answer to the conditional clause is that the Shechemites have *not* acted with integrity in a blameless and honest manner.[22]

Jotham reminds them that Gideon took great personal risk—indeed, needing the prompting of God at every moment—yet the citizens/lords of Shechem "have revolted" against Gideon's family, murdering his sons and installing Abimelech, an illegitmate son (hence a "thorn"), to the throne. Verse 19 resumes the condition ("if then you have acted honorably . . .") and concludes with a sarcastic statement, "may Abimelech be your joy, and may you be his, too!" Verse 20, however, gives the second situation and the real,

---

20. Ironically, the phrase "in your/his shade" is used in the ancient Near East to mean "under the special protection of the king"—one of the traditional roles of monarchs. Compare the following passage from an Akkadian poem: "O the shade of the cedar, the shade of the cedar, the shelter of kings! O the cypress shade of the magnates! The shade of a sprig of juniper is shelter for my darling Nabu and for my fun and games!" See A. Livingstone, "Love Lyrics of Nabu and Tashmetu," in *COS*, 1.128.

21. The thornbush (*ʾāṭād*) can be identified with the *Ziziphus spinachristi*, a plant common in the northern part of Israel, especially on the eastern slopes of the adjacent plains of Samaria or with the *Rubus species*, a thorny and prickly plant. See K. L. Younger Jr., "אָטָד," *NIDOTTE*, 1:363–64. In the "Aramaic Wisdom of Ahiqar" there is a conversation between the bramble and the pomegranate tree.

22. Thus the first conditional clause, despite its positive form, is actually a null condition. It is the second conditional clause that indicates the point Jotham wishes to make, namely, that they acted in bad faith by making Abimelech their king.

intended curse: "But if you have not [and you haven't], then let fire come out from Abimelech and consume you, citizens/lords of Shechem and Beth Millo, and let fire come out from you, citizens/lords of Shechem and Beth Millo, and consume Abimelech!"

Because the crime has already been committed and the outcomes are irrevocable, the curse is really a pronouncement of sure judgment. While Jotham's escape in 9:21 to the indeterminate Beer ("well") removes him from the narration,[23] the narrator will now show how God takes up the cause of Jotham (9:23–24). Jotham's narrative absence means God's narrative presence so that at the end of the story the retribution brought on the evildoers is described as "the curse of Jotham son of Jerub-Baal" (9:57).

The narrator's first assertion (9:22–24). This third division of the narrative's Part 1 contains an assertion of the narrator. The laconic opening statement that "Abimelech ... governed Israel three years" (9:22) is especially significant in that the time period is by far the shortest of any oppression or judgeship in the book.[24] God does not put up with Abimelech and the Shechemites very long; his retribution is the swiftest in the book. "Israel" in this verse technically only refers to those Israelites who have recognized Abimelech's authority, that is, Shechem and its environs. But its use is certainly a means of the narrator to remind the reader that it was Israel's covenantal disloyalty and unfaithfulness that have led to these events (cf. 6:1–10).

God becomes personally involved in the affairs of Shechem in order to avenge the violence committed by Abimelech and the lords of Shechem against the members of Jerub-Baal's family. He intervenes by sending an "evil spirit" (*rûaḥ rā'â*)[25] between Abimelech and the citizens/lords of Shechem (9:23). Yahweh is the architect of the estrangement between Abimelech and Shechem's folk. Former allies become mortal enemies. Undeniably, he does this in order to bring revenge on Abimelech and the citizens/lords of Shechem for the murder of Jerub-Baal's seventy sons (9:24). In this way, the polar opposites of "good" (*ṭôb*) and "evil" (*ra'*) are played out in the narration: Gideon/Jerub-Baal had done "good" (*ṭôb*) to the Israelites (8:35), who repaid

---

23. And thus the only 'legitimate heir" to Gideon's rule disappears permanently from the scene.

24. In Gen. 34 (another story of Israelites and Shechem), it is "three" days between the time that a covenant is established and a devastating calamity comes on the city.

25. The phrase *rûaḥ rā'â* appears to have the nuance of "calamitous spirit." This phrase is used elsewhere in the Old Testament (1 Sam. 16:14–23; 18:10–12; 19:9; 2 Kings 19:7) and appears to indicate that this "bad," "calamitous spirit" produces negative and destructive effects on the object, i.e., unpropitious conditions. Here this *rûaḥ rā'â* produces enmity, distrust, and bad faith between Abimelech and the Shechemites. For further discussion see Block, *Judges, Ruth*, 323–324; idem, "Empowered by the Spirit of God: The Work of the Holy Spirit in the Historiographic Writings of the Old Testament," *SBJT* 1 (1997): 42–61.

it with evil (*ra*ᶜ); what Abimelech argued was "good/better" (*ṭôb*) (9:2) became evil (*ra*ᶜ) for the Israelites (9:23).

The Fall of Abimelech (9:25–57)

PART 2 RELATES the fall of Abimelech. Like Part 1, it has a threefold division with interlinks between the divisions (9:25–41, 42–55, 56–57).

The first division (9:25–41) describes Shechem's two acts of treachery against Abimelech (9:25–41). Both acts manifest roughly the same series of components as in the first division of Part 1 (9:1–6). Shechem's first act of treachery, whose narration is truncated, is described in 9:25.

> a. People/citizens' action: Citizens/lords of Shechem ambush travelers in Manasseh (9:25a)
> b. Report: The treachery is reported to Abimelech (9:25b)

Many of the details of this incident or plot are obviously omitted in the story as it now stands. It is now nothing more than a terse summary, but it does introduce two Hebrew key words: *rōʾš* (head, mountain top, company) and *ʾārab* (ambush). To put it simply, the Shechemites initiate hostilities against Abimelech—and this happens also immediately after God sends the "evil spirit" between Abimelech and the citizens/lords of Shechem.

Shechem's second act of treachery, given in full, is narrated in 9:26–41.[26]

> a. People/citizens' action: Gaal comes to Shechem accompanied by his brothers. He claims closer genealogical ties with Shechem than those of the current ruler and incites its lords to conspire with him against Abimelech. The citizens/lords of Shechem trust the conspirator (9:26–29)
> b. Report: Treachery is reported to Abimelech by Zebul, who counsels coming at night with all his people to ambush at morning (9:30–33)
> c. Abimelech's division of his people into four companies (*roʾšîm*) to lay an ambush against Shechem (9:34)
> d. People/citizens supporting violence: interchange between Gaal and Zebul as Abimelech and his people emerge from the ambush (9:35–38)
> e. Leading to an entrance: Abimelech slays many while chasing Gaal to the entrance of Shechem (9:39–40)
> f. Fatality/depopulation: Abimelech stays in Arumah while Zebul expels Gaal and his brothers from Shechem (9:41)

---

26. Again, following O'Connell's observations (*The Rhetoric of the Book of Judges*, 143–50).

The entrance of the character Gaal is deliberately patterned after that of Abimelech in 9:1–3. This is a comment not only on the character traits of Abimelech (i.e., both Abimelech and Gaal are raw opportunists, who resort to dirty politics in their quest for power), but also on the character qualities of the citizens/lords of Shechem (disgruntled and fickle). In the midst of a reveling festival in the temple of El-Berith they curse[27] Abimelech (who has only ruled for three years). Seizing the moment, Gaal (like Abimelech earlier) uses rhetorical questions to heighten his popularity and undermine that of the current government. Gaal claims to be more of the genealogical stuff akin to the Shechemites than Abimelech: "Isn't he [Abimelech] Jerub-Baal's son, and isn't Zebul his deputy? Serve the men of Hamor, Shechem's father!" (9:28).[28]

Zebul, Abimelech's second, the governor of the city, hears of the treachery and reports it to Abimelech. Zebul advises that a night deployment may be in Abimelech's best interest with an ambush at morning (9:30–33). This is the only time in the story that anyone is recorded telling Abimelech what to do—and this coming apparently from his evil twin (so to speak).

Abimelech's response is quick. He deploys his troops (the same vagrants whom he hired [9:4b], plus whoever else among the Israelites that he can muster) into four companies (*ro'šîm*) in order to ambush the city (9:34). In the early morning, Gaal observes their movements and appeals for confirmation to Zebul, who shrugs it off as "the shadows of the mountains." But a second look causes Gaal to reassert his observation, being more specific in his description.[29] At this point, Zebul retorts: "Where is your big talk now. . .? Go out and fight them!" (9:35–38).

Gaal leads the citizens/lords of Shechem out to fight Abimelech, but Abimelech's ambush (Zebul's original idea) succeeds, and Abimelech slays many while chasing Gaal to the entrance of Shechem (9:39–40). Abimelech

---

27. This verb is the eighth and climactic verb in the series of verbs describing the activities of the Shechemites.

28. Hamor was the Hivite ruler before the Israelites ever settled in or around Shechem, according to Gen. 33:19; 34:1–31; Josh. 24:32. Thus if Abimelech could play the ethnicity card, so could Gaal.

29. Cf. Ezek. 38:12. The NIV's "the center of the land" has commonly been understood as "the navel of the earth,' which may have been a reference to Mount Gerizim, the center of the land of Canaan. Eshel and Erlich have identified the phrase used here with Ras e-Tagur, on the southwestern corridor of Jebel el-Kabir, northeast of Shechem. See H. Eshel and Z. Erlich, "Abimelech's First Battle with the Lords of Shechem and the Question of the Navel of the Land," *Tarbiz* 58 (1988–1989): 111–16. Block has recently argued that the phrase in question should be understood as "elevated ground" and refers to some "elevated plateau without external fortifications" (*Judges, Ruth*, 328–29).

stays in Arumah[30] while Zebul expels Gaal and his brothers from Shechem
(9:41). At this, one might expect the conflict between Abimelech and
Shechem to be resolved since the antagonist Gaal is out of the picture.[31] But
Abimelech is the son of Jerub-Baal—as much as he despised his father—
and his personal revenge is only now beginning.

The second division (9:42–55) narrates the fulfillment of Jotham's
curse: Abimelech's three acts of repression and his death at the hand of a
woman. Again, each act of repression uses the same series of components
as in Part 1, Division A (9:1–6). Abimelech's first act of repression is
described in 9:42–45.[32]

    a. People/citizens' action: The people go out to the field (9:42a)
    b. Report: Their vulnerability is reported to Abimelech (9:42b)
    c. Abimelech divides his people into three companies (*ro˒šîm*) to lay
        an ambush in the field (9:43a)
    d. People/citizens supporting violence: Abimelech [and his people]
        emerge from the ambush (9:43b)
    e. Leading to an entrance: Abimelech takes position at the entrance
        to Shechem while two companies (*ro˒šîm*) slay those in the field
        (9:44)
    f. Fatality/depopulation: Abimelech captures Shechem that day,
        killing its people, tearing down the city, and sowing it with salt
        (9:45)

The next day the common people (*˓am*) of Shechem resume their daily
routine and go out into the fields. Abimelech divides his troops into three
companies (*ro˒šîm*) and sets another ambush in the fields. The use of the term
"people" (*˓am*) indicates that this group includes women. Moreover, it is a
group hardly expecting battle; hence they are no doubt unarmed (except
for some agricultural implements). Abimelech's company seizes the city gate
and the other two companies (*ro˒šîm*) press the attack. The helpless victims
(not unlike Gideon's sons) are slaughtered in the fields, putting up whatever
feeble resistance that they can.

But the massacre is great, and the city is captured and destroyed. The
scattering of salt over the ground of the city is an attempt to condemn it to
perpetual barrenness and desolation (cf. Deut. 29:23; Ps. 107:33–34; Jer.

---

30. Arumah was apparently Abimelech's base of operations. Most scholars feel that
Arumah sat on top of Jebel el-˓Urmeh.

31. From the following incidents, it is clear that opponents to Abimelech are still in certain quarters of the city.

32. O'Connell, *The Rhetoric of the Book of Judges*, 148–53.

17:6; Zeph. 2:9).[33] Hence, just as Abimelech has made Jerub-Baal's family barren, so now he makes Shechem barren. Again, one might expect the conflict between Abimelech and Shechem to be resolved since the city is out of the picture. But Abimelech is the son of Jerub-Baal—as much as he despised his father—and his personal revenge is still far from over.

Abimelech's second act of repression is related in 9:46—49. It too uses the same series of components as the first act.[34]

a. People/citizens' action: Citizens/lords of the tower of Shechem enter the stronghold of the temple of El-Berith (9:46)

b. Report: Vulnerability of the citizens/lords of the tower of Shechem is reported to Abimelech (9:47)

c. Abimelech and his people ascend Mount Zalmon, where he cuts off branches and sets them on his shoulder (9:48a)

d. People/citizens supporting violence: Abimelech orders his people to imitate him in cutting off and carrying branches (9:48b—49a[1])

e. Leading to an entrance: Abimelech, followed by his people, sets fire to the stronghold (9:49a[2])

f. Fatality/depopulation: A thousand men and women of the tower of Shechem die (9:49b)

On hearing of the demise of the people, the citizens/lords in the tower of Shechem (= Beth Millo) enter the stronghold of the temple of El-Berith (9:46).[35] On hearing this, Abimelech perceives their vulnerability (9:47). He and his people ascend Mount Zalmon. He cuts off branches and sets them

---

33. For the destruction and salting of cities in the ancient world, see S. Gevirtz, "Jericho and Shechem: A Religio-Literary Aspect of City Destruction," *VT* 13 (1963): 52–62. Compare the Roman salting of the land after the destruction of Carthage in the Third Punic War.

34. O'Connell, *The Rhetoric of the Book of Judges*, 148–53.

35. L. E. Stager has recently reassessed the archaeological data concerning the temple structures at Shechem and concluded that G. E. Wright's temple 2, which he associated with the temple of El-/Baꜥal-Berith, was actually part of a ninth-eighth century B.C. building known as the "Granary" (Building 5900) and that Wright's temple 1, the great fortress (or *migdāl*) was the temple of El-/Baꜥal-Berith. See L. E. Stager, "The Fortress-Temple at Shechem and the 'House of El, Lord of the Covenant,'" in *Realia Dei: Essays in Archaeology and Biblical Interpretation in Honor of Edward F. Campbell, Jr. at His Retirement*, ed. P. H. Williams Jr. and T. Hiebert (Atlanta: Scholars Press, 1999), 228–49. For Wright's earlier discussion, see G. R. H. Wright, "Temples at Shechem," *ZAW* 80 (1968): 26; G. E. Wright, *Shechem: The Biography of a Biblical City* (New York: McGraw Hill, 1965), 95–100. For further discussion, see E. F. Campbell Jr., *Shechem II: Portrait of a Hill Country Vale* (ASOR Archaeology Reports 2; Atlanta: Scholars Press, 1991), 107–9; idem, "Judges 9 and Archaeology," in *The Word of the Lord Shall Go Forth: Essays in Honor of David Noel Freedman in Celebration of his Sixtieth Birthday*, ed. C. Meyers and M. O'Connor (Winona Lake, Ind.: Eisenbrauns, 1983), 263–67.

on his shoulders (9:48a). Now, for the first time since 9:2, Abimelech speaks. As before it is a command: "Quick! Do what you have seen me do!" (cf. Gideon's instructions in 7:17). His troops imitate him as though in a trance (9:48b–49a). They pile these branches up against the stronghold and set them on fire (9:49a). All of the people, men and women—one thousand in number—die in the conflagration (9:49b). Once again, one might expect the conflict between Abimelech and Shechem to be resolved since the stronghold of Beth Millo has been removed from the picture. But Abimelech is the son of Jerub-Baal—as much as he despised his father—and his personal revenge is still far from over. In fact, one is beginning to wonder if anything can stop it![36]

Abimelech's third act of repression is given in 9:50–55. It also uses the same series of components as the first act, although with variation as the conflict finds its resolution in Abimelech's death at the hand of a woman.[37]

> Abimelech besieges and captures Thebez (9:50)
> a People/citizens' action: The men and women and the citizens/lords flee to the tower and ascend to the roof (9:51)
> c Abimelech comes to the tower and fights against it (9:52a)
> e Leading to an entrance: Abimelech approaches the tower entrance to burn it with fire (9:52b)
> Abimelech's skull (*rōʾš*) is crushed by a stone thrown by a woman (9:53)
> Abimelech orders his servant to kill him lest a woman be credited with his death (9:54a)
> f Fatality/depopulation: Abimelech is stabbed and dies (9:54b)
> The men of Israel see that Abimelech is dead and return home (9:55)

In Blitzkrieg fashion, the narrative states that Abimelech goes, besieges, and captures Thebez (9:50).[38] All the people (men and women) flee to the tower and ascend to the roof. Abimelech attacks the tower and approaches the entrance to the tower in order to burn it (9:52). Based on the repetition of the previous reprisals, the reader's expectations are set for another of

---

36. Cf. the destruction of the tower of Peniel (Judg. 8:17).

37. O'Connell, *The Rhetoric of the Book of Judges*, 160–62.

38. Cf. 2 Sam. 11:21. The location of Thebez (*tēbēṣ*)) is uncertain. Some identify it with modern Tubas, thirteen miles northeast of Shechem. Others understand the name to be a corruption of "Tirzah" (*tirṣâ*), six miles northeast of Shechem. Campbell has recently suggested a tell about 2 km north of modern Tubas and that the name shifted to its present location during the Roman period. See Campbell, *Shechem II*, 107.

Abimelech's massacres. However, unexpectedly the narrative introduces "a woman" (lit., "one woman," or "a certain woman," [iššâ ʾaḥat]), who drops an upper millstone on Abimelech's head and cracks his skull (rōʾš) (9:53). Stunned, Abimelech orders his servant to kill him lest a woman be credited with his death. He is stabbed and dies (9:54). Then, when the troops see that Abimelech is dead, they return home without completing the attack on Thebez (9:55).

The climax of the Abimelech account is clearly found in 9:53. This verse is the point of convergence for several phrases. Abimelech argued, "Which is better for you: to have all seventy of Jerub-Baal's sons rule over you, or just *one man* (ʾîš ʾeḥād)?" Ironically, it is now stated in 9:53 that "a woman" (lit., "one woman" [ʾiššâ ʾaḥat]) drops (or perhaps better "heaves," since lit. in Heb., "throws") an upper millstone on him. Abimelech had slaughtered the sons of Gideon on a single stone (ʾeben ʾeḥāt, 9:5, 18), and his skull is crushed by this single "upper millstone" (lit., "a stone of riding," pelaḥ rekeb).[39]

The upper millstone, made of basalt or sandstone, was heavy (though its weight varied, depending on whether it was part of a "hand mill" or a "grinding house mill," with the latter being the heavier). Grinding was delegated to slaves in larger households and wives in smaller ones. For most women, grinding was a daily recurring domestic task. It was humiliating for a man to do such work (cf. the humiliation of Samson grinding in 16:21).[40] Therefore, it was also humiliating to be struck by such a stone hurled by a woman. As in the case of Jael in 4:21, this woman uses what is normally a domestic, everyday-type object and turns it into weapon (cf. also Shamgar in 3:31).

The fire with which Abimelech destroys the tower of Shechem in 9:47–49 is obviously the fulfillment of Jotham's curse about fire consuming the citizens/lords in 9:20. But what about the fulfillment of Jotham's curse about Abimelech being consumed by fire? The answer appears to be in a pun on the word "woman" (ʾiššâ). The word for fire is ʾēš. Thus, the words for woman (ʾiššâ) and fire (ʾēš) form a wordplay.[41] Abimelech's attempt to burn the tower of Thebez with fire (ʾēš) "backfires" when a woman (ʾiššâ) drops a stone on his head (rōʾš).

That verse 53 is the climax is also reinforced by a numeric depreciation in conjunction with another wordplay. The millstone that crushes the despot's head (rōʾš) denotes the end of a decreasing series of numbers. When Abimelech quells Gaal's rebellion, he has "four" companies (rōʾšîm) at his disposal (9:34). The next day he sends "three" companies (rōʾšîm) against the She-

39. O'Connell, *The Rhetoric of the Book of Judges*, 161.
40. K. van der Toorn, "Mill, Millstone," in *ABD*, 4:831–32.
41. See further Fokkelman, "Structural Remarks on Judges 9 and 19," 38–39.

chemites, with "two" of the companies (ro'šîm) slaughtering the citizens/lords in the field (9:43–44). For a short while Abimelech may think he is powerful, but then, ironically, the "one" woman drops her upper millstone and smashes his ("one") head (rō'š) (9:53).[42]

Abimelech's preoccupation with his image is played out in his death. Fearing that a stigma will be attached to him, he commands his armor-bearer to stab him "so that they can't say, 'A woman killed him.'" Ironically, this did not happen, for even in another biblical passage, his death is credited to the "certain woman" (see 2 Sam. 11:21). Not all that many years later, the first king of Israel will make a similar request to his armor-bearer on Mount Gilboa, not many miles from Thebez, to spare him the disgrace of being captured alive by the Philistines, though this armor-bearer, in contrast to Abimelech's, refuses (1 Sam. 31).

In the end, the man who had shamelessly played the female card to seize the throne (9:1–2) shamefully falls victim to a representative of this gender. In fact, the story of Abimelech, the macho man, is framed by two women: the first, who gave him life (8:31), the second, who took it (9:53).[43]

The narrator's second assertion (9:56–57). The last division (C) is the narrator's final assertion. God has repaid the evil committed by Abimelech[44] and the evil committed by the men of Shechem. The curse of Jotham, son of Jerub-Baal, comes on them. By attributing Abimelech's death to God, the narrator interprets the nameless woman of Thebez both as a divine agent by which the curse is fulfilled and as a surrogate for the Shechemites, whom the curse has identified as the source of Abimelech's demise.[45]

Ironically, the Baal name (Jerub-Baal) is conjoined with the Yahwistic name (Jotham) in 9:57.[46] At the end of the Gideon account and especially at the beginning of the Abimelech account, it looked as if Baal had, in fact,

---

42. The term rō'š is a key word in the story (vv. 7, 25, 34, 36, 37, 43, 44[2x], 53, 57). Its range of meanings ("head," "mountain top," "company") allows it to serve as another binding element for the story as well as to hint at this final denouement, when Abimelech is struck on the head and mortally wounded while the evil of the Shechemite leaders also falls (like a stone) upon their heads. See Ogden, "Jotham's Fable: Its Structure and Function in Judges 9," 302.

43. Block, *Judges, Ruth*, 334.

44. Fokkelman ("Structural Remarks on Judges 9 and 19," 34) points out that Abimelech has desperately craved to prove himself a worthy successor to his father by living up to one interpretation of his name ("the king [Gideon] is my father"), only to experience the original intention of the name ("The king [divine] is my father").

45. Though it must be remembered that the Shechemites were unquestionably the (twice) instigators of Abimelech's demise that eventually led to his death.

46. O'Connell points out the structural (chiastic) as well as thematic parallels between 9:23–24 and 9:56–57 (*The Rhetoric of the Book of Judges*, 167–69).

contended and won. But as the sequel to the Gideon story—the finale to the Gideon/Abimelech cycle—ends, Yahweh proves himself never to have abdicated his throne. Rather, he is the ultimate King, who can easily undo both the egotistical ambition of an Abimelech—the outgrowth of Gideon's sin— and the impotent Baalism, with which the Israelites so quickly apostasize (as manifested in Joash's Baal altar or the Shechemites' temple of Baal/El-Berith, both of which lie destroyed by the end of the cycle).

The primary theme of the Abimelech account is the notion of revenge: "getting even" (when in the human context) or "retribution" (when in the divine context). The pattern of divine retribution in the cycles section so far has been one of sin → punishment → compassion → deliverance. In the Abimelech narrative, however, the pattern appears to be sin → exact retribution. Ironically, the Israelites as a whole benefit from the retribution worked upon their bramble king: "When the Israelites saw that Abimelech was dead, they went home" (9:55).

The process of retribution has had the precision of a surgical operation. Those directly responsible have been destroyed. Retribution brings the evil to an end, and normal life can be resumed. As though waking from a nightmarish zombie state, the Israelites see that Abimelech is dead and go home. It is Israel's salvation from itself (and in this, it foreshadows the catastrophic need of the same in the double conclusion in Judges 17–21).

Yahweh himself has had to resolve two complications that result from Gideon's covenantal failings—his ephod production with its consequent return to Baalism and his conjugal relations with a Canaanite woman. The moral degeneration within this major judge cycle underscores how great the unmerited favor of the Lord is toward Israel.

Bridging Contexts

DIVINE LEVEL. Whereas the course of events may seem to be determined by the free decisions and stratagems of the characters in the story, this is not the case. Through a few well-placed evaluative comments, the narrator makes clear that God is in charge. He is in sovereign control whether the Israelites acknowledge him or not. If Shechem is torn by civil war and Abimelech himself is slain, the narrator attributes this to God, whose hand may be hidden to those involved in the story but in retrospect is obvious to the biblical (or more precisely the Deuteronomic) perspective. Thus the events in the story move unswervingly toward God's intended outcome.

In the larger context of the whole Gideon/Abimelech cycle, God demonstrates his kingship in spite of the Israelites' rejection of him and worship of

Baal, whether before Gideon or after him. At the end of Judges 8 and the beginning of Judges 9, it may appear as though Yahweh has lost, with Gideon making his ephod and the Israelites returning to the worship of the Baals as soon as Gideon is dead. But Yahweh has not abdicated his throne.

After the death of Gideon, the Israelites do not show covenant loyalty or faithfulness to God or other humans. They demonstrate disregard for God's covenant and for the house of the leader whom the Lord raised up on their behalf. Humanity's tendency is to quickly forget all the good that others (human or divine) may do for them. When the Israelites make Baal/El-Berith their god, breaking their covenant with Yahweh to enter into a covenant with a Canaanite deity, they become spiritually Canaanites. In such a situation, with the enemy being within rather than external, God withdraws his gracious hand. God gives the Israelites the king they deserve, and he gives Abimelech the people he deserves. What characterized the Israelites in general characterizes their leader, Abimelech, who manifests no regard for familial loyalty and certainly none for God. Certainly the culture in which we live today does not encourage loyalty to either family or God.

Human level. On the human level, Abimelech's problem runs much deeper. His problem is not simply a disregard of or an apathy toward human and heavenly fathers. Rather, it is a profound hatred of both. Rooted in hatred for his father, Gideon, he is dominated by a ruthless craving to change his marginal existence. His total disdain for the fifth commandment ("honor your father and mother") motivates him to plot the demise of all seventy of his half-brothers on his father's side. He attempts to compensate for his marginality through the seizing of power. Thus anyone who opposes him becomes the focus of his anger and hatred. But as much as he despises and hates his father, he is nevertheless the son of Jerub-Baal, and his personal, unbridled revenge will only increase until he is slain by the "one woman."

Abimelech's appeal to the "citizens/lords" of Shechem in 9:2—"Remember, I am your flesh and blood" (*^{c}sm + bśr*)—has an ironic parallel in the Israelites appeal to David to be their king in 2 Samuel 5:1: "We are your own flesh and blood" (*^{c}sm + bśr*). Clearly in the case of Abimelech kinship is not a good principle to act on politically (well-illustrated by Jotham's fable). A far better principle is that of God's election, which David had and Abimelech did not.

While the Israelites are guilty of covenant disloyalty and act without integrity in their siding with Abimelech (who is the embodiment of guile), Yahweh appears blameless, having utter integrity in his dealings with human beings. Even in his sovereign opposition to Abimelech this is true. As an adversary to the wicked, God raises up opponents to wicked people.

It is important to remember that all of the slaughters and destructions that are described in chapter 9 are the result of Gideon's sins in 8:27–32.

What a comment on how destructive sin is! Gideon's sins have impacted his own family in the generation immediately after him in ways that he could not have remotely predicted. Serious reflection on this chapter of the book of Judges alone ought to encourage us to lay aside our sin.

DIVINE LEVEL. Sometimes it may appear as though evil is in control and that God has taken a vacation. Injustice dominates and wicked people, morally empty and reckless like Abimelech's hirelings, seem to prevail. Anyone living at the time of Abimelech's rule must have felt this way. Certainly many Christians living in Nazi Germany felt this way,[47] as does anyone living in a similar totalitarian state. And when believers forget the Lord and live according to the world's dictates, this only intensifies the power of the wicked. When believers choose this path, becoming functionally unbelievers, they may find that God allows them to get what they deserve, just as the Israelites experienced in the Abimelech story.

Believers' apostasy can never negate God's sovereignty. He is in control whether they acknowledge him or not, just as he is in control whether unbelievers acknowledge him or not. The Lord moves things to his intended outcome, and whatever gods have been used to replace him will prove to be worthless in the day of trouble, just as Baal/El-Berith proved to be for the Shechemites, who took refuge in his temple from Abimelech.

Human level. This story clearly demonstrates that any leader who raises himself or herself up through evil processes can expect that the Lord will eventually bring retribution. This may be much sooner than later; but whatever the case, it will take place.

Our society today is indoctrinated to quickly forget all the good things that may have been done for them. The entertainment business and the sports industry in particular create an environment where hard work and subsequent achievement are short-lived. This has even crept into the church pulpit, where one outstanding sermon after another may be the expectation,

---

47. There are some interesting parallels between Abimelech and Hitler. Both had severe hatred for their fathers, which manifested itself in the hatred of others. Both rose to power through the brutal elimination of their potential rivals. Both used morally empty and reckless men to aid their rise to power and in the maintaining of that power. Both made pacts with elite power structures: Abimelech with the lords of Shechem and Hitler with the German industrialists and bankers. Both of these elite power structures realized soon after their pacts that they had misjudged their coconspirator and had gotten much more than they had bargained for. Both Abimelech and Hitler brought almost total destruction on their lands. Both died ignominious deaths, leaving their lands in ruins.

and good overall ministry may be devalued. This is serious, but how much more dangerous it can be when a leader quickly forgets the good done for him or her. What characterizes the society in general often characterizes its leaders.

When individuals today act without loyalty and integrity, they may side with a leader who acts without loyalty or integrity. But the Lord, who is blameless and always acts with utter integrity in his dealings with human beings, will raise up sovereign opposition to such individuals. As an adversary to the wicked, God raises up opponents.

This text certainly underscores the results of sin. Our sins cannot be measured in a lifetime. They have an impact on the next generation and beyond. Whether it is our families or our communities or our nation, the impact will be felt. The harvest of the seeds of sin may not necessarily come in our generation but in innumerable ones beyond us.

Judges 10:1–5

AFTER THE TIME of Abimelech a man of Issachar, Tola son of Puah, the son of Dodo, rose to save Israel. He lived in Shamir, in the hill country of Ephraim. ²He led Israel twenty-three years; then he died, and was buried in Shamir.

³He was followed by Jair of Gilead, who led Israel twenty-two years. ⁴He had thirty sons, who rode thirty donkeys. They controlled thirty towns in Gilead, which to this day are called Havvoth Jair. ⁵When Jair died, he was buried in Kamon.

Original Meaning

WITH THE COMPLETION of the Gideon/Abimelech cycle the narrative now introduces two non-cyclical/minor judges: Tola son of Puah and Jair of Gilead.

Tola (10:1–2)

THE NOTICE ABOUT Tola immediately raises a question: From whom did Tola save (yšᶜ) Israel? Some scholars argue that Tola saved Israel from Abimelech's rule. Thus Webb states:

> Such details as are given of Tola's activity, together with the explicit reference to Abimelech's career which had immediately preceded strongly suggest that it was the disastrous effects of Abimelech's rule that Israel needed saving from, and that Tola did this by providing a period of stable administration. Tola saved Israel from disintegration.[1]

However, in my opinion, there is nothing in the text that indicates that Tola provided "good administration." This is not stated, nor can it be inferred from the statement that Tola "led [šp̄ṭ] Israel twenty-three years," since this is used for all the judges from Tola on, including Jephthah and Samson—hardly "good administrators!"[2] Underlying this interpretation is the presup-

---

1. Webb, *The Book of the Judges*, 160. See also Boling, *Judges*, 187.
2. This statement may be a type of replacement for the component statement "and the land had rest for X years," which occurs with the four cyclical judge narratives prior to the introduction of Tola.

position that there are "saving/delivering" judges and "administrative" judges, and Tola is forced into the latter even though the text describes him as "saving" (*yšʿ*) Israel. The verb *yšʿ* is used specifically with Othniel, Shamgar, Deborah, and Tola. Nothing in the text indicates that the other three are "good administrators." If, as we have discussed previously (see comments in the introduction), the judges (*šōpʿṭîm*) were to be both "deliverers" or "saviors" of their people from their enemies and "instigators," "catalysts," or "stimuli" for godly living (2:16–17), then these criteria should be applied to Tola (and the rest of the noncyclical/minor judges).

While it is true that the phrase "after ... Abimelech"[3] is special in that it provides a proper name in the slot after the preposition, the syntax is actually similar to that of Jair (10:3). The syntax argues for a one-two-three sequence in the minor judge presentations as described in the introduction (see p. 43).

While Tola and Puah are clearly clan names in the genealogy of the "sons of Issachar" in 1 Chronicles 7:1 (cf. also Num. 26:23), the fact that Tola is specified in Judges 10:1 as "a man of Issachar" seems to reflect an awareness of the possible confusion of the personal and clan names and that this is a personal name.[4] Also listed in 1 Chronicles 7:1 is a brother of Tola named Shimron (MT) or Shomron (LXX^L). The place name Shamir of Judges 10:2 is thought by some scholars to be identical with the site of Samaria (Shamir = Shemer = Shomron), since the clan may have bequeathed its name to the hill.[5]

However, there are difficulties with this view. (1) According to 1 Kings 16:24, Omri paid a considerable amount for the estate of Shemer—two silver talents (= 6,000 silver shekels) and then named the site Samaria after Shemer.[6]

---

3. As pointed out in the introduction, this phrase functions as a literary device, signaling narratorial rather than strict historical sequence.

4. The name appears to mean "worm," which Block suggests invites the reader to interpret this "lowly person" against the backdrop of the ambitious and pretentious Abimelech (*Judges, Ruth*, 338).

5. See Boling, *Judges*, 187; L. Stager, "Shemer's Estate," *BASOR* 277/278 (1990): 93–108. See also Z. Gal, "The Settlement of Issachar: Some New Observations," *Tel Aviv* 9 (1982): 79–86. According to excavations, the site of ancient Samaria was apparently occupied from an early period. Numerous oil and wine presses have been discovered, which appear to be a small part of a large and impressive estate with vineyards and olive yards occupying the surrounding slopes of the hill of Samaria. See R. E. Tappy, *The Archaeology of Israelite Samaria* (HSM 44; Atlanta: Scholars Press, 1992); Stager, "Shemer's Estate," *BASOR* 277/278 (1990): 93–108.

6. Based on noun pattern, it is more likely that Samaria (*šōmrôn*) is derived from Shemer (*šemer*) than from Shamir (*šāmîr*). For an analogy of the same name pattern in the book of Judges, note "Samson" derived from "Shemesh," i.e., "sun" (*šemeš šimšôn*).

(2) The site in Judges 10:2 is identified as being in Mount Ephraim, whereas Samaria was located in Manasseh.[7]

Whatever the case, what is "a man of Issachar" doing living (*yšb*) outside of his tribal allotment (whether in Ephraim or Manasseh)?[8] According to 10:1–2, Shamir was the ancestral estate of Tola. He lived, died, and was buried there. Obviously, some of the clans of Issachar had given up on occupying their own allotment (cf. Josh. 19:17–23) and had moved to another site, one they could easily occupy (cf. the Danite movement in Judg. 18).

In any case, Tola's socioeconomic status may be reflected in the fact that he is the only judge (cyclical or noncyclical) for which a genealogical connection is given back to a third generation: Tola, the son of Puah, the son of Dodo. Often in the Old Testament such a genealogical statement is an evidence of high social standing.

Yet the verb "to live" (*yšb*) is also reminiscent of the early career of Deborah ,who sat/presided (*yšb*) under her palm tree in Mount Ephraim and judged Israel (4:4–5). She, too, is said to have "arisen" when Israel was in disarray (5:7). Hence, Tola's career has positive links.

But from whom did Tola save Israel? As we have already pointed out, the text is deliberately ambiguous. Surely the narrator could have been more direct. But if the noncyclical/minor judges evince the same moral decline that the major judges do, then Tola's activity is likened to that of Ehud or Deborah/Barak. He is not of the same quality as a Shamgar, who "saved" Israel from a specific enemy. One can wish that the narrator supplied more information or was less ambiguous, but then such might have obscured his one-two-three pattern of minor judges and/or distracted from the cycles message of moral degeneration.

Jair (10:3–5)

THE SECOND OF the two noncyclical/minor judges mentioned in this section is Jair. The information about him is initially straightforward. Jair is Transjordanian (Gilead is located on the east side of the Jordan), and he "led [lit., judged] Israel twenty-two years." But then somewhat puzzling statements

7. From the biblical and archaeological evidence it seems that some of the tribe of Issachar may have settled together with Cisjordanian Manasseh, at least in the latter's territory in the northern Samarian hills (see Gal, "The Settlement of Issachar," 82–85). The strong connections of Issachar to this region are illustrated by the outstanding position this tribe held in the history of Israel. Several important kings came from Issachar, while Manasseh, a much larger tribe, contributed not even one king.

8. The choice to live in another tribal allotment will be encountered again in the double conclusion.

follow (lit. trans.): "He had thirty sons, who rode on thirty donkeys; thirty towns belonged to them. Their towns are called Havvoth Jair, which are in the land of Gilead to this day."[9] One thing is certain: Jair is a powerful man. In order to have thirty sons,[10] one has to have a harem. Following as it does so soon after the Gideon/Abimelech cycle, the issue of kingship seems to be clearly in view.

Thus the same problems with this that were encountered in the Gideon narrative seem to apply. (1) The accumulation of wives was the custom of ancient Near Eastern monarchs, and (2) the support of such a harem and its sons required monarchic-type resources. The statement that they "rode on thirty donkeys" seems humorous to modern, Western readers, but in its ancient Near Eastern context, monarchs in the Levant often rode on donkeys.[11] Appropriately, the sons of Jair ride on donkeys as evidence of their royal-type power. They have (i.e., possess and control) thirty cities, and this area has attained a regional name from Jair himself: Havvoth ("settlements of") Jair.

The obvious alliterative play on words between Jair (*yāʾîr*), donkey (*ʿayir*), and city/town (*ʿîr*) creates a humorous irony in the passage. Jair's concerns are not with "saving" Israel from anyone; instead, they are in building a power base for himself and his sons. This self-interest motif will recur throughout the remaining judges (both cyclical and noncyclical).

Ironically, Jair's power base quickly succumbs to the Ammonite oppression described in 10:6. As Webb puts it: "Small use Jair's pampered sons will be when the Ammonites invade! Then the Gileadites will search desperately for a fighter (10:17–18)." The description of Jair in 10:3–5 illuminates the offer made by the elders of Gilead to Jephthah ("you will be our head over all who live in Gilead" [11:8]) and explains why Jephthah finds it so attractive. The reality, however, is different for Jephthah from what it has been for Jair. Jephthah has to maintain his position by force (12:1–6) and has no family to parade his greatness; he is rendered childless by his own rash, manipulative vow (see next section).

---

9. The Hebrew text is difficult at this point. See Boling's discussion (*Judges*, 188).

10. Boling understands the "sons" to be metaphoric for "confederates." However, the notice concerning Ibzan (12:8–10) seems to argue convincingly that these were literal "sons," though the number "thirty" may, of course, be symbolic of an ideal royal family, though the narrator does not make this connection.

11. For biblical evidence see 2 Sam. 13:29 (David's sons on mules [*pered*]); 18:9 (Absalom as an acting king on his mule); 1 Kings 1:33 (Solomon on David's mule); cf. Gen. 49:11 (the donkey [*ʿayir*] of the one to whom the scepter belongs); Zech. 9:9 (a king will come riding on a donkey [*ʿayir*]); Matt. 21:5; Luke 19:30 (Christ's riding on a donkey). Cf. also Judg. 5:10. Evidence from the ancient Near East can be seen from Mari and elsewhere; see, e.g., ARM, 6:76:20–25; for discussion, see A. Malamat, *Mari and the Early Israelite Experience* (Oxford: Oxford Univ. Press, 1989), 2–4, 80.

While Jair is an anticipatory foil of Jephthah, Ibzan is a resumptive foil (12:8–10). Thus with only one child, a daughter at that, Jephthah is sandwiched between Jair with his thirty sons and Ibzan with his thirty sons and thirty daughters.

SEE THE COMMENTS at the end of the last three minor judges (12:8–15, pp. 278–79 below).

SEE THE COMMENTS at the end of the last three minor judges (12:8–15, p. 280 below).

Judges 10:6–12:7

🔥

Introduction to the Jephthah Cycle

THE JEPHTHAH NARRATIVE consists of five sections, with specific dialogues contained in each one.[1] Each of these dialogues contains a confrontation and a resolution. Thus, the power of the spoken word is a major motif in the cycle, in certain ways climaxing in Jephthah's vow. As a narratival link between the episodes, the Hebrew word ʿābar (with its full range of meanings, "to cross over," "to transgress") is used with increasing frequency.

"Contention" is also a major element in this cycle.[2] It begins with contention within Jephthah's own family, leading to his disinheritance. Next there is contention with his own tribe concerning his involvement in delivering them from the Ammonite oppression, which leads to his becoming the "head" of Gilead. This is followed by contention with another people, the Ammonites, which results in the defeat of the Ammonites but the sacrifice of his daughter. Finally, there is contention with another Israelite tribe, which results in the defeat and destruction of the Ephraimites. The fivefold structure appears to be:

A Israel vs. Yahweh (10:6–16) with specific dialogue in 10:10–16

   B The Ammonite threat—the elders' ill-considered oath, leading to the elders vs. Jephthah (10:17–11:11) with specific dialogue in 11:5–11

      C Jephthah vs. the Ammonite king (11:12–28) with specific dialogue in 11:12–28

   B′ The Ammonite defeat—Jephthah's ill-considered oath leading to him vs. his daughter (11:29–40) with specific dialogue in 11:34–38

A′ Jephthah vs. the Ephraimites (12:1–7) with specific dialogue in 12:1–4a

Judges 10:6–16

⁶Again the Israelites did evil in the eyes of the LORD. They served the Baals and the Ashtoreths, and the gods of Aram, the gods of Sidon, the gods of Moab, the gods of the Ammonites and the gods of the Philistines. And because the Israelites forsook the LORD and no longer served him, ⁷he

---

1. Webb, *The Book of the Judges*, 41–78. See also Polzin, *Moses and the Deuteronomist*, 176–81.
2. Block, *Judges, Ruth*, 381–82.

became angry with them. He sold them into the hands of the Philistines and the Ammonites, [8]who that year shattered and crushed them. For eighteen years they oppressed all the Israelites on the east side of the Jordan in Gilead, the land of the Amorites. [9]The Ammonites also crossed the Jordan to fight against Judah, Benjamin and the house of Ephraim; and Israel was in great distress. [10]Then the Israelites cried out to the LORD, "We have sinned against you, forsaking our God and serving the Baals."

[11]The LORD replied, "When the Egyptians, the Amorites, the Ammonites, the Philistines, [12]the Sidonians, the Amalekites and the Maonites oppressed you and you cried to me for help, did I not save you from their hands? [13]But you have forsaken me and served other gods, so I will no longer save you. [14]Go and cry out to the gods you have chosen. Let them save you when you are in trouble!"

[15]But the Israelites said to the LORD, "We have sinned. Do with us whatever you think best, but please rescue us now." [16]Then they got rid of the foreign gods among them and served the LORD. And he could bear Israel's misery no longer.

THE FIRST SECTION of the Jephthah account records a confrontation between Israel and Yahweh (10:6–16). The specific dialogue is carried out in 10:10–16. As in the previous cases of Ehud (3:7a) and Deborah/Barak (4:1a), the frame component statement ("Again the Israelites did evil in the eyes of the LORD") opens the cycle. In fact, of all the major judge cycles other than Othniel, the one concerned with Jephthah is the most abounding in cycle frame components. Thus the exposition narrative of 10:6–16, which sets the stage for the appearance of Jephthah, adds that the Israelites "served the Baals and the Ashtoreths [i.e., Astartes]" and other gods, and Yahweh "became angry with them" (10:6–7a; cf. 3:7).

Seven groups of foreign deities are listed in verse 6 (see table below). Interestingly, in Yahweh's response seven groups of oppressors[3] are listed in

---

3. Yahweh's remarks in 10:11–14 demonstrate that there were other oppressions that Israel suffered during the judges' era that are not fully narrated (or for that matter alluded to). The oppressions of the Egyptians, Amorites, Sidonians, and Maonites have no corresponding narration in the book. See the comments and discussion in the introduction (pp. 28–30). The attempt to root these oppressions in the history of the nation (esp. to the period of the judges) is to force the data beyond its intention.

verses 11–12, and there have been exactly seven judges up to this point in the book: Othniel, Ehud, Shamgar, Barak, Gideon, Tola, and Jair. The list of foreign oppressors is reminiscent of the seven-member stereotyped "list of nations" in Deuteronomy 7:1 (cf. Judg. 3:5), which may emphasize the complete spiritual corruption to which Israel has succumbed. This detailed description of Israelite apostasy serves double duty for both the Jephthah cycle and the Samson cycle (note the pairing) since the Ammonite and Philistine oppressions are perceived to have occurred simultaneously (10:7), although they lasted different lengths (eighteen years and forty years respectively, 10:8b; 13:1b).

Foreign deities (10:6)	Foreign oppressors (10:11–12)	List of "nations" (Deut. 7:1; cf. Judg. 3:5)
Baals	Egyptians*	Hittites
Ashtoreths (Astartes)	Amorites*	Girgashites
gods of Aram	Ammonites	Amorites
gods of Sidon	Philistines	Canaanites
gods of Moab	Sidonians*	Perizzites
gods of Ammonites	Amalekites	Hivites
gods of Philistines	Maonites*	Jebusites

*These oppressors/oppressions are not known from the book of Judges.

Only the Ammonites, Philistines, and Sidonians are mentioned in both the god and oppressor lists. The Ammonites and Philistines are specified as the current oppressors in 10:7, although it is the Ammonites who are especially in view in the narration of Jephthah's judgeship. This initial emphasis on the Ammonites and the fact that the Israelites are worshiping their gods (which include Milcom) sets the stage for the particular irony of this cycle, since Milcom was worshiped by child sacrifice (cf. the prohibitions of Lev. 18:21; 20:2–5).

As in the case of Gideon earlier, the severity of the oppression is detailed. Yahweh sells them into the hands of the Philistines and Ammonites, who shatter (*rāʿaṣ*) and crush (*rāṣaṣ*) them. These two alliterative and interrelated terms (*rāʿaṣ* and *rāṣaṣ*) form a hendiadys with the meaning something like "crushingly oppress" or "really crush." The term "crush" (*rāṣaṣ*)[4] is also used specifically in God's promised "curses" that he would bring on Israel in the event of covenantal unfaithfulness (Deut. 28:33). This oppression continues

---

4. This word is used in 9:53 of the "crushing" of Abimelech's head by the upper millstone.

in Gilead for eighteen years. The Ammonites even cross over the Jordan and fight against Judah, Benjamin, and the house of Ephraim. Israel is "in great distress" (cf. Judg. 2:15).

In the previous Gideon/Abimelech cycle, the Israelites' cry to the Lord (a standard frame component) is met, not with the raising up of a deliverer, but with Yahweh's confronting the Israelites' sinfulness through his prophet (6:7–10).[5] This time, however, it is Yahweh himself who chides and threatens not to deliver the Israelites since they seem to assume that Yahweh should more or less instantaneously restore them whenever they cry out to him even though they are so repeatedly given to idolatry (10:10–14). Hence, Yahweh's rebuke foreshadows the ironic consequences for Jephthah, the elders, and the nation—all of whom try in a mechanical manner to manipulate him to serve some private end. The statements in 10:14, "Go and cry out to the gods you have chosen. Let them save you ..." reveal the divine humor and sarcasm. The words are deftly chosen to mimic the people's pleas and to highlight the fundamental perversion in Israel's thinking and behavior. In this response to their cry from their distress, Yahweh demonstrates "the purely utilitarian and manipulative nature of their cry."[6]

What follows in 10:15–16 (Israel's confession of sin and removal of the foreign gods) seems on the surface to reflect a genuine repentance. But the use of similar wording in Yahweh's reprimand (10:12b–13a) demonstrates that "the putting away of foreign gods is part of the routine with which he has become all too familiar from previous experience."[7] Yahweh's explicit complaint in 10:12b–13a is not that Israel has failed in the past to remove foreign gods but that, after every saving intervention, they again forsake Yahweh and revert to serving other gods.[8] Thus, in this instance, Israel is attempting again to manipulate him to meet their immediate specific need of deliverance. Their hearts are not really devoted to God except for convenience.

The NIV's translation "And he could bear Israel's misery no longer" might better be translated "and his soul/person was short because of the efforts of Israel."[9] That is, far from being a statement that Yahweh is overcome with compassion once more and intends to deliver Israel (as in previous cycles), in this context the phrase "the soul is short" (*qṣar npš*) expresses the frustration, exasperation, and anger in the face of an intolerable situation.[10] Yahweh is

---

5. Cf. also the previous confrontation of the messenger of Yahweh in 2:1–5.
6. Block, *Judges, Ruth*, 347.
7. Webb, *The Book of the Judges*, 46.
8. O'Connell, *The Rhetoric of the Book of Judges*, 187.
9. Block, *Judges, Ruth*, 348.
10. See R. D. Haak, "A Study and New Interpretation of QṢR NPŠ," *JBL* 101 (1982): 161–67.

dismissing the Israelite actions as further evidence of their iniquitous condition and manipulative ways. This is why we are met with only his silence and a reminder (10:17) that the Ammonites are renewing their threat. Yahweh's silence seems to be an indication of his anger[11] or, at least, displeasure.

In light of the values of the Law (Torah), Jephthah will not be a fitting judge for the nation, and yet that seems to be just the point. With each round of apostasy, the nation seems to plunge deeper, God's response is more serious, and the "judge" for the nation is less qualified for the role. There is a correspondence between the nation's unfaithfulness to Yahweh and his Torah, and the "quality" of the judge raised up to deliver them.

Bridging Contexts

WHAT DOES THIS episode tell us about God's people? What does it tell us about God himself and how he deals with people? The description of the apostasy is the most detailed yet in the book. Seven foreign deities or sets of deities are detailed to emphasize how completely the Israelites have departed from Yahweh. This time God himself (not a prophet) confronts the Israelites. This also witnesses to the severity of their apostasy.

We must also look at the degree to which God has revealed himself in the preceding cycles. God has poured out his heart into the Israelites. In spite of his gracious compassion and goodness to them, delivering them time and time again from their enemies (hence the listing of seven oppressors), they have readily turned away and are worshiping other gods (hence the listing of seven groups of foreign deities). And with the most recently narrated cycle, they have done this before the cycle is even completed. In their fickleness the Israelites have made a mockery of God's grace; they have taken advantage of his character and attributes in an attempt to manipulate him.

This is why God is so angry and sarcastic in his dealings with the Israelites in this episode. This is not arbitrary anger, but well-informed, perceptive, purposeful, and focused anger. God is so used to their pattern of repentance that he sees right through their insincerity. As humans we think that because we can hide our sinfulness from other people, somehow we can hide it from God. But God examines the hearts of human beings (Ps. 17:3–5; 139:23–24; Jer. 17:9–10) and sees the wickedness, improper motives, and so on that reside within the soul.

---

11. Block, *Judges, Ruth*, 349; O'Connell, *The Rhetoric of the Book of Judges*, 187–88; Webb, *The Book of the Judges*, 75, 230 n. 75; Klein, *Triumph of Irony*, 95; Polzin, *Moses and the Deuteronomist*, 178.

No wonder Israel's vain attempt at manipulating God through insincere repentance fails. Their devotion is only for convenience (i.e., they want God to end their trouble that has come as a result of the oppression, but they also want to continue living according to their own desires).

OFTEN AS CHRISTIANS we want God to perform when we want him to. We want him when we need him. Otherwise, we don't want to be bothered by him. We want a god who will perform according to our criteria, according to our timing and agenda.

Even when we are the ones who have acted unfaithfully and are reaping the consequences of those actions, this is the kind of god we want. Yet we are the ones who have turned away from the Lord God to the materialistic gods. We are the ones who have disobeyed his Word in seeking the gratifications of the flesh. Yet when the consequences of worshiping these other gods come upon us, we want God to deliver us immediately. At times in the past, he has bailed us out. For example, he has provided for the reckless credit card debt that we ran up. In his grace he worked on our behalf. Yet we do it all again and expect his performance one more time. And with enough prayer and repentance, he will bail us out again, right? After all, isn't his grace infinite?

What's wrong with this picture, with this theology of God? The present passage demonstrates that it doesn't work this way. Believers are entirely capable of going through the motions, of offering God insincere and superficial repentance. They can do the right rituals, play their parts, and certainly put on a convincing performance, at least as far as other human beings are concerned. But the Lord sees through the charade; he knows our hearts. He will not be manipulated by us.

Judges 10:17–11:11

¹⁷When the Ammonites were called to arms and camped in Gilead, the Israelites assembled and camped at Mizpah. ¹⁸The leaders of the people of Gilead said to each other, "Whoever will launch the attack against the Ammonites will be the head of all those living in Gilead."

¹¹:¹Jephthah the Gileadite was a mighty warrior. His father was Gilead; his mother was a prostitute. ²Gilead's wife also bore him sons, and when they were grown up, they drove Jephthah away. "You are not going to get any inheritance in

our family," they said, "because you are the son of another woman." ³So Jephthah fled from his brothers and settled in the land of Tob, where a group of adventurers gathered around him and followed him.

⁴Some time later, when the Ammonites made war on Israel, ⁵the elders of Gilead went to get Jephthah from the land of Tob. ⁶"Come," they said, "be our commander, so we can fight the Ammonites."

⁷Jephthah said to them, "Didn't you hate me and drive me from my father's house? Why do you come to me now, when you're in trouble?"

⁸The elders of Gilead said to him, "Nevertheless, we are turning to you now; come with us to fight the Ammonites, and you will be our head over all who live in Gilead."

⁹Jephthah answered, "Suppose you take me back to fight the Ammonites and the LORD gives them to me—will I really be your head?"

¹⁰The elders of Gilead replied, "The LORD is our witness; we will certainly do as you say." ¹¹So Jephthah went with the elders of Gilead, and the people made him head and commander over them. And he repeated all his words before the LORD in Mizpah.

THE SECOND SECTION of the Jephthah account (B, see introductory comments on 10:6–12:7) narrates the Ammonite threat, in which the elders make their ill-considered oath leading to their negotiation with Jephthah. The specific dialogue is carried out in 11:5–11. Whereas in every other cycle Yahweh is involved in the raising up of the deliverer, Jephthah's emergence is treated as a purely human development. It is true that Yahweh is invoked as a witness to the covenant between Jephthah and Israel, but this is a far cry from earlier episodes.

The Ammonite oppression comes to a head in the military activity in 10:17. What will happen? The leaders or elders of Gilead[12] are pictured as taking the initiative to maintain their social and political status. They state: "Whoever will launch the attack against the Ammonites will be the head

---

12. In this section, *śārê gilʿād* ("leaders of Gilead") is parallel to *ziqnê gilʿād* ("elders of Gilead").

[*rōʾš*] of all those living in Gilead" (10:18). The use of the term "head" (*rōʾš*) forms an obvious link with the previous story of Abimelech. The phraseology of this verse is reminiscent of the situations of divine inquiry at the beginning and end of Judges, yet no one here calls on Yahweh for a decision about the battle or for guidance in the process of choosing a leader (cf. 1:1–2; 20:18, 23, 26–28).[13] In fact, these men are pictured as irreligious opportunists, who seize the role of commissioning Jephthah, a role that belongs to Yahweh alone.

The ill-considered oath of these leaders of Gilead that the one who initiates the attack against the Ammonites will be the "head" (*rōʾš*) of everyone living in Gilead shows that only under extreme duress is Jephthah appointed as the leader of the Israelites. Presumably this is why it is not said of Jephthah that Yahweh raises him up to deliver Israel. The absence of such a statement only reinforces how ill-advised the elders' oath is to choose "whoever" to be head of their clan. With an ironic twist, the elders' ill-considered oath is anticipatory of Jephthah's later ill-considered oath.

Jephthah[14] is introduced in a parenthetical flashback (11:1–3).[15] The first thing emphasized in the narrative introduction is that "Jephthah ... was a mighty warrior [*gibbôr ḥayil*, cf. Gideon in 6:12]."[16] This is exactly what the elders of Gilead need and are looking for (10:18). Moreover, he is one of them, a Gileadite. Perfect. Why don't they just go get Jephthah?

But the second part of the verse adds a problem: His father was a man named Gilead, but his mother was a prostitute (*zônâ*).[17] In addition, Gilead's wife had sons, and when they grew up, they drove Jephthah away. The issue is inheritance, as the brothers make clear: "You are not going to get any inheritance in our family ... because you are the son of another woman [a prostitute]" (v. 2). It seems as if Jephthah had originally been adopted by Gilead (otherwise, the issue of inheritance would not exist). But when his father died, his brothers went to court—to the elders—to sue on the grounds that Jephthah's adoption was not valid because, in their opinion, the son of

---

13. O'Connell, *The Rhetoric of the Book of Judges*, 188.

14. The name Jephthah means "He [DN] has opened [the womb]" or "May he [DN] open [the womb]." As a personal name, it is attested in the form *ypthʾl* in Old South Arabic and as a place name in the Heb. *yiptaḥʾēl* (Josh. 19:14, 27).

15. Indicated by the circumstantial clause at the beginning of 11:1.

16. Block correctly notes: "The narrator's characterization of Jephthah as a 'valiant warrior' (*gibbôr ḥayil*, 11:1) hardly commends him spiritually for the role of savior of Israel. Indeed, he was a most unlikely candidate for leadership, being the ostracized son of a harlot and leader of a band of brigands in the mountains of Gilead (11:1–3)" ("The Period of the Judges: Religious Disintegration Under Tribal Rule," 50).

17. For a discussion of this term in v. 1, see Block, *Judges, Ruth*, 353.

a prostitute could not be adopted. The elders ruled in favor of the brothers and legally disinherited Jephthah.[18]

Verse 3 explains how Jephthah became known as a "mighty warrior" (*gibbôr ḥayil*). He had fled from his brothers, settled in the land of Tob,[19] and formed a gang. The NIV's translation "a group of adventurers" (*ʾanāšîm rêqîm*, lit., "empty men") misses the narrator's negative assessment of these men. Jephthah is not a Walt Disney Robin Hood-type character. He is the leader of a group of vagrants, morally empty men, and is thus pictured in the same terms as Abimelech (cf. the use of *ʾanāšîm rêqîm* [lit., empty men] in 9:4 to describe Abimelech's cut-throat hirelings). In this respect, the characterization of Jephthah is that of a Gileadite renegade or outlaw, an *ʾApiru*, in the vernacular of the day.[20]

Block points out the parallel structure of the dialogue between Yahweh and the Israelites in 10:10–16 and the dialogue between Jephthah and the elders in 11:4–11.[21]

The dialogue between Yahweh and the Israelites (10:10–16)	*The dialogue between Jephthah and the elders (11:4–11)*
The Ammonite oppression (10:7–9)	The Ammonite oppression (11:4)
Israel appeals to Yahweh (10:10)	Gilead appeals to Jephthah (11:5–6)
Yahweh retorts sarcastically (10:11–14)	Jephthah retorts sarcastically (11:7)
Israel repeats the appeal (10:15–16a)	Gilead repeats the appeal (11:8)
Yahweh refuses to be used (10:16b)	Jephthah seizes the moment opportunistically (11:9–11)

---

18. D. Marcus, "The Bargaining Between Jephthah and the Elders (Judges 11:4–11)," *JANES* 19 (1989): 95–110, esp. 98; idem, "The Legal Dispute Between Jephthah and the Elders," *HAR* 12 (1990): 107–11. In addition, one might surmise from the text that Jephthah was older than his brothers, otherwise there would not be any need to specify "when they were grown up." See also T. M. Willis, "The Nature of Jephthah's Authority," *CBQ* 59 (1997): 33–44.

19. Ironically, after the Israelites plead with Yahweh, "Do with us whatever you think best [*ḥaṭṭôb*, lit., good]" (10:15), Yahweh arranges that their deliverer comes from the land of Tob (*Ṭôb*, 11:3a)—the land to which his Gileadite half-brothers had unjustly banished him! See Webb, *The Book of the Judges*, 50, 223 n. 19.

20. For a discussion of this term, see A. F. Rainey, "Who Is a Canaanite?" 1–15; and "Unruly Elements in Late Bronze Canaanite Society," in *Pomegranates and Golden Bells: Studies in Biblical, Jewish, and Near Eastern Ritual, Law and Literature in Honor of Jacob Milgrom*, ed. D. P. Wright, D. N. Freedman, and A. Hurvitz (Winona Lake, Ind.: Eisenbrauns, 1995), 481–96.

21. Block, *Judges, Ruth*, 354.

The elders' initial offer of 10:18 was that "whoever" saved them would become the "head" of all those living in Gilead. But in their first approach to Jephthah (11:4–5), they make the lesser offer of *qāṣîn* (commander, 11:6). It may be that the elders first offer Jephthah the title *qāṣîn* instead of the title *rōʾš* (head) because he had been disinherited. It may be that being disinherited somehow disqualified him from being *rōʾš* over Gilead.[22]

But the essence of Jephthah's response in 11:7 is a rejection of their offer: "Didn't you hate me and drive me from my father's house? Why [*maddûaʿ*] do you come to me now, when you're in trouble?" The use of the term "why" (*maddûaʿ*) in this rhetorical question's context has particular force, the essence of which is:

> The Gileadites have undeniably rejected Jephthah and expelled him. Given these facts, how, he asks, can you now come to me when you need help? People do not go to those they have rejected for help, nor does the victim of rejection help his rejecters. Nobody in his right mind would come to ask for help in such circumstances: your plea is rejected; I will not help you.[23]

In other words, Jephthah rejects the elders because they have previously rejected his case in court and have annulled an adoption agreement that his father made in his favor. Moreover, their offer of making Jephthah commander (*qāṣîn*) is rightly perceived for what it is.

Only after Jephthah's objection (11:7) do they raise the offer to its initial level (i.e., "head" [*rōʾš*] instead of simply "commander" [*qāṣîn*]). Their haggling shows how unprincipled these opportunists are. They seek to hire Jephthah "cheap" by offering him less than what they offered a full citizen of Gilead (10:18). They would gladly abuse him to accomplish their ambitious ends. But Jephthah is negotiating out of a position of strength. Thus the connotation in the elders' answer in 11:8 is (in paraphrase): "Nevertheless [*lākēn*] we do not disagree with you; what you say is true. We did disinherit you, but now we are coming to you as a gesture of reconciliation and are offering you the position of leader."[24]

---

22. Willis, "The Nature of Jephthah's Authority," 35.

23. Marcus, "The Bargaining Between Jephthah and the Elders," 98. Marcus shows that (1) the clauses before *maddûaʿ* always state undeniable facts and (2) the *maddûaʿ* clause either calls into question a situation or assumption, or indicates incredulousness that, given the preceding facts, certain acts could be carried out. Thus nobody in one's right mind would think that such a thing could happen (pp. 97–98).

24. Marcus, "The Bargaining Between Jephthah and the Elders," 99. Marcus argues that the dispute between Jephthah and the elders in Judges 11 centers only on the issue of Jephthah's disinheritance and reinstatement. He argues against the view of a distinction in the elders' offer between "commander" (*qāṣîn*) and "head" (*rōʾš*). I feel that it is not an either/or in this context,

Jephthah lays down the condition for which he was willing to go fight the Ammonites (11:9): Reinstate me to my rightful inheritance and make me not just commander (*qāṣîn*) but also and affirmatively "head" (*rōʾš*).[25] If they could have obtained Jephthah without reinstating him to his inheritance, they would have. But they also have no hesitation to reverse their earlier decision and disinherit Jephthah's brothers in order to "get their man." In the end, because of their desperation, the elders give in, reinstate Jephthah, and commission him as both "head" (*rōʾš*) and commander (*qāṣîn*) (11:11).[26] However, as Willis points out, Jephthah's authority does not cut across or supersede the authority of the elders; his authority is controlled by theirs. The traditional authority of the elders is apparently still intact.[27] Thus the text paints the elders of Gilead as truly unscrupulous (anticipatory of ch. 21).

Furthermore, the elders will get a leader like themselves. Jephthah, seeing his chance for promotion in Gilead, is equally as ready to perform an illegitimate cultic vow to guarantee the military victory he needs to retain the status that he acquires through his negotiations with the elders. The error in both cases is the same: placing ambition above covenantal loyalty, familial loyalty, and proper cultic performance. The elders of Gilead get the leader they deserve, for, like them, Jephthah is a person who is willing to utilize "whomever" by whatever means in order to pursue a private agenda. Both the elders and Jephthah are calculating opportunists and are using each other.

The ratification ceremony takes place at Mizpah, where Jephthah swears "the oath of office" and becomes officially the "head" (*rōʾš*) and the "commander" (*qāṣîn*) of Gilead. Jephthah's inauguration at Mizpah foreshadows that of Saul (1 Sam. 11:15). This ceremony raises two questions. (1) Why is Jephthah sworn in at Mizpah in Gilead? There has been no indication that this site is a sacred site. Block argues that

> it is difficult not to conclude that, like Jephthah's reference to Yahweh in v. 9 and the elder's appeal to him in v. 10, the entire ceremony represents a glib and calculated effort to manipulate Yahweh. In reality the witness Jephthah is concerned about is not Yahweh, but the army of Gilead, camped at Mizpah.[28]

---

but a both/and. Jephthah wants to be reinstated, and he wants more than just *qāṣîn*; he wants *rōʾš*. The heightened employment of *rōʾš* in the pericope, the elders' attitude described below, as well as other factors seem to indicate that both issues are present in the text's dialogue.

25. Block righty observes: "Jephthah's appeal to Yahweh sounds pious—a tacit recognition of Yahweh as the national deity—but like Abimelech he was driven only by self-interest" (*Judges, Ruth*, 355).

26. Malamat, "The Period of the Judges," 158.

27. Willis, "The Nature of Jephthah's Authority," 41.

28. Block, *Judges, Ruth*, 356.

(2) Is Yahweh really engaged in this process of installing Jephthah as the military commander (hence deliverer) and head (i.e., chief) of the Gileadite region? Unlike past instances where he played the decisive role in raising up the deliverers, Yahweh is relegated to the role of silent witness to a purely human contract between a desperate but opportunistic people and an ambitious, opportunistic outlaw. In 10:10–16, Yahweh had refused to let himself be used by Israel. Nevertheless, Jephthah and the Gileadites have no hesitation in using him to seal their agreement.

THE ELDERS OF Gilead are irreligious opportunists. They do not care about true worship of the Lord for they willingly usurp Yahweh's role in raising up a deliverer. There is no prayer to God from these men, no seeking his will, no trust in him to guide. They can do it themselves because in so doing they can guarantee their positions of authority (or at least they think they can). They seek to hire Jephthah "cheap" by offering him less than what they would offer a full citizen of Gilead. These are the kind of leaders who would gladly abuse whomever they can to maintain or gain more power. There is nothing that they wouldn't do to anyone to this end.

How ironic that they get a leader like themselves. Jephthah is willing to do anything to anyone in order to seize power and to maintain that power and status. He wants so desperately to be restored and accepted, to be the head, that he will do anything and deal with anyone (including the unscrupulous elders) in order to achieve his goals. The error in both cases is the same: a placing of blind ambition above covenantal loyalty, familial loyalty, and proper worship of God. Thus the elders and Jephthah deserve one another. Selfish ambition drives them all.

Yahweh is passive here. While both the elders and Jephthah use his name to legitimate their actions, he is not active in raising up a deliverer for the Israelites. Rather, he allows them to proceed in their own plans and devices. As we will see, he can work his will even in spite of these.

IN THE WORLD TODAY, there are plenty of those who are driven by blind ambition to achieve their goals. In business, sports, entertainment, and political contexts (to name a few), we see time and again individuals who are raw opportunists. They will do whatever it takes to accomplish their ends. And frequently our society lauds such persons as "single-minded" individuals who serve as wonderful success stories to be imitated. For many, a Jimmy Johnson, winner of two Super Bowls as the former head coach of the Dallas Cowboys, is the model to be emulated. Wife and family must be put aside for the exclusive goal of "winning." Players are expendable if you can achieve the objective of "winning." The end justifies the means if it brings "winning." Or take a Vince Lombardi orientation, "Winning isn't everything; it's the only thing." Such a perspective is unfortunately ingrained into us and our children at many levels and in many ways.

What is especially disturbing in this passage is that the raw opportunists are the political and spiritual leaders of Israel! Could such raw opportunists be found in the church today? It is a chilling thought, but the better part of wisdom recognizes the fact that such situations can and do exist. And unfortunately they can be found in every area of Christian ministry activity. They are our modern-day Balaams that Peter warns about (2 Peter 2:1–22). Ironically, as in the case of the elders of Gilead, they often get the same kind of person, a Jephthah, just like them in their blind ambition orientation. Fortunately, the Scriptures clearly teach that there is a more excellent way. As Philippians 2:1–11 (esp. vv. 3–5) advocates, believers should "do nothing out of selfish ambition or vain conceit, but in humility consider others better than yourselves.... Your attitude should be the same as that of Christ Jesus."

At certain points in his dealings with humankind, Yahweh is passive. He does not actively work to bring deliverance but allows men and women to attempt their own machinations even though the motives in these designs are less than godly. In other words, he gives them over to their own plots and schemes. God refuses to be predictable in the sense that this can be used by humans to manipulate him. He is not a raw machine of deliverance who can be used whenever one wants or needs to use it. When God is passive to human beings' machinations, it is not a sign of his endorsement but rather a signal that things may be amiss. In allowing men and women to proceed in their own plans and devices, God permits them to reap the consequences of these. Nevertheless, in every case, the Lord can accomplish his will in spite of evil motives and intents.

Judges 11:12–28

¹²Then Jephthah sent messengers to the Ammonite king with the question: "What do you have against us that you have attacked our country?"

¹³The king of the Ammonites answered Jephthah's messengers, "When Israel came up out of Egypt, they took away my land from the Arnon to the Jabbok, all the way to the Jordan. Now give it back peaceably."

¹⁴Jephthah sent back messengers to the Ammonite king, ¹⁵saying:

"This is what Jephthah says: Israel did not take the land of Moab or the land of the Ammonites. ¹⁶But when they came up out of Egypt, Israel went through the desert to the Red Sea and on to Kadesh. ¹⁷Then Israel sent messengers to the king of Edom, saying, 'Give us permission to go through your country,' but the king of Edom would not listen. They sent also to the king of Moab, and he refused. So Israel stayed at Kadesh.

¹⁸"Next they traveled through the desert, skirted the lands of Edom and Moab, passed along the eastern side of the country of Moab, and camped on the other side of the Arnon. They did not enter the territory of Moab, for the Arnon was its border.

¹⁹"Then Israel sent messengers to Sihon king of the Amorites, who ruled in Heshbon, and said to him, 'Let us pass through your country to our own place.' ²⁰Sihon, however, did not trust Israel to pass through his territory. He mustered all his men and encamped at Jahaz and fought with Israel.

²¹"Then the LORD, the God of Israel, gave Sihon and all his men into Israel's hands, and they defeated them. Israel took over all the land of the Amorites who lived in that country, ²²capturing all of it from the Arnon to the Jabbok and from the desert to the Jordan.

²³"Now since the LORD, the God of Israel, has driven the Amorites out before his people Israel, what right have you to take it over? ²⁴Will you not take what your god Chemosh gives you? Likewise, whatever the LORD our God has given us, we will possess. ²⁵Are you better than Balak son of Zippor, king of Moab? Did he ever quarrel with Israel or fight with them? ²⁶For three hundred years Israel occupied Heshbon, Aroer, the surrounding settlements and all the towns along the Arnon. Why didn't you retake them during that time? ²⁷I have not wronged you, but you are doing me wrong by waging war against me. Let the LORD, the Judge, decide the dispute this day between the Israelites and the Ammonites."

²⁸The king of Ammon, however, paid no attention to the message Jephthah sent him.

THIS THIRD SECTION of the Jephthah account (C, see introductory comments on 10:6–12:7) narrates the confrontation between Jephthah and the Ammonite king. Immediately after Jephthah's installation at Mizpah, he sends messengers to the Ammonite king asking why the Ammonites are attacking. In this initial communiqué there is a subtle invitation to trial by combat: (lit.) "What's between me and you. . . ?" This particular rhetorical question occurs in the exalted style of diplomatic speech and functions to render the addressee uncertain, confused, and sensing his guilt for whatever consequences ensue.[29]

The Ammonite king's response is hardly satisfying: Israel has stolen Ammon's land; surrender it, and there will be peace (11:13). In the lengthy speech that follows, Jephthah uses a common ancient Near Eastern form known as the royal covenant/treaty disputation (in biblical materials this is known as the *ri̇̂b*; cf. the account of Gideon's naming as Jerub-Baal, 8:35). A common element in these disputations is the rehearsal of past historical relations between the parties. In his speech, Jephthah gives an extensive history of the area in dispute (11:15–22), which serves as the basis for his conclusions in 11:23–27. This recounting coincides with the accounts of the region's history recorded in Numbers 20–24 and Deuteronomy 2–3.[30]

Jephthah starts the speech with the assertion that Israel did not take the land of Moab or the land of the Ammonites (11:15). This assertion (if true, and it is) undercuts the Ammonite claim right from the beginning. Israel cannot give back to Ammon that which was never Ammon's. After the exodus from Egypt and after Israel had come into the region, the Israelites sent messengers to the king of Edom, asking permission to go through his land, but the Edomite king refused. The same happened with the king of Moab. As a result, Israel eventually traveled around Edom and Moab to the east, exposed to the desert, and came into the land north of Moab, north of the Arnon river. They never entered Edomite or Moabite territory, since the land north of the Arnon was not Moabite at the time.

Israel then sent messengers to Sihon king of the Amorites (note, not king of the Ammonites), who ruled in Heshbon and who had only recently taken over this territory from the Moabites. These messengers again appealed to Sihon for permission to pass through his territory. But Sihon attacked Israel (a very serious mistake); Yahweh gave him into the Israelites' hands, and the Israelites completely defeated him and his troops and took over his land. This is how Israel obtained the area in dispute, and this is why the Ammonite claim is illegitimate.

---

29. See O. Bächli, "'Was habe ich mit Dir zu schaffen?' Eine formelhafte Frage im Alten Testament und Neuen Testament," *TZ* 33 (1977): 69–80.

30. See esp. the extensive discussion in O'Connell, *The Rhetoric of the Book of Judges*, 193–203.

Not only does Jephthah's rehearsal of the area's history function to undercut the Ammonite claim—he will further the argument shortly—it also functions as a mocking warning to the Ammonite monarch. Just as Israel sent messengers to the Transjordanian kings, so Jephthah has sent messengers. Just as the Transjordanian kings chose a negative response (especially Sihon), so the Ammonite king may choose a negative response. But just as Yahweh gave Sihon into the Israelites' hands, so will he give the king of Ammon into their hands. Just as Israel utterly defeated Sihon and his army, so the Israelites will defeat the Ammonite king and his army (if he chooses the same response as Sihon).[31]

Through a series of loaded rhetorical questions based on the history of the area just rehearsed, Jephthah concludes his disputation against the king of Ammon in 11:23–27. Since Yahweh drove out the Amorites from this disputed area and gave the land to Israel, what right does the Ammonite king have to take it over? The question contains a wordplay that literally is more like: "Since Yahweh dispossessed [*yāraš*] . . . will you [king of Ammon] now dispossess [*yāraš*]?" (11:23). The implied answer is, of course, no.[32]

Next, Jephthah poses a double question (11:24): "Will you not take what your god Chemosh gives you? Likewise, whatever the LORD our God has given us, we will possess [lit., will we not possess it]?" Jephthah uses what appears to be a "logical" argument—an argument commonly asserted in the ancient Near East: A people must accept the will of its god. Therefore, the Ammonites will possess the lands that Chemosh, their god, gives them, and the Israelites will possess the lands that Yahweh, the God of Israel, gives them (in this case, the disputed area!).

But his "logical" argument conflates the religious facts and even transposes the Moabite and Ammonite national gods.[33] Even though he is logical, deeply emotional, and articulate, in the end Jephthah demonstrates his great factual ignorance. For all his apparent piety, Jephthah identifies faith in Yahweh with the *practices* of the surrounding national cults rather than the *ideals* of biblical faith. He localizes Yahweh as though he is just like Chemosh, Milcom, Baal, and so on (i.e., gods can only exercise their power in their particular localized areas). Jephthah's theological error is compounded by the fact that Deuteronomy 2:19 specifically states that *Yahweh* has given the Ammonites their own land as their "possession" (noun form of *yāraš*).[34] This

---

31. For the deliberate patterning of Judg. 11 along the lines of Num. 20–24 and Deut. 2–3, see O'Connell, *The Rhetoric of the Book of Judges*, 199.

32. There may have been some emotional charge in the tone of this question, since Jephthah has personally been "dispossessed" or "disinherited" by his half-brothers.

33. See Soggin, *Judges*, 210.

34. This is esp. ironic since Jephthah has deliberately patterned his speech along the lines of Num. 20–24 and Deut. 2–3. Yahweh alone determines the boundaries of nations (cf. Deut. 32:8–9; Amos 9:7).

is a comment on Jephthah's ignorance of the Law (the Torah) and will have implications later with reference to his vow and his daughter.

In all probability, this theological error as an ignorance of God's Law is not perceived by the Ammonite king. To him the logic is fine. Jephthah has used the common logic of the day to be convincing in his disputation. However, the Ammonite king is likely surprised to be told that his god is Chemosh (who was the god of the Moabites).[35] First Kings 11:33 clarifies the issue with the phrase "Chemosh the god of the Moabites, and Molech [better, Milcom] the god of the Ammonites." Thus, the national deity of the Ammonites[36] was Milcom,[37] not Chemosh.[38] This is an error, and it hardly impresses the Ammonite king![39]

---

35. Some scholars (see most recently O'Connell, *The Rhetoric of the Book of Judges*, 196–99) take the view that the disputation was against a king of Ammon who had recently taken part of the Moabite territory and was thus entitled, by diplomatic protocol, to claim Moabite land rights and to defer to Moabite deities. While this is a remote possibility, it is really begging the question. There is no evidence for such an assumption. Ammonite inscriptions do not refer to Chemosh, and to assume that this was permissible with the Ammonite king is a great assumption indeed without any evidence. The fact that Jephthah has committed a theological error in his statement opens the door to the possibility that he has committed a factual error. While it would be wrong to conclude that Jephthah was an inept negotiator (inept is certainly too strong a term), it is certainly true that Jephthah, for all his verbal facility, opens his mouth too quickly in other places in the narration of his story and thus likely has committed a bungle here.

36. Recently, Aufrecht proposed that the national deity of the Ammonites was El, not Milcom, since Milcom does not appear as a theophoric element in Ammonite personal names. The evidence, however, is small for Ammonite personal names, and I believe it is better to reserve judgment on this issue until more data are produced. See W. E. Aufrecht, "The Religion of the Ammonites," in *Ancient Ammon*, ed. B. MacDonald and R. W. Younkers (Leiden: Brill, 1999), 152–62.

37. Milcom (*mlkm*) is attested 1 Kings 11:5, 33 and 2 Kings 23:13. Some of the Greek manuscripts and other versions read Milcom in seven other passages (many of which modern English translations opt to read as Milcom): 2 Sam. 12:30; 1 Kings 11:7; 1 Chron. 20:2; Jer. 49(30):1, 3; Amos 1:15; Zeph. 1:5. According to 2 Sam. 12:30, Milcom, like a number of deities, was depicted by an anthropomorphic image. There are a number of extrabiblical attestations from Ammon, most notably the Amman Citadel Inscription (see *COS*, 2.24), and seals and bullae (see *COS*, 2.71).

It has been commonly thought that Milcom is another form of the god Molech/Malik (*mlk*). See, e.g., R. de Vaux, *Ancient Israel* (2 vols.; New York: McGraw-Hill, 1965), 2:444–46. The facts that both deities' names derive from the same Semitic root *mlk* (to rule, reign) and 1 Kings 11:7 (MT has *mlk*; LXX has *mlkm*) have added to the possible confusion. Many recent scholars understand the two as separate deities with only Milcom being definitely identified with the Ammonites as their national deity. Second Kings 23:10–13 seems to treat the two separately. Yet both deities appear to have had connections to the netherworld and with fire (see E. Puech, "Milcom," *DDD*. col. 1078; G. C. Heider, "Molech," *DDD*, col. 1096).

38. Chemosh is not only attested as the Moabite national deity in a number of biblical texts (e.g., 1 Kings 11:5, 7, 33), but is also attested in the Mesha Inscription (see *COS*, 2.23) and Moabite seals (e.g., *COS*, 2.72).

39. Block takes this to be a deliberate, intentional error on the part of Jephthah to insult him and start the war.

Now Jephthah follows up with a series of questions related to Balak: "Are you better than Balak, the son of Zippor, the king of Moab? Did he ever quarrel [*rāb*] with Israel or fight with them?" These on the surface seem strong arguments. Technically, Jephthah is right. Balak never quarreled with Israel (as the Ammonite king is doing), and Balak never actually fought with Israel (although he did intend to attack Israel after Balaam had cursed them; he only refrained from this because Yahweh intervened, causing Balaam's blessing of Israel).[40]

Jephthah's last rhetorical question is preceded by an assertion: "For three hundred years Israel occupied Heshbon. . . . Why [*maddûaʿ*] didn't you retake them during that time?" This is the same grammatical construction as found in Jephthah's response in 11:7 (see comments). Accordingly, the essence of the argument is this: Since no Ammonite king (or Moabite either, for that matter) has ever attempted to claim the land area in dispute for over three hundred years,[41] nobody in his right mind would claim them now. Thus your claim to this territory is rejected.

Jephthah's conclusion is found in 11:27: "I have not wronged [*ḥṭʾ*] you, but you are doing me wrong [*rʿh*] by waging war against me. Let the LORD, the Judge, decide the dispute this day between the Israelites and the Ammonites." This brings the disputation to its climax. Often such disputations were but a preamble to the violence of the battlefield.

The Ammonite king is unable to offer a reasonable rebuttal to Jephthah's arguments. In the narrator's view, those arguments leave the Ammonite king speechless (11:28). This has two effects: It shows that Jephthah's argument is in the main correct and therefore unanswerable, and it shows that the Ammonite king had his heart set beforehand and really did not care about "truth and accuracy"; he is going to war.

Jephthah mocks the Ammonite king for pondering war with the Israelites, since war with them is war with Yahweh. His mockery only compels the Ammonite king onto the battlefield, where he will be, like Sihon, greatly

---

40. Cf. Num. 22–24. That this mention of a Moabite king is evidence that the king of Ammon has taken Moabite land is doubtful (see comments in note 35). In that Jephthah has rehearsed the history including the other identifiable characters, it is not surprising that he mentions the next character in the historic narration of the book of Numbers after Sihon.

41. Soggin observes that this has an approximate analogue in the Mesha Inscription (*Judges*, 211). Line 10 states: "Now the Gadite [lit., man of Gad] had settled in the land of ʿAḥarot from antiquity; and the king of Israel had fortified for him [the Gadite] ʿAḥarot." One must be cautious in accepting Jephthah's number "three hundred" as an accurate number. Since Jephthah has been wrong on a number of points in the speech already, this may also be erroneous (see the discussion of Block, *Judges, Ruth*, 363).

humbled. As in his dealings with the elders (11:9), Jephthah voices a recognition that the victory belongs to Yahweh (11:21, 27). But like his negotiations with the elders, this is only a tacit recognition, for Jephthah is a pragmatic Yahwist. He is the sort of man whom we wonder whether God will use but who has no reservations about manipulating God for his own use (this becomes clear in the next section).

JEPHTHAH USES LOGIC, emotion, and great articulation in his dispute with the Ammonite king. Using the common logic of the day in order to persuade his opponent, Jephthah demonstrates that these are no substitutes for truth. In his ignorance, he makes a serious theological error in equating the worship of Yahweh with the worship of other gods. It is this theological error that leads him to execute a religious practice used in the worship of these other gods—child sacrifice! In other words, ignorance of God's Word leads him to emulate a pagan religious practice.

Theological accuracy is important. What one thinks about God is important. Wrong thinking about God is reprehensible. Job's three "friends" stand out as examples of those who argued with great articulation, logic, and emotion—they were indeed sincere—but in the end, they were very wrong. In the epilogue of Job, God declares his anger with them because they did not speak correctly about him (Job 42:7–9).

THEOLOGICAL IGNORANCE and error lead to devastating results. In addition, we live in a world that has, over the course of a century, continually depreciated the worth of theological matters. A knowledge of the Bible is not considered important today. In our drive for technology, knowing God's Word is seen as having little or no value. Knowing the Bible doesn't put bread on the table, so the argument goes.

But whether it is Jonestown following Jim Jones's teachings or the Heaven's Gate group searching for paradise with outer space extraterrestrials, such ignorance of God's Word opens the way to religious exploitation and, literally in these two cases, death and destruction. The error of Jephthah—making the worship of Yahweh equal to the worship of the Ammonite god—is an error that can easily be repeated in generation after generation. If we accept such a premise—maybe in the guise of ecclesiastical harmony—the door lies open for endorsement of wrong theological practices.

Judges 11:29–40

²⁹Then the Spirit of the LORD came upon Jephthah. He crossed Gilead and Manasseh, passed through Mizpah of Gilead, and from there he advanced against the Ammonites. ³⁰And Jephthah made a vow to the LORD: "If you give the Ammonites into my hands, ³¹whatever comes out of the door of my house to meet me when I return in triumph from the Ammonites will be the LORD's, and I will sacrifice it as a burnt offering."

³²Then Jephthah went over to fight the Ammonites, and the LORD gave them into his hands. ³³He devastated twenty towns from Aroer to the vicinity of Minnith, as far as Abel Keramim. Thus Israel subdued Ammon.

³⁴When Jephthah returned to his home in Mizpah, who should come out to meet him but his daughter, dancing to the sound of tambourines! She was an only child. Except for her he had neither son nor daughter. ³⁵When he saw her, he tore his clothes and cried, "Oh! My daughter! You have made me miserable and wretched, because I have made a vow to the LORD that I cannot break."

³⁶"My father," she replied, "you have given your word to the LORD. Do to me just as you promised, now that the LORD has avenged you of your enemies, the Ammonites. ³⁷But grant me this one request," she said. "Give me two months to roam the hills and weep with my friends, because I will never marry."

³⁸"You may go," he said. And he let her go for two months. She and the girls went into the hills and wept because she would never marry. ³⁹After the two months, she returned to her father and he did to her as he had vowed. And she was a virgin.

From this comes the Israelite custom ⁴⁰that each year the young women of Israel go out for four days to commemorate the daughter of Jephthah the Gileadite.

THIS FOURTH SECTION of the Jephthah account (B', see introductory comments on 10:6–12:7) narrates the Ammonite defeat along with Jephthah's ill-considered oath, which leads to his confrontation with his daughter. A special dialogue is carried out in 11:34–38.

The first sentence of this section is a narrative frame component: "Then the Spirit of the LORD came upon Jephthah" (11:29a). As pointed out in the discussion of the Spirit of Yahweh "clothing" Gideon (6:34–35), this does not presuppose any particular level of spirituality on the part of the recipient. It affirms Yahweh's involvement in empowerment but does not guarantee the recipient's spirituality. Otherwise, it is difficult to explain how someone empowered by the Spirit could make so many wrong choices (certainly a question that also will apply to Samson). Being empowered does not mean that Yahweh overwhelms Jephthah's personality, forcing him to only perform a certain way. Jephthah still makes choices, and these choices are, unfortunately, because of his ignorance, not based on God's Word (see discussion on pp. 186–87).

Following this statement is a fourfold repetition of the same verb (ʿbr, variously translated in the NIV) in 11:29b–32a, which serves to link Jephthah's endowment with Yahweh's Spirit with his Yahweh-given victory.

He crossed [ʿbr] Gilead and Manasseh (11:29a²),
he passed [ʿbr] through Mizpah of Gilead (11:29b),
and from there he advanced [ʿbr] against the Ammonites (11:29b²).

Then Jephthah went over [ʿbr] to fight the Ammonites (11:32a),
and Yahweh gave them into his hands (11:32b).

His "crossing," "passing," "advancing," and "going over" are in fact segments of one movement of which Yahweh's Spirit is the motive force. His "tour" of Gilead and Manasseh (11:29a²-b) was probably related to preparation for battle such as recruitment and morale building.[42] In any case, the fourfold employment functions to intensify Jephthah's actions, building up to the climax of Yahweh's giving the Ammonites into his hands (11:32b).

Unfortunately, there are two verses inserted between verses 29 and 32 that not only disrupt the narration of what should have been repetition of the judge's deliverance of his people as recounted in the previous cycles, but actually supplant the climax with Jephthah's vow. It is very tragic that almost immediately after the Spirit of Yahweh comes on Jephthah, he disrupts the flow toward the climax in Yahweh's victory by vowing to perform a sacrifice if Yahweh should give the Ammonites into his hand (11:30–31). This vow and its implementation now dominate the focus of the narrative. In a sense, Yahweh's victory over the Ammonites is usurped by the vow.[43]

Jephthah is negotiating with Yahweh as he had with the Gileadite leaders and with the king of Ammon, seeking to acquire concessions and favors from

---

42. Webb, *The Book of the Judges*, 63–64. Willis argues that the actions of Jephthah beginning in 11:29 indicate that he has stepped over the line of traditional authority into the arena of charismatic authority. He is no longer leading Gileadites alone; he is attempting to expand his authority to include all the other clans of Manasseh and even Ephraim ("The Nature of Jephthah's Authority," 42).

43. Gideon usurps the victory after the battle(s) and does so subtly. But Jephthah does so before the battle in a blatant manner.

him as he had from others in the past. But his success in negotiating steadily declines. With the Gileadites he achieved all he wanted (11:4—11); with the Ammonites he received a verbal if negative response (11:12—28); with Yahweh there is only silence, indicating that God disregards Jephthah's vow.

While some scholars have interpreted Jephthah's vow as rash and hastily worded,[44] others have seen it as manipulative.[45] In fact, Jephthah's vow is both rash and manipulative.[46] (1) In light of his manipulating character as noted in other sections, the vow is another attempt to manipulate the circumstances to his own advantage. In this sense, then, it is not impulsive but has a specific intent (i.e., to get Yahweh to perform: "If you give the Ammonites into my hands ..."). Ironically, this shrewd attempt to manipulate Yahweh demonstrates both folly and faithlessness in the character of Jephthah.

(2) The vow is, however, also rash and imprudent. If Jephthah had said simply, "I will offer a burnt offering [ʿôlâ] to you when I return safe and secure[47] from the Ammonites," then, of course, there is nothing rash in this (though it still would have been calculating and manipulative). The problem is in the qualification "whatever comes out of the door of my house to meet me when I return in triumph from the Ammonites." This imprudent element leads to disaster (see 11:39).

There is little doubt that Jephthah's vow is nothing short of making a deal with the deity, an attempt to exert control over God—a practice familiar to pagans, who believed in the manipulation of the gods for human purposes.[48] In fact, the irony is stark. Jephthah delivers the Israelites from the Ammonites, who along with their neighbors sacrifice their children to their gods; then he sacrifices his daughter to Yahweh, who does not accept human sacrifice! In this way, Jephthah exhibits his ignorance of God's Law (Torah) as he did in his disputation speech to the Ammonite king (see comments on 11:14—27). In addition, he demonstrates his confusion again with deities, conflating what Milcom or Chemosh accept with what Yahweh might accept.

---

44. E.g., Klein, *Triumph of Irony*, 95; Boling, *Judges*, 215—16; D. Marcus, *Jephthah and His Vow* (Lubbock, Tex.: Texas Tech Univ. Press, 1986), 54—55.

45. Webb, *The Book of the Judges*, 64; O'Connell, *The Rhetoric of the Book of Judges*, 180—81; Soggin, *Judges*, 215—16; Block, *Judges, Ruth*, 367—72. Block states: "Although some may interpret the vow as rash and hastily worded, it is preferable to see here another demonstration of his shrewd and calculating nature, another attempt to manipulate circumstances to his own advantage" (p. 367). But he also states: "Ironically, the one who appeared to have become master of his own fate has become a victim of his own rash word" (p. 372).

46. Manipulation speaks to its intent; rashness to its content.

47. The Heb. *bᵉšālôm* carries this connotation (Soggin, *Judges*, 213). The NIV's "in triumph" is not as accurate.

48. Cf. Mesha's action in 2 Kings 3:27. See Block, "The Period of the Judges: Religious Disintegration Under Tribal Rule," 50.

Does Jephthah intend to imply a human sacrifice in his vow? Some believe the vow does intend human sacrifice.[49] Others, however, believe that the text is ambiguous as to human or animal sacrifice.[50] The narrative's shock[51] as to who comes out of his house to meet him after his return may imply the latter, for whom else does he expect? His wife (assuming she is alive)? These are the only human possibilities. The fact that Jephthah uses in the apodosis of his vow (v. 31) the masculine gender as an indeterminate reference "whoever/whatever" rather than the feminine gender, which would have specified either his daughter or wife (assuming that she is alive), seems to underline his expectation for something other than his daughter or wife. Sheep or cattle (things usually offered as a burnt offering) would then be in view.[52] It may seem odd to Western readers for sheep or cattle to come out of one's house. But the typical "four-room house" of this period contained a room that housed animals.[53] Hence in his vow, Jephthah most likely had this in mind.

It is interesting to observe that there is a striking similarity between the vow formula in 11:30b–31 and the vow formula in Numbers 21:2. The latter states: "Israel made this vow to the LORD: 'If you will deliver these people into our hands, we will totally destroy [ḥrm] their cities.'" Hence, Jephthah's daughter becomes like those in the cites of Numbers 21:2, even though she has no direct involvement in the issue at hand.

Narrative frame components relate that Yahweh gives the Ammonites into Jephthah's hands as expected (11:32b) and that he slaughters twenty of their towns (11:33a). Israel subdues the Ammonites (11:33b). Thus, in this context, Jephthah's vow is completely empty,[54] totally unnecessary. His last words to the Ammonite king are sufficient: "Let the LORD, the Judge, decide the dispute this day between the Israelites and the Ammonites" (11:27). If he believed his own words, the argumentation is convincing: Yahweh will

---

49. See Webb, *The Book of the Judges*, 64, 227 nn. 51, 52; Klein, *Triumph of Irony*, 91 (cf. 221 n. 13); Block, *Judges, Ruth*, 367.

50. Marcus, *Jephthah and His Vow*; Boling *Judges*, 208–9.

51. Note in this instance the clear use of *wᵉhinnēh* to denote surprise and shock.

52. Gen. 14:17 appears to be a parallel, where the verbs *yṣʾ* and *qrʾ* are used to describe someone (here the king of Sodom) "going/coming out to meet" someone after a military victory (Abram's victory over the kings of the east). However, there is a difference in referent (in Judg. 11:31 it is indeterminate) and a difference between a straightforward narrative and the direct speech of a vow. In my opinion, the context—esp. in its relating of the grievous surprise of Jephthah—must come into consideration so that the combination of the verbs *yṣʾ* and *qrʾ* are not limited only to human beings but also include animals. In any case, this ambiguity only heightens the irony of the passage.

53. See Y. Shiloh, "The Four-Room House: Its Situation and Function in the Israelite City," *IEJ* 20 (1970): 180–90; A Mazar, *Archaeology of the Land of the Bible*, 340–45; 485–89.

54. Compare the empty word *shibboleth*, below.

deliver the Ammonite king into Jephthah's hands just as he did in the earlier case of Sihon.

And Yahweh does just that. Therefore, since the reader already knows that Yahweh would have given Jephthah success in battle even without his vow, the vow and its negative consequences seem all the more unnecessary. It achieves nothing in the story except to mar the accomplishment of Yahweh's victory and to characterize Jephthah negatively. In this callous gesture, Jephthah shows his willingness to brutalize even his closest kin in order to rule over a tribe of half-brothers (cf. Abimelech). This is why his vow to Yahweh overwhelms what should have been the climactic victory over the Ammonites because it is so unnecessary, illegitimate, and horrific.

The irony of this passage is multiplied by the way in which Jephthah's daughter is introduced (11:34). When he returns home, the surprise is emphatic in 11:34b (lit.): "Look [*hinnēh*]! His daughter [*bitô*] came out to meet him!" The narrator uses the term *hinnēh* to convey a sense of surprise and shock on the part of the character—a sense related to Jephthah's show of emotional recoil when he sees her. He clearly is *not* expecting *her*. But she appears in order to celebrate her father's victory, dancing to the sound of tambourines (cf. Ex. 15:19–21; 1 Sam. 18:6–7). How wrenchingly pathetic! Moreover, the text adds that she is an only child. And if not clear enough, the text adds, "Except for her he had neither son nor daughter."

The dialogue in this episode between Jephthah and his daughter concerns this vow and its implications. Verses 11:35b[1] and 11:36a[1] are juxtaposed to heighten the contrast.

11:35b[1] "I have opened my mouth to Yahweh"   *wᵉ'nky pṣyty py 'l yhwh*
11:36a "You have opened your mouth to Yahweh"   *pṣyth 't pyk 'l yhwh*

As Webb aptly notes:

> . . . the expression is striking enough in itself, involving both alliteration (*p-p*) and assonance (*ī-ī*), and its repetition at this crucial point in the narrative throws it into special prominence. It gains thematic significance from the *Leitmotif*, "the words of Jephthah," which links the previous two episodes. His negotiations with the elders, his diplomacy with the king of Ammon, and his vow have amply displayed Jephthah's facility with words. Jephthah, we know, is good at opening his mouth (how ironical that his name should be *yptḥ* "he opens"). What has precipitated the crisis with his daughter is that he has opened his mouth to *Yahweh*, that is, he has tried to conduct his relationship with God in the same way that he has conducted his relationships with men. He has debased religion (a vow, an offering) into politics.

It is the sequence of dialogues in episodes 2–4 which gives the point its dramatic force. The same point is made by the "parallel" dialogues of episodes 1 and 2: Israel has debased repentance into negotiation.[55]

Despite the sympathy created by the reluctance of both daughter and father to carry out the vow (11:37–38), both eventually submit to it. The verses that describe her mourning her virginity only serve to heighten what transpires by emphasizing her innocence. In verse 39, there is an alternation between the daughter and Jephthah (lit.): "She returned to her father, and he did to her his vow which he had vowed; and she had never known a man."[56] The focus is on the daughter's innocence and Jephthah's ignorance.

While it was sin to break a vow (Num. 30:2), God did provide for the redemption of vows, vows made without full reflection of their ramifications. Tragically, had he known about this, Jephthah could have redeemed his daughter (Lev. 27:1–8)![57] Klein remarks:

Jephthah's daughter is not only virginal, she is unknowing, innocent; and "innocence" is a kind of "ignorance." The daughter is innocent, the father is ignorant. The daughter is already a victim of her father's ignorance and that ignorance will victimize him. Jephthah loses his daughter and he loses contact with Yahweh, both through ignorance.[58]

Ironically, Jephthah transposes the values of Yahweh with those of other gods, gods for whom a vow must be kept even if it involves human sacrifice. In so doing, he implicitly acknowledges polytheism.[59] In fact, Jephthah's action is directly condemned in Deuteronomy 12:31 (again underscoring his ignorance): "You must not worship the LORD your God in their way, because in wor-

---

55. Webb, *The Book of the Judges*, 74.

56. Only by overlooking the plain meaning of ʿôlâ, and overestimating Jephthah's spirituality by not taking into account the macrostructure of the cycles section can one argue that Jephthah did not sacrifice his daughter but devoted her to some kind of perpetual virginity (for this interpretation, see G. L. Archer, *Encyclopedia of Bible Difficulties* [Grand Rapids: Zondervan, 1982], 164–65). The phraseology of the Hebrew here eliminates this interpretation: "He did his vow to her," namely, "whatever comes out is Yahweh's, and I will burn it up as a burnt offering [haʿªlîtîhû ʿôlâ]."

57. The Jewish sources struggled with Jephthah's vow. *Targum Jonathan* states: "And at the end of two months she returned to her father and he fulfilled on her his vow, which he had vowed. She had not know any man. And it became a decree in Israel that no one may offer up his son or his daughter for a burnt offering, as Jephthah the Gileadite did, who did not ask Phinehas the priest. For if he had asked Phinehas the priest, he would have rescued her with a monetary consecration." For a translation and discussion, see W. F. Smelik, *The Targum of Judges* (OTS 36; Leiden: Brill, 1995), 555–57.

58. Klein, *Triumph of Irony*, 93.

59. Ibid., 96.

shiping their gods, they do all kinds of detestable things the LORD hates. They even burn their sons and daughters in the fire as sacrifices to their gods."[60]

Ironically, Yahweh's giving the Ammonites into Jephthah's hand (11:32b) has two different meanings: one for Israel, the other for Jephthah (not to mention his daughter!). For Israel, it means salvation, deliverance from the Ammonite threat; for Jephthah, it means that he must fulfill the gruesome requirements of his self-imposed vow. This raises a real question: Is Gilead truly saved from foreign oppression when deliverance comes at the expense of making a foreign-style sacrifice of one of its number?[61] Thus, Jephthah's vow and its execution dissolve the stability achieved by the victory over the Ammonites. The vow turns Jephthah from deliverer into another oppressor. Joined to the slaughter of the Ephraimites in 12:1–6, Jephthah functions as the catalyst for Israel's destabilization on two fronts: religious and political (the same two fronts that were the problems at the beginning of the cycle).

Violence is often the way in which a spiritually flawed character compensates for his or her sense of inferiority. In this case, Jephthah's sense of inferiority derives from his having been victimized by past rejection. The irony is that what Jephthah perpetrates on his daughter is more violent than the victimization he himself suffered at the hands of his half-brothers![62]

Along this same line it is helpful to compare Jephthah to Abimelech. Abimelech was an outsider (the son of a [Canaanite] concubine). He attempted to compensate for this by a great display of power, especially directed against his father's side of the family. Jephthah is not only an outsider but also an outcast—literally so, on the grounds that he is the son of a prostitute and has been disinherited (11:1–3). He also seeks to compensate by gathering power. First, he does so by becoming the leader of a band of vagrant no-counts in a far-off land. Then because of a crisis, he returns as the strong man ("head and commander")—although the call comes not from God but from the elders of Gilead. Nevertheless, he gathers the troops and mightily defeats the Ammonites. But he undercuts his own victory through an unnecessary manipulative vow and violently sacrifices his only daughter in order to fulfill his imprudent vow—all the result of an attempt to compensate for a perceived inferiority. Ironically, "in this way Jephthah's life is determined and ruined by the connection of the two poles: whore and virgin."[63]

---

60. Cf. also Lev. 18:21: 'Do not give any of your children to be sacrificed to Molech, for you must not profane the name of your God. I am the LORD."

61. O'Connell, *The Rhetoric of the Book of Judges*, 181.

62. Note the contrast between the despicable behavior of Jephthah and the sensitivity and submissiveness of his daughter.

63. Fokkelman, "Structural Remarks on Judges 9 and 19," 40. Cf. also Abimelech with the two women, one of whom gives him life, the other death.

Why doesn't Yahweh intervene to prevent Jephthah from fulfilling his vow?[64] The text implies that Jephthah alone is the agent of violence against his daughter. The vow is not Yahweh's doing. In arrogance, Jephthah attempted to manipulate Yahweh to give him the victory in order to fulfill his own selfish ambition. Yahweh did give the victory, not because of Jephthah's vow but because of his compassion and grace in saving Israel. Thus Jephthah's action in fulfilling the vow is due to a misunderstanding and ignorance on his part for the role the vow even played in the victory over the Ammonites.

Yahweh's nonintervention permits Jephthah's machinations to take their natural consequences with the loss of his line (11:39). "Thus, ironically, through Jephthah's seeking to attain permanent social status in Gilead through an act of human sacrifice, the atrocity of that act, coupled with the fact that it is his inaugural act as Gilead's head, forever characterizes him as an agent of atrocity in Gilead" (11:39b—40).[65] There are no memorials for Jephthah, but the memory of his daughter is immortalized, at least in Gilead, for her honor.

Bridging Contexts

IN HIS ARROGANCE, Jephthah attempts to manipulate Yahweh to give him the victory in order to fulfill his own selfish ambition. The subject of manipulation was also discussed in the Bridging Contexts and Contemporary Significance sections in 10:6—16, although there the emphasis was on the corporate level, whereas here it is on the individual level.

Circumstances and situations sometimes arise in which individuals resort to rash and manipulative vows to God. The more dire the situation, the more apt for vows to be made. War has for centuries been a sure context for such utterances. But for the Christian such maneuverings are unnecessary, as they were for Jephthah. At the foundation of faith is the conviction that God is sovereign; he is in control of each circumstance and situation. Therefore, rash vows are senseless since God will order things in accordance with his will.

Faith is the combination of two basic characteristics. Faith should seize the initiative to act in dependence on God, yet sometimes it must be patient. In one sense faith is full speed ahead; in another it is waiting on the Lord. Our lives require a vibrant faith applied to the affairs of life, but it also requires a patient waiting on the Lord, for the Father does know best.

---

64. No doubt for the same reason that he does not intervene in stopping the slaughter of Gideon's sons by Abimelech.

65. O'Connell, *The Rhetoric of the Book of Judges*, 182.

Moreover, God also understands our humanity, our fragility. In the Law, the making of vows is a serious matter (contrast our attitude today), and to break a vow was sin. God made provisions for rash vows (Lev. 27), and intercession of the Holy Spirit in the New Testament context aids in the interpretation of our utterances to God in the midst of dire circumstances today.

However, in the case of manipulative petitions and vows, God also understands these, but not with compassion and possible positive results. He has no toleration for this very human propensity to try to call the shots, to be in control. He will not allow us to be the ones who determine the outcomes. He will not allow us to orchestrate the processes of our lives. And sometimes, as in the case of Jephthah, we suffer at our own hands because of our lack of faith and manipulative devices. The irony is that just as Jephthah's vow accomplished nothing in the process of Yahweh's victory except to mar it, so our manipulative vows do nothing to promote God's kingdom (because they are merely motivated by our self-interest).

Jephthah wants to rule over his clan so desperately that he attempts to manipulate Yahweh to give him the victory. Thus in the fulfillment of his vow, Jephthah shows how callous he really is to anyone or anything that is not part of his life's goal of ruling over his clan of half-brothers. He is willing to brutalize his own daughter for this (see Contemporary Significance section of 10:17–11:11). When we manifest the win-at-all-cost attitude, those closest to us are frequently the ones so unnecessarily, illegitimately, and horrifically brutalized. Blind ambition that tries to manipulate God brings only disaster.

THE DIVINE LEVEL. Our Western materialistic culture ingrains in us the notion that we somehow deserve things. The "I-deserve-it" mentality manipulates to gain what it determines it has coming to it. The attitude "I-deserve-it-as-much-as-that-other-guy" permeates much of modern society. Many in our culture value the one who can manipulate the system or other people to obtain the good life (cf. any daytime TV talk show). Like Jephthah, those raised in this culture often deal with God the way they deal with others to get what they think they deserve.

But there is abundant Scripture to demonstrate that God, the true and living God, does not work according to human dictates. God will never be manipulated by any human being for one simple reason: If that ever happens, just once, he is no longer God. There comes a point at which God does not answer prayers—prayers that at their very roots are manipulative. It may appear as though God answered Jephthah's prayer by giving him victory over the Ammonites (certainly Jephthah thought so). But Yahweh gave the victory because as Judge of all the earth he defended his people and brought defeat on the Ammonite king. As outlined above, Jephthah's prayer (and hence vow) was utterly unnecessary. God worked out of pure grace on Israel's behalf, not because he was manipulated by Jephthah's prayer and vow. Ultimately, therefore, God's silence means that he did not really respond to Jephthah at all.

When all is said and done, we must end our petitions to God with "not my will, but yours be done." As Christians we can become subject to the error that somehow God owes us or is in a sense obligated to do such and such on our behalf. Illness, economic stress, familial problems, and so on are things that each of us—even ministers, teachers, and missionaries—think that God ought to fix because, well, we're Christians. Of course, pagan, nonchurch attending persons cannot expect God to answer their prayers because they don't worship him. But we're Christians, who are involved in service to him. Surely he ought to do something to solve our problems.

Beside the fact that God may be doing something in our lives beyond our understanding in this world during our lifetime (cf. Job's experience), it may be that we are hiding a personal manipulative motive in our prayer. Until we recognize that God is not obligated by our actions to do anything on our behalf, until we recognize that whatever he does is on the basis of his grace— that is, we don't deserve it—we will experience frustrations in our relationship to him. We don't worship him because of what we can get out of him, but because he is our God!

Hurt people. The tragedy of this passage is repeated again and again in our modern society. Hurt people hurt people.[66] Jephthah came from a dysfunctional background. He was an illegitimate son, born of a prostitute, rejected and disinherited by his family, leader of a gang. He became a man who was hurt, angry, bitter, ambition-driven, ready to fight, manipulative, ignorant of God's Law, abusive of his daughter, lacking boundaries, contentious, emotionally reactionary, revengeful, and doing what is right in his own eyes for his own gain. He made his daughter responsible, blaming her for the disaster that he would inflict on her and making himself the victim of his rash vow. In many ways this nameless daughter represents all the courageous daughters of abusive fathers. Jephthah performs on her the ultimate abuse, for killing one's own child is the worst form of murder.

More than any time in the history of Western civilization, there is a cognizance of the dysfunctional abuse of children. More literature on the subject has been produced in the last few decades and more money and effort have been expended in the attempt to curb this awful testimony to human

---

66. Sandra Wilson, *Hurt People Hurt People* (Nashville: Thomas Nelson, 1993).

depravity than in any previous generation. Yet, there is evidence that this is an increasing trend. The more hurt people, the more hurt people.

No congregation in America is free from the horrific acts of wife and/or child abuse. Unfortunately, the recent kidnapping of an eleven-year-old girl by her Christian school principal in Gary, Indiana, only underscores this. What can be done to arrest this plague? People need to get into the Word of God and follow it. Soaking up the love of God in Christ, they need to let the Lord meet their needs. They may need to seek professional counseling—which more and more churches are providing. But most important they need to remove their ignorance of God and his Word on a broad level, for ignorance of God's Word is not bliss, it is disaster. Only a knowledge of the truth—in particular, the very embodiment of truth, Jesus Christ—can make one free (John 8:32)! Only a knowledge of God's Word can break the bonds of sin and oppression and the cycle of hurt people hurting people.

On another level, Jephthah's callous sacrifice of his daughter as a burnt offering is paralleled by the modern abortion of sons and daughters by a culture that, like Jephthah, is driven by selfish ambition.[67] Granted none of these modern sacrifices is to Milcom, Chemosh, or Baal, but as we have already examined (see esp. ch. 2), the gods of this age are no less demanding and oppressive than their ancient Near Eastern counterparts. Having repudiated the authority of Scripture, the modern narcissistic society is utterly consumed with its "rights" and has no place for the concept that humankind is created in the image of God and that from conception on, the human embryo is a human being made in that image.

Judges 12:1–7

[1]The men of Ephraim called out their forces, crossed over to Zaphon and said to Jephthah, "Why did you go to fight the Ammonites without calling us to go with you? We're going to burn down your house over your head."

[2]Jephthah answered, "I and my people were engaged in a great struggle with the Ammonites, and although I called, you didn't save me out of their hands. [3]When I saw that you wouldn't help, I took my life in my hands and crossed over to fight the Ammonites, and the LORD gave me the victory over them. Now why have you come up today to fight me?"

---

67. We recognize that some abortions are the tragic result of the hard choice in favor of the life of the mother. But the vast bulk of abortions performed throughout the world are not for this reason.

⁴Jephthah then called together the men of Gilead and fought against Ephraim. The Gileadites struck them down because the Ephraimites had said, "You Gileadites are renegades from Ephraim and Manasseh." ⁵The Gileadites captured the fords of the Jordan leading to Ephraim, and whenever a survivor of Ephraim said, "Let me cross over," the men of Gilead asked him, "Are you an Ephraimite?" If he replied, "No," ⁶they said, "All right, say 'Shibboleth.'" If he said, "Sibboleth," because he could not pronounce the word correctly, they seized him and killed him at the fords of the Jordan. Forty-two thousand Ephraimites were killed at that time.

⁷Jephthah led Israel six years. Then Jephthah the Gileadite died, and was buried in a town in Gilead.

THE FINAL SECTION of the Jephthah account (A', see introductory comments on 10:6−12:7) narrates the confrontation between Jephthah and the Ephraimites (12:1−7). A special dialogue is carried out in 12:1−4a. Instead of congratulating Jephthah for his accomplishment and thanking him for delivering them from the Ammonite threat, in their jealousy and wounded sense of self-importance the Ephraimites are determined to destroy the deliverer. They call out their forces, cross the Jordan, and accuse Jephthah of not calling them out to fight the Ammonites (12:1a-b¹). The parallel with the action of the Ephraimites in the Gideon episode is evident (cf. 8:1−3).

The Ephraimites also level a threat against Jephthah (12:1b²). Given the importance to Jephthah of his being the "head" (rō'š), even to the extent of uttering and fulfilling his vow in order to get and maintain the position, the Ephraimite curse must have been especially personal: "We're going to burn down your house over your head [lit., over you]!" Jephthah has just incinerated his only daughter, the first thing out of "his house" to meet him. Now the Ephraimites threaten to incinerate Jephthah's "house" with him in it!

It is clear that the Ephraimite accusation and threat come from the ancient Near Eastern context of the covenant disputation. They have the same rhetorical effect as the earlier threat of the king of Ammon (11:13). It is as though, having delivered Gilead from the external threat of the Ammonite king, Jephthah must now face this internal threat from one of the tribes of Israel. It is ironic that the Ephraimites, who did not become involved in the battle with the Ammonites even though they too were oppressed by them (10:9), now want to fight Jephthah![68] They are depicted here as "bratty upstarts who want to be included where they do not belong."[69] In fact, during this period, it is possible that Ephraim controlled some territories east of the Jordan (cf. 2 Sam. 18:6, which mentions the "forest of Ephraim").[70] In this way, this final story of the Jephthah account may be a "satire" on the "arrogant and insufferable Ephraimites."[71]

Jephthah's reaction is not, however, like Gideon's. He does not cow to the Ephraimites. While he does appear to seek a diplomatic resolution ("I and my people were engaged in a great struggle"),[72] he is particularly concerned with exonerating himself from any personal responsibility (12:2–3a). The diplomacy that follows lacks the same high quality of divine righteousness as that which characterized Jephthah's diplomacy with the king of the Ammonites. Jephthah's claim that he did summon the Ephraimites is in fact doubtful, since there is no confirmation of it in the narrative.[73] If he had appealed to the Ephraimites (and this is not proven), they rejected him and his authority as invested by the elders of Gilead. Why, he asks them, have they come up to fight him?

There is no solemn appeal here to Yahweh, the Judge, to decide the issue. In fact, Jephthah mentions Yahweh only to enhance his own authority vis-à-vis the Ephraimites (a tactic he used with the elders of Gilead, cf. 11:9). His argument that he is in the right is not, in this case, to establish an entitlement to divine help but rather to gain a psychological advantage over his opponents. Jephthah is "still the same skillful practitioner with words, but he appears more eager for the fight on this occasion, and more confident."[74]

---

68. Willis argues that the "squabble did not erupt until Jephthah had claimed authority beyond Gilead. The Ephraimites did not object (indeed, had no right or reason to object) to the Gileadite elders making Jephthah *qāṣîn* and *rōʾš*, because that right was beyond Ephraimite 'jurisdiction': by intertribal tradition it was confined to Gilead's sphere of control. Only when matters moved beyond the traditional were objections raised" ("The Nature of Jephthah's Authority," 43 n. 33). While this may have been a factor, the text states that the Ephraimite disquiet is caused by the noninvitation of Jephthah to participate in the war against the Ammonites.

69. Brettler, "The Book of Judges: Literature As Politics," 408.

70. According to Malamat, the heavy Ephraimite losses may indicate that Jephthah exploited this opportunity to clear Gilead of all the Ephraimites who had settled there ("The Period of the Judges," 159–60).

71. D. Marcus, "Ridiculing the Ephraimites: The Shibboleth Incident (Judg 12:6)," *Maarav* 8 (1992): 95–105, esp. 100.

72. Lit., "I was a *rîb* man, I and my people, with the Ammonites." Jephthah asserts that he resorts to diplomacy first, in contrast to the Ephraimites, "who would fight first and negotiate later" (Boling, *Judges*, 212).

73. He may have appealed to the Ephraimites during his movements in 11:29, but this is purely conjecture.

74. Webb, *The Book of the Judges*, 71.

But the problem is that the Ephraimites are not prepared to recognize any leader of Israel who acts independently of Ephraim. Their wounded, selfish pride leads them to reject him outright. Thus, just as his half-brothers rejected him, so now his tribal "brothers" seem to have rejected him. And both parties are smarting to bring the other down.

Without waiting for a response to his rhetorical question at the end of verse 3, Jephthah calls out the Gileadites and fights against the Ephraimites, who have made another bad remark: "You Gileadites are renegades [i.e., fugitives, *pᵉlîṭê ᵉprayim*] from Ephraim and Manasseh" (i.e., "you illegitimates, you bastards," 12:4). The implications of the Ephraimite taunt are not lost on the man who has suffered most of his life with the tag "illegitimate," "son of a prostitute."[75] Ironically, the Gileadites answer the Ephraimite taunt by putting them to a shameful rout and thus make them the true fugitives of Ephraim (*pᵉlîṭê ᵉprayim*, 12:5).

Interestingly, Yahweh is not involved in this battle in any way. Just as in the second (Transjordanian) battle in the Gideon account (8:4–21), so here Yahweh is not mentioned anywhere. This is an intertribal feud that God has hardly sanctioned. This episode is a foretaste of the intertribal war that erupts in Judges 19–21.

The Gileadites seize the fords of the Jordan and administer a great slaughter of the Ephraimites. The tactic of seizing the fords of the Jordan was utilized by the Ephraimites previously in the battle against the Moabites under Ehud (3:27–30) and against the Midianites under Gideon (7:24–25). Now, ironically, it is used against Ephraim.

Fleeing from the Gileadites, the Ephraimites try to mingle with the regular travelers at the fords and, when asked if they are Ephraimite, deny it. So to facilitate the Ephraimites' demise, the Gileadites employ a word: *šibbōlet*.[76] In a polite request to the Ephraimites, the Gileadites say: "All right, say 'Shibboleth.' If he said 'Sibboleth,' because he could not pronounce the word correctly, they seized him and killed him" (12:6).

It is possible to translate the phrase "because he could not pronounce the word correctly" three ways.[77] (1) The phrase could be translated as indicating a lack of preparation: "because he was not prepared to pronounce it correctly." (2) The phrase could be translated as indicating an inattention: "because he was inattentive to pronounce it correctly." (3) The phrase could be translated as indicating an inability: "because he did not have the ability to pronounce it correctly." But no matter how this phrase is interpreted—whether it be lack of

---

75. Cf. Josh. 22, where the Transjordanians feared this very thing, namely, that they would be considered second-class citizens of Israel.

76. The etymology of the word is uncertain, possibly "ear of wheat" or "current of water." See Marcus, "Ridiculing the Ephraimites," 99.

77. Marcus, "Ridiculing the Ephraimites," 100–101.

preparation, inattention, or inability—it clearly indicates the incompetence of the Ephraimites. They are deficient in language skills and cannot properly repeat the test word spoken by the Gileadite guards. The high and mighty Ephraimites cannot "speak the Queen's English," and so fail the Shibboleth test. Instead of saying "God save the Queen!" they say "God shave the Queen!"[78]

Thus the word *šibbōlet* was chosen because it exposed the incompetence of the Ephraimites to pronounce it, not because of any lexical significance inherent in the word. It is truly an irony that life or death is made to revolve on this "completely empty word," *šibbōlet/sibbōlet*.[79] Consequently, the dialectal difference[80] is not the main emphasis of the test. The Shibboleth episode ridicules "the Ephraimites who are portrayed as incompetent nincompoops who cannot even repeat a test-word spoken by the Gileadite guards."[81]

Gilead's slaughter of its tribal "brother" Ephraim (12:1−6) parallels Jephthah's slaughter of his daughter (11:39−40). Just as Jephthah through his word (11:30−31) murders a daughter within his tribe—in fact, within his own family—so Gilead through a word (*šibbōlet/sibbōlet*) murders a confederated tribe. One can see vividly the further escalated parallel between the effects of a misspoken word on Jephthah's daughter and the Ephraimites. It is, therefore, no surprise that the "justice" wrought on Ephraim by Gilead is as violent as that which Jephthah, their new ruler, has wrought on his own daughter. This intertribal feud under Jephthah is part of a thematic development (progressive internal disintegration) that reaches its climax in the civil war involving the whole of Israel at the end of the book (chs. 19−21).

Verse 7 records the fact that Jephthah judged Israel for six years and then died; he was buried in a town of Gilead. Thus ends the cycle devoted to the "mighty warrior" (*gibbôr ḥayil*) Jephthah.

Bridging Contexts

AS IN 11:29−40, two entities are vying for power. In 11:29−40, it was Jephthah and the Ammonite king; in this section, it is Jephthah and the Ephraimites. The Ephraimites question Jephthah's authority, and the fighting begins. Nothing positive in a spiritual sense comes out of this strug-

---

78. For this illustration, see J. A. Emerton, "Some Comments on the Shibboleth Incident (Judges XII 6)," in *Mélanges bibliques et orientaux en l'honneur de M. Mathias Delcor*, ed. A. Caquot, S. Légasse, and M. Tardieu (AOAT 215; Neukirchen-Vluyn: Neukirchener Verlag, 1985), 155−56.

79. G. von Rad, *Gottes Wirken in Israel* (Neukirchen-Vluyn: Neukirchener Verlag, 1974), 41.

80. For the dialectal issues, see A. Faber, "Second Harvest: *šibbōlet* Revisited (Yet Again)," *JSS* 37 (1992): 1−10.

81. Marcus, "Ridiculing the Ephraimites," 100.

gle. As in the intertribal fighting at the end of the Gideon story and anticipatory of the intertribal warfare at the end of the book (chs. 20–21), this intertribal feud only serves to destroy Israelites—in this case, the Ephraimites.

The Ephraimite threat is met with self-exoneration from any personal responsibility on the part of Jephthah. Insult is countered by insult, and fighting rather than diplomacy follows. Just as Jephthah willingly slaughtered his daughter, now he leads the Gileadites to slaughter their tribal brothers. His unbridled blind ambition has come to its full maturation.

VIOLENCE IS OFTEN the way that a spiritually flawed character compensates for his or her sense of inferiority. In this case, Jephthah's sense of inferiority derives from his having been victimized by past rejection. Ironically, Jephthah victimized his daughter and now victimizes a brother tribe in a more violent way than his own victimization at the hands of his half-brothers. In a society so prone to victimizing others, what kind of violence are we inducing for the next generation? If blind ambition is unbridled and comes to full maturation, the product will be devastating.

Contentious people produce contention. The Ephraimites are contentious, but so is Jephthah. The Ephraimites ought to be happy that their sons did not have to fight and die in this war against the Ammonites. They should thank God for their deliverance from the oppression. And note that Jephthah is far more contentious with the Ephraimites, his own people, than with the Ammonite king. He is diplomatic with the Ammonites and yet astonishingly impatient with his own countrymen.

This is an unnecessary war. But jealousy, envy, and every sort of evil (James 3:14–18) can consume God's people. So it is with the petty, unimportant, and unnecessary fights that consume many a church. And while forty-some thousand may not die,[82] the emotional and physical damage can be astronomical—especially in its long-term effects. There is a need for humility and repentance.

Note the great contrast with the Lord Jesus. He too was despised and rejected. Even those in his only family thought he was crazy. He received no end of criticism from the Pharisees, Sadducees, and religious rulers of the day, even though he knew infinitely more about God and his Word than they did. He was betrayed and utterly abandoned, being crucified with common criminals, even though there was no guile in him. Certainly the Lord Jesus can serve as a model for overcoming dysfunctionality.

---

82. Perhaps in some cases, only because we have a civil government that prevents it.

Judges 12:8–15

AFTER HIM, IBZAN of Bethlehem led Israel. ⁹He had thirty sons and thirty daughters. He gave his daughters away in marriage to those outside his clan, and for his sons he brought in thirty young women as wives from outside his clan. Ibzan led Israel seven years. ¹⁰Then Ibzan died, and was buried in Bethlehem.

¹¹After him, Elon the Zebulunite led Israel ten years. ¹²Then Elon died, and was buried in Aijalon in the land of Zebulun.

¹³After him, Abdon son of Hillel, from Pirathon, led Israel. ¹⁴He had forty sons and thirty grandsons, who rode on seventy donkeys. He led Israel eight years. ¹⁵Then Abdon son of Hillel died, and was buried at Pirathon in Ephraim, in the hill country of the Amalekites.

Original Meaning

AFTER THE JEPHTHAH cycle the narrative introduces three noncyclical/minor judges: Ibzan of Bethlehem, Elon the Zebulunite, and Abdon son of Hillel. The introductory formula (v. 8) unites these three noncyclical/minor judges distinctively from the prior one- and two-minor judge enumerations (see the introduction).

Ibzan (12:8–10)

AFTER THE TWO Transjordanian Gileadites, Jair and Jephthah, the judgeship returns to the Cisjordan (i.e., the west bank of the Jordan). Most scholars refer the Bethlehem mentioned in connection with Ibzan (12:8–10) to the northern Bethlehem of Joshua 19:15, on the Asher-Zebulun border, though there is no consensus here.[1]

A personal detail is given about Ibzan: "He had thirty sons and thirty daughters." This is, on the one hand, similar to the information given about Jair ("thirty sons"), but on the other hand, contrastive to the facts about Jephthah (thirty daughters vs. one daughter). Thus, the just-completed tragic story of Jephthah and his "one daughter," an only child, is followed by this short note about a judge who has "thirty daughters" and brings in a further

---

1. Boling, *Judges*, 215–16. But see Block, *Judges, Ruth*, 389.

"thirty daughters" from outside his clan as wives for his thirty sons! Of all the judges, daughters are mentioned only in connection with these two, Jephthah and Ibzan. After Jephthah's barrenness comes Ibzan's fecundity; the contrast serves to underscore the tragic barrenness suffered by Jephthah in consequence of his vow.

After the Gideon account and its complementary sequel about Abimelech, the references to the number of sons of the judges seems to indicate that from Gideon on judgeship is always on the verge of turning into kingship, with sons succeeding fathers to office.[2] Again, in order to have thirty sons and thirty daughters (sixty children!),[3] one must have a substantial harem (between thirteen and twenty-four wives) and the resources to support such a harem (i.e., monarchic-type resources).

The marriages mentioned here are not just a trivial note. Ibzan deliberately arranges for marriages of all his children to individuals outside his family or clan.[4] In a tribal societal context, this is clearly a means of building and securing one's power base. These marriages cement clan alliances and extend the scope of Ibzan's political influence. Like Jair before him, Ibzan is not concerned with "saving" Israel from anyone; rather, his interests are in building an endowment for himself and his sons. Thus, the self-interest motif continues in both the cyclical/major and noncyclical/minor judges.

Elon (12:11–12)

NOTHING IS REALLY reported about Elon the Zebulunite except the length of his judgeship and the place of his burial. His name is usually interpreted to mean "oak" or "terebinth." The name Elon is also that of a clan in the tribe of Zebulun (Gen. 46:14; Num. 26:26).[5] There may be a wordplay between the name Elon (*ʾêlôn*) and the judge's burial place Aijalon (*ʾayyālôn*) (the two words are spelled the same in the unpointed, consonantal Hebrew script).[6] This may indicate that Elon gave his name to the town from which he governed.[7]

---

2. Webb, *The Book of Judges*, 161.

3. There is a Hittite parallel for these thirty sons and thirty daughters, though the Hittite story is quite different. See H. A. Hoffner Jr., "The Queen of Kanesh and the Tale of Zalpa," COS, 1.71; M. Tsevat, "Two Old Testament Stories and Their Hittite Analogues," *JAOS* 103 (1983): 35–42.

4. Lit., "to the outside" and "from the outside." Family or clan is implied in the ellipsis.

5. The name Elon is also the name of Esau's "Hittite" father-in-law (Gen. 26:34; cf. 36:2).

6. It is also possible that there is a wordplay here with *ʾayil* (despot; cf. Ex. 15:15) (see KBL², 37–38). If so, then the name Elon (*ʾêlôn*) is punned with "little despot" (*ʾayilôn*).

7. Block, *Judges, Ruth*, 390.

Abdon (12:13–15)

ABDON'S JUDGESHIP IS centralized in "Pirathon in Ephraim" (12:15).[8] Like Jair, he has sons who ride on donkeys; but unlike Jair, he has forty, not thirty, and he has grandsons who ride donkeys too (thirty in number). Like Gideon, his total progeny comes to "seventy."

As in the notice about Jair in 10:4, the statement that they "rode on seventy donkeys" may seem humorous to Westerners, but in its ancient Near Eastern context, monarchs in the Levant often rode on donkeys (see comments on 10:4). Thus, like Jair's sons, Abdon's sons riding on donkeys is evidence of their royal-type power over their region. But, unlike Jair, Abdon has extended the control to another generation. Nevertheless, they are no more than royal wannabes—parodies of kingship.

The notice about Abdon's death and burial completes the noncyclical/minor judge notes. There is, however, a tremendous irony at this point. The final phrase of verse 15 states that this last of the noncyclical/minor judges is buried not in Israel but "in the hill country of the Amalekites."[9] Whose land is this? Have the Israelites dropped to such a level of living that they are being absorbed into the peoples of the land? This is not the note we would have hoped the noncyclical/minor judges' presentations to end on.

Bridging Contexts

WHILE THESE NONCYCLICAL/MINOR judge notices are all brief, they seem to play a role in the cycles section of the book. Generally commentators do one of two things with the noncyclical/minor judges. Either they comment briefly on the notices without any attempt at tying them into the interpretation of the larger context, or they understand them as notices of short periods of peace within the many wars documented primarily in the cyclical/major judge narratives.

If the definition of a "judge" (*šōpēt*) as we have posited it is correct (see the introduction, pp. 21–22), and if the criteria for evaluating the judges apply to both the cyclical/major judges and these noncyclical/minor judges, then it seems that the noncyclical judges function literarily through their one-two-three pattern to reinforce the overall message of the cycles section (see the introduction, pp. 42–43). In other words, they strengthen the message of moral declivity that is communicated in the cycles section.

---

8. For the identification of Pirathon, see G. Galil, "Pirathon, Parathon and Timnatha," *ZDPV* 109 (1993): 49–53; E. A. Knauf, "*Pireathon—Farʿaṭ*," *BN* 51 (1990): 19–24; and N. Naʾaman, "Pirathon and Ophrah," *BN* 50 (1989): 11–16.

9. Cf. the ironic border description given in Judg. 1:36.

With Shamgar (3:31), there are many questions but few answers. For example, did Israel do evil in the eyes of the Yahweh? Did God sell/give them into the hands of the Philistines? What is clear is that Shamgar—though a non-Israelite—saved Israel. Israel's salvation came from an unexpected source, in an unexpected manner. Despite the brevity of the vignette, Shamgar is the most successful of the noncyclical/minor judges in fulfilling the role of judge. Like Othniel (first cyclical/major judge), while the account is limited, what is recorded argues for his ideal position among the minor judges.

With Tola (10:1–2), there are also more questions than answers. He saves Israel, but from whom? He is a man of Issachar, but why does he live in Shamir in the hill country of Ephraim? The former question can be evaluated positively—he did save Israel—but not as positively as the statement about Shamgar since at least some basic details are given for his delivering activity. The latter question is difficult to answer, but the fact that the text naturally raises this question in the minds of ancient readers seems to merit some reservations.

In the case of Jair (10:3–5), matters are much clearer. He is interested in wealth and power. He has a harem with thirty sons, who ride on thirty donkeys (a clear sign of rulership and power) and who control thirty towns in a district named after him. This is raw wealth and power. It strongly hints at a materialistic orientation. In this respect, he is pictured in the mold of Gideon.

With Ibzan (12:8–10), the trend set by Jair is extended. He has a harem with thirty sons and thirty daughters. His great concern is to make sure that these sons and daughters marry individuals outside his clan in order to build alliances and his base of power. This too paints a picture of self-interested power and materialism in the mold of Gideon.

In the case of Elon (12:11–12), we have no definite information. But if his name is meant as a pun on the place name Aijalon, indicating that he gave it its name, or if his name is a pun with "little despot" (ʾayilôn, see footnote 6), then he is a further comment on the declivity of the noncyclical/minor judges. But this is uncertain.

With Abdon (12:13–15), however, the trend started with Jair (and Gideon before him) comes to its climax. He has forty sons and thirty grandsons who ride on seventy donkeys. Abdon has extended his power to another generation. Ironically, however, this last noncyclical/minor judge is buried in the hill country of the Amalekites (which strongly hints at Israel's inability to possess the land).

After Gideon, it seems as if judgeship is always on the verge of turning into kingship, with sons succeeding fathers in office.[10] From the little information given, these judges seem to be dominated by power and wealth concerns.

---

10. This notion appears again in the debate between the Israelites and Samuel over the issue of judgeship versus monarchy (with special reference to Samuel's sons); see 1 Sam. 8:1–5.

Contemporary Significance

THE NONCYCLICAL/MINOR JUDGES give evidence (like their major judge counterparts) of a spiritual and moral degeneration. Rather than living up to their responsibilities in "saving" Israel and "stimulating Israel to godly living," aside from Shamgar and Tola, they are, in the main, characterized as self-interested materialists hungry for power. Such a negative characterization serves as a warning to us today. In a culture that promotes self-interest and materialism and that worships power, such activity does not work the works of God.

Judges 13:1–16:31

ℳ

Introduction to the Samson Cycle

THE SAMSON CYCLE is composed of three distinct sections: the birth account (13:1–25), the paralleled life accounts (14:1–15:20), and the death account (16:1–31). The first section narrates the double theophany to Manoah's wife that leads to Samson's birth. The second section recounts Samson's initial exploits emanating from his marriage to a Philistine woman at Timnah. The third section narrates his downfall and death emanating from Samson's rendezvous with two women: a prostitute at Gaza and Delilah.[1] Thus the structure of the Samson cycle is:

I. **Birth Account: Double Theophany to Manoah's Wife (13:1–25)**
   Narrative Frame (13:1–2)
   First Theophany to Manoah's Wife (13:3–7)
       Prediction: Deliverer's Birth As Nazirite (13:3–5)
       Result: Communication of Theophany to Incredulous
           Manoah (13:6–7)
   Second Theophany to Manoah's Wife (13:8–23)
       Prediction: Deliverer's Birth As Nazirite (13:8–14)
       Result: Sacrifice By Incredulous Manoah (13:15–23)
   Narrative Frame (13:24–25)
II. **Paralleled Life Account: Accounts Linked to Samson's Timnite Wife (14:1–15:20)**
   First Account (14:1–20)
       Episode 1: Samson Goes Down to Timnah: Engagement
           to Timnite Wife (14:1–4)
       Episode 2: Action Involving an Animal: Samson's Prowess
           (14:5–7)
       Episode 3: Action Involving Honey, a Gracious Act
           (14:8–9)
       Episode 4: Smiting of Thirty Philstines (14:10–20)
   Second Account (15:1–20)
       Episode 1: Samson Goes Down to Timnah: Attempted
           Consumation with Timnite Wife (15:1–3)
       Episode 2: Action Involving an Animal: Samson's Prowess
           (15:4–6a)

---

1. Webb, *The Book of the Judges*, 160.

Episode 3: Action Involving Retaliation, a Vicious Act
(15:6b−8)
Episode 4: Smiting of One Thousand Philistines
(15:9−19)
III. Death Account: Downfall and Death Linked to the Gazite and Delilah (16:1−31)
Downfall (16:1−22)
Prostitute of Gaza (16:1−3)
Delilah's Deception (16:4−22)
Death (16:23−31)
Death of Samson/Death of Dagon

The entire Samson account is framed by two paradoxes: "birth from a barren wife" (13:1−25) and "death from a disabled warrior" (16:23−31).[2] Furthermore, it is marked by Samson's relationships with four women: mother (Manoah's wife), wife (the Timnite), prostitute (the Gazite), and antagonist (Delilah). Ironically, only the last of these—the treacherous, destructive woman who brings about his downfall, the one he "loves"—is named.

There are also three sets of narrative framings that unite the cycle. The first inclusio, framing chapter 13, is found in the only references to the Danites in the cycle: "the clan of the Danites" (13:2) and "Mahaneh Dan" (13:25). The second framing is found in the mentioning of Zorah and Eshtaol in 13:25a and 16:31a, which frame the second and third sections. The third inclusio, surrounding all three sections of the cycle, is found in the references to Samson's father, Manoah, and Zorah in 13:2 and 16:31a. Moreover, as O'Connell notes, it may be "a result of deliberate design that these three inclusios are triangulated among the three verses (13:2, 25a; 16:31a), so that each verse contains only two inclusio elements."[3]

The layout of the Samson cycle is similar to that of the Gideon cycle. In both, the angel of the Lord commissions his agents. In Judges 6, he commissions Gideon directly; in Judges 13, he commissions Samson indirectly through his mother (this may anticipate the significant role that women will play in his career). In both cycles, the motif of fire plays a major role: the torches (*lappīdîm*) of Gideon and his three hundred men (7:16, 20) and the torches (*lappîdîm*) used by Samson with his three hundred foxes (15:4). Both cycles evince two major movements with their respective climaxes. The Samson story begins and ends at Zorah (and Eshtaol), as the Gideon narrative began and ended at Ophrah.

---

2. See J. A. Freeman, "Samson's Dry bones: A Structural Reading of Judges 13−16," in *Literary Interpretations of Biblical Narratives*, ed. K. R. R. Gros Louis (2 Vols.; Nashville: Abingdon, 1974, 1982), 2:145−60.

3. O'Connell, *The Rhetoric of the Book of Judges*, 223.

The second and third sections show a number of parallels in movement and development of the plot: Samson sees a woman (the Timnite, the prostitute of Gaza), becomes involved with a woman who betrays him by revealing a secret (the Timnite, Delilah), is bound and given into the hands of the Philistines (by the Judahites, by Delilah), and is then empowered by Yahweh to slaughter them in great numbers. The second section climaxes in the slaughter of the Philistines at Ramath Lehi in 15:14–19. The third section climaxes in his slaughter of the Philistines and Samson's own death in the temple at Gaza in 16:30 (in fact, this third section begins and basically ends at Gaza).

The Samson cycle has more than one dramatic climax (just as the cycles of Deborah/Barak/Jael, Gideon/Abimelech, and Jephthah). While many scholars find only two major climaxes in the Samson cycle, O'Connell argues that the Samson account has nine moments that achieve at least a partial resolution, each one building on the intensity of those that precede (14:19a; 15:4–5, 8a, 15; 16:3 [9b, 12b, 14b], 30a).

> Of these, three climaxes involve the destruction of some object of material or cultural worth to the Philistines: the burning of their wheat crop (15:4–5), the destruction of the gate at Gaza (16:3), and the destruction of Dagon's temple at Gaza (16:30a). Four climaxes entail the killing of Philistines: thirty men at Ashkelon (14:19a), a great slaughter (at Timnah?) (15:8a), a thousand men at Ramath Lehi (15:15), and all the "tyrants" and people at the temple of Gaza (16:30a). Only in the last climax do both material destruction and mass homicide combine so that the last climax of the account is unmistakably the most intense. But the final climax of 16:30a has the ironic distinction of being the moment of Samson's suicide.[4]

Judges 13:1–25

[1]Again the Israelites did evil in the eyes of the LORD, so the LORD delivered them into the hands of the Philistines for forty years.

[2]A certain man of Zorah, named Manoah, from the clan of the Danites, had a wife who was sterile and remained childless. [3]The angel of the LORD appeared to her and said, "You are sterile and childless, but you are going to conceive and

---

4. Ibid., 221–22. According to O'Connell, the Othniel and Ehud accounts have only one climax each, and the cycles of Deborah/Barak/Jael, Gideon/Abimelech, and Jephthah have two each. All together these cycles have eight climaxes. But the Samson cycle has nine all by itself.

have a son. [4]Now see to it that you drink no wine or other fermented drink and that you do not eat anything unclean, [5]because you will conceive and give birth to a son. No razor may be used on his head, because the boy is to be a Nazirite, set apart to God from birth, and he will begin the deliverance of Israel from the hands of the Philistines."

[6]Then the woman went to her husband and told him, "A man of God came to me. He looked like an angel of God, very awesome. I didn't ask him where he came from, and he didn't tell me his name. [7]But he said to me, 'You will conceive and give birth to a son. Now then, drink no wine or other fermented drink and do not eat anything unclean, because the boy will be a Nazirite of God from birth until the day of his death.'"

[8]Then Manoah prayed to the LORD: "O Lord, I beg you, let the man of God you sent to us come again to teach us how to bring up the boy who is to be born."

[9]God heard Manoah, and the angel of God came again to the woman while she was out in the field; but her husband Manoah was not with her. [10]The woman hurried to tell her husband, "He's here! The man who appeared to me the other day!"

[11]Manoah got up and followed his wife. When he came to the man, he said, "Are you the one who talked to my wife?"

"I am," he said.

[12]So Manoah asked him, "When your words are fulfilled, what is to be the rule for the boy's life and work?"

[13]The angel of the LORD answered, "Your wife must do all that I have told her. [14]She must not eat anything that comes from the grapevine, nor drink any wine or other fermented drink nor eat anything unclean. She must do everything I have commanded her."

[15]Manoah said to the angel of the LORD, "We would like you to stay until we prepare a young goat for you."

[16]The angel of the LORD replied, "Even though you detain me, I will not eat any of your food. But if you prepare a burnt offering, offer it to the LORD." (Manoah did not realize that it was the angel of the LORD.)

[17]Then Manoah inquired of the angel of the LORD, "What is your name, so that we may honor you when your word comes true?"

¹⁸He replied, "Why do you ask my name? It is beyond understanding." ¹⁹Then Manoah took a young goat, together with the grain offering, and sacrificed it on a rock to the LORD. And the LORD did an amazing thing while Manoah and his wife watched: ²⁰As the flame blazed up from the altar toward heaven, the angel of the LORD ascended in the flame. Seeing this, Manoah and his wife fell with their faces to the ground. ²¹When the angel of the LORD did not show himself again to Manoah and his wife, Manoah realized that it was the angel of the LORD.

²²"We are doomed to die!" he said to his wife. "We have seen God!"

²³But his wife answered, "If the LORD had meant to kill us, he would not have accepted a burnt offering and grain offering from our hands, nor shown us all these things or now told us this."

²⁴The woman gave birth to a boy and named him Samson. He grew and the LORD blessed him, ²⁵and the Spirit of the LORD began to stir him while he was in Mahaneh Dan, between Zorah and Eshtaol.

THIS FIRST SECTION of the Samson cycle (13:1– 25)[5]—the birth account—has a narrative frame at the beginning that introduces the cycle events *before* the narration of the two theophanies (13:1–2) and a narrative frame at the end that relates information that transpires *after* the theophanies (13:24–25). In between these two is the recounting of the two theophanies of the angel of Yahweh (13:2–7, 8–23). Both theophanies come initially to Manoah's wife and contain both the prediction of Samson's birth as a Nazirite for the purpose of delivering Israel (13:3–5, 8–14) and the results of the theophanies, each of which heightens the incredulity of Manoah (13:6–7, 15–23).

Opening Narrative Frame (13:1–2)

THE WELL-FAMILIAR OPENING narrative frame components begin the narration of the cycle. "Again the Israelites did evil in the eyes of the LORD, so the

---

5. See J. Cheryl Exum, "Literary Patterns in the Samson Saga: An Investigation of Rhetorical Style in Biblical Prose" (Ph.D. diss.; Columbia University, 1976), 83; idem, "Promise and Fulfillment: Narrative Art in Judges 13," *JBL* 99 (1980): 43–59, esp. 44–45.

LORD delivered them into the hands of the Philistines for forty years." Yahweh's utilization of the Philistines[6] has already been anticipated in the introduction to the Jephthah story (10:7): Yahweh "sold them into the hands of the Philistines and the Ammonites." This may imply that the Ammonite and Philistine oppressions were simultaneous. The length of the oppression is forty years, double the next longest oppression (Deborah/Barak: twenty years; see the introduction, pp. 34–43). This may speak to its severity.

Instead of the usual third component, "and the Israelites cried out to the LORD," there is only silence. The Israelites do not make an appeal to Yahweh in this cycle! In the last two cycles (Gideon/Abimelech and Jephthah), this issue of crying out to Yahweh has come under close scrutiny. Israel does not deserve to be delivered (cf. the indictment of 6:7–10) and cannot manipulate Yahweh to intervene through false repentance (as Yahweh himself emphasizes in 10:10–16). In the Samson episode, the Israelites show no indication of even wanting to be delivered. Manoah and his wife are happy simply to avoid contact with the Philistines (14:3). And Samson does not want to fight the Philistines; he wants to copulate with their women![7]

The Judahites (note the tremendous contrast with ch. 1!) are willing to accept the Philistine dominance as the status quo (15:11). Yahweh's willingness to help demonstrates that it is his kindness alone, and not the nation's repentance, that is the ultimate basis for Israel's deliverance. Yahweh, and Yahweh alone, "was seeking an occasion to confront the Philistines" (14:4).

In light of Israel's stubborn rebellion at this time, it is much more remarkable that Yahweh will not only intervene but will do so in the context of a miraculous birth reminiscent of Abraham and Sarah (Gen. 11:30; 16:1; cf. also Rebekah in 25:21, the almost contemporary story of Hannah in 1 Sam. 1:2, and the much later story of Elizabeth in Luke 1:7).[8] This intervention in the days of Samson demonstrates the tremendous long-suffering grace of God so that, in spite of Israel's lack of response, he will act purely out of faithfulness to his covenant with them.

The introduction to Samson's father and mother is given in 13:2. He is "a certain man of Zorah" (this phrase serves as an anticipatory link with the Danites, who will migrate to Laish from this same town [18:2, 8, 11]). Thus Zorah's mention serves as a link between the renegade judge and the renegade tribe of which he was a part. Samson's father is Manoah, a name mean-

---

6. See D. M. Howard Jr., "Philistines," in *Peoples of the Old Testament World*, ed. A. J. Hoerth et al. (Grand Rapids: Baker, 1994), 231–50.

7. Webb, *The Book of the Judges*, 163.

8. Familiar motifs and themes found throughout Israel's literary corpus occur in the Samson narrative. See J. L. Crenshaw, *Samson: A Secret Betrayed, a Vow Ignored* (Macon, Ga.: Mercer Univ. Press, 1978), 20, 41–50.

ing "resting (place)" (cf. Noah, which has the same root); his wife (who remains nameless) is barren and has no children. The double mention of her situation (13:2–3) is intentional and emphatic.[9] The present concern for progeny provides an obvious link with the Jephthah narrative, in which the tragedy was not barrenness but virginity. Jephthah's daughter dies not having known a man.[10]

First Theophany to Manoah's Wife (13:3–7)

IN THE FIRST THEOPHANY to Manoah's wife, the angel of Yahweh makes an unsolicited appearance to offer two predictions: (1) Manoah's barren wife will bear a son who will be a Nazirite from conception (13:3b–5a); and (2) this son will *begin* to deliver Israel out of the hand of the Philistines (13:5b).[11] The first prediction is fulfilled in 13:24, when "the woman gave birth to a son and named him Samson." The second prediction is fulfilled progressively over chapters 14–16. The unsolicited nature of this first appearance underscores the fact that the raising up of this deliverer is a gracious act of God from beginning to end.

The Nazirite vow is described in Numbers 6:1–21. It could be voluntarily taken by a male or female for a period of time or for a lifetime. It included three basic prohibitions:

- to refrain from consuming wine (*yayin*) or other intoxicating drink (*šēkār*), in fact anything from the vine (i.e., grapes, raisins, wine, and any other fermented drink like wine-vinegar, cf. Ruth 2:14; also Num. 6:1–4)
- to refrain from cutting one's hair for the duration of the vow (Num. 6:5–8)
- to avoid coming into contact with a dead body (Num. 6:9–12)

These three marks of Samson's separation are curiously split between the mother and the son she is to bear, with only the prohibition against the cutting of hair being specifically applied to Samson himself. Moreover, Samson's vow is not voluntary (usually the Nazirite vow was voluntary) and is to be applied to his entire life (usually it was only for a specific period of time).[12]

---

9. It is important to remember that barrenness is one of the specific Deuteronomic curses for lack of covenantal fidelity to Yahweh (Deut. 28:18).

10. Block, *Judges, Ruth*, 396.

11. The phrase "and he will begin the deliverance of Israel" recalls the phrase concerning Tola in 10:1a, "Tola ... rose to save [deliver] Israel" (10:1a). Whereas Tola apparently succeeded, Samson will only begin the process of deliverance. The delivering activities of Samuel, Saul, Jonathan, and David are yet future.

12. Technically Samson's Nazirite status begins at his conception.

In addition to these three marks, the angel of Yahweh appends the prohibition for Samson's mother to consume any unclean food during her pregnancy. Since all Israelites were subject to this law, not just Nazirites, this testifies to the condition of the nation as a whole. This law, like many others, seems to have been generally disregarded by the Israelites (or at least the Danites). Thus, the fact that the woman needs to be reminded of this law suggests that it was not being observed in the manner that Yahweh intended. Interestingly, in contrast to the order in Numbers 6 (fruit of the vine, no cutting of the hair, no contact with a dead body), the prohibition concerning the hair comes last in Judges 13. This is anticipatory of the climax of the narrative.

Twice in this first divine manifestation Manoah's wife is assured that she "will conceive and give birth to a son" (13:3, 5). Interestingly, Samson is twice sacred to Yahweh: first, in being the firstborn, and second, in being consecrated to Yahweh as a Nazirite at conception.

After this initial theophany, Manoah's wife relates its message to her husband. Three items in her description are revealing. (1) She describes the angel of Yahweh as "a man of God [*ʾîš hāʾĕlōhîm*][13] ... [who] looked like an angel [or messenger, *malak*] of God, very awesome." In this, she speaks better than she knows. As in other contexts, the divine name is used in narrative description, and the generic noun "God" is used to signal a subjective conviction. Thus there is irony in saying that "the man of God" (previously introduced by the narrator as "the angel [messenger] of the LORD") looked just like God's angel (messenger). Thus, Manoah's wife only perceives this to be a divine being but does not comprehend that this *is* the angel of Yahweh, Yahweh himself.[14]

(2) She states: "I didn't ask him where he came from, and he didn't tell me his name." She does not ask the envoy's origin, for if she had, she may have been surprised at the answer. The issue of the "name" is also connected to origin (see below). The narrator has Manoah's wife come close to the truth in her groping way, but she does not comprehend it.

(3) She states: "The boy will be a Nazirite of God from birth *until the day of his death*." The words in italic were not part of the original message as given in 13:3–5; they are her own. Once again she speaks better than she knows. So this too is anticipatory of the climax, for her phrase "until the day of his death" is, in fact, her substitution for the angel of Yahweh's "and he will begin the deliverance of Israel from the hands of the Philistines." Her failure to

---

13. Often this expression describes a prophet (cf. Deut. 33:1; 1 Sam. 2:27; 9:6–10; 1 Kings 12:22).

14. Boling, *Judges*, 220.

mention the Nazirite prohibition against haircutting is understandable. The cutting of the Nazirite's hair belonged to the completion of one's "consecration," the return to normal, secular life (Num. 6:13–20). Since Samson is a Nazirite "until the day of his death," logically his vow is never over and he should never cut his hair.

Second Theophany to Manoah's Wife (13:8–23)

MANOAH IS INCREDULOUS, even cynical, about his wife's report of this first angelic visit. Apparently resentful and jealous (cf. the repeated use of the pronoun "us") that the angel of Yahweh has appeared to his wife rather than to him, he prays for another angelic visit so that *he too* may inquire how they should treat the boy to be born (cf. 13:8). Obviously, he is unwillingly to trust the Lord's word already revealed through his wife's testimony, and as a result, he unnecessarily delays the fulfillment of God's plan. In this sense, Manoah's request is similar to Gideon's fleecings (6:36–40): Both are unnecessary because God's will has already been revealed. If knowledge is power, then Manoah is determined to recapture the power in his household.[15]

Remarkably but graciously, God responds to Manoah's request and sends the angel back. Ironically, in this second theophany, the angel of the Lord reappears once again to his wife and not Manoah (13:9). She goes and excitedly tells her husband, "He's here! The man who appeared to me the other day!" But Manoah's question to the man, "Are you the one who talked to my wife?" (13:11), demonstrates that he still doubts his wife's words.[16] His next question still reflects his doubts: "When your words are fulfilled, what is to be the rule for the boy's life and work?" The angel of Yahweh has already revealed this to Manoah's wife, and so he tells Manoah this in no uncertain terms.

No additional revelation concerning Samson is communicated through the angel's second visit.[17] In the end, it only reveals Manoah's unwillingness to believe what was announced in the first visit to his wife. Thus in contrast to his wife, Manoah obstructs the development of God's plan and delays its implementation by requiring a second annunciation performed simply for his own verification. Manoah's characterization is "designed to foreshadow the

---

15. Block, *Judges, Ruth*, 407.

16. The answer "I am" in such a theophanic context is reminiscent of Ex. 3:14.

17. The mentioning of the prohibition against haircutting is also lacking in the Lord's answer here, as it was in the explanation of Manoah's wife to her husband (13:6–7). Is it because Manoah's wife speaks better than she knows? There is a tightening of the dietary restrictions concerning the consumption of the product of the vine, but this is only in closer agreement with the Nazirite restriction.

characterization of Samson, who, while disregarding the angelic commission that he should perpetually be a Nazirite, nevertheless unwittingly fulfils its purpose."[18]

Manoah's hospitality to the angel of Yahweh in 13:15–23 is clearly parallel to the pattern of Gideon's hospitality in 6:11–24 (cf. also Gen. 18:1–8). But in contrast to the theophany to Gideon, where Yahweh himself gives the reassurance (cf. 6:23), here the reassurance that they will not die comes from Manoah's wife (13:23), who thus chides Manoah for not comprehending the purpose of the divine visits.[19] And she says this not because of brilliant theological insight on her part but from basic common sense: Why would the angel of the Lord appear twice repeating his prediction and the requirements concerning the son to be born if he was planning to kill them? That would be truly stupid. Poor Manoah still does not truly believe!

Like Gideon (6:36–40), Manoah requires a sign.[20] However, unlike Gideon, this incident reveals Manaoh's spiritual dullness and his attempt at manipulating Yahweh. Manoah's attempt at hospitality ("we would like you to stay until we prepare a young goat [i.e., kid] for you)" receives a rebuff ("Even though you detain me, I will not eat any of your food").

Apparently, Manoah's intention is to detain and obligate his divine visitor through feeding, a concept well-attested in ancient Near Eastern religions, where feeding a deity or his envoy provided the basis for the supplicant's expectation of divine action on his behalf. Yahweh states that he will have none of this. Here a contrast with Abraham in Genesis 18 is informative: Abraham's motives were genuine and proper, not like Manoah's. The angel of Yahweh will not accept Manoah's manipulative, pagan attempt, but instead instructs him to offer a burnt offering to Yahweh. The last sentence of 13:16 is parenthetical and reveals Manoah's spiritual perceptions: He does not "realize that it was the angel of the LORD" (i.e., a theophany of Yahweh himself).[21]

But Manoah is not done with his attempted manipulation. He now asks the question, "What is your name, so that we may honor [*kbd*] you when your word comes true?" This question contains a number of problems. (1) In the ancient Near Eastern context, knowing the name of a heavenly being provided power over that being. So Manoah is still seeking manipulative power through special knowledge. (2) Manoah asks his name in order to honor

---

18. O'Connell, *The Rhetoric of the Book of Judges*, 214 n. 304.

19. Ibid., 218.

20. For a detailed comparison of the sacrifices of Gideon and Manoah, see Block, *Judges, Ruth*, 410–16; Webb, *The Book of the Judges*, 164–68; O'Connell, *The Rhetoric of the Book of Judges*, 218–19.

21. See Polzin, *Moses and the Deuteronomoist*, 181–87.

---

him—not immediately but *after* "[his] word comes true." In other words, Manoah still is doubtful about Yahweh's words. Significantly, Manoah does not honor the occasion and the site with a Yahweh-honoring altar name.[22] (3) Manoah, having not perceived whom he is talking to, nevertheless would honor (*kbd*) this person, when only Yahweh is to be honored (*kbd*).

The angel of Yahweh's answer confirms these problems: "Why do you ask my name?" On the one hand, the question seems to say, "Think, and you will know the answer!" It presumes that Manoah knows better than to ask.[23] On the other hand, the question demonstrates the theophanic visitor's unwillingness to release his name for Manoah's control. The divine name cannot be had on demand or taken in vain; otherwise it could be exposed to magical manipulation. Manoah is denied power through special knowledge.

The angel of Yahweh's answer to Manoah's question is a question. This question is verbatim the same as the questions asked to Jacob in Genesis 32:20, where Jacob asked for the name of the divine wrestling partner but received only this question. The "angel" here does add, however, that the name "is beyond understanding" (*peli'y*; for this root, cf. Gen. 18:14; Isa. 9:6). The root of the verb *pl'* is frequently used to refer to God's marvelous acts in judgment and salvation (Ex. 3:20; Judg. 6:13; 1 Chron. 16:9, 24; Ps. 9:1; 26:7; 139:6; etc.). Although the divine messenger provides Manoah with all the connotated hints, he is still unaware of the messenger's divinity.

As the theophany approaches its climax, Manoah prepares a sacrifice and offers it on a rock "to the LORD. And the LORD did an amazing thing" (13:19; cf. Ex. 15:11). As the flames rise up from the altar, the angel of Yahweh goes up in them, and Manoah and his wife go face down on the ground (13:20). They know that they have seen God, and the experience leaves Manoah in a state of mortal fear: "We are doomed to die! . . . We have seen God!"[24]

But his nameless wife understands more than her husband. She sensibly stills her husband's fear by sound logic, straightforward common sense. The first clause of her response, "if the LORD had meant to kill us," begins with *lû*, a particle that in this construction introduces a contrary-to-fact statement.[25] Thus, the logical statements that follow (13:23) reinforce the illogical notion that Yahweh would reveal and predict all this (twice), only to kill them.

---

22. This sets a precedent for Samson's more flagrant violations of Yahweh's grace. See Klein, *Triumph of Irony*, 122.

23. Ibid., 124.

24. Theologically correct (Ex. 33:20; Isa. 6:1–5), but logically incorrect.

25. *IBHS* §§30.5.4b; 38.2e.

Closing Narrative Frame (13:24–25)

THIS LAST SECTION contains the fulfillment of the promise of Yahweh in the birth of Samson. Exum rightly brings out the emphasis on the child in the structure of the verse (italics hers):

> The woman bore a *son*
> and she called his name *Samson*
> And the *boy* grew,
> and Yahweh blessed *him* (v. 24).[26]

Ironically, it is his mother who gives the baby the name Samson (13:24a), a name related to the Hebrew noun šemeš ("sun"), which is also the name of the sun deity in Canaanite (as well as in other Semitic) languages. The ending is probably a diminutive (thus, "Little Sun/Shemesh"). This is hardly a name that would be expected after such a double theophany of Yahweh to his mother! Certainly one would have expected a Yahwistic name, one starting or ending with the divine name (e.g., Zechariah [*zkryhw*], Jehoash/Joash [*yhw'š/yw'š*], etc.). It is incredulous indeed! Even so, by God's grace, the boy grows up, and Yahweh blesses him (cf. 1 Sam. 2:26 [Samuel]; Luke 2:52 [Jesus]).

The statement in 13:25 that Yahweh's Spirit begins (*ḥll*) to impel or stir (*pᶜm*) Samson in Mahaneh Dan,[27] between Zorah and Eshtaol, introduces motifs that will be important throughout the account. Yahweh will accomplish what he has predicted (cf. 13:5).

This account of Samson's miraculous birth discloses that the issues of barrenness and fertility, life and death, are in the hands of Yahweh. Samson will call on Yahweh two times in the course of the narrative, and in both instances his call will be answered. In the first case he will be granted life (15:18–19), and in the second case death (16:31). In dying he will bring down Dagon and demonstrate the supremacy of Yahweh.

This double theophanic story reveals directly much more about Samson's parents and their character than it does about him (though obviously his character is determined to some extent by theirs). The fact that this is a

---

26. Exum, "Promise and Fulfillment: Narrative Art in Judges 13," 57.

27. Mahaneh Dan mentioned in 13:25 and 18:12 is problematic. The location of Mahaneh Dan in 18:12 is specifically west of Kiriath Jearim in Judah. It may be that there were two specific places called Mahaneh Dan, one west of Kiriath Jearim and the other between Zorah and Eshtaol, a general enclave wherein were settled the remnants of the tribe of Dan (subsequent to the migration of Judg. 18). It is also possible that the reference in 13:25a is not a proper name but simply a reference to "a Danite camp between Zorah and Eshtaol." See O'Connell, *The Rhetoric of the Book of Judges*, 215 n. 307.

theophany and that Samson is to be a Nazirite from birth create in the reader an expectation that perhaps this will be a significant delivering judge.[28] In fact, chapter 13 raises the highest level of expectation by virtue of the two theophanic visits, which not only promise the wonder of birth to a barren woman but a chosen son, dedicated to Yahweh before his very conception and emergence into life.[29] Moreover, Yahweh's special hand will be on the child (13:24b) as he grows to adulthood. Virtually every spiritual advantage is afforded this deliverer!

The theophanic story will, however, only reinforce the negative characterization of Samson. Even with his special, miraculous birth and Nazirite status, Samson will prove to be the judge who is least interested in being a deliverer. He is portrayed as a "self-gratifying brute," "a prankish womanizer," "whose acts of deliverance are rarely better than by-products of his spiteful nature."[30] The last hope of Israel in Judges is, then, a "judge/deliverer" who chases women instead of enemies and who avenges personal grievances instead of delivering his nation from the oppression.[31]

AS PREVIOUSLY MENTIONED, as a preliminary to the interpretation and application of each cycle, it is important to place the particular cycle within the larger macrostructure of the cycles section (see the introduction, pp. 34–43). This ensures that the cycle will be interpreted in its proper overall context within the downward moral movement of this section. With the Samson cycle, the cycles section enters the climactic conclusion and the moral nadir of the period.

Apathy. What is especially striking about this cycle is the incredible apathy of the Israelites toward both spiritual matters and the oppression in general. It is hard to understand how a people who have experienced God's grace and tasted the good gifts he gives can be so unresponsive, dull, and indifferent about their spiritual lives. For example, the fact that Manoah's wife needs to be reminded about the law concerning the eating of unclean things suggests that this law is not being observed in the manner Yahweh intended. The Israelites seem to have a total lack of interest in the things of God and in particular their covenant relationship to him.

---

28. Compare also how the theophany in the Gideon account raised reader expectations.
29. Klein, *Triumph of Irony*, 116.
30. O'Connell, *The Rhetoric of the Book of Judges*, 214.
31. Klein, *Triumph of Irony*, 118.

This makes Yahweh's intervention in the situation at the time of the Philistine oppression that much more amazing. It is *not* due to any repentance by Israel, because Israel doesn't even want deliverance from the oppression! It is based solely on his kindness and faithfulness to his covenant. It is his act of pure grace toward them.

The Israelites' apathy to the Philistine oppression will manifest itself in Samson's apathy to the Philistine oppression. If the Israelites do not want to be saved, he certainly has no motivation to do it. But God will intervene in order to accomplish his plan. Even if Samson will not live for God, God will use his sinful lifestyle to accomplish the beginning of the deliverance of his people.

Unfortunately, apathy about spiritual matters is hardly a thing of the past. Many Christians today suffer the same lethargic attitude toward the things of God. They don't want to be saved from this lethargy any more than the Israelites wanted to be saved from theirs! As in the past, however, God intervenes today to arouse his people from their dormant state. Just as he stirred up Philistine opposition to stimulate Israel, God may need to stir up opposition to his people to spur them on. And even in doing this, God will be manifesting his grace toward his people.

Lack of spiritual perception. Like their countrymen, Samson's parents evince a lack of spiritual perception. (1) His father Manoah is skeptical and unbelieving. He tries to manipulate God through obtaining special knowledge of God's name in order to give him power. But Yahweh will not give Manoah that knowledge. He will not allow his name to be misused. But in attempting to gain the upper hand over God, Manoah unnecessarily delays God's work not just in his life but in the life of the nation. (2) Samson's nameless mother is more spiritually perceptive than his father, but only somewhat. She gives him his inappropriate name, especially in light of the fact that she has experienced the two theophanies of Yahweh that revealed the coming birth of the child.

Special status. Samson has a special status. The double theophany and his Nazirite call from conception stress this status. Moreover, he has Yahweh's special blessing as he grows up. All this creates the highest level of expectation for this deliverer, since he has so much spiritual advantage. But this will only heighten the tragedy of lost potential, of squandered gifts, of failure to achieve. Certainly, this speaks to the lost opportunities for believers, who, like Samson in particular and the Israelites in general, have a special status with God and who have received a calling and spiritual gifts and abilities from God. What will we do with these?

ATTITUDE CHECK. This passage calls us to an attitude check. Have we grown apathetic in our Christianity? Are we sensitive to God's calling in our lives? Has compromise with the world caused us to be unresponsive to God's Word, to his standards of morality, to his promises and expectations for our lives? Have we become dull, not being able to discern his voice? Do we demand personal verification, unwilling to trust his self-revelation in his Word?

A cynical and unbelieving attitude (as in the case of Manoah) results in a desire for personal verification at every turn. Our society demands verification, evidence, or proof. In many settings, especially in religious ones, this must be personal evidence or proof. The very notion of objective truth is insufficient in our postmodern culture. Unless we can personally touch, feel, see (i.e., "know" through our senses), we do not want to believe. Yet even the subjective aspect of Christianity, the internal witness of the Holy Spirit, is deemed insufficient evidence to a demanding, self-consumed, modern world. Today's culture has desensitized men and women to spiritual matters, and the church itself has not escaped from being influenced in this desensitizing process.

No doubt spiritual apathy to God and his church contributes also to this self-verification mentality. Disinterest in God's Word, fostered to some degree by lifeless, uncreative teaching and preaching, is reflected in various aspects of church life from giving to participation in service. Many pastors and churches are more interested in numeric growth and success as the world judges it than in a depth of commitment to God, generated through the renewal of the mind by the Word of God. When pastors and churches succumb to administering God's people as if it were just one more multinational corporation in the modern world, there should be no surprise when there is so little interest in the Bible and biblical theology.

God's grace. Fortunately, as in the days of Manoah and the Israelites of the Philistine oppression, God will not leave people in this state. In this passage, the Lord demonstrates his incredible grace by saving the Israelites when they least deserve it. He will, as before, continue to evince to human beings his marvelous grace in spite of their lack of commitment to him, even if this means stirring up opposition to his people.

No other deliverer in the book of Judges matches Samson's potential. Yet in spite of all these advantages and special attention, he accomplishes less on behalf of his people than any of his predecessor deliverers. We live in an exciting time in that there are so many opportunities for the spread of the gospel. The potential with the many resources at the disposal of Christians—spiritual and otherwise—is immense. Yet, tragically much of these resources are being squandered in self-interested waste. We too need to have an attitude check and to look to God's amazing grace.

Judges 14:1–15:20

¹Samson went down to Timnah and saw there a young Philistine woman. ²When he returned, he said to his father and mother, "I have seen a Philistine woman in Timnah; now get her for me as my wife."

³His father and mother replied, "Isn't there an acceptable woman among your relatives or among all our people? Must you go to the uncircumcised Philistines to get a wife?"

But Samson said to his father, "Get her for me. She's the right one for me." ⁴(His parents did not know that this was from the LORD, who was seeking an occasion to confront the Philistines; for at that time they were ruling over Israel.) ⁵Samson went down to Timnah together with his father and mother. As they approached the vineyards of Timnah, suddenly a young lion came roaring toward him. ⁶The Spirit of the LORD came upon him in power so that he tore the lion apart with his bare hands as he might have torn a young goat. But he told neither his father nor his mother what he had done. ⁷Then he went down and talked with the woman, and he liked her.

⁸Some time later, when he went back to marry her, he turned aside to look at the lion's carcass. In it was a swarm of bees and some honey, ⁹which he scooped out with his hands and ate as he went along. When he rejoined his parents, he gave them some, and they too ate it. But he did not tell them that he had taken the honey from the lion's carcass.

¹⁰Now his father went down to see the woman. And Samson made a feast there, as was customary for bridegrooms. ¹¹When he appeared, he was given thirty companions.

¹²"Let me tell you a riddle," Samson said to them. "If you can give me the answer within the seven days of the feast, I will give you thirty linen garments and thirty sets of clothes. ¹³If you can't tell me the answer, you must give me thirty linen garments and thirty sets of clothes."

"Tell us your riddle," they said. "Let's hear it."

¹⁴He replied,

> "Out of the eater, something to eat;
> out of the strong, something sweet."

For three days they could not give the answer.

¹⁵On the fourth day, they said to Samson's wife, "Coax your husband into explaining the riddle for us, or we will burn you and your father's household to death. Did you invite us here to rob us?"

¹⁶Then Samson's wife threw herself on him, sobbing, "You hate me! You don't really love me. You've given my people a riddle, but you haven't told me the answer."

"I haven't even explained it to my father or mother," he replied, "so why should I explain it to you?" ¹⁷She cried the whole seven days of the feast. So on the seventh day he finally told her, because she continued to press him. She in turn explained the riddle to her people.

¹⁸Before sunset on the seventh day the men of the town said to him,

> "What is sweeter than honey?
> What is stronger than a lion?"

Samson said to them,

> "If you had not plowed with my heifer,
> you would not have solved my riddle."

¹⁹Then the Spirit of the LORD came upon him in power. He went down to Ashkelon, struck down thirty of their men, stripped them of their belongings and gave their clothes to those who had explained the riddle. Burning with anger, he went up to his father's house. ²⁰And Samson's wife was given to the friend who had attended him at his wedding.

¹⁵:¹Later on, at the time of wheat harvest, Samson took a young goat and went to visit his wife. He said, "I'm going to my wife's room." But her father would not let him go in.

²"I was so sure you thoroughly hated her," he said, "that I gave her to your friend. Isn't her younger sister more attractive? Take her instead."

³Samson said to them, "This time I have a right to get even with the Philistines; I will really harm them." ⁴So he went out and caught three hundred foxes and tied them tail to tail in

pairs. He then fastened a torch to every pair of tails, ⁵lit the torches and let the foxes loose in the standing grain of the Philistines. He burned up the shocks and standing grain, together with the vineyards and olive groves.

⁶When the Philistines asked, "Who did this?" they were told, "Samson, the Timnite's son-in-law, because his wife was given to his friend."

So the Philistines went up and burned her and her father to death. ⁷Samson said to them, "Since you've acted like this, I won't stop until I get my revenge on you." ⁸He attacked them viciously and slaughtered many of them. Then he went down and stayed in a cave in the rock of Etam.

⁹The Philistines went up and camped in Judah, spreading out near Lehi. ¹⁰The men of Judah asked, "Why have you come to fight us?"

"We have come to take Samson prisoner," they answered, "to do to him as he did to us."

¹¹Then three thousand men from Judah went down to the cave in the rock of Etam and said to Samson, "Don't you realize that the Philistines are rulers over us? What have you done to us?"

He answered, "I merely did to them what they did to me."

¹²They said to him, "We've come to tie you up and hand you over to the Philistines."

Samson said, "Swear to me that you won't kill me yourselves."

¹³"Agreed," they answered. "We will only tie you up and hand you over to them. We will not kill you." So they bound him with two new ropes and led him up from the rock. ¹⁴As he approached Lehi, the Philistines came toward him shouting. The Spirit of the LORD came upon him in power. The ropes on his arms became like charred flax, and the bindings dropped from his hands. ¹⁵Finding a fresh jawbone of a donkey, he grabbed it and struck down a thousand men.

¹⁶Then Samson said,

> "With a donkey's jawbone
>   I have made donkeys of them.
> With a donkey's jawbone
>   I have killed a thousand men."

¹⁷When he finished speaking, he threw away the jawbone; and the place was called Ramath Lehi.

[18]Because he was very thirsty, he cried out to the LORD, "You have given your servant this great victory. Must I now die of thirst and fall into the hands of the uncircumcised?" [19]Then God opened up the hollow place in Lehi, and water came out of it. When Samson drank, his strength returned and he revived. So the spring was called En Hakkore, and it is still there in Lehi.

[20]Samson led Israel for twenty years in the days of the Philistines.

THE SECOND MAJOR portion of the Samson cycle is the paralleled life account that contains accounts linked to Samson's Timnite wife (see introductory comments on 13:1–16:31). Chapters 14–15 narrate in relatively parallel form the initial exploits of Samson emanating from his marriage to a Philistine woman at Timnah. There are general parallels in the four episodes[32] of these chapters (see the table on the following page.)[33] While this parallelism is general and should not be pressed too far,[34] its presence is observable and contributes to the build up to the climax of 15:14–19.

First Account Linked to Samson's Timnite Wife (14:1–20)

ALL OF THE problems narrated in this entire second section stem from the first episode (14:1–4), which starts with Samson's "going down" to Timnah[35] and "seeing" a young Philistine woman (14:1). On his return home, Samson states literally, "A woman I have seen in Timnah. . . ." He demands that his parents "get her for me as my wife."

This verse clearly reveals the character of Samson. The text's emphasis on "seeing" stresses that Samson is a man dominated by his senses, not logic. He follows his sensual instincts, instincts that find foreign women more intriguing than those of Israel. These carnal proclivities overwhelm his perception of matters that any thinking man would know better. Samson's personality

---

32. Alternatively, one could understand the paralleled accounts to contain three episodes (14:1–4, 5–9, 10–20) parallel to three others (15:1–3, 4–8, 9–19).

33. The table generally follows the discussions of C. Exum, "Aspects of Symmetry and Balance in the Samson Saga," *JSOT* 19 (1981): 3–29; and Webb, *The Book of the Judges*, 163–64.

34. O'Connell rejects any parallels between chapters 14 and 15. While the parallels are not identical, there seems, in my opinion, to be some basic parallels between the episodes.

35. Timnah has been identified with Tell Batash in the Sorek Valley, west of Beth Shemesh.

Chapter 14		Chapter 15	
1 14:1–4	Samson went down to Timnah and he saw a woman at Timnah (14:1)	**1** 15:1–3	Samson visited (15:1a)
	Conversation between Samson and parents/ father (14:2)		Conversation between Samson and parent/ woman's father (15:1a²)
	Parental objection (14:3)		Parental objection (15:1b)
	A question is raised about the possibility of another woman, which Samson rejects (14:4)		A question is raised about the possibility of another woman, which Samson rejects (15:2–3)
2 14:5–6	Samson went down (and his father and mother) to Timnah, and they came to the vineyards of Timnah (14:5a–b¹)	**2** 15:4–6a	Samson went (15:4a)
	Action involving an animal (lion) calling for prowess on Samson's part (14:5b²–6)		Action involving animals (foxes) calling for prowess on Samson's part (15:4b–6a)
3 14:7–9	And he went down and spoke to the woman (14:7)	**3** 15:6b–8	The Philistines came up (15:6b)
	Action involving honey, a gracious act (14:8–9)		Action involving retaliation, a vicious act (15:7–8)
4 14:10–20	His father went down to the woman (14:10a)	**4** 15:9–19	The Philistines came up (15:9a)
	Conversation between Samson and Philistines; Philistines and the Timnite; the Timnite and Samson; Philistines and Samson (three main characters) (14:10b–14)		Conversation between Judahites and Philistines; Judahites and Samson (three main characters) (15:9b–14a)
	Samson's first riddle (14:14)		Samson's second riddle (15:16)
	Philistines threaten third party in order to gain advantage over Samson (14:15–18)		Philistines threaten third party in order to gain advantage over Samson (15:9b)
	Spirit of Yahweh comes upon Samson and he smites Philistines (14:19–20)		Spirit of Yahweh comes upon Samson and he smites Philistines (15:14b–19)

seems to be a degeneration of the other Out-group judges (see the introduction, pp. 38–39).³⁶ Gideon is ruled by logic, Jephthah by uninformed
belief, and Samson by lust, which can—and does in Samson's case—over-
rule all reason, all sense, all faith.

Moreover, Samson's demand to his parents reveals a total disregard for
authority in his life, whether parental or divine. The emphasis in verse 2 is
on "now." This reveals his unwillingness to delay his gratifications, to let reason, and more importantly God's Word, have a chance.

Samson's demand for his parents to get for him a Philistine wife from
Timnah (14:2) is at odds with both his parents' social preferences, biblical
legal injunctions, and his divine election to Nazirite status. His parents' objection is understandable within their tribal/clan context (cf. the disappoint-
ment of Esau's parents in Gen. 26:35; 27:46; 28:1). Manoah emphasizes the
woman's unacceptability by using the phrase "uncircumcised Philistine," a
pejorative, derogatory, scornful appellation.³⁷ The biblical prohibition is seen
in Exodus 34:16 and Deuteronomy 7:1–3. According to Judges 3:5–6, the
Israelites directly disobeyed the prohibition. In contrast, it should be noted,
Othniel, the ideal judge, married the "ideal" Israelite woman, Acsah (see
comments on Judges 3:7, above). Now, in the case of Samson, we find an
Israelite judge who blatantly disregards the prohibition. In this, Samson is the
polar opposite of Othniel.

None of this persuades Samson. His mind is made up.³⁸ Stubbornly, he
insists, "Get her for me; she's the right one for me" (lit., "for she is right [yāšar]
in my eyes"). The last statement is an anticipatory link with the double conclusion's refrain (lit.), "and every man did what was right [yāšār] in his own
eyes" (17:6; etc.). Samson is insensitive and disrespectful toward his parents
and their grief over the matter. Moreover, he is totally calloused toward the
theological implications of his demand, let alone the implications for his
calling as a Nazirite.

However, in the parenthetical statement of 14:4, the narrator assures the
reader (with information to which Samson's parents are not privy, Samson
too for that matter) that the circumstance of Samson's desire to marry the

36. See Klein, *Triumph of Irony*, 125.
37. The Israelites were not the only ones in the ancient Near East to practice circumcision, but their practice was different in that it was tied to the covenant (Gen. 17). Unfortunately, there is nothing in the text that indicates that Samson's parents were remotely
interested in covenantal issues.
38. Compare Samson's characterization with that of the "fool" (kᵉsîl) in Proverbs. In particular, note how the fool brings sorrow to his father and mother (Prov. 10:1; 17:21), bitterness (17:25), and calamity (19:13). He has little regard for them (15:20). See also 10:23;
13:20; 14:7; 17:12; 18:6; 29:11.

Philistine woman in Timnah is "from the LORD, who was seeking an occasion [opportunity] to confront the Philistines; for at that time they were ruling over [*mšl*, cf. Abimelech in ch. 9] Israel." Yahweh's seeking does not imply that he is inciting Samson's lustful desire for the Timnite woman. Rather, it suggests that Samson's sinful actions accord with Yahweh's will. God uses Samson in spite of his wrong motives and actions (cf. Gen. 50:20). From the following stories it becomes clear that left to himself, Samson would never have become involved in God's or even Israel's agenda. Left to themselves, the Israelites would have been satisfied to continue to coexist with the Philistines. But Yahweh has other plans.[39]

In the second episode of chapter 14 (14:5–7), Samson's parents capitulate and go down to Timnah with Samson to arrange the marriage. Evidently some time before they reach their destination, Samson becomes separated from his parents, for what transpires occurs without witnesses. At the vineyards of Timnah, suddenly (*hinnēh*) a young lion (lit., "a young lion of lions") roars. Empowered by the Spirit of Yahweh, Samson easily tears the lion in two. While this is a truly marvelous feat, Samson deliberately withholds any mention of this incident to his parents. Why? Shouldn't Yahweh be praised and glorified for enabling Samson to deal with the lion?

Samson has, in dealing with the lion, produced a corpse. There is nothing wrong in protecting himself, but according to the Nazirite vow, "if someone [something] dies suddenly in his presence, thus defiling the hair he has dedicated," one had to go immediately to the tabernacle and undergo a lengthy restoration ritual. This was an eight-day ritual that included shaving one's head, offering a sin offering and a burnt offering, rededicating oneself for the period of the Nazirite vow, and offering a year-old male lamb as a guilt offering (Num. 6:9–12).

But to do all this would really cramp Samson's style! It is inconvenient to travel to the tabernacle, and it would waste time, money, and resources. Besides he has a woman on his mind. So, instead of keeping the Nazirite requirement concerning defilement through uncleanliness, Samson "went down and talked with the woman, and he liked her" (lit., "she was right [*yāšar*] in his eyes"). Quite simply, God and his law are not important to Samson, only what is "right" in his eyes.

This is even clearer in the next episode (14:8–9). Some time later Samson returns to marry the Timnite. On the way, he deliberately turns aside to "see" the lion's carcass in flagrant violation of his Nazirite status. What he finds is truly unusual. Bees do no normally inhabit corpses; flies and maggots do.

---

39. Block, *Judges, Ruth*, 424.

But in this decay and decomposition, Samson discovers a "swarm" or community (*ʿēdâ*) of bees, not only existing but producing sweetness. Apparently God has provided this as a further means of "stirring" Samson. As an ordinary Israelite, Samson should have left the honey in the corpse alone (Lev. 11:24–25, 39); as a Nazirite even more so. But instead, he scoops out some honey that the bees have made, eating it and giving some to his parents to eat. And, of course, he does not tell them about the corpse for the same reason as before. Not only does he not care about his own ritually unclean status, but he cares little for that of others, including his parents, who are now ritually unclean because of his action. The only thing that matters to Samson is the satisfaction of his own appetites and cravings.

Samson makes a marriage feast (*mišteh*). Such feasts were common in the ancient Near East (cf. Gen. 29:22). They often lasted seven days (as here) and included the consumption of wine.[40] Samson likely violated this part of his Nazirite vow.[41]

Samson receives thirty Philistine "companions,"[42] whom he challenges with a riddle and a bet. At the end of the seven days, if they can tell him the answer, he will provide them thirty linen garments and thirty sets of clothes. But if they cannot answer the riddle, they must give him thirty linen garments and thirty sets of clothes.[43] He gives them this enigmatic riddle (14:14, lit.):

From the eater comes out something to eat,
and from the strong comes out something sweet.

Of course, after three days of frustration—and they cannot possibly derive the answer since they have no inkling of the prior events of Samson with the lion—the companions turn to Samson's wife. Through threat and intimidation ("we will burn you and your father's household [(*bêt*]"[44]; and "did you invite us here to rob us?"), they cajole and coerce the woman to find out the answer.

Ironically, Samson, who refused to tell his own mother and father about the lion, gives in to his bride's hounding on the final day. She promptly tells

---

40. Cf. the much later example in John 2:1–11.

41. The most common types of pottery found by archaeologists in Philistine settlements is the strainer-spout "beer jug." See T. Dothan and M. Dothan, *People of the Sea: The Search for the Philistines* (New York: Macmillan, 1992), 90, 134.

42. Cf. the use of the number "thirty" in the power contexts of Jair (10:3–5), Ibzan (12:8–10), and Abdon (12:13–15). Cf. also David's "thirty" men, warriors of great exploits (2 Sam. 23:13–39; 1 Chron. 11:15).

43. Long robes or capes and tunics. See M. Görg, "Zu den Kleiderbezeichnungen in Ri 14,12f," *BN* 68 (1993), 5–9.

44. Cf. the similar threat of Ephraimites to Jephthah (12:1).

the companions, "her people" (her loyalties are with her people more than her husband). Thus the companions are able to give the answer in their own poetic form (14:18):

> What is sweeter than honey?
>> What is stronger than a lion?

While this too is a riddle, Samson discerns the meaning immediately: a woman's allure. His reply is proverbial:

> If you had not plowed with my heifer,
>> you would not have solved my riddle.

In other words, if you hadn't messed with my wife, you couldn't have solved my riddle; hence you cheated.[45] Empowered by the Spirit of Yahweh,[46] Samson goes to Ashkelon (twenty miles away)[47] and strikes down thirty Philistine men in order to get their clothes so that he can pay his debt to his companions for losing the bet over his sure winner of a riddle.

Two observations are in order. (1) It is Samson's own fault that he lost the bet. It was a sure winner if he had just persevered and kept his mouth shut. But instead, despite his great physical strength, he is completely helpless when confronted with the love of women, and he cannot resist divulging the answer. (2) The act of killing the thirty men—which is no doubt a mighty achievement—is motivated by Samson's anger and vengeance. This is murder and larceny. The motive is not to deliver Israel from the Philistines or even to bring judgment on them. It only serves his purposes. But even this does not placate his rage; Samson burns with anger and returns home.

While the Philistines initiated this through their coercion of Samson's wife, Samson's slaughter of the thirty men in Ashkelon launches a whole series of increasingly severe acts on the part of the Philistines. They manifest disloyalty to covenants (14:20—15:2), violence (15:6), increasing violence (15:9—10a), ambush to commit murder (16:2), and a proneness to use bribery (16:5). These actions of the Philistines are met by Samson's own retaliatory actions.

---

45. Heifers were not normally used for plowing; so the thirty have not played fair. See H. Wolf, "Judges," *EBC*, 3:470.

46. Although Samson is gifted with the empowerment of the Spirit of Yahweh, it is clear from the contexts that he misuses this special empowerment for his own ends again and again.

47. Apparently he hoped to conceal his actions by going such a long distance from Timnah.

Philistine trespass	Samson's retaliation
14:15	14:19
14:20—15:2	15:3—5
15:6	15:8a
15:9—10a	15:15
16:2	16:3
16:5	16:30a

It is the acts of injustice by the Philistines that are the main cause of the escalation of violence in the account and that justly culminate in the destruction of Gaza's temple, the Philistine rulers, and their subjects. But Samson's retaliations prove that he is operating on the same principle as they are. Working backward, Polzin summarizes that

> the Philistines want Samson for slaughtering their own people; but he had done this because they had killed his wife and father-in-law; but they had done this because he had burned their fields; but he had done this because his father-in-law had given away his wife; but he had done this because Samson had gotten angry and left; but he had done this because his wife had given the riddle's answer to her kinsmen; but she had done this to avoid being burnt up by them....[48]

Thus, while Samson is at home sulking, his wife is given to his companion who attended him at his wedding (14:20). In other words, his father-in-law sees an opportunity to marry his daughter to one of his own people—no doubt a better social move on his part (cf. Laban's actions in Gen. 29:14–30, esp. vv. 26–27; 1 Sam. 18:19–21). Such a move is stimulated by Samson's return to his father's house, which leads his father-in-law to assume that Samson is displeased with his daughter and has divorced her (he uses the term "hate," which can technically connote divorce).

Second Account Linked to Samson's Timnite Wife (15:1–20)

WITH SAMSON'S BELATED return (15:1),[49] the plot thickens. He suddenly shows up in Timnah with a young goat,[50] assuming that nothing has changed. His father-in-law stops him at the door (literally) and proposes a new arrangement,

---

48. Polzin, *Moses and the Deuteronomist*, 188.

49. The mention that this happens at the time of the wheat harvest (i.e., May-June) is anticipatory of the burning of the grain that will take place later in the story.

50. Boling explains this as "the ancient counterpart of the box of chocolates" (*Judges*, 234). Note also the use of a young goat by Judah as payment to the "prostitute," Tamar, in Gen. 38:17–20, as observed by Moore, *Judges*, 340.

his younger daughter, who is more attractive than her older sister (15:2). For someone who operates according to "what seems right in his eyes," this offer should have been appealing. But Boling aptly observes that no one can tell Samson how to find a wife.[51] Even though he left the wedding in a rage, this does not seem to Samson to be a good reason to give his wife to someone else. Apparently, he expects to return to his wife and resume life as if nothing has happened.[52] Thus, Samson swears revenge: "This time I have a right to get even with the Philistines; I will really harm them" (15:3).

Samson then captures three hundred foxes (šûʿālîm, cf. Song of Songs 2:15),[53] ties them tail to tail in pairs, and fastens a torch to every pair of tails—an act of prowess on his part! Lighting the torches, he lets them loose in the standing grain[54] of the Philistines, burning the shocks, standing grain, vineyards, and olive groves[55]—a thoroughgoing destruction! While truly an amazing feat, it is motivated purely on Samson's desire for retaliation and is wrong. Note Exodus 22:6: "If a fire breaks out and spreads into thornbushes so that it burns shocks of grain or standing grain or the whole field, the one who started the fire must make restitution." Once again, Samson disregards God's Law in order to do what is "right" in his eyes (i.e., get revenge).[56]

Not that the Philistines are so good. They, in turn, now inquire as to the arson and, having determined that it is Samson, burn his wife and father-in-law.[57] Needing a scapegoat, the Philistines may simply have concluded that it was easier to deal with the Timnite than with Samson. But the Philistines underestimate Samson's commitment to his wife, and so the conflict escalates even more as Samson declares: "Since you've acted like this, I won't stop

---

51. Boling, *Judges*, 235.

52. Wolf suggests that this may be evidence of a visit-type marriage, in which the wife would stay in her father's house and be visited periodically by her husband ("Judges," 470–71). He appears to follow de Vaux (*Ancient Israel*, 28–29), based on a Middle Assyrian law that describes this (see M. Roth, "The Middle Assyrian Laws," *COS*, 2.132, law A §27). However, the context of Samson's departure in rage (14:19) and the actions and comments of the woman's father (14:20; 15:2) suggest that Samson's return was not expected.

53. Block argues that these are jackals (as in Ps. 63:10; Lam. 5:18; Ezek. 13:4) (*Judges, Ruth*, 441 n. 368). See also Boling, *Judges*, 235; Soggin, *Judges*, 246.

54. Hence the earlier mention of the wheat harvest (15:1).

55. For the structure of this verse, see D. N. Freedman, "A Note on Judges 15,5," *Bib* 52 (1971): 535.

56. The destruction of all these food items, esp. the very basic commodity of wheat grain, had significant implications for an ancient dry-farming society that lived so often on the edge of hunger, where rationing was a common part of life. The potential for famine and death was quite serious.

57. By referring to him as "the son-in-law of the Timnite," the Philistines recognize Samson's status as the husband of the man's daughter and discredit Samson's father-in-law's action in giving his wife to the second man.

until I get my revenge on you."[58] He attacks them viciously and slaughters many of them (lit., "he struck them leg on thigh—a tremendous slaughter," 15:8).[59] All of this is the result of a personal vendetta for revenge. While revenge was a common modus operandi in the ancient Near East, Yahweh had declared that vengeance belongs to him (Deut. 32:35).[60]

Perhaps tired, the lone-ranger-judge escapes to a cave in the rock of Etam (a Heb. word meaning "place of the birds of prey," which may anticipate what will transpire as a result of Samson's soon-to-be-narrated feat). The Philistines, intent on finding Samson, come and camp near Lehi ("jawbone," an anticipatory mentioning since the name was received after the incident that now unfolds).

The series of dialogues between the Judahites and Philistines and between the Judahites and Samson is revealing. All three parties are concerned about *what is being or has been done to them.* The Judahites fearfully inquire, "Why have you come to fight us?" The Philistine reply demonstrates their concern: "We have come to take Samson prisoner ... *to do to him as he did to us*" (emphasis mine). Turning to Samson, the three thousand Judahites[61] question him: "Don't you realize that the Philistines are rulers over us? *What have you done to us?*" Samson replies: *"I merely did to them what they did to me"* (emphasis mine). For the Philistines, Judahites, and Samson, the only thing that matters is reprisal and counterreprisal.

Having obtained an oath from the Judahites that they will not kill him, Samson allows them to tie him up with two new ropes. The Judahites lead him from the rock to the Philistines near Lehi ("jawbone," a second anticipatory mentioning). Empowered by the Spirit of Yahweh, the binding of the ropes is easily broken. His loosing is entirely the work of Yahweh. Yet,

---

58. Boling (*Judges*, 234) translates: "If this is the sort of thing you do, I swear I will be vindicated against you! But thereafter, I quit!"

59. "He left them a tangle of legs and thighs" (ibid., 235).

60. Note how the Lord purposely designated six cities of refuge in Israel in order to prevent the endless and senseless cycle of revenge killings (see Deut. 19:1−14).

61. Apparently, the tribe of Judah is under the Philistine oppression and is willingly content to accept this. The Judahite force is mustered not to support Samson, whom they obviously respect for his reputed strength (they do not attempt to tie him up without his consent); but it is mustered to capture Samson for the Philistines. The Judahites are simply interested in maintaining the status quo.

Interestingly, there are three thousand Judahites. Only one thousand Philistines are killed by Samson! The implication is clearly that the Judahites outnumber the Philistines, since even if Samson killed half of them and the other half escaped, there would have been only two thousand Philistines near Lehi. In fact, there seems to be no other reason in the narrative for giving the numeric size of the Judahite force. Thus in spite of numeric superiority, the Judahites are motivated purely by self-interest.

he immediately finds an unclean object, a "fresh" jawbone of a donkey, and slaughters a thousand Philistines.

Samson utters his second riddle (though this riddle is hardly enigmatic, as opposed to his first riddle that he gave to his companions). Literally, it reads:

> With the jawbone of a donkey,
>> heaps upon heaps [lit. "one heap, two heaps, *ḥᵃmôr ḥᵃmōrātāyim*];[62]
> With the jawbone of a donkey,
>> I have struck down a thousand-man contingent.

This four line ditty with repetitive parallelism is relatively straightforward. Only the second line needs comment. It seems to be a wordplay involving the Hebrew words for donkey and heap, which are consonantally identical (*ḥmr*).[63] Thus Samson is tauntingly counting "one heap (of donkeys), two heaps (of donkeys)." Block points out:

> Although the song is extremely effective poetically, it is quite perverse in substance. In contrast to the Song of Deborah in chap. 5, not a word is said about God. Samson claims all the credit for himself, which causes the reader to wonder if he is even aware of God's involvement in his life.[64]

The term "fresh" implies that the jawbone is still strong, not dry and brittle.[65] But it also implies that the jawbone is from a recently slain donkey (i.e., a polluted carcass). Practically speaking, Samson uses what is available. However, in picking up this item, he again implicitly shows disregard for his Nazirite vow. After finishing his grisly business and chanting his taunting ditty, Samson discards the jawbone, and the place receives the name, Ramath Lehi ("jawbone hill").

This single-handed slaughter of a thousand Philistines with the jawbone of the donkey in 15:15 cannot help but recall to mind the remarkably similar exploit of Shamgar, who "struck down six hundred Philistines with an oxgoad" (3:31). But the difference is pronounced. Shamgar saved Israel; Samson did not. Shamgar's motive was to aid Israel; Samson's motive is personal revenge.

---

62. This reading is supported by a similar phrase in Ex. 8:14[Heb. 10] and the reading in the LXX: "A heap I heaped them"). It is preferred over the NIV ("I have made donkeys of them"), which relies on repointing the MT reading of *ḥᵃmōrātāyim* as *ḥᵃmartîm* (see Soggin *Judges*, 247; Boling, *Judges*, 239; Block, *Judges, Ruth*, 446; Gray, *Joshua, Judges, Ruth*, 333).

63. See Boling, *Judges*, 239. According to Boling, the line is also an example of archaic poetic progression used to convey impassioned speech (cf. Judg. 5:30 "one girl, two girls").

64. Block, *Judges, Ruth*, 446.

65. See Boling, *Judges*, 239.

The epilogue to this climactic slaughter of the Philistines records Samson's first prayer, the first time that he calls on Yahweh. But it is immediately plain that this is only due to the exhaustion from the massacre, a desperation of thirst. From the tone of Samson's prayer it seems clear that this is little more than "an impudent harangue."[66]

> You have given into the hand of your servant this great victory,
> and *now* will I die of thirst,
> and will I fall into the hands of the uncircumcised? (pers. trans.)

In the first line, Samson speaks better than he knows. In the next two lines, he rants at Yahweh to do something about his thirst! The suspense is sustained to the very end as Samson uses the same pejorative ("uncircumcised") as his parents (14:3) to describe the Philistines (15:18). Purely out of his grace, God provides water through a rocky place at Lehi. Samson drinks and is revived. So the spring is called En Hakkore ("the spring of the caller").

This incident is similar to those in which God provided water for Israel in the desert (Ex. 17:1–7 [Massah and Meribah] and Num. 20:2–13 [Meribah]). Just as Israel's attitude was wrong in those contexts (selfish, murmuring or grumbling against God), so Samson's is wrong here. In spite of this, God provides in each instance. Yet Samson does not infer from this incident that he ought to serve Yahweh's interests before his own,[67] as the next chapter will demonstrate.

The second section concludes with a note that Samson "led" (i.e., judged) Israel for twenty years in the days of the Philistines. The phrase "in the days of the Philistines" is the only time that the statement of the length of "judging" is qualified in the book of Judges, and it is a qualification that is negative in scope.

Bridging Contexts

MOTIVATED BY SELF-INTEREST. The picture of Samson that emerges from this section is anything but positive. What is morally right in Samson's life is determined by Samson himself, not by God or his Law. Samson is driven by the sensual: his instincts, his lusts, his appetites, his gratifications. He manifests a total disregard for human or divine authority. He shows no regard for God's Law, for his special Nazirite status. Even Samson's first prayer is motivated by self-interest and personal gratification.

---

66. Ibid., 239.
67. O'Connell, *The Rhetoric of the Book of Judges*, 216.

In matters of motivation, Samson is no different from the Philistines! He is motivated by revenge and retaliation, and he commits murder, destruction of private property, and so on. In many respects Samson manifests a number of characteristics of the fool in the book of Proverbs (Prov. 10:1, 23; 13:20; 15:20; 17:12, 21, 25; 18:6; 19:13; 29:11).

And the Judahites are no better. Everyone—Philistines and Israelites—are only concerned about what is being or has been done to them. The section seems to be nothing but reprisals and counterreprisals. The point is that God's people are working on the same principles and exhibiting the same behavior as the unbelieving, "uncircumcised" Philistines. Is it possible that God's people today might be doing the same?

Yahweh's involvement. While it is unquestionably a difficult verse, 14:4 documents Yahweh's involvements in this section. As pointed out above, Yahweh's "seeking" does not imply that Yahweh "incites" Samson's lustful desire for the Timnite woman. Rather, it suggests that Samson's sinful actions nevertheless accord with Yahweh's will. Thus, God uses Samson in spite of his wrong motives and actions (cf. Gen. 50:20). The fact that Yahweh works his will in spite of our sinful motives and actions has been demonstrated over and over again—in the case of every cyclical judge except for Othniel. It just happens in the case of Samson to a much greater extent since his sinfulness is so great.

Thus, it is abundantly clear that without God's involvement behind the scenes, left to himself, Samson would never have become involved in God's plan for delivering Israel. In fact, left to themselves, the Israelites would have been satisfied to continue to coexist with the Philistines. Hence in this context God's people seem perfectly content to maintain the status quo in relationship to unbelievers. But the Lord has other plans for his people, both then and now.

WARNING. The passage is a warning to us concerning what characteristics we should not want in our lives. In Samson, Israel has a judge who determines what is right and wrong purely based on his senses. Today we are encouraged to live life in this way. We are persuaded by commercials to "just do it," that if we like something to go for it. Ads are directed to our senses—appearance is everything. If you don't have the right stuff, you're nothing. Sex is used to sell everything from cars to ice cream, even "rice"! Samson lived in a fashion that our culture would endorse—at least in his willingness to gratify every inclination of his heart.

Authority issues. Unfortunately, in Samson, we also see the disrespect for authority, particularly in parental authority. Never has parental authority been as low as in our present society. God has given us parents so that we can learn about authority. If we cannot respect parental authority, how can we submit to the authority of God? If we are chosen by God to lead, it is important that we learn submission to authority first, and respecting our parents is the first step in such a process. It is not insignificant that the fifth commandment, "honor your father and your mother," is the pivotal commandment between the God-oriented commandments (the first four commandments) and the human-oriented commandments (the last five commandments).

And as for the authority of God, in many respects we might say, what God? For many, if there is a God, he is either unable or not interested in doing anything in the world. His self-revelation in his Word is denied. His Law ignored. Samson could certainly find his place among many folk in our society today who live life as though there were no true and living God—and certainly no coming judgment by this God.

The thing that is so sad about Samson is that he obviously believes that there is a God—even that this God is Yahweh, the God of Israel (since he prays to him). In the ancient Near East, there were no atheists; everyone believed in God or the gods. But in spite of a theological acknowledgment of this on Samson's part, he lives his life like those who do not believe that there is a God. There is perhaps nothing more tragic than seeing a believer live his or her life this way.

Samson and his contemporaries care about what is done to them. They count up his atrocities and even the score when the opportunity presents itself. Samson, the Philistines, and the Judahites all are motivated by revenge and retaliation. In our inner cities today this is unfortunately the way things are as well. Moreover, disregard for private property, life, and limb is paramount.

The passage is obviously also a warning of the imminent destructive aspects that result from such characteristics. Those in present culture who live according to the "Samsonite" code—"what's right in my eyes, I do"—face the grim prospect of much suffering in this world and in the world to come. There cannot be a greater contrast between the "Samsonite" code and Jesus' code—"others first" (cf. Othniel).

Judges 16:1–31

¹One day Samson went to Gaza, where he saw a prostitute. He went in to spend the night with her. ²The people of Gaza were told, "Samson is here!" So they surrounded the place and lay in wait for him all night at the city gate. They made no move during the night, saying, "At dawn we'll kill him."

³But Samson lay there only until the middle of the night. Then he got up and took hold of the doors of the city gate, together with the two posts, and tore them loose, bar and all. He lifted them to his shoulders and carried them to the top of the hill that faces Hebron.

⁴Some time later, he fell in love with a woman in the Valley of Sorek whose name was Delilah. ⁵The rulers of the Philistines went to her and said, "See if you can lure him into showing you the secret of his great strength and how we can overpower him so we may tie him up and subdue him. Each one of us will give you eleven hundred shekels of silver."

⁶So Delilah said to Samson, "Tell me the secret of your great strength and how you can be tied up and subdued."

⁷Samson answered her, "If anyone ties me with seven fresh thongs that have not been dried, I'll become as weak as any other man."

⁸Then the rulers of the Philistines brought her seven fresh thongs that had not been dried, and she tied him with them. ⁹With men hidden in the room, she called to him, "Samson, the Philistines are upon you!" But he snapped the thongs as easily as a piece of string snaps when it comes close to a flame. So the secret of his strength was not discovered.

¹⁰Then Delilah said to Samson, "You have made a fool of me; you lied to me. Come now, tell me how you can be tied."

¹¹He said, "If anyone ties me securely with new ropes that have never been used, I'll become as weak as any other man."

¹²So Delilah took new ropes and tied him with them. Then, with men hidden in the room, she called to him, "Samson, the Philistines are upon you!" But he snapped the ropes off his arms as if they were threads.

¹³Delilah then said to Samson, "Until now, you have been making a fool of me and lying to me. Tell me how you can be tied."

He replied, "If you weave the seven braids of my head into the fabric ⌞on the loom⌟ and tighten it with the pin, I'll become as weak as any other man." So while he was sleeping, Delilah took the seven braids of his head, wove them into the fabric ¹⁴and tightened it with the pin.

Again she called to him, "Samson, the Philistines are upon you!" He awoke from his sleep and pulled up the pin and the loom, with the fabric.

¹⁵Then she said to him, "How can you say, 'I love you,'
when you won't confide in me? This is the third time you have
made a fool of me and haven't told me the secret of your great
strength." ¹⁶With such nagging she prodded him day after day
until he was tired to death.

¹⁷So he told her everything. "No razor has ever been used
on my head," he said, "because I have been a Nazirite set apart
to God since birth. If my head were shaved, my strength would
leave me, and I would become as weak as any other man."

¹⁸When Delilah saw that he had told her everything, she sent
word to the rulers of the Philistines, "Come back once more; he
has told me everything." So the rulers of the Philistines returned
with the silver in their hands. ¹⁹Having put him to sleep on her
lap, she called a man to shave off the seven braids of his hair,
and so began to subdue him. And his strength left him.

²⁰Then she called, "Samson, the Philistines are upon you!"

He awoke from his sleep and thought, "I'll go out as before
and shake myself free." But he did not know that the LORD
had left him.

³¹Then the Philistines seized him, gouged out his eyes and
took him down to Gaza. Binding him with bronze shackles,
they set him to grinding in the prison. ²²But the hair on his
head began to grow again after it had been shaved.

²³Now the rulers of the Philistines assembled to offer a
great sacrifice to Dagon their god and to celebrate, saying,
"Our god has delivered Samson, our enemy, into our hands."

²⁴When the people saw him, they praised their god, saying,

> "Our god has delivered our enemy
>   into our hands,
>   the one who laid waste our land
>   and multiplied our slain."

²⁵While they were in high spirits, they shouted, "Bring out
Samson to entertain us." So they called Samson out of the
prison, and he performed for them.

When they stood him among the pillars, ²⁶Samson said to
the servant who held his hand, "Put me where I can feel the
pillars that support the temple, so that I may lean against
them." ²⁷Now the temple was crowded with men and women;
all the rulers of the Philistines were there, and on the roof
were about three thousand men and women watching Samson

perform. ²⁸Then Samson prayed to the LORD, "O Sovereign LORD, remember me. O God, please strengthen me just once more, and let me with one blow get revenge on the Philistines for my two eyes." ²⁹Then Samson reached toward the two central pillars on which the temple stood. Bracing himself against them, his right hand on the one and his left hand on the other, ³⁰Samson said, "Let me die with the Philistines!" Then he pushed with all his might, and down came the temple on the rulers and all the people in it. Thus he killed many more when he died than while he lived.

³¹Then his brothers and his father's whole family went down to get him. They brought him back and buried him between Zorah and Eshtaol in the tomb of Manoah his father. He had led Israel twenty years.

THIS THIRD AND final section of the Samson cycle has two parts: Samson's downfall (16:1–22) and his death (16:23–31). The first part contains two episodes that recount Samson's involvement with two women who contribute to his demise: the Gazite prostitute (16:1–3) and Delilah (16:4–22). It narrates his final exploits emanating from a rendezvous with a prostitute at Gaza that leads to his death. It has numerous parallels to the second section (14:1–15:20) as it builds up to the climax of the slaughter of the Philistines and Samson's own death in the temple of Dagon at Gaza in 16:30.

Downfall of Samson (16:1–22)

THE GAZA PROSTITUTE (16:1–3). This short episode is packed with significance. Just as all of the problems of the second section (14:1–15:20) stemmed from Samson's "going" to Timnah and "seeing" a Philistine woman, so the problems in this final section stem from Samson's "going" to Gaza and "seeing" a prostitute (ʾiššâ zônâ, cf. Prov. 6:23–35). Samson's "going to a prostitute" is once again indicative of his lack of regard for God's law. Moreover, he goes to Gaza, a Philistine city, which requires his traveling through the length of Philistia. This certainly speaks to intent. This is not a slip-up, a case of falling into sin. This is a deliberate rebellious act on Samson's part.

His insolent act endangers him (16:2). The people of the city discover his presence even though "going to a prostitute" usually involves stealth. Is he so blatant in his approach to the prostitute that he gives himself away?

The feat in 16:3 is impressive, a truly miraculous exploit. City gates were not light objects, and to haul this gate for some considerable distance to the hill opposite Hebron multiplies the magnitude of the act. The distance between Gaza and Hebron is about forty miles and involves an ascent of more than two thousand feet. While Samson does not carry the gate structure all the way to Hebron, he must have carried it some considerable distance. Hebron was the chief city of Judah, and so this seems to be Samson's rebuttal for what the Judahites did to him (15:11–13).

But the feat is completely self-serving. Not that Samson should not have acted to save himself. But it is precisely this: Samson *only* acts to save himself. He has not delivered *one* Israelite from the hands of the oppressors, the Philistines. The feat is unnecessary—at least carrying the gate any distance. Simply breaking down the gate would have been sufficient.

Delilah's deception (16:4–22). In 16:1–3, Samson escapes *from* Gaza. In this next episode, he ends up being taken *down to* Gaza after having been seized and overcome (16:21). There he will be enslaved, grinding away at a mill. Chapter 16 begins with a marvelous deed and will end with a mighty deed, but neither one really delivers Israel from the Philistine oppression.

While many view the incident involving the prostitute of Gaza (16:1–3) as unrelated to that of Delilah (16:4–22), the former furnishes the Philistines with the motive for seeking vengeance on Samson through their intrigues with Delilah. Moreover, the fact that the Philistines seek to humiliate Samson at the city of Gaza (16:21b) suggests that, through Delilah, they are seeking an opportunity to retaliate especially for the humiliation that they have suffered through Samson's nocturnal gate removal (16:3).[68]

In fact, after Samson humiliates the Gazites by this feat, they become specifically preoccupied with discovering the secret of his strength so that they, in turn, might humiliate him (16:5; cf. 16:6–7, 10–11, 13, 15–17). Once again, it is Samson himself who supplies the Philistines with the opportunity through his sensual weakness: "He fell in love with a woman in the Valley of Sorek whose name was Delilah" (16:4). Thus while Samson may be able to uproot the gates of the city of Gaza and carry them almost forty miles uphill, he cannot withstand the wiles of a woman.[69]

While there is uncertainty concerning the derivation and meaning of the name Delilah,[70] there is likely a paronomastic correspondence between

---

68. Ibid., 217.

69. Block, *Judges, Ruth*, 451.

70. Some scholars explain the name through an Arabic root *dalla* (to flirt, be flirtatious; e.g. Boling, *Judges*, 248). In my opinion, a preferable explanation with abundant attestations from the entire period of the Old Testament's corpus is to relate the root *dll* to Akkadian *dalālum* (to praise, glorify), which is an element in a number of personal names—e.g., Lud-lul-Sin, Sin-ludlul, Adalal-Sin, Adalal, Idlal-Dagan (Mari), Dilīl-Adad, Dilīl-Aššur, Dilīl-Issār). See *CAD* D, 46–47; and *PNA*, 1/2:384.

"Delilah" (*dᵉlîlâ*) and "the night" (*hallaylâ*).[71] Ironically, the Philistine fail to ambush Samson at Gaza at night (note the four uses of *hallaylâ* in the "night" scene of 16:2–3). This foreshadows their four subsequent attempts to capture him through Delilah (note the seven uses of *dᵉlîlâ* in 16:4, 6, 10, 12, 13, [14] 18).[72]

Significantly, Delilah is the only woman in the Samson cycle whose name is supplied (cf. the wife of Manoah, his Timnite wife, and the prostitute of Gaza). By only supplying Delilah's name and using it seven times, the narrator singles her out as the most portentous of the four females in the story. While the text does not specify whether Delilah is Israelite or Philistine, the latter seems more likely in the context of the Samson cycle.[73] Samson's preferences have been for "foreign" women, not Israelites (at no time does Samson evince the slightest interest in Israelite women).

The rulers (lit., "tyrants")[74] of the Philistines make the most of this opportunity. This time, there is no threat or coercion (as there was in the case of Samson's wife); rather, they offer Delilah an extraordinary bounty for information concerning the secret of Samson's strength (lit., "see in what his strength is great" [*kōaḥ gādôl*]) and "how we may tie him up [*ʾāsar*]" so that "[we may] subdue [*ʿānâ*] him" (16:5). They each offer her 1,100 shekels of silver, giving her a total of 5,500 shekels (an absurdly fantastic amount for this time period).[75]

At this point, a word is in order concerning the myth of Samson's size. Samson is most commonly pictured as a hulk, a mammoth of incredible size and strength. While there is obviously in the biblical text a satirical characterization of the Philistines as ignorant, culturally challenged morons, they cannot be so stupid as to not recognize the obvious. If Samson were a Goliath-type behemoth, then obviously the "secret" to his strength would be

---

71. Note that Samson ("Little Sun") will be reduced by Delilah (sounds like "night").

72. O'Connell, *The Rhetoric of the Book of Judges*, 217 n. 310.

73. Some scholars have argued that Delilah is an Israelite rather than a Philistine woman. This is usually based on three points: (1) Her name is thoroughly Semitic, (2) the geographic location is the Sorek Valley, and (3) she is the only paramor of Samson who is named. See J. M. Sasson, "Who Cut Samson's Hair? (And Other Trifling Issues Raised by Judges 16," *Prooftexts* 8 (1988): 334–35. None of these is compelling. Recent Philistine inscriptions demonstrate a strong tendency among them to adopt Semitic names; Philistine incursions up the Sorek Valley certainly make it possible for them to be living there; and the fact that she is named is a literary feature of the story, not an ethnic indicator.

74. This is a technical political title that connects the social organization of the five great Philistine cities on the southern coastal plain with an Aegean homeland (see Boling, *Judges*, 148).

75. These 5500 shekels would equal 550 times the average annual wage. Assuming a figure like $25,000 as an average annual wage today, the Philistine offer would be in the $15 million category. Eleven hundred shekels is the same amount of silver that Micah's mother has in 17:2.

in the size of his muscles! So the Philistines would be foolish to keep trying to overcome him (cf. the experience at Lehi). The Philistine rulers would be even dumber to pay such a price for the obvious, and Delilah would be the mother of all dummies if Samson were a man with fifty-inch biceps.

But Samson must have been a relatively ordinary-looking man in size and weight. His strength is not even in his long, seven-braided hair. Therefore, his strength is not in the obvious; it is in Yahweh, who is working through his special Yahweh-called, Nazirite status. Moreover, it is clear in what transpires that the Philistines are convinced that Samson's strength lies in supernatural or magical contexts. This is seen in that Samson offers the Philistines magical solutions, and they accept each and every one of his suggestions. In the ancient Near East, certain materials were thought to have magical properties in and of themselves or in the right quantity or combination.

Four attempts to subdue Samson follow in which Delilah unleashes a verbal attack on Samson in order to subdue him and receive her payment. The chart on the following page helps visualize these four attempts.

In the first attempt, Delilah's speech is precisely that of her employers: "Tell me the secret of your great strength [kōaḥ gādôl] and how you can be tied up [ʾāsar] and subdued [ʾānâ]." Samson's answer is teasing and untrue: "If anyone ties me with seven fresh [sinews/bowstrings, yᵉtārîm] that have not been dried, I'll become as weak as any other man." "Sinews/bowstrings" is here preferable over the NIV's "thongs." The inferior, unprocessed sinews[76] were probably used for magical reasons, which lay behind all of the other proposals of Samson (i.e., new ropes, weaving hair into the fabric on the loom and tightening it with a pin). The result, however, is that Samson is free; he snaps the bowstrings as easily as a piece of string snaps when it comes close to a flame.

In her second attempt, Delilah steps up the pressure: "You have made a fool of me [or ridiculed me, tālal]; you lied to me [kᵉzābîm]. Come now, tell me how you can be tied [ʾāsar]." Samson's answer to this second attempt is again teasing and untrue: "If anyone ties me securely with new ropes that have never been used, I'll become as weak as any other man." Apparently, the Philistines do not know that this method was already tried but failed at Lehi (15:13–14).[77] The result is that Samson is free; he snaps the ropes off as if they were threads.

In her third attempt, Delilah repeats the same line as the second: "Until now, you have been making a fool of [ridiculing, tālal] me and lying to me [kᵉzābîm]. Tell me how you can be tied [ʾāsar]." Samson's answer is again teasing and

---

76. His specification of "fresh" and "undried" sinews/bowstrings means that once more he is trivializing his Nazirite vow.

77. This may imply that there were no Philistine survivors of this earlier incident.

#		Verse			
1	Delilah's first speech	16:6	great strength (*kōaḥ gādôl*)	binding (*ʾāsar*)	subdue (*ʿānâ*)
	Samson's first answer	16:7	seven fresh bowstrings—teasing and untrue		
	Result	16:8–9	Samson is free		
2	Delilah's second speech	16:10	ridicule/make a fool (*tālal*)	lies (*kᵉzābîm*)	binding (*ʾāsar*)
	Samson's second answer	16:11	new ropes—teasing and untrue		
	Result	16:12	Samson is free		
3	Delilah's third speech	16:13a	ridicule/make a fool (*tālal*)	lies (*kᵉzābîm*)	binding (*ʾāsar*)
	Samson's third answer	16:13b	seven braids woven into the fabric, tightened with pin—teasing and untrue		
	Result	16:14	Samson is free		
4	Delilah's fourth speech	16:15	love (*ʾāhab*)	ridicule/make a fool (*tālal*)	great strength (*kōaḥ gādôl*)
	Samson's fourth answer	16:17	razor to head—exasperated and true		
	Result	16:21	Samson is blinded, bound, and set to work grinding		

untrue: "If you weave the seven braids of my head into the fabric ˪on the loom˩ and tighten it with the pin, I'll become as weak as any other man." Samson's answer is perilously near the truth since it concerns his hair. This may indicate that his will is breaking. The following helps elucidate what is involved in loom weaving:

> There were two types of looms used in this period: the horizontal loom and the vertical loom. From the description given of Delilah's loom it appears to be the former type. Four stakes were driven into the ground in a rectangular pattern. The threads that would make up the warp of the fabric were tied at regular intervals to sticks on both ends, and the sticks were then used to stretch out the threads between the stakes. When the ends of each stick were braced behind the stakes the threads would be stretched horizontal to the ground, taut for weaving. A shuttle would then be tied to the thread that was to be woven in as the woof of the fabric with a bar being used to separate alternating threads of the warp to allow the shuttle with the woof thread to pass through. Once the woof thread was in place the pin would be used to tighten that row against the previous rows. Samson has now become quite creative for he is suggesting that his hair be substituted for the woof thread. This would, however, be a logical magical procedure in that the hair was considered to contain one's life essence and the weaving would be a binding action. When Samson jumps up he pulls the whole loom with him snapping the end sticks off the four stakes between which the fabric was stretched.[78]

Delilah's tightening (*tāqaᶜ*) of Samson's hair with a pin (*yātēd*) (16:14) recalls Jael's striking (*tāqaᶜ*) the tent peg (*yātēd*) into Sisera's temple (4:21). Both scenes take place in a woman's private quarters, and the sleeping Samson of 16:19 recalls the sleeping Sisera of 4:21.[79] There can be no doubt of intentional depiction with its rich irony. But what has happened that the Israelite judge endowed with the greatest physical strength ends up being portrayed as Sisera, the Canaanite abuser of God's people? In any case, the result is that Samson is free; he pulls up the pin and the loom, with the fabric.

In her final attempt, Delilah crowns her attack: "How can you say, 'I love [*ʾāhēb*] you,' when you won't confide in me?" The rhetorical question must have particularly struck Samson hard since he is in love (*ʾāhab*) with Delilah (16:4). 'This is the third time you have made a fool of [ridiculed, *tālal*] me and

78. J. Walton, V. Matthews, and M. Chavalas, *The IVP Bible Background Commentary: Old Testament* (Downers Grove, Ill.: InterVarsity, 2000), 269.
79. Webb, *The Book of the Judges*, 164.

haven't told me the secret of your great strength [*kōaḥ gādôl*]." Like his earlier Philistine wife, she nags him continually until he is "tired to death" (16:16, tragically anticipatory).

Samson's answer to this fourth attempt is exasperated and true: ". . . I have been a Nazirite. . . . If my head were shaved . . . I would become as weak as any other man." Just as he gave in to his Timnite wife and explained the riddle that he had not even explained to his parents, so he gives in to Delilah and explains the secret to his strength that he has not entrusted to anyone else. Ironically, he bears his soul on this most intimate of matters to a pagan woman, one who isn't even his legal wife! Sadly, Samson's "confession" demonstrates that he has known all along that he is a Nazirite. This is a powerful comment on all of Samson's previous acts in which he has demonstrated total disregard for his Nazirite status.

The most important element in Delilah's verbal attack is "binding" (*ʾāsar*), which she repeats three times. The least important element to Delilah, mentioned only once, is "love." Yet this is the thing that makes Samson "weak" to her. Samson's position is hopeless. Delilah wants only to bind Samson; love is literally one of the last things that occurs to her. Samson, like many another lover, hears only what he wants to hear. The writer has created a dialogue of dramatic irony in which the reader knows more than the protagonist.[80]

Samson's confession is foolish. Yes, Delilah has worn him down. But Samson is so absorbed *with her* that he, like Eglon, makes himself an easy dumb animal sacrifice for the wily Delilah. The reversal of judgeship is preeminent here. Instead of the judge overthrowing the oppressor (Ehud vs. Eglon),[81] the judge is undone by the oppressors' hired gun. Delilah has succeeded in obtaining the information she was hired to do. The victim is lulled to sleep, and she calls "a man to shave off [better, snip off[82]] the seven braids of his hair." His strength leaves him.

Perhaps one of the most tragic verses in the Hebrew Bible follows: "He awoke from his sleep and thought, 'I'll go out as before and shake myself free.' But he did not know that the LORD had left him." The Spirit of Yahweh is no longer empowering him. As each of the seven braids is cut, so is the Nazirite status finally severed. The gap between the breaking of the first two Nazirite prescriptions and the breaking of the third has provided the narrator with time to underline God's long-suffering. God has continually stood by and invigorated Samson "so long as he clings to the one last strand of the naziriteship, the prohibition against shaving."[83]

---

80. Klein, *Triumph of Irony*, 138.
81. Contrast Judg. 3:12–30 above.
82. See Boling, *Judges*, 250.
83. E. L. Greenstein, "The Riddle of Samson," *Prooftexts* 1/3 (1981): 237–60.

As a result, Samson is blinded and bound, and after being taken to Gaza, he is set to work grinding. Grinding grain was considered a slave or female occupation (cf. Ex. 11:5; Judg. 9:53), and so the Philistines greatly humble their nemesis. From their perspective there is ironic justice in Samson's grinding the grain since he burned up their grain earlier. Perhaps also there is some irony in Samson's loss of his eyes in which his Philistine women had seemed so right (*yāšar*) (14:3, 7), and now he labors at their usual domestic task.

Places of enforced labor like the one in which Samson spends the last months of his life were equipped with a number of handmills for grinding.[84] These were "saddle-querns," consisting of two complementary stone slabs: the lower millstone (proverbial for its hardness) was usually a basalt stone imported from the Hauran region, and the upper millstone made of basalt or sandstone was quite heavy.[85] Kneeling in front of the quern, the miller moved the upper millstone up and down the lower stone, thus grinding the grain between the two. It was difficult labor, especially in the prison-type mills like the one Samson is in.

The section ends in 16:22 with a transition to the climax. This has been aptly described as "one of those pregnant sentences that is the mark of genius": "But the hair on his head began to grow again after it had been shaved." Because of the associations that Samson's hair has acquired in the course of the narrative, this brief sentence raises the reader's expectations that perhaps one crowning act is still in Samson.

Death of Samson/Death of Dagon (16:23–31)

THE OPENING VERSES of this final section of the Samson cycle introduce a new twist: The Philistines lay claim to the supremacy of their god Dagon (16:23–24). Dagon is the Hebrew form of the important Upper Mesopotamian and West Semitic deity Dagan. The Philistines apparently adopted, no doubt in some syncretistic form, the deity from the local Semitic population.[86] In the biblical texts, he appears as a grain deity.[87] In this connection, Samson's

---

84. K. van der Toorn, "Mill, Millstone," in *ABD*, 4:831–32. As van der Toorn points out, these were likely similar to the one discovered at Ebla, where sixteen grindstones were found in their original places.

85. Ibid., 831. Cf. the discussion of the upper millstone in 9:53, which was used by "a [certain] woman" to kill Abimelech.

86. Two other prominent Canaanite deities are now attested in Philistine inscriptions: "Asherah" and "Baal." Dedicatory inscriptions to both deities have been found at Ekron.

87. According to Healey, this does not mean that the name was taken from the West Semitic word for "grain." The word for "grain" probably comes from the name of the god and not *vice versa*. Also the etymology of the name from the word *dāg* "fish" is quite doubtful, although a sarcastic wordplay is not out of the question. For further discussion, see J. F. Healey, "Dagon," in *DDD*, cols. 407–13.

burning of the grain stocks is seen to be more serious. Likewise, in their excitement over the capture of Samson, it is understandable why the Philistines in their victory song[88] give the credit for this to Dagon (note esp. the third line):

> Our god has delivered our enemy
> > into our hands,
> the one who laid waste our land
> > and multiplied our slain.

The Philistines have, perhaps unknowingly, raised the issue to another level. It is now Yahweh versus Dagon! They are, of course, wrong. The Philistines do not understand that it is precisely Yahweh who gave Samson into their hands. By deserting Samson at the cutting of his hair, Yahweh permits the Philistines to confirm their belief that Samson's strength is merely a magical-mechanical fetish that can be manipulated at will by humans. The satire of the Philistines in this section is particularly rich.

To complete the humiliation, the Philistines bring Samson out of prison to the temple to perform. Samson requests to be placed near to the pillars that support the temple, a request that is anticipatory of what is to come. The temple is fully crowded with men and women, plus all the "tyrants" of the Philistines. Some three thousand are on the roof (to get a better view of Samson?). In this context, Samson utters his second prayer to Yahweh (16:28), which literally states:

> O Lord Yahweh, please remember[89] me.
> > Please strengthen me! Just this once! O God!
> And let me revenge [*nqm*] myself[90] with one revenge [*nqm*] on the
> > Philistines for my two eyes.

The first line of this prayer raises expectations that perhaps finally Samson is genuinely turning to Yahweh in humility and proper faith. But the next two lines dash this. Samson is portrayed as repeatedly putting personal ambitions ahead of Yahweh's interests. There is virtually no difference between Samson and the Philistines with respect to seeking revenge. Rather than praying, "O Yahweh, let me deliver Israel," Samson's prayer is for personal revenge for *his* eyes. Self-interest dominates him to the end. Yet Yahweh

---

88. Ironically, the Philistines are singing a victory song, when, had Samson delivered the Israelites, it would have been the Israelites singing a victory song.

89. As in other instances, the term *zākar* (to remember) is not the opposite of "to forget," as if God has forgotten him. Rather, the verb means "to take note of, to act on behalf of" (see Block, *Judges, Ruth,* 467).

90. For the reflexive verbal usage, see Boling, *Judges,* 251.

controls the "circumstances so that Samson becomes an unwitting (if not unwilling) agent of counterattack upon the Philistines."[91]

This is truly an egocentric prayer. Although ostensibly addressed to Yahweh, it is dominated by first-person pronouns, which occur five times in this short prayer. In this it is similar to the Philistines' song[92] that contains five first-person references in its few lines (16:24). But unlike the Philistine song, Samson's prayer has no corporate sense. His preoccupation is with himself as an individual. There is no thought for the nation he is supposed to be delivering, let alone for Yahweh whose name has been denigrated. Samson isn't concerned about Yahweh's reputation, only his personal revenge on the Philistines for his eyes.[93]

Gropingly finding the two support pillars, Samson bellows his last words, "Let me die with the Philistines!" Pushing the columns out of their sockets he brings down the temple structure on the Philistines and himself. The excavation of a Philistine temple at Tell Qasile reveals a structure with "a long room whose roof was originally supported by two wooden pillars set on round, well-made stone bases, placed along the center axis."[94] Webb adeptly summarizes the transpiring spectacle:

> The ensuing scene of death and destruction is for Dagon a debacle of the greatest magnitude. The words of praise for their god must have died coldly on the lips of his devotees. Subtly, and without any crude fanfare of the explicit, the narrator underlines the power of Yahweh, the irrelevance of Dagon. The victory is unquestionably Yahweh's, even if it is only achieved through the suffering of his servant.[95]

Samson kills more in his death than during his life. This is especially true since the dead in the temple include a god! Thus in spite of Samson's personal motive of revenge, Yahweh uses Samson to begin to deliver Israel, not so much in the political sphere as in the theological sphere. There can be no doubt as to who is the true and living God. Yet the tragedy is tremendous: Samson accomplishes more for God dead than alive.

Samson's body is recovered by his family and is buried in "the tomb of Manoah his father." The cycle concludes with the statement: "He had led [lit., judged] Israel twenty years." After the climax of both the second and third sections, there is a note about Samson's judgeship (15:20; 16:31). This is

---

91. O'Connell, *The Rhetoric of the Book of Judges*, 225.

92. Block, *Judges, Ruth*, 468.

93. Contrast David in his encounter with Goliath, who is concerned about Yahweh's name and reputation (1 Sam. 17).

94. A. Mazar, "A Philistine Temple at Tell Qasile," *BA* 36 (1973): 43.

95. Webb, *The Book of the Judges*, 165.

likely a case of a type of resumptive repetition meant to convey symmetry of narration.[96] With this statement, the cycles section of the book of Judges comes to an end.

In the Samson cycle, three Philistine women play an important role. Samson marries a Philistine woman, has an affair with a Philistine harlot, and loves another Philistine, Delilah. All this was in contrast to God's Law. Though he does inflict casualties on the Philistines, he does not deliver Israel from their oppression. In fact, Samson never led the Israelites in battle.[97]

Samson serves as a microcosm of Israel for its respective failures to fulfill their obligations to Yahweh. Just as

> he repeatedly neglects his Nazirite obligations to YHWH by engaging in impure acts and relations with foreign women, so the tribes of Israel [are] negligent of their obligations to YHWH as an elect people by engaging in cultically disloyal acts and by neglecting to expel foreigners from the land.

Hence, in the context of the cycles section, "Samson's struggle between loyalty to his parents and erotic attraction to foreign women is [a reflection] of the struggle of . . . his nation between religious devotion to YHWH and attraction to foreign cults."[98]

All the major episodes from Othniel to Jephthah have involved a competition between Yahweh and other gods for the allegiance of Israel. But it has been in the Out-group judges (Gideon, Jephthah, and Samson) that this theme has manifested itself more particularly. But only in the Samson cycle is the god itself physically destroyed (with its obvious theological ramifications).

Ironically, Samson, the strong man of the book, reveals himself as essentially the weakest, weaker than any of his predecessor judges, for Samson is subject, a slave to physical passion—the lowest kind of subjugation. Because his passions demand women, he is at the mercy of womankind—a deplorable situation from the point of view of a patriarchal society.[99]

---

96. Webb (ibid., 171) correctly notes that the two notices are symmetrical but not identical. He concludes from these statements that Samson's judgeship began effectively at Ramath Lehi and concluded with his death at Gaza.

97. The much more godly Samuel will subdue the Philistines (1 Sam. 7).

98. O'Connell, *The Rhetoric of the Book of Judges*, 224.

99. Klein, *Triumph of Irony*, 118.

A TYPE OF **Christ?** Samson presents one of the real cruxes of bridging the contexts in the book of Judges. It has been popular within Christian circles to interpret Samson positively. It is not uncommon to hear Samson interpreted and preached as a type of Christ. Many children learn about Samson in Sunday School classes that hold him up as a role model for his dedication to God in being willing to follow God even in death. This understanding of Samson is richly embedded in Christian tradition. The reasons for this are plethora, though two seem to be more determinative than others.

(1) The first major factor in this interpretation of Samson is undoubtedly the hermeneutic of the Christocentric principle. Christians tend to read the Bible Christocentrically, to see the person of Jesus Christ in every passage of the Bible, Old and New Testaments. Thus, to many Christians, the statement of 16:30, "Thus he killed many more when he died than while he lived," is commonly understood as a vindication of Samson. According to this interpretation, while he may have wasted his life, in the end he does succeed in saving Israel from the Philistines.

This interpretation has been greatly reinforced by the English poet John Milton in his work *Samson Agonistes* (1671). This work is a tragedy formed on the Greek model, being composed partly in blank verse and partly in unrhymed choric verse of varied line length. In it, Milton employs the Old Testament story of Samson to inspire the defeated English Puritans with the courage to triumph through sacrifice. Thus Milton has Samson, the tragic hero, emerging from his disastrous blindness and powerlessness enriched and ennobled, willing to sacrifice his own life for the sake of the divine mission.[100] In an ironic way, according to this interpretation, Samson is successful as a savior, conquering more in death than in life, proving "that the 'other gods' are no gods at all, and that Yahweh alone is worthy of Israel's devotion."[101]

The analogy of Samson to Christ is easy to make. Emphasizing what may appear as parallels between Samson and Christ, this way of understanding Samson can quickly overshadow the vast bulk of the biblical narrator's characterization of the final "deliverer." Thus Samson, like Christ, was raised up by God, announced by an angel, conceived miraculously, rejected by his people, and handed over to pagan overlords, and his saving work was

---

100. See E. Browne, "Samson: Riddle and Paradox," *TBT* 22 (1984): 161–67. Cf. also the oratorio *Samson* (1743) by the German-born composer George Frederic Handel.

101. B. Webb, "A Serious Reading of the Samson Story (Judges 13–16)," *RTR* 54 (1995): 110–20, esp. 116.

consummated in his death. In this way, he was a "forerunner of the greatest Savior of all."[102]

(2) The second major factor in this interpretation of Samson is the *singular* occurrence of Samson in the New Testament.[103] In Hebrews 11:32, Samson is listed along with a number of other "heroes" of the faith. In fact, this passage in the book of Hebrews has been commonly designated by preachers and teachers as "the hall of faith chapter." In this understanding, Samson must have been a spiritual person in order to be listed here. This interpretation of Hebrews is then read back into the story of Samson and serves as a filter to interpret the Samson cycle.

What can be said in response to these two perspectives? I will deal with them in reverse order. (1) The above-mentioned interpretation of Hebrews 11 is based on a superficial reading of the text. In a closer reading, it is apparent that the writer of Hebrews is simply making a list for homiletic reasons of those individuals with which his audience is most familiar. The writer is not making evaluative statements concerning each and is not ranking them in any order of spirituality. Hebrews 11:32 reads: "And what more shall I say? I do not have time to tell about Gideon, Barak, Samson, Jephthah, David, Samuel and the prophets." Beside the obvious rhetorical question (which plays a clearly homiletic role), it is worth mentioning the order. This order is in pairs, with the first individual chronologically following the second. Thus

	Historically second	Historically first	
1st Pair	Gideon	Barak	
2nd Pair	Samson	Jephthah	
3rd Pair	David	Samuel	and the prophets

This indicates that the writer is giving a stylized list for homiletic reasons. As the writer summarizes the history of God's dealings with the human race, especially in the history of the nation of Israel, he telescopes his presentation of the material between Moses (whom he has developed in detail) and "the last days" (i.e., the present context of the writer) in order to drive home his main point: All these were commended for their faith; therefore, let believers lay aside every encumbrance and live for the Lord (11:39–12:2). The writer does not intend for his readers to assume that all these individuals have the same spirituality, level of faith, and maturity.

---

102. Ibid., 120.

103. Besides this single occurrence in the New Testament, Samson is not mentioned elsewhere in the Bible, with the possible exception of 1 Sam. 12:11, where there is textual confusion between the reading of the last named judge (LXX[L] and Syriac: Samson; MT and others: Samuel). For further discussion of this verse, see the introduction, p. 25.

By far the most developed in Hebrews 11 are Abraham and Moses, and the author hardly intends to equate Samson with these two in spirituality issues. The latter barely has enough faith to call on him who empowered him; Abraham and Moses manifest faith on another level altogether. The point is not that all these individuals have attained a "hall of fame" level of faith, but that all, *even to the smallest degree,* manifested faith.[104] Therefore, the traditional understanding of Samson as a prime example of faith based on Hebrews 11 is founded on a misinterpretation of Hebrews 11 that has been read back into Judges. This is hermeneutically unsound.

(2) With regard to the Christocentric reading as outlined above, let us start with the interpretation of Judges 16:30. Samson's last words after his narcissistic prayer (v. 28) are literally: "Let my person die with the Philistines!" With this utterance Samson declares his total and final identification with the enemy. What a tragic inversion of the office to which he had been called! The Nazirite, set apart for the service of God, wants to die with the uncircumcised (unclean) Philistines! Samson wanted to "live" with the Philistines in life and wants to die with them in death. As Block points out, the statement concerning Samson's killing more Philistines in his death than in his life is not a vindication of Samson but rather is a tragic note on which this squandered life ends.[105] This man, with his unprecedented high calling and with his extraordinary divine gifts, has wasted his life. Indeed, he accomplishes more for God dead than alive—not because of Samson but because of Yahweh.

But more important, the Christocentric reading of Samson is also hermeneutically flawed in that it fails to read the Samson cycle in its larger narrative context. The downward spiral of the cyclical/major judges that is clearly evident in the overarching structure of the section is ignored in such an interpretation that makes Samson a type of Christ (see the introduction, pp. 34–37).

The clear and lengthy portrayal of Samson in Judges 13–16 is hardly a characterization that parallels the person of Jesus Christ. In the context of Judges, Samson is far from the standard of Christ. He is one of the most narcissistic persons in all the Bible. Self-gratification is what drives this man. Never in the Samson narrative does he operate in anyone's interest but his own. He does not care about God's plan or any of the divine standards of either his place as an Israelite or his Nazirite status. He does not care about the will of his parents or the hearts of the "lovers" with whom he consorts. All are to be manipulated for his sake.

---

104. Samson's faith is seen in his trust in Yahweh to hear his prayer and strengthen him once more, even though Samson's motives are only for personal vengeance. Yahweh answers the prayer in spite of Samson's sinful motives, because he will vindicate and glorify his name and can even use a Samson to accomplish this.

105. Block, *Judges, Ruth,* 469.

Nevertheless, in spite of his wrong motives (revenge), God uses Samson to prove that he, not Dagon, is God. *Only God's grace makes something positive come out of his life—in every case in spite of Samson.* Ironically, by the exercise of his own immoral will, Samson serves as an agent of the Lord's ethical will,[106] and by the narrator's own acknowledgment he accomplishes more dying than living.

Very simply, Samson is not a type of Christ. Nowhere is this implied in the Old or New Testaments. Instead, if anything, Samson is a foil to Christ. Yes, there are some similarities, but the contrasts are much greater. The similarities only heighten the contrasts all the more. There is no way that such an ego-driven, narcissistic, immoral man is, in any way, a real type of Christ, the one who was the ultimate *kenosis*[107]—the sinless, real deliverer!

Samson and Christ are polar opposites in attitude and action. Christ's attitude was one "emptied" of self-interest, self-determination, and self-glorification, and was focused on doing the will of God, the Father, even unto death on a cross (Phil. 2). Even in Christ's death, therefore, self-interest was laid aside for the Father's plan to be fulfilled. But in his death, Samson's concerns were about Samson—his personal revenge, not about God's plan to deliver the Israelites from the Philistines, not to mention how this might benefit the Israelites, his own people. It is truly amazing and ironic that this multifornicator, who delivered no one, is made to typify the Lord Jesus Christ, who gave his life that we might be delivered, *really* delivered, from the worst death, spiritual death!

Therefore, those who make Samson a type of Christ do so by emphasizing the similarities and utterly ignoring the tremendous differences. Just because there are a few similarities does not mean that we are dealing with a type of Christ.[108]

Samson's foolish, self-gratifying actions. This entire chapter (Judg. 16) is full of Samson's foolish, self-gratifying actions. His act of copulation with the Gaza prostitute is a deliberate, rebellious act against God's Law. His escape is a marvelous exploit, but like all his great exploits it is self-motivated.

Samson is consumed in his "love" for Delilah. Yet Delilah is just like Samson: Her motivations are driven by self-interest! "Love" is the last thing on her mind. Instead, money is the predominant subject in her thought processes. "For the love of money is a root of all kinds of evil. Some people, eager for money, have wandered from the faith and pierced themselves with many griefs" (1 Tim. 6:10). Delilah's spiritual descendants are present today, ready to receive their bribes for any and all reasons.

---

106. Klein, *The Triumph of Irony in the Book of Judges*, 118.

107. The voluntary emptying of the second person of the Godhead (Phil. 2).

108. It is also fruitful to contrast Samson with John the Baptist. Once again the similarities only heighten the contrasts.

Contemporary Significance

THE DANGERS OF SELF-INTEREST. Here in the literary climax and moral nadir of the book, amazingly Yahweh once again works in spite of the tremendous sinfulness of Samson. Throughout this cycles section, God has intervened on behalf of his people to accomplish his will, though in this case, it is only to begin the deliverance of Israel. With the death of Samson, Israel has not been freed from the Philistine oppression. The ironic tragedy is that one so gifted has cared so little for doing God's will in his life that only in his death is the process of deliverance begun.

Samson's spiritual apathy is truly stupefying. Spiritual apathy concerning one's calling can lead to open rebellion, as Samson's union with the prostitute of Gaza illustrates. And throughout the Samson cycle self-interest serves as the motivation, not only for his exploits but also for Delilah, the one who brings him down. When self-interest serves as the motivational factor in one's life, eventual devastation will come—in some cases, not surprisingly from another person whose motivation is also driven by self-interest.

In general, temptation for a plethora of sins may be the greatest to those who are most gifted. The Lord Jesus Christ and his temptations are a testimony to this. Samson's extraordinary strength is proverbial. His giftedness of exceptional physical power came through his special Nazirite status, which was conveyed to his parents through a double theophany. Unfortunately, like many contemporary divinely called and gifted leaders, Samson squandered his life playing with his God-given gifts and indulging in every sensuality. In this regard, there is no need to document the yearly succumbing to sexual sin of this pastor, this missionary, this TV evangelist, this Christian professor, this youth worker, and so on.

Sexual issues. Samson's lust led him to the abuse and exploitation of women. Biblical standards of male conduct call for the highest respect for women, who are equally created in God's image and endowed with majesty and dignity. The biblical texts communicate that God regards sex and sexual activity as sacred, as something that he established for a man and woman within the context of marriage. Anything less is perverse, demeaning, and exploitative.

Sexual purity was clearly not a concern to Samson. Yet this is hardly a minor concern for a believer, let alone a leader of God's people. The commandment against adultery (Ex. 20:14) is not simply against the act but also against the issues involving the inner person: thought, intent, and motive. It is impossible to commit adultery without thought, intent, and motive being contrary to God's will. Thus, God demands purity in our thought life as well as in our action. Jesus explains this in Matthew 5:28 by pointing out that if anyone looks at a woman lustfully, he has already committed adultery with her in his heart.

In the present-day context, when Internet pornography is so easy to access (not to mention easy access to hard copy, too), a significant number of God's servants have become addicted to it (including pastors). But sexual sin does not *just happen!* There is a conscious decision made every time before the act is committed. It does not happen without our mental involvement. Therefore, it is important that we safeguard ourselves so that we are pure before the Lord Jesus Christ at his judgment. Through the power of the Holy Spirit and the renewing of the mind (Rom. 12:2), it is possible to overcome this sin.

There is no doubt that sex and money are powerful, seductive attractions. Plethora are the number who have and who will succumb to their potency. But God's Word is a storehouse of injunctions and encouragements to avoid both, and in so doing to live (cf. Ex. 20:14; 23:8; Deut. 27:25; Prov. 5:1–21; 7:6–27). In a world where the temptations for both are as prevalent as in any other time in history, we need to inculcate these Scriptures and make them our life.

In the end, God can be counted on to vindicate his name, to demonstrate that all those things that humanity in whatever era worships and venerates are not gods. They cannot save on the day of judgment for they are not gods to begin with.

Judges 17:1–18:31

 ❦

OW A MAN named Micah from the hill country of
Ephraim ²said to his mother, "The eleven hundred
shekels of silver that were taken from you and about
which I heard you utter a curse—I have that silver with me; I
took it."

Then his mother said, "The LORD bless you, my son!"

³When he returned the eleven hundred shekels of silver to
his mother, she said, "I solemnly consecrate my silver to the
LORD for my son to make a carved image and a cast idol. I will
give it back to you."

⁴So he returned the silver to his mother, and she took two
hundred shekels of silver and gave them to a silversmith, who
made them into the image and the idol. And they were put in
Micah's house.

⁵Now this man Micah had a shrine, and he made an ephod
and some idols and installed one of his sons as his priest. ⁶In
those days Israel had no king; everyone did as he saw fit.

⁷A young Levite from Bethlehem in Judah, who had been
living within the clan of Judah, ⁸left that town in search of
some other place to stay. On his way he came to Micah's
house in the hill country of Ephraim.

⁹Micah asked him, "Where are you from?"

"I'm a Levite from Bethlehem in Judah," he said, "and I'm
looking for a place to stay."

¹⁰Then Micah said to him, "Live with me and be my father
and priest, and I'll give you ten shekels of silver a year, your
clothes and your food." ¹¹So the Levite agreed to live with
him, and the young man was to him like one of his sons.
¹²Then Micah installed the Levite, and the young man became
his priest and lived in his house. ¹³And Micah said, "Now I
know that the LORD will be good to me, since this Levite has
become my priest."

¹⁸:¹In those days Israel had no king.

And in those days the tribe of the Danites was seeking a
place of their own where they might settle, because they had
not yet come into an inheritance among the tribes of Israel.
²So the Danites sent five warriors from Zorah and Eshtaol to

spy out the land and explore it. These men represented all
their clans. They told them, "Go, explore the land."

The men entered the hill country of Ephraim and came to
the house of Micah, where they spent the night. ³When they
were near Micah's house, they recognized the voice of the
young Levite; so they turned in there and asked him, "Who
brought you here? What are you doing in this place? Why are
you here?"

⁴He told them what Micah had done for him, and said, "He
has hired me and I am his priest."

⁵Then they said to him, "Please inquire of God to learn
whether our journey will be successful."

⁶The priest answered them, "Go in peace. Your journey has
the LORD's approval."

⁷So the five men left and came to Laish, where they saw
that the people were living in safety, like the Sidonians, unsuspecting and secure. And since their land lacked nothing, they
were prosperous. Also, they lived a long way from the Sidonians and had no relationship with anyone else.

⁸When they returned to Zorah and Eshtaol, their brothers
asked them, "How did you find things?"

⁹They answered, "Come on, let's attack them! We have seen
that the land is very good. Aren't you going to do something?
Don't hesitate to go there and take it over. ¹⁰When you get
there, you will find an unsuspecting people and a spacious
land that God has put into your hands, a land that lacks nothing whatever."

¹¹Then six hundred men from the clan of the Danites,
armed for battle, set out from Zorah and Eshtaol. ¹²On their
way they set up camp near Kiriath Jearim in Judah. This is
why the place west of Kiriath Jearim is called Mahaneh Dan to
this day. ¹³From there they went on to the hill country of
Ephraim and came to Micah's house.

¹⁴Then the five men who had spied out the land of Laish
said to their brothers, "Do you know that one of these houses
has an ephod, other household gods, a carved image and a
cast idol? Now you know what to do." ¹⁵So they turned in
there and went to the house of the young Levite at Micah's
place and greeted him. ¹⁶The six hundred Danites, armed for
battle, stood at the entrance to the gate. ¹⁷The five men who
had spied out the land went inside and took the carved image,

the ephod, the other household gods and the cast idol while the priest and the six hundred armed men stood at the entrance to the gate.

¹⁸When these men went into Micah's house and took the carved image, the ephod, the other household gods and the cast idol, the priest said to them, "What are you doing?"

¹⁹They answered him, "Be quiet! Don't say a word. Come with us, and be our father and priest. Isn't it better that you serve a tribe and clan in Israel as priest rather than just one man's household?" ²⁰Then the priest was glad. He took the ephod, the other household gods and the carved image and went along with the people. ²¹Putting their little children, their livestock and their possessions in front of them, they turned away and left.

²²When they had gone some distance from Micah's house, the men who lived near Micah were called together and over-took the Danites. ²³As they shouted after them, the Danites turned and said to Micah, "What's the matter with you that you called out your men to fight?"

²⁴He replied, "You took the gods I made, and my priest, and went away. What else do I have? How can you ask, 'What's the matter with you?'"

²⁵The Danites answered, "Don't argue with us, or some hot-tempered men will attack you, and you and your family will lose your lives." ²⁶So the Danites went their way, and Micah, seeing that they were too strong for him, turned around and went back home.

²⁷Then they took what Micah had made, and his priest, and went on to Laish, against a peaceful and unsuspecting people. They attacked them with the sword and burned down their city. ²⁸There was no one to rescue them because they lived a long way from Sidon and had no relationship with anyone else. The city was in a valley near Beth Rehob.

The Danites rebuilt the city and settled there. ²⁹They named it Dan after their forefather Dan, who was born to Israel—though the city used to be called Laish. ³⁰There the Danites set up for themselves the idols, and Jonathan son of Gershom, the son of Moses, and his sons were priests for the tribe of Dan until the time of the captivity of the land. ³¹They continued to use the idols Micah had made, all the time the house of God was in Shiloh.

AS POINTED OUT in the introduction (see pp. 30–33), the double introduction of Judges is balanced by a double conclusion, which thus forms a type of inclusio. In contrast to the second introduction (B; 2:6–3:6), which describes the difficulties that Israel had with foreign religious idols, the first conclusion (B') describes the difficulties that Israel had with its own domestic idols (17:1–18:31). This first conclusion is made up of three episodes with expanding foci: the idolatry of Micah the Ephraimite (focus: Micah; 17:1–5), the installation of the Levite at Micah's shrine (focus: Micah and the Levite; 17:7–13), and the migration of the Danites (focus: Micah and the Levite and the Danites; 18:1b–31). The double conclusion's refrain occurs at two nodal points (17:6 and 18:1a), functioning as a transition in the plot's development.

The specific episodes escalate through parallels and complications with the previous episodes and climax in the promotion of Micah's family-cult apostasy to the level of tribal-cult apostasy by the Danites (18:30a, 31). Just as Samson's attraction to intermarry with a Philistine woman served as the catalyst for the whole series of events in Judges 14–15, so Micah's seemingly inconsequential theft of silver from his mother served as the catalyst that eventually led to the Danites' renaming a city and establishing a cult center after their slaughter of the people of Laish.[1]

The entire double conclusion is unified by the four-time repetition of the refrain (lit.): "In those days there was no king. . . . Every man did what right in his own eyes" (17:6; 18:1; 19:1; 21:25). This refrain emphasizes through a double entendre that during the period of the judges there was no physical king, but more importantly no spiritual king! Thus, "everyone did as he saw fit" (lit., "every man did what was right in his own eyes").[2]

The fact that the two conclusions deal with the bad decisions and moral failures of both Levites and tribal leaders reinforces the significance of the refrain. These should be the two sources of national leadership, and their failures complement the downward spiral already portrayed in the book. Their derelictions only stress the complete failure of Israel to adhere to the theocracy and its covenant.

In light of Samson's doing what was right in his own eyes, the narrator, by use of the second verse of the refrain (i.e., "every man did what was right

---

1. Block, *Judges, Ruth*, 477.

2. The NIV's translation of this line obscures the literary links back into the cycles section of the book. Therefore, I will use the literal translation throughout in order to facilitate the commentary.

in his own eyes"), has established a link back into the cycles section. In fact, this phrase is the functional equivalent to "Israel did what was evil in Yahweh's eyes" (i.e., the first formulaic statement of the judge cycles). Both statements are related to the issue of apostasy from Yahweh, especially the evil of idolatry.[3]

The perversion of idolatry leads to all manner of sexual and social perversion; nothing is left unscathed. Perversion of the relationship with God represented by idolatry leaves no other relationship whole either, whether between individuals, groups of individuals, races, or nations. Because humans are unwilling to acknowledge God as God, that same God then allows his creatures to reap the results of their idolatrous actions.[4] Thus, the moral depravity documented in the double conclusion, especially the second conclusion, is the natural outcome of the idolatry the Israelites have engaged in.

The first conclusion (17:1–18:31) should be read in the light of Deuteronomy 12:1–13:1. The entire section contains several thematic elements and concerns in common with this passage, though Judges 17:1–18:31 usually portrays them antithetically:[5] Note the following chart.

Theme	Deut. 12:1–13:1	Judg. 17:1–18:31
Cult sites on hills	to be destroyed (12:2)	constructed (17:3–4)
Idols	to be cut down (12:3a)	manufactured (17:3–4)
Ideal of central shrine	repeatedly endorsed (12:4–7, 11, 13–14, 17–18, 26–27)	repeatedly and ironically ignored (17:2b–5, 13; 18:31b)
What is right in … own eyes	prohibited (12:8)	practiced (17:6b)
Support of Levites	at central shrine (12:12, 18, 19)	at private shrines (17:7–13; 18:19–20, 30b)
Inheritance not yet settled	Israel excused (12:9–10a)	Micah (settled)/Danites (unsettled) unexcused (17:1; 18:1b)
Yahweh to let live in safety	future Israel (12:10b)	not Dan but Laish (18:7b, 10a, 27a)
Yahweh to extend territory	future Israel (12:20a)	not Dan but Laish (18:7b, 10b, 28)

3. M. K. Wilson, "As You Like It: The Idolatry of Micah and the Danites (Judges 17–18)," *RTR* 54 (1995): 73–85, esp. 74–76.

4. P. J. Achtemeier, "Gods Made with Hands: The New Testament and the Problem of Idolatry," *Ex Auditu* 15 (1999): 50.

5. O'Connell, *The Rhetoric of the Book of Judges*, 239–40.

Each point of antithesis between Judges 17:1–18:31 and Deuteronomy 12:1–13:1 heightens the rhetorical point that, in doing what was right in their own eyes, the characters of this account are acting in defiance of the cultic ideals set forth in Deuteronomy 12. It is probably not just fortuitous that Judges 17–18 concludes and culminates (18:30–31) with a contrast between the Danite cult and the cult of YHWH at Shiloh, the only cult endorsed by the narrative of chs. 17–21 (cf. 21:19).[6]

The Idolatry of Micah the Ephraimite (17:1–6)

WHEREAS AT THE beginning of the period of the judges the Israelites had difficulties with the foreign gods of the peoples in the land (2:6–3:6), the Israelites are presented now, in the first conclusion, as perfectly capable of manufacturing their own idols.

The narrative introduces a man named Micah from the hill country of Ephraim, who confesses that he has stolen[7] eleven hundred shekels of silver from his unnamed mother (obviously a woman of substantial wealth). The name "Micah" is a short form of *Mikayahu*, meaning "Who is like Yahweh?" This is ironic since Yahweh is so absent from this story. His overt disregard for the fifth and eighth commandments demonstrates a brazen attitude to Yahweh and his Law.

This sum (1,100 shekels of silver) provides a tangible link to the foregoing narrative, where Delilah takes precisely this amount from each of the five Philistine lords (cf. 16:5). Some interpreters have wrongly interpreted this sum to indicate that Delilah is the mother of Micah. But besides the fact there is nothing to support this interpretation, it obscures the important function of this literary link. In the Micah narrative, the money is stolen, not exchanged between consenting parties. Worse, Micah betrays the trust of blood-tie, of the mother-son kinship, not the betrayal of an ethnic enemy. And even worse, Micah's theft is not a business transaction for services rendered (as in the case of Delilah); it is nothing but the product of raw covetousness. "Delilah, the gauge of evil—foreigner, seductress, betrayer—is surpassed by Micah, Israelite betrayer of Israelite values without reason against the most intimate sphere, the family."[8]

Micah's mother utters a curse, and this seems to motivate Micah to return the stolen silver principally because he is afraid of the fulfillment of this

---

6. Ibid., 240.

7. Lit., "taken." The same verb will be used of the Danite action in 18:17 so that Micah's "stealing" is anticipatory of the Danites' "stealing." The first conclusion moves from family sin to community idolatry to tribal apostasy.

8. See Klein, *Triumph of Irony*, 143–44.

---

curse. But the reaction of his mother is to counteract the curse with a blessing: "Yahweh bless you, my son!" (17:2). What seems to underline Micah's mother's curse and blessing is the ancient Near Eastern concept of magic.[9] This becomes clearer from what will transpire in the story.

At this point, according to the Law prescribed in Leviticus 6:1–6, Micah— who has confessed his sin of stealing and repaid the principal (i.e., the exact amount stolen from his mother)—should do two more things. (1) He should acknowledge his sin before Yahweh at the tabernacle by paying restitution to his mother for the crime (i.e., one fifth of the principal involved). (2) He should sacrifice a guilt offering through the priest for atonement. But it is more than obvious that the Law is not being followed in this story. Israel has no spiritual king.

This is amplified by the dedication recorded in 17:3. After the promised return of the silver, Micah's mother solemnly consecrates the silver[10] to Yahweh in order for her son to make an idolatrous object (or objects). She contributes, however, only two hundred shekels of silver toward this project (evidently pocketing the rest?). There is some disagreement concerning the precise meaning of the phrase *pesel ûmassemkâ*. Some scholars argue that this phrase reflects two separate objects: "a carved image and a cast idol" (e.g., NIV, NEB). Other scholars argue that this phrase is a hendiadys signifying "a cast image" (i.e., one object, namely, "a carved image overlaid with molten metal," e.g., NRSV).[11]

In addition, verse 5 notes that Micah made *ʾēpôd ûtᵉrāpîm* (an ephod and teraphim[12]; NIV translates "some idols"; lit., "household gods"). These terms (*pesel ûmassēkâ; ʾēpôd ûtᵉrāpîm*) are more than a hendiadys[13]; they are two fixed pairs[14] used to encompass all aspects of idolatrous worship. The mother contributes the silver for production of the pair *pesel ûmassēkâ*, emphasizing the

---

9. See Block's discussion, *Judges, Ruth*, 478–80.

10. In the ancient Near East, silver often took on magical connotations.

11. See Block, *Judges, Ruth*, 480 n. 19; Boling, *Judges*, 256; J. D. Martin, *The Book of Judges* (CBC; Cambridge: Cambridge Univ. Press, 1975), 180. Cundall argues that the two words *pesel ûmassēkâ* reflect the manner of making an idol. The word *pesel* means the carving of the wood or stones by the craftsman, while *pesel ûmassēkâ* means the melting down of the metal and overlaying it on the carved sculpture (Cundall, *Judges*, 184).

12. The biblical *teraphim* appear to have been ancestor figurines that were most often used in divination, see K. van der Toorn and T. J. Lewis, "תְּרָפִים," *ThWAT*, 8:765–78.

13. Klein, *Triumph of Irony*, 150. While her discussion is helpful, she confuses the term *massēkâ* (found in Judg. 17–18) with the term *maṣṣēbâ* (not found in Judg. 17).

14. This is clear in their initial formulations in verses 4 and 5 and reinforced in 18:14, where the five Danites list the items in Micah's house as *ʾēpôd ûtᵉrāpîm ûpesel ûmassēkâ*. In 18:17–18, in the description of the Danites' theft, the pair *pesel* and *massēkâ* is split for rhetorical reasons: *ʾet-happesel wᵉʾet-hāʾēpôd wᵉʾet-hattᵉrāpîm wᵉʾet-hammassēkâ*.

---

fabricated aspect of the image. Micah contributes the material for the production of the pair *ʾēpōd ûtrāpîm*, emphasizing the *oracular* aspect of the cult shrine. The terms, as used in the Judges narrative, stress humanity's part in either *making* the idol or in *using* it.[15]

In any case, the production of the first pair is in obvious violation of the second commandment (see Ex. 20:4, 23; 34:17; Lev. 19:4), not to mention the specific Deuteronomic curse, "Cursed is the man who carves an image [*pesel*] or casts an idol [*massēkâ*]" (Deut. 27:15).[16] The making of an ephod was wrong for the same reasons that it was wrong in the case of Gideon (see comments on Judg. 8:27). The use of *trāpîm* (household gods) for divinatory purposes is attested elsewhere (Gen. 31:19; Ezek. 21:21; Zech. 10:2). Thus there is also a violation of the first commandment (Ex. 20:3; Deut 5:7) as well.

Micah places all the cult paraphernalia in his own house, where he makes a shrine (lit., "a house of god[s]", *bêt ʾělōhîm*). He installs one of his sons as the shrine's priest. The installation of someone other than a Levite as a priest was obviously in violation of the Law (Ex. 29:9; Num. 16:10). This action undercut the divinely ordained priestly authority at Shiloh.

Disregard for parental well-being, thief, homemade idolatrous objects of pilfered silver, private shrines, personal priests, self-made religious paraphernalia—these are hardly the proper trappings of one whose name means "Who is like Yahweh?"[17] Ironically, while thinking that they are doing right, both Micah and his mother perform actions contrary to Yahweh's cultic requirements as prescribed in Deuteronomy 12. In addition, it is ironic that this production of an illegitimate cult shrine takes place in the "hill country of Ephraim" (17:1), not that far from the legitimate place of worship during the period of the judges, Shiloh! Small wonder this initial story ends with the first occurrence of the refrain, "In those days Israel had no king; every man did what was right in his own eyes" (17:6). This refrain, of course, serves as a transition to the next section.

The Installation of the Levite at Micah's Shrine (17:7−13)

IN THE NEXT EPISODE, a young Levite traveling from Bethlehem in Judah finds his way northward to Micah's house. He has been living (lit., sojourning) in Bethlehem. Why is a young Levite living in Bethlehem in Judah? Bethlehem is not a Levitical town in Judah (Josh. 21:9−16). Moreover, Judges 18:30

---

15. Klein, *Triumph of Irony*, 150.

16. Cf. the golden calf incident (Ex. 32).

17. G. Yee, "Ideological Criticism: Judges 17–21 and the Dismembered Body," in *Judges and Method: New Approaches in Biblical Studies*, ed. G. A. Yee (Minneapolis: Fortress, 1995), 158.

states that this Levite is a descendant of Gershom, the son of Moses (Ex. 2:22; 6:18–20), which means that he is a member of the Kohathite clan of the Levites, who were allotted ten towns in Ephraim, Dan, and Cisjordanian Manasseh (Josh. 21:5, 20–26). Thus this Levite should not have been living in Bethlehem in Judah. The failure of the Israelites to obey the Law has probably resulted in a lack of support for the Levites and may explain the man's wandering in search of subsistence.

In his search, he comes to Micah's house (17:8). The dialogue is technically unnecessary in 17:9 since the information gained by Micah's question to the Levite has already been given in the previous verses. The restatement, however, reinforces the fact that the Levite is a wandering opportunist. In light of the offer that Micah makes to him in verse 10 ("live with me and be my father[18] and priest, and I'll give you ten pieces of silver a year, your clothes and your food"), it is clear that the Levite is motivated primarily by material concerns. The fact that later he accepts an even more attractive offer (18:19–20) confirms his materialistic motivation.

This seems "right" in the eyes of the Levite. Micah treats him like one of his sons (i.e., quite well, 17:11). Installing the Levite as his priest probably means the demotion of his own son. But having a genuine Levite as his priest gives Micah's shrine an air of legitimacy and prestige. This conclusion is supported by the statement of Micah in verse 13: "Now I know that the LORD will be good to me, since this Levite has become my priest." Like Jephthah's ignorance of God's Law, Micah evinces an ignorance of the Law in its most basic teachings.

What makes the passage even more ironic is the setting. All the action (the making of the carved image and a cast idol, the making of Micah's son a priest, the hiring of a wandering Levite, etc.) takes place in the hill country of Ephraim, the very tribe where the tabernacle of Yahweh is located (i.e., Shiloh). It should be stressed, however, that even before the Levite enters the story, the implicit assessment of Micah's shrine is negative since, according to Deuteronomy 12, the mere existence of a cult other than the one endorsed by God at the central shrine is condemned.

Both of these first two sections follow a similar pattern. Both start with the introduction of a principal character (Micah, the young Levite) and end with an addition being made to Micah's shrine (cult objects, Levitical priest). Thus they envision a progression of expansion and prosperity for Micah's

---

18. The term "father" is used here as a title of honor by which Micah acknowledges his willingness to subordinate himself to and be dependent on the Levite in spiritual matters. This is ironic in that the Levite is described as a *na^{c}ar* ("boy, youth") but is made a "father" by Micah's perversion of the God-ordained priestly ministry.

shrine that leads to his ironic expression of confidence in Yahweh's blessing (17:13). The narrator is setting us up for what will follow, when Micah's confidence is overturned.[19]

The Migration of the Danites (18:1–31)

THIS STORY OF the Danite migration starts with a partial repetition of the refrain, "In those days Israel had no king." The ellipsis of the second line of the refrain forces the reader to supply that thought echoed in the events narrated throughout the rest of the chapter: "Every man did what was right in his own eyes."

Just as the wayward Levite sought a place to settle, so now the text describes a wayward tribe seeking a place to settle. This is the initial link between the two stories. The tribe of Dan had had the least success in conquering any of its allotment (Judg. 1:34). In order to find another place to settle, the Danites send out five warriors from Zorah and Eshtaol (note the link here with the earlier Samson narrative) "to spy out the land and explore it."

Just as the Levite happened to come to Micah's house, so the Danite spies happen to come to Micah's house and spend the night. And just as the Danites' quest for new territory is illegitimate, so is their quest for a cult other than that of Yahweh.

The narration backs up slightly to the time of their approach to Micah's house when they recognize "the voice" of the young Levite servicing Micah's shrine. The word "voice" (*qôl*) probably refers to the Levite's accent.[20] Consequently, they bombard the Levite with questions about how he got there, what he is doing there, and why he is there (18:3).

The Levite replies that Micah "has hired me and I am his priest." The answer does not disturb the Danites in the least (i.e., a priest serving in non-Yahwistic context). Instead, they solicit an oracle (probably through the divination of the ephod and *t*ᵉ*rāpîm* (household gods): "Please inquire of God to learn whether our journey will be successful." Notice that they use the term "God," not Yahweh. Ironically, God has already revealed his will by the allotments given to the tribes, including Dan (Josh. 19:47–48, 51). There is no need for another inquiry.

The Levite gives them exactly what they want to hear: "Go in peace, your journey has the LORD's approval" (18:6). Ironically, the Levite, who has barely found his own way, now confidently pronounces Yahweh's approval

---

19. P. Satterthwaite, "'No King in Israel': Narrative Criticism and Judges 17–21," *TynBul* 44 (1993): 75–88, esp. 78.

20. Boling, *Judges*, 263. Perhaps his Kohathite connection gives him away (cf. the accent or dialect distinctions in the Shibboleth incident, 12:1–6).

of theirs. Yahweh, of course, would not sanction a slaughter of the town of Laish, since his will concerning the Danite allotment was already revealed. Nevertheless, the Levite's oracle will provide the Danites with a rationale for slaughtering all the inhabitants of Laish (cf. 18:10).[21] Profanely, the Levite pronounces the name of Yahweh, thus breaking the third commandment. One can hear the echo, "Every man did what was right in his own eyes."

Presumably, the next day the spies leave and go to Laish. The town is unsuspecting of the disaster that is soon to fall on it.[22] The spies return to Zorah and Eshtaol (18:8) and give their report, which stresses the prosperity of the land and the vulnerability of its inhabitants (18:9-10).

While the sending out of spies is reminiscent of the Israelite tribes sending out spies in Numbers 13 (cf. also Judg. 1:23), this Danite quest for new territory is illegitimate. In many ways, the story is contrastive to that of the Israelite spies in Numbers 13. The Danite spies do not give a negative report about the inhabitants of their scouted territory. Instead, with repeated stress on the insecurity and defenselessness of their victims (Judg. 18:7a, 10a, 27a), the writer portrays the Danites and their spies not only as too fearful to conquer their own territory (cf. 1:34-36) but also as willing to cruelly conquer a defenseless territory (18:7b, 10b, 28a) and to victimize the weaker Micah (18:14-26). Thus, unlike the Israelites in Numbers 13, the Danites respond to the spies' report without hesitation (Judg. 18:9b). Thus they are characterized as eager perpetrators of injustice.[23]

Six hundred men of the Danites set out to attack the unsuspecting town.[24] Their camp near Kiriath Jearim receives the name Mahaneh Dan—"Camp Dan." Arriving at Micah's house the five scouts inform their tribesmen that the house contains a shrine with all the trappings. The five men enter the house and start taking the cultic materials while the six hundred, armed for battle, stand at the lookout. The Danites, who properly should have destroyed Micah's cult (according to Deut. 12:2-3), instead find it worthy of acquisition, even if by means of theft (Judg. 18:15-17).

The Levite priest questions them, but they make him an offer: "Come with us, and be our father and priest. Isn't it better that you serve a tribe and

---

21. Thus indirectly the Levite's words are the cause or, at least, the legitimation of the slaughter. Ironically, in the second conclusion below, another Levite's words will be the cause for the civil war's great slaughter.

22. The meaning of two clauses of the Hebrew text of Judg. 18:7 are uncertain (see NIV text notes). For the most recent discussion, see O'Connell, *The Rhetoric of the Book of Judges*, 477-80.

23. Ibid., 237.

24. The number "six hundred" is anticipatory of the six hundred men that make up the remnant of the tribe of Benjamin in 20:47 (cf. the six hundred Philistines killed by Shamgar, 3:31).

clan in Israel as priest rather than just one man's household?" (18:19). The Levite's reaction is immediate and positive: "Then the priest was glad" (18:20). The appeal to his vanity and materialism are sufficient to obtain his commitment. In case they are attacked, the Danites put the little children, livestock, and possessions in front of them (18:21).

The men who live near Micah are called out to help recover the pilfered gods. When they catch up with the Danites, the Danites' response is to question Micah's motives: "What's the matter with you that you called out your men to fight?" (18:23). This response surprises Micah (as it surprises the reader!). "You took the gods I made," Micah exclaims. Ironically, Micah is concerned about the loss of gods who could not even protect themselves or their maker. His anguish is that of one whose life is centered on powerless gods: "What else do I have?" Not only has he been robbed and betrayed, but also without any divine and priestly support of his gods, he feels naked, completely vulnerable to the forces of evil and disaster, the very thing he was seeking to avoid by making the idolatrous objects in the first place. Micah, who at the beginning of the story was portrayed as a thief, is himself the victim of theft.

Coercingly, they reply, "Don't argue with us, or some hot-tempered men [i.e., they themselves] will attack you ."[25] Their intimidation works; Micah departs without his gods, and the Danites continue on their quest. With the cultic materials and priest securely in their possession, the Danites confidently attack the unsuspecting town of Laish, which was in a valley near Beth Rehob.[26] In the same ruthless manner that they had stolen the powerless gods from the helpless Micah, who had manufactured them, the Danites exterminate the powerless, helpless inhabitants of Laish. Thus the Danite conquest is described as a human achievement without any insinuation of God's involvement in the enterprise whatsoever.

The Danites rebuild the city and rename it Dan,[27] after their forefather. They also set up the image that Micah made and install "Jonathan son of Gershom, the son of Moses" as priest (cf. Ex. 2:22; 18:3; 1 Chron. 23:14–15). The Levite's Yahwistic name, Jonathan ("Yahweh has given"), and his genealogical connections to Moses[28] heighten the irony of the entire story. Thus, the problems of religious syncretism and spiritual decay have infected the very institution designed to combat these problems, not to mention one of the most revered households in ancient Israel.

---

25. Ironically, in their threat to kill Micah, the Danites inadvertently threaten to do the punishment that the Deuteronomic law demanded for the crime of idolatry.

26. Cf. Num. 13:21.

27. For the archaeological context, see A. Biran, *Biblical Dan* (Jerusalem: Israel Exploration Society/Hebrew Union College-Jewish Institute of Religion, 1994).

28. In an effort to prevent desecration of the name of Moses, later scribes modified the name slightly, making it read "Manasseh" (see NIV text note).

If Jonathan were the "grandson" of Moses, the events depicted in the chapter occurred early in the period of the judges. If so, then the events of this section (17:1−18:31) may historically precede and furnish the background for the story of Samson (13:1−16:31). But the expression used here may simply be understood as the "descendent" of Moses, so that the chronological time frame remains ambiguous.

It is interesting that Judges 17−18 concludes with a reference to the legitimate "house of God" (*bêt hā*ᵉ*lohîm*) at Shiloh[29] (18:31). This is a clear condemnation of Micah's illegitimate "shrine" (*bêt* ᵉ*lohîm*) and the cult objects he made (17:5), which have now become the Danites' cult materials (18:30a, 31a).[30] The story as a whole contains a number of specific criticisms of the Danite sanctuary: Its cult is syncretistic, its priesthood mercenary, and its (indirect) founder a thief turned idol maker.

Just as Judges 13:1−16:31 culminates in a portrayal of Samson's personal failings, so Judges 18 (as well as 1:34−36) depict Dan's tribal failings. As Samson moves from physical strength to weakness because of ritual impurity, so Dan moves from a position of military weakness to one of strength, albeit at the expense of cultic and covenantal loyalty.

MANIPULATING GOD. If Samson did what was right in his own eyes, so much more the Israelites in the double conclusion. Each conclusion is full of admonitions of what not to do, given through example after example. None of the activities of chapters 17−18 is sanctioned by God. In fact, quite to the contrary.

From the beginning we are confronted with one evil after another, all done by a person whose name means "Who is like Yahweh?" (Micah):

- disregard for parental well-being
- thief (from a parent)
- magical curse
- magical blessings (made in the name of Yahweh!)
- homemade idols of pilfered silver
- production of a private shrine

---

29. For Shiloh, see I. Finkelstein, ed., *Shiloh: The Archaeology of a Biblical Site* (Publications of the Institute of Archaeology 10; Tel Aviv: Tel Aviv University/Institute of Archaeology, 1993).

30. Three times at the end of ch. 18 (18:24, 27, 31) the text states that the cult objects that the Danites place in their shrine at Dan are man-made, obviously condemning the Danite shrine as false in every respect.

- making of a personal priest (son)
- adopting of a personal priest (Levite)
- self-made religious paraphernalia

Micah evinces an ignorance of God's Law and covenant in their most basic teachings. His confident assertion (17:13) that Yahweh will prosper him because he has a Levite for a priest reveals the false confidence that people often have that they know God and that they can manipulate him by cultic and institutional means and so secure their own futures.

The Danites make essentially the same error as Micah, and their shrine eventually suffers an even worse fate (2 Kings 15:29). The treatment of this theme is satirical throughout the story. This issue of a human attempt to manipulate Yahweh links the first conclusion with the cycles section, especially the Outgroup judges' attempts to manipulate the Lord (see esp. Gideon and Jephthah).

It is ironic that the Danites even bother to inquire of God's will when God had already revealed his will in the allotments to the tribes. There is no need for another inquiry. Micah's illicit ephod and the *t'rāpîm* (household gods) with their inherent ties to divination determine that the inquiry will automatically be considered unauthorized and unlawful. And while the Levite's oracle declared in the name of Yahweh is what they want to hear, it is patently not from Yahweh, who condemns these practices. Modern interest in the future, especially as secured through divinatory means, has increased significantly in the last few decades. The growth of the use of psychics and horoscopes are just two examples.

Motivated by materialism. It is clear that the Levite is totally motivated by material concerns. The fact that later he accepts an even more attractive offer (18:19–20) confirms his materialistic impetus. In this he is a continuation of the motif of the person who can be bought (cf. comments on Delilah, esp. in the Contemporary Significance in 16:1–31).

The Danites, who properly should have destroyed Micah's cult shrine (according to Deut. 12:2–3), instead find it worthy of acquisition, even if by means of theft (18:15–17). They have no more integrity than Micah. Thus, the syncretism and paganism that permeates this first conclusion determine its moral bankruptcy.

MORAL BANKRUPTCY. What kind of son steals from his own mother? What kind of mother leads her son into idolatry? What kind of a Levite serves at an idolatrous shrine and then happily moves to serve at a bigger idolatrous shrine? And what kind of people plunder their own people while on their way to annihilate a peaceful city in a region outside the boundaries of their God-ordained allotment?

When God's Word is unknown or ignored, the results are human-manufactured, culturally conditioned innovations. Self-consumed individuals (and a group) dominate this passage, which itself, at its very root, is immersed in the misconception of human manipulation of deity (i.e., idolatry). The participants in both parts of the story in this first conclusion appear quite silly in all their efforts and activities. Don't they realize what they are doing?

This would be humorous if it weren't so real. But when humankind rejects God's Word, then all activities ultimately appear foolhardy. The massive efforts by people today to substitute all kinds of things in the place of God— idols of their own making—appear the same way in the light of Scripture. Such things include riches, pleasures, security, human wisdom, advancement, personal happiness, and so on. Certainly the writer of Ecclesiastes has more than adequately shown the futility, meaninglessness, and frustration of any worldview that does not rise above the horizon of a human being. Happiness can never be achieved by pursuing it, since such a pursuit involves the absurdity of self-deification. So all these things that our current society seeks as God-substitutes—its idols—are allusions and materialistic props that are ultimately nothing but absurdities (for more, see comments in the introduction, pp. 45–47, and on 2:6–3:6, pp. 95–99).

Determining God's will. Amazingly, people will, like the Danites, inquire again and again to know God's will when God has already revealed it. For example, one hears from time to time a Christian asking this question: Is it God's will for me to marry this person (and the person is an unbeliever)? God has revealed his will on this in both the Old and New Testaments. But because of emotional involvements, this clearly revealed will of God is often ignored and rationalized away, and the inquirer marries the unbeliever anyway.

Attempts to divine God's will or the future are certainly not limited to the context of ancient Israel. The human race has used a vast array of illicit methods to inquire about the future throughout history. The increase of access to psychics and horoscopes has impacted the church too. In the last decade, more Christians are making inquiries via these means than in the prior generation. Since it has become more socially acceptable, more and more Christians find themselves becoming reliant on these practices in spite of the clear condemnation in Scripture.

The allurement of sin. A striking feature of this passage is how one sin leads to another (this is also observable in the Samson account and the second conclusion). This is not something we tend to reflect on. Yet some reflection on the interlocking nature of sin may help us see how we have gotten to where we personally are. In this passage, what is needed among the different characters is repentance (which, unfortunately, is not forthcoming). But as we reflect on the pattern of sin in our own lives, we should call out to the Lord in repentance and seek his forgiveness, so that God can intervene to break the power and pattern of sin with all of its destructive force.

In Judges 17−18, various sinful activities achieve success. We will mention only a few examples. Micah's theft, in a number of ways, becomes positive for him. Not only was there no punishment or restitution for the crime, but Micah receives a blessing! In the end the aimlessly wandering Levite succeeds in becoming the high priest of the Danite cult shrine. The Danites, who have failed to trust Yahweh in possessing their God-ordained allotment, succeed in possessing their own allotment without any trust in Yahweh. None of the characters in this section acts with integrity, yet they succeed in most of their agendas and machinations.

Thus in this section there is an important warning for the modern church. Success, especially as the world judges this concept, is not necessarily a sign of righteousness or an indication that we must be doing something right or the way that God would want things done. In fact, it may be the opposite. God does not squelch every corrupt motive, thought, or scheme of human beings (whether unbeliever or believer). Just because there is the appearance of success does not signify that the means or methods to this apparent success are godly. The issue of personal and corporate integrity matters, and the ultimate evaluation of success will be based on God's judgment of men's and women's hearts.

It is interesting that the Danites manifest attitudes and actions that are nothing short of raw paganism, brutalizing Micah in the process. In the same way, one cannot help but think of how some Christians treat other Christians. Every Christian counselor can share stories in which God's people have been or are brutalizing one another. This subject, in particular as manifested in the brutalization of women, becomes fully blown in the final section of Judges.

The double conclusion's refrain, "In those days Israel had no king; everyone did as he saw fit," emphasizes there is no spiritual king in Israel and life is a free-for-all (see comments above). Perhaps the modern expression of this is found in the famous song of the late Frank Sinatra, "I Did It My Way." While the song is about being stoic and heroic in the face of difficulties, its emphasis on self to the complete neglect and omission of the sovereign Lord proclaims the essence of modern society's orientation. Sinatra's song could have been the theme song for the Israelites in the days of the judges.

Judges 19:1–21:25

❧

Introduction to Conclusion 2

AS WE HAVE EXPLAINED in the introduction (see pp. 30–33), the balance of the double introduction by the double conclusion forms a type of inclusio. Thus, section A (Foreign wars of subjugation with the ḥērem being applied, 1:1–2:5) is parallel with A' (Domestic wars with the ḥērem being applied, 19:1–21:25).

The structure of Conclusion 2 is chiastic, being made up of five episodes.[1] The initial episode (a) that narrates the rape of the concubine (19:1–30) corresponds to the final episode (a'), which narrates the rape of the daughters of Shiloh (21:15–25). The second and fourth episodes (b and b') relate the application of the ḥērem first in the destruction of Benjamin (20:1–48) and then of its application in attempted preservation of Benjamin through the destruction of Jabesh Gilead (21:6–14). The critical and ironic oaths that are pivotal in the outcomes of b' and a' are narrated in episode c (21:1–5). Thus the structure is as follows:

a The Rape of the Concubine (19:1–30)
    b ḥērem of Benjamin (20:1–48)
        c Problem: The Oaths—Benjamin Threatened with
           Extinction (21:1–5)
    b' ḥērem of Jabesh Gilead (21:6–14)
a' The Rape of the Daughters of Shiloh (21:15–25)

The various episodes escalate through parallels and complications with the previous episodes and climax in the rape of the daughters of Shiloh (21:15–25). Just as Samson's attraction to intermarry with a Philistine woman served as the catalyst for the whole series of events in Judges 14–15, and just as Micah's seemingly inconsequential theft of silver from his mother served as the catalyst that eventually led to the Danites' renaming a city and establishing a cult center after their slaughter of the people of Laish, so what first appears as nothing more than a personal family crisis escalates into a citywide problem, then becomes a crisis for the entire tribe, and ultimately a disaster for the entire nation of Israel. Here, in an almost unbelievable manner, the problem between one man and one woman leads to a full-scale civil war.[2]

---

1. Webb, *The Book of the Judges*, 196.
2. S. Niditch, "The 'Sodomite' Theme in Judges 19–20: Family, Community, and Social Disintegration," *CBQ* 44 (1982): 365–78, esp. 366–67; Block, *Judges, Ruth*, 515.

In addition, as pointed out previously, the refrain (see the introduction, p. 31) emphasizes through a double entendre that during the period of the judges there was no physical king, but more importantly that there was no spiritual king (17:6; 18:1; 19:1; 21:25). Thus "every man did what was right in his own eyes" (17:6; 21:25). Conclusion 2 opens[3] and ends with this refrain, stressing the importance of its theological overtones for the entire passage. Also, as mentioned at the beginning of the discussion of Conclusion 1 (see comments on pp. 334--35), the second verse of the refrain "every man did what was right in his own eyes" is related to the issue of apostasy from Yahweh, especially the evil of idolatry.[4] There is little doubt that the tremendous moral depravity exhibited in this final conclusion to Judges confirms the inherent moral dangers in idolatry and polytheism.

While in previous narratives minor figures are often named, even when a knowledge of their identity is not crucial to the story, in this second conclusion anonymity is the rule. The only person named in the entire passage is a minor figure, the priest who officiates at Bethel, Phinehas (20:28). The main characters are all anonymous. This anonymity appears to have two functions.[5] (1) It permits the characters to stand for a wider group. Thus the Levite can stand for all Levites; the concubine can represent every woman, the father-in-law every host, and the old man residing in Bethel every outsider in a Benjamite town. Because everyone does as he or she sees fit, every host is capable of committing the atrocities of the Benjamites; every woman is a potential victim of rape, murder, and dismemberment; and so on. Thus, anonymity is a deliberate literary device adopted to reflect the universality of Israel's Canaanization.[6]

(2) The anonymity of the characters reflects a dehumanization of the individual. To have a name is to be somebody, to have identity. Moreover, since names are given and used by others, to have a name is to have significance within the community. Thus the anonymity of this section also reflects the disintegration of an individual's value as a human being. It denies individuality and humanity to both the criminals and the victims in the story. Ironically, in the world of the story, which is remarkably secular and where the individuals live as though they are the center of the universe, the individual counts for nothing. Thus, the use of anonymity for the characters enhances the achievement of this on a literary level and proves reinforcement for the portrayal of a malignant, fallen world.

---

3. The two repetitions at the center of the double conclusion (i.e., 18:1a and 19:1a) are intrinsically bound together by a chiasm, *ʾên melek* versus *melek ʾên* respectively.

4. Wilson, 'As You Like It," 73–85, esp. 74–76.

5. D. M. Hudson, "Living in a Land of Epithets: Anonymity in Judges 19–21," *JSOT* 62 (1994): 49–66, esp. 59–65.

6. Block, *Judges, Ruth,* 517.

Judges 19:1–30

¹In those days Israel had no king.

Now a Levite who lived in a remote area in the hill country of Ephraim took a concubine from Bethlehem in Judah. ²But she was unfaithful to him. She left him and went back to her father's house in Bethlehem, Judah. After she had been there four months, ³her husband went to her to persuade her to return. He had with him his servant and two donkeys. She took him into her father's house, and when her father saw him, he gladly welcomed him. ⁴His father-in-law, the girl's father, prevailed upon him to stay; so he remained with him three days, eating and drinking, and sleeping there.

⁵On the fourth day they got up early and he prepared to leave, but the girl's father said to his son-in-law, "Refresh yourself with something to eat; then you can go." ⁶So the two of them sat down to eat and drink together. Afterward the girl's father said, "Please stay tonight and enjoy yourself." ⁷And when the man got up to go, his father-in-law persuaded him, so he stayed there that night. ⁸On the morning of the fifth day, when he rose to go, the girl's father said, "Refresh yourself. Wait till afternoon!" So the two of them ate together.

⁹Then when the man, with his concubine and his servant, got up to leave, his father-in-law, the girl's father, said, "Now look, it's almost evening. Spend the night here; the day is nearly over. Stay and enjoy yourself. Early tomorrow morning you can get up and be on your way home." ¹⁰But, unwilling to stay another night, the man left and went toward Jebus (that is, Jerusalem), with his two saddled donkeys and his concubine.

¹¹When they were near Jebus and the day was almost gone, the servant said to his master, "Come, let's stop at this city of the Jebusites and spend the night."

¹²His master replied, "No. We won't go into an alien city, whose people are not Israelites. We will go on to Gibeah." ¹³He added, "Come, let's try to reach Gibeah or Ramah and spend the night in one of those places." ¹⁴So they went on, and the sun set as they neared Gibeah in Benjamin. ¹⁵There they stopped to spend the night. They went and sat in the city square, but no one took them into his home for the night.

¹⁶That evening an old man from the hill country of Ephraim, who was living in Gibeah (the men of the place were Benjamites), came in from his work in the fields. ¹⁷When he

looked and saw the traveler in the city square, the old man
asked, "Where are you going? Where did you come from?"

¹⁸He answered, "We are on our way from Bethlehem in
Judah to a remote area in the hill country of Ephraim where I
live. I have been to Bethlehem in Judah and now I am going to
the house of the LORD. No one has taken me into his house.
¹⁹We have both straw and fodder for our donkeys and bread
and wine for ourselves your servants—me, your maidservant,
and the young man with us. We don't need anything."

²⁰"You are welcome at my house," the old man said. "Let me
supply whatever you need. Only don't spend the night in the
square." ²¹So he took him into his house and fed his donkeys. After
they had washed their feet, they had something to eat and drink.

²²While they were enjoying themselves, some of the wicked
men of the city surrounded the house. Pounding on the door,
they shouted to the old man who owned the house, "Bring out
the man who came to your house so we can have sex with him."

²³The owner of the house went outside and said to them,
"No, my friends, don't be so vile. Since this man is my guest,
don't do this disgraceful thing. ²⁴Look, here is my virgin
daughter, and his concubine. I will bring them out to you
now, and you can use them and do to them whatever you
wish. But to this man, don't do such a disgraceful thing."

²⁵But the men would not listen to him. So the man took his
concubine and sent her outside to them, and they raped her
and abused her throughout the night, and at dawn they let her
go. ²⁶At daybreak the woman went back to the house where
her master was staying, fell down at the door and lay there
until daylight.

²⁷When her master got up in the morning and opened the
door of the house and stepped out to continue on his way,
there lay his concubine, fallen in the doorway of the house,
with her hands on the threshold. ²⁸He said to her, "Get up;
let's go." But there was no answer. Then the man put her on
his donkey and set out for home.

²⁹When he reached home, he took a knife and cut up his
concubine, limb by limb, into twelve parts and sent them into
all the areas of Israel. ³⁰Everyone who saw it said, "Such a
thing has never been seen or done, not since the day the
Israelites came up out of Egypt. Think about it! Consider it!
Tell us what to do!"

CONCLUSION 2 (19:1–21:25) opens and closes with the refrain (partial in the first instance): "In those days Israel had no king; every man did what was right in his own eyes." Although the Israelites claim to be the people of Yahweh, their beliefs, conduct, and consequent fate contradict this claim. In this passage, God's people are in their most hypocritical state, driven by selfishness.

The structure of this initial episode of the Conclusion 2, "The Rape of the Concubine," is composed of nine parts, which are punctuated by three journeys arranged in a chiastic manner.[7]

A Introduction: "Small Separation" (19:1–2): The Levite is separated from his concubine by her going to her father's house.

B Journey 1: Departure from home on trip to Bethlehem (19:3–4): Reversal of disjunctions and conjunctions between the Levite and his concubine: wife runs away (v. 2) + reunion (v. 4)— three days; they all eat and drink and spend the night together.

C Stay: Fourth day—male carousing (19:5–7): The presentation of the tarrying on the fourth and fifth days is syntactically different from that of the previous three days. Two of them (Levite and father-in-law) eat and drink; the Levite is encouraged by his father-in-law to "enjoy yourself" (*twb lb*); Levite spends the night there.

D Stay: Fifth day—male carousing (19:8–10a): Two of them (Levite and father-in-law) eat and drink; the Levite is encouraged by his father-in-law to "enjoy yourself" (*twb lb*); Levite not willing to spend the night.

E Journey 2: Trip to Gibeah (19:10b–14): Concentric structure of speeches in vv. 11–13 points to v. 12 as the pivotal element (see further below).

D' Stay: Night at the old man's house—male carousing (19:15–22a)—miniquest: Unit begins with seeking shelter and ends with having found it; they eat and drink; they enjoy themselves (*twb lb*). Three speeches: old man, Levite, old man.

---

7. This analysis is based upon my own observations in connection with those of J. P. Fokkelman, "Structural Remarks on Judges 9 and 19," in *"Sha'arei Talmon": Studies in the Bible, Qumran, and the Ancient Near East Presented to Shemaryahu Talmon*, ed. M. Fishbane and E. Tov with W. W. Fields (Winona Lake, Ind.: Eisenbrauns, 1992), 33–45, esp. 40–45.

        C′ Stay: Night at the old man's house + somewhere in the
            city—male carousing (19:22b–26)—miniquest: The
            horde that seeks homosexual gratification with the Levite
            ends having sexual gratification with the concubine.
      B′ Journey 3: Arrival home from trip to Bethlehem via Gibeah
        (19:27–28): Reversal of disjunctions and conjunctions between
        the Levite and his concubine: reunion of man and wife (v. 26)
        but separation by death.
    A′ Conclusion—The appeal: "Big Separation" (19:29–30): The Levite
      is separated from his concubine by his cutting her up and sending
      her parts to the tribes of Israel.

As in Conclusion 1, a Levite plays a significant role in the narration of this second conclusion. By focusing on Levites in the concluding episodes, the narrator communicates the extent of Israel's moral decline. The corruption that has infected the people and their deliverers has even spread to those entrusted with the Yahwistic instruction and with upholding Yahweh's holiness in their lives.

In this case, in the introduction (Part A, vv. 1–2), the Levite lives in a remote area of the hill country of Ephraim. As in the first conclusion, this certainly indicates support problems for the Levitical priests since he is not living in one of the Levitical towns. This Levite "took a concubine [*pîlegeš*] from Bethlehem in Judah" (again a link with the first conclusion). A concubine was a second-class wife—a woman who performed marriage duties without the same legal rights as a full wife (cf. Gideon's concubine in 8:31). This may imply that the Levite has another wife, but the text contains no record of that.

His concubine "was unfaithful to him" (NIV, lit., "prostituted against," *znh* *ʿl*). The more likely reading based on the ancient versions is "his concubine was angry or quarreled with him."[8] The text does not explicitly blame either party for this separation. But in light of the Levite's later conduct, it seems most likely that the blame rests with the Levite. The young woman goes straight for her father's house in Bethlehem. Thus, the introduction of this

---

8. The MT's phrase is problematic. In ancient Near Eastern culture, it is doubtful that she would have played the prostitute and then gone home to her father. It is possible that the phrase is meant to be understood figuratively (i.e., the concubine plays the harlot by walking out on her husband—this seems to be the NIV's rationale). However, the phrase is not used with this nuance elsewhere in the Hebrew Bible. The phrase *znh* *ʿl* does not appear anywhere else in the Hebrew Bible. The ancient versions, however, preserve a different reading. LXX^A reads: *ōrgisthē autō*, "she was angry with him," and *Targum Jonathan* reads: *wbsrt ʿlwhy*, "she despised him." As Block argues, it is best to understand the MT's *znh* either as a scribal error for *znḥ*, "to reject, detest," or, more likely, to retain the Hebrew and recognize a second root, *znḥ*, meaning "to be angry, quarrel." See Block, *Judges, Ruth*, 523.

story (Part A) presents a "small separation," namely, a familial squabble in which the Levite is separated from his concubine by her departure to her father's house. This will contrast to the "big separation" (19:29–30).

In Part B (vv. 3–4), the Levite's first journey is narrated. After a four-month delay (which the text does not explain), the Levite goes to Bethlehem to win her back. He speaks kindly to her (NIV translates "to persuade her," 19:3). This may suggest that she has not left without some provocation on his part (his later callousness towards her seems to be a strong indication of this).

His father-in-law gladly welcomes him, probably because the separation of his daughter and her husband is a matter of disgrace for the family, and he gladly welcomes the prospect of the reunion of the two. The father-in-law shows normal hospitality over a three-day period.

In Parts C and D (vv. 5–7,8–10a), the writer introduces a different pattern of narrating the stay. While a note of male carousing is signaled in the previous part (v. 4), it is especially emphasized in Parts C and D, where the text stresses that the Levite and father-in-law eat and drink, and twice (once in each part) the father-in-law encourages the Levite to "enjoy yourself" (lit., "make good your heart," *twb lb*).[9] The father-in-law's hospitality borders on the excessive: Six times he offers hospitality, persuading the Levite to spend five days with him. In fact, the father-in-law's delays explain why the Levite and his party end up in Gibeah, only halfway home by nightfall at the end of the fifth day.[10]

This hospitality of the father-in-law, however, serves as one of two foils against the Gibeahite actions in the latter part of the story. The model of hospitality enjoyed by the Levite while in Bethlehem heightens the contrast with the treatment received in Gibeah. Thus, while bordering on the excessive, its redundancy conveys the potentially endless hospitality that the Levite may have enjoyed had he chosen to remain in Bethlehem of Judah as over against that which he gets in Gibeah.[11] It will heighten the contrast between the male carousing of the father-in-law and Levite and the hell-raising of the men of Gibeah.

---

9. Fokkelman correctly observes that much space is given to enjoying hospitality—C, D, and D'—and at first the reader wonders what all this trivial hospitality has to do with the crime and its horrors. The answer is that the story signifies how much the Levite is attached to "carousing" (*ytb lb* and synonyms) and that such hedonism and materialism lead to a situation in which throwing women out as a sexual prey for the rabble seems right to the Levite. See Fokkelman, "Structural Remarks on Judges 9 and 19," 43.

10. Niditch, "The 'Sodomite' Theme in Judges 19–20," 366–67. See also S. Lasine, "Guest and Host in Judges 19: Lot's Hospitality in an Inverted World," *JSOT* 29 (1984): 56–57 n. 34.

11. O'Connell, *The Rhetoric of the Book of Judges*, 249.

Part E (vv. 10b–14) is the pivotal point of the story. Interestingly, the structure of Part E, which narrates the second journey, contains three speeches arranged in chiastic form.

a Trip from Bethlehem to Jebus (vv. 10b–11a)
    b Speech 1: Servant to Levite suggesting they spend the night in Jebus (vv. 11b)
        c Speech 2: Levite to servant rejecting Jebus and dictating travel to Gibeah (v. 12)
    b′ Speech 3: Levite to servant asserting where they spend the night (v. 13)
a′ Trip from Jebus to Gibeah (v. 14)

Speeches 1 and 3 have the same structure. Both begin with an imperative of *hālak* (go) plus a cohortative of a verb of movement (*sûr* [turn aside] and *qārab* [draw near], respectively) plus a place name; and both close with a form of *lîn* (spend the night) plus the preposition *bᵉ* (in) plus a spatial term. These two speeches point to the center speech (speech 2). Thus the content of this speech is the axis for the entire narrative. This speech is composed of two antithetical statements: (1) the decision to not "go into" (*sûr*) this "alien"[12] city that does not belong to the Israelites, and (2) the decision to "go on" (lit., traverse, *ᶜābar*) to Gibeah. They do so (cf. *ᶜābar* in v. 14a) and "there they stopped" (lit., turned aside, *sûr*, v. 15a) in Gibeah.[13]

Thus the nonevent (staying in Jebus/Jerusalem) furnishes the grounds for the evaluation of the event and action in Gibeah. "What seems right proves to be wrong, and what seems bad might very well have had a fortunate ending."[14] The master is wrong and the servant is right. As a result, the delayed departure from Bethlehem forces the fateful decision of verse 12: "No. We won't go into an alien city, whose people are not Israelites. We will go on to Gibeah."[15] Only the subsequent events will reveal the full irony of this decision.

---

12. This term often has negative, even pejorative connotations.

13. The term *ᶜābar* can mean not only "to cross over, pass over, traverse," but also "to violate (a commandment or the covenant)" (cf. Judg. 2:20). This may be subtly anticipatory of the "violation" that will take place in Gibeah. The term *sûr* can also have moral connotations and may hint at the moral "turning aside" that takes place in Gibeah.

14. Fokkelman, "Structural Remarks on Judges 9 and 19," 44.

15. It is only about 9 kilometers (5.6 miles) between Bethlehem and Jerusalem (Jebus) and only another 6 kilometers (3.7 miles) or 9 kilometers (5.6 miles) between Jerusalem (Jebus) and Gibeah, depending on the location of ancient Gibeah (Tell el-Fûl or modern Jabaᶜ respectively). The total distance is well within the average distance that could be traversed in a day; but with the late start, the three would have had to travel at a much faster rate and must have been quite tired when they arrived in Gibeah.

The Levite's aversion to Jebus (i.e., Jerusalem), a non-Israelite enclave to be avoided, is the second foil. It is a significant point in the narrative that the rapists are Israelites. The "foreign" status of Jebus implicitly redounds to the discredit of Benjamin (cf. 1:21). Ironically, by seeking to avoid the potential inhospitality of a foreign city, the Levite and his party suffer that very fate, or even worse, in Gibeah, an Israelite city.

Parts D' and C' (vv. 15–22a, 22b–26) describe the Levite's stay in Gibeah and the outrage that takes place there. Each part contains a miniquest: Part D' is centered on seeking and finding shelter for the night[16]; Part C' describes the men of the city of Gibeah seeking homosexual gratification with the Levite, but ending up with capitalizing their gratifications on the Levite's concubine. In both parts the theme of carousing is evident: In D', "they were enjoying themselves [*twb lb*]," and C', the horde does "good [*twb*] in their eyes" (NIV "whatever you wish") with the concubine (vv. 24a[2] + 25b).

At sunset the little group reaches Gibeah. The narrator goes to great lengths to demarcate the atrocity itself by the signposts of sunset and daybreak: Night falls upon arrival at Gibeah, and the ordeal begins (19:14); daybreak marks the end of both the outrage and the victim (19:26).[17] Entering the city the group sits in the city square waiting for someone to show hospitality and take them home with them for the night. No one offers. This crude impertinence of the citizens of Gibeah is an ominous harbinger of the far worse abuse of the travelers that follows. The last clause of verse 15 would have been shocking anywhere in the ancient Near East, but it is especially shocking in Israel. The social disintegration has infected the very heart of the community of God's people. Thus the people of Gibeah abuse in general the Levite and his party passively (by refusing basic hospitality) before the rapists abuse them actively (19:15, 22).

Finally, an old man from Ephraim, a temporary resident in Gibeah and not a Benjamite, comes by and questions the party. In his response, the Levite presents himself as a weary traveler returning home (the NIV reads: "the house of the LORD"[18] in verse 18) after a visit to Bethlehem. He does not mention

---

16. For a discussion of the motif of "night as danger," see W. W. Fields, "The Motif 'Night As Danger' Associated with Three Biblical Destruction Narratives," in *"Sha'arei Talmon": Studies in the Bible, Qumran, and the Ancient Near East Presented to Shemaryahu Talmon*, ed. M. Fishbane and E. Tov with W. W. Fields (Winona Lake, Ind.: Eisenbrauns, 1992), 17–32, esp. 21–32.

17. O'Connell, *The Rhetoric of the Book of Judges*, 250.

18. The LXX reads: "to my house," not "to the house of the LORD." If the MT's "to the house of the LORD" is accepted, then this would convey the Levite's attempt to further legitimate himself to the Ephraimite old man. However, it is more likely that the LXX preserves the better reading here (as most modern versions translate). For a discussion see O'Connell, *The Rhetoric of the Book of Judges*, 483.

the reason for the visit since this might raise questions about the good character of himself and/or his concubine. Rather, he emphasizes that they do not need anything except a place to sleep. The deferential "me, your maidservant and the young man with us" is calculated to win the host's favor while conveying minimal information.[19]

The old man welcomes them to spend the night at his house, "only don't spend the night in the square" (19:20). The latter clause—and for that matter the entire scene at Gibeah—is reminiscent of the story of Lot in Sodom in Genesis 19:1–11. As Lasine points out, "Judges 19 uses Genesis 19 to show how hospitality is turned upside down when one's guests are not angels, and one lives in an age governed by human selfishness."[20] At his house, the old man at first appears to be the model host. He fodders the Levite's donkeys, provides the people with water to wash their feet, and gives them food and drink (19:21).

Then, suddenly (*hinnēh*), everything is overturned. While they are enjoying themselves, some wicked men (lit., "sons of Belial")[21] of the city surround the house and demand the host to bring out the Levite so that they can rape him. Unexpectedly, the irony of the decision to travel on to Gibeah becomes apparent. Having eschewed the hospitality of foreigners and entrusted himself to Israelites, the Levite "finds himself in a virtual Sodom"![22] The old man's response in 19:23–24 is Lot-like:

> No, my friends, don't be so vile. Since this man is my guest, don't do this disgraceful [foolish thing]. Look, here is my virgin daughter, and his concubine. I will bring them out to you now, and you can use [rape/humiliate/abuse][23] them and do to them whatever you wish [lit. "what is good in your eyes"[24]]. But to this man, don't do such a disgraceful [foolish] thing.

This is, as Webb calls it, "a comedy of correctness; the old man is a conscientious host to the last."[25] Thus the old man, who appears initially to be

---

19. Webb, *The Book of the Judges*, 262 n. 32.

20. Lasine, "Guest and Host in Judges 19," 40. Also see D. I. Block, "Echo Narrative Technique in Hebrew Literature: A Study of Judges 19," *WTJ* 52 (1990): 325–41.

21. The meaning of the phrase is still uncertain. See T. J. Lewis, "Belial," *ABD*, 1:654–56; S. D. Sperling, "Belial," *DDD*, cols. 322–27.

22. Webb, *The Book of the Judges*, 189.

23. The NIV's "you can use them" is a poor translation of the verb *'innâ* (to humiliate, do violence to), which in such a context as this can have the technical nuance of "rape." Cf. Gen. 34:2; 2 Sam. 13:12, 14, 22, 32; Lam. 5:11.

24. Cf. the double conclusion's refrain (lit.): "Every man did what was right in his own eyes"; also the initial cyclical component: "The Israelites did evil in the eyes of the LORD" (e.g., 2:11).

25. Webb, *The Book of the Judges*, 189.

the model host, ends up being the one who comes up with the idea of throwing the concubine (and his own daughter) to the horde at the door. That he should volunteer his own daughter is one thing; that he should volunteer the Levite's concubine is another; but that he volunteer either is unimaginable. But then, he is only doing what is right in his own eyes!

"Good" and "bad" are confused in the old man's speech. He begins well with a double prohibitive: "Don't be so vile [rā'â] don't do this disgraceful thing"; or more strongly "Do not commit such a wicked *bad* thing . . . do not perpetrate this foolish outrage!" But when the second half of the speech comes to *good* (ṭôb, NIV "whatever you wish"), he is already confused morally and says something unbelievable in the face of the imminent crime (lit.): "Have your pleasure of them; do to them what is good [ṭôb] in your eyes."

Perhaps the old man thinks that proper hospitality only applies to male guests (e.g., he does not offer the Levite's young servant). But this certainly is a mistaken way of viewing matters. Or perhaps he is simply doing the best he can: Two women instead of one man; at least he will save his principal guest. Thus, hospitality and honor become more important than doing what is right in Yahweh's eyes. The man condemns the horde for thinking of doing this disgraceful (lit., "foolish") act upon the Levite and yet, ironically, ends up doing a foolish thing in making such an offer.

Amazingly, there is no protest from the Levite! Ironically, just as the Levite is unwilling to accept the argument of his father-in-law to spend the night (v. 10a), so the horde is unwilling to accept the argument of the old man (v. 25). When they refuse to listen to the old man, *it is the Levite* who seizes his concubine and hands her over to the horde. Obviously this selfish act in the extreme saves him from the horde but reveals the depths of depravity in his heart. Rapidly and graphically, the narrator declares they rape (yd') her, abuse ('ll) her, and discard (šlḥ) her (v. 25). At daybreak, the forsaken concubine collapses at the door of the old man's house, apparently too weak to knock or even cry out.

Concerning the Old Testament law of rape in an urban area, if a woman screams, she is deemed innocent. While the text does not state that she screamed, it does stress her innocence, which leads to the conclusion that she must have screamed. If this was the case, then the citizens of Gibeah are guilty of not rescuing her from these "sons of Belial." It is a troubling thought, but the image of this young woman being raped and abused—crying out for help, screaming in pain—fall on deaf ears. No one takes any action to save her.

Part B' (19:27–28), which narrates Journey 3, opens with the Levite (described as the concubine's *master*[26]), almost simultaneously to the concubine's

---

26. The narrator's choice of term here is powerful.

collapse at the door, "getting up" (*qûm*) inside the house. As Webb points out, the expression is chilling in what it implies by its sheer ordinariness.[27] Having tossed his concubine to the pack of men and being assured that he himself was no longer personally threatened, the Levite went to bed! He now rises without any apparent remorse for what he has done or concern for his concubine. In fact, he appears to give no thought to her at all until he practically trips over her as he goes out the door. The narrator's statement "with her hands on the threshold" heightens this pathetic tragedy, causing the reader to bleed with compassion for the exploited and abused woman.

This statement, in turn, heightens the next one. Her master, the Levite, commands her with almost unbelievable callousness to "get up" (*qûm*) because *he* is ready to go. How can he be so cold-hearted? There is no answer. Rather matter-of-factly, he picks her up, puts her on his donkey, and completes the journey home. Ironically, the Levite, having been reconciled to his concubine, should have returned in peace to his home in Ephraim. In fact, both the Levite and his concubine return home to Ephraim, but with the gruesome twist that she is dead (or at least appears to be). This is hardly a desirable resolution to the problem introduced at the beginning of the narrative (19:1–2). The reader is left wondering if, when, and how justice will be executed on these "sons of Belial" in Gibeah.

The answer comes quickly and appallingly in Part A' (vv. 29–30). Immediately after his return home, the Levite—with the same self-centered callousness that had delivered his concubine into the hands of the horde at the door[28]—takes a knife and cuts her up, limb by limb, into twelve parts and sends these into every tribe in Israel (cf. 1 Sam. 11:7).[29] In the beginning of the story, there was a "small separation," in that the Levite was separated from his concubine by her going to her father's house. But at the end of the story, there is a "big separation," for the Levite is separated from his concubine by cutting her up and sending her parts to the tribes of Israel.

The intention of the dismemberment, on the surface, seems to have been to awaken Israel from its moral lethargy and stimulate justice. But what are the real motives of this nameless Levite? The act of dismemberment is a graphic means of calling everyone to arms. It is highly ironic that the one who issues such a call for justice is himself so selfishly insensitive and self-involved in the crime itself. But the outrageous dismemberment achieves its intended outrageous response.

---

27. Webb, *The Book of the Judges*, 190.

28. Both verses 25 and 29 use the verb *ḥzq* (seize) to emphasize the callousness of the Levite.

29. See Lasine's discussion of the 1 Sam. 11 passage ("Guest and Host in Judges 19," 52–56).

The most agonizing question that confronts the reader is: Was the woman dead when the Levite found her on the doorstep? Two of the ancient versions answer the question. The LXX and the Vulgate offer "but she was dead" as the answer to the Levite's commands to his concubine when he comes out the door in the morning. Yet in the Hebrew text it is not clear in verses 29–30 whether the Levite simply dismembers a corpse or whether he himself murders his concubine in a fit of rage (see further comments on 20:1–48).

IF THINGS WERE bad in Conclusion 1, they get much worse here. A quick listing of the characters reveals a Levite of questionable character/callous husband, a victimized concubine, an excessively hospitable father-in-law, an inhospitable city, a questionable host, rapists/abusers, and a dismembered corpse. Isn't this the stuff of a modern movie plot?

Two misinterpretations. There are two misinterpretations and misapplications that have become popular in the recent scholarly literature on this passage. (1) The first is tied to an overemphasis on hospitality as the major problem within the passage. There is little debate that the inhospitality of the people of Gibeah toward the Levite, his concubine, and his servant is wrong. It is certainly a part of the overall portrayal of significant degeneration within Israelite culture that the passage paints.

Yet the ultimate "wrong" in the passage is the outrage that transpires that night in Gibeah. The rapists/abusers come that night and demand the host to give them his guest, the Levite, so that they can "have sex with" (lit., "know," yd^c) him. A few commentators have attempted to interpret yd^c in this passage (as well as in Gen. 19:5) as meaning something other than sexual knowledge.[30] They overstress the inhospitality problem so that the horde's attempt at homosexual rape is reinterpreted as purely a matter connected to the inhospitality issue. Behind this is an effort to argue that the Scriptures do not condemn homosexuality as sin.

This interpretation is untenable in light of Judges 19:24–25, where the host offers the Gibeahites the concubine and his daughter as alternatives (with rather obvious sexual overtones), and the men reject this offer and attempt to press home their desire for the man. Furthermore, the verb yd^c has

---

30. E.g., D. S. Bailey, *Homosexuality and the Western Christian Tradition* (London: Longmans, Green, 1955). Bailey argues that the men of Sodom (and Gibeah) were not wanting intercourse with Lot's guests, but simply credentials by which to judge that the strangers posed no threat to the town and that the host and the men evince an improper manner of inhospitality.

the clear nuance of rape, where the narrator describes the sexual actions taken against this helpless woman by the horde in terms of a heterosexual gang rape. The type of homosexual union that is clearly presented in the context of Judges 19 is that of homosexual gang rape.[31] After the Levite "seized" his concubine and handed her over to these men—which in itself is quite a sin (see comments below)—the sins of Judges 19 that can be charged to the wicked men are heterosexual gang rape, apparent physical abuse and beating, and in the end, murder (although the hand of the Levite in this must also be acknowledged).

Thus, it is important not to judge the sin of Gibeah as simply homosexual rape, since while this was the intent of these wicked individuals, it did not in fact occur. But this in no way removes the initial homosexual intent and its condemnation in the narrative, nor does this remove the clear condemnation in the rest of Scripture concerning homosexual union.[32]

(2) The second misinterpretation and misapplication of this passage is found among some contemporary feminist approaches,[33] which tend to see in this account evidences for the fundamental injustice of patriarchy or, more specifically androcentric ideology. Thus P. Trible claims that this chapter "depicts the horrors of male power, brutality, and triumphalism; of female helplessness, abuse, and annihilation. To hear this story is to inhabit a world of unrelenting terror that refuses to let us pass by on the other side."[34]

A good representative of the feminist approach to this passage is found in the recent work of C. Exum.[35] Exum gives the unnamed woman, the Levite's concubine, the name *Bat-shever*, signifying her dismemberment by her husband and the role feminist interpretation plays in breaking open the text's androcentric ideology and exposing the buried and encoded messages it gives to women. She argues that the issue in Judges 19 is "male ownership of women's bodies, control over women's sexuality."[36] The aim of the passage is to circumscribe and control women's behavior.[37] Opting for the Hebrew textual reading in 19:2 that "his concubine played the harlot against him" (NIV

31. J. G. Taylor, "The Bible and Homosexuality," *Themelios* 21/1 (1995): 4–9, esp. 5.

32. For the excellent discussion of homosexuality, see ibid., 4–9.

33. I recognize that feminist literary criticism is remarkably pluralistic and diverse. It is not monolithic in the interpretation of this passage. Nonetheless, it is accurate to say that this is the primary approach to the passage by most feminist interpreters.

34. P. Trible, *Texts of Terror: Literary-Feminist Readings of Biblical Narratives* (OBT; Philadelphia: Fortress, 1984), 65.

35. J. Cheryl Exum, "Feminist Criticism: Whose Interests Are Being Served?" in *Judges and Method: New Approaches in Biblical Studies*, ed. G. A. Yee (Minneapolis: Fortress, 1995), 65–90, esp. 83–88.

36. Ibid., 84.

37. Ibid., 87.

"was unfaithful to him") instead of the more likely reading (based on the ancient versions) that "his concubine was angry or quarreled with him"[38] (see comments above), Exum argues that this phrase is androcentric ideological code for the woman asserting her physical/sexual autonomy, which to the narrator is tantamount to an act of harlotry. Exum puts it this way:

> A woman who asserts her sexual autonomy by leaving her husband—and whether or not she remains with him is a sexual issue—is guilty of sexual misconduct. This is the ideology that determines the way gender relations are understood and evaluated in this story. In the end, the woman is raped by a mob and dismembered by her own husband. As narrative punishment for her sexual "misconduct," her sexual "freedom," she is sexually abused, after which her sexuality is symbolically mutilated.[39]

Thus, the dismemberment is a coded message to women about sexual behavior. By leaving her husband the woman makes a gesture of sexual autonomy so threatening to patriarchal ideology that it requires her to be punished sexually in the most extreme form. "Decoded, the message the story of Bat-shever gives to women is that any claim to sexual autonomy (presented as unfaithfulness or misconduct) has horrendous consequences."[40] Furthermore, Exum argues this is connected by the writer to the issue of woman's responsibility:

> By insinuating that women, by the way they behave, are responsible for male sexual aggression, the narrator relies on a fundamental patriarchal strategy for exercising social control over women. Using women's fear of male violence as a means of regulating female behavior is one of patriarchy's most powerful weapons.[41]

Thus, the message of Judges 19 is a cautionary one to women: "If you do anything that even remotely suggests improper sexual behavior, you invite male aggression."[42]

It seems to me that Exum has missed the point of the passage. Besides the methodological problem of building an entire interpretation around a variant reading, is the purpose of this passage (esp. in the larger context of the double conclusion) "to control women's behavior"? Is the issue in Judges 19 "male ownership of women's bodies, control over women's sexuality"? It seems

---

38. Interestingly, Fewell argues for the versional reading: "The young woman 'resists' him (reading *zanach* instead of *zanah*) . . ." ("Judges," 75).
39. Exum, "Feminist Criticism," 84.
40. Ibid., 85.
41. Ibid.
42. Ibid.

to me that this is difficult to sustain from the text. Is the cutting up of the woman's body a hidden patriarchal code for exercising control over women through threat and terror, or is it the depraved perversion of this murderous, hedonistic Levite? The latter seems to be what the text is communicating. Even if one accepts the variant reading and Exum's interpretation of 19:2, it does not necessarily follow that the woman is blamed in the text for what transpires. In fact, the text blames the men: the men of Gibeah, the Levite, and the host. The woman is the victim of evil men. Good, godly men treat women differently—even in a patriarchal world!

Exum has read into the text what she wants to say from a modern agenda.[43] No doubt Exum would reply that I am declaring her understanding of the passage a misinterpretation on the basis of the long history of androcentric criteria for determining legitimate and illegitmate interpretations.[44] In this, I am only reinforcing the male-dominated interpretation of the Bible and the oppression of women. But this is really only a smokescreen that permits any reading that subverts the text and that divorces a person from any responsibility to the *integrity* of the text. The text simply does not say what Exum says it says.[45]

---

43. All of us who interpret the text of the Scriptures need to be aware of how we too often do this.

44. Ibid., 67, esp. n. 4.

45. I would like to quote one final example of how Exum violates the integrity of the text of the book of Judges. She states: "One of the ways men deny their responsibility for violence is by scapegoating women, blaming women for violence of which they are the victims. We can see this tactic at work in the texts we have examined. But the violence unleashed against Bat-shever is not her fault, any more than it was Bat-jiftah's fault (as Jephthah implies) that she became the sacrificial victim, or the Timnite woman's fault that the Philistines retaliated against her when Samson burned their fields, or Delilah's fault that Samson was captured by the Philistines (he didn't have to tell her his secret). Attention to the gender politics of Judges enables us to expose the phenomenon of scapegoating women for what it is: a strategy patriarchy uses to avoid facing and having to deal with its own violent legacy" (ibid., 87).

According to the text of Judges, Jephthah does blame his daughter when it is clearly not her fault but his. And he wrongly and ignorantly carries out his vow on this innocent victim. But other than this case, Exum's statements are patently *inaccurate to what the text says*. As I have argued above, the text does not fault the concubine; it blames the men of Gibeah, the Levite, and the host. The Philistines burn Samson's wife because of what her father-in-law did (15:6); the text does not fault her. The text paints a vivid portrait of Samson's foolish handling of Delilah's attempts to get the information concerning his strength. The text does paint Delilah guilty of taking the bribe and betraying Samson; but it is ultimately Samson's fault for telling Delilah, and he suffers the consequences for the flippant revelation of his special spiritual giftedness and status with Yahweh. Thus, it is Exum who has made the text a scapegoat rather than the text scapegoating the women in it. An interpretation that violates the integrity of the text is an invalid interpretation, whether androcentric or otherwise.

Degeneration in Israelite society. It is tempting to interpret this passage only or primarily as a commentary on the abusive violation of male power and honor.[46] But Block rightly notes that there is much more in the story than this:

> From it one might conclude simplistically that in a patriarchal system it is generally preferable for men to rape women rather than to rape men. Specifically, the rape of women is acceptable if male honor is thereby served. But this is to misconstrue the broader goal of the book: to chronicle the increasing Canaanization of Israelite society.[47]

What about this questionable host who proposes the alternative to the rape of the Levite? He is promising at first with his authentic hospitality, but when the rapists/abusers show up, he fizzles out. It becomes clear that he is dominated by the principle of expedience, not by God's ethical system. While he rightly recognizes the wrong of the rapists/abusers, his mores are culturally dictated: The concubine is not as important as his male guest; therefore, he will opt to protect him. Rather than run the risk of personal disaster, he will regrettably offer a lesser substitute (at least according to the societal dictates in Benjamin at this time, which are far away from God's standards in the first place). Fokkelman's words are important in this regard:

> Many commentators write high-toned words in connection with Gen 19:8 (Lot's daughters as a sexual sell-off) and Judg 19:24, in the sense that hospitality was such a valued asset in Israel, that people would even give up their women if necessary. To me, this seems to be not only a terrible cliché, but worse: it might well be incorrect. On the one hand the two chapters are exceptional (no lawgiver can foresee such situations) and on the other hand they show something that happens all over the world: under the pressures of terror and crime, good manners and morals crumble like a house of cards. We find a variant of the cliché in Trible, *Texts of Terror*, 75: Genesis 19 and Judges 19 "show that rules of hospitality in Israel protect only males." I do not believe this.[48]

Thus, the host is doing what is right in his own eyes, what is expedient, what may be culturally conditioned (esp. in the debased period of the judges). This is the very point of the narrative: God's Word demands much higher standards of morality, but Israel has degenerated into the mire of deep depravity where lewd and base behavior dominate, and *no one* is doing what is right in Yahweh's eyes.

---

46. K. Stone, "Gender and Homosexuality in Judges 19: Subject-Honor, Object-Shame," *JSOT* 67 (1995): 91–103.

47. Block, *Judges, Ruth*, 543.

48. Fokkelman, "Structural Remarks on Judges 9 and 19," 44 n. 20.

The concubine is the victim. She is a pawn of a callous husband, the rapists/abusers, and once again the callous husband. Unfortunately, as with so many victims, she remains nameless. The narrator paints her in colors that cause us to associate with her and to have compassion and pity on her. As a victim she deserves nothing less. We can easily say that in the narrator's world she fares better than in her real world.

The Levite is, in some ways, more to be despised than the wicked rapists/abusers. He is dominated by self-interest, having absolutely no concern for the welfare of others, especially his concubine (this becomes more evident in ch. 20). The morning scene in the aftermath of the night's wantonness is absolutely chilling. He is so nonchalant, matter-of-fact in his callousness that we are stunned. How can he be so indifferent? Is he really that self-absorbed? Apparently he is.

DECLINING MORALS. The inhospitality of the people of Gibeah is clearly wrong. Unfortunately, inhospitality is not simply a problem in ancient Israel during the period of the judges. We live today in a growing hostile world. Forty to fifty years ago people hitchhiked with little fear, but today, because of the tremendous crimes that have occurred to hitchhikers or to those picking up hitchhikers, the practice has generally disappeared (and understandably so). Even in the church inhospitality can exist. Because of time pressures on families in the modern urban, mobile society, the interconnectedness of many churches has declined. It is not uncommon to hear people remark that they have been attending such-and-such church for a number of months and have not received an invitation to visit someone's home.

Homosexuality. While one might think that the homosexual issue is a Christian versus unbeliever issue, this is not the case. A recent article in the *Chicago Tribune* documented the struggle within many mainline denominations over the homosexual issue.[49] While evangelical and black Protestant churches along with Roman Catholic and Orthodox churches do not debate homosexual behavior, a number of mainline Protestant denominations are having a vigorous debate on this issue within their leaderships. All who support homosexual marriages and ordination of homosexual individuals argue that the Scriptures do not condemn homosexuality as sin and interpret Judges 19 as centering on the inhospitality problem. During the first

---

49. Richard N. Ostling, "Era's New Dividing Line," *Chicago Tribune* (July 21, 2000): sec. 2, p. 8.

half of 2000, three major mainline churches with 14.4 million members have had these showdowns.[50]

- In May 2000, the United Methodist Church's General Conference voted by a two to one ratio to retain a ban on blessing ceremonies for homosexual couples, almost guaranteeing future disobedience and church trials. Delegates opposed openly gay and lesbian clergy by a similar margin.
- In late June 2000, the Presbyterian Church (U.S.A.) General Assembly gave narrow approval (51.6 percent) to a Methodist-style ban on same-sex ceremonies. To become law, the measure must now be ratified by 87 of the church's 173 regional units.
- In mid-July 2000, the Episcopal Church's General Convention overwhelmingly endorsed a new policy acknowledging there are Episcopal couples, "acting in good conscience," in lifelong committed relationships outside marriage who should receive "prayerful support, encouragement and pastoral care." The wording covers both gay and lesbian couples, and unwed heterosexual couples, prompting new warnings from conservatives within the denomination that toleration of homosexual behavior will unglue Christian sexual morality as a whole.

Some mainline denominations have approved homosexual relationships. The United Church has long promoted toleration of same-sex couples and in 1983 declared that sexual orientation should not be a barrier to ordination. Apparently some mainline churches are more influenced by their culture than by Scripture.

Living in self-interest. There are many victims like the concubine in our world today. They are the hapless, ill-fated casualties of a world that either ignores God or outright rejects him. These victims most often are the "lesser important" people in our society; or better, what our society, in one way or another, deems the less important people: women, children, minorities—that is, people with no power to defend themselves. They deserve our compassion. They need Jesus Christ's love.

During the Nuremberg trials, a natural question arose as to how men who seemed so normal in their other human relationships could be so different, so demonic, in their attitudes and actions towards the Jews. How could these men be so kind to women and children on the one hand and then murder so many women and children on the other? While this is a complex question without a simple answer, one factor that came out in the trials was the

50. Ibid.

ability of these men to compartmentalize their emotions and hence at certain times function with the absence of any empathy and compassion. By removing all possibility of compassion, these men were able, from a purely emotional standpoint, to perpetrate incredible evil, and yet go home at night to their families. As Christians, when we lack the compassion of Christ for people, no matter who they are, we run the risk of compartmentalizing our emotions and of going down this same path.

Unfortunately, many of us are infected with the self-interest cancer. Just like the host in Judges 19, most of us can provide reasonable hospitality, but we are programmed by our societal principles to function along the axis of expedience. When confronted with a moral dilemma, too often we function on what is expedient, on what we have been culturally conditioned to do. Thus, we don't even see these victims, even though they are all around us. At the work place, school, supermarket, and church, they are there. But until we remove the self-interest cancer that diminishes our vision, we won't see them. We won't help them. But God's Word demands much higher standards of ethics and morality.

How many today make ethical decisions on the basis of the societal, cultural strictures rather than God's Word? Or even worse, how many make ethical decisions purely on the basis of how they feel, what they think is best for the enhancement of their interest? No wonder there are so many victims when every person is doing what is right in his or her own eyes. Moral relativism prevails. And the more it prevails, the worse the atrocities that people perpetrate on people. Our technological culture does not make human beings better; instead, it provides new ways for them to explore and enact their perversions and evil designs. Neo-pagan America leads the way.

Judges 20:1–48

¹Then all the Israelites from Dan to Beersheba and from the land of Gilead came out as one man and assembled before the LORD in Mizpah. ²The leaders of all the people of the tribes of Israel took their places in the assembly of the people of God, four hundred thousand soldiers armed with swords. ³(The Benjamites heard that the Israelites had gone up to Mizpah.) Then the Israelites said, "Tell us how this awful thing happened."

⁴So the Levite, the husband of the murdered woman, said, "I and my concubine came to Gibeah in Benjamin to spend the night. ⁵During the night the men of Gibeah came after me and surrounded the house, intending to kill me. They raped my

concubine, and she died. [6]I took my concubine, cut her into pieces and sent one piece to each region of Israel's inheritance, because they committed this lewd and disgraceful act in Israel. [7]Now, all you Israelites, speak up and give your verdict."

[8]All the people rose as one man, saying, "None of us will go home. No, not one of us will return to his house. [9] But now this is what we'll do to Gibeah: We'll go up against it as the lot directs. [10]We'll take ten men out of every hundred from all the tribes of Israel, and a hundred from a thousand, and a thousand from ten thousand, to get provisions for the army. Then, when the army arrives at Gibeah in Benjamin, it can give them what they deserve for all this vileness done in Israel." [11]So all the men of Israel got together and united as one man against the city.

[12]The tribes of Israel sent men throughout the tribe of Benjamin, saying, "What about this awful crime that was committed among you? [13]Now surrender those wicked men of Gibeah so that we may put them to death and purge the evil from Israel."

But the Benjamites would not listen to their fellow Israelites. [14]From their towns they came together at Gibeah to fight against the Israelites. [15]At once the Benjamites mobilized twenty-six thousand swordsmen from their towns, in addition to seven hundred chosen men from those living in Gibeah. [16]Among all these soldiers there were seven hundred chosen men who were left-handed, each of whom could sling a stone at a hair and not miss.

[17]Israel, apart from Benjamin, mustered four hundred thousand swordsmen, all of them fighting men.

[18]The Israelites went up to Bethel and inquired of God. They said, "Who of us shall go first to fight against the Benjamites?"

The LORD replied, "Judah shall go first."

[19]The next morning the Israelites got up and pitched camp near Gibeah. [20]The men of Israel went out to fight the Benjamites and took up battle positions against them at Gibeah. [21]The Benjamites came out of Gibeah and cut down twenty-two thousand Israelites on the battlefield that day. [22]But the men of Israel encouraged one another and again took up their positions where they had stationed themselves the first day. [23]The Israelites went up and wept before the LORD until

evening, and they inquired of the LORD. They said, "Shall we go up again to battle against the Benjamites, our brothers?"

The LORD answered, "Go up against them."

²⁴Then the Israelites drew near to Benjamin the second day. ²⁵This time, when the Benjamites came out from Gibeah to oppose them, they cut down another eighteen thousand Israelites, all of them armed with swords.

²⁶Then the Israelites, all the people, went up to Bethel, and there they sat weeping before the LORD. They fasted that day until evening and presented burnt offerings and fellowship offerings to the LORD. ²⁷And the Israelites inquired of the LORD. (In those days the ark of the covenant of God was there, ²⁸with Phinehas son of Eleazar, the son of Aaron, ministering before it.) They asked, "Shall we go up again to battle with Benjamin our brother, or not?"

The LORD responded, "Go, for tomorrow I will give them into your hands."

²⁹Then Israel set an ambush around Gibeah. ³⁰They went up against the Benjamites on the third day and took up positions against Gibeah as they had done before. ³¹ The Benjamites came out to meet them and were drawn away from the city. They began to inflict casualties on the Israelites as before, so that about thirty men fell in the open field and on the roads—the one leading to Bethel and the other to Gibeah.

³²While the Benjamites were saying, "We are defeating them as before," the Israelites were saying, "Let's retreat and draw them away from the city to the roads."

³³All the men of Israel moved from their places and took up positions at Baal Tamar, and the Israelite ambush charged out of its place on the west of Gibeah. ³⁴Then ten thousand of Israel's finest men made a frontal attack on Gibeah. The fighting was so heavy that the Benjamites did not realize how near disaster was. ³⁵The LORD defeated Benjamin before Israel, and on that day the Israelites struck down 25,100 Benjamites, all armed with swords. ³⁶Then the Benjamites saw that they were beaten.

Now the men of Israel had given way before Benjamin, because they relied on the ambush they had set near Gibeah. ³⁷The men who had been in ambush made a sudden dash into Gibeah, spread out and put the whole city to the sword. ³⁸

The men of Israel had arranged with the ambush that they should send up a great cloud of smoke from the city, [39] and then the men of Israel would turn in the battle.

The Benjamites had begun to inflict casualties on the men of Israel (about thirty), and they said, "We are defeating them as in the first battle." [40]But when the column of smoke began to rise from the city, the Benjamites turned and saw the smoke of the whole city going up into the sky. [41]Then the men of Israel turned on them, and the men of Benjamin were terrified, because they realized that disaster had come upon them. [42]So they fled before the Israelites in the direction of the desert, but they could not escape the battle. And the men of Israel who came out of the towns cut them down there. [43]They surrounded the Benjamites, chased them and easily overran them in the vicinity of Gibeah on the east. [44]Eighteen thousand Benjamites fell, all of them valiant fighters. [45]As they turned and fled toward the desert to the rock of Rimmon, the Israelites cut down five thousand men along the roads. They kept pressing after the Benjamites as far as Gidom and struck down two thousand more.

[46]On that day twenty-five thousand Benjamite swordsmen fell, all of them valiant fighters. [47]But six hundred men turned and fled into the desert to the rock of Rimmon, where they stayed four months. [48]The men of Israel went back to Benjamin and put all the towns to the sword, including the animals and everything else they found. All the towns they came across they set on fire.

JUST AS THERE is a satirical treatment of Israelite hospitality in the previous section (19:1–30), so there is a satirical treatment of the Israelite assembly in this section. This chapter records a massive turnout "from Dan to Beersheba and from the land of Gilead." The Israelites assemble in unparalleled unity, "as one man," before the Lord in Mizpah (20:1). It is truly ironic that this nameless Levite, so selfish and callous, is the one who gets the greatest response from the greatest number of tribes in Israel *in the entire book of Judges!* The Levite, who calls the tribes to muster by the grotesque mutilation of his concubine, has become a "self-appointed judge."[51]

---

51. Boling, *Judges*, 275.

Incitement to Battle (20:1–17)

THE READER KNOWS more about both the convener of this assembly and the details of the atrocity at Gibeah than the members of the assembly. Thus, to the reader, the Levite's systematic dismemberment of the concubine—all very businesslike—is nothing but an expression of the self-centered callousness he displayed toward her at Gibeah; however, to those at the assembly who have received the ghastly pieces it is interpreted as a zealous act of covenant fidelity and a call to religious war.

Not only is the turnout massive, but also impressive: 'The leaders of all the people of the tribes of Israel took their places in the assembly of the people of God [*ʿam hāʾlōhîm*], four hundred thousand soldiers⁵² armed with swords." Benjamin is aware of the assembly but is not apparently called out as a participant. The Levite is called upon as the *sole* witness. The leaders of the assembly hear and accept his testimony *alone*, which will have a devastating impact on all Israel.

Very simply, the Levite bears false witness. It is not a grossly distorted account. The general story line is correct. But the intended impression is different from the picture conveyed in chapter 19. Any possible culpability of the Levite in the incident at Gibeah is eliminated by his testimony.

"Some wicked men" (lit., "sons of Belial") in 19:22 become in his testimony "men of Gibeah" (lit., "the citizens/nobles/lords of Gibeah," *baʿālê haggibʿâ*) in 20:5 (cf. 9:2, etc.). Thus the members of the assembly apparently understand that the crime has been committed by the leading men of the city (*baʿālê*, cf. 9:2), not some lower class men of the baser sort. In the previous account the wicked men demanded the old man to bring the Levite out so that they could have sex (*ydʿ*) with him (19:22). The Levite now testifies (lit.): "Me they intended to kill" (20:5). While this may be a reasonable inference based on what happened to the concubine, the Levite's choice of words stresses the threat to himself, thereby diminishing his own responsibility by implication.⁵³

In other words, the Levite's report glosses the sexual danger to him (which resulted in his ruthless substitution of his concubine for himself) and yet at the same time heightens his status as an innocent intended victim of murder. He conjures up the view that his life was threatened and that he escaped, but his concubine was caught and raped. He later recovered her body and, in outrage for the crime, he sent the dismembered pieces to the tribes.

---

52. The number given is 400,000 soldiers armed with swords, which is huge even by modern standards. This could be hyperbole stressing the massive number, or perhaps the term *ʾelep* should be understood as unit or contingent (hence 400 units or contingents)—still a considerable number compared to the Benjamites. Whatever the case, the fact that this callous, self-interested Levite is able to produce this kind of response is amazingly paradoxical—a larger response than any of the major/cyclical judges!

53. Webb, *The Book of the Judges*, 191.

The previous account is ambiguous about whether the concubine died solely as a result of the rape or as a result of the combined effects of the rape and the Levite's subsequent treatment of her. Was she unconscious or dead on the doorstep? Did she die while the Levite was sleeping, during his preparations to leave, or on the journey home? The account even allows the reader to envision the possibility that having turned her out to the mob the Levite considered her as good as dead, but then, having conceived the possibility of using her corpse to avenge himself on the men of Gibeah, deliberately contributed to her death or even caused it directly with his knife when they got home.[54] This would explain the extraordinary callousness he displays.

The Levite's testimony to the assembly is deceptively simple in assigning guilt for her death to the men of Gibeah: "They raped [ʿnh] my concubine, and she died" (20:5). By telescoping the action into the single verb ʿnh (to humiliate, violate sexually), the Levite diminishes the licentious action against his concubine. The narrator had supplied a graphic threefold verbal description: "They raped [ydʿ, emphasizing sexual violation] her and abused [ʿll, emphasizing severe and wanton abuse] her throughout the night, and at dawn they let her go [šlḥ, discarded]" to struggle back to the old man's house (19:25). Thus in 20:5, the Levite undercuts the crime against the concubine and, at the same time, implies that she died solely as a result of the rape. The Levite's speech to the assembly does not arouse any of the suspicions that the narrator's account does. Ironically, the Levite has sacrificed his concubine to save himself and now is willing to sacrifice the "sons of Israel" to get his personal revenge on these Gibeahite "sons of Belial."

The assembly is duly impressed by the Levite's speech. They arise "as one man" and resolve at once on united punitive action against Gibeah (20:8–11). The action they take may well be justified in principle. The narrator has implied that the outrage at Gibeah is an act that challenges the very concept of "Israel" as a distinctive people (19:12). Such behavior is not expected among a tribe in Israel. However, the rest of Israel—the massive assembly—is not appreciably more faithful to the covenant stipulations. What will become of Israel when its assembly can be convened and manipulated by a person of such dubious morals as this nameless Levite? In fact, the Levite now disappears completely without trace. The convener and manipulator of the assembly will not be present to give an account or be held responsible for what now transpires. The self-appointed leader and deliverer disappears.

While the term ḥērem does not occur in the description of the action against Benjamin, the concept is present. It seems that the procedure for placing Gibeah under the "ban" (ḥērem) derives from a law recorded in

---

54. Polzin, *Moses and the Deuteronomist*, 200–202.

Deuteronomy 13:12–18. While the law there specifically applies to idolatry (cf. also Deut. 17:2–7), the abomination committed by the wicked men ("sons of Belial") of Gibeah may have been understood as contrary to proper covenantal behavior. Antisocial behavior breaks the covenant with God as much as idolatry.[55] The fact that Deuteronomy 13:13 describes idolaters as "wicked men" (lit., "sons of Belial") and Judges typesets the story in terms of Genesis 19:1–11 seems to strengthen the connection of Judges 19–20 with Deuteronomy 13:12–18.

Unfortunately, while this may be the case, the Israelites do not adhere to the stipulations of this law in their implementation. The leadership of the assembly does not follow the clear stipulation that "you must inquire, probe and investigate it thoroughly" (Deut. 13:14a). They simply accept the Levite's version of what has happened. Moreover, they determine a military course of action *before* they attempt diplomatic overtures. In fact, rather than dealing directly with the city of Gibeah, they raise the issue to a higher intensity level by sending men throughout the entire tribe of Benjamin, demanding that they hand over the wicked men so that the evil may be purged from Israel (Judg. 20:12–14). This, no doubt, causes a hardening of the resolve of the deep tribal loyalties rather than accomplishing the resolution of the conflict. The Benjamites will not listen to their fellow Israelites (20:13c), just as the "sons of Belial" of Gibeah would not listen to the old man (19:25a). The very fabric of Israel is being threatened.

The Benjamites mobilize their men for battle, including a elite contingent of left-handed slingers. It is ironic that these heroes of Benjamin (whose name means "son of the right hand") are set forth as "left-handed" (20:16; cf. Ehud, 3:15) and can "sling a stone at a hair and not miss [*ḥṭʾ*, lit., sin]." It is, in fact, the sin of the Benjamite men of Gibeah that has caused the war, and ironically these left-handers will be the ones who inflict even greater death on their fellow Israelites.

Three Battles (20:18–48)

THIS SECTION NARRATES a sequence of three battles in which the Israelites attempt to overcome the Benjamites. What is particularly noticeable is the cycle of four items: preinquiry actions, inquiry, Yahweh's response, and result. The three prebattle inquiries exhibit a pattern of incremental repetition, which expresses a growing anxiety of the inquirers (see the chart below).[56]

---

55. Niditch, "The 'Sodomite' Theme in Judges 19–20," 377.

56. For some of the literary aspects of the narrative, see E. J. Revell, "The Battle with Benjamin (Judges xx 29–48) and Hebrew Narrative Techniques," *VT* 35 (1985): 417–33; P. E. Satterthwaite, "Narrative Artistry in the Composition of Judges xx 29ff.," *VT* 42 (1992): 80–89.

Battle 1 (20:18–21). In the preinquiry actions, the Israelites make plans against Gibeah and threaten the city (20:8–13a). All of the prebattle inquiries are made at Bethel (from the parenthetical statement in 20:27, it appears that the ark of the covenant has been brought to Bethel for the war as a "good luck charm"; for a similar type of context, see 1 Sam. 4). Bethel had a long-standing history as a sacred site in Israelite tradition, although much of it is a negative tradition (cf. 1 Kings 12:25–33). In the overall context of the book Bethel's mention here corresponds to its mention in Judges 1:22–23, where the story of its capture is related, a capture that took place through treachery on the part of one of its former citizens, induced by a bribe by the Ephraimites.

The Israelites' first inquiry is, "Who of us shall go [*'lh*] first to fight against the Benjamites?" (20:18a). This first inquiry reflects the Israelites' confidence regarding the rightness and eventual outcome of their cause. They are already committed to the war and Yahweh's approval is assumed. They therefore raise a purely procedural matter: How is the campaign to be conducted? Yahweh's response is that Judah is to go first,[57] but there is no promise of victory (20:18b). Though the Israelites attack Gibeah en masse, they are severely defeated (20:19–21).

Battle 2 (20:22–25). In the preinquiry actions, the Israelites encourage one another and again take up their positions (20:22). They also weep before Yahweh (20:23a). The Israelites' second inquiry is, "Shall we go up [*'lh*] again to battle against the Benjamites, our brothers?" (20:23a²). The second inquiry shows the drastic loss of confidence the inquirers have suffered as a result of their disastrous defeat. They are now doubtful about the wisdom, and perhaps also the rightness, of continuing the war. A conciliatory note is struck by the reference to the Benjamites as "our brothers" (also in the third inquiry). Yahweh again replies, "Go up against them" (20:23b). The Israelites once again attack en masse, and once again they are defeated severely by the Benjamites, though not quite as badly (20:24–25).

Battle 3 (20:26–48). Before the second battle, the Israelites wept before Yahweh; now in their preinquiry actions, they weep and fast and offer sacrifices (20:26). Their third inquiry properly goes through the high priest, Phinehas[58]: "Shall we go up [*'lh*] again to battle with Benjamin our brother, or not?" (20:28a²). Here they explicitly ask whether they should desist, a possibility that now looms large in their minds. Yahweh responds "Go, for tomorrow I *will give* them into your hands" (20:28b). Although Yahweh sends them again into battle, this time he does so with an assurance of victory. In

---

57. Yahweh puts Judah in the van, appropriately so, since the ravished concubine is a Judahite (Webb, *The Book of the Judges*, 193).

58. Not to be confused with a later Phinehas the son of Eli (1 Sam 1–4).

the ensuing battle the fortunes of the two sides are suddenly reversed (20:34–35). The Israelites set an ambush and *ḥrm* the Benjamites—except for 600 men (20:47, the same number as the Danites in 18:11). They destroy all the towns, including the animals.

Thus Yahweh intentionally allows Israel to lose two battles. Yahweh's will is done, and it is done through the tribes of Israel even though the people's intent may be far different from Yahweh's. Only when a humbled Israel appeals to Yahweh do the goals of Israel and Yahweh, however briefly, coincide.[59]

Judges 20

Preinquiry Actions	Israelites' Inquiry	Yahweh's Response	Result
Make plans against Gibeah and threaten city (20:8–13a)	Inquiry #1 "Who of us shall go [*ᶜlh*] first to fight against the Benjaminites?" (20:18a)	"Judah shall go first" [but no promise of victory] (20:18b)	Israelites attack Gibeah en masse; are defeated severely by Benjamites (20:19–21)
Israelites encourage one another and again take up their positions (20:22) Israelites weep before Yahweh (20:23a)	Inquiry #2 "Shall we go up [*ᶜlh*] again to battle against the Benjamites, our brothers?"—a hint of doubt? (20:23a²)	"Go up against them" (20:23b)	Israelites attack en masse; are defeated severely by Benjamites (though not quite as badly) (20:24–25)
Israelites—all the people—weep, fast, and present sacrifices (20:26)	Inquiry #3 Inquiry through Phinehas, the high priest, "Shall we go up [*ᶜlh*] again to battle with Benjamin our brother, or not?"—uncertainty expressed (20:28a²)	"Go, for tomorrow I *will give* them into your hands" (20:28b)	Israelites set ambush and *ḥrm* Benjamites—except for 600 men.

59. Klein, *Triumph of Irony*, 179. Cf. the "Cuthean Legend," in which Naram-Sin is defeated three times before the fourth inquiry is "an affirmative yes."

One should compare this with Judges 1, where a similar pattern occurs:

Judges 1

Preinquiry Actions	Israelites' Inquiry	Yahweh's Response	Result
None	"Who will be the first to go up [ʿlh] and fight for us against the Canaanites?" (1:1)	"Judah is to go; I *have given* the land into their hands" (1:2)	Men of Judah make a deal with the Simeonites, but victories come over the bulk of Canaanites (except in the ʿmq) (1:3−20)

What is especially horrific about this war is that it is against one of the tribes of Israel and is executed with a determination and a thoroughness surpassing anything evidenced in Israel's wars with the Canaanites elsewhere in Judges. The men on both sides are called "valiant fighters" or "swordsmen" (20:2, 15, 17, 25, 35, 44, 46). The tragedy is that these are all valuable soldiers whom Israel cannot afford to lose in their occupation of the land of Canaan—a task that seems all but forgotten.

Bridging Contexts

HUMAN LEVEL. There is a tremendous contrast between the Israelite reaction to the outrage at Gibeah and the idolatry and other sins of Conclusion 1. The disproportionate numbers that turn out against Gibeah is in significant contrast to the absence of anyone turning out against Micah, the Levite, or the Danites and what they did. In addition, the enormous indignity and anger over the Gibeahites is the opposite of the indifference over actions taken by the characters in chapter 19. It is truly amazing which things will really set people off and which things they tolerate or ignore. While they rightly should be upset with the Gibeahites—it is a moral atrocity—they should equally be upset with Micah, the Levite, and the Danites in Conclusion 1 (serious spiritual deviations). There is an imbalance here.

In the same way, there is an imbalance in the difference in Israel's implementation of the ḥērem. The ḥērem is executed with a greater determination and more thoroughly than in any of Israel's wars with the Canaanites as narrated at the beginning of Judges. In other words, they are willing to follow God more in destroying other Israelites than they are in destroying Canaanites!

One of the greatest ironies of this book is that it is a *nameless* Levite, so self-centered and callous, who gets the greatest response from the Israelites. The Israelites are incited to almost a frenzy level by this Levite—they are willing to sacrifice their sons in a war to "revenge" a man whose testimony is false and motivated by self-interest. In contrast, at the end of Introduction 1 (1:1–2:5, esp. 2:1–5), the Israelite assembly is moved to tears by *the angel* of Yahweh's speech (God's special envoy), which is fully true and accurate, yet the people quickly depart from God's way. There is little real resolve to follow God.

The Israelite leaders uncritically accept the Levite's testimony; they neglect their responsibility to investigate the truth. He is the sole witness, a false witness at that, and yet his testimony is accepted. Truth is not their interest, and a dubious individual dupes them. Godly leadership must do better.

Divine level. On the divine level, this section presents an interesting portrait of Yahweh. He chastises the Israelites by speaking; in the next episode, he chastises them by remaining silent. In every case, Yahweh demonstrates his justice to a people who are not following him according to his dictates. (1) He is invoked as a silent, passive witness to the assembly of the people at Mizpah (not much different from the assembly that invested Jephthah with power before the Lord at Mizpah—though a different Mizpah). In other words, the use of his name here is basically to legitimate or validate what the people have already decided they want to do.

(2) Yahweh serves as the respondent to the Israelites' oracular inquiries concerning battle strategy—as though he were a god like the other deities. His sarcastic replies in the first two instances evinces his disapproval of the Israelites' methodology as they attempt to manipulate his approval for their strategy when they are not walking with him. He punishes them through the outcomes of the first two battles.

(3) Yahweh punishes the Benjamites for defending the perpetrators of such perversion and gross violence in Israel. They are wrong, and justice demands that they be punished too—though hardly to the extreme that is implemented. God is the only one who does "right" in this passage.

THE IMBALANCE THAT Israel manifests in its reaction to the outrage of Gibeah, in contrast to the sins of Conclusion 1 (17:1–18:31), is not unlike the imbalance some churches manifest. It is not infrequent that slanderous gossip about someone in the church is tolerated—the phone lines can burn up—but a divorced person is not allowed to teach a Sunday school class. It is not that the latter may not be an issue, especially in certain circumstances; but the former is a serious sin with God (Prov.

6:16–19).[60] It is truly a human tendency to elevate particular sins that God does not elevate and to devalue other sins that God considered grievous. Sin should be shunned and God's Word followed. In every case, God's grace is imparted.

It is not uncommon today that the religious charlatan, the spiritual quack (like the Levite in this narrative), gets the biggest response from gullible Christians who do not inquire about the real credentials of the imposter. Some of these frauds tell convincing stories to invoke action on the part of their listeners. They can inspire many to an almost frenzied level (as this Levite did the Israelites), to the point that they are willing to sacrifice their hard-earned money to support a man whose testimony is false and motivated by self-interest. Yet the truly biblical preacher will find the assembly perhaps emotionally moved, but with no real resolve to follow God.

There is little question that accepting one individual's testimony as the sole witness is a dangerous process. The Israelite leaders uncritically accept the Levite's testimony; they neglect their responsibility to investigate the truth. They are duped. Certainly this serves as a warning to be cautious in the acceptance of certain statements of a negative variety. For example, when a husband or wife shares negative problems of their spouse, it is unwise simply to accept the single witness without hearing the other side. This seems basic, but amazingly it is often not done, and the devastation that is wrought can be immense.

This is equally as true at work, at school, and within all kinds of situations. Whenever someone says "did you know such-and-such about so-and-so ...," the better part of wisdom should warn us against accepting this as unquestionably true. It may be so, but it needs verification. The leaders of Israel do not verify the testimony of the Levite, and thousands lose their lives as a result. In what ways are Christian leaders today making the same type of mistake?

Judges 21:1–25

[1]The men of Israel had taken an oath at Mizpah: "Not one of us will give his daughter in marriage to a Benjamite."

[2]The people went to Bethel, where they sat before God until evening, raising their voices and weeping bitterly. [3]"O LORD, the God of Israel," they cried, "why has this happened to Israel? Why should one tribe be missing from Israel today?"

[4]Early the next day the people built an altar and presented burnt offerings and fellowship offerings.

---

60. Note that out of the seven "sins" listed that God "hates," at least three apply to slanderous gossip. Divorce is not mentioned in this list in Proverbs.

⁵Then the Israelites asked, "Who from all the tribes of Israel has failed to assemble before the LORD?" For they had taken a solemn oath that anyone who failed to assemble before the LORD at Mizpah should certainly be put to death.

⁶Now the Israelites grieved for their brothers, the Benjamites. "Today one tribe is cut off from Israel," they said. ⁷"How can we provide wives for those who are left, since we have taken an oath by the LORD not to give them any of our daughters in marriage?" ⁸Then they asked, "Which one of the tribes of Israel failed to assemble before the LORD at Mizpah?" They discovered that no one from Jabesh Gilead had come to the camp for the assembly. ⁹For when they counted the people, they found that none of the people of Jabesh Gilead were there.

¹⁰So the assembly sent twelve thousand fighting men with instructions to go to Jabesh Gilead and put to the sword those living there, including the women and children. ¹¹"This is what you are to do," they said. "Kill every male and every woman who is not a virgin." ¹²They found among the people living in Jabesh Gilead four hundred young women who had never slept with a man, and they took them to the camp at Shiloh in Canaan.

¹³Then the whole assembly sent an offer of peace to the Benjamites at the rock of Rimmon. ¹⁴So the Benjamites returned at that time and were given the women of Jabesh Gilead who had been spared. But there were not enough for all of them.

¹⁵The people grieved for Benjamin, because the LORD had made a gap in the tribes of Israel. ¹⁶And the elders of the assembly said, "With the women of Benjamin destroyed, how shall we provide wives for the men who are left? ¹⁷The Benjamite survivors must have heirs," they said, "so that a tribe of Israel will not be wiped out. ¹⁸We can't give them our daughters as wives, since we Israelites have taken this oath: 'Cursed be anyone who gives a wife to a Benjamite.' ¹⁹But look, there is the annual festival of the LORD in Shiloh, to the north of Bethel, and east of the road that goes from Bethel to Shechem, and to the south of Lebonah."

²⁰So they instructed the Benjamites, saying, "Go and hide in the vineyards ²¹and watch. When the girls of Shiloh come out to join in the dancing, then rush from the vineyards and

each of you seize a wife from the girls of Shiloh and go to the land of Benjamin. ²²When their fathers or brothers complain to us, we will say to them, 'Do us a kindness by helping them, because we did not get wives for them during the war, and you are innocent, since you did not give your daughters to them.'"

²³So that is what the Benjamites did. While the girls were dancing, each man caught one and carried her off to be his wife. Then they returned to their inheritance and rebuilt the towns and settled in them.

²⁴At that time the Israelites left that place and went home to their tribes and clans, each to his own inheritance.

²⁵In those days Israel had no king; everyone did as he saw fit.

CHAPTER 21, the last chapter of this increasingly disappointing book, where everyone does what is right in his or her own eyes, records the aftermath of the *ḥērem* slaughter of the Benjamites. The chapter divides easily into three sections.

Oaths at Mizpah (21:1–5)

THE ISRAELITES HAVE sworn two oaths at Mizpah. The first, given in parenthetical flashback in verse 1, is that the Israelites had promised not to give their daughters in marriage to the Benjamites. The fact that this oath was taken before the battle is clear by the reference to the assembly at Mizpah (cf. 20:1). Moreover, though not stated here, apparently a curse was also connected to it (see 21:18b). It is somewhat understandable if such an oath were taken in the heat of battle when passion for revenge might be running high after the first or second battle after the Benjamites had inflicted heavy losses on the other tribes. However, this oath was almost certainly taken before any engagements in battle narrated in the previous chapter.

But the excessive slaughter of the Benjamites and the endangerment of tribal extinction expose the rashness of the oath. In this respect the oath is parallel to Jephthah's vow (also taken before the battle). With the passion of battle spent and with all the Benjamite women having been slaughtered (20:47–48; 21:16), the Israelites suddenly realize that because of their oath the six hundred male survivors will die childless and the tribe will become extinct (21:6; cf. 20:23, 28). Ironically, the daughters of Benjamin suffer the same fate as the concubine.

The people assemble at Bethel raising their voices and weeping bitterly. The wording of their inquiry is notable:

> O LORD, the God of Israel . . .
> why has this happened to Israel?
> Why should one tribe be missing from Israel today?

The threefold reference to Israel, with Yahweh being addressed as "the God of Israel," implies that the matter in hand is ultimately his responsibility.[61] Their inquiry is not a request for information. Rather, it is an oblique form of protest and an attempt by the inquirers to absolve themselves of any responsibility. But Yahweh does not answer. In the previous episode he chastised them by speaking; here he chastises them by remaining silent. Yahweh will not be used by them.[62]

Early the next day the Israelites resume the inquiry by building an altar and presenting burnt offerings and fellowship offerings (21:4). They shift their inquiry to ascertain "who from all the tribes of Israel has failed to assemble before the LORD?" Again, Yahweh is silent; they will not obtain this information from him, for Yahweh knows their motive in asking the question: "They had taken a solemn oath that anyone who failed to assemble before the LORD at Mizpah should certainly be put to death." This is the second oath the Israelites had taken at Mizpah *before* the battle. This, too, was a rash oath.

Wives for the Benjamites: Part 1 (21:6–14)

SUDDENLY THE ISRAELITES' mood changes. Instead of the strong tone of the oaths, they begin to feel sorrow for the Benjamites. The impact of the application of the *ḥērem* on Benjamin finally begins to dawn on the Israelites. Through the disjointed style at the beginning of this paragraph, the narrator captures the Israelites' frustration at God's silence in the face of their inquiry.

Verses 6–7 record the Israelites emotional dilemma created by their first oath: "How can we provide wives for those who are left?" The repetition of the question of who among the tribes did not participate emphasizes the direction that their solution will take. Ironically (and certainly unfortunately for those in Jabesh Gilead), it is discovered that Jabesh Gilead did not send any contingent to the war. But this is discovered, not by revelation from Yahweh—he remains silent—but by the pragmatics of a roll call (21:9).

So the second oath sworn at Mizpah (v. 5) is now conveniently implemented. Since the city of Jabesh Gilead did not send warriors for the war

---

61. Webb, *The Book of the Judges*, 195.
62. Ibid.

against Benjamin, they are not bound by the oath not to give their daughters to the Benjamites; hence, the Israelites can legally give the daughters of Jabesh Gilead without any danger of breaking the first vow.

Thus, a force of twelve thousand (one thousand from each tribe, cf. Num. 31:5) is dispatched at once with instructions to put the defaulters under the ban (*ḥērem*), all the inhabitants of the town except the virgins (21:10–11). This is a selective application of the ban (*ḥērem*), for which there was Mosaic precedent according to Numbers 31:17–18. However, the present instance is a clear case of using one oath in order to circumvent another—legally justifiable but morally dubious, to say the least.[63] Just as the Danites had attacked the unsuspecting town of Laish, putting it under the *ḥērem* (Judg. 18:27–28), so the Israelites attack the unsuspecting town of Jabesh Gilead, putting it under the *ḥērem*. The difference, however, is that in the latter case the unsuspecting town is inhabited by fellow Israelites.

The operation yields only four hundred young women, who are brought back to Shiloh "in Canaan" (21:12) and are "given" to the Benjamites as an offer of peace (21:13–14). But they are two hundred short of the required total. This shortfall will lead the Israelites to their final solution (see next section). The addition of the phrase "in Canaan" at the end of verse 12 heightens the irony that the *ḥērem*, which was designed for application to the Canaanites (which Israel did not fully obey, cf. Judg. 1), here is being applied to an Israelite city because it did not participate in the civil war against Benjamin (one of Israel's own tribes); and it is applied to almost utter extinction.

It is truly ironic that "united Israel exterminates Jabesh-Gilead of all but virgin females for the very covenant crime of which Benjamin had earlier been guilty [killing a woman] and does so in order to evade exterminating Benjamin from the nation. As a result, intertribal unity is preserved at the cost of loyalty to the terms of YHWH's covenant."[64]

Wives for the Benjamites: Part 2 (21:15–25)

FOR A SECOND time the Israelites grieve for Benjamin. It is interesting that in this last scene the elders of Israel play a critical role. The only other time that the elders of the entire nation of Israel[65] are mentioned in this book is 2:7, where it describes the elders under whom the Israelites served Yahweh. In contrast, the elders in 21:15–25 are the devisers of a shameful plan to supply the Benjamites with the necessary women to make up the shortage from Jabesh Gilead.

---

63. Ibid.
64. O'Connell, *The Rhetoric of the Book of Judges*, 260.
65. Not the elders of a tribe, as in the story of Jephthah, but of the entire nation.

Verses 15–18 are repetitious of verses 6–7 (i.e., the Israelites are grieved and concerned about how they can provide wives for the remaining Benjamites, since they have taken an oath). The repetition links the two erroneous solutions. This time, rather than exercising a ḥērem ban against an Israelite city, the elders devise a plan that is nothing short of another rape! Interestingly, here the oath's curse is included: "Cursed be anyone who gives a wife to a Benjamite" (21:18b). It is this curse element that will now provide the elders with the legal maneuvering necessary to do their sinister deed.

The annual festival of the Lord provides the context. This festival may have been a local one, or in light of the reference to vineyards (21:20), it may refer to the Feast of Tabernacles.[66] Block suggests that because of the ambiguity on the part of the narrator, this festival may have been a further indication of the Israelite move towards Canaanization.[67] The elders instruct the Benjamites to hide in the vineyards, and when the girls of Shiloh come out to dance, seize[68] a wife from these girls of Shiloh. The Benjamites need not worry about the girls' fathers.[69] The elders have anticipated this and have a plan. They will use the Mizpah oath against the girls' fathers: "Do us a kindness by helping them, because we did not get wives for them during the war, and you are innocent, since you did not give your daughters to them" (21:22). Isn't this big of the elders?! The implication is that if the fathers do not accept the abductions, the elders will hold them guilty of "giving" their daughters to the Benjamites, and they will come under the oath's curse (cf. 21:18b).

As in the previous case of Jabesh Gilead, this is a case of using one aspect of the oath in order to circumvent another aspect—again, legally justifiable, but morally reprehensible. With the Benjamites "seizing"[70] wives, the fathers are not technically "giving" them to the Benjamites. The legal intimidation of the threat of the oath's curse eliminates the fathers from making any objection (and none is registered in the text). In effect, the men of Shiloh are

---

66. The detailed description of the festival's location at Shiloh may indicate that this passage was written at a time when Shiloh was in ruins, having been destroyed in the connection with the battle of Aphek (1 Sam. 4:1–11).

67. Block, *Judges, Ruth*, 580–81. He observes that the mention of the girls dancing and the emphasis on the vineyards may indicate a grape-harvest festival characterized by revelry, music, and dance—indicators of a Canaanized society.

68. The verb ḥṭp, translated "seize" in the NIV, is a verb that appears in only one other place in the Old Testament (Ps. 10:9). It occurs twice in that verse, describing a wicked and violent man's ambush of an innocent person and comparing it to that of a lion pouncing on its prey to devour it.

69. Families, esp. brothers, were responsible for demanding legal satisfaction in cases of a girl's being abducted (Gen. 34:7–31; 2 Sam. 13:20–38).

70. In this verse the verb is gzl, a violent action reflected in its use in 9:25 to describe highway robbery.

asked to accept the rape as a fait accompli, just as Micah had to accept the plundering of his shrine by the Danites (18:22–26).

So, with consummate irony, this episode reaches its climax with the "elders" (*zᵉqēnîm*) doing, in principle, the same thing as both the "old man" (*zāqēn*, the host) and the Levite had done in Gibeah. The rape of the daughters of Shiloh is an ironic counterpoint to the rape of the concubine, just as the campaign against Jabesh Gilead is an ironic counterpoint to the war against Benjamin.

On top of this, the Benjamites return and rebuild their cities (21:23) so that the entire implementation of the *ḥērem* has been undercut.[71] In the end what has been accomplished? The textual ambiguity leaves the reader with the unpleasant feeling that in spite of all this flurry of legal judgments and executions, some of the men of Gibeah (the very "sons of Belial") who committed the atrocity may, in fact, be among the six hundred Benjamite survivors. In the meantime, the Levite, whose untested testimony led Israel to the brink of disaster, has utterly disappeared. In such an instance, not only has justice not been served, but many injustices have happened in the feeble attempt to implement justice for the atrocity. No positive thing has really occurred in all the outcomes of the narrative. Not only have many wrongs occurred, but no rights have ultimately been championed.

Fittingly, the reader is told that "at that time the Israelites left that place and went home to their tribes and clans, each to his own inheritance" (21:24). Like at the end of the story of Abimelech, the Israelites, as though waking from a nightmarish zombie state, see that all the action is finished and simply go home.

Conclusion 2 bookends with the powerful refrain, "In those days Israel had no king; every man did what was right in his own eyes" (21:25; cf. 19:1). Sadly, the accuracy of the second line of the refrain is forcefully made in this final story.

Bridging Contexts

IN A SENSE Judges is the antithesis to Joshua. In Joshua, the Israelites attempt to Hebraize Canaan; in Judges they Canaanize themselves. Thus, the reader will find no "Hollywood" ending in the final chapter. Instead, one is left with an overburdening sense of discomfort. Israelite degeneracy has reached its nadir. When the book finally ends, the reader can breathe a sigh, but more because the discomforting story is finished than because he or she experiences a final, positive feeling.[72]

---

71. Cf. Deut. 13:12–18.
72. The book of Lamentations produces this same reading experience.

Pharisaism. Conclusion 1 started with an individual stealing, making idols, and hiring a Levite to serve in his household shrine. It developed into a corporate theft of the idolatrous materials, the extermination of a peaceful people, and the establishment of a tribal shrine with a Levite hired to serve. Conclusion 2 started with a family dispute between a Levite and his concubine that ended in the rape and murder of the concubine. It escalated into a corporate level with a tribal war in which the ḥērem was applied selectively to Benjamin (male survivors). Because of two rash oaths, the narrative deteriorated into a ridiculous display of pharisaical legalism by the elders of Israel, culminating in the selective ḥērem of Jabesh Gilead (female survivors, i.e., virgins) and the rape of the daughters of Shiloh. The rape and mutilation of an individual has multiplied into the rape of four hundred virgins (the survivors and victims of violent carnage) and the rape of two hundred innocent women dancers through the violent seizure at a festival that, at least in name, was dedicated to Yahweh.

This final chapter could be described as a comical tragedy of legalism. Israel has gone after the letter of the law with great vengeance in order to save its national integrity and keep from breaking either of its rash vows in the process. However, in the process they have abandoned the spirit of the law, a problem that Jesus Christ dealt with much later in the Gospel accounts. These Israelite elders, were, in many ways, precursors to the first-century Pharisees. They strove to justify themselves; they strove to sustain themselves; and ultimately, they strove to save themselves. The letter of the law stands on self-vindicating righteousness; but self-vindicating righteousness leads to disaster, tragedy, and death.

A wrong application of this passage is to see in it simply the problems of androcentric social structures. What happens in this chapter is not normal androcentrism any more than Joash's backyard Baal altar and Asherah pole, Gideon's ephod, Jephthah's vow, Micah's image, and so on are proper reflections of normative Yahwism.[73] As mentioned in the previous section, godly men do not do these things. God's standards for male and female relations is much, much higher, where mutual submission and love in Christ prevail.

The folly of rash oaths. This passage demonstrates the folly of rash oaths. "It is a trap for a man to dedicate something rashly and only later to consider his vows" (Prov. 20:25). The Israelites have made two rash oaths. Only later, after the battle is over, does the full import of each one become apparent. Interestingly, the Levitical, sacrificial system made a provision for a rash vow (Lev. 5:4−6):

---

73. Block, *Judges, Ruth*, 584.

Or if a person thoughtlessly takes an oath to do anything, whether good or evil—in any matter one might carelessly swear about—even though he is unaware of it, in any case when he learns of it he will be guilty.

When anyone is guilty in any of these ways, he must confess in what way he has sinned and, as a penalty for the sin he has committed, he must bring to the LORD a female lamb or goat from the flock as a sin offering; and the priest shall make atonement for him for his sin.

Consequently, it seems that the rash oath was not the final word. If the Israelites here had confessed their sin (i.e., the rash oath) and sacrificed a sin offering as prescribed, there would have been atonement for the rash vow. There is no reason why the Israelites could not have done so in this instance. So what they did in placing Jabesh Gilead under the ḥērem and in allowing the rape of the daughters of Shiloh are hardly justified morally, or for that matter legally (even within their own system).

Believers, when not walking with God, have a tendency of attempting to work things out by technical, legal means that are often morally wrong. Using one law or oath to circumvent another is not justifiable in God's estimation. The Lord's silence in this passage and the fact that the Israelites resort to a simple roll call to identify the nonparticipants are evidences of God's disapproval. Moreover, by doing this they end up perpetrating the same crime as the wicked men of Gibeah had done: murder (all the inhabitants of Jabesh Gilead except the virgins) and rape (the virgins of Jabesh Gilead and the daughters of Shiloh, who are allowed to be taken by the rest of the Benjamites).

The elders of the Israelite nation in this last story in the book of Judges are as unscrupulous as the tribal elders in the Jephthah cycle (see comments). They are willing to use the rash oaths and curse to their advantage, no matter what kind of destruction this may bring in the lives of the people that they use. Notice how conveniently the "curse" is remembered.

BLOCK SUMS UP in an outstanding way the place that the book of Judges plays in the modern church context:

No book in the Old Testament offers the modern church as telling a mirror as this book. From the *jealousies* of the Ephraimites to the *religious pragmatism* of the Danites, from the *paganism* of Gideon to the *self-centeredness* of Samson, and from the *unmanliness* of Barak to the *violence against women* by the men of Gibeah, all the marks of Canaanite degeneracy are evident in the church and its leaders today. This book is a wake-up call for a church moribund in its own selfish pursuits. Instead of heeding the call of truly godly leaders and letting Jesus Christ be Lord of the church, everywhere congregations and their leaders do what is right in their own eyes. (emphasis mine)[74]

A word to leaders. Block's summary does not come close to mentioning all of the sins of God's people found in the book. The fact is that much of this book, and particularly these last chapters, is a comment on the *leadership* within ancient Israel. While the people in general follow the other gods and goddesses of the land of Canaan, it is the leadership that is singled out for critique again and again. If you are a leader in the church today (whether pastor, youth worker, worship/music director, elder, deacon, teacher), this book applies primarily to you! In a sense, the leaders of Israel practiced "the ends justifies the means" in their attempts to save Benjamin from extermination—which was their doing in the first place.

Therefore, in the contemporary setting, we should be careful of our words and the oaths that we take. Rash oaths can lead to destruction, as they did in ancient Israel. Certainly the words of Jesus that one should avoid complications connected with oaths are liberating (Matt. 5:33–37). These words are wise advice for how to live today.

Whenever religious reasons are used to justify actions, there is room for a closer look. If in the process God's moral laws are broken, the actions are invariably wrong. We should be careful never to use one law or oath to circumvent another, for destructive tragedy will surely follow. Yet, perhaps one of the greatest areas in which Christians fail in this is in the area of financial matters. Plethora are the Christian organizations that play with the accounting books or the way they market their ministries. Fifth Avenue may be impressed, but the Lord of the universe isn't.

When God's kingship is unacknowledged, when his law is ignored, when the morality that he advocates is circumvented, incredible, appalling disasters are the outcome. When rash oaths in his name are used to manipulate and abuse people, when leaders use the ends to justify the means, when God doesn't exist in the lives of his people, the consequences are outrageously appalling.

Like the concubine, the young virgin women of Jabesh Gilead and Shiloh are victims (see Contemporary Significance section of 19:1–30). Their victimization, like that of so many in today's context, is the sad result of soci-

74. Ibid., 586.

ety's departure from God. Only with the spread of the gospel will these victims see redemption, and only through its spread will there be any chance that the victimization will decrease. For only if our society, like any other, will embrace the true and living God and his teachings will there be a possibility that righteousness will prevail.

Our worst enemy. In certain ways Judges 21 uncovers the real source of our sin. At the beginning of the book, Israel failed to implement the *ḥērem* and was influenced by the Canaanites into idolatrous worship and apostasy. Throughout the cycles section, there was a progressive Canaanization of the cyclical judges, climaxing in the moral nadir of the self-absorbed, revenge-driven Samson. But in the final chapters of Judges, and especially in chapter 21, the Canaanites are absent. Thus Block concludes: "This book and the history of the nation that follows serve as eternal testimony to the grim reality that God's people are often their own worst enemy. It is not the enemies outside who threaten the soul but the Canaanite within."[75]

Israel was influenced by Canaan, to be sure, but the source of the problem lay in their own hearts. The problem was in their inherent sinfulness and rebellion, which the Canaanite influences only amplified. So it is with us. The ultimate root of the problem in the church today is not in the influence of the culture around us; rather, it is in our unwillingness to believe, to take God at his Word, and then to obey. We need to submit ourselves, our inherent sinfulness, to the transforming work of the Spirit (Rom. 12:1–2).

From another angle, it is evident that while God is silent in this last chapter, he has not utterly abandoned Israel. In spite of the awful machinations and atrocities recorded here, in his grace God does not bring full judgment on his people. They are not completely consumed by his righteous implementation of justice. He will accomplish his plan of redemption for humankind through and in spite of Israel. While in those days there was no king in Israel, God would eventually establish his ideal king, one after his own heart, David. From David, he has now established his ultimate ideal king, the Lord Jesus Christ, who reigns forever. Some day, humanity will no longer do what is right in their own eyes, for every knee will bow and every tongue confess that he is Lord—the King of kings—to the glory of God the Father.

---

75. Ibid., 585.

Introduction to Ruth

THE BOOK OF RUTH contains a wonderful love story, which, while set in the period of the judges, contrasts greatly with the general chaos and disobedience of that period. In a refreshing way the book provides an antithesis to the incessantly negative message about the conditions in Israel during that time by underscoring God's tremendous blessing in the midst of great familial distress.

Authorship and Date of Composition

THE BABYLONIAN TALMUD attributes authorship of the book to Samuel (*b. B. Bat.* 14b–15a), but the suggestion is doubtful.[1] The book, in fact, does not identify the author either explicitly or implicitly. Quite simply, the author of the book of Ruth is unknown. Recently, A. J. Bledstein has argued that the book of Ruth is the work of a female author, namely, Tamar, the daughter of David.[2] But this is problematic internally[3] as well as culturally.[4]

The date of the book's composition is, in many ways, a more difficult matter. Much of the argument concerning the book's date revolves around linguistic evaluations, which are not always objective and are often difficult

---

1. See R. L. Hubbard Jr., *The Book of Ruth* (NICOT; Grand Rapids: Eerdmans, 1988), 23. Luter pursues this possibility (see Luter, "Ruth," in A. B. Luter and B. C. Davis, *God Behind the Seen: Expositions of the Books of Ruth and Esther* [Expositor's Guide to the Historical Books; Grand Rapids: Baker, 1995], 14–15). See also A. B. Luter and R. O. Rigsby, "An Alternative Symmetrical Structuring of Ruth, with Implications for the Dating and Purpose Questions," *JETS* 39 (1996): 15–28. But this is doubtful, see the discussion in F. W. Bush, *Ruth, Esther* (WBC 9; Dallas: Word, 1996), 25–35.

2. A. J. Beldstein, "Female Companionships: If the Book of Ruth Were Written by a Woman ...," in *A Feminist Companion to Ruth*, ed. A. Brenner (Sheffield: Sheffield Academic Press, 1993), 116–35.

3. The opening paragraph and the concluding episode and genealogy obviously represent traditional male perspectives. See R. Bauckham, "The Book of Ruth and the Possibility of a Feminist Canonical Hermeneutic," *BibInt* 5 (1997): 29–45.

4. While there were literate females throughout the ancient Near East, the bulk of writers through the history of the region were males. Certainly the scribes in any redactional stage or copyists were males. See C. Meyers, "Returning Home: Ruth 1.8 and the Gendering of the Book of Ruth," in *A Feminist Companion to Ruth*, ed. A. Brenner (Sheffield: Sheffield Academic Press, 1993), 89.

to assess.[5] Moreover, the corpus of extrabiblical Hebrew, while thankfully growing through archaeological activities, is still small. Thus, possible contemporaneous documents of the same type are not really available for comparison. Nevertheless, the most recent evidence seems to suggest a late preexilic to early postexilic date.[6]

Canonical Status and Position

WHILE THE CANONICITY of Ruth has been almost unanimously accepted, the book's position in the canon has varied widely. Its canonical place divides broadly along two great traditional lines: the order generally found in the Hebrew Bible's textual traditions and the order found in the Septuagint (LXX), the Greek translation of the Old Testament.

In the vast majority of Hebrew manuscripts, Ruth is one of the five festal scrolls (Megilloth), which were part of the third division of the Hebrew Bible, the Ketubim or Writings. The grouping of these five scrolls or books was for functional, liturgical reasons.

But even so, in the Megilloth two different liturgical orders were used. The first grouping was a liturgical arrangement that followed a preconceived chronological/historical sequence:

Ruth (pertaining to David)
Song of Songs (Solomon's younger years)
Ecclesiastes (Solomon's older years)
Lamentations (exilic period)
Esther (postexilic/Persian period)

Generally in this tradition, the Megilloth follows Psalms, Job, and Proverbs. This tradition is the historically earlier one (rooted in the Tiberian Masoretic tradition of the ninth-tenth centuries A.D.). This order seems to be not only chronological but also thematic. In this arrangement, Ruth follows directly on the heels of Proverbs 31:10–31 (which focuses on *ʾēšet ḥayil*, "a woman of strength of character"). Ruth is called an *ʾēšet ḥayil* ("a woman of

---

5. For example, the linguistic evidence of Aramaisms is not particularly convincing; see P. T. Nash, "Ruth: An Exercise in Israelite Political Correctness or a Call to Proper Conversion?" in *The Pitcher Is Broken: Memorial Essays for Gösta W. Åhlstrom*, ed. H. G. Åhlstrom and L. K. Handy (JSOTSup 190; Sheffield: Sheffield Academic Press, 1995), 347–54.

6. For thorough recent discussions, see Bush, *Ruth, Esther*, 18–30 (slightly favoring an early postexilic date); and Hubbard, *The Book of Ruth*, 23–35 (favoring a preexilic date). Block argues at length for a late preexilic date, specifically by a northern author during the days of Josiah (*Judges, Ruth*, 590–98), while E. Zenger argues for a second-century B.C. date in the time of the Hasmoneans (*Das Buch Ruth* [ZBAT 8; Zurich: Theologischer Verlag, 1986], 28).

strength of character") in Ruth 3:11.[7] Obviously, this order has probably developed from thematic associations.

The second grouping was a liturgical arrangement that followed the order of the calendar of the festive year:

Song of Songs (*Passover*: Nisan = March-April)
Ruth (*Pentecost*: Sivan = May-June)
Lamentations (*Ninth of Ab*: Ab = August-September)
Ecclesiastes (*Tabernacles*: Tishri = September-October)
Esther (*Purim*: Adar = February-March)

In this tradition, the Megilloth follows Psalms, Proverbs, Job. This tradition is the historically later liturgical ordering.

Regardless of whether the arrangement is calendaric or historic/chronological/thematic, the liturgical ordering in the Hebrew Bible tradition is relatively late. It could not have arisen until after the period in which it became customary to read these five books at the major festivals of the Jewish year—a custom that arose during the sixth to the tenth centuries A.D.

A third ordering within the Hebrew Bible tradition is observed in the Babylonian Talmud (*b. B. Bat.* 14b). The tradition that it quotes appears to come from the first or second centuries A.D. Here the book of Ruth is placed at the beginning of the Writings, immediately before the book of Psalms. The Megilloth are not grouped together in this arrangement.[8]

The other major textual tradition is that of the LXX, in which Ruth is placed in the Former Prophets, immediately after Judges. Such a placement is understandable for at least two reasons. (1) The primary reason is that Ruth 1:1 ("In the days when the judges ruled [judged]") provides a natural linkage with the book of Judges.

(2) There appears to be contrastive thematic connections with the final story of Judges. In Judges 19–21, everything is done wrongly (see commentary on these chapters). Old institutions are thoroughly misapplied. Dismembering his concubine, a Levite calls the tribes to muster, acting as a self-appointed judge. The result is a civil war that nearly wipes out one of the tribes, the Benjamites. In order to keep the letter of their sworn oath not to supply wives for the remnant of the Benjamites—whose idea was that?—they put Jabesh Gilead to the sword and round up their virgin daughters; that

---

7. The book of Proverbs (esp. in Prov. 1–9) develops a contrast between two feminine personifications: "lady wisdom" and the "foolish woman" (ʾēšet kʾsîlût), the "prostitute" (zônâ), or the "strange woman" (ʾiššâ zārâ). Thus Ruth stands in clear contrast to these personifications of foolishness/folly.

8. For further discussion, see Bush, *Ruth, Esther*, 6–7.

proving insufficient, they allow the Benjamites to thoroughly disrupt the annual festival of Yahweh at Shiloh. In the whole miserable performance, the nation has obviously lost track of Yahweh completely!

Striking in this connection, perhaps, is the designation given to the Benjamites, who have fallen in 20:44, 46; after all sorts of military designations throughout the narrative, here they are *ʾanšē ḥāyil* (valiant fighters), recalling the description of Boaz (Ruth 2:1) and Ruth (Ruth 3:11). It is ironic that the victims of all this chaotic action are given the only accolades. One more thing: In the Israel of which Judges 19–21 tells, the only person who will give the Levite and his concubine hospitality in Gibeah is a sojourner (19:16).

The contrast with the Ruth story is striking. Older commentators often observed that the placement of the Ruth story after Judges is not due simply to their chronological connection, but also to the contrast between the two portrayals. That contrast, however, really pertains to Judges 19–21 only. Here are covenant, custom, and institutions gone awry, contrasted with a scene in which things go as they should, people make the right decisions, and Yahweh is anything but lost.[9]

Much debate has centered on which of these two traditions is older and original. It seems that they both arose among different elements of the Jewish community and existed side by side until the fourth century A.D. While there is no definitive evidence to discern which of the two has priority, it seems clear that the earliest Jewish traditions treated the book as an entity. Thus, it is difficult to see why the book would have been "demoted" from the Prophets to the Writings, while a "promotion" in the opposite direction is more easily understood.[10]

Unity

ALTHOUGH SOME SCHOLARS disagree, there is a general consensus that the story—at least through 4:17—exhibits an evident unity. Whether the extended genealogy of 4:18–22 is an inherent part of the book is another matter. Many scholars regard it as a later addition to an already finished story; to them, the "original" story had nothing to do with David and his lineage but was only later adapted for this purpose. The argument for this centers, in part, on the book's date (i.e., if the bulk of the book is dated to a preexilic context, then the genealogy is a later addition). If, however, the book

---

9. E. F. Campbell Jr., *Ruth* (AB 7; Garden City, N.Y.: Doubleday, 1975), 35–36.

10. Bush, *Ruth, Esther*, 7–9; Campbell, *Ruth*, 34–35. The Davidic genealogy at the end of Ruth perhaps served as an impetus in this "promotion."

comes from the time period implied above, there is practically no reason for the genealogy to be considered late.[11]

Recently, numerous scholars have argued for integrative connections of 4:18–22 with the rest of the book.[12] It seems clear that the genealogical section balances the narrative "family history" of the introduction (1:1–5). It also serves to link the short genealogy of 4:17b with the mention of Perez in 4:12 and confirms the blessing uttered in 4:11b–12. The genealogy functions as a coda, a story conclusion that completes the narrative discourse by relating it to the reader's own time in a variety of ways.[13] Moreover, it presents the story's characters receiving their just rewards, in being part of the long, blessed line of David. Finally, the genealogy honors Boaz, not only by including him but also by placing him in the seventh position.

Some have argued that the genealogy clashes with the story itself. In the story, Obed, who is the offspring of the levirate marriage, should be counted in the genealogical line of Elimelech-Mahlon; but in the genealogy, Obed is counted in the line of Boaz. However, the evidence gleaned from recent study of genealogies in the ancient Near East and the Bible demonstrates that genealogies change in structure and content when their function changes (see the section on Genealogy, below). Thus, in order to express David's right to exercise kingship, the descent has been traced through Boaz.[14]

The Concept of *Ḥesed*

THE CONCEPT OF *ḥesed* is important to understanding the book of Ruth since it is used to describe both secular and divine-human relationships. Unfortunately, it is a Hebrew word that no one English word can begin to convey accurately. Being expressive of relationships, the term connotes altogether the notions of covenantal loyalty, faithfulness, kindness, goodness, mercy, love, and compassion.[15] While paired with a wide range of other Hebrew words,

---

11. See the extended discussions of Hubbard, *The Book of Ruth*, 8–23; Bush, *Ruth, Esther*, 10–16.

12. See among others, Campbell, *Ruth*, 14–18; J. M. Sasson, *Ruth: A New Translation with a Philological Commentary and a Formalist-Folkorist Interpretation*, 2d ed. (Sheffield: Sheffield Academic Press, 1989), 179–83; and A. Berlin, *Poetics and Interpretation of Biblical Narrative* (Sheffield: Almond, 1983), 107–10.

13. The genealogy, then, is the work of the narrator, as spokesman for the Israelite narrative tradition, viewing the story of Ruth and putting it in the proper context in that narrative tradition. It is a kind of prologue and epilogue rolled into one, providing material that surrounds the story. This does not mean, however, that it is a late addition (Berlin, *Poetics*, 110).

14. Hubbard, *The Book of Ruth*, 19–20.

15. See most recently, G. Clark, *The Word Ḥesed in the Hebrew Bible* (JSOTSup 157; Sheffield: Sheffield Academic Press, 1993); R. Routledge, "Ḥesed As Obligation: A Re-examination," *TynBul* 46 (1995): 179–96; D. A. Baer and R. P. Gordon, "חסד," *NIDOTTE*, 2:211–18.

no single word can replace it in its relationship to the others, and thus none can provide an exact synonym. A summary of a number of major points concerning *ḥesed* is helpful:

- *Ḥesed* springs from and is based on relationship, usually some sort of prior relationship. Because of this, it is inherently tied to the concept of covenant (*bᵉrît*)[16] and is expressive of the deep and abiding loyalty and commitment between the parties of that covenant.
- While *ḥesed* contains an emotive quality that highlights issues of motive,[17] it is fundamentally an action. *Ḥesed* recognizes and acts to relieve an urgent essential need on the part of the recipient. It is not just something nice for someone to do gratuitously or because it expresses "special favor." When it is a specific act, the essential need it meets is normally "deliverance from dire straits"; when it is a series of acts, it comes out as ongoing protection "from similar dangers."[18] *Ḥesed* refers to an act performed for the benefit of a person in real and desperate need, in the context of a deep and enduring commitment between the parties concerned.[19]
- It is performed for a situationally weaker person by a situationally more powerful person. This is most clearly illustrated in God's acts of *ḥesed* for his people.
- It is a voluntary act of extraordinary mercy or generosity, a "going beyond the call of duty."[20] Because it is performed by a situationally more powerful person who has options, *ḥesed* is something such a person can decide not to do. No sanction can really force it. However, because some sort of prior relationship is clearly or assumedly the background for *ḥesed*-acts, side-by-side with the option *not* to act is a clear-cut responsibility *to* act.[21]

Yahweh is the one who models *ḥesed* (over two-thirds of the word's total number of occurrences are God's *ḥesed* to humans). Clark argues that it is "a

---

16. It is clear that acts of *ḥesed* can precede the establishment of a covenant (*bᵉrît*) and do not require the establishment of a covenant. However, the establishment of a covenant enhances the facilitation of acts of *ḥesed* because the covenant secures the continuation of mutual acts of *ḥesed*. The existence of a covenant assures the permanence of *ḥesed*.

17. Hence its semantic overlap with terms like *raḥᵃmîm* (maternal compassion). True *ḥesed* should act out of pure motives. See A. Jepsen, "Gnade und Barmherzigkeit im Alt Testament," *Kerygma and Dogma* 7 (1961): 266. Contra K. D. Sakenfeld, *The Meaning of Ḥesed in the Hebrew Bible: A New Inquiry* (Missoula, Mont.: Scholars Press, 1978), 73.

18. Sakenfeld, *The Meaning of Ḥesed*, 24, 44–45.

19. Clark, *The Word Ḥesed in the Hebrew Bible*, 192.

20. Sakenfeld, *The Meaning of Ḥesed*, 233–34.

21. E. F. Campbell Jr., "Naomi, Boaz, and Ruth: Ḥesed (חֶסֶד) and Change," *Austin Seminary Bulletin* 105 (1990): 64–74, esp. 67.

---

characteristic of God rather than human beings; it is rooted in the divine nature."[22] It is not only the basis on which the divine-human relationship is established, but the means and enablement for its continuance. *Ḥesed* precedes, and indeed gives rise to, the covenant (*bᵉrît*), which then provides additional assurance that God's promise will not fail. While the righteous may call for help based on a relationship in good order, there can also be appeal for help based not on any human merit, but rather on the faithfulness of God to help the undeserving to bring forgiveness and restoration. In this, there is a connection with God's *raḥᵃmîm* (maternal compassion). The manner of caring, committing, initiating, and responding that God demonstrates in the concept of "doing *ḥesed*" becomes the definition of responsible human behavior. The *ḥesed* of Yahweh that is experienced and known in the community comes to define what human *ḥesed* can be, ought to be, and sometimes is.[23]

In human contexts, *ḥesed* is loving commitment within a relationship, most often, though not exclusively, within the setting of the family or clan. It represents the social bonds of loyalty toward others within the community of God's people. *Ḥesed* is mutual: Those who are shown *ḥesed* are expected, not by law but by social and moral convention, to reciprocate.[24] This has particular implications for the social life of God's people where *ḥesed*, expressed in right conduct toward one another, is expected both because of the mutual relationship established through membership of the covenant community and as a proper response to the *ḥesed* shown by God. Because *ḥesed* is ultimately voluntary, it is not a legal obligation, though its failure is taken seriously.[25]

The book of Ruth employs *ḥesed* on both the divine and human levels. The word occurs three times in the book. In Ruth 1:8, there is a clear reference to Yahweh's *ḥesed* (the passage also contains a reference to human *ḥesed*). The Lord's *ḥesed* is the factor that eventually leads to the successful remarriage of Naomi's daughter-in-law, so that it cannot help but be recognized in the provision of a "kinsman-redeemer" (*gōʾēl*) for Ruth (cf. 4:14). Moreover, while not stated, Yahweh's act of "giving" a child in Ruth 4 should certainly be understood as an act of *ḥesed*.

Interestingly, the only human actors who are *explicitly* said to have exercised *ḥesed* are Orpah (once) and Ruth (twice) (1:8; 3:10). Thus, ironically, Moabites (in particular Ruth) are the people who most clearly manifest *ḥesed* in this book.

---

22. Clark, *The Word Ḥesed in the Hebrew Bible*, 267.
23. Campbell, "Naomi, Boaz, and Ruth: Ḥesed (חסד) and Change," 69–70.
24. Routledge, "*Ḥesed* As Obligation: A Re-examination," 179–96.
25. Ibid., 182.

Boaz's acts of *ḥesed* are only seen by way of allusions. In Ruth 2:20 the text is ambiguous as to whether Boaz's or Yahweh's *ḥesed* is in view. The NIV translates: "'The LORD bless him!' Naomi said to her daughter-in-law. 'He has not stopped showing his kindness [*ḥesed*] to the living and the dead.'" This translation seems to understand the reference to be to Boaz (though not necessarily). The NRSV, however, translates: "Then Naomi said to her daughter-in-law, "Blessed be he by the LORD, whose kindness [*ḥesed*] has not forsaken the living or the dead!'" This translation clearly understands the reference to be to Yahweh.[26]

Could this be a case of deliberate ambiguity?[27] Whatever the case, throughout the book, *ḥesed* is the underlying factor in various acts of loyalty and mercy. It is the issue of *ḥesed* that serves as the basis for the discussion between Boaz and Ruth as negotiations are made (3:9–13).

Thus, the *ḥesed* that humans show to one another is among the most fitting means God can use to display his own *ḥesed*. This is certainly a contrast to the book of Judges, where loyalty within the bounds of the covenant is scarce.

Genre and Purpose

SCHOLARLY OPINION CONCERNING the genre and purpose of the book of Ruth is diverse. *Genre* classifications attached to Ruth include such labels as "folktale," "novella," "short story," and "edifying short story."[28] The determination of the genres of Old Testament narrative is a notoriously difficult task. This is especially true when there are no clear ancient parallels (as in the case of Ruth).[29] Modern genre categories are not adequate and can be invariably misleading. Nevertheless, perhaps most helpful is Bush's designation of Ruth

---

26. The general consensus of scholars is that the reference is to Yahweh's, not Boaz's, *ḥesed*. See, e.g., Hubbard *The Book of Ruth*, 50–51, 186, 212–13; Bush, *Ruth, Esther*, 134–36; Block, *Judges, Ruth*, 611, 672–73.

27. The possibility of deliberate ambiguity (so that both Yahweh and Boaz can be inferred) should be considered. Cf. the case with Othniel in Judg. 3:9 (see commentary above). While Sakenfeld concludes that the reference is to Yahweh's, not Boaz's, *ḥesed*, it is interesting that she closes her discussion by asking whether there just might be deliberate ambiguity here (*The Meaning of Ḥesed*, 106). See also Campbell, "Naomi, Boaz, and Ruth: Ḥesed (חסד) and Change," 67.

28. See Sasson, *Ruth*, 197–221; W. Humphreys, "Novella," in *Saga, Legend, Tale, Novella, Fable: Narrative Forms in Old Testament Literature*, ed. G. Coats (JSOTSup 35; Sheffield: JSOT Press, 1985), 82–96; Campbell, *Ruth*, 4–10; Hubbard, *The Book of Ruth*, 47–48; Bush, *Ruth, Esther*, 30–47.

29. There are short stories in the extant literature of the ancient Near East; but none in which the major characters are women, especially a foreign woman, with familial and societal issues playing such important roles.

as an edifying short story, since it gets at the didactic or instructional aspects of the book.[30]

The book's *purpose* is likewise difficult to assess. Part of the difficulty is in how much weight of consideration should be given to the genealogy of Ruth 4:18–22. On a number of levels, different purposes are discernible. On one didactic level, the short story seems to present Naomi, Ruth, and Boaz as models for emulation.[31] On another, its theme of the continuity of God's people in the land demonstrates intentional links with the patriarchal narratives as well as with the postexilic experiences of the Israelites.[32] On a completely different level (esp. based on the coda, the final part of the book), the book functions as a legitimization of the Davidic monarchy, an apology for his kingship.[33]

The Structure of the Book of Ruth

THE BOOK OF RUTH is comprised of six units and a coda. The first and last units function as a prologue and epilogue respectively. These evince numerous thematic parallels. The remaining four units form four balanced acts that communicate the story. Acts 1 and 4 have two scenes each and demonstrate remarkable parallels. Acts 2 and 3 have three scenes each, structured along similar lines. The turning point of the book occurs exactly midway through it (2:20; see Outline).

The Prologue (1:1–5) provides the setting and predicament. A Judahite family's males have died in Moab so that the main character of the book, Naomi, is without a male to care for her.

In the acts that follow Naomi's emptiness is developed. Act 1 narrates her return (1:6–22). It has two scenes: Scene 1, in which Naomi and her daughters-in-law are on the road to Judah (1:6–19a), and Scene 2, in which Naomi and Ruth arrive at Bethlehem (1:19b–22).

Act 2 narrates the developments between Ruth and Boaz in the fields (2:1–23). It is divided into three scenes: Scene 1, in which Ruth gleans in a field that happens to belong to Boaz, Naomi's relative (2:1–3); Scene 2, in

---

30. Bush, *Ruth, Esther*, 30–47.

31. Ibid., 52. Some scholars have claimed that the book of Ruth is focused on the significance of *ḥesed*.

32. A. Berlin points out many of these connections ("Big Theme, Little Book," *BRev* 12 [1996]: 40–43, 47–48).

33. Hubbard, *The Book of Ruth*, 42; M. D. Gow, *The Book of Ruth: Its Structure, Theme and Purpose* (Leicester: Apollos, 1992), 207–10. Block has recently argued that the book is an edifying short story functioning as an apology to the northern Israelites for the Davidic dynasty, legitimating Josiah's kingship (*Judges, Ruth*, 599–616).

which Ruth and Boaz meet on the harvest field and Boaz is exceedingly generous (2:4–17a); and Scene 3, in which Naomi evaluates the meeting: Boaz is one of their kinsman-redeemers (2:17b–23).

Act 3 narrates further developments in the relationship of Ruth and Boaz at the threshing floor (3:1–18). Like Act 2, it is divided into three scenes: Scene 1, in which Naomi discloses her plan for Ruth and Boaz (3:1–5); Scene 2, in which Ruth executes Naomi's plan and Boaz offers to be the kinsman-redeemer (3:6–15); and Scene 3, in which Naomi evaluates the encounter: Boaz will act (3:16–18).

Act 4 narrates Boaz's arrangements to marry Ruth (4:1–12). It has two scenes: Scene 1, in which Boaz confronts the unnamed kinsman (4:1–8); and Scene 2, in which Boaz acquires the right to redeem Naomi and Ruth (4:9–12).

The Epilogue (4:13–17) narrates the conclusion and resolution to the main character Naomi: A son is born to Ruth and Boaz, which restores Naomi to life and fullness.

Finally, there is a coda to the story—a genealogy that traces the ten generations from Perez to David (4:18–22; see section on Genealogy, below).

It is abundantly clear that the writer of the book of Ruth uses space, time, and circumstance to build the central message of the book—Naomi's restoration from emptiness to fullness through the selfless acts of loyal love (*ḥesed*) by Ruth and Boaz. This takes place first in connection with Naomi's return from Moab to the Promised Land and to Bethlehem ("house of food"). It then progresses with the harvest season, when the fullness of the land is gathered in. All aspects of the story keep the reader's attention focused on the central issue. Consideration of these and other literary devices enhances one's understanding of the book.

Contrast is also used to good effect: pleasant (the meaning of "Naomi") and bitter (1:20), full and empty (1:21), and the living and the dead (2:20). This use of contrast is most strikingly developed between two of the main characters, Ruth and Boaz: The one is a young, foreign, destitute widow, while the other is a middle-aged, well-to-do Israelite securely established in his home community. For each, there is a corresponding character whose actions highlight, by contrast, her or his selfless acts: Ruth versus Orpah, Boaz versus the unnamed kinsman-redeemer.

One significant aspect to the book is the issue of initiative. After the disasters of the prologue and the lamentful bitter emptiness expressed in Act 1, each of the main characters seizes the initiative. In Act 2, it is Ruth who seizes the initiative, since Naomi is engrossed in self-absorbing bitterness and despair. She goes out to glean, to meet the needs of the two destitute widows. In Act 3, it is Naomi who seizes the initiative. She concocts a plan to meet the needs of her daughter-in-law. In Act 4, Boaz seizes the initiative. He secures the rights of redemption for the field and for the marriage of Ruth. In all three cases, the initiator is acting out of or motivated by issues of *ḥesed;* and in all three cases, unexpected positive results occur.

Some scholars contend that the coda of the book of Ruth (i.e., the genealogy of 4:18–22) is the structural counterpart of 1:1–5. Certainly there are indications that the two sections might mirror each other thematically. For example, as the book opened with names associated with tragedy, so it closes with names associated with triumph ("diminishment" versus "fullness" of progeny).[34] Similarly, Porten observes how the book opens with the judges and Elimelech ("My God is King") and closes with God's appointed king, David.[35]

Consequently, the coda anticipates a future beyond the story's immediate time period. The genealogy has been trimmed unmistakably to place the story's main male character, Boaz, in the favored seventh slot, thereby conveying a moral of particular interest to the historically minded Hebrews: Common people achieve uncommon ends when they act unselfishly toward each other.[36]

Background Issues

The Gōʾēl and the Levirate Marriage

A "KINSMAN-REDEEMER" (*GŌʾĒL*) was the nearest adult male blood relative who served as an advocate for any vulnerable and/or unfortunate clan member in order to correct any disruption to clan wholeness, well-being, or *šālôm* (especially through the redemption or restoration of property, persons, or lineage).[37] The "clan" (*mišpāḥâ*) or "linear descent group"[38] seems to have been the focus of the law of the *gōʾēl* (Lev. 25:48–49).[39] Apparently, this clan "wholeness" encompassed both living and deceased members of the clan or kinship group.[40]

---

34. Hubbard, *The Book of Ruth*, 17.

35. B. Porten, "The Scroll of Ruth: A Rhetorical Study," *Gratz College Annual* 7 (1978): 23–49, esp. 24–25.

36. J. M. Sasson, "Ruth," in *The Literary Guide to the Bible*, ed. R. Alter and F. Kermode (Cambridge, Mass.: Harvard Univ. Press, 1987), 321.

37. R. L. Hubbard Jr., "The Gōʾel in Ancient Israel: Theological Reflections on an Israelite Institution," *BBR* 1 (1991): 3–19.

38. See the discussion of Israelite social structures in the introduction to the book of Judges, pp. 25–28.

39. Mullen feels that the order of kinship by which the *gōʾēl* was determined is given in Lev. 25:48–49. See E. T. Mullen Jr., "Gōʾēl," in *DDD*, cols. 706–8.

40. Hubbard, *The Book of Ruth*, 51.

Since there is no similar institution in modern Western societies, there is no word in English remotely equivalent. Moreover, while similar social functionaries are attested in other tribal cultures, the terminology associated with the *gōʾēl* is almost exclusively Hebrew, and its basic meaning of "redeem, buy back, recover, restore" is derived from its use in law and custom of the Israelite clans.[41]

There are a number of specific sociolegal contexts in which the kinsman-redeemer (*gōʾēl*) takes upon himself the duties of *gᵊʾullâ* (redemption, recovery):[42]

- to redeem (i.e., reclaim through monetary payment) property once owned by an impoverished clan relative but sold out of economic necessity (Lev. 25:24–34; Jer. 32:1–15)
- to redeem impoverished clan relatives who were forced to sell themselves into servitude to a resident alien or another Israelite (Lev. 25:47–55)[43]
- to act as the blood redeemer (*gōʾēl haddām*—lit., kinsman redeemer of the blood) to avenge the killing of a clan relative, restoring clan wholeness (Num. 35:12, 19–27; Deut. 19:6, 12; Josh. 20:2–3, 5, 9)
- to act as recipient of money paid as restitution for a wrong committed against a clan relative now deceased, hence restoring clan wholeness (Num. 5:8)
- to assist a clan relative in a lawsuit so that justice is done (Job 19:25; Ps. 119:154; Prov. 23:11; Jer. 50:34; Lam. 3:58—note that the Lord is the *gōʾēl* in some of these passages)
- to redeem the wife of the deceased[44] (i.e., acquire legal right) in order to "raise up the name of the deceased upon his property" by acquir-

---

41. Mullen, "*Gōʾēl*," col. 706.

42. J. Unterman, "The Social-Legal Origin for the Image of God as Redeemer גואל of Israel," in *Pomegranates and Golden Bells: Studies in Biblical, Jewish, and Near Eastern Ritual, Law, and Literature in Honor of Jacob Milgrom*, ed. D. P. Wright, D. N. Freedman, and A. Hurvitz (Winona Lake, Ind.: Eisenbrauns, 1995), 399–405.

43. While there may have been a social hierarchy (from top to bottom): *gēr* (foreigner) → *tôšāb* (temporary resident) → *śākîr* (hired worker) → *ʿebed* (slave), since Yahweh alone owned the land, the Israelites are ironically likened to "foreigner" (*gēr*) and "temporary resident" (*tôšāb*) (Lev. 25:23–24). See R. Rendtorff, "The *Gēr* in the Priestly Laws of the Pentateuch," in *Ethnicity and the Bible*, ed. M. G. Brett (Biblical Interpretation Series 19; Leiden: Brill, 1996), 77–87, esp. 79.

44. Brichto observes: "The *gōʾēl* was not merely a close-kinsman obligated to blood-vengeance or privileged to redeem property. The *gōʾēl* is he who redeems the dead from the danger of his afterlife by continuing his line." See H. C. Brichto, "Kin, Cult, Land, and Afterlife—A Biblical Complex," *HUCA* 44 (1973): 1–54, esp. 21.

ing "the wife of the deceased" (see comments below on the law of the levirate marriage in Deut. 25:5–10).[45] This restores clan wholeness

- to redeem or restore a clan widow facing old age alone without anyone to care for her (Ruth 4:14–15)

The word *'āḥ* (brother) is used in some of these contexts with the nuance of "clan relative" (i.e., any relative of "the linear descent group" [*mišpāḥâ*]). In all seven instances, *mišpāḥâ* wholeness or restoration is accomplished by the actions of the *gō'ēl*.

Important to the understanding of Ruth is the realization that the *gō'ēl*, while having a responsibility to perform "redemption/restoration" (*gᵉʾullâ*), was not obligated to do so. The fact that there was an apparent hierarchy of response (Lev. 25:48–49) indicates that volition, choice, determination, and so on were involved.[46] Thus the *gō'ēl* must be willing to perform *gᵉʾullâ*. This is a crucial aspect to the role or function of the *gō'ēl*, which is often overlooked. The same aspect of volition is present in the levirate marriage (see below).

In Leviticus 25, the activity of the *gō'ēl* is portrayed as a follow-up to Yahweh's redemption of the Israelites from Egypt.[47] The actions of the "Great Kinsman-redeemer" in the Exodus from Egypt is the basis for the *gō'ēl*'s actions. Thus the activity of the *gō'ēl* perpetuates the first redemption from Egyptian slavery and also, at the same time, provides a redemption from unending servitude to later pharaohs within Israel's own ranks. Thus the human *gō'ēl* carries out the redemption policy of the "Great *Gō'ēl*," Yahweh himself. The human *gō'ēl* personally represents Yahweh in such transactions.[48]

Consequently, it is not difficult to see how the New Testament could interpret Christ's death in terms of the *gō'ēl*. Jesus' function as the ultimate *gō'ēl* is highlighted by the fact that he is not ashamed to call us "brothers" (Heb. 2:11; see comments on 4:1–12).

The levirate marriage is found in three passages[49]: (1) Deuteronomy 25:5–10 (legal statements), (2) Genesis 38 (Judah and Tamar), and (3)

---

45. Scholars usually refer to the marriage of Boaz and Ruth as a levirate marriage. However, Hubbard (*The Book of Ruth*, 50–51, 57) argues for a distinction between the levirate (*yābam*) and "redemption" (*gᵉʾullâ*) marriages. But there seems to me to be clear overlap with the issue being family or clan wholeness and continuity.

46. The very conditional framing of the laws of the *gō'ēl* also indicate that volition is involved. It is in this volitional aspect of the *gō'ēl* that the concept of *ḥesed* comes into play.

47. Hubbard, "The Go'el in Ancient Israel," 11–12.

48. Interestingly, in Isaiah, *gō'ēl* refers exclusively to Yahweh.

49. Often these three passages are thought to come from different sources and/or traditions and are arranged chronologically by commentator preferences. For a discussion and evaluation, see R. Westbrook, "The Law of the Biblical Levirate," *Revue Internationale des*

Ruth 4 (Boaz and Ruth). "The purpose of the levirate was to prevent extinction of the deceased's title to his landed inheritance."[50] Through it, family or clan "wholeness" was restored. Thus it was clearly a legal fiction, insofar as the offspring from the levirate belonged fictionally to the deceased line. Westbrook argues: "It is clear, therefore, that the levirate is a great sacrifice on the part of the brother, for he might just let the deceased remain without issue and take over the inheritance for himself and his progeny."[51] Though the offspring from the levirate belonged fictionally to the deceased's line, the offspring took their name from the *levir* (as Gen. 38 and Ruth 4 manifest).

In light of this, the reluctance of the *levir* in Deuteronomy 25 and Genesis 38 are understandable. However, in Genesis 38, had Onan refused outright, he would have gained nothing, since either his father or younger brother could have performed the levirate and thus produced an heir to Er. Moreover, as the firstborn, Er was entitled to a double share, as would be his fictional son, so Onan's potential loss was even greater. Thus, Onan devised a subterfuge or trick. He ostensibly undertook the responsibility given to him but took care that no heir could possibly result from the union. He had intercourse with Tamar but made sure that he did not impregnate her. By doing this (i.e., performing the duty in form but not in fact), he hoped to gain for himself his dead brother's inheritance (along with his own). Greed for property was thus Onan's motivation. Hence, God judged him. But amazingly, God's grace at the end of the narrative is even the greater when we realize that Tamar gives birth to twins—conveniently and ironically—one for the "name" of each dead brother!

While a simple conclusion might be that it is the deceased's memory that is to be preserved and that the levirate achieves this purpose by attributing offspring to him, in Genesis 38 and Ruth 4 the offspring of the levirate union is subsequently referred to as the issue of the *levir* (Judah and Boaz respectively) and not of the deceased (Er and Mahlon). This realization demonstrates clearly that the memory of the deceased is not the primary purpose of the levirate marriage. Rather, it is *property inheritance* that is at the root of the levirate marriage.[52]

Droits de l'Antiquité 24 (1977): 65–87, esp. 65–68; idem, *Property and the Family in Biblical Law* (JSOTSup 193; Sheffield: Sheffield Academic Press, 1991), 69–89. Variations of this type of marriage are found in other ancient Near Eastern cultures.

50. Westbrook, *Property and the Family*, 73. He concludes that all three biblical sources reflect an institution with this single legal object.

51. Ibid.

52. For further discussion of the detailed legal aspects of the levirate, see K. L. Younger Jr., "Two Comparative Notes on the Book of Ruth," *JANES* 26 (1998): 128–31.

In the case of Ruth, where the land has already been alienated, redemption of it "triggers" the levirate duty.[53] Since Boaz is not an heir, he must redeem the land—as well as perform the levirate marriage. In Genesis 38 and Deuteronomy 25, the *levirs* are already heirs and so there is no need for land redemption.

In Ruth, the narrator is also careful to mention that the land belonged to Elimelech. Elimelech (or his wife Naomi for him) sold the land and went to Moab with his two sons. All three died in Moab. Thus the two sons, Mahlon and Chilion, never came to own the family property at all. The redeemer of the land would receive his right to purchase from Elimelech, and the two sons would again drop out of the picture (since they had never actually inherited it).[54]

There is no point in discussing whether Naomi could have owned the land or not, as it states plainly in 4:3 that Elimelech owned the land and Naomi merely sold it. If a woman did not have the capacity to own land, it does not mean that she could not act as agent for her husband to acquire (or alienate) on his behalf (see Prov. 31:16).

I am not sure it is necessary to distinguish between a levirate marriage and a *gōʾēl* marriage, as Hubbard does.[55] The term "levirate" is a Latin imposition on a Hebrew custom that may have been more *extended* in a clan or linear descent group (i.e., the *mišpāḥâ*) than just brothers in a nuclear family. In fact, the law of the *gōʾēl* is clearly linked to the *mišpāḥâ*. Westbrook's observation that in Genesis 38 and Deuteronomy 25 the individuals are already heirs of the property whereas Boaz in Ruth 4 is not an heir seems important. The "redemption" of the land "triggers," so to speak, the levirate obligation.

Genealogy

RECENT STUDIES HAVE clarified the function and role of genealogies in the tribal societies of the ancient Near East and the Bible. Linear genealogies[56] functioned to legitimate claims to position, authority, or power in various political and societal contexts.[57] Moreover, they also served didactic or instructional purposes. They display two features: depth (i.e., the number of names in the list) and fluidity (flexibility in which names are included).

---

53. See Westbrook, "Redemption of Land," *Israel Law Review* 6 (1971): 371; H. Brichto, "Kin, Cult, Land and Afterlife," 15–16.

54. Westbrook, "The Law of the Biblical Levirate," 77.

55. Hubbard, *The Book of Ruth*, 50–51, 57.

56. In contrast to segmented genealogies (i.e., the "family tree" genealogies).

57. R. R. Wilson, *Sociological Approaches to the Old Testament* (Philadelphia: Fortress, 1984), 57–61.

Normally, there was a tendency to limit the maximum length of a written genealogy to five to ten generations.[58] This is the case with many biblical linear genealogies (cf. Gen. 4:17–24; 5:1–32; 11:10–26; 25:12–15; 1 Sam. 9:1). Consequently, it is not uncommon to find Near Eastern genealogies being modified by the addition or omission of names.[59] Though there are many reasons for fluidity, the most common reason results from the loss of names as new generations are added. The names at the end are the well-known recent generations, and the names at the beginning are the revered, honored founders, whose prestige and power the genealogy is often intended to invoke. Hence, loss of names, often termed "telescoping" or "gapping," usually occurs in the middle of the list.[60]

In its depth (ten members), the genealogy of Ruth 4:18–22 is paralleled by other biblical linear genealogies as well as by the extant ancient Near Eastern linear genealogies. Ruth 4:18–22 also manifests the "telescoping" characteristic of such genealogies.[61] At the beginning of the list, for example, Perez and Hezron are the firmly established founding ancestors of the tribe of Judah (cf. Gen. 46:12; Num. 26:21). At the end of the list, Boaz, Obed, Jesse, and David represent the well-known recent generations. Furthermore, Boaz and Obed are germane to the story, and the sequence Jesse-David is well known elsewhere (e.g., 1 Sam. 16:1–23; 17:12; 22:9; 25:10; 1 Kings 12:16). The sequence Amminadab-Nahshon is fixed in the Mosaic traditions. It is perhaps, then, significant that Ram and Salmon, which exhibit the widest variation in form and spelling in all the versional attestations (and for Salmon in the MT as well), are the two names that link, on the one hand, the patriarchal generations to those of the Mosaic era (i.e., Ram), and, on the other hand, the names of the Mosaic era to those of the recent generations.

Since genealogies functioned to legitimate claims to position, authority, or power in various political and societal contexts, a persuasive case can be made that 4:18–22, rather than being an insipid anticlimax, brings closure to the whole by underlining the significance of the story's resolution: Naomi's return to life and fullness through the birth of Obed. That resolution led two generations later to David.

---

58. R. R. Wilson, *Genealogy and History in the Biblical World* (New Haven, Conn.: Yale Univ. Press, 1977), 133–34.

59. Cf. the New Testament situation in the impositional structure of Matthew's genealogy of Christ.

60. In Gen. 5 and 11, there are exactly ten generations. These also evince examples of "telescoping" or "gapping" of names (e.g., compare 1 Chron. 6:3–14; Ezra 7:1–5). The didactic function of genealogies is also observable in Gen. 5 and 11. See T. D. Alexander, "Genealogies, Seed and the Compositional Unity of Genesis," *TynBul* 44 (1993): 261–67.

61. See Bush, *Ruth, Esther*, 14–16.

Outline

Prologue: Misery and Emptiness (1:1–6)
  (Setting and predicament: A Judahite family's males die in Moab: Naomi is without a male to care for her)

  Act 1. Naomi's Return (1:7–22)
     (responsibilities inherent in ties of kinship)

  Act 2. Ruth and Boaz in the Fields (2:1–23)
     (the character of Boaz and Ruth: he is a *gibbôr ḥayil*)

  Act 3. Ruth and Boaz at the Threshing Floor (3:1–18)
     (the character of Boaz and Ruth: she is an *ʾēšet ḥayil*

  Act 4. Boaz Arranges to Marry Ruth (4:1–12)
     (responsibilities inherent in ties of kinship)

Epilogue: Satisfaction and Fullness (4:13–17)
  (Conclusion and resolution: son born to Ruth and Boaz; Naomi is restored to life and fullness)

Coda: Genealogy (4:18–22)

Bibliography of Ruth

Alexander, T. D. "Genealogies, Seed and the Compositional Unity of Genesis." *TynBul* 44 (1993): 261–67.

Ashbel, D. "There Was a Famine in the Land . . . (Ruth 1:1)." *Yediot* 29 (1965): 221–26 (in Hebrew).

Baer, D. A., and R. P. Gordon. "חסד." *NIDOTTE*, 2:211–18.

Bauckham, R. "The Book of Ruth and the Possibility of a Feminist Canonical Hermeneutic." *BibInt* 5 (1997): 29–45.

Beattie, D. R. G. *The Targum of Ruth.* Aramaic Targum 19. Collegeville, Minn.: Liturgical, 1994.

Beldstein, A. J. "Female Companionships: If the Book of Ruth Were Written by a Woman. . . ." Pp. 116–35 in *A Feminist Companion to Ruth.* Ed. A. Brenner. Sheffield: Sheffield Academic, 1993.

Berlin, A. "Big Theme, Little Book." *BRev* 12 (1996): 40–43, 47–48.

_____. *Poetics and Interpretation of Biblical Narrative.* Sheffield: Almond, 1983.

Bernstein, M. J. "Two Multivalent Readings in the Ruth Narrative." *JSOT* 50 (1991): 15–26.

Block, D. I. *Judges, Ruth.* NAC 6. Nashville: Broadman & Holman, 1999.

Borowski, O. *Agriculture in Iron Age Israel.* Winona Lake, Ind.: Eisenbrauns, 1987.

Brichto, H. C. "Kin, Cult, Land, and Afterlife—A Biblical Complex." *HUCA* 44 (1973): 1–54.

Bush, F. W. "Ruth 4:17: A Semantic Wordplay." Pp. 3–14 in *"Go to the Land I Will Show You": Studies in Honor of Dwight W. Young.* Ed. J. E. Coleson and V. H. Matthews. Winona Lake, Ind.: Eisenbrauns, 1996.

_____. *Ruth, Esther.* WBC 9. Dallas: Word, 1996.

Campbell, E. F., Jr. "Naomi, Boaz, and Ruth: Hesed (חסד) and Change." *Austin Seminary Bulletin* 105 (1990): 64–74.

_____. *Ruth.* AB 7. Garden City, N.Y.: Doubleday, 1975.

Carasik, M. "Ruth 2,7: Why the Overseer Was Embarrassed." *ZAW* 107 (1995): 493.

Clark, G. *The Word Ḥesed in the Hebrew Bible.* JSOTSup 157. Sheffield: Sheffield Academic Press, 1993.

Fewell, D. N., and D. M. Gunn, "'A Son Is Born to Naomi!': Literary Allusions and Interpretation in the Book of Ruth." *JSOT* 40 (1988): 99–108.

Gow, M. D. *The Book of Ruth: Its Structure, Theme and Purpose.* Leicester: Apollos, 1992.

_____. "The Significance of Literary Structure for the Translation of the Book of Ruth." *BT* 35 (1984): 309–20.

Hertzberg, H. W. *Die Bücher Josua, Richter, Ruth.* 5th ed. Das Alte Testament Deutsch 9. Göttingen: Vandenhoek & Ruprecht, 1973.

Hiebert, P. S. "Whence Shall Help Come to Me?: The Biblical Widow." Pp. 134–37 in *Gender and Difference.* Ed. P. L. Day. Minneapolis: Fortress, 1989.

Howell, J. C. "Ruth 1:1–8." *Int* 51 (1997): 281–84.

Hubbard, R. L., Jr. *The Book of Ruth.* NICOT. Grand Rapids: Eerdmans, 1988.

_____. "The *Goʾel* in Ancient Israel: Theological Reflections on an Israelite Institution." *BBR* 1 (1991): 3–19.

_____. "Ruth IV.17: A New Solution." *VT* 38 (1988): 293–301.

Huey, F. B., Jr. "Ruth." Pp. 509–49 in vol. 3, *Expositor's Bible Commentary.* Ed. F. E. Gaebelein. Grand Rapids: Zondervan, 1992.

Humphreys, W. "Novella." Pp. 82–96 in *Saga, Legend, Tale, Novella, Fable: Narrative Forms in Old Testament Literature.* Ed. G. Coats. JSOTSup 35. Sheffield: JSOT Press, 1985.

Hyman, R. T. "Questions and Changing Identity in the Book of Ruth." *USQR* 39 (1984): 190.

Jongeling, B. "*HZʾT NʿMY* (Ruth 1:19)." *VT* 28 (1978): 474–77.

Kalmin, R. "Levirate Law." *ABD*, 4:296–97.

Kennedy, A. "The Root *GʿR* in the Light of Semantic Analysis." *JBL* 106 (1987): 47–64.

Layton, S. C. "Leaves from an Onomastician's Notebook." *ZAW* 108 (1996): 608–20.

Leggett, D. A. *The Levirate and Goel Institutions in the Old Testament with Special Attention to the Book of Ruth.* Cherry Hill, N.J.: Mack, 1974.

Loader, J. A. "Of Barley, Bulls, Land, and Levirate." Pp. 123–38 in *Studies in Deuteronomy in Honour of S. J. Labuschagne on the Occasion of His Sixty-fifth Birthday.* VTSup 53. Leiden: Brill, 1994.

Luter, A. B. "The Chiastic Structure of Ruth 2." *BBR* 3 (1993): 49–58.

_____. "Ruth." In A. B. Luter and B. C. Davis, *God Behind the Seen: Expositions of the Books of Ruth and Esther.* Expositor's Guide to the Historical Books. Grand Rapids: Baker, 1995.

Luter, A. B., and R. O. Rigsby, "An Alternative Symmetrical Structuring of Ruth, with Implications for the Dating and Purpose Questions." *JETS* 39 (1995): 15–28.

Meyers, C. "Returning Home: Ruth 1.8 and the Gendering of the Book of Ruth." Pp. 85–114 in *A Feminist Companion to Ruth.* Ed. A. Brenner. Sheffield: Sheffield Academic Press, 1993.

Morris, L. "Ruth." Pp. 217–318 in A. Cundall and L. Morris, *Judges, and Ruth.* TOTC. Downers Grove, Ill.: InterVarsity, 1968.

Murphy, R. E. *Wisdom Literature: Job, Proverbs, Ruth, Canticles, Ecclesiastes, and Esther.* FOTL 13. Grand Rapids: Eerdmans, 1981.

Nash, P. T. "Ruth: An Exercise in Israelite Political Correctness or a Call to Proper Conversion?" Pp. 347–54 in *The Pitcher Is Broken: Memorial Essays for Gösta W. Åhlstrom.* Ed. H. G. Åhlstrom and L. K. Handy. JSOTSup 190. Sheffield: Sheffield Academic Press, 1995.

Nielsen, K. *Ruth: A Commentary.* OTL. Louisville: Westminster John Knox, 1997.

Parker, S. B. "The Birth Announcement." Pp. 133–49 in *Ascribe to the Lord: Essays in Honor of P. C. Craigie.* Ed. L. Eslinger and G. Taylor. JSOTSup 67. Sheffield: JSOT Press, 1988.

Porten, B. "The Scroll of Ruth: A Rhetorical Study." *Gratz College Annual* 7 (1978): 23–49.

Rauber, D. "Literary Values in the Bible: The Book of Ruth." *JBL* 89 (1970): 27–37.

Riesener, I. *Der Stamm ʿbd in Alten Testament: Eine Wortuntersuchung unter Berücksichtigung neuerer sprachwissenschaftlicher Methoden.* BZAW 149. Berlin and New York: de Gruyter, 1979.

Routledge, R. "*Ḥesed* As Obligation: A Re-examination." *TynBul* 46 (1995): 179–96.

Rudolph, W. *Das Buch Ruth, Das Hohe Lied, Die Klaglieder.* 2d ed. KAT 17.1–3. Gütersloh: Mohn, 1962.

Sakenfeld, K. D. *The Meaning of Ḥesed in the Hebrew Bible: A New Inquiry.* Missoula, Mont.: Scholars Prtess, 1978.

Sasson, J. M. "Ruth." Pp. 320–28 in *The Literary Guide to the Bible.* Ed. R. Alter and F. Kermode. Cambridge, Mass.: Harvard Univ. Press, 1987.

_____. *Ruth: A New Translation with a Philological Commentary and a Formalist-Folkorist Interpretation.* 2d ed. Sheffield: Sheffield Academic Press, 1989.

Schultz, R. "אָמָה" and "שִׁפְחָה." *NIDOTTE*, 1:418–21; 4:211–13.

Trible, P. *God and the Rhetoric of Sexuality.* Philadelphia: Fortress, 1978.

Unterman, J. "The Social-Legal Origin for the Image of God As Redeemer גּוֹאֵל of Israel." Pp. 399–405 in *Pomegranates and Golden Bells: Studies in Biblical, Jewish, and Near Eastern Ritual, Law, and Literature in Honor of Jacob Milgrom.* Ed. D. P. Wright, D. N. Freedman, and A. Hurvitz. Winona Lake, Ind.: Eisenbrauns, 1995.

van der Toorn, K. "The Significance of the Veil in the Ancient Near East." Pp. 327–39 in *Pomegranates and Golden Bells: Studies in Biblical, Jewish, and Near Eastern Ritual, Law, and Literature in Honor of Jacob Milgrom.* Ed. D. P. Wright, D. N. Freedman, and A. Hurvitz. Winona Lake, Ind.: Eisenbrauns, 1995.

Westbrook, R. "The Law of the Biblical Levirate." *Revue Internationale des Droits de l'Antiquité* 24 (1977): 65–87.

_____. "Redemption of Land." *Israel Law Review* 6 (1971): 371.

_____. *Property and the Family in Biblical Law*. JSOTSup 193. Sheffield: Sheffield Academic, 1991.

Wilson, R. R. *Genealogy and History in the Biblical World*. New Haven, Conn.: Yale Univ. Press, 1977.

_____. *Sociological Approaches to the Old Testament*. Philadelphia: Fortress, 1984.

Younger, K. L., Jr. "Two Comparative Notes on the Book of Ruth." *JANES* 26 (1998): 121–32.

Zenger E. *Das Buch Ruth*. ZBAT 8. Zurich: Theologischer Verlag, 1986.

Ruth 1:1–22

❦

IN THE DAYS when the judges ruled, there was a famine in
the land, and a man from Bethlehem in Judah, together
with his wife and two sons, went to live for a while in the
country of Moab. ²The man's name was Elimelech, his wife's
name Naomi, and the names of his two sons were Mahlon and
Kilion. They were Ephrathites from Bethlehem, Judah. And
they went to Moab and lived there.

³Now Elimelech, Naomi's husband, died, and she was left
with her two sons. ⁴They married Moabite women, one named
Orpah and the other Ruth. After they had lived there about
ten years, ⁵both Mahlon and Kilion also died, and Naomi was
left without her two sons and her husband.

⁶When she heard in Moab that the LORD had come to the
aid of his people by providing food for them, Naomi and her
daughters-in-law prepared to return home from there.
⁷With her two daughters-in-law she left the place where she
had been living and set out on the road that would take them
back to the land of Judah.

⁸Then Naomi said to her two daughters-in-law, "Go back,
each of you, to your mother's home. May the LORD show
kindness to you, as you have shown to your dead and to me.
⁹May the LORD grant that each of you will find rest in the
home of another husband."

Then she kissed them and they wept aloud ¹⁰and said to
her, "We will go back with you to your people."

¹¹But Naomi said, "Return home, my daughters. Why
would you come with me? Am I going to have any more sons,
who could become your husbands? ¹²Return home, my daughters; I am too old to have another husband. Even if I thought
there was still hope for me—even if I had a husband tonight
and then gave birth to sons—¹³would you wait until they
grew up? Would you remain unmarried for them? No, my
daughters. It is more bitter for me than for you, because the
LORD's hand has gone out against me!"

¹⁴At this they wept again. Then Orpah kissed her mother-
in-law good-by, but Ruth clung to her.

¹⁵"Look," said Naomi, "your sister-in-law is going back to
her people and her gods. Go back with her."

¹⁶But Ruth replied, "Don't urge me to leave you or to turn back from you. Where you go I will go, and where you stay I will stay. Your people will be my people and your God my God. ¹⁷Where you die I will die, and there I will be buried. May the LORD deal with me, be it ever so severely, if anything but death separates you and me." ¹⁸When Naomi realized that Ruth was determined to go with her, she stopped urging her.

¹⁹So the two women went on until they came to Bethlehem. When they arrived in Bethlehem, the whole town was stirred because of them, and the women exclaimed, "Can this be Naomi?"

²⁰"Don't call me Naomi, " she told them. "Call me Mara, because the Almighty has made my life very bitter. ²¹I went away full, but the LORD has brought me back empty. Why call me Naomi? The LORD has afflicted me; the Almighty has brought misfortune upon me."

²²So Naomi returned from Moab accompanied by Ruth the Moabitess, her daughter-in-law, arriving in Bethlehem as the barley harvest was beginning.

RUTH 1:1–6 SERVES as a prologue to this edifying short story; what follows in 1:7–22 is Act 1. Naomi is the key person in this act. In the following chapters, Ruth, Naomi, and Boaz take the initiative in chapters 2, 3, and 4, respectively.

The Prologue (1:1–6)

THIS PROLOGUE PROVIDES the setting and predicament that will dominate the book: Since the Judahite males of the family of Naomi die while living in Moab, she is without a male to care for her. In staccato style, the story compresses a number of years into a few verses in order to confront the reader with the book's main problem: Naomi's emptiness. The prologue divides into three subsections.[1]

The setting (1:1–2). The story is set in the period of the judges (1:1a). Such an allusion must have conjured up for the original audience visions of the moral and spiritual declivity with the consequent oppressions and chaos that prevailed in that time.[2] In identifying the story with the period before

---

1. See Bush's discussion of the structural parameters (*Ruth, Esther*, 59–60).
2. Hubbard states: "While certainty eludes us, the Ruth story most likely falls between Ehud and Jephthah since, except for Eglon, Israel dominated Moab" (*The Book of Ruth*, 84). But the

the monarchy, a period that the book of Judges depicts as a rough and violent era, the book of Ruth offers a significant contrast, for it presents a serene and pastoral picture. This opening clause forms an inclusio with the historical reference to David in 4:17b so that the leadership vacuum evident during the period of the judges is answered in the ideal king, David.[3]

Verse 1 quickly adds that "there was a famine [*rāʿāb*] in the land, and a man from Bethlehem in Judah ... went to live for a while [lit., to live as a foreigner, *gûr*] in the country of Moab." Since "there was a famine in the land" occurs elsewhere only in Genesis 12:10 and 26:1,[4] this phrase clearly alludes to the famines of the patriarchs: Abram, who left the land to live as an foreigner (*gûr*) in Egypt, and Isaac, who left the land to live (*gûr*) in Gerar among the Philistines. In both of these instances, in spite of the tragic famines and patriarchs' false witnesses concerning their wives, Yahweh's sovereign plan brought blessing on his people. The text infers this may happen again here.

Bush remarks concerning this famine during the period of the judges:

There is not the faintest suggestion that the famine is Israel's punishment for her sin. Especially there is not the slightest hint that the tragic deaths of Elimelech and his sons in any way resulted from their having forsaken their people in a time of trouble or their having moved to Moab where the sons married Moabite women. Later rabbinic exegesis used such themes of retribution and punishment to the full, but they are read into the story, not out of it.[5]

There is no doubt that rabbinic excesses should be avoided at all cost, but the tendency among recent commentators to interpret the famine, the move to Moab, and the subsequent deaths as nothing other than matter-of-fact items[6] seems to miss the implication of the first two statements in verse 1.

Even a cursory knowledge of the Deuteronomic blessings and curses and the general moral degeneracy of the period of the judges raises the interpretive

---

book supplies no real indication or hint within the story of a precise date, nor any evidence that this is of concern to the meaning of the book.

3. Interestingly, the ideal judge, Othniel, was also a Judahite like David. See commentary on Judges 3:7–11.

4. For a discussion of the literary links between these passages, see K. Nielsen, *Ruth: A Commentary* (OTL; Louisville: Westminster John Knox, 1997), 40–41.

5. Bush, *Ruth, Esther*, 67. For a detailed evaluation of the rabbinic excesses, see Campbell, *Ruth*, 58–59.

6. E.g., one writer states: "Suffering happens; there is no underlying reason given. The deaths are reported, not explained." See J. C. Howell, "Ruth 1:1–8," *Int* 51 (1997): 281–84, esp. 282.

expectations here. The argument that the Deuteronomic passages are later and therefore irrelevant to the interpretation of Ruth 1:1 does not hold since the date of Ruth may not be as early as some scholars have argued.[7] Even if the famine is not the result of drought (which most interpreters innately presume) but of the military destructions during the period of the judges, this too still has its inherent connections to the Deuteronomic covenant's blessings and curses section.[8] Finally, the very mention of the period of the judges before the mention of the famine means that the story of Ruth is not a completely self-contained literary piece. The reader (and originally hearers) must fill in the narrative gaps here. Moreover, the literary links with Genesis 12 and 26 demand a fuller reading.

Although no such famine is recorded in the book of Judges, the canonical linkage presumably implies that the famine is the result of disobedience to Yahweh's covenant, a disobedience pervasive during that era (Judg. 2:20). Deuteronomy 28:48 includes famine ($r\bar{a}^c\bar{a}b$) in the list of curses (cf. also Lev. 26; Deut. 28:16–24)[9] that God would bring on the Israelites if they served other gods rather than him (which they did, cf. Judg. 2:10–19). The fact that there is famine in Israel and not in Moab[10] is significant to the plot, not only in providing a context for the heroine to be a Moabitess rather than a Judahite so that the motif of $\d{h}esed$ works,[11] but for underscoring the overall negative portrayal of the situation that brings Naomi to her complete emptiness.

Ironically, the man comes from Bethlehem ($b\hat{e}t$ $le\d{h}em$),[12] which means "house of bread," but there is no "bread/food" in that city. And this man, together with his wife and two sons, go to live as resident foreigners in the country of Moab—a traditional enemy of Israel throughout biblical history.[13] As Hubbard aptly notes:

---

7. And Deuteronomy, or parts of it, may be earlier than typically thought.

8. Note the concise remarks of Sasson, "Ruth," 322.

9. See the discussion in Block, *Judges, Ruth*, 624–27.

10. Moab could fare better in drought years than Judah due to evaporation from the Dead Sea, as demonstrated by actual rainfall measurements during the first half of the twentieth century. See D. Ashbel, "There Was a Famine in the Land . . . (Ruth 1:1)," *Yediot* 29 (1965), 221–26 (in Hebrew).

11. A. Berlin, *Poetics*, 103: "Had Ruth been a Judahite, there would have been nothing remarkable in her actions."

12. The phrase "man from Bethlehem in Judah" also recalls the "young Levite from Bethlehem in Judah who lived ($g\hat{u}r$) with Micah in Ephraim" (Judg. 17:7–11). See Porten, "The Scroll of Ruth," 25.

13. Although as a number of commentators observe this does not mean that there was nothing but utter hatred and constant war between the two. There were periods of peace and coexistence.

This family left the familiar for the unfamiliar, the known for the unknown. The foursome was legally a "stranger" (Heb. *gēr*), and so was its world. Further, to seek refuge in Moab . . . was both shameful and dangerous.[14]

Such a move to the territory of Moab is not outside the plausible, since there are occasions even in modern times when more rain falls in southern Moab than in Bethlehem.[15] The specification of Judah in connection with Bethlehem is necessary since there was another city with the same name in Zebulun (Josh. 19:15). The narrator gives the reader the impression that out of all the Bethlehemites caught up in this famine, only this man and his family seek refuge in the "country" (*śādeh*) of Moab. The term *śādeh* is an "arable, cultivatable land or field." Later the reader discovers that ironically this man "alienated" a *śādeh* in Bethlehem in order to go sojourn in a *śādeh* in Moab.

Verse 2 relates that the man's name is Elimelech ("My God is king") and his wife's name is Naomi (derived from the root *nʿm* [beautiful, pleasant, good]).[16] The meanings of both names play a role in the story: Elimelech with the coda, Naomi with 1:20. The names of their two sons are Mahlon and Kilion. Both names are etymologically uncertain and presently unattested in the ancient Near Eastern onomastica.[17] They may be coined names meaning "sickly one, sickness" and "finished or spent one, [hence] destroyed, death" used as "ominous names,"[18] implicitly pointing to the intensification of the crisis about to strike Naomi.[19]

The mention in verse 2 that the foursome were Ephrathites from Bethlehem Judah is significant to the development of the story. It seems very

---

14. Hubbard, *The Book of Ruth*, 87. Ironically, the Israelite family goes to live in Moab and suffers the deaths of all of the males; Ruth, the Moabitess, goes to live in Judah and has the pleasure of giving birth to a son.

15. See Block, *Judges, Ruth*, 624–27; Hubbard, *The Book of Ruth*, 87 nn. 19, 22; see also note 10.

16. Block comments concerning Naomi's name: "This may be an abbreviated name, missing the theophoric element and thereby suppressing the role of God" (*Judges, Ruth*, 625). But it is common for biblical female personal names to lack theophoric elements, so it is highly questionable that there is any "suppressing of the role of God" in her name.

17. The Ugaritic personal name *ki-li-ia-nu* (alphabetic equivalent *klyn*) is most likely Hurrian and thus a false lead to explicating the unrelated Hebrew *kilyôn*. See S. C. Layton, "Leaves from an Onomastician's Notebook," *ZAW* 108 (1996): 608–20, esp. 615–20. See also R. Zadok, *Pre-Hellenistic Israelite Anthroponymy and Prosopography* (OLA 28; Leuven: Peeters, 1988), 13, 80, 113, 130.

18. It is preposterous to suggest that parents would name their children "sickly one" or "destruction." Compare comments on the name of Cushan-Rishathaim in Judg. 3:8–10.

19. See S. Layton, *Archaic Features of Canaanite Personal Names in the Hebrew Bible* (HSM 47; Atlanta: Scholars Press, 1990), 215–16.

probable that the "clan" (*mišpāḥâ*) of the Ephrathites (the clan of which Elimelech and Boaz were part) was only a subsection of larger Bethlehem population. If the entire population of Bethlehem derived from one *mišpāḥâ* or part of a still more widely dispersed *mišpāḥâ*, then the singling out of Boaz as "known kinsman" of the same clan as Elimelech is foolish. If all Bethlehemites were from the same clan as Elimelech, then all Bethlehemites would have been "known kinsmen" of Elimelech. The excitement and suspense of the story depends on the fact that only some Bethlehemites are of Elimelech's *mišpāḥâ*.[20]

Verses 1–2 describe the setting, the characters, and the initial circumstances of the book. They are framed by the contrast between "went ... from Bethlehem in Judah" in verse 1 and the summary statement at the end of verse 2: "They went to Moab and lived there."[21]

Double bereavement (1:3–5). The family's double bereavement is powerfully conveyed, which forms a chiasm with an identically parallel inclusio (lit. trans.):[22]

A Then died Elimelech, the husband of Naomi, and she was left alone with her two sons.
  B They took Moabite wives, the name of one Orpah and the other Ruth,
  B' And they lived there about ten years.
A' Then died also both Mahlon and Kilion, and the woman was left alone without her two boys and without her husband.

The writer's terse, staccato style adds to the disaster of the double deaths and the resultant "aloneness" of Naomi. Although tragic is the loss of her husband, Naomi's aloneness is mitigated by the fact that her two sons are alive. As Hubbard notes, the sons' marriages must have fanned Naomi's flickering hope into brighter flame,[23] although the text does not offer an evaluation of these marriages to Moabite women. In fact, the narrator does not specify who married Orpah[24] and who married Ruth.[25] Does he approve or disapprove of these marriages or does he not care?

20. N. Gottwald, *The Tribes of Israel* (Maryknoll, N.Y.: Orbis, 1979), 269. The description of David in 1 Sam. 17:12 as "the son of an Ephrathite ... from Bethlehem in Judah" adds significance to the coda's genealogy in Ruth 4:18–22.

21. Bush, *Ruth, Esther*, 60.

22. Ibid., 60.

23. Hubbard, *The Book of Ruth*, 93.

24. The meaning of the name is uncertain. The meaning of "nape (of the neck)" is doubtful. Equally problematic are the meanings "cloudy" or "scented." See Hubbard, *The Book of Ruth*, 94 n. 14.

25. The meaning of her name is also uncertain. See Hubbard, *The Book of Ruth*, 94 n. 15; Block, *Judges, Ruth*, 628. The attempt to explain Ruth's name from a root meaning "friend" is doubtful.

Marriages to the people of the land (i.e., Canaanites) were strictly forbidden (Deut. 7:3; cf. Judg. 3:6). Deuteronomy 23:3[4] does not prohibit marriages to Moabites and Ammonites; it only prohibits that the offspring of such unions from entering the assembly of the Lord until the "tenth" generation.[26] Ironically, the marriages of Mahlon and Kilion lasted ten years, until their deaths. Both marriages, however, are marked by infertility: ten years, but no children (1:4). The covenantal implications are clear: As Yahweh withheld the rain and thus produced the famine, so he withheld fertility, hence no children (Deut. 28:4, 18; cf. 1 Sam. 2:5–6).

Although the sons die after a ten-year period,[27] the story compresses this time interval. The narrator creates the impression that Naomi is left battered by the relentless onslaught of one tragic event after another (cf. the battering of Job, Job 1:6–2:10).[28] But this second bereavement is overwhelming for Naomi. She has lost her children (1:5; cf. the play on the word *yeled* in the epilogue, 4:16). Now there is only "aloneness" without any mitigation, since she is alone "without her two boys and her husband." The author focuses on Naomi's emptiness and misery.

The family of Elimelech teeters on annihilation. Thus, while the threat of starvation plays a large role in the story (1:1, 6, 22; ch. 2; 3:15, 17), it is only secondary to the problem of the family's survival. In ancient Israel, the loss of a family from existence was a great tragedy. When a family died out physically, it ceased to exist metaphysically. That robbed Israel of one of her most prized possessions, namely, clan and tribal solidarity.

Hubbard points out that another crisis is the possibility that Naomi now faces old age without anyone to care for her.[29] As a widow, Naomi lacks the

---

Perhaps a derivation from the root *rwb* (to soak, irrigate, refresh), hence "refreshment, satiation" is possible. But Ruth will serve as the bridge from Naomi to Boaz, from the past to the future.

26. However, this is hardly a favorable wording; nor is the context, which mentions Balaam (Deut. 23:4–5) and forbids treaties with them (23:6). The prohibition against treaties with the Moabites is parallel to the prohibition against treaties with the people in the land (i.e., the Canaanites).

27. The Targum (1:4–5) explicitly attributes the deaths of the two sons to the sin of marrying Moabites. The Midrash (*Ruth Rabbah* 2.10) relates the deaths to the earlier sin of leaving Judah. But the biblical text is silent on this issue.

28. There are also important differences between Job and Naomi. Job's integrity is immediately and explicitly set forth, whereas Naomi's is only established over the course of the book. The divine reason for Job's trials is explicitly stated, whereas the divine reason for Naomi's is only inferred. The reactions of the two to the trials is different (at least as far as the prologue of Job is concerned).

29. That potential tragedy is implicit in her angry outcries (1:11–13, 20–21) and explicit in the joyous exclamation of her neighbors (4:14–15), who rejoice that the newborn will "renew [her] life and sustain [her] in [her] old age." In short, as in Lev. 25, here the *gōʾēl* delivers an unfortunate Israelite, not from loss of land or lengthy servitude, but from annihilation.

---

provision and protection of a husband in the male-dominated ancient Near East. Moreover, it must be remembered that she lives in a foreign land. Because of her age and poverty, she is effectively cut off from the three options that might normally be open to a widow:[30]

1. There was the possibility of returning to the house of her father. But her parents are most likely already dead. If the disaster had come earlier in life, she could have returned to her father's house like an ordinary young widow. But this is not the case here.
2. There was the possibility of remarriage, perhaps even a levirate marriage (Deut. 25:5–10). But this seems to be out of the question since she is beyond child-bearing years.
3. There was the possibility of supporting herself through some kind of craft or trade. But this is unlikely since she has none (the vast majority of women in antiquity did not have such an option).[31]

Furthermore, she is an old widow without children—the worst fate that an Israelite woman might experience. "She faces her declining years with no children to care for her and no grandchildren to cheer her spirits."[32] Naomi is a stranger in a foreign land—a victim of death and of life.[33]

Hint of change (1:6). Through these initial verses of the story, the introduction has set the stage by showing that all possible lines of ḥesed in the ancient world available to Naomi have been effectively severed. But verse 6 gives a hint that this may change if empty Naomi returns to the newly filled land of promise since Yahweh has come to the aid of his people, providing food for them. Verse 6 is antithetically parallel to verse 1, providing a chiastic contrast in content:[34]

A "there was a famine"
   B "went to ... Moab"
   B' "return ... from there [lit., Moab]"
A' "the LORD ... [provided] food"[35]

---

30. See Hubbard, *The Book of Ruth*, 96–97; and P. S. Hiebert, "Whence Shall Help Come to Me?: The Biblical Widow," in *Gender and Difference*, ed. by P. L. Day (Minneapolis: Fortress, 1989), 134–37.

31. H. A. Hoffner Jr., "אַלְמָנָה," *TDOT*, 1:290.

32. Hubbard states: "If a woman is 'saved through childbirth' (1 Tim. 2:15; cf. Rachel's cry, Gen. 30:1), Naomi is lost. With Sarah, Hannah, and Elizabeth she suffers the painful shame of childlessness" (*The Book of Ruth*, 97).

33. P. Trible, *God and the Rhetoric of Sexuality* (Philadelphia: Fortress, 1978), 167–68.

34. The NIV inverts the clauses of verse 6 and obscures this chiasm.

35. Note that in the Hebrew text, the mention of the Lord's providing food comes after the decision to return to Moab in a *kî* (for) clause.

Thus verse 6 rounds off and brings to a conclusion the prologue of verses 1–2 by balancing "went to Moab" :: "returned from Moab," and "famine" :: "food."[36] This is the first time Yahweh is mentioned in the story, and it is in the context of his compassionate provision for his people.[37] The language of verse 6 is also rich with assonance and alliteration (*lātēt lāhem lāhem*), ending with the word for food (*lehem*), which unsubtly directs Naomi, as well as the reader, back to Beth*lehem*, "(store)house of bread/food." As Yahweh has provided food for his people, will he yet provide fertility to Ruth and an offspring for Naomi? Finally, verse 6 also acts as a transition and a preview to what follows. It accomplishes this through the use of the key word *šûb* (return).[38]

Act 1: Naomi's Return (1:7–22)

ACT 1 (1:7–22) is comprised of two scenes: Scene 1: Naomi and her daughters-in-law on the road to Judah (1:7–19a); and Scene 2: Naomi and Ruth arrive at Bethlehem (1:19b–22). The opening line intimates the development of this act, and the closing sentence serves as transition to what follows in Act 2. The section emphasizes the responsibilities inherent in the ties of kinship—in particular, to the elderly widow (i.e., the past).

Scene 1: Naomi and her daughters-in-law on the road to Judah (1:6–19a). No longer does the writer convey the story through the terse, staccato style of the prologue. Rather, he now relates certain incidents in considerable detail; indeed, in this scene he brings the action to a full halt partway on the journey home and relates to us an extended conversation between Naomi and the two young Moabite widows. Moreover, he utilizes his favorite literary device here as well as in the rest of the book: dialogue. More than half the book is in dialogue (55 verses out of 85). In three separate dialogues, Naomi urges her daughters-in-law to "go back" (*šûb*) to their Moabite people and leave her (secs. B, D, and B', 1:8, 11, 15). The section appears to be chiastic in structure.[39]

---

36. Bush, *Ruth, Esther*, 60.

37. But the mention here implicitly argues for his involvement earlier, an involvement that Naomi perceives (1:13b[2]—"the LORD's hand has gone out against me!"). See discussion below.

38. Berlin ("Big Theme, Little Book," 43) points out "in chapter 1 the repetition of the root *šûb* 'return' twelve times as Naomi bids her daughters-in-law return to their families in Moab and as she returns to Judah with Ruth. Technically, Ruth cannot return to Bethlehem, since the Moabite woman has never been there. Her return is really Naomi's return."

39. See Bush for a full explanation (*Ruth, Esther*, 72). The analysis here is indebted to his observations.

A Narrative introduction: Naomi and daughters-in-law "leave" (*yṣʾ*) and begin to go (*hlk*) to the land of Judah (1:7)

   B Dialogue 1: Naomi urges the women to return home (1:8–9a)

      C Narrative transition: kissing good-bye and weeping loudly; Naomi kisses them (1:9b)

         D Dialogue 2: The young women refuse, insisting that they go with her; Naomi impassionately urges them again to return home (1:10–13)

      C' Narrative transition: weeping loudly and kissing good-bye. They continue weeping, Orpah kisses Naomi good-bye, but Ruth clings to her (1:14)

   B' Dialogue 3: Naomi urges Ruth to follow Orpah's example and return home; Ruth refuses and impassionately reaffirms her commitment to Naomi (1:15–18)

A' Narrative conclusion: Naomi and Ruth travel (*hlk*) and arrive (*bwʾ*) at Bethlehem (1:19a)

In section A (1:7), the three women leave Moab and head for the land of Judah. The terms "leave" (*yṣʾ*) and "go" (*hlk*) correspond and contrast to section A' (1:19a), where Naomi and Ruth "go" (*hlk*) and "come" (*bwʾ*) to Bethlehem.

In Section B (1:8–9a), the first dialogue of the book, Naomi urges her daughters-in-law to return "each of you, to your mother's home." Having come to Moab as a foreigner, Naomi certainly understands the problems and difficulties her daughters-in-law will face if they accompany her back to Bethlehem. She intends to spare them such grief. The phrase "mother's house/home" is unusual, since most often the Hebrew Bible refers to a widow returning to her father's house. While many different explanations have been given, the emphasis here seems to be on the contrast Naomi wishes to make—a widow should return to her mother and not stay with her mother-in-law.[40]

Naomi's urging must have been with some mixed feelings. To urge Orpah and Ruth to return to Moab necessitates that she will travel home completely alone. But to have them return to Judah with her requires them to renounce all hope and effectively consign them to the life of a poor old widow. Thus she sees no other choice but to encourage them to return. To the calamity of losing home, husband, and sons, she must now add another, this one self-inflicted: She must return home alone.[41]

---

40. Porten, "The Scroll of Ruth," 26; Trible, *God and the Rhetoric of Sexuality*, 169; Bush, *Ruth, Esther*, 75.

41. Campbell, *Ruth*, 82.

Naomi pronounces a blessing on the women (1:8): "May the LORD show kindness [*ḥesed*] to you, as you have shown to your dead and to me." Naomi invokes a proportionate blessing of *ḥesed* on the women because of their *ḥesed* to the deceased (see the discussion of *ḥesed* in the introduction). As the women have shown covenantal loyalty, kindness, goodness, mercy, love, and compassion in voluntary acts of extraordinary mercy or generosity toward Naomi and her two sons, so Yahweh will show *ḥesed* to them. The reference to the dead is simply Naomi's way of referring to her two sons, to whom Ruth and Orpah have shown loyalty and faithfulness during the ten years of their marriages. Naomi concludes with an additional blessing: "May the LORD grant that each of you will find rest [repose, *mᵉnûḥâ*] in the home of another husband." She recognizes that in the world in which they live, security and well-being are dependent on a link with some male.

In section C (1:9b), Naomi kisses her daughters-in-law good-by, and they all weep loudly. The verb *nšq* can mean simply "to kiss," but it is also used as a gesture of farewell (cf. Gen. 31:28; 1 Kings 19:20). It is clear that all three weep. This pattern of kissing plus weeping will be inverted below in C'.

Section D (1:10–13) is the second dialogue and the pivotal point in Scene 1 of Act 1. The young women refuse to leave Naomi alone, insisting that they will go with her: "We will go back with you to your people" (1:10). But Naomi impassionately urges them again to return home. She does this through three distinct dialogue units (vv. 11, 12–13a, 13b), which consist of carefully balanced couplets.[42] These are ordered in intensity, climaxing in the final clause: "The LORD's hand has gone out against me!"

(1) The first dialogue unit (1:11) contains a pair of rhetorical questions:

Return home [*šûb*], my daughters!
Why would you come with me?
Am I going to have any more sons, who could become your husbands?

Naomi is not eliciting facts or seeking an explanation; she is expostulating.[43] Her appeal is logical: Hope for a better future is not to be found with her. The probability of her having more sons is remote. Notice that Naomi does not argue: "Can I find you husbands?" Her logic is linked to the levirate marriage possibilities, as the next dialogue unit will explain.

(2) The next dialogue unit (1:12–13a) answers the initial rhetorical questions and then continues with a balanced conditional sentence that concludes

---

42. Porten, "The Scroll of Ruth," 27–28.

43. Bush correctly observes the nature of the questions in the dialogues (*Ruth, Esther*, 77–78). See also R. T. Hyman, "Questions and Changing Identity in the Book of Ruth," *USQR* 39 (1984): 190.

with another pair of rhetorical questions, each pair introduced by the same Hebrew particle (lit. trans.):

> Return home [*šûb*], my daughters! Go!
>> For [*kî*][44] I am too old to have a husband!
>> Even [*kî*] if I thought [or said] there was still hope for me—
>>> even [*gam*] if I had a husband tonight
>>> and then [*wᵉgam*] (actually) gave birth to sons—
>> would [*bᵉlāhēn*] you wait until they grew up?
>> Would [*bᵉlāhēn*] you remain unmarried for them?

Naomi's logic of this hypothetical scenario heightens the argument developed in the first dialogue unit, that is, the improbability of her having more sons. For in her hypothetical scenario of becoming pregnant with sons that very night (utterly impossible anyway, since she has no husband), logic again dictates that the two Moabite women would be foolish to wait for these sons to grow up in order to marry them (they would be elderly women themselves by that time). Hence, Naomi's invocation to return to their families has even greater force of argument.

(3) The third dialogue unit contains a couplet that reaches an irrefutable conclusion by moving from the foolishness of the previous rhetorical questions to the statement of Yahweh's past action. Again the same Hebrew particle introduces the pair of statements:

> No, my daughters.
>> [For, *kî*][45] it is more bitter for me than for you,[46]
>> because [*kî*] the LORD's hand has gone out against me!

Naomi concludes her argument with emphatic, climatic force with two statements that are meant to convince the two Moabite women not to stick with her. Things are far worse in her state than theirs. To stick with her is to doom oneself to her fate. And this is a fate that the hand of the God of Israel, Yahweh, has brought against her.[47] Thus to stick with her is to put oneself in the same situation in which Yahweh will be against that person. To be connected to a person who has God opposed to them is a situation that few would desire. One ought to shun such a person to escape the maelstrom of her mis-

---

44. The NIV does not translate the particle *kî* as causal, but from the logic of the argument it seems appropriate.

45. Again, the NIV does not translate the particle *kî*.

46. On the interpretation of this clause, see the discussions of Hubbard (*The Book of Ruth*, 112) and Campbell (*Ruth*, 70–71).

47. With this statement, Naomi is implicitly acknowledging Yahweh's sovereign activity in the earlier tragedies: famine, exile, bereavement, childlessness, etc.

fortune. What better argument to make return to Moab attractive? Naomi has built an airtight case for not being connected to her.

While the text has only subtly alluded to this fact and the reader may not have fully recognized it, Naomi makes it abundantly clear that, at least in her understanding, the earlier famine in Bethlehem, her family's sojourn in Moab, the deaths of her husband and sons, and the barrenness of her daughters-in-law are all evidences of God's hand as the cause of her hardships. She feels she is the target of God's overwhelming power and wrath. That God is actively behind these events will be affirmed throughout the story; that he is punishing Naomi—at least as Naomi feels is the case—is not necessarily correct. God is not "out to get her" (see further comments below).

In section C' (1:14), there is an inversion of the action of section C (weeping + kissing). They all weep loudly once again. This weeping indicates the women's concurrence with Naomi: The only sensible course of action is to leave Naomi and return to Moab.

Consequently, Orpah kisses Naomi good-bye. Naomi's powerful argument has convinced her that a normal life back in Moab is preferable to life with Naomi in Israel. She chooses the "sensible" track. But this only heightens Ruth's reaction. She clings (*dbq*) to Naomi. The order of the clauses expresses the simultaneity of Ruth's and Orpah's actions as a contrast between them. The expression "cling to" (*dbq* + prep. *b*) implies firm loyalty and deep affection. It implies leaving membership in one group to join another. In Genesis 2:24 this expression is used along with its opposite (*ᶜzb*):

> For this reason a man will leave [*ᶜzb*] his father and mother,
> and be united [cling, *dbq* + *b*] to his wife
> and they will become one flesh.

Thus Ruth's gesture illustrates her commitment to "abandon" (*ᶜzb*) her Moabite father's house and permanently remain with or cling to (*dbq* + *b*) Naomi.

While Orpah serves as a foil to Ruth in the story heightening the contrast, the narrator does not criticize Orpah's decision. She is not portrayed negatively; the reader is given good reason for her decision and little other information. It is not that Ruth is right and Orpah is wrong per se. Rather, the actions of Orpah make Ruth appear that much more the positive (the unnamed nearer kinsman-redeemer will serve the same function in relation to Boaz in ch. 4). Berlin puts it this way:

> In the case of Orpah, both she and Ruth initially react the same way, expressing reluctance to leave Naomi. Only after prolonged convincing does Orpah take her leave, and, of course, Ruth's determination to remain with Naomi becomes, in the eyes of the reader, all the

more heroic. The two were first made to appear similar—they were both Moabite wives of brothers, both childless widows, both loyal to their mother-in-law. Only gradually is the difference between them developed, and when it is, the effect is dramatic and moving.[48]

Section B' (1:15–18) contains the third dialogue. Naomi urges Ruth to follow Orpah's example and return home: "Look [*hinnēh*] . . . your sister-in-law [*yᵉbēmet* is going back to her people and her gods [*ᵉlōhêhâ*].[49] Go back with her [lit., sister-in-law, *yᵉbāmâ*]." The term *yᵉbēmet* is connected with the levirate marriage (see Deut. 25:7–9). Since the word *ᵉlōhîm* can be understood as a "plural of majesty," a number of commentators opt for a singular sense so that the word refers to Chemosh, the national god of the Moabites. Actually, the context leaves this open so that the term may refer to Chemosh (sing.) or to the numerous deities worshiped in that country (plural). In either case, the contrast is consequently heightened with Ruth's words that her spiritual commitment is to *the* God of Israel.

Ruth refuses to go back and impassionately reaffirms her commitment to Naomi. There is a chiastic structure to her affirmation speech (lit. trans. of 1:16–17):

a Do not press/urge me to leave you,
　　or to turn back from following you.
　　　b For wherever you go, I will go;
　　　　And wherever you stay, I will stay.
　　　　　c Your people will be my people,
　　　　　　And your God, my God.
　　　b' Where you die, I will die;
　　　　And there shall I be buried.
a' Thus may Yahweh do to me and more so—
　　Nothing but death will separate me from you!

The terms in b, "go" (*hlk*) and "stay" (*lwn*), are opposites, creating a merism, equivalent to saying "all of life."[50] Ruth swears her commitment to Naomi in the name of Israel's God, thus acknowledging him as her God.

---

48. Berlin, *Poetics*, 85.

49. Block interprets this as an indication that Naomi is acknowledging the existence of the Moabite god(s) and is therefore an evidence of her lack of orthodoxy (*Judges, Ruth,* 638–39). But this seems to be taking the phrase too literally. Literarily, the phrase "back to her people and her gods" is part of the foil. In contrast to Orpah, Ruth will choose the God of Israel. The phrase can be just as easily understood as a tacit recognition that in turning back to Moab this automatically meant that Orpah would be back in a society that worshiped these gods, and that's all.

50. Bush, *Ruth, Esther,* 82.

In the conclusion to her speech of affirmation (1:17b), Ruth uses a self-imprecatory oath formula. There is a difference of opinion regarding how this phrase should be translated. The following are the three possibilities:

> if anything but death separates you and me (NIV)
> if even death separates you and me (RSV; Campbell, *Ruth*, 74–75;
>   Hubbard, *The Book of Ruth*, 119–20)
> nothing but death will separate me from you (Bush, *Ruth, Esther*, 82–83)

Whatever the case, the essence of the oath is that only death will separate Ruth from Naomi. Her commitment to Naomi transcends even the bonds of racial origin and national religion: Naomi's people and Naomi's God will henceforth be hers. With such a speech of affirmation, Naomi realizes that Ruth is determined[51] to go with her, so she stops urging her to leave and go back to Moab. All the power of Naomi's logic and argument has been ineffective. Ruth's faith defies human logic and wisdom.[52]

Section A' (1:19a) contains the narrative conclusion: Naomi and Ruth go on (*hlk*) until they come (*bw'*) to Bethlehem. Thus Scene 1 ends.

Scene 2: Naomi and Ruth arrive at Bethlehem (1:19b–22). This scene describes the arrival of Naomi and Ruth in Bethlehem and the interaction between the women of Bethlehem and Naomi. This is presented by the narrator in dialogue that Naomi once again predominates. The first clause of the scene ("When they arrived [*bw'*] in Bethlehem") not only repeats the information of 1:19a ("until they came [*bw'*] to Bethlehem,"), but forms an inclusio with the closing statement of Act 1, "arriving [*bw'*] in Bethlehem" (1:22b).

This closing statement of 1:22 emphasizes the return in the context of the "barley harvest," which confirms the statement in 1:6 that Yahweh has provided food for his people and brings resolution to the famine mentioned at the beginning of the prologue (1:1). While providing closure for Act 1, this mention of "the barley harvest" links with and previews Act 2, in which Ruth gleans in the fields of this same harvest.

---

51. The participle expresses durative action in past time, stressing the continuous nature of Ruth's resolve, a nuance difficult to bring out in translation. See Bush, *Ruth, Esther*, 83.

52. Block comments: "Although some would interpret Ruth's declaration as a sign of conversion, it is better viewed as an affirmation of a transfer of membership from the people of Moab to Israel and of allegiance from Chemosh to Yahweh. How much she knew about the implications of claiming Yahweh as one's God we do not know. She had indeed been observing Naomi for more than a decade, but from what we have seen of her in this chapter she hardly qualified to be a missionary of orthodox Yahwistic faith and theology. But this is a start, a noble beginning" (*Judges, Ruth*, 641). Not only is this again unduly harsh on Naomi; it is far too demanding on Ruth. That Ruth is a believer in Yahweh is confirmed by her actions; in this, with her confession, she is analogous to Rahab with her confession and confirming actions (Josh. 2; cf. James 2).

As in Scene 1, the narrator prefers dialogue rather than narrative to communicate his message. This entire passage consists simply of the dialogue between Naomi and the women of Bethlehem (1:19b²–21) with a narrative statement at the beginning (1:19b¹) and at the end (1:22). Thus the structure of the scene appears to be:

Prologue (1:19)   When they arrived in Bethlehem, the whole town was stirred because of them, and the women exclaimed, "Can this be Naomi?"

	"Don't call me Naomi," she told them. "Call me Mara ["Bitter"],
	A because the Almighty [Shaddai] has made my life very bitter.
Naomi's Bitter Speech (1:20–21)	B I went away full, but the LORD [Yahweh] has brought me back empty.
	Why call me Naomi?
	B' The LORD [Yahweh] has afflicted me; A' the Almighty [Shaddai] has brought misfortune upon me."

Epilogue (1:22)   So Naomi returned from Moab accompanied by Ruth the Moabitess, her daughter-in-law, arriving in Bethlehem as the barley harvest was beginning.

The scene opens with the glad reception of the women of Bethlehem for Naomi ("the whole town was stirred[53] because of them"). The question "Can this be Naomi?" is not addressed by the women to Naomi but rather to one another, creating excited commotion. It is a rhetorical question having the force of an exclamation.[54]

This question of the women is followed by Naomi's sarcastic double response, in which she utilizes two wordplays on her name, the first in the form of a command and the second in the form of a question. In the first wordplay (1:20), she denies the meaning of her name, demanding that she be called Mara, "Bitter" (*mārāʾ* comes from the root *mārar*, "to be bitter"),

---

53. The root and meaning of this term is uncertain. It can be taken to express agitation and consternation, or delighted excitement. The context determines the meaning, which, in this case, seems to make the latter preferable (cf. 1 Sam. 4:5; 1 Kings 1:45).

54. See B. Jongeling, "HZ'T NᶜMY (Ruth 1:19)," *VT* 28 (1978): 474–77.

instead of the antonym "Naomi" ("pleasant, beautiful, good").[55] In the second wordplay (1:21b[1]), she employs a rhetorical question ("why") that is intended to reject the identity that her name implies.

Both wordplays give the twofold reasons for the denial of her name in the design of a couplet. The two couplets, in turn, form a chiasm A:B and B′:A′. A and A′ utilize the divine name "Shaddai"[56] and are parallel in structure and content; B and B′ are parallel in their use of the divine name "Yahweh," although they are different in structure and content.

In B, Naomi states (lit.): "Full was I when I went away; but empty has Yahweh brought me back." The emphasis is clearly on full (*ml'h*) and empty (*ryqm*). The two statements are chiastic.[57] In B′, the expression *'nh b* means "to respond/speak against." It is usually used in a juridical context, where it has the technical force "to testify against" (e.g., Ex. 20:16; Num. 35:30). The NIV's "afflicted" attempts to capture this nuance. In Hebrew thought, one's name was often understood to be expressive of one's character, being, and personality. Thus, Naomi challenges the tone and content of the women's glad and delighted cries by twice denying the meaning of her name.

In urging the women of Bethlehem to call her "Mara" ("Bitter") "because the Almighty [Shaddai] has made my life very bitter [*hēmar*],"[58] there is an interesting parallel in one of Job's speeches in which he states:

As surely as God lives, who has denied me justice,
    the Almighty [Shadday], who has made me taste bitterness [*hēmar*]
    of soul. (Job 27:2)

In addition, Naomi's feeling that Yahweh is making her a target for his arrows is also paralleled by a feeling that Job expresses:

---

55. The reason Naomi gives for calling herself Mara instead of Naomi is strikingly parallel to the reasons she gave in verse 13 for refusing Ruth and Orpah's announced intention to accompany her to Judah: "[Life] is more bitter for me than for you."

56. Naomi uses the divine name *šadday* as a synonym for Yahweh. The meaning of this name is still obscure. English translations have generally followed the LXX and the Vulgate in translating the word "the Almighty." The name appears mostly in passages involving blessing and cursing, frequently in contexts expressing judgment (cf. Job 5:17; Isa. 13:6; Joel 1:15).

57. Bush, *Ruth Esther*, 83.

58. It seems that Naomi may be drawing from the Song of Moses that documents some of Yahweh's promised curses on the Israelites when they do not follow him, but worthless idols instead. Deut. 32:23 and esp. 24a state:

"I [Yahweh] will heap disasters upon them;
    spend my arrows against them;
wasting hunger [famine],
    burning consumption,
    bitter [*m'rîrî*] pestilence." (NRSV)

The arrows of the Almighty [Shadday] are in me,
my spirit drinks in their poison;
God's terrors are marshaled against me. (Job 6:4)

Thus, "Naomi returned along with Ruth the Moabitess, her daughter-in-law—she who returned from the territory of Moab" (Ruth 1:22, lit.). By the structure of this sentence, the narrator gives Ruth's "return" prominence.[59] This is further heightened by the identification he gives her, using her full name "Ruth the Moabitess," hence underlining her foreign origin.

Not only has Naomi returned home, so has Ruth. Naomi has returned home empty, unfulfilled, and bitter. Her journey has been a journey into the depths, and she can see nothing else. But there is more. In Naomi's anguished response to the delighted cries of the women of Bethlehem—all absorbed in her own world of pain and bitter affliction—she fails even to acknowledge Ruth's presence with her, a presence whose accomplishment transcends the call of religion and home and hope! Her whole complaint is voiced in the singular: "... bitter indeed has the Almighty made *my* life ... empty has Yahweh brought *me* back ... the Almighty has pronounced disaster upon *me*!" (1:20–21, lit.).

In a subtle touch of the narrator, Naomi utters her complaint as though Ruth, whose words of loving commitment still ring in the readers' ears, has never pronounced these words at all! Yahweh has indeed not brought Naomi back empty, and the final word to this effect lies with the narrator when, in his closing summation, he gives all the prominence to describing Ruth's arrival as a "return."[60] Thus, "we know that Naomi is not alone and will not be."[61]

The last sentence of verse 22 is anticipatory of the means by which Yahweh will provide for the two widows: It's the beginning of the barley harvest when they arrive in Bethlehem. The timing is providential (one more example of Yahweh's sovereignty) for this means that the barley and wheat harvests are just beginning to take place (late April–early May by our calendars).

Bridging Contexts

YAHWEH AND HIS COVENANT. Large impersonal forces appear to control the beginning of this narrative: geography, history, meteorology—circumstances beyond human control. The narrative is specific when it mentions Bethlehem, within Israel's sphere, and becomes diffuse when it speaks of the other world, Moab, where Judahites ought to

---

59. Ibid., 94.
60. Bush, *Ruth, Esther*, 96.
61. D. Rauber, "Literary Values in the Bible: The Book of Ruth," *JBL* 89 (1970): 27–37, esp. 30.

have no business. The historical situation of the period of the judges dictates a time of political, religious, and social problems. And the circumstances of a famine in Judah, a situation outside human abilities to remedy (esp. in antiquity), mandate that only disaster can follow.

Moab, where the god Chemosh reigns (so to speak), may not be experiencing famine when Elimelech and his family seek shelter there, but its fields will eventually kill a father and his sons and render their wives sterile and widowed. But behind these "forces," so to speak, is the God of circumstances and situations—Yahweh, Israel's covenant-keeping God. He is equally as faithful in keeping his covenant with regard to its curses as he is with regard to its blessings.

During the period of the judges, the Israelites lacked faith in Yahweh and broke his covenant (Judg. 2:1–5, 10–23). As seen in Judges, God chastened his people in accordance with his promised curses. He expected his people to live according to his Word in the land he had given them and not go to go and live in another land when difficult times arose. This will was clearly revealed in his Word. Elimelech, like many Israelites of his day, lacked the faith to trust God in the midst of this famine. The move to Moab was highly unusual and was outside of God's revealed will. Ironically, Elimelech parts with a field (*śādeh*) in Bethlehem, in the Promised Land, to live in the field (*śādeh*) of Moab. Furthermore, the marriages of his sons were outside of God's revealed will for his people.

All of this brought disaster on the family of Elimelech and his sons. In addition, the infertility was no accident. In light of God's covenant stipulations, this was not simply bad luck or fate. Thus, the outcomes of these tragedies were truly disastrous for Naomi. She suffered because of decisions that were not necessarily hers. Yet the same sovereign Lord has *already* begun a process whereby Naomi will not only survive but will be genealogically redeemed. He provides the stimulus to return to Bethlehem—Yahweh has given his people food (1:6).

God and the human situation. There are three human issues in the narration of the prologue that transcend time: aloneness, hopelessness in suffering,[62] and the plight of old age. Not only does Naomi suffer loneliness, but that loneliness is intensified in this short background narrative. Such loneliness is not unique to Naomi's situation in ancient Moab, nor is the double bereavement of husband and children. These, unfortunately, find modern analogues.

People in such a double tragedy often experience hopelessness. Feelings of helplessness and uncertainty are often overwhelming. Naomi, as many in

---

62. On some of these see Howell, "Ruth 1:1–8," 281–84.

similar contemporary settings, feels the anquish of having no one to help—no kinsman-redeemer—and no hope of seeing one on the horizon. There are no options. There are no alternative plans. No amount of brainstorming can come up with any options. Such feelings can be debilitating. The longer she stays in Moab, the more she feels the deep distress of these tragedies and the debilitating anxiety for the future. Yet, in the deepest distress, at just the right moment, Yahweh brings hope—even the faintest hint of an option: The famine in Bethlehem is over, so there is the possibility of provision there.

In Act 1, Naomi is the main character. Even though Ruth gives her great confession of faith and affirmation in Yahweh in this section of the book, Naomi is the focus of this chapter. She speaks more than Ruth, and it is her experience that the narrator depicts as central to the development of his plot. This in no way lessens Ruth's confession; it simply puts it in its proper context.

As in the prologue, God's sovereignty over the human situation is maintained throughout Act 1. In spite of the obvious emotional grief that is stirred up by Naomi's departure from Moab, God is sovereignly at work moving her back to Bethlehem in order to bring blessing into her life once again. Naomi, quite naturally, does not see the move with this in mind. While she knows that Yahweh can bless, as she invokes his blessing on the two younger women, she sees only disaster for herself. Yet the move back to Bethlehem is the means by which Yahweh will bring blessing into the old widow's life. God's sovereign timing is alluded to in the final statement of chapter 1, which mentions that the widows arrive in Bethlehem at the beginning of the barley harvest—a providential coincidence!

Approaching life with human logic. In Act 1, Naomi appears logical and practical. There is no reason to stay in Moab: no husband, no sons, no land, no food, no hope, no future—and she is a foreigner! The return to Bethlehem is logical. At least there is the clan to fall back on; moreover, there is food there now, so perhaps she can survive. If she remains much longer in Moab, she certainly will not survive. God has shut the doors on living in Moab any longer; there really isn't any other option.

Naomi also logically sees that it is best for her daughters-in-law to return to their families' homes. She blesses them, invoking Yahweh (twice) to show *ḥesed* and give them husbands.[63] But both daughters-in-law initially respond with commitment to Naomi; they will go with her to Bethlehem.

Naomi responds with logic and practical wisdom. No more sons are coming from her! She is too old. Even if she were already remarried and could

---

63. With an ironic twist this will definitely happen for Ruth. Yahweh will fulfill Naomi's invocation in his name. We are never told what happens to Orpah.

become pregnant that very night, logic argues against the women waiting for these hypothetical children to grow up—the women would be old ladies themselves by then. Besides—Naomi uses her most powerful argument— Yahweh is *against her*. Just look at the disasters! Anyone connected with her can *expect* the same—nothing but more cursing from Yahweh. So practical wisdom mandates that it is best to have no connection to her.

This time the logic and practical wisdom works, at least on Orpah. She returns to her family. But Ruth clings to Naomi (1:14). The narrator really does not have to relate the speech of faith and commitment of Ruth in 1:15– 16. The verb "cling" already communicates Ruth's abandonment of her father and mother, her country, and her country's god/gods. She is completely committed to Naomi. Interestingly, the very logic and practical wisdom that has driven Naomi to her decision to return to Bethlehem—the means by which the sovereign Lord intends to bring blessing back into her life—if applied completely here, will eliminate the very means by which God intends to bring the blessing back into her life. If she returns alone, the means of God's blessing will be effectively removed.

Nevertheless, Naomi (who cannot begin to perceive this means of restoration and blessing) still urges Ruth to return since Orpah has gone back. Fortunately, the narrator reports Ruth's speech (1:16–17). Orpah serves as a foil to Ruth in the action of her return to her family. What ḥesed this Ruth has toward Naomi! Not only is Orpah a foil in action, but Naomi is a foil in word. Naomi's logic is incontrovertible: There is only more disaster if Ruth continues with her. Yahweh is against her, so Yahweh will be against Ruth too. But rather than leave (as logic and practical wisdom would dictate), Ruth commits herself to *this* God of Israel.

Ruth is willing to accept whatever Yahweh may grant to Naomi and herself. Yahweh will be *her* God. Nothing but death will separate her from Naomi. Ruth was utterly determined to go with Naomi. It was her firm resolution. What ḥesed this Ruth has toward Naomi! It is truly ironic that it is the Moabite widow, Ruth—who like Naomi has lost her husband—who evinces this kind of commitment to Yahweh rather than the Israelite widow.

Naomi continues in her logic. She stops trying to convince Ruth to return. Why waste any more time and energy when someone is determined to do what she is going to do? Thus she (and Ruth) return to Bethlehem.

Naomi's reaction to the women of Bethlehem is also logical. To the women's innocent question of amazement that Naomi has returned, she challenges the tone and content of their delighted cries by twice denying the meaning of her name. Logic dictates that she was misnamed. What she has experienced mandates a name like Mara (bitter), not Naomi (pleasant). What Yahweh has done to her prescribes that her name be changed.

Finally, it is worth noting in this context that the opposite of Naomi's logic is not illogic or emotion. It is Ruth's determined commitment.

Reading Naomi's character. In general, recent commentators have been much harsher on the character of Naomi than earlier commentators. For example, Fewell and Gunn paint a picture of a rather reprehensible Naomi. To them, Naomi's silent response to Ruth's magnificient speech of commitment in 1:16—17 is an indication of her hardenness of heart toward Ruth. They state: "If Ruth's famous 'Where you go, I go; your god, my god' speech can melt the hearts of a myriad of preachers and congregations down the centuries, why not Naomi's heart?"[64]

Recent commentators are equally hard on Naomi for other silences— for example, for her failure to so much as acknowledge Ruth's presence to the women in Bethlehem as she rails against God at the end of chapter 1. Their reason for her behavior thus far is that she has got a Moabite "albatross" around her neck, whom she does not really want. Self-centered, resentful, bitter, and prejudiced, she certainly is no paragon.

While Naomi is human, with all the frailties that means, it seems to me that Fewell and Gunn have overread the narrative silences to paint a character who is far worse than the text intends to paint. This widow has gone through the awful experience of burying her husband and both of her sons in a foreign land and understandably has virtually no hope for survival. Cut her some slack! But if, for a moment, we grant Fewell and Gunn's interpretation for the sake of argument, such an understanding of the person of Naomi makes Yahweh's sovereign and providential *ḥesed* look that much greater as an act of grace toward a very undeserving widow.

However, it seems better to understand that Naomi is not evidencing little faith; rather, with the freedom of faith that ascribes full sovereignty to God, she takes God so seriously that, with Job and Jeremiah (and even Abraham, Gen. 15:2), she resolutely and openly voices her complaint. One should not minimize what this poor woman has gone through! The pain is real. Often it is commentators who have not experienced the kind of devastation and grief that Naomi experienced who sit in judgment.

The pain and anxiety, however, have indeed blurred her perception. Like many of Job's speeches, Naomi's anguished, reactive speech to the women of Bethlehem demonstrates one of the unfortunate truths of suffering: In the midst of pain, there is often self-absorption. It is "my" pain. Her entire complaint is singular in its orientation: "Bitter has the Almighty [Shaddai] made *my* life; empty has Yahweh brought *me* back; the Almighty

---

64. D. N. Fewell and D. M. Gunn, "'A Son Is Born to Naomi!': Literary Allusions and Interpretation in the Book of Ruth," *JSOT* 40 (1988): 99—108, esp. 100.

[Shaddai] has pronounced disaster upon *me!"* Such self-absorption in the midst of pain and affliction is understandable. Yet it always blinds a person from God's greater plan and the small ways in which God may be working this plan out.

Thus, Naomi is blind to the evident presence of Ruth, who stands as an outright contradiction to her bitter words. God has not brought Naomi back completely empty. She has Ruth. Granted that is not the same as returning with her husband and sons and grandchildren. But it is better than returning completely and utterly alone (as Act 2 will demonstrate, for without Ruth Naomi may have starved to death in a very short time).

A common misuse of Ruth 1:16–17. Sometimes at weddings, one hears a song or a reading of this passage—presumably on behalf of the bride to the groom—where Ruth 1:16–17 is invoked as a description of the commitment of the bride to the groom. While the declaration "Where you go I will go, and where you stay I will stay," and so on, may sound initially appropriate for a wedding, this is hardly the context of the passage in Ruth. Obviously, Ruth's commitment to Naomi to follow the God of Israel has nothing whatsoever to do with the commitment of a bride to follow the religious and social leadings of her husband (on reflection, a rather shocking idea). While commitment in marriage is laudable, even a part of the institution's very essence, there are significant differences between the commitment of the widowed Moabitess Ruth to her widowed Israelite mother-in-law and a modern bride to her groom.

RESPONDING TO HUMAN TRAGEDIES. What the world attributes to large impersonal forces of nature and chance, the Scriptures attribute to the sovereignty of God. This is a fundamental teaching of the Bible, and the book of Ruth stresses it throughout its pages. How we respond to the circumstances that God may bring into our lives often determines further outcomes. Elimelech's response to the famine was to move his family to Moab—a decision contrary to God's revealed will for his people. The sons' decision to marry Moabite women was also contrary to God's revealed will. These decisions spelled disaster for the males of the family, not to mention the grievous situation that came upon their women.

The disastrous circumstances and situations that the prologue describes are outside the control of Naomi. While the disobedience of others during the period of the judges may have brought God's judgment through the famine, Naomi had no way of controlling this. The decision to move to Moab was, undoubtedly, outside her control—Elimelech is the responsible party here. And the ensuing tragedies of the deaths of her husband and sons were all beyond her ability to intervene.

Accidents and tragedies strike Christians too. I am reminded of a former neighbor family, three born-again Christians, in which the husband and teen-age son were suddenly killed in an auto accident when the car they were in simply spun out of control. The accident left the wife completely alone. The doctrine of God's sovereignty is not especially comforting at that moment. Furthermore, the fact that others have gone through similar disasters is not usually much of a relief at the time. Yet these situations, which God in his administration of his kingdom may permit, are often the very circumstances through which God acts in compassion and *ḥesed* for his people. And it is through these conditions that the *ḥesed* of God's people themselves is evidenced.

It is easy to live out the belief in God's sovereignty when things are going well. When one good thing after another comes along, we can easily acknowledge and praise God's sovereignty over our lives. But when disasters strike, when one bad thing after another piles up, the doctrine of God's sovereignty is harder to accept and live out. The person who believes in the sovereignty of Yahweh and feels pounded by catastrophes that he or she believes God has allowed must come to terms with what God is doing in his or her life. Is God judging or chastening for some open or hidden sin? Perhaps. As the book of Job conclusively demonstrates, however, perhaps not. Sometimes disasters come, and the suffering that takes place is not the result of God's punishment of sin in the life of the believer. Sometimes it comes in order that God may glorify himself through the believer's life.

This is not the place to develop a theology of suffering, yet Naomi, like Job, faces great anguish, grief, and suffering, and not necessarily because of something that she has done wrong. There are always "friends" (like Job's) and theologians who have their "pat" answers for disasters and suffering. While God allows emptiness to come to Naomi, he does so in order to bring her fullness once again in an even more significant way and brings great glory to Yahweh, the God of Israel, who keeps *ḥesed* to a thousand generations. But while Naomi is in that state of anguish depicted in chapter 1, she registers the real pain and anguish that a person who believes in God's sovereignty sometimes feels in the midst of disaster. The tremendous pain and affliction these trials bring is real and sometimes impossible humanly to handle.

God's sovereignty over life. I am not saying Naomi (or Job, for that matter) is right in her railing against God at the end of chapter 1. Her understanding and conclusion that God is against her and has brought these disasters on her because he is against her is wrong. Similarly, Job is wrong in his view that God is arbitrarily judging him, pounding him into the turf for no good reason. What is truly amazing is that although both Naomi and Job are wrong in their assessments of God's actions, neither suffers because of their accusations of God's determined punishment on them. Their sufferings are for reasons that go beyond them—they are part of the greater plan of the Almighty in his administration of a complex universe. The stories of Naomi and Job give us a glimpse at that plan and the place that our own suffering may play in it, allowing us to face that suffering with fuller knowledge of God than we might have otherwise.

In recognizing Yahweh's sovereignty over her life, Naomi feels that this confirms that Yahweh is *against* her. But in his gracious *ḥesed*, Yahweh was not *against* her. Rather, he has provided food to his people (1:6), which serves to stimulate Naomi to return to Bethlehem. In attempting to deal with her anguish as best she can, Naomi saw logically that it is better to trek back to Bethlehem and possibly survive than to stay any longer in Moab and perish. God sometimes closes our options and leads us through "no brainer" guidance.

In addition, he has provided Ruth, who will not be shaken by Naomi's logic to return to her people, but who instead manifests incredible *ḥesed* to Naomi and faith in Yahweh. But Naomi, because of her natural self-absorption because of her pain and affliction, cannot see it.

This is certainly true for us too. Often in the pain and affliction of life our perception is obscured. We depend on our logic, which is helpful to a point (fortunately God has given us this). But human logic often breaks down in the midst of pain. In fact, if Ruth had followed Naomi's logic as Orpah did, then Naomi's logic would have completely eliminated any chance of a reversal in her fortunes. Thankfully, Ruth does not "buy into" Naomi's logic (in spite of Naomi's three attempts to dissuade her from coming). Human wisdom does not accomplish the will of God.

There are times in the life of every individual when loneliness sets in. There are two kinds of loneliness: one that we feel when there is literally no one around, and one we feel when we are with people but unable to really communicate the longings or struggles of the heart. Thus, no matter how many friends one has or how happy a marriage or how connected to the children, there are times when we all feel lonely. It is not necessary that we have gone through the same exact experience of Naomi in order to feel the depths of her aloneness, hopelessness, and despair.

For the most part, we attempt to fill the void. We have work activities and family activities and all kinds of other activities to keep going and fill that void. We have dreams and goals and achievements that keep us focused. Yet, in the quiet place of the soul can be found that sense of loneliness, that sense of "I'm not sure I fit," of "I don't feel understood or appreciated." When the things with which we have filled our lives are removed, the void caused by aloneness screams out. That void can only be soothed by one relationship—relationship with Jesus Christ.

Amazingly, our laments and complaints while going through these trials are registered. God hears them, even though we often may think not. And God has been subtly at work answering Naomi's blessing on Ruth as well as her complaint to him. This gives us assurance that he will do the same.

In an age when familial responsibilities are rationalized away, passed off, or simply ignored, Ruth's commitment is a powerful testimony. Such needs within families still exist in the modern world. Tragedy can and does strike, but it is still God's plan that the family be the structure in which comfort, commitment, and resolution to pain and anguish be found.

Moreover, in the larger context of the church, such *ḥesed* as Ruth's is desperately needed. If the Galatians 6:2 instruction to "carry each other's burdens" has any meaning, certainly Ruth's actions are an evidence of it. Where we can help ease the pain of individuals within the body of believers, we should do *ḥesed*.

Ruth 2:1–23

*

Now Naomi had a relative on her husband's side, from the clan of Elimelech, a man of standing, whose name was Boaz.

²And Ruth the Moabitess said to Naomi, "Let me go to the fields and pick up the leftover grain behind anyone in whose eyes I find favor."

Naomi said to her, "Go ahead, my daughter." ³So she went out and began to glean in the fields behind the harvesters. As it turned out, she found herself working in a field belonging to Boaz, who was from the clan of Elimelech.

⁴Just then Boaz arrived from Bethlehem and greeted the harvesters, "The LORD be with you!"

"The LORD bless you!" they called back.

⁵Boaz asked the foreman of his harvesters, "Whose young woman is that?"

⁶The foreman replied, "She is the Moabitess who came back from Moab with Naomi. ⁷She said, 'Please let me glean and gather among the sheaves behind the harvesters.' She went into the field and has worked steadily from morning till now, except for a short rest in the shelter."

⁸So Boaz said to Ruth, "My daughter, listen to me. Don't go and glean in another field and don't go away from here. Stay here with my servant girls. ⁹Watch the field where the men are harvesting, and follow along after the girls. I have told the men not to touch you. And whenever you are thirsty, go and get a drink from the water jars the men have filled."

¹⁰At this, she bowed down with her face to the ground. She exclaimed, "Why have I found such favor in your eyes that you notice me—a foreigner?"

¹¹Boaz replied, "I've been told all about what you have done for your mother-in-law since the death of your husband—how you left your father and mother and your homeland and came to live with a people you did not know before. ¹²May the LORD repay you for what you have done. May you be richly rewarded by the LORD, the God of Israel, under whose wings you have come to take refuge."

¹³"May I continue to find favor in your eyes, my lord," she said. "You have given me comfort and have spoken kindly to

your servant—though I do not have the standing of one of your servant girls."

¹⁴At mealtime Boaz said to her, "Come over here. Have some bread and dip it in the wine vinegar."

When she sat down with the harvesters, he offered her some roasted grain. She ate all she wanted and had some left over. ¹⁵As she got up to glean, Boaz gave orders to his men, "Even if she gathers among the sheaves, don't embarrass her. ¹⁶Rather, pull out some stalks for her from the bundles and leave them for her to pick up, and don't rebuke her."

¹⁷So Ruth gleaned in the field until evening. Then she threshed the barley she had gathered, and it amounted to about an ephah. ¹⁸She carried it back to town, and her mother-in-law saw how much she had gathered. Ruth also brought out and gave her what she had left over after she had eaten enough.

¹⁹Her mother-in-law asked her, "Where did you glean today? Where did you work? Blessed be the man who took notice of you!"

Then Ruth told her mother-in-law about the one at whose place she had been working. "The name of the man I worked with today is Boaz," she said.

²⁰"The LORD bless him!" Naomi said to her daughter-in-law. "He has not stopped showing his kindness to the living and the dead." She added, "That man is our close relative; he is one of our kinsman-redeemers."

²¹Then Ruth the Moabitess said, "He even said to me, 'Stay with my workers until they finish harvesting all my grain.'"

²²Naomi said to Ruth her daughter-in-law, "It will be good for you, my daughter, to go with his girls, because in someone else's field you might be harmed."

²³So Ruth stayed close to the servant girls of Boaz to glean until the barley and wheat harvests were finished. And she lived with her mother-in-law.

ACT 2 CONSISTS of three scenes. The first is a short introductory scene involving Ruth and Naomi (2:1–3). Scene 2 is a lengthy scene between Ruth and Boaz as she gleans in his field (2:4–17a). The third scene is again a short introductory scene involving Ruth and Naomi (2:17b–23). Act 2 evinces many similarities to Act 3:

(1) Both acts contain three scenes of generally the same structure (see the discussion of structure in the introduction); (2) there is a focus on the characters of Ruth and Boaz; in particular, he is a described as a *gibbôr ḥayil* (2:1); (3) the opening scene presents Naomi and Ruth, and Ruth sets out; (4) there is an encounter between Ruth and Boaz; (5) Boaz inquires about the girl's identity (2:5); (6) the opening line intimates its development; and (7) the closing sentence acts as transition to what follows (2:23).

Scene 1. Ruth Gleans in a Field Belonging to Boaz, Naomi's Relative (2:1–3)

THE STRUCTURE OF this short scene is chiastic. Bush recognizes this and outlines it in the following manner:[1]

A from the clan of Elimelech (2:1a)
  B whose name was Boaz (2:1b)
    C go to the fields to glean (2:2a¹)
      D behind someone in whose eyes I might
      find favor (2:2a²)
    C' "Go ahead, my daughter." . . . So she went and gleaned
    the fields (2:2b–3a)
  B' the field of Boaz (2:3b¹)
A' who was from the clan of Elimelech (2:3b²)

Verse 1 serves as a parenthetical digression in which one of the major characters is proleptically introduced. The name is withheld to the last possible moment. He is described first in relationship to Naomi, "a relative[2] on her husband's side." It was necessary to state that Naomi had a relative on her husband's side of the family in order to make clear that the blood relationship is with her husband and not with her (since Israelite marriage was endogamous). This relative is further described as "a man of standing" (*ʾîš gibbôr ḥayil*), from the clan of Elimelech.

The phrase *ʾîš gibbôr ḥayil* is difficult to translate into English. The word *gibbôr* comes from a root meaning "mighty" and is frequently translated "warrior." The word *ḥayil* can mean "strength, power, ability, capability, wealth," and its meaning depends on the context in which it is used. In a military setting it refers to a warrior, particularly one who has distinguished himself in armed combat. In other contexts, it can refer to wealth (2 Kings 15:20) or ability (1 Kings 11:28). It designates one who possesses social standing and

---

1. Bush, *Ruth, Esther*, 99.
2. It seems preferable to follow the majority of scholars and read here the Qere *môdaʿ* (relative).

a good reputation. In this context it connotes not only wealth and status but also ability, honor, and capability.[3] Thus it is clearly used as a description of character[4] (cf. Ruth's description below as an *ʾēšet ḥayil*, 3:11).

The clan (*mišpāḥâ*)[5] of Elimelech is stated earlier as the Ephrathites (see comments on 1:2). These were undoubtedly kinsmen, although the relationship is relatively distant, since it was the *bêt ʾāb* ("father's house," i.e., the extended family) that contained the more closely related kin group. The *mišpāḥâ* was the most important single group in the social structure in ancient Israel and formed the basis for the functions of the *gōʾēl* ("kinsman-redeemer; see comments in the introduction, pp. 399–403).

Boaz occurs as a personal name only in Ruth. Its etymology is obscure and much debated,[6] particularly since it occurs also as the name of one of the pillars stationed before the entrance of the temple of Solomon (1 Kings 7:21).

Verse 2 picks up the story where 1:22 left off. Ruth, the Moabitess—once again a reminder of her foreign and generally despised status—makes her request to Naomi to go to the fields and glean ears of grain. Although the Law (Lev. 19:9–10; 23:22; Deut. 24:19–21) provided a legal right to glean specifically to the poor, the resident alien, the widow, and the orphan, it is clear from other passages that these people were not always granted permission to glean.[7] Hence, the simplest understanding of Ruth's words in the last clause of verse 2 "behind anyone in whose eyes I find favor" is that "she wants to glean behind someone who would benevolently allow it."[8]

In the Old Testament, God established at least two ways through which widows could have their needs met. (1) On a yearly basis, special considerations in the harvesting of fields, orchards, and vineyards were to be followed. Deuteronomy 24:19–22 delineates these:

> When you are harvesting in your field and you overlook a sheaf, do not go back to get it. Leave it for the alien, the fatherless and the widow, so that the LORD your God may bless you in all the work of your hands. When you beat the olives from your trees, do not go over the branches a second time. Leave what remains for the alien, the fatherless and the widow. When you harvest the grapes in your vine-

---

3. "A real, substantial man of character" might capture the nuance here.

4. Block defines the phrase: "noble with respect to character" (*Judges, Ruth*, 651).

5. For use of this term in the social structure of ancient Israel, see the discussion in the introduction to the book of Judges.

6. See Sasson, *Ruth*, 41; Campbell, *Ruth*, 90–91.

7. See, e.g., Job 24:3, 21; Ps. 94:6; Isa. 1:23; 10:2; Jer. 7:6.

8. Bush, *Ruth, Esther*, 104.

yard, do not go over the vines again. Leave what remains for the alien, the fatherless and the widow. Remember that you were slaves in Egypt. That is why I command you to do this.

(2) A second means of provision was established through the third-year tithe. Thus Deuteronomy 14:28–29 (cf. also 26:12–15) states:

> At the end of every three years, bring all the tithes of that year's produce and store it in your towns, so that the Levites (who have no allotment or inheritance of their own) and the aliens, the fatherless and the widows who live in your towns may come and eat and be satisfied, and so that the LORD your God may bless you in all the work of your hands.

In other words, in addition to the yearly provision, there was a special provision every third year.

However, the Israelites often failed to observe these injunctions. This is clear from a number of passages (see, e.g., Deut. 27:19; Isa. 1:17; Mal. 3:5; cf. Mark 12:38–40). This underscores the dangers that Ruth and Naomi faced.

Note that Ruth is the one who takes the initiative in this first scene after the return to Bethlehem. Still absorbed with the bitter affliction and emptiness of her life, Naomi remains inactive and, except for two words, keeps her silence. Ruth initiates the decision to provide the sustenance to support them by offering to glean in the fields. In courtesy to her mother-in-law, she politely requests her consent. Naomi responds with two mere words of assent: "You-may-go, my-daughter." Naomi seems resigned to her despair. But Ruth is capable and active (cf. her description in 3:11 as *ḥayil*). It is part of her character.

Ruth goes out and begins "to glean in the fields behind the harvesters" (2:3). The storyteller then adds an important clause: "As it turned out, she found herself working in a field belonging to Boaz, who was from the clan of Elimelech." The NIV phrase "as it turned out" literally means "and her chance [*miqreh*] chanced [*wayyiqer*]." Both noun and the verb derive from the root *qrh*, which means "to meet, encounter." The phrase is used in this sentence as a rhetorical device, hyperbolic irony. By excessively attributing Ruth's good fortune to chance, the phrase points ironically to the opposite, namely, to the sovereignty of God. In the context, it indicates that Ruth (without any intention to do so) ends up gleaning in the field that belongs to Boaz. Thus God, who is constantly working behind the scenes, is pictured as directing and controlling this situation through his gracious providence.

Scene 2. Ruth and Boaz Meet on the
Harvest Field (2:4–17a)

THIS SECTION IS comprised of two episodes (2:4b–13, 14–16), which are enclosed by a narrative prologue and epilogue (2:4a and 2:17a).[9] The two episodes incorporate an A:B::B':A' chiasm. The first episode (2:4b–13) consists almost exclusively of dialogue. It divides into two parts. Part A (2:4b–7) is a conversation between Boaz and his workers about Ruth and her gleaning. Part B (2:8–13) is a conversation between Boaz and Ruth in which Boaz grants her exceptional rights. Each centers its attention on Ruth and Boaz to the exclusion of all else. Verses 5–13 consist of a tight series of stimulus-response-related dialogues that drive the dialogue of the first episode.

Episode 2 (2:14–16) contains more narrative than dialogue. It divides into two parts. Part B' (2:14) revolves around the actions of Boaz and Ruth in which Boaz grants her exceptional privileges at the noon meal. Part A' (2:15–16) is a conversation between Boaz and his workers about Ruth and her gleaning. He commands that they carry his generosity far beyond the gracious allowances he granted her previously in 2:8–9.

The narrative prologue (2:4a) begins with the important grammatical construction: *wᵉhinnēh* + subject + verb. The NIV translation, "Just then," has chronological implications that are not present in this usage. The suddenness the phrase expresses in the presentation of information to the reader "has nothing to do with the time lapse between events; it has to do with the abrupt or unexpected way in which the new fact is introduced in the narrative."[10] It expresses point of view or presentation of perception for the reader, not suddenness in the occurrence of events. Thus it emphasizes once again the providence of God that "wouldn't you know it,"[11] Boaz shows up!

The first episode (2:4b–13) begins with the conversation between Boaz and his workers about Ruth and her gleaning (Part A, 2:4b–7). The initial greetings between Boaz and his workers in the remainder of verse 4 builds suspense by focusing on Boaz, a man whose first words are a blessing on his workers in the name of Yahweh. Such a greeting speaks to his character and foreshadows his generosity.

Boaz immediately inquires from his foreman[12] about the identity of the

---

9. See ibid., 109–11.

10. Berlin, *Poetics*, 93–94.

11. This is Bush's suggested translation of *wᵉhinnēh* (*Ruth, Esther*, 113).

12. The term is *naʿar* (lit., young man), but the term is used in biblical and extrabiblical texts of a foreman or overseer.

unknown young woman[13] gleaning in his field by probing her origins (2:5).[14] The foreman identifies Ruth by national origin, a "Moabitess [lit., Moabite young woman]," and by her connection to Naomi, the one "who came back from Moab with Naomi." In verse 7 (the verse is very difficult),[15] the foreman volunteers additional information about Ruth that immediately speaks to her character in three ways: (1) It stresses that she asked permission to glean behind the reapers (not a necessity according to the Law); (2) it stresses the length of time she has been there; and (3) it emphasizes her diligence in working all morning with hardly any break.

The last clause, which the NIV translates "except for a short rest in the shelter," is difficult. Literally it reads: "this (masc.) her sitting the house (a) little."[16] The immediately succeeding verses (2:8–9) are important to explicating what these words mean.

In Part B (2:8–13) the conversation switches. Boaz addresses Ruth, not the foreman. In a series of six short statements with a final seventh conditional statement (2:8–9), Boaz outlines a beneficent program for Ruth in his field despite the fact that she is a Moabitess:

1. Don't go and glean in another field;
2. and don't go away from here;
3. Stay here with [lit., stick close to, *dbq*] my servant girls;
4. Watch the field where the men [and girls] are harvesting;
5. and follow along after the girls;
6. I have told [ordered] the men not to touch you [or hoot at you];
7. And whenever you are thirsty, go and get a drink from the water jars the men have filled.

From these statements, it is possible to conclude:

- (from points 1–3) that Ruth was leaving the field as Boaz arrived
- (from points 4–6) that something done to her by the male reapers has made her uncomfortable enough to leave
- (from point 7) that Ruth's attempt to get a drink of water had provided the occasion for the young male reapers' action

---

13. The choice of the word *nᶜrh* (young woman) is a natural means of inquiry. It implies Ruth's youth vis-à-vis Boaz.

14. For the syntax of the question, see Block, *Judges, Ruth*, 655.

15. For a full recent discussion, see Bush, *Ruth, Esther*, 113–19; Hubbard, *The Book of Ruth*, 147–52; and M. Carasik, "Ruth 2,7: Why the Overseer Was Embarrassed," *ZAW* 107 (1995): 493–94.

16. The clause is so difficult that Campbell (*Ruth*, 96) does not attempt a translation and states that "a hundred conjectures about a badly disrupted text are all more likely to be wrong than any one of them absolutely right!" See also Block, *Judges, Ruth*, 657–58.

With this in mind, it seems apparent that the last words of verse 7 record the foreman's confused and embarrassed explanation of a situation to Boaz.[17] As he is speaking, Ruth is at some distance from them, with her back turned to Boaz, and she is on her way out of the field because of an incident of what today we would call sexual harassment,[18] which she experienced when she sought a drink of water. Thus, the translation of the last words of verse 7 might be something like: "This fellow ... ah, she's just going home for a bit."[19] The foreman starts his explanation, becomes embarrassed, and tries to make some lame excuse.

Whatever the case, clearly Ruth's social status is untenable and danger-ous as long as she lacks a connection to a male provider. It is also clear that chance may have prevented Ruth and Boaz from meeting and marrying, had not providential interference invisibly guided the story along to its conclu-sion. Ruth may simply have walked away to glean in another field had not Boaz inquired when he did.

Moreover, in these seven statements Boaz is granting her more than the ordinary rights of gleanage.[20] Ruth must be careful not to inadvertently glean in some other field adjoining Boaz's property. She is to glean in that portion of the field normally off limits to poor gleaners. In order to help ensure this, Boaz instructs her to "stick close to" his young women workers, and he instructs his workers not to interfere with (lit., touch) her. Finally, if she is thirsty, she can drink from the more immediately available water jars rather than seek refreshment elsewhere and lose time in gleaning. Normally in the ancient Near East, foreigners would draw water for Israelites, and women would draw it for men. Thus Boaz's provision is extraordinary.

Verse 10 records Ruth's reaction and reply. Overwhelmed by Boaz's unex-pected protection and generosity, she falls to the ground. This gesture con-sists of dropping to the knees and touching the forehead to the ground. As Gruber has shown, this nonverbal gesture is often used as a posture express-ing gratitude.[21] Ruth asks why she has found such favor with him that he has

---

17. Here I am following Carasik's explication ("Ruth 2,7," 493−94).

18. This is not to claim that sexual harassment was a category of behavior recognized in the Israelite legal system, or even one that had a name in biblical Hebrew. But the phe-nomenon of sexual language or contact that could make a woman uncomfortable existed in the realities of the ancient world, just as today. That Boaz orders/commands (*ṣwb*) his young male workers not to touch or hoot at Ruth confirms this interpretation. The com-mand of Boaz to his workers in 2:16 as a warning against even a remark that would make Ruth uncomfortable reinforces this interpretation. Cf. also the incident of the shepherds dri-ving away Jethro's daughters from the well until Moses' arrival (Ex. 2:17).

19. Carasik, "Ruth 2,7," 494.

20. See Bush, *Ruth, Esther,* 121−22.

21. M. I. Gruber, *Aspects of Nonverbal Communication in the Ancient Near East* (2 vols.: Studia Pohl 12; Rome: Biblical Institute Press, 1980), 187−99, 303−10.

paid any attention (*l*ᵉ*hakkîrēnî*) to her—a foreign woman (*nokrîyâ*).²² There is a play on words between the two opposing meanings of the root *nkr* in *lhkyr* (to recognize, pay attention to) and *nkryh* (foreign woman).²³ This word-play heightens Ruth's surprise reaction to Boaz's graciousness: "Why have I found such favor in your eyes that you notice me—a foreign woman!?" (*nokrîyâ* often has negative connotations, especially in the book of Proverbs).²⁴ Both Ruth's action and her accompanying words exhibit that she is completely surprised at what Boaz has said to her. This confirms that he has granted her far more than she has requested. Boaz's action is once again an evidence of God's providence (Yahweh has answered her wish in v. 2).

Boaz's reply is the high point of the scene (2:11–12). In a concise and straightforward manner, permeated with praise and admiration, he affirms what Ruth has solemnly vowed to Naomi in her stirring words of commitment in Moab (1:16–17): "You left [*ᶜzb*, abandon] your father and mother and your homeland [*môledet*] and came to live with a people you did not know before" (2:11).²⁵ Boaz then wishes that Yahweh will "repay" (*šlm*) Ruth for her actions and prays that she "may be richly rewarded by the LORD, the God of Israel, under whose wings you have come to take refuge" (2:12). Boaz specifies that Yahweh is the God "under whose wings" (*k*ᵉ*nāpîm*) Ruth has sought refuge/asylum. The word *kānāp* can mean "wing" or "corner of a garment." In 2:12, it connotes the image of a bird tenderly protecting its young. Like a defenseless starling, Ruth sits securely under Yahweh's mighty wings.²⁶

Knowing now why this unknown landowner has been so kind and generous, Ruth expresses her gratitude (2:13). Boaz has certainly relieved Ruth's mind and encouraged her. As a destitute foreign woman (*nokrîyâ*) who went out to glean, she had no idea what she might encounter; in fact, the possibility of trouble of one sort or another was a real possibility (and may have already occurred before Boaz's appearance on the scene). Boaz's kindness has greatly assured her that her mission will succeed.

Ruth refers to herself here as "servant" (*šiphâ*), although she does not really even have this status (she is officially a *nokrîyâ*). Although *šiphâ* and *ʾāmâ* (another word translated "maidservant" or "servant girl," which Ruth uses in 3:9, see comments) are frequently synonymous, it appears that *šiphâ*, when used distinctively, is the more deferential term since it refers to women

22. The clause is concessive in force, "though I am a foreigner." See Bush, *Ruth, Esther,* 123.
23. There is also alliteration of the consonants *n* and *k*. See Campbell, *Ruth,* 98–99.
24. See, e.g., Prov. 2:16; 5:20; 6:24; 7:5; 23:27. Also see Gen. 31:15; 1 Kings 11:1, 8; Ezra 10:2.
25. The statement, esp. with its use of *ᶜzb* and *môledet,* is reminscient of Abram's migration (Gen. 11:28–12:4). Thus Ruth is indirectly likened to Abram.
26. There are further implications connected to this term in ch. 3.

belonging to the lowest rung of the social ladder (cf. 1 Sam. 25:41).[27] The term is thus an expression of Ruth's humility.

The second episode (2:14–16) bears witness to Boaz's magnanimity, extended to an even greater degree. In Part B' (2:14), he grants Ruth exceptional privileges: He welcomes her to the intimacy of the noon meal, invites her to partake ("Have some bread and dip it in the wine vinegar"[28]), and bestows so much roasted grain[29] on her that she eats all she wants and has some left over. Thus Boaz transformed a rather ordinary occasion—the noontime meal—into another demonstration of his compassion and generosity (i.e., his *ḥesed*).

Part A' of this episode (2:15–16) consists of a conversation between Boaz and his workers about Ruth and her gleaning. When Ruth resumes gleaning, Boaz orders his workers to let her glean between the sheaves themselves without trouble[30] and even commands them without fail to pull out stalks of grain from the handfuls the men cut and leave them behind for her—an unheard-of favor. He concludes by charging them once again not to drive her away.[31]

The narrative conclusion to Scene 2 (2:17a) telescopes the rest of the day into a single sentence: "So Ruth gleaned in the field until evening." The irony is rich. Ruth has received extraordinary favor and privileges from a landowner who treats her like a member of the family, but the significance of his identity remains hidden to her.

Scene 3. Naomi Evaluates the Meeting (2:17b–23)

SCENE 3 CONSISTS of a narrative prologue (2:17b–18) and epilogue (2:23), which enclose a dialogue between Ruth and Naomi that exhibits a chiastic structure. The high point of this is at the center: Naomi's revelation to Ruth of Boaz's family and social relationship to them. The structure of the scene appears to be:

---

27. Berlin, *Poetics*, 88–89. A *šipḥâ* is of lower status than an *ʾāmâ*. Thus in 1 Sam. 25:41, Abigail states: "Look, your *ʾāmâ* is but a *šipḥâ* to wash the feet of the servants of my lord." Abigail is an *ʾāmâ* but wants to further reduce herself to a *šipḥâ* vis-à-vis David.

28. The exact nature of the word *ḥōmeṣ* that the NIV translates "wine vinegar" is not known. Cf. Num. 6:3; Ps. 69:21; Prov. 10:26. Perhaps it is some kind of refreshing sour condiment (cf. Hubbard, *The Book of Ruth*, 173).

29. "Roasted grain" (*qālî*) was a staple of Old Testament society (cf. 1 Sam. 17:17; 25:18; 2 Sam. 17:28).

30. This clause is variously interpreted. See Bush, *Ruth, Esther*, 126.

31. Kennedy argues that this clause means, "Don't hoot at her or treat her in such a way as to send her away frightened and helpless" (A. Kennedy, "The Root GʿR in the Light of Semantic Analysis," *JBL* 106 [1987]: 47–64, esp. 60–64).

Narrative prologue (2:17b–18)
  A Naomi's inquiry and blessing (2:19a)
    B Ruth's response—she worked with a man named Boaz (2:19b)
      C Naomi's blessing of Boaz and a revelation—he is a relative and one of their redeemers (2:20)
    B′ Ruth's response (2:21)
  A′ Naomi's endorsement (2:22)
Narrative epilogue (2:23)

The narrative prologue sets the stage for the exclamatory dialogue that ensues (2:17b–18). Verse 17b stresses the large quantity of grain Ruth has threshed[32] from her gleanings in the field of Boaz—"an ephah" of barley. Commentators, with the exception of Sasson,[33] usually give some kind of conversion figure for an ephah and end at that. Nielsen in her commentary concludes: "Of course, the important thing is not to find out exactly the actual weight but to be overwhelmed by Boaz's generosity to Ruth."[34] While the text is obviously giving this data in order to demonstrate Boaz's ḥesed towards the two widows, Ruth and Naomi, what are the practical, real-life implications? Certainly this note about the significant amount of grain gleaned by Ruth is not given to the reader in order "to add to her list of virtues that she was as strong as an ox."[35] It must have had some tangible, utilitarian value.

An ephah was one-tenth of a homer. The homer was apparently the amount that one donkey could carry, which lies somewhere about ninety kilograms (two hundred pounds), fixing the assload of barley at about 150 liters or the assload of wheat at about 120 liters. Even allowing for uncertainties and upward adjustment by redefinition of norms, the "natural" assload can hardly have exceeded two hundred liters. Because of diachronic and political circumstances, it seems likely that there were a number of homer norms in the preexilic period. The probable parameters of the preexilic Old

---

32. The Hebrew literally states: "She beat out what she had gleaned." In order to thresh small quantities, the stalks and ears of the grain were beaten with a stick (cf. Judg. 6:11; Isa. 28:27). For such threshing techniques, see O. Borowski, *Agriculture in Iron Age Israel* (Winona Lake, Ind.: Eisenbrauns, 1987), 63.

33. In a one-sentence comment, Sasson links the interpretation of this verse to the data from Mari, but not to all the Ration Lists evidence. He states: "Given the fact that at Mari of the Old Babylonian period, the ration of a male worker rarely exceeded one to two pounds per day, we are impressed by Ruth's ability to gather enough to last her and her mother-in-law a few weeks" (Sasson, *Ruth*, 57). Hubbard follows Sasson (*The Book of Ruth*, 79).

34. Nielsen, *Ruth: A Commentary*, 61–62.

35. Campbell, *Ruth*, 104.

Testament dry measures from smallest to greatest were: *omer* → *ephah* → *homer* :: 1–2 liter → 10–20 liters → 100–200 liters respectively.[36]

The ancient norm for a daily food ration seems to have been widely regarded as approximately one liter, usually of barley.[37] Therefore, if Ruth's ephah equaled about ten to twenty liters of barley, she has threshed roughly enough for the two women to eat for a little more than a week.

The epilogue of Scene 3 (2:23) states that Ruth continues to glean in Boaz's fields "until the barley and wheat harvests were finished." According to Deuteronomy 16:9–12 and the Gezer Calendar,[38] the time period from the beginning of the barley harvest to the end of the wheat harvest was normally seven weeks, concluding at Pentecost. If Ruth averages the same each day (i.e., one ephah, cf. 2:21 below) and works the entire seven weeks, she gleans enough barley and wheat to feed the two women, at the minimum rate, approximately two-thirds of a year, or at the maximum rate, more than an entire year.[39] Thus, it is most likely that ancient hearers of this book would have perceived the import of this gleaning detail as heightening the generosity of Boaz toward the two widows on a scale greater than modern readers of the story have even begun to perceive.

The large quantity and leftovers from the noon meal clearly lead into Naomi's surprised reaction and excited questions in 2:19a, which comprise section A of the scene. It is clear from Naomi's two questions that she is not concerned about finding out a particular geographic location where Ruth has gleaned but is concerned about who the owner of the field is.[40] Naomi

---

36. The even larger capacity measure for a ephah that is sometimes listed in commentaries (i.e., 36.4 liters) is a measure based on much later sources and would produce a homer (364 liters) that no donkey could carry! See the detailed discussion of M. A. Powell, "Weights and Measures," in *ABD*, 6:897–908, esp. 903–5. It may be that early Hebrew norms for the homer were not much different from those of the contemporary Mesopotamian homer. Thus Mesopotamian *qû* → *sūtu* → *imēru* :: omer → ephah → homer :: 1 liter → 10 liters → 100 liters respectively. The NIV text note states that the ephah is "probably about 3/5 bushel (about 22 liters)." This seems to be too high in light of recent research.

37. Ibid., 904. For a full discussion, see L. Milano, "Food and Diet in Pre-Classical Syria," in *Production and Consumption in the Ancient Near East: A Collection of Essays*, ed. C. Zaccagnini (Budapest: Chaire d'Egyptologie de l'Université Eötovos Loránd de Budapest, 1989), 201–71; F. M. Fales, "Grain Reserves, Daily Rations and the Size of the Assyrian Army: A Quantitative Study," *SAAB* 4 (1990): 23–34.

38. According to this extrabiblical Hebrew inscription (lines 4–5), a month was devoted to harvesting barley and a month was devoted to harvesting wheat. See the discussion and bibliography in D. Sivan, "The Gezer Calendar and Northwest Semitic Linguistics," *IEJ* 48 (1998): 101–5; Borowski, *Agriculture in Iron Age Israel*, 31–44.

39. For a more detailed discussion of the ration data and the implications of the ephah, see K. L. Younger Jr., "Two Comparative Notes on the Book of Ruth," 121–25.

40. Zenger, *Das Buch Ruth*, 60.

---

then utters a general blessing on whoever this man is who has taken notice of Ruth.[41]

Ruth's response (section B) in 2:19b gives a lengthy and somewhat redundant reply to Naomi's questions, which allows the narrator to delay the revelation of the name. Thus, Ruth leaves the climactic name, Boaz, to the very end of her sentence. The narrator can thus build anticipation and place emphasis on the name of the man whom Naomi will recognize.

At the center of the chiasm of Scene 3 (C, 2:20), Naomi pronounces a specific blessing on Boaz: "The LORD bless him! . . . [He] has not stopped showing his kindness [*ḥesed*] to the living and the dead." The Hebrew text contains two grammatical ambiguities that have fueled scholarly debate over the meaning of the text (see discussion in the introduction, pp. 395–96). It may be that the ambiguity is deliberate in order to stress that both Boaz and Yahweh (through Boaz) have shown *ḥesed*, that is, compassionate, covenantal loyalty, kindness, goodness, and love toward the widows.

Naomi also now adds some crucial information: "That man is our close relative; he is one of our kinsman-redeemers [*gōʾēl*]" (see discussion of *gōʾēl* in the introduction, pp. 399–401). In one sense, Boaz has already acted as a *gōʾēl*: He has redeemed Ruth and Naomi from their destitute hunger through his kindness in the field. But Naomi's revelation of Boaz's relationship to them is important to the plot because it creates anticipation of events to come. It heightens what was revealed at the beginning of Act 2 (2:1): Boaz is a relative on Naomi's husband's side, from the clan of Elimelech (i.e., Ephrathah). However, he is not the only one (as Naomi's use of the plural in 2:20 indicates). There are, in fact, others, as the story will confirm.

In section B' of Scene 3 (2:21), Ruth gives her response to Naomi's blessing and revelation of Boaz. It is interesting that the narrator at this point suddenly refers to Ruth as the "Moabitess."[42] The narrator continues to remind his audience of the foreignness of Ruth, which serves in his ultimate scheme to stress the astonishing act of *ḥesed* by Boaz on her behalf, which will eventually be played out. In 2:21, Ruth is not adding a new piece of information to her report to Naomi. Rather, having learned Boaz's identity, Ruth is, through her excitement, expressing understanding of Boaz's actions, now that she knows of his relationship to them, including the fact that he has accorded her the same extraordinary gleaning privilege throughout the rest of the harvest.[43]

---

41. This particular form of blessing is only found in 1 Kings 10:9 (= 2 Chron. 9:8) and Prov. 5:18.

42. In one sense, this is Ruth's full name, similar to, e.g., Uriah the Hittite (2 Sam. 11:3) or Ebed-Melech the Cushite (Jer. 38:7). See Bush, *Ruth, Esther*, 138.

43. Ibid. This may reinforce the possible conclusion that Ruth averaged an ephah per day.

Finally, in section A' of Scene 3 (2:22), Naomi gives her endorsement: "It will be good for you, my daughter, to go with his girls, because in someone else's field you might be harmed." Naomi is clearly concerned with Ruth's safety since she uses a much stronger word than Boaz in reference to possible "harm"[44] (cf. comments on 2:9).

In the narrative epilogue to Scene 3 and closing to Act 2 (2:23), the phrase "until the end of the barley harvest" (lit.) also carries us back to the end of Act 1, Scene 2, when Naomi and Ruth arrived at Bethlehem "at the beginning of the barley harvest" (lit.) and completes the cycle. Again, for the completion of both harvests, approximately two months would be required.

At the end of this two-month period, 2:23b stresses that Ruth is still living with her mother-in-law. This is significant to the plot of the story. The ancient readers (well aware of the length of time involved in the agricultural year) would have quickly recognized that Ruth has gleaned for both the barley and wheat harvests in the fields of Boaz (where presumably there was further contact with Boaz), but there has been no development in their relationship. What looked like a clear solution to their widowed situation seems to have died out. While the provision of food is significant to their immediate need and somewhat beyond, it does not solve the long-term problem of their destitute widowhood. What appeared to be a promising relationship has evaporated. Ruth and Naomi still live together in the same status as when the chapter opened.[45]

THIS CHAPTER CONTINUES the picture of Yahweh's sovereignty and providence in the lives of the widows. The text does not accomplish this with conspicuous declarations but through the apparent coincidence of timing, place, and relationship of the events and human interrelations. Through the unfolding of the events of the story, God's sovereign, providential hand is perceived. He has a plan for Naomi and Ruth, and he will provide for them as he brings this plan to completion.

Doing *ḥesed*. Few of us will be in fields harvesting the edges, and few of us will find foreign widows gleaning in our fields. Thus few of us will have an opportunity to do *ḥesed* in an exactly similar manner as in Ruth 2. However, the ways in which we can manifest *ḥesed* are all around us: at home, at work, in church, to name just a few. The *ḥesed* that Ruth and Boaz do is a

---

44. The word *pāgaʿ* (with the prep. *b*) means "to physically attack" or "molest physically" (cf. Judg. 8:21; 15:12; 18:25; etc.).

45. Bush, *Ruth, Esther*, 140.

reflection of the type of *ḥesed* God does. It is through the doing of *ḥesed* that people will know that we are Christ's disciples, if we do *ḥesed* one to another (cf. John 13:35).

The introduction of Boaz as a *gibbôr ḥayil* (a man of strength of character, 2:1) heightens the expectation that he is one who can act to solve the widows' destitution. That this is the case will be seen in Act 3 as Boaz interacts with Ruth. The present chapter depicts two people of extraordinary character. Interestingly, the phrase *gibbôr ḥayil* is used to describe Boaz as well as Jephthah! The contrast in personality and character can hardly be greater. The ambition-driven, wheeling-dealing Jephthah is no match in ethical character to Boaz, who lives out the essence of *ḥesed*.

In this chapter, it is Ruth who takes the initiative to do *ḥesed*. Naomi is paralyzed—understandably to a point—by her despair. Fortunately for Naomi, her last words (1:20–21) were not entirely accurate, for she has not returned totally "empty"; she has Ruth. Ruth immediately demonstrates that she is capable and active (a woman of *ḥayil* [strength] to accomplish the needed task, cf. 3:11). Rather than allowing the debilitation of mother-in-law to infect her, Ruth recognizes the immediate need and acts to remedy it. Her response is extraordinary, for she voluntarily assumes responsibility for the care of Naomi. Doing *ḥesed* requires taking the initiative; it will not get done if we sit back and wait for someone else to do what needs to be done.

Doing *ḥesed* for others does not mean that it will always be a piece of cake. Gleaning the edges of the fields, especially if one were a female foreigner, entailed the possibility of danger.[46] This is one more way in which the narrative pictures Ruth as a woman of exceptional quality and outstanding character: She is willing to risk the dangers in order to do what is right, to do what is needed for another. Ruth is selfless in her attitude—and this will be perceived by Boaz (and others).

The sovereign hand of God. Little does Ruth know that "by chance" she will end up in Boaz's field. One must be careful not to read modern secular conceptions of "fate" or "chance" into the wording here. Rather, the paradoxical wording is used with an ironic twist: What some call chance, luck, or fate, the Hebrew Bible attributes to the sovereign hand of God. The clear implication is that in some way Ruth's choice of field has been superintended by God.[47] This is reinforced by 2:4a, where Boaz unexpectedly happens to

---

46. The very fact that Boaz stresses to his male workers not to "touch" or "hoot at" or in any way dispute Ruth is a clear indication that such things happened.

47. Cf. the "chance" finding of Joseph by the man in the field at Shechem in Gen. 37:15–17. If Joseph had not been "found" by this man, there would be no nation of Israel! Joseph would never have found his brothers, been sold into slavery, risen to vizier of Egypt, and saved his family from famine and the moral corruption of Canaan.

show up. Once again the sovereign hand of God is implicated. The narrator, however, presents this subtly. It is for those who have eyes to see, that is, the community of faith, to perceive. The world attributes such things to chance, the random events of a complex universe that simply produce the occasional coincidence. But the eyes of faith are able to perceive the hand of God in these apparent coincidences.

Quality of character. The remainder of the chapter emphasizes the quality of character of both Boaz and Ruth. The fact that the first words Boaz speaks are a blessing in the name of Yahweh is a precursor of all that he is, for it is from the heart that such an attitude toward his workers comes.

Ruth's quality traits are viewed next through the evaluation of the foreman. The focus is on her unassuming attitude (she asks permission to glean before she starts) and her work ethic (she has worked hard from the early morning until that time without a break).

Boaz's quality traits then come into focus again in the narration. Boaz calls her over and grants her extraordinary rights of gleanage. She is not only given permission to glean that part of the field normally off limits to poor gleaners, she is given the same opportunity as Boaz's other female workers—and beyond. Even Ruth recognizes (as the ancient readers certainly did) that this is very unusual, especially since she is a foreign woman (*nokrîyâ*).

Boaz's words also contribute to the narrator's portrayal of him. He acknowledges Ruth's tremendous act of *ḥesed*: "You left your father and mother and your homeland and came to live with a people you did not know before" (2:11). This description of her actions validates the analogy between Ruth and Abraham that her previous words to Naomi implied (i.e., 1:16–17).[48] Like Abraham, who was willing to leave father and mother and his homeland and go to a land that he did not previously know, so Ruth has done. Boaz also desires Yahweh to repay Ruth for her acts of *ḥesed* and to protect her in a special and intimate way (placing Ruth under his wings). He realizes that only Yahweh can really do this. Little does he expect that Yahweh will use him to do it!

Ruth's humility is evinced in her response to his speech. Her very use of the word *šipḥâ* (rather than *ʾāmâ*) demonstrates her presumption of a lower status.

Boaz's magnanimity is magnified even more (2:14–16). He provides Ruth with an overabundant lunch and even more special gleaning privileges—all from a man who treats her like family but ironically whose identity remains hidden from Ruth for the moment. Even this speaks to Boaz's quality. He does not reveal to Ruth that he is giving her these privileges because he is Naomi's

---

48. Trible, *God and the Rhetoric of Sexuality*, 177.

clan relative—it would have been easy to slip such information into his dialogue with her. But Boaz is not interested in how he looks in Ruth's eyes as much as in genuinely helping her and Naomi. This man is a true *gōʾēl* in his attitude towards the two widows.

That Ruth is able to glean an ephah is exceptional indeed. With the implication of 2:21, the provision of grain to the widows through Boaz's extraordinary gleaning rights amounts to close to a year's supply. The two women could not have imagined in their wildest dreams such a provision when they initially returned from Moab.

Such amazing provision, not surprisingly, enlivens Naomi. Her specific blessing on Boaz (2:20) rightly emphasizes that both Boaz and Yahweh (through Boaz) have shown *ḥesed* to them. Naomi's revelation that Boaz is among their *gōʾēls* builds the anticipation of the reader. But it is an anticipation that will not be immediately fulfilled (in fact, some question concerning whether it will happen is left at the end of Act 2).

The narrator means to imply that behind Boaz and his acts is Yahweh (who is engendering the *ḥesed* of Boaz toward the widows). This is because, at the end of the day, Yahweh is the protector and provider for widows, as Deuteronomy 10:17—19 states:

> For the LORD your God is God of gods and Lord of lords, the great God, mighty and awesome, who shows no partiality and accepts no bribes. He defends the cause of the fatherless and the widow, and loves the alien, giving him food and clothing. And you are to love those who are aliens, for you yourselves were aliens in Egypt.[49]

It is apparent that Boaz knows these laws and observes them. He is a man who cares for a helpless, defenseless widow—a man whose focus is not on himself but on others and their needs. He is truly a *gibbôr ḥayil*.

GOD IN SOVEREIGN CONTROL. We live in a world that denies God's sovereignty. Events are seen as the result of the purely independent action of "free" agents or as simple random events in the universe. That something may be ordained, patterned by the divine Creator, does not receive much consideration. Therefore, life is what we make of it. We "free agents" can control our destinies through a determination of our wills.

---

49. Cf. also Ex. 22:22—24; Deut. 24:17—18; Ps. 68:4—5; 94:1—6; 146:9.

But Ruth 2 demonstrates that if it were just left up to us, we would, in all likelihood, not make it. While Ruth took positive action (on which we will see its application shortly), she could not determine—she couldn't have even known—that she will end up in the field of Boaz, who will show her incredible kindness and will eventually marry her. If this book teaches anything, it is that the Lord is in sovereign control. While we are called on to live our lives in accordance with his Word, it is the Lord who providentially supplies our needs and orders our lives for good (Rom. 8:28). God superintends in the details of life.

Hesed. It is certainly the case that Boaz and Ruth represent ideal models of extraordinary character. As Ruth seizes the initiative to do *ḥesed*, so the text encourages its readers to take the initiative in doing *ḥesed*. There are risks involved, but Ruth's selfless attitude, action, and hard work result in God's honoring her.

It is not in some religious setting that Ruth or Boaz manifest their *ḥesed*. Rather, it is in the daily workplace, the place where too often *ḥesed* is lacking. Such manifestations of *ḥesed* are the result of commitment to the Lord, and both Ruth and Boaz exhibit *ḥesed* qualities to those around them. Certainly the writer intends that his readers (both ancient and modern) look to these two individuals as didactic models for life.

The New Testament clearly continues the injunction for the care of widows. James 1:27 states: "Religion that God our Father accepts as pure and faultless is this: to look after orphans and widows in their distress and to keep oneself from being polluted by the world." It is unfortunate that in the church today even the activity of ministry can infringe on this important need as it did in the early church. But as in the early church, provision can and must be made to implement it (Acts 6:1–4).

The apostle Paul gives a detailed treatment of this situation in 1 Timothy 5:3–16. There he outlines the need to rank the widows according to their situation in order to make sure that each is adequately taken care of. Thus, those who have children or grandchildren should be taken care of by their own families. This is obviously a continuation of the Old Testament requirements in the clan-based laws as well as in the unambiguous teaching of the fifth commandment. Moreover, by doing this, the body of believers is freed to help those in real need without using vital resources for those who can and should be cared for by others.[50] Paul also specifies that any believer who has widows in the family should help them. Again this is for the purpose of free-

---

50. In fact verse 8 states: "If anyone does not provide for his relatives, and especially for his immediate family, he has denied the faith and is worse than an unbeliever." This is a continuation of the care for relatives as seen in the Old Testament context.

ing the church to help those widows who are really in need. Paul even outlines a differentiation between younger widows and older widows and what should be done in these different instances.

Finally, the book of Ruth demonstrates that peace and well-being (i.e., šālôm) are possible in the midst of personal catastrophes and amid societal degeneration as in the days of the judges. The strength of character in Boaz and Ruth demonstrates this lesson—a lesson vitally needed by individuals in the church today, which finds itself in an analogous societal declivity.

Ruth 3:1–18

❧

O NE DAY NAOMI her mother-in-law said to her, "My daughter, should I not try to find a home for you, where you will be well provided for? ²Is not Boaz, with whose servant girls you have been, a kinsman of ours? Tonight he will be winnowing barley on the threshing floor. ³Wash and perfume yourself, and put on your best clothes. Then go down to the threshing floor, but don't let him know you are there until he has finished eating and drinking. ⁴When he lies down, note the place where he is lying. Then go and uncover his feet and lie down. He will tell you what to do."

⁵"I will do whatever you say," Ruth answered. ⁶So she went down to the threshing floor and did everything her mother-in-law told her to do.

⁷When Boaz had finished eating and drinking and was in good spirits, he went over to lie down at the far end of the grain pile. Ruth approached quietly, uncovered his feet and lay down. ⁸In the middle of the night something startled the man, and he turned and discovered a woman lying at his feet.

⁹"Who are you?" he asked.

"I am your servant Ruth," she said. "Spread the corner of your garment over me, since you are a kinsman-redeemer."

¹⁰"The LORD bless you, my daughter," he replied. "This kindness is greater than that which you showed earlier: You have not run after the younger men, whether rich or poor. ¹¹And now, my daughter, don't be afraid. I will do for you all you ask. All my fellow townsmen know that you are a woman of noble character. ¹²Although it is true that I am near of kin, there is a kinsman-redeemer nearer than I. ¹³ Stay here for the night, and in the morning if he wants to redeem, good; let him redeem. But if he is not willing, as surely as the LORD lives I will do it. Lie here until morning."

¹⁴So she lay at his feet until morning, but got up before anyone could be recognized; and he said, "Don't let it be known that a woman came to the threshing floor."

¹⁵He also said, "Bring me the shawl you are wearing and hold it out." When she did so, he poured into it six measures of barley and put it on her. Then he went back to town.

¹⁶When Ruth came to her mother-in-law, Naomi asked, "How did it go, my daughter?"

Then she told her everything Boaz had done for her ¹⁷and added, "He gave me these six measures of barley, saying, 'Don't go back to your mother-in-law empty-handed.'"

¹⁸Then Naomi said, "Wait, my daughter, until you find out what happens. For the man will not rest until the matter is settled today."

ACT 3 CONSISTS of three scenes. Scene 1 (3:1–5) is a short introductory scene that takes place at the home of Naomi during the day, with Naomi disclosing her plan for Ruth and Boaz. Scene 2 (3:6–15) is a lengthy scene that takes place at the threshing floor that evening, midnight, and dawn, with Ruth executing Naomi's plan and Boaz offering to be the kinsman-redeemer. Scene 3 (3:16–18) is a short concluding scene that takes place at the home of Naomi at dawn, in which Naomi evaluates the encounter (i.e., Boaz will act).

This Act evinces many similarities to Act 2: (1) Both contain three scenes of generally the same structure (see discussion in the introduction, pp. 397–99); (2) there is a focus on the characters of Ruth and Boaz—in particular, she is an *ʾēšet ḥayil* (3:11, "woman of noble character"); (3) the opening scene presents Naomi and Ruth, and Ruth sets out; (4) there is an encounter between Ruth and Boaz; (5) Boaz inquires about the girl's identity (3:9); (6) the opening line intimates its development (3:1—finding a home for Ruth); and (7) the closing sentence (3:18) acts as transition to what follows.

Scene 1. Naomi Discloses Her Plan for Ruth and Boaz (3:1–5)

SCENE 1 IS clearly enclosed by the statements: "One day Naomi ... said to her" (3:1) and "Ruth answered" (3:5). It takes place at the home of Naomi during the day. With the setting established (3:1a), Naomi's proposal (3:1b–2a) is given in the form of a pair of negative questions that actually constitute strong affirmations. The first question states the problem, the second the solution. "My daughter, should I not try to find a home [*mānôaḥ*] for you, where you will be well provided for?" The word *mānôaḥ* here means "a place of tranquility and repose" and refers to the condition of security and rest afforded a woman in Israelite society by marriage (cf. 1:9).[1]

---

1. Bush, *Ruth, Esther*, 147.

Commentators are split as to what is implied in this initial question of Naomi.[2] Is she concerned with providing an heir for the family line of Elimelech, or is she simply concerned (in a narrow sense) with Ruth's welfare? In other words, is she proposing here a levirate marriage that will possibly provide an heir or simply a marriage that will relieve Ruth of her destitute widowhood and provide security for her? The latter seems to be the primary focus of Naomi. Hubbard observes:

> Besides seeing Ruth happily settled, Naomi probably also wanted to provide for Ruth's uncertain fate after Naomi's death. It would be one thing for Ruth to endure widowhood in a strange land during Naomi's lifetime, quite another to do so after she was gone.[3]

Naomi's second question (3:2a) proposes that Boaz may be the answer to Ruth's need for a home (*mānôaḥ*): "Is not Boaz, with whose servant girls you have been, a kinsman of ours?"[4] It is worth noting that Naomi does not ground her presentation of Boaz as the answer to Ruth's problem of security on the fact that he is a kinsman-redeemer (*gōʾēl*), but only on his position as a relative.[5]

The fact that Boaz is a clan relative is here used to imply degree of success. In other words, since Boaz is a clan relative, the chances are increased that he will be receptive to a marriage proposal (as opposed to someone outside the clan). He already knows Ruth, and there is a reasonably good chance that he will respond positively to marriage overtures. Moreover, the opportunity is right: "Tonight[6] he will be winnowing barley on the threshing floor." In other words, he will be alone, and the circumstances will be perfect for a marriage proposal.

Winnowing barley consisted of throwing the mixture of straw, chaff, and grain up into the wind by means of a fork with large teeth. The chaff was blown away farthest from the winnower, the straw less far, while the heavier kernels of grain fell back onto the threshing floor.[7]

---

2. Campbell, in fact, suggests that the verbal construction here alludes to other unspecified efforts by Naomi behind the scenes (*Ruth*, 116).

3. Hubbard, *The Book of Ruth*, 198.

4. The NIV translation does not reflect the conjunction + particle (*wᵉʿattâ*) that regularly introduces a logical step in an argument, often a consequence or a conclusion. Thus the question should be translated: "So then, is not Boaz a relative of ours?"

5. Bush, *Ruth, Esther*, 148.

6. The choice of "tonight" rather than "this evening" may have been dictated by thematic considerations, i.e., to orient the audience to the timing of the scene about to unfold in the dark of the night. See Campbell, *Ruth*, 119; and Hubbard, *The Book of Ruth*, 201 n. 16.

7. Borowski, *Agriculture in Iron Age Israel*, 65−66.

Naomi formulates a risky and fragile scheme. She instructs Ruth to do three things: bathe, put on perfumed oil, and put on her "dress" (*śimlâ*). The NIV translates *śimlâ* as "best clothes." However, as Bush and others have rightly observed, the *śimlâ* was simply a generic piece of clothing worn by both men and women (although there were apparently differences between the two, Deut. 22:5).[8]

A number of commentators understand Naomi's instructions to be a bride's preparations for marriage, so that Ruth comes to Boaz as a bride. But this is not borne out by comparison with other bridal contexts in the Old Testament. This is not to say that Ruth is not "making herself more presentable," but she is not "decking herself out" either (e.g., note that no jewelry or dress of fine linen is mentioned). The most likely explanation of Naomi's instructions is that they mean that Ruth should end her period of mourning and so signal her return to the normal activities and desires of life, which, of course, would include marriage. This change in her appearance, with its symbolic meaning, will indicate to Boaz both her availability and the seriousness of her intentions.[9]

Naomi also gives Ruth further instructions on what to do at the threshing floor. (1) "Don't let him know you are there until he has finished eating and drinking." Naomi's intention here is probably to make sure that the mood is the best for receptivity as possible.

(2) When he lies down, Ruth is to note that place and then go and uncover his feet (or legs)[10] and lie down close beside him (probably not simply "at his feet," as is often understood),[11] so that "both lie beside one another as husband and wife."[12] That sexual overtones are present in the action of a woman uncovering a man's legs in the dark of the night and lying down, there can be no doubt. But that our author intends the explicitly sexual sense of "uncover his genitals and lie down" is in my opinion utterly improbable.[13]

(3) Thus, Ruth's action of uncovering Boaz's legs and lying down is a nonverbal, apparently customary means of requesting marriage. That this is the case is reinforced by Naomi's final instruction: "He will tell you what to do."

---

8. Bush, *Ruth, Esther*, 150–52; Block, *Judges, Ruth*, 683. According to Ex. 22:25–26, poor people used this garment for a blanket at night. Since Ruth is a poor person going out to spend the night in the field, she certainly will need this to stay warm.

9. Bush, *Ruth, Esther*, 152. Block points out that this is confirmed by the interesting analogy of 2 Sam. 12:20, in which David ceased his mourning, washed himself, applied perfumed oil, put on his *śimlâ*, and went to the temple to worship—i.e., resumed normal life.

10. This particular term (*marg°lôt*), derived from *regel*, is used only in Ruth (3:4, 7, 8, 14) and Dan. 10:6. It probably has the same range of meaning as *regel* (foot, lower leg, leg), although in Dan. 10:6 it clearly refers to the legs as a whole (there it is paired to arms).

11. See, e.g., L. Morris, "Ruth," in *Judges, and Ruth* (TOTC. Downers Grove, Ill.: Inter-Varsity, 1968), 286; Hubbard, *The Book of Ruth*, 121.

12. See Bush, *Ruth, Esther*, 152; Zenger, *Das Buch Ruth*, 67.

13. Bush, *Ruth, Esther*, 153.

Ruth's response demonstrates her willingness to engage in this risky endeavor: "I will do whatever you say" (3:5). It should be remembered that things could go wrong in the plan. For example, Boaz could mock her request for marriage to him—a wealthy and powerful Israelite landowner—as a vain attempt at social climbing for a poor widowed "Moabitess." Or, since Ruth has not secured a new marriage contract and is technically still the wife of Mahlon (cf. 4:5, 10), Boaz could charge her with failing in her family responsibilities, branding her an adulteress. Or even worse, Boaz could use the night's opportunity for his sexual pleasure, bringing on her great humiliation, and then malign her (charging her with entrapment) or even charge her with prostitution. Yet Ruth responds, "I will do whatever you say," which demonstrates her radical commitment to and trust in Naomi. Fortunately, there is the possibility that Boaz will wake up and recognize immediately the true meaning of Ruth's actions and respond favorably to her.

Scene 2. Ruth Executes Naomi's Plan and Boaz Offers to Be Kinsman-Redeemer (3:6–15)

SCENE 2 IS enclosed by two statements: "So she went down to the threshing floor" (3:6), and "then he went back to town" (3:15). It takes place at the threshing floor during the evening, midnight, and dawn, with Ruth executing Naomi's plan and Boaz offering to be the kinsman-redeemer. The scene divides basically into two parts: Ruth's implementation of Naomi's plan (3:6–9) and Boaz's response to the plan (3:10–15). It is chiastically arranged:[14]

A Ruth's symbolic actions of petition (narrative) (3:6–7)
  B Ruth's words of petition (dialogue) (3:8–9)
  B′ Boaz's words of consent (dialogue) (3:10–13)
A′ Boaz's symbolic actions of commitment (narrative) (3:14–15)

In section A, verse 6 forms a transition between Scenes 1 and 2. Moreover, it summarizes and previews the entire Scene 2 by emphasizing that Ruth "went down to the threshing floor and did everything her mother-in-law told her to do." Verse 7 narrates that Boaz is in good spirits (lit., "his heart was good"). Thus, he will be receptive to the request communicated by Ruth's symbolic actions. In addition, the verse mentions that Boaz lies down to sleep "at the far end of the grain pile." This "minor detail" is suggestive. Earlier Ruth "happened" to come to the field of Boaz (2:3); now it is Boaz who "happens" to lie down at the opportunistic corner of the threshing floor where the symbolic actions can transpire without interruption or misinter-

---

14. For a fuller discussion, see Bush, *Ruth, Esther,* 159–61.

pretation. Hence, stealthily Ruth approaches, uncovers his legs, and lies down. The narrator has built the suspense to a peak.

The next section of the scene (B, 3:8−9) records a dialogue between Boaz and Ruth in which Ruth verbalizes her petition for marriage. But the writer introduces this dialogue from Boaz's perspective: In the middle of the night he is startled,[15] and he turns over and discovers that someone—a woman—is lying beside him!

The utter surprise of Boaz is captured in the narration. Quite naturally he probingly exclaims: "Who are you?" Ruth's words are carefully chosen. She begins by identifying herself: "I am your servant [*ʾāmâ*] Ruth." Earlier in 2:13, Ruth referred to herself as Boaz's *šipḥâ*, although she does not really have even this status (she is officially a *nokrîyâ*, "foreign woman"; see comments on 2:13). Now she uses *ʾāmâ*; the choice of the socially higher term is doubtless Ruth's attempt to suggest that she is within the class of women who might be married. This word seems to emphasize a slave's feminine qualities (need for protection, weakness, sexual attractiveness, etc.), while *šipḥâ* seems to be used when the female is viewed as a possession and a laborer.[16]

Both terms can be used as self-designations. When used this way, *ʾāmâ* suggests a female petitioner's weakness and need for help or protection when presenting a request before a more powerful male, never before another female. When *šipḥâ* is used as a self-designation, it signifies the woman's subservience and readiness to serve or obey instructions.[17] The word *ʾāmâ* does show respect to a superior to be sure, but even a woman of high rank, married to a man of wealth, might use this word to put herself in a subordinate position (cf. Abigail in 1 Sam. 25:41).[18] Thus, in her nocturnal visit Ruth's reference to herself as an *ʾāmâ* is appropriate in the context of a request of marriage[19] to a *gibbôr ḥayil* like Boaz.

---

15. Block notes that the notion of fear is not inherent in the word *ḥrd* used here (*Judges, Ruth*, 690, n. 34). Cf. Ex. 19:16; 1 Sam. 14:15; Isa. 32:11. The Targum reads, "and he was afraid, and his flesh became soft like a turnip from fear" (see discussion by D. R. G. Beattie, *The Targum of Ruth* [Aramaic Targum 19; Collegeville, Minn.: Liturgical, 1994], 26 n. 5). Block adds: "Any effort to attribute the 'startling' to a dream or a midnight apparition or a visit by a night demon (Lilith) is unnecessarily speculative." For further discussion see Bush, *Ruth, Esther*, 162.

16. I. Riesener, *Der Stamm ʿbd in Alten Testament: Eine Wortuntersuchung unter Berücksichtigung neuerer sprachwissenschaftlicher Methoden* (BZAW 149; Berlin and New York: de Gruyter, 1979), 76–83.

17. R. Schultz, "אָמָה" and "שִׁפְחָה" *NIDOTTE*, 1:418–21; 4:211–13.

18. This nuance seems to be confirmed in extrabiblical Hebrew inscriptions; see the discussion in Younger, "Two Comparative Notes on the Book of Ruth," 126–28.

19. Hubbard, *The Book of Ruth*, 211.

Next, Ruth invokes Boaz to "spread the corner of your garment [*kānāp*] over me, since you are a kinsman-redeemer [*gōʾēl*]." The choice of the term *kānāp* is purposeful as it carries a number of nuances. (1) It can be construed as a general plea for protection. Thus, Ruth is invoking Boaz's usage of the term *kānāp* ("wings") in 2:12.[20] Like the "wings" in 2:12, this gesture probably also symbolizes protection of the woman (and perhaps sexual readiness as well). By repeating the key word from his own lips, Ruth essentially asks Boaz to answer his own prayer![21]

(2) The term *kānāp* may also refer to the "corner of his garment" and hence be a more specific reference to the symbolic investment connected with marriage. The term *marriage* is not spoken, but the intentions of Boaz are clear. The next morning he officially redeems the land and acquires Ruth as his wife (4:9–10). The "spreading of the hem" of one's garment over a woman appears to be a variant of the ceremonial covering of the head of the bride by the husband.[22]

> An obvious correspondence between the two acts is the symbolical use of clothes. The idea behind each of the rites seems to be that clothes are a symbol of appurtenance, while nakedness is a symbol of social ejection. The public investiture, whether with a veil or another garment, established the new family situation of the woman.[23]

Hubbard concludes that the repetition of *kānāp* in 2:12 and 3:9 implies a relationship between the two.

> Thus, by covering Ruth with his *kānāp*—that is, to marry her—Boaz implements Yahweh's *kānāp*—that is, his protection of Ruth. Or to weave a thread dropped earlier, the *ḥesed* of Boaz toward Ruth is the form in which Yahweh conveys his *ḥesed* to her.[24]

In addition, Ruth's choice of the term "kinsman-redeemer" (*gōʾēl*) is not fortuitous. Contrary to some interpreters, Ruth is not going beyond Naomi's instructions in appealing to Boaz's *gōʾēl* status. Naomi herself revealed that

---

20. The idiom *pāraś kānāp ʿal* ("to spread a garment-cover over [someone]") means "to marry" (Ezek. 16:8; cf. Deut. 22:30 [23:1]; 27:20; Mal. 2:16).

21. L. Morris puts it this way: "Ruth had put herself under Yahweh's 'wing' when she came to Judah. Now she seeks also to put herself under that of Boaz." See Morris, *Ruth*, 290.

22. K. van der Toorn, "The Significance of the Veil in the Ancient Near East," in *Pomegranates and Golden Bells: Studies in Biblical, Jewish, and Near Eastern Ritual, Law, and Literature in Honor of Jacob Milgrom*, ed. D. P. Wright, D. N. Freedman, and A. Hurvitz (Winona Lake, Ind.: Eisenbrauns, 1995), 327–39, esp. 334–35.

23. Ibid., 335.

24. Hubbard, "The *Gōʾel* in Ancient Israel," 17.

Boaz is among the *gōʾēls* for herself and Ruth (2:20). The possibility of the success of the marriage invitation is dependent on the clan relative/*gōʾēl* status[25] of Boaz (cf. again 2:20; 3:2). There are other clan relatives/*gōʾēls*, but Ruth is invoking this status of Boaz as a basis for *his* response.

Ruth's actions and words seem to achieve the desired effect. In section B' (3:10–13), Boaz issues his words of consent. Clearly he understands her actions and words to mean something other than "Sleep with me!" He takes them to be an invitation to marriage. Instead of cursing her and shooing her off as some immoral whore, he blesses her.[26]

There is no doubt that this scene on the threshing floor is sexually provocative. But the narrator constantly and consistently depicts both Ruth and Boaz as individuals of unmatched integrity (*ʾēšet ḥayil* and *gibbôr ḥayil*), whose lives exhibit that faithful loyalty to relationships described by the Hebrew word *ḥesed*. It is evident that his silence means to imply here that they meet this moment of choice with the same integrity. The sexual connotations of the scene are used by the narrator to convey the sexual and emotional tension felt by the characters.[27]

Boaz's first words are a blessing: "The LORD bless you, my daughter" (3:10). He then states: "This kindness [*ḥesed*] is greater than that which you showed earlier: You have not run after the younger men, whether rich or poor." Literally the Hebrew reads, "You have made your last *ḥesed* better than the first." Ruth's first act of *ḥesed* obviously refers to her compassionate loyalty and kindness to Naomi, which Boaz has already noted (2:11). Ruth's latest *ḥesed*, in this context, seems to refer to her proposal of marriage to Boaz. This is evident from the second clause where Boaz asserts, "You have not run after the younger men, whether rich or poor."

That Ruth could have sought marriage with any of the men of the town means that she is under no legal obligation to become the wife of Mahlon's

---

25. The two descriptions are interconnected and establish his status and role. As pointed out in the introductory remarks on the *gōʾēl*, there was a hierarchy of response, and while it was a role that should be carried out, it was not a must.

26. Block, *Judges, Ruth*, 692.

27. Bernstein aptly puts it this way: "The narrative tells us straightforwardly that no sexual intercourse has taken place on the threshing floor, that final resolutions await the scene at the city gate. All the while, however, the vocabulary of the scene indicates that it might have, that the atmosphere was sexually charged. Thus the ambivalence. The words point, beneath the surface, to the might-have-been which the characters felt might be, while the combinations of the words emphasize the opposing reality. The author of Ruth is relying upon ambiguity in language to depict the tension of emotion, enabling him to convey the atmospherics of the scene without digressing from his narrative to describe them." See M. Bernstein, "Two Multivalent Readings in the Ruth Narrative," *JSOT* 50 (1991): 15–26, esp. 19–20.

closest relative in order to raise up an heir for her dead husband (i.e., carry out the levirate as prescribed in Deut. 25:5–10). And vice versa, the closest relative of Mahlon is not obligated to perform a levirate marriage—and apparently none of the relatives (close or otherwise) has given any thought to implementing a marriage to Ruth.[28]

Boaz goes on to assure Ruth, "And now, my daughter, don't be afraid. I will do for you all you ask." While the last clause may be formulaic, it nevertheless stresses Boaz's commitment to Ruth. He then adds: "All my fellow townsmen know that you are a woman of noble character [*ʾēšet ḥayil*]." This phrase clearly emphasizes "the quality of Ruth's person."[29] Boaz's attribution of this quality to Ruth matches the narrator's attribution of this quality to him in 2:1 (see comments). Block sums it up this way:

> Boaz could have treated her as Moabite trash, scavenging in the garbage cans of Israel, and then corrupting the people with her whorish behavior; but with the true *ḥesed* of his own, he sees her as a woman equal in status and character to himself.[30]

Boaz's next statements provide additional support for the narrator's earlier assessment of his quality as a *gibbôr ḥayil*: "Although it is true that I am near of kin [lit., kinsman-redeemer, *gōʾēl*], there is a kinsman-redeemer [*gōʾēl*] nearer [or more closely related] than I." Boaz acknowledges his responsibility, but he also recognizes the fact of hierarchy within the clan structure. He will not misappropriate that hierarchy but will give opportunity to the nearer kinsman to act first. On this, Campbell aptly remarks:

> From a story-telling point of view, this has the marvelous effect of creating one more suspenseful moment, in which Boaz is given his opportunity to show his worthiness; for it is one feature of Boaz's valor that he will not even usurp another man's right to act responsibly![31]

Boaz concludes his response to Ruth's marriage invitation with some instructions to her. "Stay here for the night, and in the morning if he [this nearer *gōʾēl*] wants to redeem, good; let him redeem. But if he is not willing, I vow that, as surely as the LORD lives, I will do it. Lie here until morning."

The final section of Scene 2 (A′, 3:14–15) takes place the next morning, when Boaz engages in a symbolic action that signifies the genuineness of his

---

28. The request to Boaz reflects *ḥesed* loyalty to Naomi for as a *gōʾēl*, Boaz is a relative who can ensure security for Naomi, not just Ruth.

29. Campbell, *Ruth*, 125. Hence the attraction of the book to the final poem of the book of Proverbs in some of the canonical orderings (see the introduction).

30. Block, *Judges, Ruth*, 695.

31. Campbell, *Ruth*, 137.

promise (in parallel to Ruth's symbolic actions that previous evening). After remaining the night, Ruth arises early before anyone else, after which Boaz expresses the thought: "Don't let it be known that a woman came to the threshing floor." The writer is communicating the idea that both Boaz and Ruth now take the initiative in the progress toward resolution of what has become their common cause.

Boaz's symbolic action of promise (3:15) is parallel to his first act of generosity in 2:14–17. Asking Ruth for her shawl,[32] he measures out six measures of barley and gives it to her (3:15). The exact amount of his gift of barley is unknown since there is uncertainty concerning what measure is involved (certainly not an ephah since no shawl could support such a volume and weight). It is clear from the gift, however, that this is meant as a symbol of his commitment to the relationship. He will do what is right. As though the symbol were not enough, the narrator adds, "Then he went back to town," which notes his immediate attention to the matter at hand (i.e., no delay in fulfilling his commitment to Ruth).[33]

Scene 3. Naomi Evaluates the Encounter (3:16–18)

THIS BRIEF SCENE contains Naomi's question, Ruth's reply, and Naomi's conclusion. It takes place at Naomi's home at dawn (with a reference to an expected conclusion the next day, 3:18). Naomi evaluates the encounter of the previous night (i.e., Boaz will act).

Scene 3 begins with the statement, "Ruth [lit., she] came to her mother-in-law." This contrasts with the concluding statement of the previous scene, "He went to the city." Then Naomi's question begins the dialogue, "How did it go, my daughter?" (lit., "Who are you, my daughter?").[34]

The narrator telescopes all of the events from the previous night into one statement, "Then she told her everything Boaz had done for her." This allows the narrator to focus attention on only one of the things that Boaz said—in fact, something attributed to Boaz only through a quote by Ruth in her response to Naomi's question: "He gave me these six measures of barley, saying, 'Don't go back to your mother-in-law empty-handed'" (3:17).

There can be little doubt that the writer's use of the word "empty" is meant to reflect the reversal of Naomi's "emptiness" expressed in 1:21: "I went away full, but the LORD has brought me back empty." By putting it on

---

32. The term *miṭpaḥat* is used only here and in Isa. 3:22, where it appears to have the nuance "cloak."

33. For a discussion of the textual problem in this verse, see Block, *Judges, Ruth,* 698.

34. The question is not concerned about identification but about Ruth's situation; the NIV translation attempts to reflect this.

the lips of Ruth (rather than on the lips of Boaz in the previous scene), there is a rich irony since it was Ruth who heard the word used for the first time by Naomi as an expression of her deep despair, even though Ruth was present and already foreshadowed Naomi's relief. Campbell reasons: "With a single word the resolution of one part of Naomi's plight is accomplished."[35] Moreover, the narrator is able to throw all the stress on the gift and, in particular, on the reason for it.

> This stress is intended to communicate to us (and to Naomi!) the seriousness of Boaz's intentions. Surely, then, he intends to imply that this really is Boaz's purpose in giving the gift of grain and not just Ruth's impression of the same.[36]

Naomi's response to Ruth reveals that she fully understands the meaning of Boaz's symbolic gift. She counsels Ruth to sit tight. Her confidence in Boaz's integrity is undiminished, even greater than when she sent Ruth to the threshing floor. But there is another *gōʾēl* (kinsman-redeemer), and there is some uncertainty on how things will transpire. Thus it is best for Ruth to patiently wait and see.

This dialogue between Ruth and Naomi comprises the last words that either of them utter in the story. Poised on the threshold of fulfillment, they both step aside with Boaz taking center stage. His action will now dominate the story's resolution.

Bridging Contexts

DIVINE AND HUMAN ACTIONS. Enlivened by the amazing amount of grain that Ruth was able to glean in a day at the field of Boaz, Naomi is restored to life. This is the beginning of resolution of Naomi's emptiness (it had been hinted at in 1:22b, namely, that they were arriving as the barley harvest was beginning). It is marvelous the way in which Yahweh restores his people. Naomi's outlook changes radically from self-absorption to concern for her daughter-in-law's well-being. Naomi's response here is extraordinary because she is under no obligation to do anything of this sort for Ruth. God is truly gracious in his restoration of his people.

In this chapter it is Naomi who takes the initiative to do *ḥesed*. She clearly wants to see a new marriage for Ruth and the attendant security, permanence, and belonging it will provide Ruth. In fact, before leaving Moab

---

35. Campbell, *Ruth*, 129.
36. Bush, *Ruth, Esther*, 186.

Naomi had voiced that desire for Ruth (1:8–9). At that point, Naomi expressed this as something that Yahweh would carry out. Now, however, she seizes upon a providentially given opportunity. God has provided the possibility for her prayer to be answered.

Thus Naomi "models one way in which divine and human actions work together: believers are not to wait passively for events to happen; rather, they must seize the initiative when an opportunity presents itself," knowing that God presents the opportunity. "In Naomi's case, any success presumably would be part of Yahweh's 'full payment' of Ruth (cf. 2:12). If so, then, theologically Yahweh acts *in* Naomi's acts. That is, what Naomi does constitutes at the same time God's acts. Her acts execute God's plans."[37]

The plan is risky, but Ruth is willing to take the risk in order to see the relief of Naomi. Any number of things could go wrong (see the possibilities at the end of the discussion of Scene 1). But Ruth is radically committed to Naomi. Such commitment goes beyond what is usually found.

Acting honorably. Ruth's deeds and words at the threshing floor are honorable. Her motives are pure. She simply follows Naomi's instructions in what was apparently a customary way of making a marriage proposal. Why does Ruth take the initiative in this matter? Boaz himself comprehends one reason: age. Boaz is older vis-à-vis Ruth, and so Boaz has assumed that she will not be interested in marriage to him. Another reason is tied to the change of clothing that Naomi orders; that is, Ruth needs to put away the signals of widowhood and demonstrate that she is available. In any case, Boaz's reaction to Ruth's deeds and words shows that he interprets them as nothing but honorable.

Boaz too is pictured in this scene as acting honorably. To be awakened by the presence of a woman may cause a weaker man to succumb to temptation. But not Boaz. At this point, the contrast of Boaz on the threshing floor with Ruth and Samson with all of his sexual escapades could not be more pronounced. Both Boaz and Ruth are individuals of *ḥayil* (strength of character). In fact, Boaz attributes to Ruth the highest of compliments by calling her an *ʾēšet ḥayil* (a real, substantial woman of character). It is interesting to note that Boaz is willing to take on the "risk" of marrying Ruth when the nearer kinsman later does not.

Sexual issues. Obviously the point of this part of the story is not to give us a model on how marriage proposals should be made. In our culture the threshing floor is not the paragon of romantic settings. Rather, the point is to emphasize how God works circumstances providing the private context in which Ruth can approach Boaz concerning this matter of marriage. The

---

37. Hubbard, *The Book of Ruth*, 199.

setting also provides the context in which the motives of both Ruth and Boaz become clear so that they are beyond question.

In the midst of a sexually charged setting where the potential for sin and abuse is high, this couple demonstrate their honor and integrity in their words and actions. Neither takes advantage of the other for personal gain or gratification. In a world obsessed with taking advantage of every opportunity for personal gratification—rare indeed is the movie that shows characters in sexually charged circumstances not fulfilling their self-interest—we need encouragement that to act with integrity is not only possible but preferable.

Both Boaz and Ruth take the initiative after the threshing-floor incident to accomplish the marriage; it is now their common cause. But because of the legal context, it will be Boaz who assumes the major role in bringing about its fulfillment.

Boaz's gift and words are significant. The keyword is the word "empty." It signals the next stage in the removal of Naomi's emptiness. If Ruth's first day of gleaning is the beginning of the resolution of Naomi's emptiness, the gift and word from Boaz are one more step toward its complete resolution—and one more way that God demonstrates his *ḥesed* to the widows.

 INTEGRITY. Act 3 of the book of Ruth displays three individuals acting on behalf of others, even when there is no obligation to do so. Naomi has no obligation or duty to find Ruth a husband. The easy route for her is to enjoy her final years knowing that Boaz will let Ruth glean enough for them to live. There is a real risk in sending Ruth on such a mission. She might jeopardize the whole situation. Boaz might become irritated or offended by Ruth's symbolic actions and cut the two widows off. True, because he is a man of integrity, the risk is lessened, but any small mistake or misrepresentation could destroy even the relatively good, though still impoverished, situation that the two women enjoy now by ruining the relationship to Boaz.

Ruth is also not obligated to follow Naomi's plan. She runs a number of risks in this plan. Again, one misrepresentation, one misplaced word could undo all the good that has been developed over the last two months.

Finally, Boaz is not obligated to respond the way he does. There are risks for him too. But in all three individuals we see models of decisive action in doing what is right. Each one acts honorably and with integrity, even in (or especially in) difficult or tempting contexts. For Ruth and Boaz, integrity is on the line on the threshing floor. But because their motives are pure, they respond in accordance with God's standards.

All of this speaks volumes in a world where integrity seems to be a forgotten character quality. Whether one is looking at the political scene or at the world of business, there seems to be a great shortage of integrity. People seem to be more concerned with whether they are liable than whether they are doing the right thing. They are concerned more with not suffering personal loss than with living by godly, biblical principles.

In many ways Ruth and Boaz demonstrate their pure motives in this chapter. And it is the issue of purity in motives that is the very heart of the issue of integrity. Human beings, whether believers or unbelievers, have difficulty with pure motives. James makes it clear to his readers that many of them were trying to deal with God in their prayers with improper motives (James 4:3). And naturally, if they were dealing with God with impure motives, it isn't hard to imagine that they weren't dealing with their fellow Christians or others in their community any differently.

One of the important ways in which the Scriptures attempt to encourage and stimulate us to proper motives is the reality of a future judgment that will consider this issue. Thus, for example, Proverbs 16:2 points out that "all a man's ways seem innocent to him, but motives are weighed by the LORD." Lest Christians forget this important stimulus, Paul reminds believers that when the Lord Jesus Christ returns, "he will bring to light what is hidden in darkness and will expose the motives of men's hearts." And at that time "each will receive his praise from God" (1 Cor. 4:5).

Another important teaching that encourages proper motives is the One whom we as Christians serve. Once again Paul explains:

> For the appeal we make does not spring from error or impure motives, nor are we trying to trick you. On the contrary, we speak as men approved by God to be entrusted with the gospel. We are not trying to please men but God, who tests our hearts. (1 Thess. 2:3–4)

As Christians, ultimately we are called to serve the Lord and therefore ought to speak and act out of pure motives that will bring honor and glory to his name. Honesty with God and honesty with ourselves as we reflect on what we are doing and why we are doing it goes a long way in helping us to evaluate our motives and to act with integrity with others.

Ḥesed. Ruth is characterized by Boaz as an *ʾēšet ḥayil* (a real, substantial woman of character). And the character that she (and Boaz) displays is nothing short of the standard of *ḥesed*. Loyalty and love are at the root of their actions. The character that they manifest and that we are called to imitate is summed up in the following: love, joy, peace, patience, kindness, goodness, faithfulness, gentleness and self-control (i.e., the fruit of the Spirit, Gal. 5:22–23). The apostle Paul outlines this *ḥesed* quality in 1 Corinthians 13:4–7:

Love is patient, love is kind. It does not envy, it does not boast, it is not proud. It is not rude, it is not self-seeking, it is not easily angered, it keeps no record of wrongs. Love does not delight in evil but rejoices with the truth. It always protects, always trusts, always hopes, always perseveres.

What Ruth and Boaz manifest is what Jesus puts in the form of a command: "My command is this: Love each other as I have loved you" (John 15:12). He then models this for us: "Greater love has no one than this, that he lay down his life for his friends" (15:13).

True covenant faith is expressed by concern for the welfare of others. In our story this concern is expressed by loving actions of *ḥesed* that promote the other person's well-being and by verbal expressions of prayer for the other person. How many Christians expect the pastor to minister to them without once considering that God expects Christians to be ministering to one another? Through this story about these long-ago folk from Bethlehem, the narrator is able to flesh out for the modern reader what the life of faith should look like. The measure of a person's faith is not found in the miracles that he or she can wrest from the hand of God nor in his or her personal health and prosperity, but in demonstrating ethical character. As James points out, "faith without deeds is dead" (James 2:26), and this book, especially in the acts of *ḥesed* in chapters 2–4, paints a vivid picture of a virtuous theology and a powerfully vibrant faith. In this, it has a timeless message to readers of every age.

Ruth 4:1–22

M EANWHILE BOAZ WENT up to the town gate and sat
there. When the kinsman-redeemer he had mentioned came along, Boaz said, "Come over here, my
friend, and sit down." So he went over and sat down.

²Boaz took ten of the elders of the town and said, "Sit
here," and they did so. ³Then he said to the kinsman-
redeemer, "Naomi, who has come back from Moab, is selling
the piece of land that belonged to our brother Elimelech. ⁴I
thought I should bring the matter to your attention and suggest that you buy it in the presence of these seated here and
in the presence of the elders of my people. If you will redeem
it, do so. But if you will not, tell me, so I will know. For no
one has the right to do it except you, and I am next in line."

"I will redeem it," he said.

⁵Then Boaz said, "On the day you buy the land from
Naomi and from Ruth the Moabitess, you acquire the dead
man's widow, in order to maintain the name of the dead with
his property."

⁶At this, the kinsman-redeemer said, "Then I cannot redeem
it because I might endanger my own estate. You redeem it
yourself. I cannot do it."

⁷(Now in earlier times in Israel, for the redemption and
transfer of property to become final, one party took off his
sandal and gave it to the other. This was the method of legal-
izing transactions in Israel.)

⁸So the kinsman-redeemer said to Boaz, "Buy it yourself."
And he removed his sandal.

⁹Then Boaz announced to the elders and all the people,
"Today you are witnesses that I have bought from Naomi all
the property of Elimelech, Kilion and Mahlon. ¹⁰I have also
acquired Ruth the Moabitess, Mahlon's widow, as my wife, in
order to maintain the name of the dead with his property, so
that his name will not disappear from among his family or
from the town records. Today you are witnesses!"

¹¹Then the elders and all those at the gate said, "We are
witnesses. May the LORD make the woman who is coming into
your home like Rachel and Leah, who together built up the

house of Israel. May you have standing in Ephrathah and be famous in Bethlehem. ¹²Through the offspring the LORD gives you by this young woman, may your family be like that of Perez, whom Tamar bore to Judah."

¹³So Boaz took Ruth and she became his wife. Then he went to her, and the LORD enabled her to conceive, and she gave birth to a son. ¹⁴The women said to Naomi: "Praise be to the LORD, who this day has not left you without a kinsman-redeemer. May he become famous throughout Israel! ¹⁵He will renew your life and sustain you in your old age. For your daughter-in-law, who loves you and who is better to you than seven sons, has given him birth."

¹⁶Then Naomi took the child, laid him in her lap and cared for him. ¹⁷The women living there said, "Naomi has a son." And they named him Obed. He was the father of Jesse, the father of David.

¹⁸This, then, is the family line of Perez:

> Perez was the father of Hezron,
> ¹⁹Hezron the father of Ram,
> Ram the father of Amminadab,
> ²⁰Amminadab the father of Nahshon,
> Nahshon the father of Salmon,
> ²¹Salmon the father of Boaz,
> Boaz the father of Obed,
> ²²Obed the father of Jesse,
> and Jesse the father of David.

THIS FINAL CHAPTER of Ruth is composed of three elements: Act 4 (4:1–12), in which Boaz takes the initiative to act as kinsman-redeemer; an epilogue (4:13–17), which balances the prologue as it shows how Naomi's emptiness has been resolved with fullness; and a coda (4:18–22), which gives a genealogy from Perez to David.

Act 4: Boaz Arranges to Marry Ruth (4:1–12)

THIS ACT IS amazingly parallel to Act 1 (esp. Scene 1, 1:7–19a); Boaz here has a dialogue with the nearer kinsman-redeemer and then with the legal assembly. In the course of this dialogue, the nearer redeemer withdraws. This is like the dialogue between Naomi, Ruth, and Orpah, in the course of which Orpah departs for home. Boaz's acquisition of the right to marry Ruth in 4:9–12 resolves the question of a home and husband for her. This, of course, was the very problem on which the dialogue between Naomi and the two young women centered and which Ruth appeared to forfeit when she committed her life to Naomi and Yahweh.

Act 4 is comprised of two scenes. In Scene 1 (4:1–8), Boaz confronts an unnamed kinsman-redeemer (*gōʾēl*) who has the legal first right of redemption. In Scene 2 (4:9–12), Boaz acquires the right to redeem the field of Elimelech with its implications concerning Ruth and Naomi.

The opening line intimates the development of this Act—the decisive event at the gate (4:1). The closing sentence acts as transition to what follows in the epilogue (4:12). The section emphasizes the responsibilities inherent in ties of kinship, in particular to the levirate marriage (i.e., the future). Just as Orpah served as a foil to heighten the character of Ruth in 1:7–19a, so the unnamed kinsman-redeemer serves as a foil to heighten the character of Boaz in 4:1–12. Finally, the initiative for action shifts to Boaz in this act. Without his positive, purposeful, and skillful maneuvering, the story will not see its favorable resolution.

Scene 1. Boaz confronts the unnamed kinsman (4:1–8). Scene 1 divides into two clearly discernible parts: Boaz's convening of the legal assembly (4:1–2) and Boaz's negotiations with the nearer redeemer (4:3–8). The first part sets the stage for the dialogues of negotiation in the second part. After Ruth gave Naomi her report (3:16–18), Boaz, true to his words, "went up to the town gate and sat there" (obviously with the intent of resolving the matter concerning Ruth).

The NIV's translation of 4:1a ("When the kinsman-redeemer he had mentioned came along") completely obscures the impact of the Hebrew grammatical construction, which is better translated here as "and just then" (*wᵉhinnēh* + subj. + part.). It is meant to convey surprise. Campbell states:

> Here, as there [2:4], the scene is set (Boaz taking his place at the gate), where upon at just the right moment along comes just the right person. Commentators who point out that virtually every male in town was bound to go out through the gate at some time during the morning on the way to work in the field are missing the impact of the Hebrew construction, which at least in Gen 24:15 and in Ruth conveys a hint of God's working behind the scenes.[1]

Thus this is not simply coincidence but the hidden hand of Yahweh at work.

Boaz calls to this individual to come over and sit down ("Come over here, my friend [*pᵉlōnî ʾalmōnî*], and sit down"). Again, the NIV translation misses the

1. Campbell, *Ruth*, 141. Cf. 2 Kings 8:5 for an interesting and clear analogy.

impact of the sentence. The phrase $p^e l \bar{o} n \hat{i}$ $^{\flat} alm \bar{o} n \hat{i}$ is an example of a wordplay termed *farrago*.[2] The best translation is "So-and-So." The same expression is used in 1 Samuel 21:2 and 2 Kings 6:8, where the narrator does not wish to give the name of the place, so that the translation "such and such a place" is appropriate.[3]

This phrase originates with the narrator, not with Boaz. Boaz would surely know the name of a fellow citizen in a small town like Bethlehem, not to mention a relative who is the $g\bar{o}^{\flat} \bar{e}l$ just prior to him. Consequently, the narrator is underscoring the namelessness of this man in order to create a less than favorable impression and is prompting the audience to suspect a pejorative purpose in the choice of the expression.[4] Therefore, to translate the expression as "my friend" is to obscure the narrator's purposeful omission of the man's name.

Having called the man over, Boaz now procures ten elders of the city. This contrasts markedly with the way in which Boaz summoned the nearer relative. While he summoned this man over at the moment he passed through the gate, the text strongly suggests that Boaz does not simply wait in the gate with the other redeemer until ten elders of the city chance to pass through on their way to the fields. Instead, he actively seeks these individuals out so that the legal proceedings can start. As Bush puts it:

> ... it would seem that the specific statement that Boaz procured ten of the town's elders is intended to stress the care that he took to ensure that a duly constituted legal forum would be present to notarize and legitimate the civil proceedings he wished to set in motion.[5]

The second part of Scene 1 records Boaz's negotiations with the nearer $g\bar{o}^{\flat} \bar{e}l$ (4:3–8). Having convened the legal assembly, he immediately opens the negotiation with a statement to this relative of his (4:3). It introduces a totally new item to the story. Without a single prior word on the subject, the narrator has Boaz inform the nearer redeemer that "Naomi, who has come back

---

2. Sasson, *Ruth*, 106. This is a wordplay in which unrelated and perhaps even meaningless rhyming words are combined to produce a new idiom. English examples might included: "hodge-podge," "helter-skelter," "heebie-jeebies," and "hocus-pocus" (see Block, *Judges, Ruth*, 706).

3. The renderings of the ancient versions, which attempt to translate the expression by some etymological explanation, are clearly attempts to translate a difficult and unknown phrase (i.e., they are nothing more than guesses by the translators).

4. Zenger, *Das Buch Ruth*, 81; Bush, *Ruth, Esther*, 197. Bush states: "Such a device can only raise our eyebrows and make us wonder proleptically about the role this man will play in the proceedings about to take place. (One wonders indeed if the Hebrew expression we have translated 'So-and-So' was also used euphemistically in place of a stronger epithet, as the English expression is!)" (p. 244).

5. Bush, *Ruth, Esther*, 199.

from Moab, is selling the piece of land that belonged to our brother[6] Elim-elech." The understanding of this statement and the rest of Act 4 are diffi-cult, and there are uncertainties on practically every level. Time and space do not permit an explanation of all the intricacies of the text.[7] What appears to be the main thrust of the passage will be presented.

First of all, it is clear that the text is *not* describing an outright sale of land by Naomi. Instead, this refers to a transaction in which only the right of use of the land is being transferred for a stipulated value (paid completely at the beginning of the deal) for a stipulated period of time (Lev. 25:14–16). This is because the land of the family or clan could not be sold permanently (25:23; cf. 1 Kings 2:3). In this context, the word translated by the NIV "is sell-ing" (*mkr*) is best translated into English as "to surrender the right to."[8]

It also seems best to understand (as the majority of scholars do) that Naomi must have inherited rights to the field of Elimelech. The proprietary rights to the land in the Old Testament were vested in the clan, with the indi-vidual only holding the right of possession and usufruct.[9] Thus, a widow could only hold usufructuary rights to her husband's property, and she did this only until she married again or died in her turn, at which time the rights reverted to her husband's clan in the normal order of inheritance.

Since Naomi "is selling" the field, only two broad scenarios are possible explanations: (1) Elimelech did not sell the usufruct of his field before emi-grating to Moab, and Naomi now has the usufructuary rights to the field. Naomi through Boaz is calling on the nearer redeemer to acquire these rights from her. The transaction, then, is a case of preemption such as is related in Jeremiah 32.[10] (2) Elimelech sold the usufruct of his land[11] before he and his family emigrated to Moab, and the field since then has been in the possession of others. Since Naomi has no means to repurchase the field, she transfers this

---

6. Brother is used in the sense of clan relative here.

7. For a more complete recent discussion of the difficulties, see Bush, *Ruth, Esther*, 200–243. I must acknowledge my general dependence on Bush's research and argumentation at this point.

8. Ibid., 202. At issue is not the transfer of ownership of property but the acquisition of the right of holding in usufruct someone else's property until the next Jubilee Year" (E. Lipiński, "מכר," *TDOT*, 8:292).

9. The term "usufruct" means "the right of enjoying the use, profits, and advantages of another's property or estate short of the destruction, waste or impairing of its substance."

10. The absence of the seller and the failure to mention any payment or its amount ren-der it most difficult, if not impossible, to regard the transaction involved as a preemptive sale, or sale of any kind, of the field of Elimelech to Boaz by Naomi. In addition, the nearer redeemer's change of mind also makes it virtually impossible to understand the transaction as a preemption. See Bush, *Ruth, Esther*, 215.

11. Outright sale was, of course, not possible to him.

obligation/right to her nearest kinsman. Now Naomi through Boaz is calling on the nearer redeemer to repurchase the field from its present possessor. The transaction, then, is a case of redemption such as is described in Leviticus 25:25. This is the more likely scenario in this context.

Hence, Naomi is surrendering her rights to the usufruct of Elimelech's land, rights she enjoys as the widow of the deceased. Boaz then solemnly calls on the nearer redeemer to accept these rights and to redeem the field, that is, to repurchase it from the unnamed third party to whom, since it stands in need of redemption, Elimelech must have previously sold it.

Surely this nearer kinsman is aware of Naomi's return (1:19 states "when they [Naomi and Ruth] arrived in Bethlehem, the whole town was stirred because of them"[12]). Thus, it seems apparent that he has not taken any initiative to "help" Naomi and/or Ruth. In other words, in contrast to Boaz, who had already functioned as a *gōʾēl* of sorts for Naomi and Ruth, this man has done *nothing*. It seems likely that this nearer redeemer has been thinking along different lines.

In all probability he knows about the plot of Elimelech.[13] So, if he quietly ignores his voluntary family responsibility to marry Ruth (the only eligible widow of marriageable age), then he can negate the possibility of raising up an heir to the property of the deceased (see the discussion of the levirate in the introduction). Without a descendant of the line of Elimelech, the field will simply become part of his own family inheritance. The amount that he would pay to redeem it (and perhaps care for the elderly widow involved) would be offset by the value and produce of the field. With such self-interest in mind, the nearer redeemer quickly consents to redeem the field when Boaz draws his attention to it.

However, the levirate was indelibly linked to the inherited estate (*naḥălâ*).[14] Where the land has already been alienated (as in the case of Elimelech), redemption of it "triggers" the levirate duty[15] (cf. the discussion

---

12. Cf. 1 Sam. 4:5 (people rejoicing at the ark's return) and 1 Kings 1:45 (people rejoicing at Solomon's anointing). Even granting some overstatement here, the sentence, nevertheless, conveys the substantial impact of the return of Naomi and Ruth on the town. Boaz's foreman refers to Ruth as "the Moabitess who came back from Moab with Naomi." This seems also to indicate an awareness of her presence in Bethlehem.

13. It is inconceivable in a small town like Bethlehem that the ownership of a plot of land would have been forgotten after only ten years or so. Everything biblical points to a close registering of agricultural property. The detailed record-keeping in other regions of the ancient Near East also argues in favor of this man's being aware of the property's existence.

14. Westbrook, *Property and the Family in Biblical Law*, 9–89; idem, "The Law of the Biblical Levirate," 65–87.

15. See Westbrook, "Redemption of Land," 371; H. Brichto, "Kin, Cult, Land and Afterlife," 15–16.

about the levirate in the introduction, pp. 399–403). Thus Boaz now publicly calls on the nearer redeemer to take on (lit., "you acquire"[16]) the voluntary family or clan responsibility of marrying Ruth the Moabitess, in order (lit.) "to raise up the name[17] of the deceased on his inherited estate [*naḥălâ*]" (4:5).

In appealing to the nearer redeemer (*gōʾēl*) to raise up the name of the deceased, Boaz is not appealing to the letter of the law but its spirit. This is another manifestation of Boaz's *ḥesed*.[18] Neither man is legally bound by Deuteronomy 25:5–10 to marry Ruth; it is voluntary. But this does not erase all moral responsibility. As *gōʾēl*, Boaz, the reader knows, is prepared to do this. But what about this nearer *gōʾēl*?

The nearer redeemer could have agreed to take on both responsibilities. Thus for a brief moment, suspense builds. Will Boaz lose Ruth to this nearer nameless redeemer? But quickly the narrator relieves any troubling thoughts concerning this. The nearer redeemer reveals that he has neither the motives nor the character to rise to this occasion: "Then I cannot redeem it because I might endanger[19] my own estate [*naḥălâ*]. You redeem it yourself. I cannot do it."[20] Thus Bush correctly sums it up:

> His words clearly express concern only for his own interests; they show no concern for Ruth and the line of Elimelech at all. Thus unwilling to shoulder his full responsibilities as the redeemer with the prior right, he summons Boaz to acquire his rights (4:8a) and expresses the transfer symbolically by the physical act that customarily accompanied such a transfer: he removed his sandals and gave them to Boaz (4:8b).[21]

---

16. The Qere is preferred (see Bush, *Ruth, Esther*, 216, 229).

17. While "name" (*šēm*) can be used in the Old Testament as the virtual equivalent of "descendants, posterity" (cf. Isa. 66:22), in this context it has the connotation of "title." See Westbrook, *Property and the Family in Biblical Law*, 69–89.

18. For further discussion of *ḥesed* as the demonstration of the spirit of the law, see J. A. Loader, "Of Barley, Bulls, Land, and Levirate," in *Studies in Deuteronomy in Honour of S. J. Labuschagne on the Occasion of His Sixty-Fifth Birthday* (VTSup 53; Leiden: Brill, 1994), 123–38.

19. The term *šāḥat* in this context has connotations of "ruin" or "undermine."

20. The nearer redeemer is now publicly caught in an ethical and economic dilemma. He has only three options: (1) He can agree to redeem the field and marry Ruth and so raise up an heir to inherit the family property of Elimelech. If he does this, he will incur the cost of redeeming the field, only to see it become the property of the heir he must raise for the line of Elimelech. (2) He can agree to redeem the field but ignore his pledge to marry Ruth. If he does this, he will cast himself in an unfavorable light as one who is willing to meet family obligations only when they benefit him and do not cost him. (3) He can cede his rights as redeemer to the next *gōʾēl* (i.e., Boaz).

21. Bush, *Ruth, Esther*, 246.

Nonverbal action closes the scene. The nearer redeemer (*gōʾēl*) removes his sandal and hands it to Boaz as a symbolic act declaring his abdication of his own right of redemption.[22]

In this light, it is more understandable why the narrator leaves this *gōʾēl* anonymous and has Boaz address him pejoratively as "So-and-So." As Trible rightly notes, "Since he refused to 'restore the name of the dead to his inheritance,' he himself has no name. Anonymity implies judgment."[23] This is also the probable reason that Boaz assembles an "official" meeting at the city gate. As a man of strength of character (*gibbôr ḥayil*), he manifests the *ḥesed* that the spirit of the law intends.

Scene 2. Boaz acquires the right to redeem Naomi and Ruth (4:9–12). Calling the entire assembly to be his witnesses, Boaz formally declares in a full and detailed form the two obligations that the nearer redeemer has ceded to him. His sworn commitment to these obligations encompasses three expansions, as illustrated in the following table.

Item	Formulation given to nearer redeemer		Expanded formulation in Boaz's legal oath
The property	"the piece of land that belonged to our brother Elimelech" (4:3b)	→	"all the property of Elimelech, Kilion and Mahlon" (4:9a²)
Ruth's identification	"Ruth the Moabitess . . . the dead man's widow" (4:5b¹)	→	"Ruth the Moabitess, Mahlon's widow" (4:10a)
The purpose of the marriage	"in order to maintain the name of the dead and his property" (4:5b²)	→	"in order to maintain the name [*šēm*] of the dead with his property, so that his name will not disappear from among his family or from the town records" (4:10a²)

---

22. Since the singular *naʿal* is used as often as the dual to refer to the two sandals normally worn (cf. 1 Kings 2:5; Isa. 20:2; cf. Josh. 5:15 with Ex. 3:5), it is probably the usage here. Consequently, it remains uncertain who removes his sandals and gives them to the other and whether the act makes concrete a transfer of rights or legitimates the same by a symbolic payment. However, the most natural interpretation of 4:8 is to understand that the subject of the first verb, "the redeemer said," is also the subject of the following verb "and he drew off," and therefore it is the nearer redeemer who takes off his sandals and gives them to Boaz (cf. Hubbard, *The Book of Ruth*, 250). The act then symbolizes and makes concrete the transfer of rights from the one "redeemer" to the next. See Bush, *Ruth, Esther*, 234–36.

23. Trible, *God and the Rhetoric of Sexuality*, 190.

These detailed expansions are not just a formality. They irrevocably and legally obligate Boaz to the family of Elimelech as *gōʾēl*, thereby securing the restoration of clan wholeness. Through this solemn and emphatic declaration, Boaz names once again the whole family that sojourned from Judah to Moab (cf. 1:2). This reinforces the issue of restoration of the clan—the memory of the deceased may not perish.

The only character from the prologue who is not mentioned is Orpah, for obvious reasons. However, her role as a foil to Ruth has been filled by the nearer redeemer as a foil to Boaz.

> But substitution means dissimilarity. Orpah had both name and speech (1:10). She decided to die to the story by returning to her own people, and the judgment upon her is favorable (1:15). The unnamed redeemer chooses to die to the story by returning to his own inheritance, and the judgment upon him is adverse. After all, he is not a foreign woman but the nearest male kin. Thus he passes away with the infamy of anonymity.[24]

While both Orpah and the nameless *gōʾēl* are motivated by self-interest, Orpah's is a self-interest that is humanly understandable; the nameless *gōʾēl*'s is morally inexcusable. Quite simply, he has failed in every way in his *gōʾēl* functions.

The elders and all those at the gate declared their witness of the legal proceedings. They then pronounce a threefold blessing on Boaz:

1. "May the LORD make the woman who is coming into your home like Rachel and Leah, who together built up the house of Israel."
2. "May you have standing [*ʿăśē ḥayil*] in Ephrathah and be famous [*qārāʾ šēm*] in Bethlehem."
3. May your family be like that of Perez, whom Tamar bore to Judah through the offspring the LORD gives you by this young woman.[25]

In the first blessing, the elders express the hope that Ruth will be fruitful and build up the house of Boaz as Rachel and Leah did in the case of Jacob. Interestingly, Rachel is listed first, Leah second. This may be a case in which the more important person is named second, as with Ruth in 1:4, 14 and Mahlon in 4:9. Leah as the mother of Judah and her descendants are in view in the third blessing (v. 12).[26]

---

24. Ibid., 191.
25. The NIV unnecessarily reverses the clauses in this verse.
26. Bush, *Ruth, Esther*, 240. Campbell, however, notes reasons why Rachel is listed first (*Ruth*, 152): (1) because Rachel was Jacob's favorite wife; (2) because Rachel was buried traditionally at Bethlehem (Gen. 35:19); (3) because Rachel experienced a lengthy barrenness

The second blessing contains a poetic paralleling. The last clause enhances the understanding of the first. The phrase *qārā' šēm* literally means "may a name be called/given," which appears to be idiomatic for "be famous." The recurrence of the word *šēm* (name) in this blessing cannot help but be a play on the third part of Boaz's sworn declaration, "to maintain the name [*šēm*] of the dead." Thus the first clause of the blessing is best seen (as the NIV translation reflects) as dealing with standing or reputation, though the richness of the nuances of *'ašē ḥayil* cannot be overlooked.[27]

The third blessing invokes the case of Perez, the offspring of Tamar and Judah, who in spite of the machinations of his father and mother (Gen. 38)[28] proved to be a gracious blessing from God. This blessing subtly speaks to the parallel of Ruth and Tamar as non-Israelites included in the tribal delineation. Like the story of Boaz and Ruth, the story of Judah and Tamar is a story of family continuity achieved by the determination of a woman,[29] though the story of Boaz and Ruth is also a tremendous contrast to the tale of Judah and Tamar.[30]

Boaz is certainly a praiseworthy man. The threefold blessing begins and ends with a reference to the woman he has pledged himself to marry. However, she is not named in any of the three blessings. Moreover, the first blessing mentions her only so that Boaz may have a family commensurate in size with that of the patriarch Jacob/Israel. And she is alluded to in the third blessing only because she is the means through which Boaz may have a family line as significant as that of Perez. The focus and emphasis in the blessings is on Boaz. While the offspring of Boaz and Ruth will count in the family line of Elimelech, he will also count as a genuine scion of Boaz.

Epilogue (4:13–17)

EVEN THOUGH THIS epilogue is brief, its importance to the story is similar to that of its counterpart the prologue (1:1–6), for the resolution to the death

---

at first just as Ruth had in her earlier marriage; (4) because Ruth is second-named in 1:4 and was apparently married to the younger of the two sons (like Rachel, who was married to the younger of two sons: Jacob)—thus Ruth the least in rank of the story's characters is now to receive the reward of her faithfulness.

27. The range of meaning for *ḥayil* has resulted in numerous translations: "power, strength" (NEB, JB); "worth, ability" (KJV, ASV); and "wealth, possessions" (NASB, RSV).

28. Tamar bears twins, Perez and Zerah, after she masquerades as a prostitute to seduce her father-in-law, Judah, who had failed to fulfill his promise to give her his youngest son, Shelah, as husband after his two older sons died while married to her.

29. A. Berlin, "Big Theme, Little Book," 47.

30. Note also the huge contrast between Boaz and Ruth and the Levite of Bethlehem and his nameless concubine (Judg. 19).

and emptiness that have afflicted Naomi are truly resolved in these few verses. In staccato style, the story compresses about an entire year into a few verses in order to bring resolution to the book's main problem: Naomi's emptiness.[31] In contrast to the ten years of infertility in Moab, Yahweh "enables" Ruth to conceive; she does so almost immediately (4:13). While Naomi's "children" (*yelādîm* in 1:5; NIV "sons") died in Moab, a "child" (*yeled*) is born to Ruth and Boaz in Bethlehem (4:16).

The epilogue (4:13–17) is also strikingly parallel to Scene 2 of Act 1 (1:19b–22). In the epilogue the women of Bethlehem joyously celebrate the son born to Ruth and Boaz as the one who restores life and fullness to Naomi. This is parallel to 1:19b–22, where the women of Bethlehem joyously greet Naomi only to hear her bitter lament of bereavement and emptiness.

The epilogue divides into two parts, which evince parallel structuring:[32]

Part 1 (4:13–15)	A	Narrative Statement (4:13)
	B	Speech of the Women (4:14–15)
Part 2 (4:16–17)	A'	Narrative Statement (4:16)
	B'	Action of the Women (4:17)

Each narrative statement results in a response on the part of the women. Both A (4:13) and A' (4:16) are parallel in form and content. The resultant actions of the women B (4:14–15) and B' (4:17) are also parallel in form and content in that each involves a statement made by the women of the city; both center their attention on the relationship between the newborn child and Naomi; and each contains the idiom "call his name" (*qārā' šēm*; NIV "may he become famous," 4:14; "they named him," 4:17). In fact, the last statement of verse 17, "he was the father of Jesse, the father of David," provides the fulfillment of the prayer of the women for the newborn infant in 4:14b.

The narrative statement of Part 1 (4:13) relates in a straightforward manner the marriage of Boaz and Ruth, her pregnancy (credited to Yahweh), and the birth of a son. All of this, which certainly takes at least a year to transpire, is telescoped into one verse. It is not the events themselves that the narrator is concerned with but their meaning and significance, especially for Naomi.

In the statement that it is Yahweh who enables Ruth to conceive and bear a son, there is a dramatic fulfillment of Boaz's petition to Yahweh on behalf of Ruth in 2:11–12, for in the realization of home, husband, and child is surely to be seen both her being "richly rewarded" (2:12) and her repayment for the good deed of leaving father, mother, and country for Naomi

---

31. Naomi is "the person whose 'trial' holds the whole story together" (Campbell, *Ruth*, 168).
32. Bush, *Ruth, Esther*, 250–52.

(2:11). In fact, Ruth now sees restored all that she has given up—and more, for the instant fertility that Yahweh provides stands in stark contrast to the ten years of barrenness in Moab. In this same terse statement, the conception granted by Yahweh marks the immediate fulfillment of the prayer of the legal assembly for fruitfulness for Boaz's bride, and the birth of the child constitutes the beginning of the fulfillment of their wish for an abundance of descendants for Boaz (4:11b–12).

The speech of the women (B) is threefold and provides the commentary on and meaning of the events just related. This speech devotes itself almost exclusively to describing Naomi's restoration to life and fullness. Appropriately, it is the women of Bethlehem (cf. 1:19b) who interpret the significance of the boy's birth. While they praise Yahweh, their focus is on Naomi and the infant boy. He is Yahweh's provision to Naomi as a kinsman-redeemer (*gōʾēl*). The meaning of this is given in the following statement: "He will renew [restore] your life and sustain [support] you in your old age." As a *gōʾēl*, the infant boy—despite his age—through his birth provides restoration and wholeness to the family. The resolution is perfect. Death and emptiness (1:3–5, 21) have given way to life and fullness—a kind or type of resurrection.

The use of the term *šûb* ("renew") in verse 15 also heightens the significance. When Naomi returned from Moab, she bitterly lamented (lit.): "Full was I when I went away, but empty has Yahweh brought me back [*šûb*]" (1:21). Now, ironically, the jubilant women describe the child as one who will bring back (*šûb*) life (4:15).

The women base their conviction that this child will do all these things because "your daughter-in-law, who loves you and who is better to you than seven sons, has given him birth." The love they speak of has been demonstrated by Ruth both in words (1:16–17) and in deeds (2:11). Thus, Ruth's "own love for Naomi will be bequeathed to him."[33] These words also enshrine the story's ultimate evaluation of Ruth by stating that she has meant more to Naomi than seven sons—the ideal number in the Old Testament (1 Sam. 2:5; Job 1:2; 42:13; Acts 19:14–17).[34]

The term translated "love" is *ʾāhēb*, which is essentially a term of covenantal commitment that is expressed in acts of *ḥesed*. Block observes:

> More than anyone else in the history of Israel, Ruth embodies the fundamental principle of the nation's ethic: "You shall love your God with all your heart" (Deut. 6:5) "and your neighbor as yourself (Lev.

---

33. W. Rudolph, *Das Buch Ruth, Das Hohe Lied, Die Klaglieder* (KAT 17.1–3, 2d ed.; Gütersloh: Mohn, 1962), 70.
34. Campbell, *Ruth*, 168.

19:18). In Lev. 19:34 Moses instructs the Israelites to love the stranger as they love themselves. Ironically, it is this stranger from Moab who shows the Israelites what this means.[35]

It is also important at this point to note that the concerns that dominate 4:14–15 are not male concerns but female concerns. Therefore, Yahweh is celebrated by the female chorus

not because he has not left the line of Elimelech without a descendant but because he has not left Naomi without a redeemer to care for her in her need. And the female chorus sees the meaning of this child not in his identity as the heir of Elimelech and all his property but in his role as the restorer of Naomi to life who will support her in her old age.[36]

Parallel to Part 1, Part 2 (4:16–17) of the epilogue opens with a narrative statement (A'): "Then Naomi took the child, laid him in her lap and cared for him" (4:16). The picture here is that of a fulfilled grandparent enjoying her grandchild. Such a picture is in utter contrast to the bitter lamentation scene in Act 1, in which Naomi decries her emptiness (= childless situation).[37] She who was left alone without her two sons (*yᵉlādîm*, 1:5) now takes the boy (*yeled*), holds him, and becomes the one who cares for him (4:16).

The narrative statement stimulates a female response in B' (4:17). They proclaim: "'Naomi has a son.' And they named him Obed."[38] Just as the women proclaim the significance of the birth in B (4:14–15) with reference to Naomi above, now in B' (4:17) they joyfully proclaim the meaning of his name. The narrator is using poetic license here. He does not expect to be taken literally as if the women of the neighborhood really are the ones who give the child his name! Rather, these women "name" him in the sense of providing the explanation for his name with their glad cry, "Naomi has a son." Thus the narrator intends a semantic wordplay:[39] The "son born

---

35. Block, *Judges, Ruth*, 729.

36. Bush, *Ruth, Esther*, 264.

37. There does not seem to be any reason to understand this act as a legal adoption of the child by Naomi. Naomi has no need to adopt the infant; he is already hers through the legal fiction of the levirate. See the discussion of Bush, *Ruth, Esther*, 257–58.

38. Bush has surveyed the syntactic structures of name giving in the Old Testament and convincingly argues that this is a case of semantic wordplay. See F. W. Bush, "Ruth 4:17: A Semantic Wordplay," in *"Go to the Land I Will Show You": Studies in Honor of Dwight W. Young*, ed. J. E. Coleson and V. H. Matthews (Winona Lake, Ind.: Eisenbrauns, 1996), 3–14.

39. Bush, *Ruth, Esther*, 261. The fact that Obed is in all probability a hypocoristic (an abbreviated form) for a name without a theophoric element (cf. ᶜ*bdyhw*/ᶜ*bdyh*, a common name in the Old Testament [e.g., Obadiah]) does not speak against this view since such a semantic play totally ignores scientific etymology.

---

to Naomi"[40] receives the name "Obed/server," understood here in the sense of "provider, guardian" (cf. Mal. 3:17), since he will show kindness to his grandmother.

The normal setting for this type of proclamation was in the context of an announcement to the father of a child, who was waiting nearby to hear the news of the birth.[41] Exercising his literary license, the author emphasizes the happy significance of this child for Naomi—she who was childless now has a son—by applying to her the very language of the joyous birth announcement that commonly came to a waiting father.

Finally, a surprise identification is given. The child is "the father of Jesse, the father of David." This surprise is all the more delightful because the narrator at the beginning subtly hinted at some such connection by his identification of the family as "Ephrathites from Bethlehem, Judah" (1:2). This, of course, was the very clan and city of David used in the introduction to the narrative in 1 Samuel 17:12: "Now David was the son of an Ephrathite named Jesse, who was from Bethlehem in Judah." It is at this point that the reader can perceive how precarious the situation was: Without Ruth the line of Elimelech would be extinguished, as too the line of Boaz, and hence no David.

This last statement of the epilogue serves as a logical link to the genealogy of the coda (4:18). It also serves as a link to the earlier speech of the women when they pronounced, "May he become famous throughout Israel!" (4:14).

Coda (4:18–22)

THIS CODA (SEE the discussion in the introduction on unity as well as the structure, pp. 397–99) is linked to the preceding by the personal names Perez, Obed, Jesse, and David and by the skillful use of the number seven.[42] The ten names in the genealogy are contrasted with the ten infertile years in Moab.

---

40. "The announcement is addressed to the larger community outside the family, which is invited, not to claim the child for itself, but to appreciate what this means for Naomi. Hence, Naomi, as the primary beneficiary of the birth, is cited as the one to whom the child is born." See S. B. Parker "The Birth Announcement," in *Ascribe to the Lord: Essays in Honor of P. C. Craigie*, ed. L. Eslinger and G. Taylor (JSOTSup 67; Sheffield: JSOT Press, 1988), 133–49, esp. 139.

41. R. Hubbard Jr., "Ruth IV.17: A New Solution," *VT* 38 (1988): 293–301, esp. 296.

42. See Porten, "The Scroll of Ruth: A Rhetorical Study," 48. He states: "Ruth is said to be better to Naomi than 'seven' sons (4:15). The descendent of Perez who married Ruth appeared in the *seventh* generation (4:21). The young widow Ruth, worth more to the old widow Naomi than seven sons, married the seventh generation Boaz. The elders had blessed Boaz that his house be like the house of Perez (4:12). The reader is now shown what the house of Perez meant—seven generations to Boaz (4:18–21) and ten to David."

One of the three blessings of the legal assembly in 4:11–12 was that Yahweh might make Boaz flourish and give him renown in Bethlehem through a family line whose size would be as great as that of the patriarch Jacob/Israel and whose significance would match that of Perez (the premier clan of Judah). This genealogy, which leads from Perez through Boaz to David, bears testimony to the fulfillment of the blessing of the legal assembly of Bethlehem.

The genealogies at the end of the book lift the story to a national level. The first genealogy (at the end of the epilogue, 4:17) begins with Obed, son of Boaz and Ruth, and culminates two generations later in David; the second (here in the coda) goes back to Perez, the son of Judah and Tamar, then leads to Salmon, father of Boaz, and after ten generations also culminates in David. The double emphasis on David moves the book to the national level.

The genealogy also provides a fitting end to the story because it adds a striking significance to the story's resolution—Naomi's return to life and fullness. The writer intends the genealogy to portray the significance of the resolution of the story, for that resolution has meaning not only by virtue of all that was discussed in the previous section (i.e., the epilogue), but also by virtue of the fact that it provided an integral link in the family line that led two generations later to David. In this way, the narrator is able to show the "greater" significance of the characters' decisions and actions and to tie this together with God's sovereign, providential care.

In other words, the *ḥesed* shown by Ruth, Naomi, and Boaz has repercussions, not just for themselves in their lifetime, but for the nation of Israel for many generations to come. The long-term impacts of their personal piety has ramifications far beyond their lifetimes. This is because in the sovereignty and providence of God there are implications for a person's covenantal fidelity often extended for many generations to come (Ex. 34:7a; Deut. 7:9).

Consequently, the original point of the narrative is extended beyond showing God's providence and care in the life of one family. It now concerns the life of the entire nation, for in the son born to Naomi the history of God's rule through David has begun. Furthermore, God's rule through his ultimate ideal king, a son of David and God's own Son, will come through Naomi's son. This has ramifications throughout both history and the future.

Thus the theme of family continuity becomes the theme of national continuity. The book of Ruth is the bridge between the era of Israel as family or tribe and Israel as nation. Far from being peripheral to the main narrative sequence of the Bible, Ruth dramatizes its principal theme: the continuity of the people Israel in their land. Moreover, in Yahweh's providence, the *ḥesed* of Boaz, Ruth, and Naomi lays the foundation for a salvation that extends to the ends of the earth for a lost world.

IN THIS CHAPTER God demonstrates one final time his sovereignty and providence. The series of "coincidences" in the chapter and the way in which Yahweh weaves the actions of the human characters together for his purposes reinforce this. The timing of the nearer redeemer's entering the gate at the precise moment that Boaz is preparing the legal action and the sudden ability of Ruth to get pregnant come to mind (see more on this below). Moreover, God demonstrates once more his *ḥesed* to the two widows through the *ḥesed* of Boaz.

The *ḥesed* and integrity of Boaz. Obviously, the cultural customs contained in this chapter are foreign to our modern context. The *gōʾēl* function, the levirate marriage, and the custom of removing the sandal as a token of transfer of legal rights are practices unknown to our culture (the last item was removed even from the Old Testament culture at the time Ruth was written). Nevertheless, we can understand the roles of these customs in Israel's tribal/clanish society and appreciate the motivation of *ḥesed* that was the underlying stimulus to action. Furthermore, we can appreciate the ways in which such customs might be used in ancient times to reflect God's character, in particular, his *ḥesed*.

In Act 4, Boaz is presented as one who takes the initiative to do *ḥesed*. His voluntary act of *ḥesed* is greatly heightened by the nearer kinsman's unwillingness to do *ḥesed*. The fact that Boaz mentions the existence of a nearer *gōʾēl* to Ruth and takes it on himself to find that person and apprise him of the situation, thereby risking his own chance to marry Ruth, greatly adds to the characterization of Boaz as an honest, upright man. He is a man of integrity. Boaz will not obtain Ruth as a wife by a backdoor maneuver.

While Boaz is loyal to the interests of the family (i.e., Naomi and Ruth) as manifested in his willingness to fulfill his obligation as redeemer, his loyalty is seen to be exponentially greater than this since he is willing to relinquish that privilege if law or custom demand it (i.e., if the nearer redeemer acts to redeem the field and marry Ruth). Yet, the nearer *gōʾēl's* declining for reasons other than legal necessity makes Boaz's putting legal requirements ahead of personal desires stand out all the more sharply.[43] This is a man of integrity, a man without guile.

Thus, in Act 4, Boaz is portrayed as knowing the law and of wisely/cleverly implementing it. The other *gōʾēl* is depicted as selfish, perhaps even greedy and unable to maneuver in legal matters like Boaz. Boaz is unquestionably depicted as "knowing" more than the other *gōʾēl*, of understanding the implications better than him, and of having a willingness beyond that of

---

43. Berlin, *Poetics*, 86.

the other *gōʾēl*. In a word, Boaz is wiser than the *gōʾēl*, just as Ruth is wiser than Orpah. While Orpah's motivations are pictured as practical, the nearer *gōʾēl*'s motivations seem to be selfishly driven. In contrast, Ruth and Boaz are depicted as being motivated by devoted loyalty to others.

Thus on the one hand, as in the case of Orpah, we may not pursue acts of *ḥesed* on behalf of others because those acts don't seem logical/practical/realistic. In other words, they don't make sense. On the other hand, as in the case of the nearer *gōʾēl*, we may not pursue acts of *ḥesed* toward others because our motives are selfishly driven.

If the book of Judges (esp. in the latter part of the book) presents people doing what is right in their own eyes, being self-absorbed and self-driven, then the book of Ruth presents the very opposite, where Boaz and Ruth in particular are driven by concerns for others, by the issues of *ḥesed*. An interesting contrast that can be drawn from this is the contrast between Samson and Boaz—the contrast could not be greater.

God's sovereignty and providence. In Act 4, God restores Naomi—a remarkable testimony to God's providential care for his people. Gradually, first through subtle hints, then through daily provisions, and finally overtly through the levirate marriage and birth of a baby, God brought Naomi back (*šûb*). As from the beginning, God is sovereignly in control. He "gives" Ruth an immediate pregnancy (in contrast to the ten years of barrenness).[44] The very issues of life and death in this short book are clearly portrayed as in the hands of the Almighty (Shaddai).[45]

Furthermore, Yahweh provides Naomi with another *gōʾēl*. There were things that Boaz could do as *gōʾēl*, and there were things beyond his ability to remedy. Boaz could give provisions to the two widows, he could redeem the land, and he could acquire Ruth as his wife. But he could not, by himself, restore Naomi's emptiness as a result of childlessness. But through his grace, God is able to do this by means of the birth of Obed. It is he who "brings back" Naomi in this final regard. God's ability to fulfill prayer and petition is especially emphasized in this birth.

Ruth's decision to commit her life to Naomi and Yahweh bears results that she cannot have possibly imagined. This is especially true in the context of what God will do through her descendants.

In some ways, God hardly seems present at all in the story of Ruth. He directly intervenes only two times—he gives the Israelites in Bethlehem

---

44. While, in certain ways, this could have had more to do with Mahlon and Boaz than Ruth, the text presents it as a specific way of God's blessing Ruth.

45. In the biblical way of understanding, Elimelech's, Mahlon's, and Kilion's deaths were not the result of fate. In his sovereignty Yahweh determines the timing. Cf. 1 Sam. 2:6: "The LORD brings death and makes alive; he brings down to the grave and raises up."

food (1:6) and gives Ruth conception (4:13). Closer inspection, however, reveals that God is very much present. Though hidden behind the scenes, his sovereign hand is quietly guiding the events of the book. Using Hubbard's analogy, it can be said:

> On stage, Ruth and Boaz faithfully live the life-style of *ḥesed*. Backstage, however, behind them, moves the Great *gōʾēl*, pained by famine, death, and old age, gently acting to alleviate them. His broad, powerful wings protect those, like Boaz and Ruth, who please him.[46]

Thus, God is very much at work in this story and in life. Even this genealogy of Perez demonstrates his sovereign plan and work. The goal to which the story moves and has fulfillment is in David. But David serves as part of the link in the genealogy of Judah to Christ in Matthew 1, and so the implications for the Christian who reads this genealogy is ultimately found in Christ. It points to the ultimate *Gōʾēl*, who would redeem the world.

Thus, in many ways, the coda with its ten-person genealogy anticipates a future beyond the story's immediate time period. This genealogy has been trimmed unmistakably to place the story's main male character, Boaz, in the favored seventh slot. By doing this, it relates a moral that was of particular interest to the historically minded Hebrews: When common people act unselfishly toward each other in accordance with God's standards of *ḥesed*, they achieve uncommon results. Through this genealogy the narrator of the book of Ruth expounds the faithfulness of God in two marvelous ways: (1) in his preservation of the family that will bear the royal seed in the midst of the dark, troubled period of the judges, and (2) in his reward to those who lived genuine godly lives manifesting his *ḥesed* through their deeds.

The issue of typology. Undoubtedly, one of the most common and vexing problems that one faces in the interpretation of the book of Ruth is the issue of typology, an issue linked to the difficult question of the relationship between the Old and New Testaments. Unfortunately, the book of Ruth serves as one of the prime examples of far-fetched Christological exegesis of the Old Testament. Moreover, this typological focus and emphasis has predominated in many devotional commentaries on the book of Ruth to the exclusion of many other important lessons and applications that the book offers its readers. It is important to emphasize all that this important book teaches, especially with reference to God's providential care.

Consequently, it is illegitimate to draw elaborate parallels between Boaz as Christ and Ruth as the bride of Christ, as is not infrequent within certain

---

46. Hubbard, "The *Gōʾēl* in Ancient Israel," 18.

Christian circles.[47] Boaz is not mentioned once in the New Testament and so obviously is never declared a type of Christ. Just because Boaz is a *gōʾēl* and the New Testament describes Christ's death in terms of redemption does not mean that the interpreter is free to draw all kinds of parallels between the two individuals.

It must be remembered that in the Old Testament, Yahweh is identified as Israel's divine *Gōʾēl*, an identification particularly derived from his redemptive action in delivering Israel out of Egyptian bondage (e.g., Ex. 15:13).[48] Interestingly, the Old Testament, by identifying Yahweh as Israel's divine *Gōʾēl*, is stressing the covenant, in which God has bound himself to his people. Therefore, it is natural that Christ's work of redemption be likened to Yahweh's work of redemption. Since Yahweh is the divine redeemer, any human (whether Boaz or someone else) who functions as a redeemer will, to some extent, parallel Yahweh.

Hence, Boaz's action is simply a human outworking of *gōʾēl* activity as the agent of Yahweh's divine activity. So instead of being a type with a clear antitype, Boaz is an agent—a human mirror—of the divine work.

DOING *ḤESED* AND LIVING **with integrity before God.** Boaz is a man who knows the law (Torah) and is obedient to it. He is unwilling to bypass its directives that give priority to the nearest relative just to fulfill his own gratifications (cf. 3:12). What a powerful testimony! Christians can learn much from Boaz. Because we live in a world that demands to get its own way and is often more than willing to bypass or short-circuit any ethical issue that stands in the way, the church finds itself infected with this way of living. Clear scriptural directives for reconciliation are ignored in order to achieve one's goals. Unsupported testimony (i.e., gossip) filters its way throughout congregations in order to gain its intended aims. The very idea of "doing *ḥesed*" does not cross the minds of many a church attendee who is more interested in having his or her needs met.

But just because the law demands that the nearer redeemer have the first option does not mean that Boaz should wait it out. Here he is the initiator; he knows the situation and the law, and not only is he able, but he is willing to do what is right in God's eyes. Many of our difficulties and problems are

---

47. A. Gaebelein, *As It Was—So Shall It Be: Sunset and Sunrise: A Study of the First Age and Our Present Age* (New York: "Our Hope," 1937); M. R. DeHaan, *The Romance of Redemption: The Love Story of Ruth and Boaz* (Grand Rapids: Zondervan, 1958).

48. Cf. the analogy of the divine *gōʾēl*, whose redeeming activity in at least one instance (Isa. 54:5) is described in terms of a marriage with a childless widow.

the result of not "knowing" God's Word—in particular, his moral standards as reflected in the Torah. The blessed (Ps. 1) are those who know this law and have inculcated it into their lives. The wise seize the initiative that God gives; they do not wait or hesitate.

The role of the *gōʾēl*, in one sense, is foreign to our culture. But in another sense, the examples of Boaz and Jesus certainly give us illustrations and models that we can emulate. There are many around us, whether in our families, extended families, or in the church, who desperately need a *gōʾēl*, that is, someone who can redeem them and restore them to wholeness. This is true in many physical contexts but also in numerous spiritual contexts.

At the root, however, there must be *ḥesed*. This rich term enables us to act with loyalty, love, and compassion. It provides the basis and proper motives for the action of the *gōʾēl*. As clearly illustrated in Boaz and Jesus, *ḥesed* sees the world in a different way. It is selfless, not like the nearer *gōʾēl*, who is apparently dominated by self-interest.

Finally, the role of *gōʾēl* among one's family or church requires *ḥayil* (strength of character). Just as Boaz and Jesus demonstrated their *ḥayil* in their integrity and willingness to actually do what was right, so in our modern contexts *ḥayil* will see that the right thing is done, not just thought about. It provides the fortitude to accomplish as well as the stamina to maintain integrity in the midst of temptations.

The faithfulness of God. In a fallen world that has lost all direction and certainty, the book of Ruth reaffirms time and again the sovereignty and providence of God. At the beginning of the third millennium, modern Western culture has produced a highly mobile urban society in which ties of extended families have, in many cases, disappeared. The norm has become the two-parent working family that is greatly in debt and significantly stressed by the issues of raising children in a more and more promiscuous and violent society. It is easy in the midst of such life stresses to forget that the Lord is sovereignly in control and still providentially cares for his people. Just as God demonstrated his *ḥesed* through Boaz to the two widows, he demonstrates his loving faithfulness and loyalty to his people today through individuals living out the spirit of his Word, motivated by loving commitment to people in need.

God's *ḥesed* restored Naomi, and it restores us. As with Naomi, sometimes the process seems slow from a human standpoint, but gradually and definitely, God acts to "bring us back." God is sovereignly in control, whether in life or in death. The Lord often provides us with a *gōʾēl*, sometimes in a form that we would least expect—as he did in the case of Naomi through Obed. In this process, God inevitably demonstrates his ability to answer our prayers and petitions.

In general, our culture does not care much about familial links with the past, with its implications for the future. In fact, our narcissistic society cares little for anyone other than self. But the genealogy at the end of this important little book has not only important links with the past but with the future. The *gōʾēl* in the seventh place in the genealogy serves as a wonderful type of the *gōʾēl* who would come—even from among his descendants. This ultimate *gōʾēl*, who laid down his life to redeem his "brothers" in the great redemption of all time, is the end to which the genealogy moves.

This coda should instill in us hope. When we live a life of personal piety, doing *ḥesed* to others, loving one another within the community of faith, and loving our neighbors, there is the expectation that through God's sovereignty and providential care such a life will have impacts that go on far beyond our lifetimes. Because he is a faithful God keeping *ḥesed* to those who love him, this is not a vain expectation.

Scripture Index

Subject Index

Subject Index

Author Index

We want to hear from you. Please send your comments about this book to us in care of zreview@zondervan.com. Thank you.

ZONDERVAN.com/
AUTHORTRACKER
follow your favorite authors